Christian
Dogmatics

VOLUME 1

Christian Dogmatics

Carl E. Braaten, *editor*

Gerhard O. Forde

Philip J. Hefner

Robert W. Jenson, *editor*

Hans Schwarz

Paul R. Sponheim

FORTRESS PRESS   PHILADELPHIA

Technical editors: John M. Stroup and Margaret B. Hoover

Chapter 4 of Locus 1 is based in part on *Principles of Lutheran Theology* by Carl E. Braaten (Philadelphia: Fortress Press, 1983).

Locus 2 is based in part on *The Triune Identity* by Robert W. Jenson (Philadelphia: Fortress Press, 1982).

Locus 3 is based in part on an article in *Word and World* 1:3 (Summer 1981), "Word and World: The Experience of God, Self, and World," pp. 252–61.

Chapter 7 of Locus 6, "The Uniqueness and Universality of Jesus Christ," was originally a paper read at the 1979 meeting of the American Society of Missiology and was published by the *Occasional Bulletin of Missionary Research* and by *Missiology*, January 1980, and by *Mission Trends* 5, ed. by Gerald H. Anderson and Thomas F. Stransky (New York/Ramsey: Paulist Press; Grand Rapids, Mich.: Wm. B. Eerdmans, 1981), pp. 69–89.

Biblical quotations, unless otherwise noted, are from the Revised Standard Version of the Bible, copyright 1946, 1952, © 1971, 1973 by the Division of Christian Education of the National Council of the Churches of Christ in the U.S.A. and are used by permission.

Library of Congress Cataloging in Publication Data

Main entry under title:

Christian dogmatics.

Includes index.
1. Theology, Doctrinal.   2. Lutheran Church—
Doctrines.   I. Braaten, Carl E., 1929–
II. Jenson, Robert W.
BT75.2.C48 1984   230'.41   83–48007
ISBN 0-8006-0712-0 (set)
ISBN 0-8006-0703-1 (v. 1)
ISBN 0-8006-0704-X (v. 2)

K104C83   Printed in the United States of America   1–703

Contents

VOLUME 1

CONTENTS

CONTENTS

FIFTH LOCUS
Sin and Evil
by Paul R. Sponheim
359

SIXTH LOCUS
The Person of Jesus Christ
by Carl E. Braaten
465

CONTENTS

VOLUME 2

CONTENTS

NINTH LOCUS
The Church
By Philip J. Hefner

CONTENTS

ELEVENTH LOCUS
Christian Life
by Gerhard O. Forde

Preface

The conception of this book took place in the late 1970s as the editors again remarked on the fact that almost all our usable dogmatics have been imported from Europe. In the decades since World War II we have used all or parts of the imposing volumes of the continental theologians—Emil Brunner, Karl Barth, Gustaf Aulén, Regin Prenter, and Paul Tillich. As teachers of dogmatic and systematic theology, we have had no textbooks that reflect the American context from the standpoint of the Lutheran tradition. We set out to rectify the situation by means of a team of authors.

Our intention in producing a complete dogmatics, with emphasis on information about the dogmatic tradition, is to serve two purposes above all: We hope our work will be a textbook in theological instruction and a resource for those who practice the arts of ministry. It lies in the nature of a work such as this to seek the widest possible churchly acceptance, since dogmatics speaks from the church to the church, by way of disciplined reflection on the sources of its faith and traditions. But theology at present is fragmented into an unusually large number of schools and movements. The fact of theological pluralism is inescapable. We have chosen to make a virtue out of a necessity by way of multiple authorship. A dogmatics by any one person would likely be received only as advocacy for the positions of that person's own school of thought, and thus fail to command the wide churchly use inherent in the notion of dogmatics. Hoping to avoid this fate, we offer this joint work of six authors.

Although all of us stand within the Lutheran tradition, the differences among us, and the consequent inconsistencies in the book, are considerable. Those who like to label theologians—"hope," "process," etc.—will by our calculations need seven or more labels for the six of us. The authors have different concentrations of historical knowledge; some refer most naturally to the fathers, others to the reformers, and still others to modern theologians. At some points the authors simply disagree, and this disagreement occasionally reaches the point of contradiction. We will leave it to the readers to discover the places where this occurs. Whether these differences and disagreements be taken as bane or blessing, they follow from the initial reason for multiple authorship.

Yet we do not think we are presenting a mere collection of essays. A draft of each *locus* has been read and criticized by the whole group. Perhaps more important, the likenesses among us as authors are as great as the differences. All of us understand ourselves by intention and calling to be churchly theologians; the goal of our work is primarily the liveliness and authenticity of the gospel, and only secondarily increased understanding of religion or metaphysical construction. All of us have written theological works of other kinds—exegetical, historical, apologetic, liturgical, homiletical, and so on—but here we are doing dogmatics in the classical tradition. All of us are of the same theological generation, and therefore influenced by the important theologians of the mid-twentieth century: Barth, Bultmann, Tillich, et al. We find it possible to disagree without either anathemas or relativism; the divergences between us are probably not greater than have always been usual in the theologically contentious Lutheran tradition from which we come. And we are indeed all Lutherans; this perhaps demands further comment.

It was an early decision to invite only Lutherans to write. At least so much commonality of tradition seemed essential if the book were not to be a mere collection and yet not be unified by common adherence to a current school of theology. At the same time, it is in the definition of Christian dogmatics that it aims at ecumenical validity and usefulness. None of us thinks of himself, either here or in his other works, as writing especially for Lutheran readers. The character of our Lutheranism will doubtless be detected in the book in many ways, such as a tendency to cite Luther himself when matters become earnest. But we believe that the true aim of the Lutheran movement has always been to serve the whole church, so that Lutheran commitment inherently bears an ecumenical orientation when it is true to its original nature.

The Lutheran movement has classically had two chief characteristics, as a look at the Augsburg Confession will reveal. The first is devoted affirmation of the catholic tradition. We think that our concurrence in this devotion can only make our work the more useful as a textbook, and also for those Protestants whose own relation to the catholic tradition is more distant. At some points in the history of Lutheranism, a full reception of the catholic dogmatic tradition has been hindered by an attempt of Lutheran confessionalism to deduce the whole of the church's life and teaching from the special principle of Lutheran theology—the article of justification by faith alone. Whenever this reductionistic error has been committed, it has produced a particularly inhumane form of Lutheran sectarianism. We trust that all participants in this project of dogmatics are free of it.

The second Lutheran concern is the specific Reformation proposal to the church: the doctrine of "justification by faith alone, apart from the works of the law." As will become clear at several points in the body of this work, the Reformation doctrine of justification is fundamentally a *critical* principle. It is the demand continuously to submit all preaching, liturgy, pastoral care, church administration, and so forth to this question: Does this particular act of ministry lead people to find their life's justification, their reason to be, in the fact that the crucified Jesus lives, or are people left on their own, to depend on themselves for the ultimate meaning of life? If a churchly word or practice in any way suggests the latter, it must, according to the doctrine of justification by faith, be reformed. We have tried to make this critical principle effective throughout this work for the ongoing reform of the church. And we will not conceal our opinion that the contemporary American church needs to be reformed by this criterion at least as much as that of the sixteenth century. We would only ask our readers: Is this critique not right and very much needed also in your part of the church? If readers can generally answer that it is, then adherence to this historically Lutheran specialty need not diminish the ecumenical scope and relevance of the dogmatics.

Finally, a word is in order about the organization of this work. The plan of multiple authorship suggested the usefulness of the older system of *loci*—literally, "locations." A *locus* in this sense is a point at which the historic teachings and theological investigations of the church are brought into focus. Each *locus* is developed on its own terms, without deduction from the others; and that is what mandates this more ancient method for us. Many of the traditional *loci* could be developed into entire systematic theologies. In a dogmatics organized as a set of such *loci*, some overlapping of topics is inevitable and desirable.

A sequence of *loci* is thus a set of pigeonholes intended to accommodate all the relevant and recurrent concerns of Christian dogmatics. We follow the traditional sequence of topics, arranging them in a kind of history-of-salvation order, roughly corresponding to the items in the three articles of the creed. But the set of *loci* is not derived from any particular theology of salvation-history or directly from the creeds. It reflects rather the actual history of the church to date; the *loci* mark the centers around which the church has in fact been compelled to gather its reflections. Any actual set of dogmatic *loci* is, of course, a proposal by the author or authors about the exact location of these centers. As far as we know, no previous work of Christian dogmatics has used the precise set and sequence of topics we have adopted here. This is most clearly evident in our inclusion of separate *loci* for "The Knowledge of God," "The Holy Spirit," and "The Christian Life." The extent to which this is an innovation indicates that in dogmatics, no less than in other theological disciplines, it is never a question of simply repristinating a previous achievement of the church.

CARL E. BRAATEN
ROBERT W. JENSON

xix

Abbreviations in Volume 1

The abbreviations used in this volume, as given below, are with slight variations based on Siegfried Schwertner, *Internationales Abkürzungsverzeichnis für Theologie und Grenzgebiete* (Berlin and New York: Walter de Gruyter, 1974).

AnBib	*Analecta Biblica*
ANFa	*Ante-Nicene Fathers*. New York, 1926.
AThR	*Anglican Theological Review*
BC	*The Book of Concord: The Confessions of the Evangelical Lutheran Church*. Translated and edited by Theodore G. Tappert. Philadelphia: Fortress Press, 1959.
COD	*Conciliorum Oecumenicorum Decreta*. Basel, 1962.
CP	*Classical Philology*
CQR	*Church Quarterly Review*
CR	*Corpus reformatorum*. Berlin, 1934ff.
Crit.	Criterion
Denzinger	Heinrich Denzinger, ed. *The Sources of Catholic Dogma*. Translated by Roy J. Deferrari from the 13th edition of *Enchiridion Symbolorum*. St. Louis: B. Herder Book Co., 1957.
DThC	*Dictionnaire de théologie catholique*. Paris, 1903ff.
EnchP	*Enchiridion Patristicum*. Edited by Marie Joseph Rouët de Journel. Freiburg, 1911ff.
ER	*Ecumenical Review*
EvTH	*Evangelische Theologie*
Interp.	*Interpretation: A Journal of Bible and Theology*
JEH	*Journal of Ecclesiastical History*
JR	*Journal of Religion*
JThS	*Journal of Theological Studies*
KuD	*Kerygma und Dogma*
LCC	Library of Christian Classics
LuthQ	*Lutheran Quarterly*
LW	American Edition of *Luther's Works*. St. Louis: Concordia Publishing House; Philadelphia: Fortress Press, 1955– .

ABBREVIATIONS IN VOLUME 1

NSHE   *New Schaff-Herzog Encyclopedia of Religious Knowledge.* New York, 1908ff.

Pers.   *The Personalist: An International Review of Philosophy, Religion, and Literature*

PG   *Patrologiae cursus completus.* Series Graeca. Edited by Jacques-Paul Migne. Paris, 1857–66, 1928–36.

PhB   *Philosophische Bibliotek.* Leipzig, 1868ff.

PhQ   *Philosophical Quarterly*

PL   *Patrologicae cursus completus.* Series Latina. Edited by Jacques-Paul Migne. Paris, 1850–55, 1941–49.

RelSt   *Religious Studies*

RGG³   *Die Religion in Geschichte und Gegenwart.* 3d ed. Tübingen, 1956–65.

RMet   *Review of Metaphysics*

ScEc   *Sciences ecclésiastiques: Revue philosophique et théologique*

SM(E)   *Sacramentum Mundi: An Encyclopedia of Theology.* 6 vols. New York, 1968–70.

StNT   Studien zum Neuen Testament

TDNT   *Theological Dictionary of the New Testament.* 10 vols. Edited by Gerhard Kittel and Gerhard Friedrich. Grand Rapids, 1964ff.

ThTo   *Theology Today*

ThWNT   *Theologische Wörterbuch zum Neuen Testament.* Edited by Gerhard Kittel. Stuttgart, 1933ff.

TS   *Theological Studies*

USQR   *Union Seminary Quarterly Review*

VigChr   *Vigiliae Christianae*

VT   *Vetus Testamentum*

VT.S   *Vetus Testamentum*, Supplement

WA   *D. Martin Luthers Werke.* Kritische Gesamtausgabe. Weimar, 1883ff.

ZKG   *Zeitschrift für Kirchengeschichte*

ZThK   *Zeitschrift für Theologie und Kirche*

FIRST LOCUS

Prolegomena to Christian Dogmatics

CARL E. BRAATEN

PROLEGOMENA TO CHRISTIAN DOGMATICS

Introduction

1. Theology and Dogmatics
   What is Theology?
   The Task of Apologetics
   Method in Theology

2. The Heritage of Dogmatics
   The Discipline
   The Ancient Church
   The Middle Ages
   The Reformation
   Protestant Orthodoxy
   The Dissolution of Dogmatics in Pietism and the Enlightenment
   The Revival of Dogmatics in the Nineteenth Century
   The State of Dogmatics in the Twentieth Century

3. The Fundamentals of Dogmatics
   The Concept of Dogma
   The Confessional Principle
   The Fundamentals of Dogmatics

4. The Holy Scriptures
   The Authority of Scripture
   The Interpretation of Scripture
   The Problem of Scripture Today

Introduction

Dogmatics is one of the traditional disciplines of Christian theology. Its special task is the critical interpretation of the doctrines of the church's faith in light of our knowledge of Christian origins and the challenge of the contemporary situation. The term "dogmatics," however, is no longer in vogue in our schools of theology. In ordinary language the words "dogma" and "dogmatics" conjure up the worst possible associations. A "dogmatic" person is rigid and narrow-minded. "Dogmatism" recalls the period of the inquisition and its heresy-hunting. In the present situation dogmatic thinking seems to be the trademark of the more conservative groups of Christians. In pietistic circles dogmatic theology was held in great suspicion as the intellectualistic dry bones of a dead orthodoxy, in contrast to the warm, personal faith of true biblical Christianity. No wonder the term "dogmatics" has been largely replaced by "systematic theology" or "constructive theology."

As the title of our work makes clear, we believe it inadvisable to surrender the use of the term "dogmatics." We would emphasize that there is a doctrinal core of the faith of the church. Dogmatic theologians are not autonomous philosophers of religion creating their own system of ideas. Instead, they are interpreters of the living stream of the church's traditions of faith expressed in dogmas and doctrines. Dogmaticians function within the context of the church for the sake of its mission in the world. If theologians are writing dogmatics, odd as it may sound in the current theological situation, there can be no doubt that their calling is a service performed within the church and for the church.

The shift from the word "dogmatics" to more neutral terms has been accelerated by a steady secularization of theology and its transformation into the scientific study of religion. The question today is whether theology can be a meaningful discipline in the secular academic context. "Religious studies" have preempted the place of theology. They feature the history of religion, the sociology of religion, and the like, but never specifically a theology of religion. Why not? This situation may point to a twofold crisis in theology. The first is the fall of dogmatics into theology in general, and the second is the fall of theology itself into general religious studies, raising the critical question whether theology is possible at all in the modern secular context.

INTRODUCTION

The crisis in dogmatics reflects the larger crisis in theology as a whole, and the crisis in theology as such reflects itself in the dismal state of dogmatics.

Dogmatics is a part of theology, perhaps the heart but certainly not the whole of it. For this reason it is necessary to deal with theology in general and its method before defining the nature and task of Christian dogmatics in particular. This is not a novel procedure. It was good tradition in classical dogmatics to begin with a chapter on the general subject of theology and then to consider the articles of faith in the witness of Holy Scripture and the symbols of the church.

The retrieval of the discipline of dogmatics may help overcome the trend to dissolve Christian theology into religious studies. If there is a specifically Christian foundation for the study of religious phenomena, it is well to clarify the fundamental presuppositions of what makes theology Christian. These are explicitly dogmatic presuppositions:

The self-revelation of God in judgment and grace

The person of Jesus the Christ of God

The witness of Holy Scripture

The means of grace in word and sacraments

The one, holy, catholic, and apostolic church

The faith worked by the Holy Spirit

Suspending the methodological function of these central symbols of Christian dogmatics inevitably leads to the disintegration of the unity of theology into a multiplicity of positivistic-scientific approaches to the study of religious phenomena. The outcome is the current anarchy in the academic study of religion, generating results of little interest to the Christian faith and the church's mission. Scholars of religion study and teach more and more about things of less and less importance.

Dogmatics is like a thorn in the flesh of the purely academic study of religion. The claim on which dogmatics rests speaks for the absolute truth of the one God and the final meaning of all humanity and the whole world. This is the scandalous claim of the gospel about Jesus the Christ of God. Dogmatics is a believing response of the mind to this imperious and gracious claim. It is an echo of the gospel in the realm of ideas. Where there is no church to preach this gospel of God's self-revelation in the history of Jesus the Christ, there is no such thing as Christian dogmatics. This is the abiding truth we have learned from the great dialectical theologians of the preceding era, Karl Barth and Paul Tillich. They stressed that Christian theology is a function of the church. This churchly connection is a distinctive mark of dogmatic theology. Dogmatics exists for the sake of the identity and mission of the church. Of course, it has its own special way of serving, not by repeating the doctrines of the past, but by a critical interpretation of the received doctrines in light of our biblical knowledge and our present engagement with the modern world. This means that dogmatics is done not so much to defend the church as it is, but to criticize it. This criticism occurs in the interest of discriminating between true and false preaching, as well as between church-centered activism for its own sake and kingdom-oriented praxis for the good of the world.

1

Theology
and Dogmatics

Theology deals with the knowledge of God, the *logos theou*. As
ordinarily taught, theology covers a comprehensive agenda of beliefs
and practices which the church requires for educating its ministry.
In its apologetic form theology seeks to argue the claims for Christianity to those who do not yet believe. In its dogmatic form theology
aims to clarify the contents of the Christian faith for those who
already believe.

WHAT IS THEOLOGY?

It is appropriate for dogmatics to begin with a reflection on the subject of
theology as a whole. What is theology? This question can be answered from
two different standpoints, from that of a general philosophical theory of human
knowledge or from that within a specific theological circle of Christian faith.
The one places theology within the scope of natural reason; the other links
it to the events of historical revelation. In classical dogmatics theology was
defined as the knowledge of God and divine things, to be gained partly in
a natural way by the use of reason, and partly in a supernatural way through
special revelation. In new and varied proposals theology continues to define
itself from two such perspectives, from the side of reason or from the standpoint of faith in special revelation, or perhaps a combination of both.

THEOLOGY =
REASON +
FAITH

Beginning with the period of the eighteenth-century Enlightenment,
theology gradually lost its confidence in natural reason and appealed more
and more to special revelation. As theology failed to prove its case in the general
academic setting, it became increasingly defined as an ecclesial science. This
made it primarily a function of the practical requirement to produce a professional class of leaders for the church. The question which the history of
modern theology has posed with inescapable urgency is this: Does theology
belong exclusively within the province of the *ecclesia,* or does it also fit
somehow within the framework of the universe of sciences in *academia,* where
the faculty of theology can hold its own along with the faculties of law,

medicine, science, history, literature, and the arts? Does theology have a subject matter and a method that can be rationally defended, or is it merely a matter of professional skills which the practitioners of religion must acquire to be effective?

The church has no reason to claim to hold a monopoly on theology. The word "theology" was not originally an invention of the Christian faith. In ancient Greece the poets were the first to be called theologians. Homer and Hesiod narrated the stories about the gods in the special medium of myth; theirs was a mythic theology. Then came the philosophers Plato and Aristotle, who criticized and translated the mythic theology of the poets into the medium of the philosophical *logos*. These philosophers were the first demythologizers. In addition to the poetic and the philosophical, there was a political form of theology in ancient Greece.[1] Political theology dealt with the gods of state religion. Eventually, under Constantine, the political gods were Christianized, and the Christian God became the head of the political religion of the Roman Empire.

This tripartite theology—poetic, philosophical, and political—existed before the rise of Christianity. The apologists of the second century were the first to appropriate the Greek concept of theology into Christian discourse. Though not a biblical word, "theology" referred to the truth of God and God's word of revelation. In the early apologetic situation Christian theology was set forth as the true philosophy, a *philosophia Christiana*. Christian theology and Greek philosophy both dealt with the *logos theou*, except that Christianity had the advantage of knowing the *logos* in the flesh, making its grasp of universal truth humanly and historically concrete.

In the period of medieval scholasticism, theology was understood in two ways, first, in its literal sense as the doctrine of God (*logos theou*), but second, and more broadly, as the statement of the truth concerning all the sacred teachings of the church (*sacra doctrina*). Thus theology dealt with everything from the creation of the world and the sacraments of the church to the second coming of Christ. The *Summa Theologica* of Thomas Aquinas offers the most splendid example of this twofold meaning of theology. In this massive work, Thomas dealt with all things pertaining to the Christian faith. The system combined theology in general (natural theology) and dogmatics in particular (*sacra doctrina*). Natural theology forms a part of philosophy, subject to the faculty of human reason. Sacred doctrine is based on the supernatural knowledge of God, available through the special revelation of Scripture and passed on by church tradition.

If medieval scholasticism broadened the meaning of theology to include everything that could be known of God through reason *and* revelation, Martin Luther inaugurated a trend in Protestant theology to sharpen the distinction between theology and philosophy. The interest of Luther was to base Christian theology exclusively on the Word of God. This Word was the subject of Scripture as a whole, manifest in the incarnation of Jesus Christ, and present today in the living voice of the gospel (*viva vox evangelii*). Luther's reduction of theology for the sake of the gospel was not upheld by the scholastic theologians of seventeenth-century Protestant orthodoxy. The great dogmaticians (John Gerhard, John William Baier, John Andrew Quenstedt, and David Hollaz) reverted to the pattern of medieval scholasticism, restoring the claim of natural theology to stand at the beginning of the dogmatic system, setting forth all that can be known about God by reason in general before specifying the pure doctrines of Christian faith (*sacra pura doctrina*).

The massive broadening of theology continued with the explosion of the new methods and results of historical-critical research in the eighteenth and nineteenth centuries. Theology as a whole became subdivided into various fields: Old and New Testament, church history, and the history of doctrine, dogmatics, and practical theology. The modern age of field specialization was dawning. At the beginning a theologian was liberated to specialize in one aspect of theology, using the new historical method, but this always presupposed the dogmatics of the church. Later a wedge was driven between the historical and dogmatic approaches to theology. Historical research opted for complete freedom from dogmatic controls, also in the theological seminary. The all-too-familiar anomaly developed whereby professors in the theological faculty could teach their specialty, whether in the biblical, historical, or practical field, without explicit reference to either the doctrine of the triune God or the christological faith of the church, and still be called theologians. This has led to the critical questions: What, then, is theology? And what is its proper method?

Friedrich Schleiermacher formulated a broad definition of theology to encompass the variety of studies pursued in the modern faculty of theology. In his *Brief Outline on the Study of Theology*, Schleiermacher stated: "Christian theology . . . is that assemblage of scientific and practical instruction without the possession and application of which a united leadership of the Christian Church, i.e., a government of the Church in the fullest sense, is not possible."[2]

This definition opened the door to the eventual expansion of the theological curriculum and the introduction of a host of new disciplines to supplement the traditional fourfold division of theology into its exegetical, historical, dogmatic, and practical fields. Whatever may contribute practically to the exercise of leadership in the church can be included in Schleiermacher's definition of theology. The question of truth need not arise, because theology deals descriptively with the theoretical ideas and practical rules which serve the professional and administrative needs of the church. The line from this definition to the present situation is direct. The place of dogmatics in the theological curriculum began to shrink, making room for auxiliary studies that introduce new methods and results from the social and behavioral sciences, all of practical importance to the ordained leadership of the church. Steadily this specialization led to secularization. The new disciplines—the history and phenomenology of religion, the psychology and sociology of religion, and the like—became autonomous fields of study, each conspicuously remote from classical definitions of theology as the doctrine concerning God or as the interpretation of Christian faith. A palace revolution took place in which theology as the erstwhile "queen of the sciences" was taken hostage by the guards who had once been hired to serve. This represents the situation of crisis in which the study of theology now finds itself.

THE TASK OF APOLOGETICS

Friedrich Schleiermacher claimed that "apologetics is a theological discipline which needs to be refashioned for these present times." [3] There is evidence of a renewal of the apologetic tendency in contemporary theological thought. This is a response to the critical state of theology in general and of dogmatics in particular. Dogmatics presupposes the truth of the Christian faith as a whole and aims to make it explicit. It is the task of apologetics to establish the grounds on which the truth claims of Christianity can be understood and legitimated, in the face of questions raised by both outsiders and insiders. The apologist is a defense attorney for the meaning and truth of the Christian message in the modern world. Apologetics is the organ by which the case for Christianity can be made before the bar of human reason as such.

Classically, apologetics took the form of natural theology, enjoying a place of prominence at the head of the dogmatic system, preparing the way for the treatment of the gospel, a John the Baptist pointing toward the coming of Christ. The function of apologetics was to serve as an introduction to dogmatics, but in actuality dogmatics was the heart pumping life into the apologetic organs. Today, dogmatics and apologetics are generally not so closely linked. The *Systematic Theology* of Paul Tillich stands as the monumental exception. In his method of correlation the apologetic element is built into the structure of the theological system as the Christian answer to the questions put to it by the contemporary situation.[4]

Systematic theology is often used as an interchangeable term for dogmatics. Our terminology would be clearer if systematic theology were understood more inclusively than dogmatics, embracing apologetics, dogmatics, systematics, and ethics. "Apologetics" in Protestant theology would then mean the same thing as "fundamental theology" in Roman Catholic terminology. Their common task is to explain and substantiate the formal and fundamental conditions of the possibility of responding in human experience and understanding

TILLICH ON APOLOGETICS

to the self-revelation of God. The purpose of dogmatics is to set forth the basis and contents of specifically biblical-Christian faith. Systematics goes beyond dogmatics in that it deals with the Christian doctrines in light of further questions. Systematics is more self-consciously aware of the most appropriate system of conceptualization, whether it be Platonic, Aristotelian, Cartesian, Kantian, Hegelian, Whiteheadian, or whatever the case may be. Ethics draws out the moral implications of the total Christian message in both personal and social spheres of existence. Such a comprehensive systematic theology is exceedingly rare at the present time. It is more common for apologetics and ethics to be treated separately from dogmatics, taking the form of independent monographs on special questions regarding the intellectual claims and moral praxis of Christianity.

The essence of the apologetic mode of procedure is to find common ground between Christian theology and the intellectual situation of its time. The apologist of the second century, Justin Martyr, combined the Stoic concept of the Logos with the biblical idea of the Word of God. The Alexandrian theologians, Clement and Origen, found common ground in Platonic philosophy, as did Augustine. Thomas Aquinas made use of Aristotle. Starting from common ground, the aim of the apologists was always to recommend the Christian truth to the outside pagan world, using all the evidences from history and human nature at their command. When Christianity became the majority religion of the empire, no longer a fighting minority in a pagan world, apologetics worked to clarify the reasonableness of Christian faith to those who already believed, arguing that it is perfectly reasonable to accept the biblical accounts of miracles and prophecies as proofs of the divine origin of Christianity. After the Reformation, apologetics became the defender of Christian orthodoxy against attacks from deism, rationalism, naturalism, materialism, and the like. At the same time, however, apologetics was placed on the defensive because of the findings of the natural and historical sciences. Apologetics discredited itself by looking for "God in the gaps" of our modern scientific and historical knowledge, steadily having to retreat from one outpost to another, until finally no significant ground was left to defend. There is no desire on the part of theologians to return to this self-defeating type of apologetics.

In twentieth-century theology the main apologetic way has been to latch on to the system of a leading secular philosopher and to show the "beauty" of the Christian faith in terms of its set of categories. Some biblical, kerygmatic, and confessional theologies have called for a complete separation of theology from philosophy, in the spirit of Tertullian's famous question: What does Jerusalem have to do with Athens? Careful analysis will show, however, that none of these theologies has successfully purged itself of all philosophical presuppositions and concepts, whether epistemological or metaphysical.

13

Today there are notable examples of the classical apologetic way in which theology makes use of philosophy as its handmaid. Existentialist theology has used the categories of Martin Heidegger's philosophy of existence to translate the kerygma into terms that modern people can understand. The need for translation is obvious: The kerygma is embedded in the mythical picture of the world. By demythologizing the New Testament, it is possible for Christianity to set forth a possibility of existence which philosophy also talks about. They share common ground in the understanding of human existence. Language-analysis theology has taken hold of Ludwig Wittgenstein's theory of "language games" to show that religious language has its own kind of logic. Christianity, accordingly, as every other religion, has its own rules which have to be learned to play the language game of faith. This approach has given religious language a reprieve in a secular age in which many intellectuals believed all talk about God to be literally non-sense. Process theology has adopted the metaphysics worked out by the process philosophers, most notably Alfred North Whitehead and Charles Hartshorne, in order to have the most adequate resources to express within the modern framework of the evolutionary world view what the Bible means by God and the world. The God of process metaphysics and the God of biblical revelation are supposedly one and the same. The apologetic intent is unmistakable; now it should be possible for theology and science to share the same frame of reference. A Christian can be at once explicitly theological and think scientifically without violating the canons of either side.

Contemporary apologetics has not only used twentieth-century philosophical thinkers, but has also reached back to appropriate in new ways some older nineteenth-century models. While Paul Tillich drew on the existentialist analysis of Heidegger, the influence of the absolute idealism of Friedrich Schelling was far more definitive throughout his theological system. The renaissance of G. W. F. Hegel's dialectical thought has also provided the undergirding for the universal-historical approach of Wolfhart Pannenberg. The role of Karl Marx and his concept of praxis has provided liberation theology with its main entree into the political realities of the modern world. Ernst Bloch's philosophy of hope gave eschatological theology a hermeneutical key for reading the Bible in light of the principle of hope. The transcendental Thomism of Roman Catholic thinkers, particularly Karl Rahner and Bernard Lonergan, has used the critical philosophy of Immanuel Kant and the existentialist anthropology of Heidegger as a bridge back to the Aristotelian metaphysics of Thomas Aquinas. Its direct apologetic relevance is clearly exhibited in the Thomist principle: Grace does not destroy but fulfills nature. Therefore, Christian revelation is bound to build on the natural knowledge of God and of the world.

With these examples we have barely skimmed the surface of the apologetic situation in the contemporary period. They are sufficient, however, to demonstrate the extent to which Christian theology has felt the need for an apologetic link between the Christian faith and the modern intellectual situation. In this way it is pursuing the classical line, repeating both its liabilities and assets.

It may be well for theological apologetics to proceed in a more eclectic fashion, refusing to bind itself to one particular philosophy. Kant, Hegel, Marx, Heidegger, Wittgenstein, Whitehead, and others may each have a different service to render to theology. At a minimum, we can cite three attainable goals of apologetics today. First, apologetics can thematize the ultimate questions concerning the meaning of human existence.[5] Apart from revelation, it cannot identify and name the reality of the One who is truly God. At best it can show that religious language and symbols do function in a meaningful way because they disclose dimensions of human existence which seek after the ultimate and the holy.

Second, apologetics can inquire into the formal conditions of the possibility of thought and speech about God.[6] The movement here is from human being to God, from anthropology to theology, starting from below in the human subject and leading to God as the ultimate term of human self-transcendence. Along this route it is not possible to know the will of God. But we can find traces of transcendence in the human spirit, which theology might link up with the Christian knowledge of the triune God.

Third, apologetics can relate theology to the human search for meaning in history.[7] Every particular science deals with only a part of reality. None can claim to know it all, to possess an omnicompetent method to deal with the totality of reality. Theology can be defined as that science which goes beyond partial meanings, seeking an answer to the question of the final and total meaning of all events in the history of nature and society. The human spirit, it can be shown, is inherently concerned about the totality of meaning, bent on transcending infinitely every partial embodiment of meaning, whether in secular or religious experience.

The discipline of theology can thus be justified within the framework of the hermeneutical inquiry into the conditions of possible meaning in history. There is some truth in the observation that modern hermeneutics from Schleiermacher to Gadamer is "a continuation of theology by other means."[8] Theology presses the question of the final meaning of things implied in the process of hermeneutical inquiry.

The type of apologetics we are briefly advocating seeks to raise the question of God within the philosophical framework of the general possibilities of human experience and knowledge. It may be called a "new style of natural theology."[9] It stops short of claiming to possess definitive knowledge of "God and divine things" on which human beings can base a life of faith, hope, and love. But it does ground the meaning of the *idea* of God in the structures of common human experience. In this way we may claim a certain formal continuity with the twofold approach to the knowledge of God in classical dogmatics, through natural reason *and* through special revelation.

METHOD IN THEOLOGY

The method of theology must be adequate to its subject matter. It should be evident from the division of theology as a whole into exegetical, historical, systematic, and practical disciplines that the method appropriate to theology is bound to be complex. If we define Christian theology as the "science" which deals with the self-revelation of God in the history of Jesus Christ as confessed by the faith of the Christian church, we have reason to be open to every method that proves itself through trial and error to be capable of investigating the realities to which the elements of this comprehensive definition refer. There is no one absolute approach that can do everything theology requires. Despite the relativity of method, however, we can discuss various indispensable methodological principles that continue to prove their worth for theological work.

First. *Faith* is the methodological point of departure for every branch of real theology. We may call this the existential factor at work in all theological research and reflection, hidden or manifest. Anselm of Canterbury gave us the most succinct definition of theology as "faith in search of understanding" (*fides quaerens intellectum*). Luther called for a *theologia pectoralis*, saying that it is the heart that makes a theologian. Søren Kierkegaard, the father of modern existentialism, stated, "Subjectivity is truth," explaining that religious truth can be grasped only with infinite personal passionate interest. This captured the same point the pietists made earlier, insisting on a "theology of the regenerate," in contrast to the possibility of a "theology of the irregenerate," a notion some of the orthodox party had overzealously advanced to stress the objective character of truth. Paul Tillich claimed that the theologian, in distinction from a philosopher of religion, must stand within the "theological circle," for "the object of theology is what concerns us ultimately. Only those propositions are theological which deal with their object so far as it can become a matter of ultimate concern for us."[10] Similarly, Rudolf Bultmann stated that it only makes sense to speak of God from one's concrete existential situation, from a commitment of faith.

This idea that faith is the starting point of theology must be carefully distinguished from the error of nineteenth-century theological subjectivism, rooted in Schleiermacher's definition of religion as "feeling of absolute dependence." Faith would then be not merely the starting point but the source of theology, generating religious experiences that become objectified in the form of doctrinal statements. If faith is productive of its own basis and contents, the believer is caught in a vicious cycle of egocentric subjectivism. The great Erlangen theologian J. C. K. von Hofmann tried to improve on Schleiermacher's subjectivism of religious feeling by making the consciousness of the Christian person the object of theology. However, the danger of a solipsism of faith remains, as the gaze of the believer is radically turned inward.

Faith is not religious feeling or emotion in general, nor is it specifically Christian experience or consciousness as such. Faith in the biblical sense is not a human phenomenon that can be created by exercising at will a particular faculty of religious experience. The identifying mark of Christian faith is given by its object, so that faith is always faith in the living God whose self-identification is in the person of Jesus, God's Son and our Lord. Faith is not the source of theological knowledge; it does not produce the data of historical revelation; it is a state of radical receptivity. Faith receives what revelation gives. It is the receiving side of a relationship which the Spirit of God has created.

Second. The standpoint of existential faith does not diminish the fact that theology also claims to be an academic discipline with a reasonable method. For centuries theologians have debated whether theology is a *science*, and if so, of what kind. If theology is the "science of God," its claim to knowledge is not limited to the devotees of a believing sect, but has universal validity. The idea of God, by definition, is not merely a matter of private experience, but deals with the final power which determines the being and meaning of all reality. Any God who is less than this is no God at all. Yet it has been questioned whether theology can be seriously considered a "science," that is, a discipline dealing with some field of knowledge with an appropriate method.

It should be freely acknowledged that theology does not exhibit the ideal of science prevalent in the fields of mathematics and the natural sciences, but neither do any of the other humanistic disciplines—art, literature, history, politics, economics, and numerous others. Theology, like all these, must take great care in applying the most adequate procedures in dealing with its subject matter. It should also be admitted that theology is not a science in the usual sense that its object is potentially accessible to every rational human being. Reason alone is not sufficient; faith is an indispensable presupposition of theology. But if faith refers to an attitude of special interest in its object, theology is not alone in requiring such a passionate commitment in the process of inquiry. Art and music most obviously require a similar attitude. No doubt every science calls for a dimension of insight and interest in its specific field of inquiry as a condition for finding new truth.

The most serious difficulty in defending the "scientific" character of theology arises from the common claim that true science is limited to knowledge

17

about empirical objects in the world. There can, of course, be no empirical knowledge of God, because God is not an object at the disposal of our sensory perception. However, the concept of science need not be limited to an empiricist account of human knowledge. Should theology then abandon the claim to be a science in some sense, or work together with other humanistic disciplines to broaden the understanding of knowledge, and then render a reasonable account of its method appropriate to its own subject matter? Here we can only briefly outline the elements of a workable method in theology.

Theology is a human science. The mind at work in theology is the same mind called on to perform all other kinds of mental operations. The human mind is a dynamic structure of inquiry, moving forward in a ceaseless pattern of questioning beyond all known limits. This boundless propensity of the human mind to transcend every given answer represents a thrust toward the infinite mystery of being. The image of God in the human mind (the *imago dei*) may be interpreted as the orientation of human being toward ultimate reality, toward a complete set of answers to the most complete set of questions, embracing the universal, total, and final future of all things. Theology is ultimately concerned about a total understanding of all that can be understood, because its goal is the knowledge of God, the One who determines the meaning and being of everything that exists. The *logos* of theology has universal meaning.

In Christian faith the universal *logos* has become concrete. The method of theology is intended to bring to contemporary expression the ultimate meaning of what occurred in the concrete history of Jesus the Christ of God. In Jesus of Nazareth the eschatological kingdom of God became an incarnate reality, engendering hope in a future of universal fulfillment for all humanity. The test of the adequacy of theological method is whether it can thematize the significance of the Christ-event for one's theory of knowledge and view of the world, for epistemology and metaphysics. This means that faith as the methodological point of departure and reason as the instrument of understanding do not struggle against each other, but work together in a creative way. Thus, there is a two-way movement in theology, faith in search of understanding (*fides quaerens intellectum*) and understanding of faith (*intellectus quaerens fidem*). *Intellectus* without *fides* leads to rationalism; *fides* without *intellectus* falls into emotionalism.

The anthropological presupposition of theology is the presence of the image of God in human nature. This image is the root of the possibility of understanding the self-revelation of God. It is operative as the desire to know the "not yet" known, in quest of "the knowledge of things hoped for."[11] This leads theology to stress the function of the imagination and the role of myth in the knowledge of ultimate reality. The natural scientist and the rational philosopher do not possess the only ways to the knowledge of reality. The prophet and the poet, the storyteller and the myth-maker, have nourished a dimension of the human mind moved by the logic of anticipation, exhibiting its power in the medium of images, symbols, and myths that relate to the future of all reality. The human mind possesses a *sensus divinitatis*, the uncommon sense of people who divine the realm of "the true, the good, and the beautiful." Theology draws on this power of the imagination to mediate a critique of the present situation (prophetic judgment) and participation in the promise of the future (redemptive grace). The Old Testament speaks of "knowing" in this uncommon sense of sharing the secret mystery of things beyond their obvious meaning.

When the faculty of imagination is fully operative, it makes the human mind aware that there is another dimension of reality that does not yet exist. Method in theology must be guided by this dual dimension of the mind that corresponds to the nature of an unfinished and imperfect world. The method of theology must help us read the world in a realistic way, discerning the signs of contrast between the world as it is and the coming of the new. This power of the imagination to participate in the realm of the coming future is a structural part of the human mind potentially possessed by all, though many succeed in stifling their capacity to see beyond the end of their nose. Very often the knowledge of the realm of the future takes a negative form in the present, in the awareness of darkness, misery, and evil, and in protest against these negative forces. But the knowledge of the deficiency of things as they are may be coupled with the positive desire to transcend this negative state in the power of a more promising future. Otherwise despair is granted the last word. The knowledge of theological truth focuses not only on what already existing reality contains but also on what it fails to contain. Otherwise knowledge is one-sided, merely analytical and positivistic.

Thus the anticipatory dimension of knowledge must be given an adequate place in epistemology.[12] Anticipation is an integral element of the activity of knowing. The future of reality must be envisioned in the construction of a whole frame of reference within which all the fragments of knowledge can be given a meaningful place in relation to each other. The horizon of the future is an essential condition of the universal scope of a theological project of thought. A theological statement is a projection of the imagination that pictures God as the comprehensive unity of all things in their final state of being. Without this theological frame of reference, the unity of life's meaning falls apart into bits and pieces of experience, and the idea of truth as a whole is broken into fragments and segments of information. Theology can thus be called a "science" in the sense that it makes statements about God who is conceived to be the unifying power, universal meaning, and fulfilling destiny of all things. Without this reference to God, there can be no vision of the whole. Then human confidence in the worthwhileness of life and creation is threatened by a world of facts without values, movement without meaning, process without purpose, journey without goal, and future without promise beyond the prospect of nothingness and death.

Third. The material content of theological statements about God derives from given texts and traditions of *history*. Inasmuch as Christian theology depends on historical sources, it is bound to use the critical methods of research common to historical science in general. The aim of the historical method is not only to establish facts, but also to search out their meanings in their original historical context. The latter is the primary aim of an historical hermeneutic. There are no naked facts as such that interpret themselves. Historical facts are always suspended in traditions of interpretation which keep them alive in the stream of a community's memories and hopes.

The historical criticism of the biblical texts and sacred traditions on which Christianity is based has been feared by conservative Christians as the destruction of the foundations of faith. Actually, however, the historical method is an indispensable ally of Christian theology. Paul Tillich said it well:

> The historical approach to Biblical literature is one of the great events in the history of Christianity and even of religion and human culture. It is one of the elements of which Protestantism can be proud. It was an expression of Protestant courage when theologians subjected the holy writings of their own church to a critical analysis through the historical method. It appears that no other religion in human history exercises such boldness and took upon itself the same risk.[13]

The historical-critical method is a tool which can be used by historians and believers from every school of thought. It is not essentially bound up with any particular set of presuppositions, nor do the results of its application favor any particular dogmatic position. Liberals and conservatives, naturalists and supernaturalists, use the findings of historical research to defend their own convictions. It is clear that the methods and results of critical scholarship are invoked by people on all sides of every conceivable issue. This highlights the fact that there is no such thing as a neutral appeal to the authority of modern historical science. Every historian is in fact coming from his or her own set of presuppositions, embedded in his or her own *Weltanschauung*, whether acknowledged or not. Many historians are blind to the role their own prior assumptions play in their scientific investigations. As a rule they need to have other critics open their eyes to the extent to which their own ideology controls their scholarly research. Usually scholars can see the ideological speck in the eyes of their critics more clearly than the beam of prejudice at work hidden in their own minds. The critical scholar, however, need not remain isolated, but works best within a community of scholars in a spirit of mutual criticism and freedom to pursue the path of truth wherever it might lead.

The first task of the historical method is research. Leopold von Ranke, the great German scholar, formulated the perennial ideal of the critical historian: to find out what actually happened. The historical method of research must be applied both to the texts of the Bible and to the traditions of the church. Criticism is necessary because numerous absurd beliefs claim for their support the witness of Scripture and Christian tradition. The clearing of the ground of mere opinion by discerning what really happened can help the ongoing process of reform in the church and the renewal of theology.

The second step of the historical method is interpretation. History is more than a reconstruction of naked facts of history. We always find the facts in a context of meaning, or we simply cannot grasp anything at all. In contemporary theology the task of interpretation is commonly referred to as hermeneutics. The texts and traditions of the Christian faith must be encountered for the sake of their meaning, first in terms of their original contexts and second in terms of the contemporary context of the interpreter. Without this process of interpretation in the historical method, we end up with a mere hodgepodge of names and dates and places and events. There is a living, dynamic, forward-moving history to be understood: the history of Israel among the nations, the history of Jesus and the apostolic community, the history of the life and doctrine of the Christian churches in the context of the general history of the world, right up to the present time. It is not possible to encounter the texts and traditions of all this history, from the past to the present, without taking a stand in some way, without daring to make judgments and decisions, without personal participation and self-involving encounter with the meaning of the texts and traditions of Christianity.

Traditionally, hermeneutics was defined in a narrow sense as the system of rules to be followed in biblical exegesis. In the modern discussion hermeneutics deals more broadly with all the conditions involved in the interpretation of history and historical documents.

Friedrich Schleiermacher is the father of modern hermeneutical theory. He realized that more is involved in biblical interpretation than the application of a set of principles. The gap between what a text meant in its own context and what it means now in a new context must be bridged somehow. Schleiermacher, and later Wilhelm Dilthey, proposed a psychological theory of hermeneutical understanding. The interpreter must somehow penetrate a text by an act of psychological imagination in order to reproduce the original creative moment of the author and his or her feeling for life.

Rudolf Bultmann revised Schleiermacher's hermeneutics, retaining its character as a theory of understanding at work in the interpretation of historical documents. Bultmann focused on the presupposition of all historical interpretation, the existential interest of the interpreter as one who puts a question to which the answer coming from the text will correspond. There is no research without presuppositions, without some prior understanding of what a given text is all about, else one would not be motivated to inquire into its subject matter.

Fourth. Theology has frequently suffered from a fatal separation of the historical and the dogmatic methods. There has been a dualism consisting of two tracks, the facts of history going along one and the interpretations of faith along another. Theological hermeneutics seeks to unify the two approaches so that every new and serious interpretation is a creative synthesis of the results of historical research and the life situation of the present interpreter. Dogmatics enters into the hermeneutical process because theologians approach the text neither from a neutral point of view nor even from a merely existential standpoint. It is simply not the case, as Bultmann claims, that "the interpretation of biblical writings is not subject to conditions different from those applying to all other kinds of literature."[14] In their biblical interpretation theologians do bring a prior understanding of the Word of God conditioned by the life of faith and the worship of the church. General factors of philosophical and historical understanding retain their validity throughout, but in addition there is an ecclesiological dimension which acknowledges that God continues to speak to the church through the Scriptures.

Theology approaches the Bible as canon. This is a datum of prior understanding which cannot be derived from any philosophical theory or any result of historical research. What the Bible has meant as the canon in the tradition of the church and the life of believers, namely, the medium of the unique message of God's saving history, must be taken into account in a theological treatment of hermeneutics. Dogmatics is thus directly linked to the hermeneutical concern, because the interpretation of Scripture and dogmatic reflection are both carried on for the sake of the proclamation which creates and sustains the church. One of the main tasks of dogmatics is to facilitate the movement from the Bible to present-day preaching. This hermeneutical task of dogmatics is successfully carried out when the gulf is bridged from the written text of Scripture to the audible event of preaching.

The hermeneutical process does not take place by a leap from the Bible to a present-day sermon. The traditions of the church provide hermeneutical guidelines for biblical interpretation. The creeds and confessions of the church are important links in the hermeneutical chain that connects the biblical message with the contemporary church. Theologians who choose to interpret the Scriptures apart from the mainstream of the tradition tend to produce novel teachings out of touch with the church's life and mission. Especially Protestants have been so allergic to dogma that they try to reach back to the Bible for a kerygma that will leapfrog into the present without the intermediate developments of tradition. This widespread indifference to the significance of dogma accounts for the massive attenuation of Christian substance in the multiplicity of sects and denominations in Protestantism.

The dogma of the church does not automatically guarantee the faithful transmission of the biblical message into the contemporary situation. It is the Spirit who breathes life into the texts of Scripture and the words of tradition, so that the Christian community may be empowered by the hearing of the living Word. It is finally the Spirit who closes the hermeneutical gap between the biblical Word and the human world. It is the Spirit who fills the earthen vessels with heavenly treasures. The inner witness of the Holy Spirit within the community of faith and worship is an event that cannot be controlled by a rational hermeneutic or ecclesiastical magisterium. The Spirit blows where and when he wills.

The hermeneutical circle would not be complete without mention of the liturgy as the medium in which the church receives the living presence of the biblical Christ. The Spirit makes use of the liturgy to transmit the apostolic witness to Jesus Christ. In the liturgy the history of God with the world and God's chosen people is recited, remembered, and represented in a way that links the past to the eschatological future kingdom which the sacrament of Christ's body and blood makes really present.

Fifth. The Christian faith claims to represent the absolute, ultimate, unconditional, and everlasting *truth* of God in the once-for-all event of self-revelation in the person and history of Jesus Christ. It has always been difficult to delineate the conditions under which this claim to truth can be acknowledged. The New Testament clearly states that the final truth of faith will always meet the resistance of unbelief. What is wisdom to faith is foolishness to the world; the dynamics of agape infinitely surpass the reasonable demands of the law; and hope runs contrary to all appearances at hand.

Today the theological statement of truth is complicated by certain modern forms of consciousness. (1) Historical relativism deeply conditions our modern consciousness of truth. There is nothing in the world of human history exempt from the universal flux of things. Everything without exception is thus subject to historical analysis. There are no timeless ideals or values that exist above and beyond this one-dimensional history of humankind, no suprahistorical reality free from the laws and principles that govern all other events. In light of this radical historicism, all historical life becomes profane.

(2) The modern consciousness of truth is influenced by naturalistic reductionism. Human beings exist within a closed continuum of natural causes and effects. Without exception everything in history is explained in analogy with the phenomena of nature. What is un-natural or super-natural is *a priori* excluded from the realm of possibility. The ideal of science is to explain things in the most natural, simple, probable, predictable, and exact way. An awareness

23

of truth that confines itself to the limits of nature alone will be inherently skeptical of belief in providence or miracles. Everything going on in the real world is subject to the unbreakable laws of nature. And there can be no exception.

(3) The corollary of these two aspects of the modern concept of truth—historicism and naturalism—is an autonomous view of human reason. Reason is taken to be the measure of all truth. It would be a theological error to define faith in absolute contradiction to reason. It would be equally erroneous to require that the insights of faith be proved by the operations of reason. The history of the relations between faith and reason is full of variety and change. Faith has no special interest in defending irrationalism. There is a noetic element of faith, something to be known. It is not only a matter of feeling. A split between reason and faith is as intolerable as a reduction of faith to what reason will allow. If rationalism blunts faith, fideism throws the believer helplessly into a position of blind trust or the abyss of empty feeling. In the final analysis, faith is a gift of the Spirit, not the product of reason. Faith cannot be accounted for within the limits of reason alone. Rationalism invariably discounts the effect of the fall and sin on the capacity of reason to acknowledge the truth of God and his revelation.

(4) A fourth factor in determining the modern consciousness of truth is pragmatism. Pragmatism comes from the Greek word *prattein*, "to do." According to pragmatism, the criterion of truth is "what works." In France, Maurice Blondel's philosophy of action stressed that the center of philosophy must be shifted from intellection to action. The Blondelian shift in theory, as applied to theology, means that truth becomes present through choosing and doing, that the intellect alone is not the faculty of access to the real. Existentialism followed suit in stressing the moment of decision in human existence. The analytic philosophy of language, influenced by Wittgenstein, also emphasized that the meaning of language does not lie in its correspondence to an eternal world of ideas and objects, but is tied to its function within a particular "language game."

In contemporary theology the shift to the practical criterion of truth is taking place under the impact of the Marxist theory of praxis. From the left wing of the Hegelian school in the nineteenth century arose the call for philosophy to become practical in a revolutionary sense. Marx wrote in his "Theses on Feuerbach," "The philosophers have only interpreted the world in various ways; the point is to change it."[15] The attainment of objective truth, Marx said, is not a theoretical question but a practical question.

The Marxist theory of praxis has been appropriated by German political theology and Latin American liberation theology as a new criterion of truth. Jürgen Moltmann stated, "The new criterion of theology and of faith is to be found in praxis."[16] This calls for a radically new model of truth quite unlike anything we can find in the classical Christian tradition. The heart of this novel proposal is the notion of the priority of practical activity to change the world. The Marxist idea of the priority of praxis cannot, however, be assumed into the Christian understanding of truth without utterly destroying the foundations on which it stands. In Marxist theory, the acting subject of transformative praxis is the human agent. In Christian theology the prius of fundamental change in history is the activity of God in establishing the right of divine rule. The divine indicative is prior to any human imperative. The idea of the priority of praxis has given rise to the substitution of an orthopraxis for an orthodoxy, leading to the legalization of the Christian faith.

GOD
↓
HUMAN

The power to change the world in a fundamental way is not within human control. Transformative praxis can only be the historic working out of the reconciliation that the gospel has announced for the world through God's act in Christ. Within the structure of a Christian theology, the notion of the priority of Jesus' message of the kingdom of God is the prius of transformative praxis. Ethics stems from eschatology; the ground of the possibility of a truly liberating praxis lies in the eschatological event of God's kingdom in Christ. The criterion of the gospel comes first; praxis is always a second step.

These four modern post-Enlightenment forms of consciousness concerning truth—historicism, naturalism, rationalism, pragmatism—give expression to the common underlying premise of the autonomy of the human subject: "Man is the measure of all truth." The modern trend toward autonomy can be seen as a legitimate expression of the drive toward freedom and liberation from every heteronomous system of authority, ecclesiastical or secular. Christian theology cannot locate the final criterion of the truth it seeks on either side of the conflict between autonomy and heteronomy, although its own vision of absolute freedom will place it decidedly in sympathy with all who struggle to overthrow dehumanizing structures of domination, religious or political. The criterion of truth in Christian theology is grounded in the gospel of Jesus Christ, the authorized medium of the freedom which promises to set people free from *every* kind of bondage. True authority, as opposed to heteronomous authoritarianism, has its ultimate source in the power of freedom which God exercised in raising the crucified Jesus from the dead.

The task of dogmatics is to understand and interpret the authority of Jesus Christ and the apostolic witness in relation to the later history of Christianity and the faith of the church today. Without the authority of Jesus Christ and the derivative witness of Scripture and the tradition, Christian theology is unthinkable. This clearly implies a disclosure model of truth and revelation, which does not eliminate but invites the help of auxiliary disciplines such as historical criticism, phenomenological inquiry, sociological research, and ontological reflection to interpret the connections and correlations between the texts and traditions of revelation and the conditions and experiences of human existence.

The authority of Jesus Christ in mediating the revelation of God to the generations of humankind is transmitted through Scripture and the symbols of tradition. The eschatological promise of the gospel in the history of Jesus is the basis of the unity of Scripture and the continuity of the Christian tradition. The history of doctrine, and particularly the ecumenical creeds and dogmas of the church, help transmit the message of God's saving presence in Jesus the Christ that transcends and relativizes that history itself. Nothing in the tradition of the church, not even its most crucial doctrines and offices, can be exempt from the criticism that emanates from the eschatological word of God in the person of Jesus Christ.

The final future of God is proleptically manifest in the christological foundation of the church. The church in history meets every new situation with reference to that transcendent future which has already been previewed in the coming of the crucified and risen Lord. The anticipation of this future reacts on the church's memory of the Word of Scripture and its traditional structures of faith and witness, putting the question whether they can still serve as instruments of the church's mission in the world. The fact that a structure can be traced back to the church fathers in the first five centuries, or some other period of church history, or even back to the Bible, is no sufficient reason to keep it. The authority of Scripture itself is based on what it conveys concerning Jesus Christ, not on its antiquity or sanction by church dogma. This is what it means to speak with Luther of *was Christum treibt* as the final criterion of truth in theology.

NOTES

1. Jürgen Moltmann, *The Experiment Hope*, trans. M. Douglas Meeks (Philadelphia: Fortress Press, 1975), p. 104.

2. Friedrich Schleiermacher, *Brief Outline on the Study of Theology*, trans. Terrence N. Tice (Richmond, Va.: John Knox Press, 1966), p. 20.

3. Friedrich Schleiermacher, *The Christian Faith*, ed. H. R. Mackintosh and J. S. Stewart (Edinburgh: T. & T. Clark, 1928), p. 4.

4. Paul Tillich, *Systematic Theology*, 3 vols. (Chicago: University of Chicago Press, 1951–63), 1:7.

5. An example is Langdon Gilkey's *Naming the Whirlwind: The Renewal of God-Language* (Indianapolis: Bobbs-Merrill, 1969).

6. See Karl Rahner's one-volume theology, *Foundations of Christian Faith*, trans. William V. Dych (New York: Seabury Press, 1978).

7. Wolfhart Pannenberg's program of theology as a whole is an apologetic answer

to the modern question of meaning. See esp. his *Theology and the Philosophy of Science*, trans. Francis McDonagh (Philadelphia: Westminster Press, 1976).

8. The observation is by Hans Albert, quoted by Pannenberg, *Theology and the Philosophy of Science*, p. 126.

9. I have adopted this term from John Macquarrie, *Principles of Christian Theology* (New York: Charles Scribner's Sons, 1966), p. 48, and first applied it in my own way in my *The Future of God* (New York: Harper & Row, 1969).

10. Tillich, *Systematic Theology*, 1:12.

11. See Robert W. Jenson, *The Knowledge of Things Hoped For* (New York and London: Oxford University Press, 1969).

12. This point is a major contribution of Pannenberg to theological epistemology in *Theology and the Philosophy of Science*.

13. Tillich, *Systematic Theology*, 2:107.

14. Rudolf Bultmann, "The Problem of Hermeneutics," in *Essays*, trans. James C. G. Greig (London: SCM Press, 1955), p. 238.

15. Quoted in Ernst Bloch, *On Karl Marx*, trans. John Maxwell (New York: Herder & Herder, 1971), p. 57.

16. Jürgen Moltmann, *Religion, Revolution, and the Future* (New York: Charles Scribner's Sons, 1969), p. 138.

2

The Heritage
of Dogmatics

The history of dogmatics is a specialized field of theology. There are good reasons, however, to include an overview of the heritage of dogmatics in this introduction. The primary reason is didactic: Dogmatic reflection presupposes the concrete historical development of each of its themes. There is also a methodological reason: Every dogmatics begins within the context of a particular tradition and makes its inquiries into Scripture, gospel, dogma, philosophy, and culture from that standpoint.

THE DISCIPLINE

Dogmatics, as the term suggests, is a theological discipline that deals with the church's dogmas. It was first used in the seventeenth century by Lukas Reinhard in the title of his theological system, *Synopsis Theologiae Dogmaticae* (1659).[1] It was a synonym for other commonly used titles such as "Summa," "Loci," "Institutio," "Compendium," and "Medulla." These contain summaries and interpretations of the doctrinal decisions of the church covering all the chief articles of the Christian faith. In the nineteenth and twentieth centuries dogmatics became a highly specialized discipline in both Protestant and Roman Catholic circles, exemplified most eminently by Karl Barth's *Church Dogmatics* and Michael Schmaus's *Katholische Dogmatik*.

The term "dogmatics" may be of recent origin, but its substance is not. The heritage of dogmatics reaches back into the New Testament, where Paul speaks of preserving the "truth of the gospel" (Gal. 2:5, 14). The root of dogmatics is just such insight into the content of the gospel that its preaching might be true and every false doctrine, which inhibits a clear witness to the truth, might be decisively rejected. John too speaks much about the witness to the truth, who is Jesus Christ himself. The seeds of the dogmatic concern can be found in the apostolic testimony to the wisdom (*sophia*), the knowledge (*gnosis*), and witness (*marturia*) to the truth essential for communicating the gospel of salvation in the name of Jesus Christ.

1 / PROLEGOMENA TO CHRISTIAN DOGMATICS

Works on the history of dogma have been written by many scholars, most notably Adolf von Harnack,[2] but no one has yet written a history of dogmatics. Though no such thing can be attempted here, it may still prove useful to ground this introduction to dogmatics in a brief sketch of the main characteristics of dogmatics from earliest times to the present.[3] Instruction in dogmatics can be facilitated both by a systematic analysis of its fundamental elements as well as by an historical recapitulation of its development. Each topic in this outline of dogmatics is filled with references to historical materials from different periods of church history. This sketch can serve as a map to prepare the reader for the various excursions authors take below into the vast regions of classical dogmatics.

THE ANCIENT CHURCH

There is a notable difference between the dogmatic thinking of the Greek fathers of the East and the Latin fathers of the West. The Greek fathers tended toward speculative thought, delving into the deepest mysteries into which the mind can aspire. The Latin fathers were bound more to practical activity, concerned about legitimate authority and order in the church. The cast of their mind and interest was more juridical than speculative, oriented more to church *praxis* than mystical *gnosis*.

The earliest root of dogmatics can be seen in the apologies written by some of the Eastern fathers. The apologists wrote to defend the Christian faith to the outside pagan world. Their basic apologetic motive was to present Christianity as the fulfillment of the philosophical quest for truth and to affirm Greek philosophy as a preparation for the gospel. Justin Martyr used the concept of the *logos* as the chief term of comparison between Christianity and philosophy. This implied that philosophical concepts are capable of expressing the essence of Christianity. The apologists have been falsely accused of betraying the Christian gospel into the hands of pagan philosophy. They were committed to the belief that the meaning of Jesus Christ can be expressed in categories common to both the Bible and Greek philosophy.

In addition to the apologetic we can see the speculative root of dogmatics most clearly exhibited in the Alexandrian theologians Clement and Origen. These theologians took up the idea of *gnosis* to explain the Christian revelation. Gnosticism is thought to have existed as a pre-Christian mystery religion of Oriental origin, which Christianity encountered in a form transformed by Hellenistic philosophy. Gnosticism taught that mystical knowledge was the way of salvation. The soul aspires to salvation from its bondage to the body, which exists in a radically inferior, physical, fleshly, earth-bound form. Salvation is made possible by the descent of a redeemer from the highest eon to rescue the soul here below, giving it knowledge of the way back home. The gnostic drama of salvation was half mythological and half philosophical. The similarity to the biblical story of salvation was too striking to miss. Christian gnosticism is a fusion of biblical and gnostic symbols of salvation, the most serious heresy to threaten the gospel on Hellenistic soil. The concrete historicity and true humanity of Jesus Christ came to be of secondary importance. The church in the gnosticizing view comprised two levels of Christians: mere believers with nothing but faith (*pistis*) and the truly enlightened, those possessed of knowledge (*gnosis*).

The attempt of Christian gnosticism to transform Christianity into a mystery cult was defeated by church theologians like Clement and Origen. Ordinary believers (*pistikoi*) could grasp the same *logos* of God and his revelation through faith as the gnostics could through knowledge. Admittedly, however, gnosis was the higher form. Clement and Origen were confident that the best insights of philosophy and religion could be appropriated as preparations for the full system of Christian truth. Origen was the first to produce a dogmatics in the Greek language, *Peri Archōn* (*On First Principles*). Origen's significance for dogmatics lay in his fusing of the philosophical understanding of *logos* and *gnosis* with biblical interpretation and theological teaching. The great master was able to hold together biblical exegesis and ontological specula-tion, historical events and timeless ideas (Plato), faith and *gnosis*, *logos* and Jesus. But after Origen, dogmatics found itself at a crossroads: What Origen kept together split between right- and left-wing factions. Writings in dogmatics became embroiled in the struggle of the church to formulate a christology and a doctrine of the Trinity that would keep the preaching of the gospel continuous with the apostolic witness in opposition to various heresies of the time. The writings of Athanasius and the Cappadocian fathers provide ex-amples of this type of dogmatics, but none of these produced a complete dogmatic system.

In Irenaeus we can see another root of dogmatics, the polemical concern for the truth of the gospel against the incursion of heresy inside the church. Irenaeus did not apologetically address the outside pagan world, as Justin did, nor did he speculatively accommodate Hellenistic wisdom, in the manner of Clement and Origen. Rather, he polemically attacked the gnostic heresy that had erupted inside the church itself. The power behind Irenaeus's dogmatic thrust came from the biblical history of salvation. What theology has recently referred to as "history of salvation" (*Heilsgeschichte*) is adumbrated in Irenaeus's idea of theology as a recapitulation of the economy of salvation in the Bible.

Dogmatics in the East reached its zenith in the orthodox theological system of John of Damascus, building on the chief dogmas of the church, Trinity and christology. Then the creative period of dogmatics in the Eastern church came virtually to an end. Since then the tendency in the dogmatics of Eastern

Orthodoxy has been to reproduce and preserve the traditions formulated by the ancient ecumenical councils.

The West built on the foundations of dogmatics laid in the East, but moved forward in a continual quest for a more precise system of concepts of practical relevance for the church. Tertullian was the first Western theologian to shape the Latin concepts used in later dogmatic thought. He was trained in jurisprudence and demonstrated the skills of a legal expert in choosing precise terminology, particularly in the areas of christology and anthropology. Cyprian, a follower of Tertullian and precursor of Augustine (all three of North Africa) left an indelible mark on the emerging Catholic doctrine of the church. But without doubt the greatest achievement in Western theology was reached by Augustine. Before embracing the orthodox dogmas of the church, Augustine's restless quest for saving truth led him to try the leading options of the day in Manichaean dualism, Ciceronian stoicism, and finally Neo-Platonism. Augustine's journey through the religio-philosophical systems of his epoch meant that as a theologian he would be challenged to answer their questions and to question their answers, and thus significantly broaden the heritage of Western dogmatic thought.

Augustine's dogmatic reflection on how he turned from Neo-Platonism to become a Christian placed a lasting stamp on the subsequent theology of grace in the medieval church and the Protestant Reformation. Augustine's passion was to know, as he said, "God and the soul, only God and the soul." Neo-Platonism taught him that the soul longs to make its way, through mystical contemplation, back to its origin in God. He became a Christian when he discovered the reverse movement of grace, that God in overpowering love comes, through the incarnation, down to the human soul. This is what happened in Jesus Christ, and this is what the church exists to communicate.

Once he became a Christian, Augustine found himself in a struggle against two movements within the church which seemed to threaten the meaning of grace. These movements, Donatism and Pelagianism, sought to restore the moral vigor of the church. Donatism, named after the schismatic bishop Donatus, aimed to purify the church by getting rid of clergy who had lapsed under persecution. This would make the efficacy of grace through Word and sacraments dependent on the moral worthiness of the priest and thereby spell the denial of God's unmerited grace. Pelagianism, named after the monk Pelagius, was declared a heresy because its notion of free will, coupled with the rejection of original sin, kept open the possibility of not sinning, thus denying the necessity of special grace. These movements represent the classical ecclesiological and soteriological heresies, which again and again have surfaced in church history under new guises, with the identical result of converting the gospel into law.

No other theologian in the West matched Augustine in contributing to the history of dogmatics. His teaching was so many-sided that both the reformers and the Roman theologians in the sixteenth century could appeal to Augustine for support, the reformers to his doctrine of sin and grace, law and gospel, letter and spirit, and the Romans, seemingly with equal right, to his concept of nature and grace, eros and agape, city of God and city of earth, and the hierarchical church as an institution dispensing sacraments of salvation.

Our review of dogmatics in the ancient church has given samples of different lines of development. They were the *apologetic* address to the outside pagan world, the *polemical* attack on heresies inside the church, and the *speculative* interest in building up a comprehensive system of Christian truth.

THE MIDDLE AGES

In the Middle Ages dogmatics reaped the harvest of the victory of the church in the Roman Empire. Culturally and politically paganism had given way to the Christian world. Two common prejudices need to be set aside. The first is the prejudice of the Enlightenment, which characterized this thousand-year period as the "Dark Ages" in contrast to the illumination of modern times. The second and opposite prejudice is that of romanticism, which idealized the organic unity and wholeness of religious and cultural life in the Middle Ages, in contrast to the fragmentation which Protestantism brought about. Modern scholarship has invalidated these stereotypes about the medieval period, bringing to light both the creativity and the diversity of the medieval contribution to Christian thought. It was neither as barren nor as monolithic as these distorted pictures would have us believe.

In this section we will list the most notable characteristics of medieval dogmatics, citing some of the classical works in which they were typically embodied.

1. The first is the *scholastic method.* The term "scholastic" refers to the method and doctrines taught by schoolmen in the medieval universities from the tenth to the fifteenth century. Regrettably it has come to mean pedantic quibbling about pointless issues, such as how many angels can dance on the point of a needle, or whether God, being omnipotent, can create a stone so large even God cannot move it. Actually, scholastic method was a dialectical treatment of the church's tradition, gathering opposing views and trying to harmonize the various decrees and doctrines through a process of "yes and no." Abelard's book, *Sic et Non* (Yes and No), set the pattern for all the later scholastics. This dialectical method aimed to reinforce the authority of the tradition by overcoming its apparent internal contradictions.

2. Scholastic theology presupposed the authority of the *tradition.* It proceeded by collecting the sentences of the fathers on the doctrines of faith and

then commenting on them. Peter Lombard's *Four Books of Sentences* became the manual of scholasticism and continued as a classic into the period of the Reformation and Protestant orthodoxy.

3. Scholasticism used *reason* to articulate faith and tradition. Anselm of Canterbury formulated the principle *"credo ut intelligam"* (I believe in order to understand). Faith and tradition are the prior givens; reason and theology are a second step, involving interpretation, even speculation. But not all scholastics agree with Anselm's way to harmonize faith and reason. There was the complementary model of Thomas Aquinas, in which supernatural faith supplements and completes the knowledge of God which reason can gain by natural means. In late scholasticism, the nominalist William of Ockham related faith and reason in an oppositional model. Faith becomes radically subject to authority, because reason is totally incapable of grasping the real ground and contents of faith.

4. There was, moreover, a core of *mysticism* in all of medieval theology, despite its formal allegiance to authority, tradition, and dialectics. Bernard of Clairvaux was the most eminent representative of Christian mysticism. The aim of Christian mysticism was to make the objective substance of Scripture and tradition a matter of subjective experience. Medieval mysticism was deeply nourished by the stream of Neo-Platonism in the Christian tradition, particularly as it was transmitted through the writings of Augustine and Pseudo-Dionysius. Theologically, Christian mysticism stressed the reality of God in the picture of Christ, and ethically the principle of following Jesus.

5. There was only one short step from Neo-Platonic mysticism to *pantheism*. In the early Middle Ages, Johannes Scotus Erigena wrote an outline of systematic theology, *De divisione naturae*, in which he poured the substance of Christian faith into the mystical ontological system of Neo-Platonism. Pantheistic ideas mingled with mystical piety in many of the great scholastics, including Anselm, Bonaventura, and Thomas Aquinas. In this pantheistic way of thinking, creation is conceived of as the actualization of the ideas in the divine mind; everything exists by virtue of participation in the divine being. This trend came to its fullest expression in German mysticism, particularly in the thought of Meister Eckhart.

6. Of utmost importance in the history of medieval scholasticism was the union of Augustine and Aristotle in the *Summa Theologica* of Thomas Aquinas. Thomas was undoubtedly the greatest of the dogmaticians since Augustine. He used the philosophy of Aristotle as an intellectual instrument to set forth the contents of the Christian revelation. Everything found a place in his system: faith and reason, nature and grace, the world and the church, intellectual thought and mystical piety, biblical exegesis and philosophical speculations. It is fitting that he should be called the Doctor of the Church

in Roman Catholicism, and not merely one of the church fathers, because his system is the purest expression of a Catholic vision of God and the world.

7. The introduction of Aristotle into the theological curriculum of the High Middle Ages (thirteenth century) meant that the classical conflicts in philosophy between Platonism and Aristotelianism would be renewed on theological soil. The Augustinians, steeped in Platonism, were not prepared to give way to the "modernism" (*via moderna*) of Thomas Aquinas, with his Aristotelian categories. This was a conflict between a more mystical experiential approach to theology and a more rational scientific approach. One form of this conflict became focused on the problem of universals. It is possible to refer to a whole set of individuals that belong to the same class by one word or name. What unites all the individuals is a universal. Medieval theologians battled over the ontological status of the universals. The Platonic line generally taught that the universals are the realities, existing independently and prior to their embodiment in individual entities. They exist, as it were, in the mind of God, and only thereafter become concepts in the human mind, while being actualized in the individuals of a particular class. Though this position is commonly called medieval realism, it resembles more closely what modern philosophy refers to as idealism. The extreme opposite position became known as nominalism, which holds that universals have no reality in themselves. There are only individual things that become grouped together under a common name or concept. Medieval theologians struggled with this problem of the ontological status of universals and individuals, with far-reaching repercussions in every area of dogmatics. The main schools of late medieval theology—Thomism, Scotism, and Ockhamism—were divided on the precise application of the philosophical problem of universals to theological doctrines.

Although the theologians of the High Middle Ages were receptive to philosophy, they kept it safely subordinate to the authority of the church, assigning to it at best the role of "handmaid" of theology. With confidence they developed the theory of a natural and a revealed theology, joined together in close harmony, the one as the preparation for the other.

THE REFORMATION

Martin Luther, the foremost leader of the Protestant Reformation, was not a dogmatician or systematic theologian. The starting point of Luther's reforming work was not dogma but gospel. His intention was to go deeper than dogma, down to the bedrock of gospel truth concerning how human beings really stand before God. Luther expressed his thoughts in exegetical works, such as his lectures on Romans and his commentary on Galatians, in sermons, and in an abundance of occasional and polemical writings. All this material was pre-dogmatic, the stuff of which dogma might be constructed by the church. Luther's style was to think in terms of contrasts, for example, the antithesis of law and gospel, and not to systematize his ideas into a harmonious rational synthesis.

Philip Melanchthon's *Loci Communes* of 1521 was the first dogmatics of the Reformation period, winning the praise of both Luther and Calvin. In contrast to the massive *Summas* of medieval scholasticism, Melanchthon's work was merely an outline of dogmatics. "To know Christ is to know his benefits," said Melanchthon, and he followed this principle to reduce the stuff of dogmatics to the questions of soteriology. Melanchthon's little dogmatics underwent a series of editions and achieved its final form in 1559 under the title *Loci praecipui theologici.* Melanchthon's thought had evolved in the meantime. In the earlier work Luther's influence was dominant; the impact of the gospel produced new dogmatic insights into such basic questions as free will, sin, law, justification, faith, works, baptism, and the Lord's Supper. In his latest edition, Melanchthon began to restore certain doctrines of the scholastic tradition, without revising them in light of the new insights of the Reformation. Aristotle's methods and categories, which Luther had expelled, were brought back into the theological system. Thus the later work of Melanchthon formed a bridge to the subsequent dogmatics of Protestant scholasticism.

John Calvin was undoubtedly the most accomplished dogmatician of the Reformation era. His *Institutes of the Christian Religion*, like Melanchthon's *Loci*, gradually evolved through a series of editions until it reached its final form in 1559. It was marked by its biblical orientation and its Augustinian vision of grace, set against every form of Pelagianism in the doctrine of salvation. Although Calvin's intention was to carry forward the reforming work of Luther, it became his destiny to become the theological leader of the Reformed branch of Protestantism, in many ways the polar opposite of Lutheranism.

PROTESTANT ORTHODOXY

The Protestant Reformation, both in its Lutheran and Reformed branches, achieved a highly developed dogmatic form of orthodoxy. Orthodox dogmatics gave a place of prominence once again, as in the Middle Ages, to reason and natural law, cast in Aristotelian thought forms. Yet its chief concern was to frame the central article of the Reformation, justification through faith alone, and to use Scripture alone as the criterion of all true doctrine. These two points, *sola fide* and *sola scriptura*, have been called the material and formal principles of the Reformation.

When the church divided, dogmatics had to become confessional, reflecting either the Roman Catholic theology of the Council of Trent, or the Lutheran theology of the *Book of Concord*, or the Calvinist theology of the Synod of Dort (1618) and various other confessions, such as the Heidelberg Catechism (1563) and the Westminster Confession (1647). These various confessional theologies presupposed the unity of Christian truth and therefore contended with each other's competing claims for the sake of pure doctrine. None could conceive an apology for pluralism, since the loss of consensus in doctrine led directly to political strife and division. In this light it is understandable that the great scholastic systems of the seventeenth century were produced in the midst of the catastrophic religious wars of 1618–48. The central thrust of Lutheran dogmatics was on justifying faith and its realization apart from works of the law, whereas Reformed theology centered in predestinating grace and the unfolding of God's eternal decrees in history. These were not mutually exclusive positions, however, since the Lutherans also affirmed the doctrine of predestination and the Calvinists retained Luther's teaching on justification by faith alone.

Three phases in the development of Lutheran scholastic orthodoxy can be distinguished. First, early orthodoxy was dominated by the theological problems of the Formula of Concord (1577). The leading figure was Martin Chemnitz, whose lectures on Melanchthon's *Loci* were published posthumously as *Loci Theologici*, 1591. The second phase of high orthodoxy was productive of monumental works of doctrine, such as Leonhard Hutter's *Compendium locorum theologicorum* (1610) and Johann Gerhard's *Loci communes theologici* (1610–22). The third phase, that of late orthodoxy, witnessed a massive outpouring of multivolume systems: Abraham Calov's *Systema locorum theologicorum* (1665–77), John Andrew Quenstedt's *Theologia didactico-polemica* (1685), John William Baier's *Compendium theologiae positivae* (1686), and last, David Hollaz's *Examen theologicum acroamaticum* (1707), which marks the end of orthodoxy.

The orthodoxy of Reformed Christianity was far less clearly defined than that of Lutheranism. It possessed no common confession such as the Augsburg Confession (1530) and no book of confessional writings such as the Lutheran *Book of Concord* (1580). It was beset by various movements that challenged the heart of the Calvinist predestinarian system, such as Socinianism, Arminianism, and to some extent also Amyraldism. Finally, Reformed orthodoxy was from the beginning so pluralistic, having spread into so many different countries with such varied languages and cultures, that it remains difficult for historians to define exactly what it is, except that the doctrine of predestination was exalted to the position of dogma.

One of the most significant developments within Reformed Christianity in the period of high orthodoxy was the "federal theology" of Johannes Coccejus, set forth in his *Summa doctrinae de foedere* (1648). This theology inaugurated the modern tendency to introduce the historical perspective into theology. Instead of thinking of predestination as an absolutely preordained decree which God is simply spelling out, predestination can be thought of as something God is working out in stages in the course of history. Here we find the seeds of the contemporary notion of the history of salvation (*Heilsgeschichte*). And here we find also an opening within orthodoxy to the modern historical interpretation of the Bible.

The achievement of Protestant orthodox dogmatics on the whole was considerable. It demonstrated that Aristotelian philosophy could be used as much in the service of Evangelical as of Roman Catholic theology. The great systems of Protestant scholasticism rivaled the greatest *Summas* of the medieval period. They shared many common features: the ideal of a complete system, natural theology, the *loci* method, propositional truth, the tradition of dogma, and an objective authority.

In the sphere of Roman Catholicism dogmatics was greatly stimulated by its ongoing polemical exchanges with the representatives of the Reformation. For example, the Jesuit Robert Bellarmine wrote his *Disputationes de controversiis Christianae fidei* (1586) as a challenge to Evangelical dogmatics, on the basis of the definitions of the Council of Trent (1545–63). Although the sharp differences between the leading medieval schools of theology continued in the post-Reformation period, Thomistic theology gained the upper hand in the sphere of dogma and church politics. However, it was chiefly the formulas of the system of Thomas, and not much of his spirit, that became the legacy. The Council of Trent defined the terms of Roman Catholic orthodoxy. It was not able to incorporate the leading ideas of the Protestant Reformers, but elevated the good and the bad, the wheat and the chaff, of late medieval theology to the status of ecclesiastical dogma. The shape and content of Roman Catholic dogmatics remained constant from the Council of Trent to the Second Vatican Council, where new winds of doctrine began to modify the monolithic orthodoxy of post-Tridentine Catholicism.

THE DISSOLUTION OF
DOGMATICS IN PIETISM
AND THE ENLIGHTENMENT

The objectivism of orthodoxy and its system of authority provoked the revolt of pietism and the Enlightenment. Pietism did not reject the objective truths of orthodox dogmatics as such, but reached back to the underlying faith— the subjective element—of Luther's reformation. Its interest was more in the *fides qua creditur* than the *fides quae creditur.* Orthodoxy had defined faith as *notitia, assensus*, and *fiducia. Notitia* (knowledge) involves the mind, *assensus* (assent) the will, and *fiducia* (trust) the heart. Pietism stressed faith as *fiducia*, as trust, and could appeal to what Luther said in his fight against scholastic theology, that it is the heart that makes the theologian. Pietism rightly saw that the inner power of the Reformation was its preaching of the Word, establishing a new personal relationship to God by the grace of forgiveness and not by the works of the law. Pietism produced no great works in the area of dogmatics. It was more concerned for practical religion and the Christian life, and even mistrusted the intellect at work in theology.

In the wake of pietism came the revolt of the Enlightenment against the supernaturalist dogmatics of orthodoxy. The goal of the Enlightenment was to reduce Christianity to what can be grasped by reason. Immanuel Kant wrote the religious manifesto for the Enlightenment, *Religion within the Limits of Reason Alone.* The theologians of the Enlightenment accepted the natural theology of orthodoxy, but overthrew its supernatural superstructure as beyond the principles of a reasonable religion. The specific elements of traditional dogmatics were subjected to rigorous criticism and finally dissolved into a rationalistic form of mysticism, metaphysics, and morality.

THE REVIVAL OF DOGMATICS
IN THE NINETEENTH CENTURY

The task of the nineteenth century was to go beyond rationalism and place dogmatics on a new footing. At the same time, it could not simply repudiate the achievements of the Enlightenment, particularly the new methods of biblical criticism and the emerging world view of modern science. Nor was there much chance to repristinate the confessional dogmatics of Protestant orthodoxy, although the attempt was made.

The new beginnings in nineteenth-century dogmatics took up certain trends of the times, such as romanticism and idealism, that had overtaken the flatland of rationalistic thinking, yet without surrendering the critical spirit of the Enlightenment. Friedrich Schleiermacher made the initial breakthrough in his book, *Speeches on Religion to Its Cultured Despisers.* It is an apology for the category of religion as *sui generis*, distinct from rational knowledge and moral principle. The essence of religion is "the feeling of absolute dependence." Schleiermacher could also call it "God-consciousness." This general concept of religion became the starting point of Schleiermacher's new construction of dogmatics, which he called *Glaubenslehre*, the doctrine of faith. Dogmatics is to be the description of the faith that exists in the Christian community. Hence Schleiermacher could speak of dogmatics as a positive

1 / PROLEGOMENA TO CHRISTIAN DOGMATICS

science and subsume it under historical theology. The point of this descriptive task is to show how everything that is distinctively Christian is "related to the redemption accomplished by Jesus of Nazareth."[4] Therefore Schleiermacher's dogmatics was both grounded in the church and centered in Christ, characteristics which proved decisive in almost all later schools of theology.

In 1818 Georg Wilhelm Friedrich Hegel became Schleiermacher's colleague in Berlin, but he was far from collegial. Hegel inaugurated a trend in theology in polar contrast to Schleiermacher's. Hegel was a philosopher, perhaps in his own way a theologian, but certainly not a dogmatician. Yet he produced a universal system in which all the symbols of the Christian tradition were given a philosophical interpretation, and he thus became enormously influential on the most creative minds and trends in the nineteenth century. For Hegel, religion was not essentially subjective feeling, but the symbolic representation of the dialectical self-actualization of the absolute Spirit (*Geist*) in nature and history. Theology bearing Hegel's influence split into a left-wing and a right-wing school of interpretation. The issue on which the split occurred was whether the universal meaning of history can be tied to the particular historical events on which Christian faith is based, or whether these events are merely temporary exemplifications which can in principle be phased out or transcended in the further course of history. The significance of Hegel for dogmatics thus has to do with the interpretation of history. It opened the struggle for the truly historical character of Christian faith, a fight which is still going on with no end in sight.

The remainder of the nineteenth century lived in the shadow of the three towering philosophers of religion: Kant, Schleiermacher, and Hegel. The school of mediating theology (*Vermittlungstheologie*) combined features from both Schleiermacher and Hegel. The Erlangen school, epitomized by J. C. K. von Hofmann, developed the Christian interpretation of history known as *Heilsgeschichte*. Confessional theology worked to repristinate the pre-Enlightenment dogmatics of the church. Albrecht Ritschl and his school rediscovered the philosophy of Kant, as it was then interpreted by Hermann Lotze. Ritschl's dogmatics took a sharp turn away from Hegel, rejecting all metaphysics and choosing instead a moral foundation of religion. Ritschl claimed to follow Luther in his rejection of all scholastic speculation, focusing instead on justifying faith and its vocation in the world. Ritschl's influence dominated the teaching of dogmatics for decades, until it gave way at the turn of the century to new directions, some defined by Martin Kähler and Adolf Schlatter, and others by the history-of-religions school, which had a direct impact on theology through the works of Albert Schweitzer and Ernst Troeltsch.

THE STATE OF DOGMATICS
IN THE TWENTIETH CENTURY

The optimism of the post-Enlightenment view of human progress was shattered by World War I. The leading schools of modern Protestant dogmatics came to a crashing halt. The beginnings of a new theology emerged in the context of the parish. Karl Barth, Friedrich Gogarten, and Emil Brunner were all parish pastors, who read the "signs of the times" and asked the same question, "Do we have a Word of God for the crises of our time?" Thus there arose the school of dialectical theology, sometimes called theology of crisis, which was convinced that theology could no longer proceed along nineteenth-century lines. Rudolf Bultmann and Paul Tillich also agreed with Karl Barth about the need for a new beginning. All these theologians were united in their criticism of the theology of modern Protestantism. Once they began to sketch out their own proposals for a new dogmatics, however, the school of dialectical theology began to break up into various factions.

The early period of twentieth-century dogmatics, sandwiched between the two world wars, was a time of rediscovery. Karl Barth and Emil Brunner returned behind modern Protestantism and the Enlightenment to the christocentric theology of the Word of God in Luther and Calvin. Gustaf Aulén and Anders Nygren, co-leaders of Lundensian theology (Sweden), also returned to the theology of Luther, stressing the Reformation motifs of God's agape-love, Christ's dramatic victory over the tyrants, and the justification of sinners. At the same time, Oscar Cullmann and Gerhard von Rad developed the categories for a biblical theology of the history of salvation, aiming to supplant the traditional dogmatic concepts derived from Hellenistic metaphysics.

The second period covers the time from World War II to the new departures in theology in the early 1960s. "Hermeneutics" became the common word to express the concern for a meaningful interpretation of the Christian gospel in terms that modern people can understand. Rudolf Bultmann proposed his program of demythologizing the Bible in order to grasp its message in existential terms. Paul Tillich proposed the method of correlation. Like Bultmann he used the categories of existentialist philosophy to relate the biblical message to the modern situation. The difference between them was chiefly that Tillich went beyond existentialism and drew heavily on nineteenth-century German classical idealism (Schelling and Hegel) for his ontological interpretation of theology. The concern for a meaningful interpretation of the biblical message was then programmatically intensified in the hermeneutical theology of Gerhard Ebeling and Ernst Fuchs. They constructed a theory of language to explain the transition from the Word of God in Scripture to the event of faith in contemporary existence. In a parallel development, Friedrich Gogarten extended certain of Dietrich Bonhoeffer's prison insights in the direction of a secular interpretation of the gospel. The thesis in this line is that the gospel, rightly understood, promotes the process of secularization, and is no longer dependent on a prior religious category of experience. This trend took a radical turn in the American "Death of God" theology. In different ways the radical theologians Paul van Buren, William Hamilton, and Thomas J. J. Altizer speculated on the shape of a theology without God or belief in God. The phenomenon of Christian atheism quickly revealed itself as an absurdity and is now remembered as a curious wrinkle in the theology of modern times.

The Word-of-God theology of neo-orthodoxy operated without any positive correlation with philosophy in general or metaphysics in particular. During this time, Paul Tillich continued to stress that philosophy could serve in some way as the handmaid of theology. He coined the phrase "Philosophy asks the question, theology provides the answer." Others, too, worked to formulate an appropriate philosophical theology for use in the construction of a specifically Christian theology. This is a third significant phase in the development of contemporary theology. Process theologians like Schubert Ogden and John Cobb used the metaphysics of Alfred North Whitehead and Charles Hartshorne to make explicit the meaning of Christian faith. On another front theologians such as I. T. Ramsey used the philosophy of ordinary language of Ludwig Wittgenstein to clarify the logic of religious language. The Jesuit priest Pierre Teilhard de Chardin projected the outline of an evolutionary theology, bringing theology into a close correlation with the world view of the natural sciences. In Roman Catholic circles Karl Rahner and Bernard Lonergan, both Jesuits, placed traditional Thomist thought on the new foundations of post-Kantian critical philosophy. For this reason their thought is referred to as transcendental Thomism.

It is clear that no single philosophy is now universally acceptable among theologians as a partner for theological work. At the present time there is a new affirmation of the philosophy of G. W. F. Hegel and Karl Marx. The eschatological theologians—Wolfhart Pannenberg and Jürgen Moltmann— have launched their perspectives in conjunction with a creative appropriation of Hegelian insights. As eschatological theology sought to make itself relevant to the practical situation in the world today, it became fragmented into several schools of thought. Jürgen Moltmann together with Johann Baptist Metz developed a political interpretation of the gospel. Others, seeking to be more radical, called for a theology of revolution, drawing on eschatological messianism. At the present time the theology of liberation is the new key for a complete reinterpretation of the texts and traditions of Christian faith. It draws heavily on the revolutionary ideas of Karl Marx, seeking a practical transformation of the world in accordance with the socialist vision of justice and peace.

It is no exaggeration to state that pluralism is the most fitting word to characterize the present situation in theology. There is no single reigning dogmatics for the church, no such thing as an ecumenical dogmatics that synthesizes the truths in all the bodies of Christendom. There are distinctly contradictory currents, some trying to restore old modes of orthodoxy, others reaching for equally tired ideas of liberalism, sometimes without enough knowledge of the tradition to know that some new proposals are not so new after all.

NOTES

1. Wolfgang Trillhaas, *Dogmatic* (Berlin: Alfred Töpelmann, 1962), pp. 15–16.
2. Adolf von Harnack, *History of Dogma*, trans. Neil Buchanan, 7 vols. (New York: Dover Publications, 1961).
3. The following works were consulted in this brief sketch of the history of dogmatics: Karl Barth, *Protestant Theology in the Nineteeth Century* (Valley Forge, Pa.: Judson Press, 1973); J. F. Bethune-Baker, *An Introduction to the Early History of Christian Doctrine* (Cambridge: At the University Press, 1902); Hans von Campenhausen, *The Fathers of the Greek Church*, trans. Stanley Godman (New York: Pantheon Books, 1959); Aloys Grillmeier, *Christ in Christian Tradition*, trans. J. S. Bowden (New York and London: Sheed & Ward, 1965); Gerhard Gloege, "Christliches Dogma," in RGG[3], ed. Kurt Galling (Tübingen: J. C. B. Mohr [Paul Siebeck], 1958), cols. 221–25; Harnack, *History of Dogma*, vols. 1–7; Edward Caldwell Moore, *History of Christian Thought since Kant* (London: Gerald Duckworth & Co., 1912); J. L. Neve, *A History of Christian Thought* (Philadelphia: Fortress [Muhlenberg] Press, 1946); Jaroslav Pelikan, *The Christian Tradition: A History of the Development of Doctrine*, vol. 1, *The Emergence of the Catholic Tradition (100-600)* (Chicago: University of Chicago Press, 1971); Carl Heinz Ratschow, *Lutherische Dogmatik zwischen Reformation und Aufklärung* (Gütersloh: Gerd Mohn, 1964), part 1; Reinhold Seeberg, *History of Doctrines*, trans. Charles Hay (Grand Rapids: Baker Book House, 1954), vols. 1 & 2; Heinrich Schmid, *The Doctrinal Theology of the Evangelical Lutheran Church*, trans. Charles A. Hay and Henry E. Jacobs (Minneapolis: Augsburg Publishing House, 1899); Paul Tillich, *A History of Christian Thought*, ed. Carl E. Braaten (New York: Simon & Schuster, 1972); Henry A. Wolfson, *The Philosophy of the Church Fathers* (Cambridge, Mass.: Harvard University Press, 1956), vol 1.
4. Friedrich Schleiermacher, *The Christian Faith*, ed. H. R. Mackintosh and J. S. Stewart (Edinburgh: T. & T. Clark, 1928), p. 52.

3

The Fundamentals
of Dogmatics

The aim of dogmatics is to contribute to the proper understanding of the gospel in the church. Dogmatic theology does not begin and end with an interpretation of dogma, but traces the meaning of dogma to its ground in the witness of Scripture and serves the missionary proclamation of the church. The main theme of dogmatics is the self-revelation of God in the history of God's people Israel, in Jesus Christ, and in the apostolic witness of faith.

THE CONCEPT OF DOGMA

There can be no doubt that the word "dogma" provokes an allergic reaction on the face of modern theological thought. "Dogma" conjures up a coercive teaching of an authoritarian church, a static and sterile statement of truth frozen in the manuals of ecclesiastical dogmatics. This allergic reaction can be seen throughout the Christian world today. Even at Vatican II the Roman Catholic church chose to promulgate no new dogma with a polemical bite, but only to issue teachings with a pastoral intent. No anathemas were pronounced! The age of dogmatism seemed to be over. Instead, there was growing recognition of pluralism and ecumenical openness. To many observers it seemed that Rome was going the way of Protestantism, implicitly acknowledging the thesis of Adolf von Harnack that the history of dogma has come to an end.

At the First Vatican Council dogma was defined as truth revealed by God, officially proclaimed by the teaching office of the church, and binding on all faithful Christians. The intention was clear even then that the church does not make up dogma on its own authority, but defines dogma from what is *given* in revelation.[3] Dogma is therefore binding on the faithful not primarily because of the authority of the church but because of the divine revelation which dogma contains. Protestants have often mistakenly heard only the ring of ecclesiastical authoritarianism in the notion of dogma. In any case, the Second Vatican Council and leading Roman Catholic theologians today teach that dogma is a witness to revelation,[2] a sign of the church's reception of revelation, whose truth is constant but whose formulation is subject to further development. What is permanent is the truth, but the statement of the truth is historically conditioned and open to change. Hence, a dogmatic statement points beyond itself to the mystery of God's self-communication in Jesus Christ. The dogma must make use of finite concepts to refer to what is inherently infinite and incomprehensible. The point is that the content and the meaning of the dogma must be distinguished, but not separated, from the linguistic and historical forms of expression which dogmatics utilizes at any given time.

The contemporary Roman Catholic concept of dogma makes allowance for the difference between the truth already known and the final truth yet to come. Dogma lives within the eschatological horizon of Christian faith and understanding. Walter Kasper has formulated this point very well:

> Both finality and provisionality belong to dogma. Dogma is one way in which the gospel of the eschatological coming of Christ expresses itself in the church. A dogma is the provisional occurrence of the eschatological final truth of Christ. By means of the word "provisional" the anticipatory character of the dogma should be expressed. It is not meant to be contradictory to "final." On the contrary, it is meant in the original meaning of the word as a provisional fore-conception of the eschaton, to which the church opens itself in light of the eschatological future. This means, then, that a dogma does not close history but keeps it open to the future.[3]

Dogma lives in the tension between the gospel of the kingdom which has already arrived in Jesus Christ and the final future of the promise which yet remains outstanding. The heart of dogma is Jesus Christ himself, to whom the Christian community can look back as its origin and to whom it can look forward as its destiny and goal in the future of God. This concentration of dogma on the Christ-event in current Roman Catholic teaching points to the primacy of Scripture over tradition, paving the way for possible rapprochement with the Reformation view of the relation between gospel and dogma.

The view of Adolf von Harnack that the history of dogma ended with the faith of Luther has nourished a widespread Protestant prejudice against dogmatic theology. But no one could have been more concerned than Luther for a faith clearly expressed in true doctrine. Against Erasmus, Luther cried: "Take away assertions, and you take away Christianity."[4] It is erroneous to picture Luther as placing faith on the side of feeling, opposed to pure doctrine. Luther was not opposed to the dogmas of the church as such, but only to a theology that derives dogma from the church rather than from the Word of God. The Apostles' Creed is true not because the church teaches it but because it is a true summary of the doctrine contained in Scripture. Hence, also, Luther's words concerning the creeds and councils of the church in general had the effect of relativizing their authority, but always with respect to the prior authority of Scripture, not with respect to autonomous reason. Holy Scripture is a prior norm for reading the doctrines of the fathers and decrees of the councils. The dogmatic decisions of the councils do not stand on the authority of the church, but refer back to the prior authority of Scripture. Luther wrote:

> These then are the four principal Councils and the reasons they were held. The first, in Nicaea, defended the divinity of Christ against Arius; the second, in Constantinople, defended the divinity of the Holy Spirit against Macedonius; the third, in Ephesus, defended the one person of Christ against Nestorius; the fourth, in Chalcedon, defended the two natures in Christ against Eutyches. But no new articles of faith were thereby established, for these four doctrines are formulated far more abundantly and powerfully in St. John's gospel alone, even if the other evangelists and St. Paul and St. Peter had written nothing about it, although they, together with the prophets, also teach and bear convincing witness to all of that.[5]

As we compare Luther's view of the relation between dogma and Scripture to current Roman Catholic teaching, we find that both agree in referring the content of dogma to the revelation of Scripture. It was not Luther's intent to elevate *sola scriptura* at the expense of dogma, nor do Roman Catholic theologians today place dogma on a par with Scripture. In both cases, at least in principle, the priority of the Word of God is maintained over the creeds and councils of the church.

We enter another world of thought altogether with the rise of modern Protestant theology. The use of the critical historical method eroded the very concept of dogma as a binding statement of revealed truth. Adolf von Harnack drove a sharp wedge between the gospel and dogma. In his classic *History of Dogma* Harnack stated, "Dogma in its conception and development is a work of the Greek spirit on the soil of the Gospel."[6] Harnack's view that the gospel is not dogma, but is instead falsified by it, epitomizes the modern Protestant dream of an undogmatic Christianity, one that impinges on religious feeling or moral action and abandons the claim of doctrinal truth. For Harnack the hellenization of Christianity meant the conversion of the gospel into the static and timeless realm of intellectualistic ideas. Harnack did not object, of course, to the effort of the church to make the gospel intelligible in clear statements. He was even able to state, "Christianity without dogma, that is, without a clear expression of its content, is inconceivable."[7] He seems to contradict himself, but the contradiction is only apparent. Harnack actually maintained that it was inevitable for the church fathers to give systematic intellectual expression to the gospel, but the dogmas which resulted from their effort are bound to the historical period in which they were produced and possess no binding validity for later times.

Harnack's work emphasized the historical relativity of dogma, but the generation of theologians that was to follow him did not accept his verdict at face value. Harnack's most famous pupil, Karl Barth, spent a lifetime writing dogmatics for the church and placed himself decidedly on the side of the classical dogmas. Barth, however, turned Harnack's relativization of dogma on its head. All doctrines of the church, emerging in history, are relativized primarily through their relation to the transcendent Word of God. The concrete dogmas of the church, though relativized by the revealed Word, Jesus Christ, do not lose their value as guides for our own dogmatic work.[8] They are not final and absolute, to be sure. Rather, they point beyond themselves to the *dogma* which is the perfect knowledge of the Word of God. This is never realized in the pilgrim church; it always remains an eschatological goal. Barth has not dissolved dogma in the relativities of history, like Harnack. But he has severely limited dogma in terms of the ongoing gap in time between faith and knowledge, human language and the Word of God, history and the eschatological goal. The *dogma* is a transcendent goal and model of the *dogmas*. Barth saw that the relation between the latter and the former is one of radical obedience to the Word of God revealed in Christ and Scripture and proclaimed by the church.

Emil Brunner, an early close associate of Karl Barth, defined truth in terms of encounter, appropriating Martin Buber's concept of the I-Thou relationship.[9] Brunner opposed this concept of truth to the notion of truth as a property of propositions, which fits into a subject-object scheme, an I-It relationship. Brunner argued that truth-as-encounter is the biblical concept of truth. It is difficult to fit dogma into this personalist theory of truth-as-encounter. Yet Brunner, admitting that dogma bears all the marks of legalism and is therefore alien to faith, does not wish to get rid of dogma altogether. The function of dogma or doctrine is to lead to the event of the personal encounter with God through the hearing of the Word. The purpose of dogma in the Christian faith is to lead to Jesus Christ, as the law to the gospel, as the letter to the spirit. In this way, Brunner follows Barth in subordinating church doctrine to the personal encounter with Jesus Christ. Doctrines are the setting for the jewel of the gospel.[10]

After World War II the journal *Kerygma und Dogma* was founded in Germany. It signaled a more positive turn to dogma and dogmatics. The nineteenth century, climaxing in Adolf von Harnack, rightly perceived the danger of dogma becoming a tool of an authoritarian church and a lifeless deposit of archaic beliefs. But the overreaction of Protestantism to the Catholic concept of dogma stood in need of correction. New Testament scholarship demonstrated clearly that the preaching of the kerygma in primitive Christianity was not the sole and all-sufficient medium of the knowledge of God's saving revelation in Jesus Christ.[11] Preaching was immediately accompanied by teaching (*didache*) and the transmission of tradition (*paradosis*). The New Testament does not record merely a series of existential encounters of an I-Thou type. It communicates a *subject matter* that claims the authority of God and of Jesus Christ. These are truths of revelation, meaningful events, that can be taught and learned and passed on by disciples who tell *what* they have seen and heard. New Testament Christianity is not simply concerned with personal encounters and existential relationships, let alone religious feelings; it contains the *dogmata* of the apostles which refer to the good news of salvation. There is a natural and continuous relationship between the *kerygma* which the apostles preached, the *didache* which they taught, and the *paradosis* which they passed on to their disciples. It is simply false to set these facets of early Christianity into an antagonistic relationship.[12]

Dogma is not an alienating move away from the gospel, but an intrinsic development of interpretation to a more advanced reflective level of consciousness within the Christian community. The gospel is not antidogmatic. Without dogma it would be inherently impossible to pronounce any anathema against heretical teachings which cut the nerve of the church's gospel. An undogmatic Christianity can no longer tell the difference between true and false preaching of the gospel. The point of dogma is to ensure the correct interpretation of the gospel, not to make faith legalistically dependent on church authority. As Luther put the matter:

> It is the promises of God that make the Church and not the Church that makes the promise of God. For the Word of God is incomparably superior to the Church, and in the Word the Church, being a creature, has nothing to decree, ordain, or make, but only to be decreed, ordained and made. For who begets his own parent? Who first brings forth his own maker?[13]

A dogma is not true because the church teaches it. It is true only if it brings to expression the true meaning of the gospel. Luther stated that only God's Word can establish an article of faith, no one else, not even an angel.[14] This leads to a critical, gospel-oriented notion of dogma and away from an ecclesiastical positivism which refers faith to whatever the church or its authorities happen to decree as revealed truth. The criterion to apply is whether dogma conveys the truth of the gospel, not whether it has been officially promulgated by the church. Whenever the church supports its dogmas by sheer appeal to its own authority, the hermeneutical link between dogma and gospel is weakened and the primacy of the gospel and its creative authority are surrendered.

The new affirmation of dogma as continuous with the kerygma can be found in the dogmatics of major twentieth-century theologians. We need only refer to the works of Paul Althaus, Werner Elert, Regin Prenter, Gerhard Gloege, Edmund Schlink, and Wolfhart Pannenberg. Edmund Schlink made a notable contribution to the contemporary understanding of dogma in his article "The Structure of Dogmatic Statements as an Ecumenical Problem."[15] There is more than one form of human response to divine revelation. Schlink says, "Dogmatic scholarship is obliged to consider the rich diversity of Christian responses, whether in proclamation, in demanding, in thanksgiving, in assurance, in prayer, or in doxology."[16] Dogmas and creeds are among the forms of response which the Christian community makes in confessing its faith in God. The aim of a dogmatic statement is to make a clear and definitive expression of *what* God has revealed.

Wolfhart Pannenberg, once Schlink's pupil, integrated Schlink's positive assessment of dogma into his own systematic theology.[17] Pannenberg also moves dogma away from its traditional connection with the authoritarian claim of the church to its historical ground in the concrete history of Jesus Christ whose universal meaning the Scriptures declare. The function of a dogmatic statement is to bring to the level of knowledge the universal meaning of the historical particularity of the message of Jesus Christ. Church dogmas are true and refer to what really happened, but can never be more than provisional because our grasp of the universal meaning of Jesus is always partial. We should not absolutize dogma, because there is a real distinction between revelation and dogma. Dogma is the sum of the church's knowledge of revelation accessible to faith. But neither should we minimize the importance of dogma, because it intends to express nothing less than the apostolic witness to the truth of revelation in the actual history of Jesus. On the basis of history and the modern historical-critical method we have in Pannenberg's notion of dogma a new formulation of the Reformation principle of *sola scriptura*.

One of the chief motives for the Protestant flight from dogma can be removed by rejecting its authoritarian connections. What we retain is a clear picture of the essential place of dogma in the scheme of theological knowledge. Theology inevitably goes beyond telling the gospel story. It formulates its universal meaning for our consciousness of truth and for the whole of reality. Dogmatic statements do not merely repeat the events in historical sequence. They claim to speak of God as the Creator and Eschaton of history on the basis of the particular events witnessed in Scripture. They speak of the universality and totality of meaning, but always in a provisional and proleptic way, because history is still going on and the church is not yet at the end. "The church's dogma," says Pannenberg, "which is still on the way, cannot itself be the eschatological form of revealed truth."[18] The authority of a dogmatic statement must not pretend to straddle all history from the vantage point of the eschaton.

THE CONFESSIONAL PRINCIPLE

Within the tradition of the Reformation, the churches have developed their own confessional heritage beyond the classical dogmas of the ancient church. The attempt of some Protestants to profess "no creeds but Christ" has only produced a new confessional stance, even if not pronounced in so many words. A creedless, nonconfessional, undogmatic Christianity has proven itself incapable of reproducing vital forms of witness to the New Testament gospel.

Lutheran churches have stressed the confessional principle more than the Reformed and the Radical Protestant branches of the Reformation. Yet the confessional principle has been a constant source of controversy in world Lutheranism, not least in the United States. The right wing appeals to the confessional principle to exclude all new developments in modern theology. Committed to a theology of repristination, it lifts up the *Book of Concord*,[19] sometimes coupled with seventeenth-century scholasticism, as the golden age, the once-for-all model of what theology must be. Here doctrines become laws, creating a climate of doctrinal legalism in the church, snuffing out the freedom which is the church's birthright from the gospel.

The other extreme, the heritage of liberalism, strives to dissolve the confessional principle in theology. One form of this nonconfessional attitude goes behind the confessional writings of the church to the heroic faith of the young man Luther, making his image into an object of hero worship. Much of modern Luther research was inspired by the desire to undercut the authority of orthodox confessionalism, in the hope of salvaging Luther from Lutheranism, in order to gain leverage in the clash between liberalism and orthodoxy. Another form of the anticonfessional approach reaches back to the Bible, ironically turning the confessional principle of *sola scriptura* against itself, as a principle of self-dissolution. The pietistic heritage had a strong biblicist tendency, joined with a kind of antiintellectualism that looked upon dogmas and doctrines with suspicion. Each believer with Bible in hand had a right to his or her own private interpretation, pitting the Spirit against the collective consciousness of the community expressed in its confessional teachings.

The confessional principle can be maintained within a creative tension between the pole of continuity, which grounds dogmatics in the catholic substance of the faith, and the pole of contemporaneity, which keeps the church open to modern horizons of experience and understanding. The disregard of either principle leads to a polarization of theology between orthodox confessionalism and liberal modernism. Dogmatics can look for insights in the creeds and confessions of the church without being archaistic, and it can learn new ways of thinking without becoming modernistic.

The authority the confessions claim for themselves is limited. They always speak in the indicative rather than the imperative mood. They introduce their statements with the phrase "We believe, confess, and teach," declaring not what must be believed in order to have true faith but what is already believed on the basis of faith in the gospel of Christ. They are not so much a legal requirement as an evangelical witness, not legally binding canonical norms, but human testimonies of faith in the Word of God. The confessions subordinate themselves to the Holy Scriptures of the Old and New Testaments. This means that no doctrinal dispute can be decided for the church merely by a legalistic appeal to the confessions. That would be a shortcut for a church that holds to the primacy of Scripture.

A confessional church stands for a concrete and specific witness to the truth of the gospel. Those who subscribed confessional writings in the sixteenth century were willing to stake their lives on the truth they believed and taught. They were convinced that their confession participated in the very truth of the gospel itself. The act of confessional subscription contains a risk, of course, because the church is fallible, councils can err, dogmas are provisional, and confessional statements are conditioned by the set of questions they address at a particular time of church history.

Today we may witness to the power of the confessions to liberate the church for a new hearing of the gospel. The confessions may become "emancipation proclamations" at a time when the church becomes captive to the spirit of the age. The Barmen Declaration was just such a confession, equipping the Confessing Church to withstand the heresy of the "German Christians." Non-confessional churches were impotent in face of the Aryan heresy. The church at the time derived great strength and freedom from its confession of the one Lordship of Jesus Christ against all pretenders to the throne of absolute leadership. Under persecution and attack the Confessing Christians experienced the liberating effects of a church confession. As in the past, so in the contemporary period the church was bound to formulate a new confession in a special kairos to face a particular crisis.

The particular confessions of the Lutheran church, chiefly the Augsburg Confession and Luther's Small Catechism, claim to voice the truth of the gospel that concerns the whole church. The confessional principle intends to be ecumenical, not sectarian. If the particular confessions of the Lutheran church point to the gospel, and nothing else, and if other confessions point in their own way, in their own time and place, to the same gospel, we can expect a meeting of the confessions in their common reference to the same core and substance of faith. Article VII of the Augsburg Confession states that "for the true unity of the church it is enough to agree concerning the teaching of the Gospel and the administration of the sacraments" (*BC* 32). As the various communions strive to understand their own confessional heritage, they may converge on the same point which lies at the center of the faith they hold in common. It is erroneous to conceive of the rich diversity of Christian confessions in history on the adversarial model. They may be more complementary than competitive. Each communion best serves the interest of the one, holy, catholic, and apostolic church when it remains true to the substance of its own confession and humbly calls on other communions to listen to its witness in a spirit of dialogue and mutual service.

It is the purpose of the confessional writings in the Lutheran *Book of Concord,* for example, to serve the catholic church by referring it to the unifying gospel of Christ. This gospel is summarized in terms of justification by grace alone, through faith alone, on account of Christ alone. This is a summary of the whole gospel. The stress on the word "alone" is not a denominational peculiarity, which other churches and sects may magnanimously allow to the Lutherans, while others are permitted to pursue and accent their own denominational specialty, be it papal infallibility, episcopal succession, presbyterian polity, congregational autonomy, liturgical legalism, or pentecostal spirituality. With the deletion of the *sola* the gospel itself is betrayed, not merely some Lutheran idiosyncrasy.

The crucial significance of the Reformation principle of *sola gratia/sola fide* has been confirmed by major contemporary Roman Catholic theologians, such as Karl Rahner, Hans Küng, Walter Kasper, and many others. In his *Foundations of Christian Faith,* Karl Rahner discusses the three famous "alone's" of the Reformation: grace alone, faith alone, and Scripture alone. He concludes his treatment by acknowledging that the core of the original Reformation and of Evangelical Christianity is identical with Catholic faith and doctrine. He writes, "We can and must, therefore, hold the doctrine 'by grace alone' with an ardour which is both Christian and Catholic."[20]

The chief dogma of the Reformation, justification through faith alone, is an hermeneutical proposal. It offers the key for the right interpretation of the Holy Scriptures. The decisive question to which the Scriptures provide an answer is how humanity stands before God in the ultimate dimension. If dogmaticians do not use this hermeneutical key in biblical exegesis, they will use some other one. There is no presuppositionless approach to the Scriptures. The purely scientific historian who imagines that the Scriptures can be read and understood without any presuppositions is a victim of naive positivism.

The confessions possess hermeneutical significance because they point to the central message of the Scriptures as a whole. They are like a map giving directions on how to find the way through the Scriptures. The absolute confessionalist is like one who studies the map but neglects to take the trip. The anticonfessionalist sets off on the trip with no map for guidance, and quickly gets lost on the way. The confessions are a means to an end, just that but not less than that.

The chief point of the church's creeds and confessions is not to guarantee

PREACHING IS CONFESSIONAL "true doctrine" but rather to set norms for the right preaching of the gospel. Preaching has a confessional content; it is also a confessing act. Every sound preacher is a public confessor of the faith of the church. Preaching is secularized if kerygmatic style is achieved at the expense of confessional content; this is the main temptation of modern Protestant Christianity. Conversely, preaching becomes sterile if the content is frozen in creedal propositions, lacking the existential dimension of the *credo*. This has been the tendency of orthodoxy in both its Protestant and Roman Catholic traditions. Christian preaching is not a mere report of what has been believed once upon a time; it is the announcement of what the living church believes today on the basis of the biblical witness to the gospel. Preaching thus reflects the truth of what the Samaritans said to the woman at the well: "It is no longer because of your words that we believe, for we have heard for ourselves, and we know that this is indeed the Savior of the world" (John 4:42).

The confessional life and understanding of the church need not be static. The church is free to take the risk of extending the confessional limits of her own tradition. The confessions are not the final formulation of the gospel. New confessions will need to be written and subscribed from time to time. The past creeds and confessions of the church must not be glorified, for the church is made of sinners on their pilgrim way, possessing at best imperfect and fragmentary knowledge. The church will watchfully live by faith and hope in the expectation of new light until at last she will see face to face in a state of eschatological glory. Meanwhile, the church is "at once just and sinner" (*simul iustus, simul peccator*). The eschatological perspective calls the church to repentance, in need of forgiveness also in its confessional life. Luther's distinction between a theology of the cross and a theology of glory is directly applicable to the way in which the church uses its creeds and confessions.

There is no *a priori* reason to oppose a new ecumenical council of all the churches in which a major confessional act might occasion the reunion of the divided churches. Jesus prayed to the Father that his followers might all be one. It is right that all Christians pray for the historical realization of his ecumenical prayer.

THE FUNDAMENTALS OF DOGMATICS

It is the task of dogmatics to present the truth of God's revelation as apprehended by the faith of the Christian church. Dogmatics deals with the knowledge of faith within the context of the church and the history of its traditions. There are no revealed dogmas which must be believed. The object of faith is always God, in and through the means of God's own self-revelation. "God and faith belong together," said Luther. But faith is not an empty response; it is no mere emotional reaction. When faith expresses what it has received from God's saving revelation, it gives rise to the kind of truth and knowledge of which doctrines and dogmas are made.

The knowledge of faith is a subject of deep personal interest, but it is no private matter. God's revelation has created a community of believers and therefore a common faith which belongs to the one universal church as well as to each of its members. Dogmatics deals with the fundamental dogmatic decisions the church has formulated on the basis of the divine revelation which has created its common faith.

It is necessary for the Christian church to formulate dogmatics. No other community can do it. First, the church must formulate dogmatics to ground its own teachings in the truth which God's revelation has disclosed for the knowledge of faith. Dogmatics is concerned about the *identity* of the Christian faith. Second, the church must formulate dogmatics to criticize and renew itself with reference to the source and norm of its life and message. Dogmatics is concerned for the present *vitality* of the church's proclamation. Third, dogmatics is necessary to help the missionary church distinguish between the invariant essence of the gospel and the cultural forms in which it embodies itself from time to time. Dogmatics is concerned for the *integrity* of the Christian mission in the world. Fourth, dogmatics is indispensable to help the church remain faithful to its own interior meaning through the discontinuities of time. Dogmatics is concerned for the historical *continuity* of the faith. These principles of identity, vitality, integrity, and continuity are inherent in the classical Christian belief in the *una sancta catholica et apostolica*. When they are present in the right balance, the church will be doing rightly what it is called to do: preaching the gospel, teaching the faith, interpreting the word, evangelizing the nations, and liberating the captives.

The basic doctrinal decisions of the church provide a useful outline for the organization and development of the contents of dogmatics. Dogmatics today builds on what it has received from the past, on the creedal and confessional decisions of the classical Christian tradition. To be sure, the autobiography of the individual dogmaticians—their religious experience, their confessional tradition, their scholastic training, their field of specialization, their professional achievements, and so on—will be indirectly reflected in each of the topics. But there is a certain givenness about the dogmatic tradition which commends itself even today. There are fundamental principles of dogmatics, basic decisions of the church that are common to our tradition and whose order lends itself to such a cooperative venture in dogmatics as this one.

First, there is the canonical decision of the church which has established the preeminent position of the Holy Scriptures above all other witnesses to the revelation of God. They are the "norm that has no norm" (*norma normans non normata*). The methodological significance of this decision means that dogmatic theology must always in principle begin with biblical exegesis and then exercise its critical and constructive function in correcting and interpreting the church's message to the world today. The chapter on Holy Scripture appears in this prolegomena because this canon is foundational; it is the fundament of all other witnesses in the life of the church. The canonical writings participate in the once-for-all events of revelation which founded the church and continue to perpetuate its life.

Second, the chief point of the canonical decision is to provide a framework, to set rules and limits, for the church to make the fundamental decision of its life, the theological one. This is the answer to the question Who is *theos*? Who is the God whose voice we hear within the words of Holy Scripture and through the witnesses of Christian tradition? The trinitarian dogmatic decision of the church answers that God is one being in three persons, whose names are Father, Son, and Holy Spirit, the Trinity in unity. In this decision the church decided against the gods of pagan polytheism and various forms of monotheism, religious, metaphysical, or political (Jewish, Greek, or Roman).

Third, the key to the trinitarian answer to the question of the nature and identity of God was the christological question: whether the Son incarnate as the person of Jesus of Nazareth is of the same essence as God the Father or is some subordinate intermediate being half-divine and half-human. In traditional dogmatics, the question arose as to what can be known of God apart from his special revelation in Jesus Christ and the history of salvation beginning with Israel. For this reason we include a *locus* on the knowledge of God, dealing with the significant differences between general and special revelation, or between natural and revealed theology. This issue of the knowledge of God is of particular importance today in the encounter between Christianity and the major non-Christian religions. The church has not rendered a dogmatic decision on this issue in any definitive way. It remains fluid and subject to lively controversy in the schools of theology.

Fourth, dogmatics respects the order of the creed, which in turn follows that of the Bible. Creation comes first, then the new creation. Belief in God the Creator precedes the confession of Jesus as Lord and Savior. Genesis is the first book of the Bible, and the Revelation to John is the last. The Old Testament begins with the statement "In the beginning God created the heavens and the earth." The New Testament lifts up the hope of a new creation in Christ, a new heaven and a new earth. The sequence of the law of creation prior to the gospel of redemption is a given of Scripture as well as of the nature of things.

Fifth, the doctrine of the goodness of creation is followed by the topic of sin and evil. Sin is a theological concept. It is rebellion against the Creator's will for the orders of creation. It is a contradiction of the image and likeness of God built into the created being of humanity. Evangelical dogmatics must define the confessional differences between the Reformation and the Roman

Catholic conceptions of sin. The problem of evil in Christianity has received no dogmatic solution. The Christian faith affirms the paradox that the creation is good, because God created it, and yet is radically distorted by evil for which God is not responsible. No theoretical explanation of evil has proved itself essential or crucial to the self-understanding of faith. The accent of the Christian faith is not on explaining sin and evil, but on narrating the gospel history of God's mighty acts in dealing with the conditions of a sinful and suffering world.

Sixth, the church's main christological decision was made to safeguard the mystery that we meet God in the person of Jesus Christ. At stake in the decision was the issue of what it takes to bring about a full salvation for humanity and the world. Two axioms were in control of the christological dogma: First, only God can save, no inferior half-divine figure; and second, what is not assumed cannot be saved. Therefore, Jesus Christ must unite in his very person the true meaning of being both divine and human, without one side being reduced or negated to make room for the other. To say that Jesus Christ is truly God and truly man (*vere deus et vere homo*) means that salvation does not occur the pagan way by turning humans into gods or making gods appear as humans. The incarnation represents the freedom to become truly human after the damage due to sin has been repaired.

Seventh, in addition to the "Person of Christ" dogmatic theology has dealt with christology also in a second topic, under the rubric "The Work of Christ." In the New Testament, of course, one can find no clear-cut distinction between Christ's person and work. There the emphasis is more on his function than on his being or essence. In the ancient church the reverse is true. It produced the dogma of the incarnation, defining who Jesus Christ *is* in terms of his one person and two natures. The church, however, never created a dogma of the atonement. In the history of Christian thought, there have been several distinctly different ways of interpreting the atoning death of Jesus. The early Christian communities used a host of symbols, most of them rooted in the Hebrew religion, especially the symbol of sacrifice. These symbols have given rise to the various "theories" of the atonement which Gustaf Aulén has delineated in his classic *Christus Victor.* The task of dogmatics today is to bring order out of the confusion that prevails in the teaching of contemporary Christianity on the reconciling work of God in Jesus Christ.

Eighth, the church has rendered a clear dogmatic decision on the personal being and meaning of the Holy Spirit. The first phase of this decision states that the Holy Spirit, like the Son himself, is truly God. The second phase occurred in the Western church centuries later with the statement that the Holy Spirit "proceeds from the Father *and the Son*" (*filioque*), an addition to the Nicene Creed which the Eastern church has rejected to this day. In Christian dogmatics the doctrine of the Holy Spirit is placed between Christ and his church because he is the mediator of the saving benefits of Christ to the church and the world. The pneumatological dogma is in principle the answer to the question of how Jesus Christ and his benefits can be really present and appropriated through faith here and now.

Ninth, twentieth-century theology has produced more books and treatises on the church than any previous time in its history. This is a symptom of a profound struggle for a more adequate doctrine of the church. All churches confess their belief in the "one, holy, catholic, and apostolic church," but they do not share a common understanding of the elements of that formula. Contemporary Christianity has not received an ecclesiological dogma from the classical Christian tradition which can claim to be authoritative. The New Testament offers a plurality of images that point to the mystery of the church. The empirical history of the churches has generated competing, sometimes even mutually exclusive conceptions of the nature and mission of the church, each one critical of the others. Hence, there are many ecclesiologies. The question is whether they can be unified sufficiently to give expression to the essential unity of the church, manifest in the practice of their common faith.

Tenth, the doctrine of the means of grace asserts that the Holy Spirit uses the Word and sacraments to mediate the salvation which God has worked in Jesus Christ. God does not convey the grace of salvation immediately, apart from particular means. The Word is an audible sacrament, and the sacraments—baptism and the Lord's Supper—are visible words. They mediate the same salvation, only in different forms, the same Christ *in, with,* and *under* such things as words and water and bread and wine.

Eleventh, dogmatics in the tradition of the Protestant Reformation is based on the soteriological decision of its confessional writings, which has virtually the same value as any of the dogmas deriving from the ancient church, because it concerns "the article by which the church stands or falls" (*articulus stantis et cadentis ecclesiae*), "justification through faith alone." This article forms the existential basis of the life of the church in the world and all its individual members. The article on justification is the starting point for the Christian life, the freedom to live by faith before God apart from trust in the works of the law, and the possibility of living life to the hilt in one's secular vocation, in the service of one's fellow human beings and the world.

Twelfth, the tradition of dogmatics has ended with a chapter on "the last things." This dogmatic *locus* has dealt with biblical symbols such as the resurrection of the dead, the return of Christ, the final judgment, the end of the world, eternal condemnation and eternal life, heaven and hell, and so on. There is no such thing as an eschatological dogma in the history of Christianity. There are various strands of eschatological thinking in the New Testament, each of which has provided the confessional basis for a specific type of religious experience and church structure. There is the realized type of eschatology which stresses the present tense. The kingdom of God is already fully here and now, present somehow in the depths of present experience. There is the futuristic type of eschatology, which stresses the kingdom of God still to come in the future, and perhaps very soon but not yet now. Then there is the type of eschatology which places the kingdom of God and eternal life in another world above and beyond this one. In contemporary theology these various types are sometimes sharply juxtaposed in a diastatic way, sometimes coordinated in a multidimensional synthesis. Christian eschatology has received unparalleled attention in present-day theology because it has to do with the raw nerve of primitive Christian hope and at the same time offers a point of contact with the secular visions of modern ideologies.

The fundamental principles of dogmatics outlined here delineate a double tension in the history of God with the world. There is the tension that results from the distance between the original creation of the world and the new creation. Had there been no fall into sin, the original creation would still have enjoyed a history with God, pointing forward to something new. It would not have remained static. The new creation is no mere restoration of the old. The eschatological goal of the creation was originally something to be realized through God's involvement with the world. The second tension that runs through dogmatics is constituted by the difference between sin and grace, the sharp contrast between the righteousness of God and the sinfulness of humanity. Both kinds of tension find their resolution in Jesus Christ and the kingdom of God whose coming he signaled and embodied.

NOTES

1. See Dom Cuthbert Butler, *The Vatican Council, 1869–1870* (Westminster, Md.: Newman Press, 1962).

2. Two examples will suffice: Walter Kasper, *Dogma unter dem Wort Gottes* (Mainz: Matthias-Grünewald Verlag, 1965); and Michael Schmaus, *Dogma: God in Revelation* (New York and London: Sheed & Ward, 1968), vol. 1.

3. Kasper, *Dogma unter dem Wort Gottes*, p. 128.

4. Martin Luther, *The Bondage of the Will*, trans. J. I. Packer and O. R. Johnston (Westwood, N.J.: Fleming H. Revell Co., 1957), p. 67.

5. *LW* 41:121.

6. Adolf von Harnack, *History of Dogma*, trans. Neil Buchanan (New York: Dover Publications, 1961), 1:17.

7. Ibid., p. 22.

8. Karl Barth's views on dogma can be found in *Church Dogmatics*, vol. 1, part 1, *The Doctrine of the Word of God*, trans. G. T. Thomson (Edinburgh: T. & T. Clark, 1936), pp. 284–330.

9. Emil Brunner, *Truth as Encounter*, trans. Amandus W. Loos and David Cairns (Philadelphia: Westminster Press, 1964).

10. Brunner develops a more positive statement on dogma in his dogmatics, *The Christian Doctrine of God*, trans. Olive Wyon (Philadelphia: Westminster Press, 1950), 1:50–59.

11. Cf. Heinrich Schlier, reacting to a limited existentialist view of the relation between kerygma and dogma in the Bultmann school, in "Kerygma und Sophia: Zur neutestamentlichen Grundlegung des Dogmas," in *Die Zeit der Kirche* (Freiburg: Herder Verlag, 1958), pp. 206–32.

12. For a discussion of the contemporary controversy of dogma's relation to gospel, see F. W. Kantzenbach, *Evangelium und Dogma* (Stuttgart: Evangelisches Verlagswerk, 1959), pp. 293–98.

13. *LW* 36:107.

14. Quoted by Kasper, *Dogma unter dem Wort Gottes*, p. 15.

15. Edmund Schlink, "The Structure of Dogmatic Statements as an Ecumenical Problem," in *The Coming Christ and the Coming Church* (Edinburgh: Oliver & Boyd, 1967), pp. 16–84.

16. Ibid., p. 38.

17. Wolfhart Pannenberg, "What Is a Dogmatic Statement?" in *Basic Questions in Theology*, trans. George Kehm (Philadelphia: Fortress Press, 1970), 1:182–210.

18. Ibid., p. 210.

19. *The Book of Concord: The Confessions of the Evangelical Lutheran Church*, trans. and ed. Theodore G. Tappert (Philadelphia: Fortress Press, 1959).

20. Karl Rahner, *Foundations of Christian Faith*, trans. William V. Dych (New York: Seabury Press, 1978), p. 360.

4

The Holy
Scriptures

The Holy Scriptures are the source and norm of the knowledge of
God's revelation which concerns the Christian faith. The ultimate
authority of Christian theology is not the biblical canon as such,
but the gospel of Jesus Christ to which the Scriptures bear witness—
the "canon within the ‚canon." Jesus Christ himself is the Lord of
the Scriptures, the source and scope of its authority.

THE AUTHORITY OF SCRIPTURE

The history of the church presents numerous examples of unhappy conflict
between authority and freedom. The Gospels portray Jesus of Nazareth as
a preacher of the kingdom of God in conflict with the keepers of the sacred
traditions of Israel. "The Sabbath was made for man, and not man for the
Sabbath." The apostle Paul defended the freedom of the gospel over against
the "Judaizers" who would imprison it within a ritualistic legalism. The great
Augustine of North Africa in the fifth century championed the freedom deriving from the grace of God against Pelagianism, on the one hand, which tied
salvation to a moralistic system of good works, and Donatism, on the other
hand, which based the validity of the church's ministry on the moral purity
of the clergy. In the thirteenth century Thomas Aquinas was branded a
"modernist" because he fought for the freedom to interpret the Christian
faith to his contemporaries in the categories of Aristotle, which at that time
attracted the leading minds of the universities. Church authorities attempted
to curtail his efforts by condemning no less than twenty of his teachings.[1] Later
the hierarchical authorities of Rome refused to respond to Luther's call to
reform the church by the standard of the gospel of Jesus Christ. Still another
sad chapter is how scientists had to suffer at the hands of orthodox inquisitors
for the right to discover new truth. Galileo was silenced by the inquisition.
   The theological question is whether we can grasp a concept of authority
in the church that stands on the side of freedom. Is there an authority that
releases rather than inhibits that power of the gospel which generates the

"freedom for which Christ has set us free" (Gal. 5:1)? An evangelical concept of authority calls for the freedom to renew and reform the church in accordance with the Word of God which "authored" the church in the first place. The foundational event of the church is Jesus Christ himself according to the original apostolic witness of faith. This event is no mere past-historical fact; it is the eschatological event which holds the key to the present meaning of the church and future destiny of the world. Because this event is the source of the church's faith, it is the norm of the church's doctrine. Creative authority occurs through a double movement of going "back to the sources" (*"resourcement"*) and bringing the church up-to-date (*"aggiornamento"*), as it was so well expressed by Vatican II. Every generation of believers must claim the freedom to go back to the original source of true authority as witnessed by the Holy Scriptures, open to its critical and constructive power and meaning.

The Reformation provides a paradigm case of the issue of authority and freedom in the church. What was the authority to which Martin Luther appealed against the highest authorities in the church and empire? Was it reason, conscience, religious experience, dogma, magisterium, or Scripture? The question of the ultimate authority, the final and absolutely reliable referee of matters of faith and life, is inescapable within the church. All Christians, of course, whether Protestant, Roman Catholic, or Eastern Orthodox, will begin by saying that the absolute authority can be none other than God. They will go further in agreeing that God is manifest and knowable in Jesus Christ, supremely, uniquely, and unsurpassably. Beyond this preliminary agreement, however, there are significant confessional differences, not to mention serious tensions, within each confessional position. How do we come to know the mind of Jesus Christ—God's Word of truth to us? Where do we have the trustworthy medium of God's self-communication? The answer to this question was given in the sixteenth century by the Reformation principle of *sola scriptura.* As the Epitome of the Formula of Concord tells us, "Holy Scripture remains the only judge, rule, and norm according to which as the only touchstone all doctrines should and must be understood and judged as good or evil, right or wrong." It further states that all other writings, no matter how classic and official, "are not judges like Holy Scripture, but merely witnesses and expositions of the faith, setting forth how at various times the Holy Scriptures were understood by contemporaries in the church of God with reference to controverted articles, and how contrary teachings were rejected and condemned."[2]

The Bible was the chief document of the Reformation. Luther's existential struggle to find a gracious God took place in the context of his encounter with the Bible. His ensuing call for the church to reform arose out of the gospel he discovered through his interpretation of Scripture. Luther was professor of biblical exegesis at the University of Wittenberg, not a systematic theologian like Melanchthon or Calvin. He came to possess a radical confidence in the word of Scripture for faith, proclamation, and theology.

The popular view of Luther rediscovering the Bible—or emancipating the Scriptures—is a misconception. There were many Bibles in Germany before Luther. His own Augustinian order encouraged a devout study of Holy Scripture. Thousands of copies of the Latin Bible (Jerome's translation) existed in Luther's time, mostly in churches, schools, and monasteries. There were also various translations into German in Luther's day. Humanistic scholars, like Reuchlin and Erasmus, were producing critical texts of the Bible in Hebrew and Greek, so that when Luther began to study the Bible in earnest he had access to the Bible in its original languages. Luther's unique contribution was a translation of the Bible into the language of the common people, peasants and villagers. The invention of printing made it possible to bring this popular version to the masses, so that the Reformation could be carried forward with a laity that knew the Scriptures. To advance the teachings of the Reformation, Luther provided prefaces for almost all the biblical books. Some of his sharpest and most memorable critical judgments on Scripture are found in these prefaces, for example, that he did not wish to have books like James and Revelation in the Bible.[3] Books that really belong in the canon of Scripture must clearly communicate the gospel. Books that fail to do that hold a lower rank in the canon.

Luther did not produce a new canon. He operated with the canon that had been in actual use in the church. However, he made fundamental distinctions between the books by applying *a christological canon of interpretation*: the gospel of free grace and justification through faith alone. This is the truly apostolic standard. It cannot be overemphasized that for Luther what counted was the *material* contents of the book and not its *formal* position within Scripture. Thus, although Luther retained the established canon of the ancient church, he discovered within it a canon by which all its parts could be judged. Luther says:

> And that is the true test by which to judge all books, when we see whether or not they inculcate Christ, Romans 3:21; and St. Paul will know nothing but Christ, I Corinthians 2:2. Whatever does not teach Christ is not yet apostolic, even though St. Peter or St. Paul does the teaching. Again, whatever preaches Christ would be apostolic, even if Judas, Annas, Pilate or Herod were doing it.[4]

This "canon within the canon"[5] (Käsemann) is not something that Luther brought to the biblical text out of his subjective experience. Rather, it is to be found as the clear center of the main books of Scripture itself. In the New Testament the books that most clearly convey Christ are the Gospel and First

Letter of John, the epistles of Paul, especially Romans and Galatians, and 1 Peter. The Letter of James is inferior because it preaches the law instead of the gospel. As for the Revelation of John, Luther says he can find no evidence that it was written by the Holy Spirit.

The significant thing is not Luther's critical opinions on various parts of Scripture, but the fact that he applied criticism at all. In the following period of Lutheran orthodoxy, the beginnings of biblical criticism in Luther were virtually aborted. Whereas for Luther the canon was to be found in the Bible, for orthodoxy the canon came to be equated with the inspired text. Whereas for Luther the material principle of Scripture, justification through faith alone, was primary, for orthodoxy the formal principle of Scripture, namely, that it is verbatim the inspired Word of God, took precedence.

Yet even in the period of orthodoxy some dogmaticians continued to make a distinction between the canonical and the deuterocanonical (or apocryphal) books of the New Testament. Such a distinction had been consistently maintained by all the reformers with regard to the Old Testament. But now books like 2 Peter, 2 and 3 John, Hebrews, James, Jude, and Revelation were placed in a special class. In general it can be stated that the closer the dogmaticians stood to Luther, the more they preserved this distinction. Thus Martin Chemnitz insisted on the difference between the undoubtedly canonical books and those which had been marked with uncertainty by many in the ancient church as well as by Luther. By the time of David Hollaz, who represents orthodoxy in full bloom, the meaning of the distinction had been lost.[6] This undifferentiated view of the books of the Bible finally triumphed and today survives in Protestant fundamentalism. The canon which was open and flexible in Luther's thinking became closed and rigid in the circles that inherited the doctrine of Scripture in orthodoxy.

Luther and all his fellow reformers, Zwingli and Calvin, accepted the authority of Scripture, but in this respect they were not manifestly different from their opponents. The theology of the Middle Ages also affirmed the authority of Scripture and its full inspiration. Luther's departure consisted in deriving the authority of Scripture from its *gospel content*. The gospel is a promise; therefore the Bible is a book of promises that circulated first in the Word of preaching. The living Word of preaching is the basic form of the gospel. The Scriptures are the written form which became a necessary aid in the ongoing oral proclamation of the church. Luther stated: "The fact that it became necessary to write books reveals that great damage and injury had already been done to the Spirit. Books were thus written out of necessity and not because this is the nature of the New Testament."[7] Luther's decisive break with Medieval theology rests on this massive simplification of the manifold character of Scripture: The heart of Scripture is the promise of the gospel that is brought to expression in the Christ-event. Scripture's authority is not of a juridical kind; it is not essentially a book of legal doctrines, inerrant reports, or devotional materials. Scripture conveys the life-giving Word of salvation in Christ to those who accept it through faith. Authority in matters of faith rests on the gospel of Scripture, not on the creeds and councils of the church or on the hierarchical offices, papacy and episcopacy. The Word of Scripture alone (*sola scriptura*) is to be believed and accepted as finally valid with respect to the concerns of faith and salvation.

Luther's Scripture principle is articulated most clearly in the *Book of Concord* (1580), the final collection of Lutheran confessional writings. These confessions claim to be authoritative expositions of the truth of Scripture, always acknowledging the principle of the priority of Scripture over confession. Thus the Solid Declaration of the Formula of Concord states:

> We pledge ourselves to the prophetic and apostolic writings of the Old and New Testaments as the pure and clear fountain of Israel, which is the only true norm according to which all teachers and teachings are to be judged and evaluated. . . . The Word of God is and should remain the sole rule and norm of all doctrine, and no human being's writings dare be put on a par with it, but everything must be subjected to it.[8]

This same principle was even more clearly elaborated by Zwingli, Calvin, and the confessional documents of the Reformed churches. In none of the Lutheran confessions is there an article explicitly on the authority of Scripture; rather, it is presupposed and applied in implicit terms. But, in the Reformed confessions there are explicit articles on "the Word of God" or "the authority of the Scriptures." Thus, in the Genevan Confession of Faith (1536) the very first article deals with Scripture: "We desire to follow Scripture alone as a rule of faith and religion, without mixing it with any other thing which might be devised by the opinion of men, apart from the Word of God." The Scots Confession (1560) declares: "As we believe and confess the Scriptures of God sufficient to instruct and make the man of God perfect, so do we affirm and avow the authority of the same to be of God and neither to depend on men or angels. We affirm therefore that such as allege the Scripture to have no authority but that which it receives from the Church, to be blasphemous against God and injurious to the true Church." The Westminster Confession of Faith (1647) gives a much fuller account of Scripture, stating that the Old Testament in Hebrew and the New Testament in Greek are "immediately inspired by God, and by his singular care and providence kept pure in all ages."

These brief summaries of the early Lutheran and Reformed positions on Scripture indicate two things: first, that both agree completely on the authority of Scripture, and second, that the Reformed confessions express a more detailed doctrine of Scripture. In the period of orthodoxy, however, the Lutheran dogmaticians show the same concern as the Reformed to have a complete doctrine of Scripture. This was due in part to external pressure from the Roman side, which could appeal to a full-fledged doctrine of papal authority, challenging the Protestants to produce one of equal force in the polemical situation. It was also due in part to an interior development, in which Luther's stress on the material content of Scripture—justification through faith alone—was relegated to the status of a true doctrinal proposition, along with others, which could be proved from Scripture. In this development the doctrine of the inspiration of Scripture enjoyed a great inflation in the works of the dogmaticians, both Lutheran and Reformed.

Thus in Protestant orthodoxy a shift away from Luther occurs in the account of Scripture's authority. For Luther, as we have seen, its authority resides in its gospel content. Scriptures are a means of grace. They are to be judged entirely in terms of Luther's famous formula *"was Christum treibt"* (what conveys Christ). For the seventeenth-century orthodox dogmaticians, Scriptures are authoritative because of their divine inspiration and inerrancy. Because this doctrine became the official teaching of almost all Lutheran and Reformed churches, and remains valid to this day, except where the historical-critical approach to Scripture has occasioned a new doctrine, it is well to consider some of the essential features of the doctrine of Scripture in Protestant orthodoxy.

According to this doctrine, the Scriptures are the written deposit of revelation which God communicated to the prophets and apostles by means of the inspiration of the Holy Spirit. God was the real author of Scripture; the human writers were the instruments God used to produce the Bible. The process of inspiration pertained to both the matter and the form of Scripture. God provided the correct ideas in the minds of the authors, the right words to use, as well as the stimulus to their wills to cause them to write. Hence it follows that, with the Holy Spirit in complete charge of the production of the Scriptures, they are totally free of all errors and imperfections. The final conclusion was that the difference between the Word of God and the Holy Scriptures, which Luther was able to assert, could be allowed to vanish. The activity of God in the writing of the Bible was so direct that it was likened to dictation. The Holy Spirit dictated in so many words, even the punctuation, everything to be written down. The prophets, evangelists, and apostles were but the inspired secretaries. David Hollaz writes, "All the words, without exception, contained in the Holy Manuscript, were dictated by the Holy Spirit to the pen of the prophets and apostles."[9] The ground of the authority of Scripture has been shifted from the gospel revelation to a verbal inspiration. A great fascination arises concerning the miraculous intervention of the Holy Spirit. It was even taught that everything the authors would normally know on their own had to be the subject matter of inspiration, in order to close every possible gap that might arise from human fallibility.[10]

The doctrine of inspiration continued to grow as the controversy with the Roman Catholics continued. All the weapons of Protestantism seemed to hang on this one doctrine—the absolutely inspired text of Scripture, down to the last syllable and punctuation mark. The result was the divinization of the biblical texts, the ascription of attributes which nearly rival the attributes of the Almighty. The faith and obedience which the New Testament refers to God, Christ, or the Gospel are now transferred to Scripture as the Word of God.

The authority the Scriptures possess in orthodoxy is of an authoritarian kind, commanding blind faith and obedience. This is so because it is affirmed that they are to be believed not because of *what* they say, but purely *because* they say it. The Scriptures are endowed with causative authority, so that in the language of orthodoxy it is said that the Scriptures create faith and obedience; the Scriptures create assent to the truths to be believed. This type of language indicates that the distinction between the Holy Spirit, who alone according to classical Christianity possesses such creative, regenerative, and illuminative power, and the Holy Scriptures has virtually collapsed.

Untiringly the orthodox dogmaticians drew up lists of the attributes of Scripture. They possess infallible truth and the power to interpret themselves correctly; the Hebrew and Greek texts are endowed by the providence of God with incorruptibility; and everything taught in the Bible is perfectly true. The Scriptures, in addition, have the attributes of perfection, perspicuity, and efficacy. The perfection of the Scriptures means that they are the solid Word of God and instruct us flawlessly in things that pertain to the salvation of humankind. In no way do they have to be supplemented by other sources with regard to the true knowledge of God's revelation. By the perspicuity of Scripture is meant that they are clear and plain for everyone to understand. No light outside of Scripture needs to be turned on to make its teachings explicit and meaningful. Thus Scripture has the quality of efficacy in itself, that is, "even apart from its use" (*etiam extra usum*).

In the theology of the Reformation we are thus faced with two doctrines of the authority of Scripture. For Luther and Melanchthon and their closest pupils the authority of Scripture is grounded in its witness to Christ. The Scripture is to be believed on account of Christ, its essential content. The other doctrine holds that Scripture is trustworthy because of the testimonies that prove its divine origin by means of inspiration. There are traces of this doctrine also in Luther and Melanchthon, which they inherited from a tradition going back to the early church and its Jewish antecedents. Likewise, within the Calvinist tradition the same two forms of the doctrine of Scripture exist side by side. For Calvin, Scripture's authority is communicated to believers by the internal testimony of the Holy Spirit (*testimonium Spiritus Sancti in-*

ternum); it is an immediate certainty of faith in response to hearing God's Word in Scripture. This is a certainty that only the Spirit can work, and cannot be built up inductively by rational proofs.

In later Calvinism a biblicism emerges which neglects Calvin's teaching and which petrifies the authority of the Bible in words mechanically dictated by the Holy Spirit. Testimonies in favor of Scripture, evidences of its divine origin, are enumerated, such as the miracles they report, the antiquity of the writings, the literal fulfillment of the prophecies, the moral superiority of its doctrine in comparison with the pagans, the joy of the martyrs, and so on.

This doctrine of testimonies for Scripture became the point at which the battleline was drawn between the orthodox defenders of Scripture and the critics of the Enlightenment who sought purely rational proofs for the contents of belief. The reasoning was simple: If the authority of Scripture was to be defended by rational evidences, it could be attacked on the same grounds. And so the Bible became the subject of a long, drawn-out controversy between the supernaturalism of the orthodox party and the naturalism of the biblical critics.

Luther's emphasis on the Bible as the living voice of the gospel enjoyed a revival in pietism. Pietism may be seen as a counteraction to orthodoxy, insofar as it was less concerned with having a systematic doctrine about Scripture than with reading it directly as a means of spiritual experience and growth in Christian living. This brought about an intensification of interest in the study of the Bible; here we find perhaps the origin of the modern existential exegesis of Scripture.

While Lutheran pietism recaptured the existential personal dimension of Scripture's message, the Calvinist "federal theology" of Johannes Coccejus (1669) read the Bible as a book of history and a series of interconnected covenants. This historical convenantal conception of the Bible had enormous influence on such thinkers as J. G. Herder, J. A. Bengel, J. T. Beck, and J. C. K. von Hofmann, all forerunners of the contemporary "history-of-salvation" theology. In this line the authority of the Bible rests on the meaning of the historical events which the Bible reports. The Bible itself bears witness to this meaning: All the events point to Christ as the midpoint of history. This christocentric view of the Bible again gathers up an emphasis central in the theology of Luther and Calvin.

The authority of the Bible was the basic presupposition which the Reformation held in common with the Middle Ages and with its Roman Catholic contemporaries. But already in the sixteenth century impulses of humanist criticism were beginning to be felt. These impulses increased until there was a flood tide of critical thought in the Enlightenment that applied the categories of "nature" and "reason" to wash away the foundations of biblical authority. The English deists, the French encyclopedists, and the German thinkers of the Enlightenment released such an avalanche of critical methods and insights that not only the orthodox theory of verbal inspiration was swept away, but the unique status of Scripture in theology and the church was also severely threatened. The result is that in modern theology the authority of the Bible no longer functions as an unquestioned presupposition, as it did in the theology of the reformers, but is treated precisely as that which has to be established.[11] The question of biblical authority stands or falls with the approach one takes; it has become a matter of interpretation. In the contemporary idiom it is an "hermeneutical" question.

THE INTERPRETATION OF SCRIPTURE

The church in history has always retained its identity by the ongoing activity of biblical interpretation. This essential appeal to Scripture has created a rich history of rediscovering ever-new means of grasping the biblical word. Luther's most revolutionary principle of interpretation was the insistence on the literal-historical and philological exposition of the Scriptures. Thereby he rejected the allegorical method of exegesis which had been practiced to excess since Origen. Allegorical exegesis could prove anything from Scripture. The effect was to rob Scripture of its own validity and to diminish its power to criticize the evolving traditions of the church. If Scripture was to regain its primacy in the church, the interpretation would have to be bound to the original sense as that appears in the Hebrew and Greek texts. So Luther said, "We shall not long preserve the Gospel without the languages. The languages are the sheath in which this sword of the Spirit is contained."[12] Against the spiritualists who sought hidden meanings behind the words of the text, Luther said, "The Holy Spirit is the plainest writer and speaker in heaven and earth, and therefore His words cannot have more than one, and that the very simplest, sense, which we call the literal, ordinary, natural sense."[13]

In addition to his insistence that the biblical expositor must search out the literal sense of Scripture, Luther maintained that every passage has only one authentic meaning. The allegorists had found sometimes as many as four meanings in a single verse: the physical, moral, spiritual, and mystical senses. Luther did away with this complicated apparatus, which filled medieval biblical commentaries with idle and sometimes dangerous speculations. The interpreter must not be the master and judge of Scripture, but must only bring to expression Scripture's own witness to itself. It is not the church which authorizes the meaning of Scripture; the Scripture authenticates itself. The church has only to listen and obey. "The gospel is not believed because the church confirms it, but because one recognizes that it is God's word."[14] To those who argued that at least the church determined the canon, Luther retorted that it is only the Word of God that determines what is canonical.

Luther stopped at this point. One searches in vain for a further answer to those who counter with the charge that this is circular reasoning, proving one unknown thing by appealing to another unknown thing.

A further step in Luther's hermeneutical position is the principle "the Scripture interprets itself." This means that the standard of interpretation cannot come from outside Scripture. "Scripture is therefore its own light. It is a grand thing when Scripture interprets itself."[15] This principle was applied polemically against both the Roman theologians and the Protestant enthusiasts. The Roman theologians controlled the interpretation of Scripture by the teaching office of the church; the enthusiasts read Scripture in light of their own spiritual experiences. In both cases some standard outside Scripture was used to determine what was relevant. Either way leads to the erection of an authority alongside Scripture or above it. Luther's position was that, to be sure, the Spirit of God enables the right interpretation of Scripture. The Spirit, however, does not operate apart from the scriptural word, but is mediated through it. Luther wanted nothing alien to Scripture to be permitted to determine the saving message it communicates.

Such an emphasis on the sovereignty of Scripture did not mean that the tradition of the church was rejected. This was not an exclusive biblicism, with no room for the classical creeds, dogmas, and traditions of the church. Martin Chemnitz observed that there are eight different meanings of tradition,[16] and almost all of them are positively affirmed by the Reformation theologians. First, there is the oral tradition of Christ and his apostles, written down by the evangelists. Here Scripture and tradition are identical. Second, there is the tradition of handing down the Scriptures from age to age on the part of the church. Third, there are apostolic doctrines referred to by the early fathers not written down in Scripture. Fourth, there is the exegetical tradition of expounding the Scriptures. Fifth, there is the tradition of doctrines built up by the church, taught in Scripture not in so many words but only by implication. Sixth, the term is applied to what is called the tradition of the fathers, the patristic consensus. Seventh, there is the ecclesiastical tradition of rites and customs that are very ancient. They may be observed on account of their antiquity, provided they do not conflict with the gospel. Eighth, there are traditions pertaining to faith and morals with no basis in Scripture, but which the Council of Trent commands to be revered with the "same reverence and pious affection" as Scripture itself. Only in this sense is tradition to be rejected.

The picture that emerges is one relatively conservative on tradition, calling for reform only at those points where tradition conflicts with the gospel. A wide range of freedom is permitted for new developments in church tradition, so long as the gospel message of Scripture remains clear and central.

For this reason the structures of the church and its forms of worship need not all derive from the New Testament, as some Protestants have tried to insist.

The hermeneutics of the orthodox period effected a systematization of the principles of interpretation that Luther applied. The basic premise was the clarity of Scripture; the Bible is not a dark and obscure book that only a few professors can understand. This does not mean that all the passages are clear, only that everything necessary for Christian faith and life is clearly revealed in Scripture. The rule was to clarify obscure passages by clear ones. The idea of the clarity of Scripture did not mean that unregenerate people can grasp the true meaning of Scripture. Without the aid of the Holy Spirit they can understand the words and syntax, but the real saving content of Scripture will elude them until their hearts are tuned into the Spirit. The true interpretation of Scripture is a gift of faith worked by the Holy Spirit. This was finally taken to mean the ability to hold fast to what Scripture says even if it means a break with reason and runs contrary to the evidence of the senses. It may, indeed, require a *sacrificium intellectus*.

With the full emergence of biblical criticism in the age of the Enlightenment, the pillars of orthodox hermeneutics were shattered. Yet the biblical critics, who applied the new methods of literary and historical analysis, conceived of their work as faithful to Luther's own pioneering critical insights. They could appeal to Luther's critical statements about certain books of the Bible. However, unlike Luther, they did not apply a canon of criticism from within Scripture itself, namely the free gift of justifying grace on account of Christ, but developed an autonomous scientific criticism of the biblical documents. The methods of historical-critical investigation which were applied to all ancient writings were now applied without hesitation to the biblical writings.

The history of the development and refinement of the historical-critical method covers the last two centuries and is very complex, so we can only highlight several of its main features. The first *premise* is that the orthodox doctrine of inspiration has no heuristic validity at all in the scholarly study of the Bible. The investigation must proceed without prejudice concerning the special authority of this book. The biblical writings are products of two thousand years of history and must be examined as are all other literary remains from antiquity. The startling *discovery* was that the ecclesiastical dogmas are not to be found in the Bible, but are products of a later time. In the age of Christendom, the dogmas of the Trinity and of Christ, as formulated in the Nicene and Athanasian creeds, were necessary to believe for salvation. Now the biblical critics could apply the Scripture-principle of Protestantism to show that these dogmas cannot be required for faith, since they lack solid biblical support. One of the main incentives in the history of criticism was in fact to achieve freedom for scholarly research from the oppressive authority of the church and its dogmatic controls. If the dogmas could be undermined, no field of research could be declared off-limits. Three areas of research involving the interpretation of Scripture brought the new criticism into virulent conflict with traditional modes of understanding.

First, there arose the criticism of the Gospels, the main source documents of the birth, ministry, and death of Jesus of Nazareth. The overall result of Gospel criticism was shocking to those whose faith was dependent on the utter reliability of every word of Scripture, for the words and deeds of Jesus which the Gospels report were found to be intermingled with and modified by the beliefs of the early church. The question of who Jesus of Nazareth really was and what he accomplished became a matter of research and therefore in principle an open question always subject to continuing investigation. This research affected the christological dogma because it placed in question the traditional assertion of the divinity of Christ and the notion that a person's relation to God is determined by what is believed about Jesus of Nazareth.

Second, the unity of the New Testament was challenged on the grounds that there are different and rival theologies circulating in primitive Christianity. The theology of John is different from the theology of Luke, and Paul's theology is again very different from both. The upshot of this finding was to challenge the idea that the unity of the church could be founded on the unity of doctrine, since in the New Testament itself there is a plurality of theologies. This led to the relativizing of church dogma and the traditional demand for a *consensus doctrinae*.

Third, critics were eager to show that the biblical documents are not unique, but reflect the religious ideas of the environment in which they were written. The teachings of Jesus were traced back to various strands of Judaism; the Christianity of the Pauline and Johannine congregations was shown to be an expression of the religious syncretism of late antiquity.

In view of these critical results a question was bound to arise: What then is the ground and content of Christian faith? What is the essential core of the New Testament that defines the essence of Christianity for each succeeding generation? Is an objective answer to this question possible? A critical investigation of the history of biblical criticism indicates, as Albert Schweitzer documented so clearly in his *The Quest of the Historical Jesus*, that each epoch reads and interprets the Bible through the spectacles of its own milieu and world view. Eighteenth-century rationalism was able to portray Jesus as a teacher of moral enlightenment, espousing the eternal truths of rational religion. In the nineteenth century the Tübingen school of F. C. Baur interpreted the New Testament under the spell of Hegel's dialectical philosophy of history. Thus history is the dialectical unfolding of a religious idea; in the New Testament this idea clothes itself in the christological symbols of that day. In due time it is possible to dispense with the outer symbolic language in favor of the pure concept stated philosophically. David Friedrich Strauss shocked the Christian world with his *Life of Jesus*, in which he broke through the supernaturalism on the right and the rationalistic naturalism on the left and projected the mythological hypothesis. The New Testament can be interpreted only in terms of its mythical character. The point is not to argue whether the miracles happened or how they could be explained in natural terms, but to see that myth was the language of religion of that time. It is the nature of myth to speak of the otherworldly in terms of this world; therefore it is pointless to ask whether the myths convey historical facts.

Protestant liberalism in the nineteenth century provided numerous examples of a strange irony. On the one hand, the biblical critics were zealous in their commitment to scientific historical scholarship; on the other hand, their religious commitments and philosophical presuppositions shine through all their critical scholarship. In trying to be utterly historical they wound up reading the ideas of their own time into the biblical documents. The school of Albrecht Ritschl is a case in point. The Ritschlians were deeply influenced by the Kantian moral philosophy of religion. They looked for the ethical superiority of Christianity; they tended to interpret Jesus as a religious personality with a morally persuasive impact. Adolf von Harnack's bestseller *What Is Christianity?* portrayed Jesus as a religious personality who had the power to kindle a like religiosity in others. So he called theology away from the religion about Jesus, as we find in Paul, to the simple religion of Jesus, as he himself supposedly believed and taught it. Thus Harnack's famous assertion: "The Gospel, as Jesus proclaimed it, has to do with the Father only and not with the Son."[17] By the end of the nineteenth century the critical movement in theology had brought about a crisis in the Scripture-principle of modern Protestantism.

THE PROBLEM OF SCRIPTURE TODAY

In contemporary Protestantism the burning question continues to be how to unify the historical and hermeneutical approaches to the Bible. The purely historical interest can stifle the concern for the relevance of the biblical message today. The purely hermeneutical concern can force the Scripture into the mold of modern questions, so that the historical horizon of its own questions and answers is neglected. The attempt to take the message of the Bible on its own terms and make it speak prophetically to the current situation received a special impetus in the neo-Reformation theology of Karl Barth and Emil Brunner just after World War I. The appropriate name for this new movement is the "theology of the Word of God." These theologians took the Bible with a renewed seriousness, thinking of themselves as disciples of Luther and Calvin.

Owing to Karl Barth, biblical studies have played a vital role in recent dogmatic and systematic theology.

In Barth's theology the Word of God is the central concept. The Word of God comes to us in a threefold form: the preached Word, the written Word, and the revealed Word. The Word is by nature correspondingly speech, deed, and mystery, a threefoldness present in each form of the Word of God. This threeness-in-oneness and this oneness-in-threeness provide the only analogy to the doctrine of the Holy Trinity.

The Word of God is not a remote word of antiquity. It is the Word heard in the proclamation of the church today. This motif is a recurrence of Luther's stress on preaching from the Bible. The church preaches the Word which is witness to Christ, the revealed Word. This revealed Word proclaimed in the living language of the church is attested by the Word of Scripture. Thus the three forms, preaching, revelation, and Scripture, converge on the one name of Jesus Christ, in whom God is revealed as the Lord of humanity and the world. These themes of the Word of God are developed and repeated in the many volumes of Barth's *Church Dogmatics* and from there have found their way into many branches of the modern church, including Eastern Orthodoxy and Roman Catholicism.

The controversy over the Bible was not settled in the eighteenth and nineteenth centuries. An enormous gap has opened up within the Christian denominations regarding the interpretation of Scripture. In most denominations there is an attempt to recover the authority of the Bible in precisely the terms of seventeenth-century orthodoxy, before the rise of biblical criticism. Fundamentalist biblicism has not receded in vigor, even though it does not enjoy great prestige in the great theological schools. Masses of laity and clergy wish to possess an uncomplicated answer to the question of authority. Biblicism holds to an infallible Bible that can be the absolute authority in matters of belief and morals. The ancient doctrine of verbal inspiration survives. In some Christian groups the theory of inspiration is used to vouch for the absolute reliability of the Bible on all matters that relate to cosmology, biology, geography, chronology, and history. The Bible is used as a bulwark against the evolutionary hypothesis of modern natural science. The authority of Scripture for Luther and his followers was affirmed with respect to its chief purpose of declaring the gospel of Christ for faith and salvation. In modern Protestant fundamentalism, which ironically claims to bear the legacy of the Reformation, the authority of Scripture is extended to include infallible information on all kinds of subjects.

Fundamentalist biblicism is rejected by most theologians and is out of favor in most of the seminaries that train clergy for the parish ministry. They reject biblicism not merely because historical science has disclosed errors and contradictions in the biblical writings, but rather because the authority of the

Bible is elevated at the expense of the authority of Christ and his gospel. Non-fundamentalist Protestants also accept the Bible as the Word of God in some sense, but they point out that the concept of the Word of God, as Barth made clear, cannot be confined to the Bible. We cannot say that the Bible is the Word of God in a simplistic way, for the concept of the Word of God bears many diverse meanings in the classical Christian tradition.

Paul Tillich has observed that the "Word of God" has six meanings.[18] First, the "Word of God" refers classically to the second person of the Trinity, who was coeternal with the Father. Second, the Word of God was the active agent and medium of the creation of the world. Third, the Word of God was preached by the prophets in the Old Testament. Fourth, the Word of God became flesh in the person of Jesus of Nazareth. Fifth, the Word of God was proclaimed by the apostles of Jesus Christ in creating the church. Later it was written down by the apostles and their disciples. The Bible is the written Word of God in a derived way; it is the deposit of preaching of the early church. Sixth, the Word of God is the living voice of the gospel in every generation of Christians to follow. The Protestant fundamentalist doctrine of Scripture represents a reduction of the Word of God to only its written form.

A corollary of the revival of the Reformation theology of the Word of God has been the christological interpretation of Scripture. The christocentricity of Barth's theology has made an enormous impact on modern biblical theology. All the meanings of the Word of God have one center and norm: the appearance of Jesus Christ in history. For Christians following this line, the ultimate authority in matters of faith and life must be the Word of God made flesh, who died and rose again for the salvation of humanity. The honor of his name is mediated through Scripture and now lives through his Spirit in the Christian community today. The humanity of God in Christ is emphasized, as well as the historicity of all the means of his self-communication. The Word of God is not apart from humanity; rather, he uses human words and concepts, human hands and lips, human history in its glory and tragedy. The medium of his revelation is completely incarnational. Modern theology continues to show a marked preference for stressing the humanity of God in Christ, in the spirit of Luther who insisted that one can never draw God's Son too deeply into human flesh. The Scriptures, both Old and New Testaments, are Christ-centered; they point to the revelation of God in Jesus of Nazareth. Personal religious experience cannot add any stature to the magnitude of the Christ-event.

The uniqueness, the authority, and the value of the Bible, therefore, continue to be central for contemporary theological work. By means of Scripture, Christ is pictured and proclaimed as God's message and answer to the human predicament. Subsidiary to this central idea, the Bible is *also* treated as a collection of ancient documents which give us information about the history of Israel and the beginnings of Christianity. The Bible is *also* appreciated as a library of great literature, ranking with the greatest literature of the ancient world from a humanist literary critical viewpoint. The Bible is *also* a source document for the imaginative construction of church doctrines; it provides fresh stimulus in every age to create new history in the realm of doctrine. The Bible is *also* a devotional book full of inspiring passages to cultivate the religious life. But beyond all these viewpoints, the Bible is the unique book of the church because of its original and intrinsic connection with the history of the promises of God and its astonishing climax in the career of Jesus the Christ. It is finally for the sake of Christ alone that the church continues to regard the Bible as a book without equal in the history of human literature. For this reason the churches that claim the heritage of Luther and the Reformation still affirm the Bible as the Word of God. This is not meant in the fundamentalistic sense that everything in the Bible stands directly as the Word of God. Nor is it meant in the sense that only some things in the Bible are the Word of God—the red-lettered passages in some versions of the New Testament or the most inspiring verses of anyone's choosing. The Bible is the Word of God as a whole, in its total import and impact, because it conveys the message of eschatological salvation.

This valuation of the Bible as the Word of God is asserted with greater difficulty today than in Luther's time and with greater awareness of the historical problems involved in biblical interpretation. First of all, the theological task is not so easily limited to the interpretation of the Bible, as it was for Luther. The God whom Scriptures attest is Creator and Lord of all, active in all spheres of life and human experience. Therefore, whatever theology asserts about God on the basis of Scripture must in some way be correlated with what can be learned about God's world in nature and history from other disciplines. Theology that attempts to be true to Scripture tries to relate all things to the God of the Bible, the God of history and of all humanity and of the entire world from the beginning to its future fulfillment. Modern theology is currently rediscovering and applying the universal perspective of the Bible, reasserting the implications of the monotheistic idea of God. It faces the challenge of overcoming the dichotomy between theology and the secular sciences, inasmuch as the world of life and history that the Bible talks about can hardly be totally other from the world that science explores with its different methods.

The role of the Bible in constructive theology is radically qualified today by historical consciousness. Luther believed that the literal meaning of Scripture is identical with its historical content; things happened exactly as they were written down. Today it is impossible to assume the literal historicity of all things recorded. What the biblical authors report is not accepted as a literal transcript of the factual course of events. Therefore, critical scholars inquire behind the text and attempt to reconstruct the real history that took place. In christology this has led to endless debates on the relation between the historical Jesus and the Christ of apostolic faith and preaching. This debate continues, and there seems to be no way to proceed except to make all christology an interpretation of the historical Jesus. Otherwise history and interpretation fall asunder, and theology ignores the wisdom of Kant's dictum that all concepts without percepts are empty and all percepts without concepts are blind.

Modern hermeneutics has expanded in scope and significance to come to grips with the historical problem of the distance between the historical events and written testimonies to those events. The Reformation principle that Scripture alone must interpret Scripture—*Scriptura est suipsius interpres*—is broadened to mean that the biblical texts can only be interpreted out of their historical contexts. Critical attention to the historical situation has magnified the sense of the distance between biblical and modern times. Its thought world, its symbols and myths, are felt to be utterly different from the modern ways of thinking. Therefore Bultmann's call to demythologize the biblical concepts is an attempt to interpret the biblical message in terms that moderns can understand, without taking offense at the alien modes of thought we encounter in the Bible.

Luther's principle of sticking to the single grammatical historical sense of each portion of Scripture is also applied in modern hermeneutics, but with a different result. Critical attention to what the texts actually say has exploded the notion that one orthodox dogmatics can be mined out of Scripture. There are different theological tendencies and teachings in the various texts. Ecumenically this has led to the practical conclusion that the traditional demand for a complete consensus of doctrine may be wrongheaded, if even the Scriptures fail to contain such a consensus. Perhaps the unity of the church can be realized without the kind of doctrinal uniformity demanded by the sixteenth-century theologians on both the Protestant and Catholic sides. In any case, the interpretation of the texts of Scripture can no longer be dominated by the history of dogma, so that the exegetes are compelled to produce nothing but proofs the dogmaticians require. Biblical theology and dogmatic theology are not reducible to each other. This awareness is a result of taking the historical development seriously. A deep gulf exists between the biblical world of thought and that of, say, Alexandria in the third century, Rome in the thirteenth century, Wittenberg in the sixteenth century, or New York in the twentieth century. It is the task of hermeneutics to make an intelligible transmission of meaning from the biblical text to the completely new situation here and now. This is a shared task. Theology plays a part, but so do preaching and worship, as well as the faith and the witness of the laity. For Christianity is not merely the ideas handed down from Scripture, but the life and action of Christ's people in the world. The interpretation of Scripture is not successfully confined to the academic situation. The really creative insights come out of the crucible of missionary experience as the witnesses of Christ take on themselves the burdens of humanity and the pain of the world.

NOTES

1. Etienne Gilson, *History of Christian Philosophy in the Middle Ages* (New York: Random House, 1955), p. 728 n. 52.

2. The Epitome of the Formula of Concord, *BC* 465.

3. "Prefaces to the Books of the Bible," *LW* 35:225–411.

4. Ibid., p. 396.

5. Ernst Käsemann, "The Canon of the New Testament and the Unity of the Church," in *Essays on New Testament Themes*, trans. W. J. Mantague (London: SCM Press, 1964).

6. Heinrich Schmid, *The Doctrinal Theology of the Evangelical Lutheran Church*, trans. Charles A. Hay and Henry E. Jacobs (Minneapolis: Augsburg Publishing House, 1899), pp. 80–91.

7. Quoted by Paul Althaus, *The Theology of Martin Luther* (Philadelphia: Fortress Press, 1966), p. 73 n. 2.

8. *BC* 503–4, 505.

9. Schmid, *Doctrinal Theology*, p. 45.

10. Werner Elert refers to this exaggerated aspect of the doctrine of inspiration as an *Irrlehre* (wrong doctrine) in *Der Christliche Glaube* (Hamburg: Im Furche-Verlag, 1956), p. 171.

11. See Wolfhart Pannenberg, "The Crisis of the Scripture Principle," in *Basic Questions in Theology*, vol. 1 (Philadelphia: Fortress Press, 1970).

12. Martin Luther, "To the Councilmen of All Cities in Germany That They Establish and Maintain Christian Schools," *LW* 45:360.

13. Martin Luther, "Answer to the Hyperchristian, Hyperspiritual, and Hyperlearned Book by Goat Emser," *LW* 39:178.

14. Quoted by Althaus, *Theology of Martin Luther*, p. 75.

15. Ibid., p. 76.

16. Martin Chemnitz, *Examination of the Council of Trent*, part 1, trans. Fred Kraemer (St. Louis: Concordia Publishing House, 1971), pp. 220–307.

17. Adolf von Harnack, *What Is Christianity?* trans. T. B. Saunders (New York: Harper & Brothers, 1957), p. 144.

18. Paul Tillich, *Systematic Theology*, 3 vols. (Chicago: University of Chicago Press, 1951–63), 1:157–58.

SECOND LOCUS

The Triune God

ROBERT W. JENSON

THE TRIUNE GOD

Introduction

CONTENTS

Introduction

The dogmatic *locus* about God is not and cannot be a description of God, though it often intends to state facts about God. Nor is the *locus* on God a piece of metaphysics, though it will raise and try to answer metaphysical questions. The dogmatic *locus* about God is a convenient gathering of certain questions that regularly arise in the Christian church, those that are most straightforwardly about God. These do, of course, turn out to have systematic relations to each other, and tracing these is a main task of dogmatics. But the specific set of questions that coalesce to make the *locus* "on God" is more the fruit of liturgical and catechetical history than of timeless logic.

The primary religious question is always about the identity of God: *Which* is God? Of history's putative or possible deities, which will sustain the claim? To whom may I—do I—pray?

Within biblical faith or within culture influenced by it, the question *whether* there is God can also acquire religious potency, for biblical faith poses the possibility of nihilism, of absolute distrust of reality, as not all religion does. And as long as it appears that there is only one plausible candidate for deity, that the biblical God's only competitors are such straw gods as "money" or "the belly," the awful issue between faith and nihilism is the first to claim attention. If we are sure who would be God if there were any, "Is there God?" heads our perplexity.

But history has already made clear that the "post-Christian era" will not be one of efficient and religionless secularity, but a combination of nihilist communal life, whether collectivist or chaotic, with a compensating efflorescence of non-Christian private religions. In the immediate future, Western streets will present a new divine claimant on every corner, as did those of the declining ancient world, and we will first have to make clear to ourselves which one we mean by "God" before we wager God's reality. In a religiously plural age, the question of God's identity reasserts its natural priority.

The question of *what* God is like cannot fruitfully be taken first. The big theological words—"salvific," "merciful," and so on—share a logical peculiarity: They are so determinedly analogous and open to interpretation that by themselves they mean almost nothing. "X redeems," for example, is not even an ordinary open sentence making a specific assertion about an unspecified subject, for until X is specified we do not know what "redeems" says about her/it/him. Only when "Baal," for example, replaces X does "redeems" acquire the operational value "sends rain." A theology of no-god-in-particular or of all gods at once would be, if not quite vacuous, wholly unhelpful. Prior to identification of God, all that can be said about it/him/her is "God is the object of ultimate concern" or "God is whatever you hang your heart on." The most that "X redeems" could mean is "X restores whatever state X defines as good." A doctrine that went no further would be of purely analytical use and no religious use.

We begin, therefore, and spend most of our space, with the *identity* of the gospel's God, and discuss the existence and nature of God afterward. That is, we begin with "the doctrine of the Trinity," for within Christian theology it is the identification of God which this body of teaching seeks to accomplish.[1] In following this order, we follow a minority tradition of dogmatics;[2] the minority, we claim, is right.

We must next note that the doctrine of the Trinity is no one teaching or homogeneous set of teachings, as is, for example, the doctrine of justification by faith alone. It is a complex of expressions of various forms and various relations to the identification of God. We distinguish four bodies of trinitarian discourse. Their classification makes the gross outline of the part of the following devoted to trinitarian doctrine (Chapters 1–4). Allotment of space among the four reflects relative complexity, not relative importance.

The doctrine of the Trinity is moribund in large sections of the church; indeed, it often serves as a prized example of useless theological hairsplitting. The book perhaps most frequently used in Protestant seminaries for instruction in systematic theology, Gustaf Aulén's *Faith of the Christian Church*, scarcely mentions the matter, and what it does say is inaccurate.[3] Other standard works are more informative, but little more helpful in seeing the point and vivacity of trinitarian language.[4] Such positive works as Leonard Hodgson's *The Doctrine of the Trinity*, Claude Welch's *In This Name*, or even Karl Rahner's pioneering *The Trinity* have not had the impact that might have been expected.[5] And when a "Trinity" is affirmed, it is often that of John Macquarrie or Paul Tillich, an interesting fruit of speculation but only distantly related to the church's trinitarianism here to be discussed. In general, such an enterprise as that of the present essay is a minority report in the present church.

It is to be feared that modern incomprehension of trinitarian discourse often expresses a morbidity of the faith itself; against this, dogmatics as such can do little. Error and incompleteness, both in the inherited body of trinitarian teaching and in current standard theological suppositions, play the chief role. We hope to make several contributions to overcoming these, but one suspects that the sheer bulk of inherited trinitarian discourse, of various functions and from various mostly distant times and places, also makes it hard simply to grasp what all this stuff is for. It is to the aid of this last perplexity that the organization of Chapters 1 through 4 was adopted, attempting to sort the mass of trinitarian language.

From discussion of God's triune identity, we must continue to the questions traditionally discussed as the doctrine of "the one God": what God is, whether God is, what God is like. The more clearly and dialectically specific our talk of God is, the more drastically—but perhaps also hopefully—it will in our time be challenged. The acids of modernity attack every aspect of belief. Is it even meaningful to talk of God? Is there any reason to affirm God's reality? Is it not rather evil or absurdity that is God, rather than fatherly goodness? And how do we find out what to think about God anyway? Would it not be better simply to adore God in silence or by meaningless speech?

It cannot be the task of dogmatics to complete faith's response to all challenges, but dogmatics can make a necessary contribution. In the course of theological history, three bodies of teaching have developed which seek to explicate the single reality of God. By no accident, each does in fact respond to an aspect of the modern perplexity. By no accident—for the questions just recited are historically faith's own questions, merely now reflected back in secularized form.

Doubt that talk about God makes sense is pervasive through the modern period. In the modern theological tradition, analysis of the logic of theological language has become an enterprise of its own. In response to this development, this book contains a separate *locus* on the knowledge of God, where direct discussion of the meaningfulness of God-language will be found. But the logical oddity of talk about God is not as such a modern discovery. Theology traditionally discussed it in the material mode and asked: What kind of "being" is God? How am I using "is" when I say "God is such-and-such"? These investigations have often led and may yet again lead to important material assertions about God and must therefore be pursued also in this *locus*, as Chapter 5.

The more or less biblical God of Western religion was long the only serious candidate among us. Just so, there has long been a standard topic: whether it is reasonable to think that God is. This question is often part of the present *locus*, but in this work it will be discussed in the next, epistemological, *locus* and is therefore omitted here.

Finally, since theologians must make sentences of the form "God is such-and-such," they must be concerned not only with the "is" but also with the such-and-such, with the predicate. What should we say about God? And why should we say one thing instead of another? Such questions make the problem about what are traditionally called the attributes of God and are here discussed in Chapter 6.

NOTES

1. Karl Barth made this clear. Karl Barth, *Kirchliche Dogmatik* (Zürich: Zollikon, 1932–67), 1/1:313–20.

2. Most notably represented by Peter Lombard, Bonaventure, and Barth.

3. Gustaf Aulén, *The Faith of the Christian Church* (Philadelphia: Fortress Press, 1948), pp. 245–49.

4. E.g., Regin Prenter, *Creation and Redemption*, trans. Theodore I. Jensen (Philadelphia: Fortress Press, 1967); Helmut Thielicke, *The Evangelical Faith*, trans. G. W. Bromiley (Grand Rapids: Wm. B. Eerdmans, 1967), 2:124–83.

5. Leonard Hodgson, *The Doctrine of the Trinity* (New York: Charles Scribner's Sons, 1944); Claude Welch, *In This Name* (New York: Charles Scribner's Sons, 1952); Karl Rahner, *The Trinity*, trans. J. Donceel (New York: Herder & Herder, 1970).

1

The Triune
Name of God

In functional continuity with biblical witness, "Father, Son, and Holy Spirit" is the proper name of the church's God. That God have a proper name is a demand of both the Hebrew Scriptures and the New Testament gospel. That God has *this* proper name is an immediate reflex of primary Christian experience.

THE SENSE OF "GOD"

What can be said prior to God's identification must, to be sure, be said. What do people use this word "God" for, that we ask so urgently to whom or what it is truly applied?

The horizon of life and its concerns is time, the inescapable already, no-more, still, and not-yet of all we know and will. Every human act moves from what was to what is to be; it is carried and filled by tradition but intends new creation. Just so our acts hang between past and future, to be in fact temporal, to be the self-transcendence, the inherent and inevitable adventure, that is the theme of all religion and philosophy. But also, our acts threaten to fall between past and future, to become boring or fantastic or both, and all life threatens to become an unplotted sequence of merely causally joined events that happen to befall an actually impersonal entity, "me."

Human life is possible—or, in recent jargon, meaningful—only if past and future are somehow bracketed, only if their disconnection is somehow transcended, only if our lives somehow cohere to make a story. Life in time is possible only if there is such a bracket, that is, if there is eternity. Thus in all we do we seek eternity. If our seeking becomes explicit, we practice "religion." If our religion perceives the bracket around time as in any way a particular something, as in any way the possible subject of verbs (as in, e.g., "The eternal speaks by the prophets"), we tend to say "God" instead of "eternity."

But already we are becoming intolerably indefinite, for manifestly there are many kinds of bracketing that can be posited around past and future, many possible eternities. There is, for example, the eternity of tribal ancestors who have become so old that nothing can surprise them any more and in whose continuing presence all the future's putative novelties are therefore mastered by traditional maxims. There is the eternity of nirvana, where a difference of past and future is just not permitted. There is the eternity of existentialism, in which decision brings time momentarily to a halt. So multiform is eternity that the mere assertion that it is, that there is some union of past and future, that life has some meaning, is for practice as good as the suspicion that there is none at all. Life is enabled not by a posit *that* life means but by a posit of *what* it means. The plot and energy of life are determined by which eternity we rely on, and the truth of any mode of life is determined by the reality of the eternity it posits. If we speak of "God," our life's substance is given by which God we worship, and our life's truth is given by whether this is the God that really is.

Meditating on the foundation of biblical faith, the exodus, Israel's first theologians made Moses' decisive question be: "If I come to the people of Israel and say to them, 'The God of your fathers has sent me to you,' and they ask me, 'What is his name?' what shall I say to them?" If Israel was to risk the future of this God, to leave secure nonexistence in Eygpt and venture on God's promises, Israel had first and fundamentally to know which future this was. The God answered, "Say this to the people of Israel, [Yahweh], the God of your fathers, the God of Abraham, the God of Isaac, and the God of Jacob, has sent me to you, this is my name for ever, and thus I am to be remembered throughout all generations" (Exod. 3:13–15).[1]

The answer provides a proper name, "Yahweh." It also provides what logicians now call an identifying description, a descriptive phrase or clause, or set of them, that fits just the one individual thing to be identified. Here the description is "the God whom Abraham and Isaac and Jacob worshiped." The more usual description is that found in a parallel account a few chapters later: God said to Moses, "Say . . . to the people of Israel, 'I am [Yahweh], and I will bring you out from under the burdens of the Egyptians . . . ; and you shall know that I am [Yahweh] your God, *who* has brought you out. . . . I am [Yahweh]'" (Exod. 6:2–7; emphasis added).

In general, proper names work only if such identifying descriptions are at hand. We may say, "Mary is coming to dinner," and be answered with, "Who is Mary?" Then we must be able to say, "Mary is the one who lives in apartment 2C, and is always so cheerful, and . . . ," continuing until the questioner says, "Oh, *that* one!" We may say, "Yahweh always forgives," and be answered with, "Do you mean the Inner Self?" Then we must be able to say, "No. We mean the one who rescued Israel from Eygpt, and . . . "

Linguistic means of identification—proper names, identifying descriptions, or both—are a necessity of religion. Prayers, like other requests and praises, must be addressed. Thus the typical prayer-form of Western Christianity, the collect, usually begins with some identifying description such as, "O God, who didst give thine only-begotten Son to be. . . ." The moral will of God must be proclaimed as a particular will if we are to follow it. Paul set a pattern for Christian preaching when he wrote to the Philippians: "Have this mind among yourselves, which you have in Christ Jesus, who . . ." (Phil. 2:1–11). Eschatological promise must be specified. Proclamation of a final union of humankind is gospel because the gathering is to be around Jesus, but it would be quite something else were the gathering to be around Stalin. It was precisely the wrong address of praise in which Paul saw the perversion of heathendom (Rom. 1:24–25).

Trinitarian discourse is Christianity's effort to identify the God who has claimed us. The doctrine of the Trinity comprises both a proper name, "Father, Son, and Holy Spirit," in several grammatical variants, and an elaborate development and analysis of corresponding identifying descriptions.

We live in the present; that is a tautology. But the content of present life is memory and expectation, in some union. We speak of "God" to name that union. Or rather, we speak to and from God to invoke it. Just so, we need to know who God is, to know how our lives hang together. Trinitarian discourse is Christianity's answer to this need.

ISRAEL'S IDENTIFICATION OF GOD

What the word "Yahweh" may once have meant we do not know. Since historical Israel did not know either, the loss is not theologically great. "Yahweh" was for Israel a pure proper name which no doubt had once been applied on account of its sense but had survived the knowledge thereof.[2] Indeed, in the famous passage in which Moses asks for an explanation of the name, Yahweh is depicted as replying with a play on an ad hoc etymology precisely to reject such curiosity: "I am who I am" (Exod. 3:14).[3]

It is remarkable that "Yahweh," with its variants, was the *only* proper name in ordinary use for Israel's God. Other substantives, predominantly "Elohim," were used as common terms and appelatives. Other ancient peoples piled up divine names.[4] The comprehensiveness of a god's authority was achieved by blurring the god's particularity, by identification of initially distinct numina with one another, leading to a grandly vague deity-in-general. Israel made the opposite move. Israel's salvation depended precisely on unambiguous identification of its God over against the generality of the numinous. In the Yahwistic account of Yahweh's decisive self-revelation at Mount Sinai, the central passage is "And [Yahweh] descended . . . and proclaimed the name [Yahweh]. . . : '[Yahweh, Yahweh], a God merciful and gracious'" (Exod. 34:5–6), as gods in general could not be supposed to be. Therefore it was included in Israel's fundamental description of righteousness, the ten commandments, that Israel must not demean the name of Yahweh (Exod. 20:7).

A proper place for prayer, sacrifice, or consultation of the oracles was therefore one where the name Yahweh was known (Exod. 20:24). What happens at such a holy place can be compendiously described as "calling on the name [Yahweh]" (e.g., Gen. 12:8). Blessings are "applications" of the name Yahweh (e.g., Num. 6:27), and prayers are addressed by it (e.g., 1 Kings 18:24). The worshipers' use of "Yahweh" is their reason for confidence that their offering will be acceptable and their petitions heard (e.g., Ps. 20:1–3; 25:11), for those who know God's name are God's people, to whom God is committed. When God did not want to be grasped, he withheld his name (Gen. 32:30); the heathen are heathen just because they do not know it (Ps. 79:6).

To go with the name, Israel necessarily had identifying descriptions. At the very foundation of Israel's life, the introduction to the basic Torah of the ten commandments, the two are neatly side by side: "I am [Yahweh], your God, who brought you out of the land of Egypt" (Exod. 20:2). There were many descriptions that could be used to identify Yahweh, but this one, the narrative of Exodus, was that on which Israel's faith hung.[5] The exodus was the chief content of Israel's creed: "And you shall make response before [Yahweh] your God, 'A wandering Aramean was my father; and he went down into Egypt. . . . And the Egyptians treated us harshly and afflicted us. . . . Then we cried to [Yahweh] . . . , and [Yahweh] brought us out of Egypt with a mighty hand . . . and he brought us into this place and gave us this land'" (Deut. 26:5–9; see also Josh. 24:2ff.) The entire narrative of the Hebrew Scriptures is probably best understood as an expanded version of the creedal narrative just cited.[6] And the whole Torah was explication of the exodus' consequences: "You have seen what I did to the Egyptians, and how I . . . brought you to myself. Now therefore . . ." (Exod. 19:4ff.) To the question "Whom do you mean, 'God'?" Israel answered, "Whoever got us out of Egypt."

The act of calling God by name was in Israel so tremendous that, as the identification of the true God over against other claimants ceased to be a daily challenge, and use of the name therefore ceased to be a daily necessity, actual pronunciation of the name ceased, at least for all but the mightiest occasions.[7] This is reflected in the pointing of "YHWH" in our Hebrew text with the vowel points for "Adonai" (Lord) as a signal to speak this word instead, and in the Septuagint translation of "Yahweh" by Kyrios.

IDENTIFYING GOD
IN THE NEW TESTAMENT

The gospel of the New Testament is the provision of a new identifying description for this same God. The coming-to-apply of this new description is the event, witness to which is the whole point of the New Testament. God, in the gospel, is "whoever raised Jesus from the dead."[8]

Identification of God by the resurrection did not replace identification by the exodus; it is essential to the God who raised Jesus that he is the same one who freed Israel. But the new thing that is the content of the gospel is that God has now identified himself also as "him that raised from the dead Jesus our Lord" (Rom. 4:24). In the New Testament such phrases become the standard way of referring to God.[9]

To go with this new identifying description there are not so much new names as new kinds of naming. "Yahweh" does not reappear as a name in use. The habit of saying "Lord" instead has buried it too deeply under the appellative.[10] But in the church's missionary situation, actual use of a proper name in speaking of God is again necessary in a variety of contexts. It is the naming of Jesus that occurs for all such functions. Exorcism, healing, and indeed good works generally are accomplished "in Jesus' name" (e.g., Mark 9:37ff., par.). Church discipline and quasi-discipline are carried out by sentences pronounced in Jesus' name (e.g., 1 Cor. 1:10), and forgiveness is pronounced in the same way (e.g., 1 John 2:12). Baptism is described as into Jesus' name (e.g., Acts 2:38), whether or not it was ever actually performed with this formula. Undergoing such baptism is equated with that calling on the name "Yahweh" by which, according to Joel 3:5, Israel is to be saved (Acts 2:21, 38). Above all, perhaps, prayer is "in Jesus' name" (e.g., John 14:13–14), in consequence of which the name can be posited as the very object of faith (e.g., John 1:12). Believers are those "who call on the name of our Lord Jesus Christ" (e.g. Acts 9:14).

So dominant was the use of the name "Jesus" in the religious life of the apostolic church that the whole mission can be described as proclamation "in his name" (Luke 24:47), "preaching good news about the kingdom of God and the name of Jesus Christ" (Acts 8:12), indeed, as "carrying" Jesus' name to the people (e.g., Acts 9:15). The gatherings of the congregations can be described as "giving thanks . . . in the name of our Lord Jesus Christ" (Eph. 5:20), indeed, simply as meetings in his name (Matt. 18:20). Where faith must be confessed over against the hostility of society, this is "confession of the name" (e.g., Mark 13:13). The theological conclusion was drawn in such praises as the hymn preserved in Philippians in which God's own eschatological triumph is evoked as cosmic obeisance to the name "Jesus" (Phil. 1:10), or in such formulas as that in Acts which makes Jesus' name the agent of salvation (Acts 4:12). However various groups in the primal church may have conceived Jesus' relation to God, "Jesus" was the way they all invoked God.

One other new naming appears in the New Testament, the triune name: "Father, Son, and Holy Spirit." Its appearance is undoubtedly dependent on naming God by naming Jesus, as just discussed, but the causal connections are no longer recoverable. It is of course toward this name that we have been steering. That the biblical God must have a proper name, we have seen in the Hebrew Scriptures. In the life of the primal church, God is named by uses that involve the name of Jesus. "Father, Son, and Spirit" is the naming of this sort that historically triumphed.

"FATHER, SON, AND HOLY SPIRIT" AS PROPER NAME

That "Father, Son, and Holy Spirit" in fact occupies in the church the place occupied in Israel by "Yahweh" or, later, "Lord" even hasty observation of the church's life must discover.[11] Why it came to be so is the matter of the next chapter; for now we register the fact. Our services begin and are punctuated with "In the name of the Father, Son, and Holy Spirit." Our prayers conclude, "In his name who with you and the Holy Spirit is. . . ." Above all, the act by which people are brought both into the fellowship of believers and into their fellowship with God is an initiation "into the name 'Father, Son, and Holy Spirit.'"

The habit of trinitarian naming is universal through the life of the church. How far back it goes, we cannot tell. It certainly goes further back than even the faintest traces of trinitarian reflection, and it appears to have been an immediate expression of believers' experience of God. It is in liturgy, when we talk not *about* God but to and for him, that we need and use God's name, and that is where the trinitarian formulas appear, both initially and to this day.[12] In the immediately postapostolic literature there is no use of a trinitarian formula as a piece of theology or in such fashion as to depend on antecedent development in theology, yet the formula is there. Its home is in the liturgy, in baptism and the eucharist. There its use was regularly seen as the heart of the matter.[13]

There are two New Testament occurrences of a trinitarian name-formula. The earliest is the closing benediction of Paul's second letter to Corinth (2 Cor. 13:14). The epistolary benedictions of the New Testament reflect epistolary custom, liturgy, and no doubt personal style. They occur in the opening salutations and at the closing. If we sort them out, there is a surprising result. The opening benedictions all name both "God the Father" and "the Lord Jesus Christ." The closing benedictions—with one exception—either name no one and are simple wishes of "grace," or name only the Lord Jesus. Moreover, the naming of the Lord Jesus occurs in all and only the authentic letters of Paul and is obviously Paul's idiosyncrasy. Then suddenly, in one Pauline letter (and that neither the earliest nor the latest) a trinitarian naming replaces the naming of the Lord Jesus only: "The grace of the Lord Jesus Christ and the love of God and the fellowship of the Holy Spirit be with you all."

These circumstances prohibit all thought of development from one-membered to two-membered to three-membered formulas.[14] As far as the texts let us see, all forms are equally immediate,[15] the choice depending on epistolary custom. The particular trinitarian formula that ends 2 Corinthians looks very much like Paul's creation of the moment, apropos of nothing special in the letter and done only because it was natural to do. The purely christological benediction that was Paul's habit ("The grace of our Lord Jesus Christ be with you") expands in both directions by its own logic. Or if Paul did not create it here, he took it from liturgical use in the same unmotivated and obvious fashion.

The most important New Testament trinitarian naming is the Matthean baptismal commission (Matt. 28:19). Baptism is the church's chief sacrament, its rite of passage from old reality to new. Within such a rite, the new reality must be identified, for the neophytes must be directed into it. In baptism, as often elsewhere, this is done by naming the God whose reality it is. The name stipulated in the canonical rubric for baptismal liturgy is "Father, Son, and Holy Spirit."[16]

It is often supposed that the tripartite baptismal formula developed from unitary or bipartite formulas: "In Jesus' name" or "In the name of God and of the Lord Jesus." There is evidence from the second century of baptism with such formulas. But as to an origin of the trinitarian formula from these, there is no evidence.[17] In any case, the tripartite formula was soon there, and it is the only one in the New Testament.

The trinitarian name did not fall from heaven. It was made by believers for the God with whom we have found ourselves involved. "Father" was Jesus' peculiar address to the particular transcendence over against whom he lived.[18] Just by this address he qualified himself as "the Son," and in the memory of the primal church his acclamation as Son was the beginning of faith.[19] "Spirit" was the term provided by the whole biblical theology for what comes of such a meeting between this God and a special human of his. It is involvement in this structure of Jesus' own event—prayer to the "Father" with "the Son" in the power of and for "the Spirit"—that is faith's knowledge of God. Thus "Father, Son, and Holy Spirit" summarizes faith's apprehension of God; this is the matter of the next chapter. But in the event so summarizable, "Father, Son, and Holy Spirit" came together also simply as a name for the one therein apprehended, and apparently did so before all analysis of its suitability.

One further matter must be discussed here: the masculinity of "Father." Emerging consciousness of the historic oppression of women rightly watches for expressions thereof also, or perhaps principally, in inherited interpretations of God. When such are found, Christianity has every reason to eliminate them. We will in fact find a decisive area where male sexism has shaped the

93

structure of doctrine. Trinitarian Father-language cannot, however, be one such; and the widely spread supposition that it is reflects a breakdown of linguistic and doctrinal knowledge and judgment.

The church's trinitarian naming incorporates Jesus' filial address to God. That Jesus called God "Abba," which can only be translated "Father," must settle the matter for trinitarian naming, since it is Jesus' historical reality that created the name. But of course, that we may not substitute for "Father" in the triune name may only mean that the whole name is irremediably offensive. Nor can the use of "Father" within the trinitarian name be altogether separated from its more general use in Christian speech to and about God.

For filial address to God, the choice of words is limited, for us as for Jesus. "Parent" and its natural or artificial equivalents cannot be regular filial terms of address because they do not individuate. That leaves "mother" and "father." It is decisive for Israel's God that we are not of God's own substance, that God's role as our parent is not sexual, that God is not even metaphorically a fertility God.[20] The choice between "Mother" and "Father," as terms of filial address to God, was and must be made according to which term is more easily separable from the reproductive role.

Sexuality, as the union of sensuality and differentiated reproductive roles and apparatus, is the glory of our specific humanity. It is the way in which our directedness *to* each other, both among those now living and between generations—and that precisely by differences between us—is built into our bodies, into our sheer created givenness. Moreover, within the mutuality of male and female, the female is ontologically superior. She is the more ineradicably human, for while sensuality and reproduction can socially be ripped apart in the male, by alienating economic or political structures, not even abortion can do this to the female—short, of course, of the "brave new world" or of humankind's decision to die out. In societies that value members by especially inhuman standards, as in capitalist or technocratic-socialist societies that value only by contribution to the gross national product, the female's human superiority will indeed cause suffering, and many will understandably seek to be rid of it.

In religions where the direct religious analogy from human perfection to divine perfection is undisturbed, the female gender has therefore usually been religiously dominant, even in otherwise male-dominated societies. The whole of Christianity's soteriology can be summarized in the observation that in it this analogy is broken. Vice versa, it is just the ontological inferiority of the male that offers "Father" rather than "Mother" as the proper term of address to Israel's sexually transcendent God, when a filial term is needed.

That the biblical God is sexually transcendent does not, of course, mean that God is less than sexual, but rather that what we are by sexual differentiation God is without the various relations of more and less which sexual differentiation indeed involves. That Jesus, and we after him, have called God "Father" thus involves no valuing of masculinity above feminity. On the contrary, it is the only available way to satisfy the determination of Israel and the church to attribute neither to God. As for "Father and Mother," which incredibly has actually been used in services wishing to be Christian, it is most objectionable of all since by insisting on both it makes the attribution of sexual roles entirely inescapable and repristinates the deepest fertility myth, that of divine androgyny. The biblical God is not both our begetter and our bearer; he is neither.

In general, the assumption that it is a deprivation not to address God in one's very own gender is a case of humankind's general religious assumption of direct analogy from human perfections to divine qualities. In the faith of the Bible, this direct line is, for our salvation, broken. All speech about God is of course, in a commonsensical way, by analogy. But the gospel is free to take its analogies sometimes from human perfections and sometimes from human imperfections, depending on theological need. Sometimes it takes them from death and sin. If we must, irrelevantly, worry about whether calling God "Father" is praise or dispraise of earthly fathers, the answer, in the structure of Christian language-use, must be that it will be in some contexts the one and in some contexts the other.

THE TRIUNE NAME AS DOGMA

So far we have merely noted an historically contingent fact about the church's discourse. Now we must note that it is a fact with authority, for in view of the function of canonical sacramental mandates, the biblical stipulation of a triune formula for baptism must be regarded as dogma.[21] Moreover, the impact of this dogma extends far beyond the baptismal rite itself.[22] The function of naming God in initiation, in baptism as elsewhere, is to address the initiate to new reality, to grant new access to God. In the community of the baptized, therefore, the divine name spoken in baptism is established as that by which the community has its particular address to God.[23]

It has in fact worked out so in the church, both liturgically and theologically. In the church's life of prayer and blessing, threefold invocation is established at every decisive point. And in the theological history we will trace in a following chapter, we will find the role of the baptismal formula so predominant that there would be reason to call "Go . . . baptizing in the name of the Father and of the Son and of the Holy Spirit" the founding dogma of the faith.

This dogma is not about something we are to think but about something we are to do. When we pray or give thanks or otherwise invoke God, it is by this formula that we may most precisely address our utterance. There are other such orthopractic dogmas. The very stipulation of washing in God's name as the church's initiation is one. So is the stipulation of a meal of bread and cup, with christological thanksgiving, as the church's chief gathered occasion. So, for that matter, is the stipulation that final authority in the church is to function by our reading of the Bible.

From time to time, various concerns lead to proposed replacements of the trinitarian name, for example, "In the name of God: Creator, Redeemer, and Sanctifier" or "In the name of God the Ground and God the Logos and God the Spirit." All such parodies disrupt the faith's self-identity at the level of its primal and least-reflected historicity.

Such attempts presuppose that we first know about a triune God and then look about for a form of words to address that God, when in fact it is the other way around. Moreover, "Creator, Redeemer, and Sanctifier," for example, is, like other such phrases, not a name at all. It is rather an assemblage of after-the-fact theological abstractions, useful in their place but not here. Such assemblages cannot even be made into names, for they do not identify. Every putative deity must claim, for example, somehow to "create," "redeem" and "sanctify." There are also, to be sure, numerous candidates to be Father or Spirit, but within the trinitarian name, "the Father" is not primarily *our* Father, but the Father of the immediately next-named Son, that is, of Jesus. The "Holy Spirit," within the name, is not any spirit claiming to be holy, but the communal spirit of the just-named Jesus and his Father. By these relations inside the phrase, "Father, Son, and Holy Spirit" is historically specific and can be what liturgy and devotion—and, at its base, all theology—must have, a proper name of God.[24]

These last remarks again claim that "Father, Son, and Holy Spirit" is not an arbitrary label, like "Robert" for the author of these pages. A proper name is proper just insofar as it is used independently of aptitude to the one named, but it need not therefore lack such aptitude. "Father, Son, and Holy Spirit" is appropriate for naming the gospel's God because the phrase immediately summarizes the primal Christian interpretation of God. It is this second level of trinitarianism to which we must now continue.

NOTES

1. Brackets around "Yahweh" (Hebrew: YHWH or JHWH) are used throughout this *locus* in quotations from the Revised Standard Version of the Bible. The RSV follows the Jewish custom of avoiding the proper name of God and substituting "the Lord," but in this *locus* we are speaking precisely of God's proper name and thus use the name "Yahweh."

2. Gerhard von Rad, *Old Testament Theology*, trans. D. M. G. Stalker, 2 vols. (New York: Harper & Row, 1962–65), 1:10–11.

3. On the exegesis, Walther Zimmerli, *Old Testament Theology in Outline*, trans. D. E. Green (Atlanta: John Knox Press, 1978), pp. 19–20.

4. Von Rad, *Old Testament Theology*, 2:180ff.

5. E.g., Zimmerli, *Old Testament Theology*, pp. 21–27.

6. Von Rad, *Old Testament Theology*, 1:121ff.

7. From the third century B.C. *RGG*[3], s.v. "Namenglaube," by K. Baltzer.

8. The most convenient recent marshaling of the evidence is by Peter Stuhlmacher, "Das Bekenntnis zur Auferweckung Jesu von den Toten und die biblische Theologie," *ZThK* 70 (1973): 377ff., 389ff.

9. Cf. Rom. 4:24 with Rom. 8:11; 1 Cor. 15:15; 2 Cor. 1:9; 4:14; Gal. 1:1; Col. 2:12; 1 Pet. 1:21.

10. As a name, *Kyrios* appears only in Scripture references, e.g., Matt. 4:10; 22:37. Otherwise, referring to God, it is only an alternate to *theos*.

11. For less hasty observation, see Josef A. Jungmann, *The Place of Christ in Christian Liturgical Prayer*, trans. A. Peeler (New York: Alba House, 1965).

12. Ignatius, *To the Magnesians*, xiii,1,2; Clement, *To the Corinthians*, xlii,3; xlvi,6; lviii,2; *2 Clement*, xx,5; *Martyrdom of Polycarp*, xiv,3.

13. Georg Kretschmar, *Studien zur frühchristlichen Trinitätstheologie* (Tübingen: J. C. B. Mohr [Paul Siebeck], 1956), pp. 182–216.

14. As posited by Henry A. Wolfson, *The Philosophy of the Church Fathers* (Cambridge, Mass.: Harvard University Press, 1956), 1:147–54. See also Hans von Campenhausen, "Taufen auf dem Namen Jesu," *VigChr* 25 (1971): 1–16.

15. So also J. N. D. Kelly, *Early Christian Creeds* (New York and London: Longmans, Green & Co., 1950), pp. 23ff.

16. For the second and third centuries, Kretschmar, *Studien*, pp. 196–216.

17. The passages in Acts that describe baptism "in Jesus' name" (2:38; 8:16; 10:48; 19:15) are all theological descriptions, not rubrics.

18. E.g., Günther Bornkamm, *Jesus of Nazareth*, trans. I. and F. McLuskey (New York: Harper & Row, 1960), pp. 124–29.

19. Martin Hengel, *The Son of God*, trans. J. Bowden (Philadelphia: Fortress Press, 1976).

20. Von Rad, *Old Testament Theology*, 1:24ff., 62ff.

21. Robert W. Jenson, *Visible Words* (Philadelphia: Fortress Press, 1978), pp. 6–11.

22. For an account of the spread of the baptismal formula into the rest of the primal church's worship, see Kretschmar, *Studien*, pp. 182–216.

23. The ancient church laid great stress on this point. See Basil the Great, *On the Holy Spirit*, 26, in *PG* 32:67–218: "For if baptism was the beginning of life for me . . . , clearly the address spoken to me in the grace of my adoption is for me the foremost of utterances." According to Gregory of Nyssa, *Refutation of Eunomius' Confession*, in his *Opera*, ed. W. Jaeger (Leiden: E. J. Brill, 1952), 2:313: "For we have learned once for all from the Lord to whom we must attend . . . : to 'the Father and the Son and the Holy Spirit.' Therefore we say that it is a fearful and evil thing, to contemn . . . these divine sounds."

24. This is not only our after-the-fact interpretation. The ancient trinitarian theologians who created the developed doctrine worked out this logic explicitly; e.g., Gregory of Nyssa, *Refutation*, pp. 314–15.

2

The Trinitarian
Logic and Rhetoric

"Father, Son, and Holy Spirit" is a slogan for the temporal structure
of the church's apprehension of God and for the proper logic of
its proclamation and liturgy. Within the Hebrew Scriptures' interpretation of God, trinitarian discourse remains unproblematic and
so generates new language and images but not analysis.

THE TRINITARIAN LOGIC

"Father, Son, and Holy Spirit" became the church's name for its God because
it packs into one phrase the content and logic of this God's identifying descriptions. These in turn embody the church's primal experience of God. In turning from the trinitarian name to the history and logic by which it became
the name, we therefore also move out from the church's specific life of praise
and petition, in which a name is most needed, to the wider whole of the
church's life and reflection.

The gospel identifies its God thus: God is the one who raised Israel's Jesus
from the dead. The whole task of theology can be described as the unpack-
ing of this sentence in various ways. One of these produces the church's
trinitarian language and thought.

If for any reason we attend to the temporality of "God is whoever raised
Jesus," we note certain temporal features, which have been noticed at least
liturgically, from the church's very beginning. God is here identified by a narrative that uses the tense-structure of ordinary language, whereas divine identification is more ordinarily done by time-neutral characters, as in "God is
whoever is omnipotent to bolster my weakness" or "God is whatever is immune to the time which takes my life." Nor is this narrative mythic, so that
the tenses would not be used in their ordinary way, for its power to identify
depends on mention of an historical individual and so, in turn, on the historical
narrative by which that individual—as any such individual—must be identified. Such a procedure is religiously peculiar, as has often been noticed, for
while religions often mention some historical event (a "revelation") as

epistemologically necessary for their knowledge about God, they do not normally identify the subject of this knowledge by that event.

To identify the gospel's God, we must identify Jesus. In this sense we may first say that God "is" Jesus. Every reality is somehow identifiable, and we cannot identify this God without simultaneously identifying Jesus. This also displays why religions do not normally pin their identifications of God to the identity of an historical event, for drastic restrictions are imposed on the ways in which we can go on to talk of a God so identified. If God, in any sense, is Jesus—or were Abraham Lincoln or the British Empire—we cannot rightly talk of this God in any way that would make the temporal sequences, the stuff of narration, unessential to his being, and that, of course, is just how religions normally want to talk of God. Indeed, the posit of one to whom tenses are insignificant and in whom, therefore, time may be evaded is the whole usual point of their enterprise.

God, we may therefore identify, is what happens with Jesus. But if we said only that, we would show no reason why it should be *God* that happens with Jesus and not merely, perhaps, an important religious epoch. Moreover, it is not as if we in any case knew about God, and then for some reason decided to "identify" God by reference to Jesus. It is what in particular happens with Jesus that compels us to use the word "God" of *this* Father in the first place.

Following much of the New Testament, let us use "love" as a slogan for what humanly happened with the historical Jesus. Then we may say that Jesus was a lover who went to death rather than qualify his self-giving to others; the love which was the plot of his life is an unconditional love. Of this person it is said that he nevertheless lives, that he is risen. Said of this particular person, such an assertion—whether true or not—is at least appropriate, for love means an unconditional self-giving, an acceptance of death; and a successful love would be an acceptance of death that resulted not in the lover's absence from the beloved but in his or her presence. Love *means* death and resurrection. For this particular man, resurrection, if it happened, was therefore but the proper outcome of his life.

Moreover, if this lover's resurrection happened, then there also now lives an unconditional lover with death—the limit of love—already behind him, so that his love must finally triumph altogether, must embrace all people and all circumstances of their lives. If he is risen, the human enterprise has a conclusion: a human communion constituted in its commonality by one man's unconditional self-dedication to his fellow creatures and thus embracing each individual and communal freedom established in the history so fulfilled.

Thus, if Jesus is risen, his personal love will be the last outcome of the human enterprise. If he died, his self-definition has been written to its end, as each of ours will be, but if he also yet lives, just this life so defined is not thereby a dead item of the past, but an item of living, surprising time, an item of the future and indeed of the last future. Only of a person whose life had been defined as this particular man defined his would these propositions be appropriate. And it is because they are appropriate, and in that they are made, that "God" is an appropriate word for the reality identifiable as what happened with Jesus. A God is always some sort of eternity, some sort of embrace around time, within which time's sequences can be coherent, and if Jesus is risen he is to be both remembered and awaited.

Conversely, we may identify God so, now a second time: God is what will come of Jesus and us, together. In our original proposition, "God is whoever raised Jesus," the event by which God is identified, Jesus' resurrection, is the event in which Jesus is future to himself and to us.

In the Bible generally, the "Spirit" is God as the power of the future to overturn what already is, and just so fulfill it. The Spirit is indeed a present reality. But *what* is present is that there is a goal, and that we therein are free from all bondage to what is. The Spirit is the power of the eschaton now to be at once goal and negation of what is. In the New Testament, this Spirit is identified as Jesus' spirit, as every human being has spirit. That Jesus' particular spirit is the very power of the last future is the "spirit"-form of the identification of God by Jesus from which trinitarian language begins. Therefore the biblical "Spirit" is the inevitable word for this second identification of God, although developed trinitarian doctrines, since they respond to postbiblical problems, need by no means be bound exclusively to this name.

Finally, this particular embrace around time must be universal, for it is the embrace of an unconditional love. It must grant a universal destiny. Therefore this God may also be identified so: God is the will in which all things have Jesus' love as their destiny. Jesus, we saw, "is" God only *as* God's identifiability. In our original identifying proposition, "God is whoever raised Jesus," "Jesus" is the object of an active verb. God is—a third time—identified as the one who does Jesus' resurrection, as a given active transcendence to all that Jesus is and does. As what happens with Jesus is its own and our end, so also it is its own and our given.

In the New Testament, "Father" is Jesus' address to the transcendence *given to* his acts and sufferings, the transcendence *over against* whom he lives and to whom he is responsible—addressed in trust. For Jesus' disciples, therefore, "the Father" is God as the transcendent givenness of Jesus' love, the one in whom we may trust for that love.

Thus we have a temporally three-point identification of the gospel's God. If we think of an identification as a pointing operation (as in "Which one?" "That one"), we must point with all three of time's arrows in order to point out this God: to the Father as Given, to the Lord Jesus as the present possibility of God's reality for us, and to the Spirit as the outcome of Jesus' work. The identification is triple—rather than, say, double or quintuple—because time does have three arrows. The past, present, and future of all that is, is doubtless a peculiar sort of fact, but it is also the most inescapable.

That the gospel's identification of God is threefold rests, therefore, on the way the gospel modulates a generally inescapable metaphysical fact. What is peculiar about the gospel's identification of God is not the number three but rather that it follows the three arrows of time without mitigating their difference. It is the very purpose of most discourse about gods to mitigate the threatening difference of past, present, and future. Among us Greeks, this is ordinarily accomplished by a doctrine of God's being as a timeless persistence in which past, present, and future are "really" all the same. The gospel's theology cannot produce such a doctrine, for thereby it would saw off the limb of narrative identification on which all its talk of God sits. But if such a doctrine is not produced, we are left with the three peculiar identifications of God just described and with their even more peculiar mutual relation.

The God of the gospel is the hope at the beginning of all things, in which we and all things are open to our fulfillment; this God is the love which will be that fulfillment; and this God is the faithfulness of Jesus the Israelite, which within time's sequences reconciles this beginning and this end. All else being equal, no more need be said. The rhetorical and soteriological space opened here is vast and permissive. Ignatius of Antioch was once moved to say, "We are drawn up [to God the Father] by Jesus Christ's crane—the cross—suspended by the rope that is the Holy Spirit" (*To the Ephesians* ix,1).

The temporal structure we have analyzed is the unreflected open and free temporal horizon of the church's life and proclamation. Trinitarian discourse becomes problematic, and the difficult metaphysical dialectics we first think of as "the doctrine of the Trinity" become necessary, only when mitigation of time becomes tempting, that is, only in confrontation with more normal identifications of God. The confrontation of that sort which historically occurred is the matter of the next chapter.

THE HEBREW SCRIPTURES
AS THE ROOT OF TRINITARIANISM

There is a famous saying of an anonymous first-century preacher that we must "think about Jesus Christ as we do about God."[1] The dictum formulated a principle that was immediate and self-understood through the apostolic and immediately postapostolic time,[2] for to think of God in the way this chapter has so far analyzed is to think of Christ "as of" God.[3]

Whether such thinking remains immediate and obvious or is difficult and problematic, and so also whether we just *do* such thinking or also reflect on what we do, depends on how one does in fact antecedently think about God.

As the Hebrew Scriptures, and so the earliest church, think of God, there is no problem, and none was felt. As the religion and philosophy of the Greeks and ourselves think of God, there are many great problems, which will be the matter of the next two chapters.

To be sure, superficial reflection supposes the opposite. It is commonly thought that trinitarian language about God marks Christianity's discontinuity with the Hebrew Scriptures. Increasingly Hellenist Christians were supposedly led by their devotion to Jesus to "divinize" him and so to mitigate God's uniqueness. This common supposition is false.

It is true—as we will see in the next chapter—that from about A.D. 150 Christianity's confrontation with Hellenism led to formulations which initially smacked of divinization. But—as we will also see—the whole developed doctrine of the Trinity was the church's effort to resist this temptation. And at the level of immediate trinitarian witness and experience which we are now discussing, and during the period before massive confrontation with Hellenic theology, there was not even incipient conflict between trinitarian and Hebrew interpretations of God. On the contrary, this immediate trinitarianism was the only possible fulfillment of the Hebrew Scriptures.

Israel's interpretation of God was undoubtedly the historical result of a multitude of factors, many now untraceable. But systematically and at least in part historically, Israel's theology can all be derived from the identification of God by the exodus. If God is, more than trivially, *the one who* rescued Israel from Egypt, the main characteristics of this God are immediately evident.[4]

First, Yahweh is not on the side of established order. The usual God, whose eternity is the persistence of the beginning, has as his very honor among us that in him we are secure against the threats of the future. Ancient imperial peoples poignantly experienced the fragility of their achievement: The situation in which seedtime and harvest return each year had barely been secured, and the barbarian destroyer was each year at the door. The gods of the ancient civilizations simply *were* the certainty of return, the guarantee of continuance. Marduk, for example, was *the one who* back at the beginning divided the Mesopotamian swamps into irrigated land and channeled water, and in that he was always still there the people could transcend the ever-renewed threat of relapse into precreation disorder. The damnation against which Yahweh fought for Israel was the precise opposite.

Israel understood itself not by an established order but by rescue from oppression under the archtypically standing order, that of Egypt. Throughout its history, Israel longed to become an established state "like all the nations" (1 Sam. 8:4–5). But God always saw to it that Israel would fail, and the prophets regularly denounced the very attempt (see 1 Sam. 8:7–9). Indeed, and most uncanny of all, Yahweh remained free to undo the standing order of his own people: "For, behold, [Yahweh, Yahweh] of hosts, is taking away from Jerusalem and from Judah stay and staff, the whole stay of bread, and the whole stay of water; the mighty man and the soldier, the judge and the prophet, the diviner and the elder" (Isa. 3:1–2).

Second, Yahweh's will is not identical with natural necessity—that is, Yahweh's will is indeed what we mean by "will." In great ancient myths, the beginning of the people's worship of God is in each case identical with the absolute beginning of all things. Therein lay assurance: nothing can overthrow the people's basis, since outside it there is nothing. Israel, on the other hand, knew very well of a history, including a history of Israel's own ancestors, that preceded the exodus. The great myths of other peoples tell of a primeval event which set the pattern of time and is therefore above time, which never really ceases to happen—as Marduk's primeval separation of water and land recurred at each yearly inundation and draining. Israel's story told of an event which, for all repeated cultic celebration, had happened only once, in time rather than above it.

Israel, of course, could and did attribute general creation to its God. But Yahweh's creation of the world and of Israel were two acts, not one. Israel knew that created reality did not necessarily include it, that Israel might not have been. Since Israel did nevertheless exist, by an act of Yahweh, that act was just so understood as a choice:[5] "You have seen what I did to the Egyptians, and how I . . . brought you to myself. Now therefore . . . , you shall be my own possession among all peoples" (Exod. 19:4–5).

Third, since there was history before there was Israel, and yet the God of Israel ruled that history, this question must be asked: How was Yahweh the God of Israel before there was Israel? The developed form of Israel's tradition had an answer: Between creation-times and the exodus was the time of the fathers, of Abraham, Isaac, and Jacob. But how were these Israel? The solution of the ancient narrators was that patriarchal Israel was Israel by the promise of a land and a land's possibility of nationhood.[6] Abraham and the other fathers had lived in response to the promise that their descendants would be a great people. Having as yet no established order, the fathers had lived by the word that promised one.

Thus Israel knew itself as created by God's word, in the exact sense in which we until recently spoke of "a gentleman's word." Yahweh made a promise and kept it, and so Israel came to be. From the start, salvation for Israel is given by promise of what is not yet, of the future that is real only in the word that opens it. What other nations could say of a visible and tangible presence of God in holy images and places, Israel could say only of God's utterance: "The grass withers, the flower fades, but the word of our God will stand for ever" (Isa. 40:7–8). Moreover, Israel knew of a time when Israel had been Israel only by this word, without security, when Israel's whole existence had been hope. There remains only to note that with the exile of 587 B.C., when all secure national existence was (at least until A.D. 1948) taken away, historical Israel was put in exactly the position posited for the fathers.[7]

Thus the identity of Israel's God, his difference from other gods, is precisely that Israel's God is not eternal in the way the other gods are, not God in the same way. That the past guarantees the future is exactly the deity of the gods, but Yahweh always challenges the past and everything guaranteed by it, from a future that is freedom. The key steps of the trinitarian logic described in the previous section are the very specificity of the Hebrew Scriptures' interpretation of God.

As to how, positively, Yahweh is eternal, Israel's interpretation is that he is faithful. Where other ancient religions said that God is beyond time, Israel said: "For ever, [Yahweh], thy word is firmly fixed in the heavens. Thy faithfulness endures to all generations; thou hast established the earth, and it stands fast" (Ps. 119: 89–90). *Emunah* (faithfulness) is the reliability of a promise; thus the Revised Standard Version often translates it "truth" (e.g., Prov. 12:17; Hos. 5:9), and a promise which is verified by events is "made *emun*" (e.g., 1 Kings 8:26). If God continues to bless Israel in spite of everything, it is because he "is keeping the oath which he swore" to the fathers, "because [Yahweh] is the *faithful* God who keeps covenant" (Deut. 7:8–9). And when the fulfillment comes, when "kings shall see and arise," it will be "because of [Yahweh], who is faithful" (Isa. 49:7).

In one famous passage, the interpretation of God's eternity as faithfulness approaches a metaphysical definition. Within the tradition of the covenant with David, the most beautiful statement of Israel's hope proclaims: "I will make with you an everlasting covenant, my steadfast, sure love for David" (Isa. 55:3).

Unlike the normal gods, Yahweh does not transcend time by immunity to it. The continuity of Yahweh's being is not that of a defined entity, some of whose defining characteristics persist from beginning to end. It is rather the sort of continuity we have come to call "personal." It is established in Yahweh's words and commitments, by the faithfulness of later acts to the promises made in Yahweh's earlier acts. The continuity of Yahweh's being is eternity, transcends time, in that Yahweh keeps all promises, in that time cannot take any commitments away. It is just this interpretation of God's eternity that we introduced as the logical necessity—given the resurrection and the resultant necessity to identify God by Jesus—of trinitarian identification of God.

PRIMARY TRINITARIANISM

Therefore, so long as Christian interpretation of God was in unshaken continuity with that of the Hebrew Scriptures, Christian discourse and reflection shaped themselves naturally and unproblematically to the triune logical and rhetorical space. This can be seen in the New Testament and so long thereafter[8] as the communities were not strongly confronted with Hellenic interpretation of God.

That "God" and God's "Spirit" form a rhetorical and conceptual pair for proclamation of God's work and interpretation of our life is entirely unproblematic in the New Testament. The use was imposed by the experience of Pentecost and needed no conceptual or linguistic innovation over against the Hebrew Scriptures. Also that "Christ" and the "Spirit" form such a pair in that the Spirit is *Christ's* Spirit was direct and historically legitimate interpretation of the Hebrew Scriptures, asserting merely the fulfillment of certain expectations in fact contained therein and involving no conceptual or linguistic innovation. These matters are analyzed in detail in another *locus* of this work.

That "God the Father" and "Jesus Christ his Son" form a similar pair is more complicated. It was of course the immediate consequence of that identification of God by Jesus' resurrection which is the whole import of the New Testament. But although the identification of God by historical events is fundamental in the Hebrew Scriptures, that the conclusively identifying events turn out to be the life of an individual person requires language beyond that of the Hebrew Scriptures, though in the New Testament itself never incongruous therewith. We cannot avoid a quick survey of these developments, though in detail they too belong to another *locus*.

The emergence of a semantic pattern in which the uses of "God" and "Jesus Christ" are mutually determining is fundamental. That pattern is firmly established before the earliest Pauline writings,[9] for example, the formula quoted by Paul "If you confess with your lips that Jesus is Lord and believe in your heart that God raised him from the dead, you will be saved" (Rom. 10:9). The pattern is the logical backbone of all Paul's own discourse about God.[10] In Paul the standard Hebrew theological predicates take either God or Jesus as subject, or both at once;[11] for example, "grace" is interchangeably "of God" (Rom. 5:15) or "of Christ" (Rom. 16:20) or bestowed "from God our Father and the Lord Jesus Christ" (Rom. 1:7). Parallel constructions have "God" in one part and "Christ" in the other.[12] "So we are ambassadors for Christ, God making his appeal through us" (2 Cor. 5:20). For Paul, *God* will rule the kingdom, Jesus is *Lord*, and these two circumstances are one fact only: "For the kingdom of God [means] righteousness and peace . . . ; he who thus serves Christ is acceptable" (Rom. 14:17–18, e.g.). Christ simply is "the power of God and the wisdom of God" (1 Cor. 1:24), the manifestation of that "righteousness" in which Judaism summed up the godliness of God (Rom. 3:21–22). Yet "God" and "Christ" are not simply identified; thus prayer and thanksgiving are always directed to God, through Christ or "in his name."[13]

106

This semantic pattern best displays the relation between the Father and Jesus, "the Son," as the apostolic church experienced it. The titles and images by which various groups more directly attempted to grasp the relation are for our present concern of secondary importance. We need only note primal Christianity's eclecticism in the drafting of such conceptions, and their general concord with the Hebrew Scriptures. Such mythic christology as appears, for example, in Philippians 2 or the Book of Hebrews or John's Gospel, where Christ is a "pre-" or "postexistent" heavenly being of unstipulated relation to God, displays a kind of thinking fully shared by contemporary Judaism[14] and well grounded in the Old Testament.[15] The various "christological titles" by which the risen Lord was addressed and proclaimed are without exception functional in their import. They do not say what sort of "being" Christ has, but merely what role he has. Most typical in its logic is "Lord."[16] Initially merely Jesus' disciples' term of address to their master, it was naturally resumed for their risen Lord after the resurrection. But now this Lord is enthroned in God's own power and directs their mission by a Spirit that is God's own. In these circumstances, the Hebrew Scriptures' use of "Lord" for God cannot help but resonate the in-itself still purely human title. With the experience of the ancient church in our inheritance, *we* cannot but ask what sort of being ("divine," "human," or what) this title and the others used by the primal church attribute to Jesus. It is vital to understand that they raised no such question for the primal church itself, that the analysis, for example, just given of "Lord" completely describes what it did or could do for the apostolic users.

The resurrection compelled the apostolic church to find new language. Only for us does this language raise questions over against the Hebrew Scriptures. The language once available, and given the logic of the Hebrew Scriptures' talk of God, Christian invocation, exhortation, and explanation seem to have taken triune form merely by following the path of least difficulty and quite without need for explicit reflection on the pattern itself. We will best assure ourselves of this by means of samples cited at near random from different strands of the New Testament: "But you, beloved . . . , pray in the Holy Spirit; keep yourselves in the love of God; wait for the mercy of our Lord Jesus Christ" (Jude 20–21); "But it is God who establishes us with you in Christ . . . ; he has . . . given us his Spirit in our hearts as a guarantee" (2 Cor. 1:21–22);[17] "For through him [Christ] we both have access in one Spirit to the Father" (Eph. 2:18).[18] Nor is this merely a matter of stock phrases; the essential temporal logic appears in triune formulas lacking one or another of the standard titles, for example, "I charge you in the presence of *God*, and of *Christ Jesus* who is to judge the living and the dead, and by *his appearing and his kingdom*" (2 Tim. 4:1).[19] Again, "May the *God of hope* fill you with all joy and peace in *believing*, so that by the power of the *Holy Spirit* . . ." (Rom. 15:13).

The initial place in life of such language is doubtless displayed by the writer of Ephesians at 5:18–20: "But be filled with the Spirit, addressing one another in psalms and hymns and spiritual songs, singing and making melody to the Lord . . . giving thanks in the name of our Lord Jesus Christ to God the Father." The essential Christian experience was of assemblies gripped by the dynamism of a particular future—"his appearing and his kingdom"—which dynamism the Scriptures taught them to call "the Spirit" and in which grip all prayer and praise was to "God the Father" and in the name of the one under whose lordship we are indeed God's children and share his Spirit. Given this sort of liturgical experience, it was utterly natural for the work of salvation to be compendiously described simply by reversing the order and going through the same sequence starting with God, as does the same writer to the Ephesians: "In him according to the purpose of him who accomplishes all things . . . , we who first hoped in Christ have been destined . . . to live for the praise of his glory. In him you also, who . . . have believed in him, were sealed with the promised Holy Spirit, which is the guarantee of our inheritance" (Eph. 1:11–14). Just so this writer obtains a complete framework for theology and can describe the entire Christian reality in the coordinates of "God's grace," "the mystery of Christ," and revelation "by the Spirit" (e.g. Eph. 3:2–6).

The most remarkable trinitarian passage in the New Testament, amounting to an entire theological system, is Romans 8. Its conceptual and argumentative heart is verse 11: "If the Spirit of him who raised Jesus from the dead dwells in you, he who raised Christ Jesus from the dead will give life to your mortal bodies also through his Spirit which dwells in you." The subject phrase displays in the uttermost conceptual compression the precise structure we have called "the trinitarian logic": the *Spirit* is "*of* him *who* raised *Jesus*." And from the prepositional structure of this phrase, Paul then develops a rhetoric and argument which sweeps justification and the work of Christ and prayer and eschatology and ethics and predestination into one coherent understanding. With somewhat less dialectical and rhetorical complexity than Romans 8, many other passages display what can only be called a standard Pauline trinitarian conceptuality. "God" is named as the agent of salvation, which is accomplished in an act described by such phrases as "in Christ Jesus," the purpose of which act, both eschatologically and penultimately, is a "sending" of the Spirit with "gifts" (e.g., 1 Cor. 1:4–8; Gal. 4:4).

The new thing that appears in the immediate postapostolic church is the attempt to *grasp*—mostly in mythic images—the constitution of God by Christ and the Spirit, that is, not merely to speak in a trinitarian fashion but to speak about the Trinity. What we have here to examine is the trinitarianism of what Daniélou somewhat misleadingly called "Jewish Christianity,"[20] that is, all Christianity up to the direct challenge of Hellenic thought around A.D. 150, and thereafter the Christianity of those areas not heavily so challenged.

The principle of all this trinitarianism is classically stated by the epexegetical continuation of the saying of Clement earlier cited: "as of God, *as of the judge* of the living and the dead."[21] The equation of Christ—and the Spirit—with God is in all this thinking an attribution of *function* inseparable from God.

There were many "Jewish" Trinity-images.[22] The most important evoked the Son and the Spirit as "angels." In the most ancient postapostolic church there was undoubtedly an angel christology immediately dependent on apocalyptic Judaism's angel speculation, but there was an angel pneumatology too, on the same basis.[23] And so the full trinitarian experience of God found expression, as in the apocalyptic vision of Isaiah: "And I saw him [Christ] ascend into the seventh heaven, and all the saints and angels praised him. And I saw him sit down on the right hand of the Glory. . . . And the Angel of the Holy Spirit I saw sitting on the left hand."[24] This vision of God and two great angels seems to have had great continuing importance for the later development of trinitarianism: Origen, creator of the first great trinitarian theology, repeatedly proof-texts with Isa. 6:1–3, interpreting the two great seraphim of that passage as allegories of the Son and the Spirit and explicitly attributing this interpretation to a Jewish teacher.[25]

We now find this angel christology and angel trinitarianism alarming. It seems to create a large class of demigods and to locate Christ and the Spirit among them, surely a case of "divinization," and halfhearted at that. But this happens only because we anachronistically project our question about kinds of being back on this essentially Semitic discourse, and are then disappointed[26] to find Christ and the Spirit not fully divine, and Christ not fully human either. But in this thinking itself, an "angel" is simply one to whom God gives a mission and whose own reality is constituted by this mission. *Nothing* is thereby suggested about what sort of being is possessed by either God or this manifestation.[27] It can well be that the mission is in fact God's own mission. If it is, this will simply appear in descriptions of what the angel does—judges all people, forgives sin, or whatever.[28] And that Christ and the Spirit are transcendent over "other" angels appears iconographically, as in Hermas, where Christ is bigger than the other archangels and is a seventh, when all know the full number of archangels is six, or as in the *Ascension of Isaiah* where God and the two great angels are together worshiped by the other angels.[29]

The kinds of trinitarian discourse developed in the New Testament and in the immediately subsequent period have continued through the history of the church. With use of the triune name, they are the substance of living trinitarian apprehension of God. Christians bespeak God in a triune coordinate system; they speak *to* the Father, *with* the Son, *in* the Spirit, and only so bespeak *God*. Indeed, they *live in* a sort of temporal space defined by these coordinates, and just and only so live "in God." And they represent the God with whom they have thus to do in iconography and metaphor that is functional in its attribution of deity. Where, as in the medieval and modern Western church, these modes lose some of their power to shape actual proclamation and prayer, an alienation of the church must be suspected.

Pastors often believe that the Trinity is too complicated to explain to the laity. Nothing could be more misguided. Believers *know how* to pray to the Father, daring to call him "Father" because they pray with Jesus, God's Son, and so enter into the future these two have for them, that is, praying in the Spirit. Those who know how to do this, and who realize that just in the space defined by these coordinates they have to do with God, do understand the Trinity. All the intellectual complexities we must shortly embark on are a secondary phenomenon, whose proper location is the back of teachers' and preachers' minds, determining the way they guide and, when necessary, explain, this relation to this God.

THE DOGMATIC STATUS
OF PRIMARY TRINITARIANISM

The structures of language and experience analyzed in the previous two sections are not merely in fact present in the life of the church. They are daily and explicitly acknowledged and proclaimed as fundamental by the worshiping assemblies of all Christendom, being embodied in the great liturgical creeds of the apostles, and of Nicaea. The three-article creeds are the daily education and public self-definition of the Christian community in all its branches, recited at baptism and often at the Supper or other main services. And they are acknowledged such by Eastern, Roman Catholic, and Reformation bodies alike—as, for example, in the Lutheran *Book of Concord*, where they are set in first place and aptly called "the ecumenical" creeds.

Creedal formulations are as old as the gospel.[30] For our immediate purposes, two forms are important. First, the initial preachers and catechists and their successors used and passed on narrative summaries of the chief claims and facts about Jesus (see 1 Cor. 15:1–7).[31] Second, there is the rubric that baptism is to be "in the name of the Father and of the Son and of the Holy Spirit." We do not know what liturgical form this naming initially took, or even if it took the same form in all communities. But by the time ancient baptismal practice emerges into clear view,[32] in the writings of Hippolytus at the turn of the second and third centuries, the naming is an interrogation of trinitarian confession: "Let the baptizer . . . say, 'Do you believe in God, the Father Almighty? Do you believe in Christ Jesus, the Son of God . . . ?' [etc.]."[33] There are signs that such interrogation may have been the—or an—original way of baptismal "naming"; in any case, the primal church did demand confession of faith at baptism,[34] and this confession was shaped by the triune pattern of baptismal naming, however the latter was done.

The sort of declaratory creeds we know and use, such as the Apostles' Creed or the creeds used as bases by the councils of Nicaea and Constantinople, developed from the fusion of these two forms: the baptismal questions with their canonically stipulated triune pattern, and the summaries of christological narrative.[35] It seems likely that the location of this development was catechetical discipline, which had both to prepare for baptism and to reinforce the main items of christological missionary preaching. The shift to declaratory form from interrogatory form—which was retained at baptism itself—was probably occasioned by the demand that catechumens, before baptism, report to the congregation their participation in the faith into which the congregation had been baptized: "I believe—as do you—in. . . ." It also seems likely that the earliest stable product of this development was the forerunner of the Apostles' Creed, the old creed of the church of Rome, fixed sometime toward the end of the second century. This old Roman creed was created by addition of the christological kerygma "who was conceived by" to a trinitarian baptismal interrogation about "God the Father Almighty, and . . . Christ Jesus, his only Son, our Lord, and the Holy Spirit, the holy church, the resurrection of the flesh."[36]

What is dogmatized by the classical three-article creeds is thus not only or even primarily any one list of kerygmatically vital christological events or necessary theological items. There has never, in fact, been any one universally accepted creedal list of either. Even now, when we have reduced the creeds in practical use to two, they do not present quite the same list. What is first of all dogmatized are the kerygmatically narrated history itself, the triple-name structure, and the union of the two. Moreover, the popular impression is precisely wrong, that first there is a three-step history of God's works—the "three articles"—and that then the triune name is a sort of summary and the trinitarian logic a kind of explanation thereof. The reverse is the case.

The Apostles' Creed and those like it were created by the catechetical and liturgical affinity, and the logical fit, between the triune baptismal name of God and the evangelical history narrated in the gospel. That is, it is exactly the logic analyzed in this chapter which the creeds declare to be the true and necessary logic of the gospel.

NOTES

1. See *2 Clement*, i,1–2.

2. Thus Ignatius, who has the Greek diction, a Logos concept, and treats the ascription of deity and temporality to one subject as a paradox, nevertheless refers to Jesus

simply as God, quite without noting a problem: *To the Ephesians*, viii,2; *To the Smyrneans*, i,1; *To the Romans*, viii,2; *Ephesians*, xix,2; xvii,2.

3. Thus "Clement" does exegesis on his own dictum in *2 Clement*, i,1–2: ". . . as about the Judge of the living and the dead."

4. On the following about Israel, see Walther Zimmerli, *Old Testament Theology in Outline*, trans. D. E. Green (Atlanta: John Knox Press, 1978), pp. 21–32. On the general pattern of ancient religion, see Mircea Eliade, *Cosmos and History*, trans. W. R. Trask (New York: Harper & Row, 1959), the classic study.

5. Zimmerli, *Old Testament Theology*, pp. 43ff.

6. Ibid., pp. 27–32, 64–65.

7. Walther Zimmerli, "Die Bedeutung der grossen Schriftprophetie für das alttestamentliche Reden von Gott," *VT.S*, 1972, pp. 63–64.

8. I.e., in what Jean Daniélou, *The Theology of Jewish Christianity*, trans. J. A. Baker (Chicago: Henry Regnery Co.; London: Darton, Longman & Todd, 1964), somewhat misleadingly calls "Jewish Christianity."

9. Klaus Wengst, *Christologische Formeln und Lieder des Urchristentums*, StNT 7 (Gütersloh: Gerd Mohn, 1972).

10. See Wolfgang Schrange, "Theologie und Christologie bei Paulus und Jesus," *EvTh* 36 (1976): 123–35.

11. Ibid., pp. 124–25.

12. Ibid., p. 125.

13. Ibid., pp. 127–28.

14. Wilhelm Bousset, *Die Religion des Judentums*, ed. Hugo Gressman, 3d ed. (Tübingen: J. C. B. Mohr [Paul Siebeck], 1966), pp. 302–57; Robert L. Wilken, ed., *Aspects of Wisdom in Judaism and Early Christianity* (Notre Dame, Ind.: Notre Dame University Press, 1975), pp. 1–31, 103–41; Martin Hengel, *Judaism and Christianity*, trans. J. Bowden (London: SCM Press, 1974), 1:153–75.

15. From the "angel of the Lord" in the patriarchal narratives (e.g., Gen. 22:9–19) to the great eschatological figure of Dan. 7:13–14.

16. E.g., Ferdinand Hahn, *The Titles of Jesus in Christology*, trans. H. Knight and G. Ogg (Cleveland: World Publishing, 1969), s.v. "Lord."

17. In Paul the list of such uses is long, e.g., Rom. 14:17–18; 15:30; 1 Cor. 2:2–5; 12:4–6; 2 Cor. 3:3; Phil. 3:3; 1 Thess. 5:18–20.

18. Elsewhere in this literature: Eph. 1:11–14; 1:17; 2:18–22; 3:2–7, 14–17; 4:4–6; 5:18–20; Col. 1:6–8; Titus 3:4–6.

19. It is regularly "Spirit" that is omitted as a word but present in substance; e.g., 1 Pet. 1:3.

20. Daniélou, *Theology*.

21. *2 Clement*, i,2.

22. On these images, see Daniélou, *Theology*, pp. 146–66; Aloys Grillmeier, *Christ in Christian Tradition*, trans. J. S. Bowden (New York: Sheed & Ward, 1965), 2:41–53; Jaroslav Pelikan, *The Christian Tradition: A History of the Development of Doctrine*, vol. 1, *The Emergence of the Catholic Tradition (100–600)* (Chicago: University of Chicago Press, 1971), pp. 176ff., 184ff.; Georg Kretschmar, *Studien zur frühchristlichen Trinitätstheologie* (Tübingen: J. C. B. Mohr [Paul Siebeck], 1956), pp. 20–22.

23. Daniélou, *Theology*, pp. 117–47, esp. pp. 128ff.; Johannes Barbel, *Christos Angelos* (Bonn: Hauslein, 1941), pp. 181–311; Martin Werner, *The Formation of Christian Doctrine* (New York: Harper & Row, 1957), pp. 120–61; Grillmeier, *Christ*, pp. 46ff.

24. *Ascension of Isaiah*, xi,32–35. For other documentation, Kretschmar, *Studien*, pp. 71–124.

25. E.g., Origen, *Commentary on Isaiah*, 1,2; 15; 41; *Commentary on Ezekiel*, 14,2; *On First Principles*, i,3,4; iv,3,14. See Kretschmar, *Studien*, pp. 220–23.

26. Or we may be gleeful if we oppose the later doctrines of true godhead and believe ourselves now to discover that the earliest church contradicted them. This is Martin Werner's blunder, which invalidates all the arguments of his otherwise admirable investigations.

27. Daniélou, *Theology*, pp. 117ff.

28. E.g., Hermas, *Similitudes*, viii,1–2.

29. Ibid., ix,12,7–8; *Ascension of Isaiah*, viii,16–18.

30. The standard presentation is by J. N. D. Kelly, *Early Christian Creeds* (New York and London: Longmans, Green & Co., 1950), pp. 6–29.

31. Ibid., pp. 17ff.

32. See ibid., pp. 40–49.

33. Hippolytus, *Apostolic Tradition*, 21.

34. Kelly, *Creeds*, pp. 40ff.

35. Ibid., pp. 30–130.

36. Ibid., 119ff.

3

The Nicene-
Constantinopolitan Dogma

*Over against the Hellenic identification of God, the church's
discourse about God was and still is tempted to alienation from its
proper trinitarian logic. The dogma of Nicaea and Constantinople
was a decisive victory over this temptation.*

THE GOD OF THE GREEKS

In much of this chapter we have a story to tell. The gospel mission did in
fact meet with another and fundamentally incompatible identification of God,
that of the Greeks, which could not be ignored. Christianity as we know it,
and especially our inherited body of developed trinitarian dogma and analysis,
is the result.

If the gospel had not met the challenge to its strange identification of God
in the form of the Greek interpretation, it would have met it in some other—
and indeed it did and does in those branches of the mission that lead into
great culture areas other than that in which our narrative is set. Moreover,
the clash will always be at the same point: religion's normal reluctance to take
time seriously for God. Thus any possible great non-Western theology must
contain some functional equivalent for the developed trinitarianism on which
we are about to embark. But such possibilities are beyond the scope of this
work.

From its beginning, Hellenic theology was an exact antagonist of biblical
faith.[1] Israel's interpretation of God was determined by the rescue of wandering tribes from oppression under an established civilization, Greece's by
an established civilization's overthrow by just such tribes.[2] The flourishing
religious and material world of Mycenaean Greece was swept away by the flood
of Dorian tribes from the north. But in certain areas the memory and traditions of lost glory survived. When Greek civilization began to revive in the
ninth century, it was these surviving Ionians that led the way. Thus the
historical memory of Greece began with catastrophe, with a national experience
of sheer irrational contingency and power, and of death and destruction

115

brought by it. Greek religion and reflection were tragic from their root. They were a sustained attempt to deal with the experience that we must "not reckon any mortal blessed . . . until he has reached the end of his life without suffering disaster."[3] Greek religion and reflection were thereby imprinted with five characters important for our purpose.

First, their driving question was: "Can it be that *all* things pass away?" The assurance they needed, as formulated by Aristotle, had to be: "Being as such neither comes to be nor perishes."[4] In the myth of Chronos, "Father Time" who devoured all his children, the Greeks stated their experience of time and its surprises. Their religion was the determination that "Time" not be supreme, that he be overthrown by a true "Father of gods and men." Greek religion was the quest for a rock of ages, resistant to the flow of time, a place or part or aspect of reality immune to change. The gods' one defining character was therefore immortality, immunity to destruction. Whereas Yahweh was eternal by his faithfulness *through* time, the Greek gods' eternity was their abstraction *from* time. Yahweh's eternity is thus intrinsically a relation to his creatures—supposing there are any—whereas the Greek gods' eternity is the negation of such relation.

Second, Greek religion and reflection were an act of human self-defense against mysterious power and inexplicable contingency, that is, against just what humankind has mostly called "God." The Ionian survivors willed that history have a humanly comprehensible pattern, of such a kind that its events be in principle predictable and plannable. If superhuman (i.e., immortal) actors were needed to explain some events and so vindicate their sense, these too had to be understandable and predictable in their motivations and reasons. Such were the Olympian gods, the Ionian Homer's rationalized versions of various inherited nature and clan deities, whose singular lack of holiness and mystery scholars have always noted. The Ionians rescued themselves from chaos by enlightenment, by explanation of time's seeming mysteries.

Homer's successors, as religious thinkers, were the Ionian philosophers.[5] With them the reduction of all godly characteristics to one, immortality, and the inclusion also of the gods within one comprehensible scheme of events, led (and this is the third character on our list) to the concept of "the divine," a unitary abstraction of godly explanatory power in and behind the plural gods of daily religion; for example, Aristotle reports, "The Unbounded has no beginning . . . , but seems rather to be the Beginning of all other realities, and to envelope and control them. . . . This is the Divine. So the opinion of Anaximander and most of the natural philosophers."[6] For the educated class of Greece's classic period, this abstraction, often called "Zeus," was the true religious object: timelessness simply as such. So also the word "God" is understood as an adjective, applicable to various manifestations in various degrees.

Fourth, the quest for timeless reality is never satisfied by anything directly presented in our experience. All the world we see, hear, and touch does indeed pass away. If there is the divine, it must therefore be above or behind or beneath or within the experienced world. It must be the bed of time's river, the foundation of the world's otherwise unstable structure, the track of heaven's hastening lights. Greek religion and reflection, by their inner function, were metaphysical, a quest for the timeless ground of temporal being that just so is a different sort of being than we ever immediately encounter.

And fifth, Greek religion and reflection were precisely the quest we have been calling them, for since the timeless ground is never directly presented in experience, it has to be searched for. A whole complex of motifs that will be centrally important for our story is involved here. Greek apprehension of God is accomplished by penetrating through the temporal experienced world to its atemporal ground. This theology is therefore essentially negative: The true predicates of deity are negations of predicates that pertain to experienced reality by virtue of its temporality. God is "invisible," "intangible," "impassible" (i.e., unaffected by external events), "indescribable." This theology is essentially analogical,[7] for while it consists in negations of predicates that apply to the temporal world, it cannot dispense with such predicates. The pattern is always "Deity is F, only not as other, temporal reality is F." This theology necessarily raises the question of true deity, of the characteristics marking the final and so real ground, for if deity must be searched out, we have to be able to recognize it when we find it. And finally, all this penetration is accomplished by "mind" (*nous*), that is, not by discursive analysis or argument but by instantaneous intellectual intuition, by a sort of interior mirroring, for what is to be grasped is precisely a timeless pattern.[8]

So far the essentials of Greek interpretation of God, in practiced religion and in the philosophy to which it gave birth. Before returning to the main line of our narrative, we must note one great event in the history of this religion.

The posit of timelessness was initially a sustaining posit: Deity was the reliable meaning and foundation of the human world. But only a sort of blink was needed for the value signs to reverse themselves. Timeless and temporal reality were posited as different kinds of being, defined by mutual negation. All meaning and value were located in timeless being. If we are given a metaphysical shock, we may suddenly see the line between time and eternity as a barrier, shutting us out from meaning, for we are temporal. Without attempting to assign a cause, it is enough for our purpose to note that in the transition from the local communities of classic Greece to cosmopolitan Hellenism exactly this reversal of values occurred.[9]

Thus the dominant religious apprehension of late antiquity was of deity's distance, created by the very characteristics that made it deity. We are in time and God is not, and just so our situation is desperate. Therefore the religion

117

of late antiquity was a frenzied search for "mediators," for beings of a third ontological kind between time and timelessness, to bridge the gap.[10] Already Socrates had posited such a third kind, Eros, the child of Fullness and Want, and perceived that the language appropriate to speak of this realm is myth, that is, stories about divine beings, speech about eternities as if they were in time.[11] Discourse about deity was in any case understood to be analogical; "god" is basically adjectival and thus applicable in various grades to deity itself and to any mediators one or more steps down. In cosmopolitan Hellenism, such interpretation was put into practice. All the vast heritage of the world's savior-gods, demigods, reified abstractions, and mid-beings generally were pressed into mediatorial service. It was inevitable that when the gospel appeared on this scene, Christ would be too.

THE INITIAL
CHRISTIANIZING OF HELLENISM

When the gospel mission confronts the Hellenic interpretation of God, it cannot and could not simply reject it. Israel proclaimed Yahweh as God for all peoples. In confrontation with Hellenism, this had to mean the claim that Israel's is the real God posited by Hellas' philosophers.[12] Moreover, Hellenism's interpretation of God both caused and expressed late antiquity's chief religious problem, the distance of God; the gospel had to address the problem. It was at the middle of the second century that Christian thinkers first posed the Hellenic analytic tasks to themselves as explicit matter for reflection. It is there we begin our narrative.

However the confrontation might have begun, it was in fact begun thus: Both bodies of discourse about God, the biblical and the Hellenic, were simply set alongside each other and more or less well carpentered together, depending on skill. On the one side this meant that Christians took over the procedure of penetrating to the "real" God by abstracting from time with negative analogies.[13] Accordingly, Christians also adopted the negative predicates by which Hellenism had qualified true deity, and made one composite list with items from biblical language.

Already Ignatius, in A.D. 125, adopted the central and least biblical concept of late Hellenic theology: God is "impassible," immune to being acted upon (*To the Ephesians*, vii,2). This concept was to be the clearest and most troubling mark of Hellenic interpretation within Christian theology.[14] Justin Martyr, the most influential second-century theologian, defined God as the eternally self-caused and changeless cause of the being of all other beings, (e.g., *Dialogue with Trypho*, 3), to the satisfaction of believers and unbelievers alike. For Justin and his fellows, God is therefore "unoriginated," "unutterable," "immovable," "impassible," "inexpressible," "invisible," "unchange-able," "unplaceable," "immaterial," "unnameable."[15]

Yet the same theologians could also speak of God in incisively and even creatively biblical fashion. So Justin again: God is concerned with us; God is the "just overseer" of our lives (*Apology*, ii,12); God is compassionate and patient (the flat contradiction of "impassible") (*Dialogue*, 108); God's omni-potence is exercised above all in Jesus' resurrection (*Apology*, i,19); God actively intervenes to reward and punish (*Apology*, i,12); God's course of action is determined by regard for us (*Apology*, i,28). The true God, indeed, is to be identified as the one who led Israel from Egypt (*Apology*, i,11).[16] Such language is not mediated with the negative theology; the two conceptions of God are not so much synthesized as merely added together.[17] It is this additive tactic that has, from the apologists to the present, remained standard in theology. The notion of divine timelessness, once thus given room in Christian in-terpretation, then promptly attacks liturgical and proclamatory immediate trinitarianism.

The immediate question of every Hellenist, hearing the gospel's talk of God the beginning and God who is our fellow Jesus and God the fulfillment, must be But what is the timelessly self-identical something that is all these three? What is the time-immune continuity that must be the being of the real God? If we are not firm enough to challenge the question, there are only two possi-ble answers: It is a fourth, of which the three are only temporal manifesta-tions, or it is one of the three (which must then be the Father, since the other two are "from" him), of which the other two are only temporal manifesta-tions. Historians label the first move "modalism," the second "subordina-tionism." Together, they comprise the whole list of ancient trinitarian heresies. They are heresies because they speak of God in just the way that saws off our narrative limb. They are precisely as common and contrary to the gospel now as in the second and third centuries. In history, they had to be worked through to be found out.

Modalism is the teaching that God is above time and the distinctions of Father, Son, and Spirit, but appears successively in these roles to create, redeem, and sanctify.[18] From its first recorded appearance in Rome, around A.D. 190, it was the standard theory of the congregations, as it still is. It was, indeed, a direct attempt to systematize congregational piety on the assumption of the timeless God. It keeps Father, Son, and Spirit in the same row and so stays close to liturgical use of the triune name and to the linear past, present, and future of baptismal and eucharistic life. But it was nevertheless as much a compromise with Hellenic deity as subordinationism. Indeed, it was and is the more complete submission, since the whole biblical talk of God is de-prived of reference to God. None of the three is God. This is not noticed in immediate liturgical and proclamatory experience, but it is immediately noticed upon reflection. At the levels of learned or dogmatic theology, therefore, modalism has always been rejected promptly on its appearance.[19] We hear of only two actual modalist theologians in the ancient church, Paul of Samosata and Sabellius. Of the details of their thought we know next to nothing; only their names survived, as the ancient church's labels for modalism.

Subordinationism appears able to identify at least the biblical "Father" with God. Moreover, it had the missionary advantage that it answered directly to late Hellenism's religious need. Since it puts the Father on top, and ranks the Son below the Father—in vertical order, so to speak—it makes the Son just such a middle being between God's eternity and our time as late antiquity longed for.

Whenever Christ is grasped as a halfway entity between the supposedly timeless God and the temporal world, the subordinationist scheme is established. This can be, was, and is done strictly mythologically, with a demi-God descending and ascending.[20] But it is the sophisticated subordinationism inaugurated around A.D. 150 by the so-called apologists, the famous Logos christology, which we must describe, since it created the theological system within and against which developed trinitarianism was to be worked out. Christ, said the apologists, is—almost—God in that "the Logos" is incarnate in him.

However Justin, Theophilus, and the rest derived or invented their Logos concept, what they meant by it is plain. In the Greek philosophical tradition,[21] "logos" is at once discourse and the meaningful order which discourse discloses. If then the universe has such order, this is a divine Logos which is both deity's self-revelatory discourse and the reasonable order of the cosmos. Just so the apologists spoke of "the Logos." Moreover, as the divine reason *in* our world, the Logos could become the mediator of deity *to* our world, a "second God," and with the intensifying religious anxiety of late antiquity that is just what happened.[22] With or without dependence on this extra-Christian development, the apologists paralleled it and made "the Logos" the name of a typical personalized mediator-entity of second-century religiosity, "the next power after the Father of all, a Son. . . ." [23] Right or wrong, they thought that in all this they were but continuing John's testimony to the Logos who "was in the beginning with God," "illumined every man," and came in flesh to make God known (John 1:1–14).

In that the apologists shared the interpretation of God as the one who grounds all being by negating time, they shared also late antiquity's great problem, this God's distance. If we are to be saved, God must somehow dwell in our world, all agreed. And in the Old Testament, Christians possessed a narrative of God's activity here. But God has been defined just by his elevation above temporal action. It cannot have been God himself who walked in Adam's garden or shut the door of Noah's ark or talked to Abraham and Moses, for—as Justin asked—how should he "speak to anyone or be seen by anyone or appear in a particular part of the earth. . . . ? Neither Abraham nor Isaac nor Jacob nor any other human saw the Father, the unutterable Lord . . . , but rather they saw that other, who by his will is his Son and the messenger ("angel") to serve his purpose." An "other God," one step down the hierarchy of being, is needed to bridge the chasm between God and time.[24]

This "other God" is the Logos, the self-manifesting God, "the angel of the Lord" of the Hebrew Scriptures. Subordination is explicit. The Logos is "called" God, but over against "the creator of all things, above whom there is no other God," this predication is not literal. The Logos has "come into being," unlike the Father; he is "from" the unnameable and unoriginated Father, and just so is worshiped "after him."[25]

Since God is rational, the Logos is eternally in himself, as his own rationality. Then when God moves to create, that is, to be related to a reality other than himself, his Logos becomes external to him, as the rationality of artisans is manifest in their creations, and so also as God's relation to creation, that is, as revelation. Thus the Logos is the "first originated being" or even simply "first creature,"[26] over against the Father, who has no beginning. No distinction is yet made between different ways of deriving from God, so the difference between the Logos and the world is stated by adjectives like "first." It is this divine bridge to time that is then present in Jesus,[27] thus anchoring the bridge more securely at our end. For the second God's derivation from the Father, "Son" suggests "born" and "Logos" suggests "uttered"; both appear and combine in the neutral "gone forth."[28] He is numerically distinct from the Father, yet not set off from him.[29]

Not much has been said of the Spirit, which leads us to a vital point. The Logos theology is *not* the origin of developed trinitarianism. In itself, it is not in fact trinitarian at all.[30] The primal trinitarian naming and liturgical pattern make a temporal structure horizontal to time and inherently triple as time is. The God/Mediator/World scheme is timelessly vertical to time and of itself would posit either a deity of God and God's one mediator, or of God and infinitely *many* mediators. The space between God and the temporal world may be thought of either as one space or as indefinitely divisible, but there is no reason to think of two subspaces. In fact, the status of the Spirit was ambiguous in the whole apologetic theology. Since God "*is* Spirit" according to John (4:24), Spirit can be the name of the divine in Christ.[31] But how then is "the" Spirit a third? In the trinitarian pattern itself, on the other hand, there is no problem. On the contrary, we have seen that it is precisely in the self-posit of Spirit that triune Godhead is established. It was the Spirit's lack of place within the world view to which subordinationism was an adaptation that prevented the assimilation of all three items of the baptismal faith into the subordinationist scheme and preserved the three-article formulas of baptism as the chief counterinstance against it.

Insofar as the apologists were nevertheless trinitarian, sometimes they tried to stack all three vertically to time, with little conceptual success, and sometimes they assigned the Spirit his biblical role outside their mediator scheme altogether.[32] What kept them trinitarian in intention was the presence of factors outside their system: the continuing trinitarian life of the church; the developing three-article creedal structure, based on baptismal confession as just noted;[33] perhaps the continuing availability and influence of a picture by which to imagine God in accord with this creed, the "Jewish-Christian" picture of the Father and the two great angelic advocates; and churchly critique of the religious and metaphysical basis of subordinationism.[34]

In the interplay of all these factors, apologetic theology reached its historical fulfillment in two great figures of the early third century. In the West, Tertullian taught a more creedal and terminological trinitarianism; in the East, Origen taught a more speculative trinitarianism. Each set the style of his region for centuries to come.

For Tertullian, Logos theology was not so much the solution of his own religious problems as part of the now available intellectual repertoire for use on quite a different problem: the Trinity itself, the proper explication of the Christian interpretation of God.[35] For him, the trinitarian rule of faith was already a given (*Against Praxeas*, ii,1–2). Tertullian was moved to trinitarian analysis by a propagandizing explanation of the rule, the modalism urged in Rome by one Praxeas, around A.D. 190. He rightly thought this explanation explained the creed away, and set out to refute it and offer a better. As it turned out, he set the terminology of all subsequent Western analysis: There are in God "three persons" (*personae*) who are "of one substance" (*unius substantiae*).

Tertullian's chief trinitarian concern was to show how God's "monarchy" and "economy" could be simultaneously preserved (ibid., vii,7). "Monarchy" was his opponents' slogan for the abstract oneness of God as such, which Tertullian made mean instead the uniqueness and self-consistency of God's rule, of his divine work.[35] Tertullian himself adapted "economy" to be a term of trinitarian analysis from Irenaeus, for whom it meant the historical unfolding of God's saving work; Tertullian uses it for God's own inner self-disposition to this saving history.[37] It is "the economy . . . which disposes the unity into trinity" (ibid., ii,4). Plainly, it is theological interpretation of the three-step creed that is Tertullian's task. *Both* the one and three are those of God's reality in saving history.

For the three, Tertullian used *personae*, establishing the word for all subsequent Western theology. *Persona*[38] had been first the actor's mask, through which the actor spoke, then the role the actor thus played, and by Tertullian's time was the everyday term for the human individual, established in individuality by social role, by speaking and responding. The immediate background of the word's trinitarian use was an established exegetical use. The Logos was considered by ancient theology as the agent of all revelation; therefore when Scripture attributes speech to the Father or the Spirit, this was said to be the Son speaking "in the person" (*ex persona*) of the Father or the Spirit. Exegetically, Tertullian was thus accustomed to the three, in their distinction from one another, being called "persons." The step to use in trinitarian analysis was apparently taken before Tertullian; it was in any case a short one.

Tertullian's assertion of three *personae* in God is thus the assertion against modalism that the role distinctions, the relations of address and response, found in Scripture between the Father and Jesus and the Spirit, establish reality in God, just as such relations do among human individuals.[39] Tertullian's cases of the distinction of "persons" all come down to the distinction of Father, Jesus, and Spirit in scriptural narrative (ibid., xxiff.). They are three in that they speak to and about one another (ibid., xi,9–10) in such scriptural incidents as Jesus' baptism. They are three because they have three mutually recognized proper names (ibid., iv,4). Also the inner-trinitarian eternal roles are defined by the roles in saving history; when God said, "Let us make man," "he spoke, in the unity of the trinity, with the Son, who was to put on man, and with the Spirit, who was to sanctify man, as if with ministers and councillors" (ibid., xii,3).

In his use of *substantia* for the unity of God, Tertullian followed his own philosophical tradition. This was not adhered to by later Western theology, so that "one substance" came simply to mean somehow one thing[40] and then to be interpreted within whatever philosophy was in vogue.

The resultant terminology was useful both for good and for bad. It gave the Western church language with which to get on with its daily proclamatory and disciplinary business, 175 years before this urgent necessity was filled in the East. But in its conceptual blandness, it also served to cover the very real religious and intellectual problems posed by the Christian identification of God. These were to be faced in the East.

That event was prepared by the first truly great thinker and scholar of Christian history, Origen of Alexandria, who carried subordinationist trinitarianism to its unstable perfection and created a way of thinking that dominated the Eastern church for the remainder of its theologically creative history. Though he was a far greater theologian than Tertullian, his role in our special story is so much that of the fulfiller of already-described tendencies that our treatment can be brief. One great aspect of his work may be simply noted here, for future reference: He was the creator of hermeneutically self-conscious biblical exegesis.

Origen's God the Father is Hellenic deity in purest form: sheer mind, utterly removed from the temporal material world, utterly undifferentiated, and just so unknowable (*On First Principles*, i,1,5–6). The unknowability of God is identical with the difference between the temporal and the timeless (*Fragments to John*, i,xiii). God is knowable only as ground of his works, by the intuition of *nous* (*On First Principles*, i,1,6; iv,3,15).

Accordingly, Origen's entire soteriological concern is for mediation of the knowledge of God. He succeeded in creating a consistently subordinationist system to mediate this deity that had place for the Spirit and so did not obviously clash with the trinitarian creeds and liturgies. He created a grandiose version of late antiquity's vision of a hierarchy of being—the Christian pair to Plotinus's—descending in successive mediations from God, like the rays from the sun, down finally to the material universe.[41] The "birth" of mediating deity from God is an eternal event: God just is self-mediating (ibid., i,2; i,9; lv,5). Also, the Spirit is eternal, given from God without beginning (ibid., i,3,4).

The problem of the place of the Spirit is ingeniously solved. The Spirit's work is sanctification; its sphere is the church; Origen includes the church's special reality in the mediation system. He conceives the work of Father, Son, and Spirit as three concentric circles, along the line of mediation between God and us, as an inverted, stepped cone. The Father gives being to all beings; the Son gives the knowledge of God to all beings capable of knowledge; the Spirit gives the holiness in which such knowledge is fulfilled to those among rational beings who are to be saved. Both the downward mediation of being and the upward mediation of fulfillment are thus essentially triple—if dubiously triune (ibid., i,3,5; i,3,8).

THE ARIAN CRISIS

The Origenist system was unstable, since the initial mere compromise between biblical and Hellenic interpretation of God still lay at its heart. In historical particular, it could not stand the question "Well, which *is* the Logos, Creator or creature?" The secret of subordinationist trinitarianism, perfected by Origen, was the posit of an unbroken continuity of being from the great God, through the Logos, the Spirit, and other "spiritual" beings, down to temporal beings. Across this beautiful spectrum the biblical radical distinction of Creator from creature could only make an ugly slash somewhere. But the intense and open study of Scripture which was the other great achievement of Origenism itself had sooner or later to pose the Creator-creature difference.

The intellectual and religious instability of Origenism was also a confessional instability of the Eastern church. At the turn of the third and fourth centuries, the great bishoprics and professorships of the East were almost all occupied by Origenists of one shade or another, from a left wing of those most drawn by Origen's intellectual respectability, to a right wing most drawn by his christological passion.[42]

Subordinationism's inevitable breakdown was triggered by the students and other disciples of Lucian of Antioch.[43] Lucian's theology is not well known. In the last decades of the third century and the first of the fourth, he was a great teacher in the style of Origen, a martyr, and the founder of Antioch's scholarly fame. His students learned a methodical exegesis of Scripture more devoted to the literal sense than Origen's, and therefore more likely to intrude the dangerous Creator-creature distinction. They also learned a more coolly analytical—Aristotelian—Platonism, amenable to such commonsensicalities as that each thing is itself and not another. This made Origen's spectrum of being look more like a set of steps than a glissando, and so emphasized its subordinationism. If the Logos is a distinct entity only a very, very little bit different from God, then he is, said the Lucianists, in fact different.[44]

The struggle began among the Egyptian clergy. The priest of an Alexandrian parish, a second-rate Lucianist named Arius, attacked the Origenist right wing's tendency to attribute full divine eternity to the Son.[45] Since the attack touched the bishop, Alexander, a synod of Egyptian bishops deposed Arius and a few sympathizers from office.

Thereupon Arius appealed to the old-school tie. Leaving Egypt, he and his fellow rebels sought and found place with the most notable of the Lucianists, Bishop Eusebius of Nicomedia. Eusebius launched a correspondence campaign among the Eastern bishops to have Arius restored to office. Alexander responded, and a general uproar ensued which can only be explained by the theological development being ripe for it.

What Arius and his friends were concerned about is explicit and clear in the first document of the conflict, Arius's appeal to Eusebius of Nicomedia. As Arius understands it, those who attribute to the Son coeternity with the Father must either regard the Son as some sort of emergent from within the Father's being or as a parallel unoriginated being. Both are termed "blasphemies."[46]

For Arius, and for the whole Lucianist group to which he appealed, and indeed for all the more left-wing disciples of Origen, there were only two identifying characteristics of God. First, God is "unoriginated." As we have seen, the theology deriving from the apologists did not differentiate between possible different ways of having an origin; left-wing Origenism made the catchall negative definitive of deity.[47] Second, God is altogether devoid of internal differentiation. For Arius, therefore, to say that the Son is "co-unoriginated," or anything of the sort, posits two "co-gods,"[48] while to say that the Son is an emergent from within the Father introduces differentiation into even the Father, that is, denies that there is any real God at all.[49] Arius therefore teaches: "The Son is not unoriginated, nor is he in any way a part of the Unoriginated."[50]

It is plain that what moves Arius is the late-Hellenic need to escape time, become utterly dominant. If we are to be saved, there must be some reality entirely uninvolved with time, which has no origin of any sort and whose continuity is undifferentiated and uninterrupted. Just so, it is because Christ is involved with time that he will not do as really God: "How can the Logos be God, who sleeps like a man and weeps and suffers?"[51] It had long been decided, against the modalists, that the longed-for absolute timeless and impassible One cannot be a divine essence other than Father, Son, and Spirit. Then it must be the Father. Very early, the Arians put their whole case in two sentences: "As the monad, and the Source of all things, God is before all things. Therefore he is also before the Son."[52] All other considerations must be sacrificed to this logic and the religious need behind it.

It was around the converse that the controversy was to be conducted. Arius had to say, "There was once when he [the Logos] was not,"[53] that is, the Logos is a creature. In the direction of the transcendence from which we come and into which we are to return, the way, according to the Arians, leads beyond what happens in time with Christ, to a God who is not yet the Father of the Son, who is a sheer unoriginate, above all differentiation and relation. As we climb back up the ladder of being, the Logos, so long as he is above us, is God *for us* but is not God in himself.[54] The great thinker of later Arianism (350–380), Eunomius, was finally to draw the religious conclusion: the last goal is precisely to transcend the revealer and see God as does he.[55]

In the long term of the conflict, the opposition to Arius was to be carried above all by Athanasius, Alexander's adviser and then his successor as bishop. He attacked precisely the Arian vision of God as not that of the gospel. If God is not intrinsically Father of the Son, he is not intrinsically Father, for "father" is relational (*Discourse II against the Arians*). But being fatherly defines the God Christians worship. Therefore he can no more be God without the Son than light can be without shining (*Epistle on the Decree of Nicaea*, 2;12). It is Origen's doctrine of the eternal generation of the Son—that the origin of the Son from the Father is not *in* time at all—that is here adapted. The very being of the Father would be unfinished without the Son; God's goodness is that God is Father; God's truth is the Son (*Discourse I against the Arians*, 14,28;20); and the Son cannot be a creature willed by the Father because the Son *is* the Father's will (*Discourse III*, 68). It is not too much to say that, for Athanasius, *what* the Son reveals about God is exactly that God is his Father.

Since relation to us, as the Father of our Lord, is internal to God's being, there is no need for bridge-beings between God and us. The great religious need of late antiquity is not filled by the gospel; it is abolished. Then Athanasius is free to label the adjectival and graded use of "God" as what it is: "polytheism, for since they [the Arians] call [the Son] God, because it is so written, but do not call him proper to the Father's being, they introduce a plurality of . . . forms of divine being" (*Discourse* III, 15). Assimilating created beings to God is the very principle of the non-Christian religion: "This is the characteristic of the Greeks, to introduce a creature into the Trinity" (*Discourse* III, 18). The middle realm is gone altogether: "If Son, not creature; if creature, not Son" (*Nicaea*, 13).

NICAEA AND CONSTANTINOPLE

Therefore, driven by equal and opposite ultimate concerns, the churchmen of the eastern Empire fell on one another when Arius said, "when he was not." Just at this point the first Christian emperor assumed power. Constantine came as an agent of universal peace, dreaming of the *pax Romana* restored by the new religion of love, and he found the very bishops in a brawl, the most learned in the front. After initial efforts to restore peace failed, he commanded a general council of the bishops of the eastern Empire, to meet at Nicaea in 325 in succession of an earlier Egyptian council.

Those who attended found themselves at the first great meeting of ecumenical Christianity, in a world suddenly turned from persecution to supplication. Understandably, they were in no more mood for disturbers of unity than was Constantine. They confirmed the condemnation of Arius and deposed his more intransigent supporters. And they produced a rule for talk about Christ which excluded Arius and his immediate followers but which all others, even Eusebius of Nicomedia, contrived to sign. Into a typical three-article liturgical creed, they inserted four theological explications: Christ, they said, is "out of the being of the Father," "true God of true God," "begotten not created," and *homoousios* (of one being) with the father."[56] This is the dogma of Nicaea, the first deliberately created dogma and a main object of this whole *locus*.

"Out of the being of the Father" affirms just that origin of Christ within God's own self that Arius most feared. The phrase says that the Son is not an entity originated outside God by God's externally directed choice, that he is not in any sense a creature. And it says there *is* differentiation within God, that the relation to the Son is an internal relation in the Father, a relation necessary to his being God the Father. *To be God is to be related.* With that the fathers contradicted the main principle of Hellenic theology.

"Born, not created . . ." makes exactly that distinction between two ways of being originated from God, the lack of which enabled the subordinationist glissando from God himself, who is unoriginated, to us, who are originated, through the Son, who is a bit of each. On the contrary, we are "created," the Son is "begotten," and these are just two different things. Nobody claimed to know exactly what "begotten" meant in this connection. Yet a tremendous assertion is made: There is a way of being begun, of receiving one's being, which is proper to godhead itself. To be God is not only to give being, it is also to receive being. And there went the rest of Plato.

"True God of true God" prohibits all use of the analogy principle in calling Jesus "God." He is plain God, not qualified God. What the clause prohibits is the whole Greek use of "God" as an adjective applicable in various degrees.

Finally there is the famous and fateful "*homoousios* with the Father." The history of the word *homoousios* was checkered.[57] Its first theological use was by gnostics, for the mythic emergences of their sundry divine entities. Origen used the word, but rarely, to say that the Son had all the same essential characters as the Father, but on another ontological level.[58]

We do not know how or why this came to be Nicaea's big word. Perhaps it was introduced precisely by Arius's negative use simply to contradict him. Arius had said, "The Son . . . is not *homoousios* with [the Father]" to reject Western-type trinitarianism or any notion of Father and Son being two by division of one substance.[59]

The bishops seemingly did not have any one meaning in mind when they used *homoousios*. Constantine's Western advisers at Nicaea, thinking in Latin, no doubt took *homoousios* as a simple translation of Tertullian's "of one substance" and had no further problem. For those who thought in Greek it was not so simple. Did *homoousios* mean the same as it did in Origen? The most ardent anti-Arians, such as Athanasius, suspected it might, and might therefore be a poor guard against subordinationism; they were for a time wary in their use of it. Did it mean that Father and Son both had all the characteristics of godhead, whatever these are? Then are there not two (or three) Gods? Or did it, in more Aristotelian fashion, mean that Father and Son were numerically one actual entity? But how then could modalism be avoided? The Lucianists feared modalism could not be avoided, and when one of the chief Nicene anti-Arians, Marcellus of Ancyra, turned out in fact to be a modalist, they had a horror example ever after.[60]

Yet so much was clear: *homoousios* meant that Arius was a heretic. Affirmatively, there is only one divine being, and both Father and Son have it. Whatever it means to be God, pure and simple, Christ is. And that suffices to make the needed and revolutionary point: Christ is not at all the sort of halfway entity that normal religion needs and provides to mediate time and eternity. He is not a divine teacher or example, a personal savior, a mediator of grace, or any of the beloved semigods of standard religion. He is constitutive of God, not merely revelatory—or if one develops a whole theology of revelation, then being revealed in Christ is itself constitutive of God.

Abrupt and almost instinctive though they were, the Nicene phrases make the decisive differentiation between Christian and other interpretations of God, then and now. Proclamation of a God or salvation that do not fit cannot be the gospel, however otherwise religious or beneficial. The Arian incident was the decisive crisis to date, and the Nicene Creed the decisive victory to date, in Christianity's self-identification. The gospel—Nicaea finally said unequivocally—provides no mediator of our ascent to a timeless and therefore distant God. It rather proclaims a God whose own deity is not separable from a figure of our temporal history and who therefore is not and never has been timeless and distant from us.

The bishops were not clearly aware of what they had said with this creed, except that Arius had gone too far. When they went home, they slowly became aware. Then the real fight began, to last for sixty years. In some ways, it still continues.

Subordinationist trinitarianism had not yet undone itself from within; it had only been renounced in a crude version. A variety of moves could seemingly yet be tried to combine the glissando of being with the difference between Creator and creature. In the next forty years each such move would produce a new creedal proposal and a new alignment against Athanasius. Moreover, the Nicene dogma was incomplete; what about the Spirit? So soon as the matter was noted—in Egypt again—a whole new spectrum of disputes displayed itself.

The Lucianists began the new struggle, refusing to take Nicaea as the last word and working for possession of the bishoprics and for ecumenical acceptance of a more moderate creed.[61] The lineup shifted with each new theological attempt. At one end of the spectrum were two groups: Athanasius with his followers, and the Western bishops, who stuck to Tertullian's formula, never quite understood the Easterners' problems, and supported Athanasius when they dared. It took some daring, for after Nicaea the anti-Nicene reaction usually contrived to look like the peace-loving middle of the road, and so to secure imperial support. At the other end were actual Arians, some willing to be called that and others not, sporadically recruited from the Origenist middle. In between were the majority of Eastern churchmen, whose common purpose was to preserve the traditional Origenist theology of the East. But, once the challenge of the *homoousios* was there, their ground proved slippery, and the left wing constantly slid into practically Arian positions.

After initial hesitation Athanasius made *homoousios* his slogan, to mean that the Father and the Son—and the Spirit—together make the one reality of God: It is the Trinity as such that is God.[62] Whatever sundry bishops at

Nicaea meant by *homoousios*, it is with this point that the word enters dogmatic history. The various anti-Nicene coalitions took the Father *by himself* as really God, and the Son, next down on the spectrum of being, as very closely—perhaps even altogether—assimilated to God. Confused as the terminologies were, the issue was and is clear and vital to faith. The issue is not so much about the status of Jesus as about who and what is God himself.

Anti-*homoousian* slogans waxed and waned.[63] None quite worked; then a new one would be tried. The final result of the anti-Nicene movement was the discrediting of subordinationism, by the destruction of the confessional unity of the Eastern church. For example, in Antioch just before 360 there was a complete denominational system: a congregation of out-and-out Arians, a congregation of sophisticated Arians, the official church with a Eusebian bishop, a pro-Nicene group that had submitted to the bishop but held their own meetings, and a separate congregation of intransigent Nicaeans.[64]

As the weary creed-making went on, many not originally of Athanasius's party began to see that the vision of God evoked by *homoousios*—as used by Athanasius—was theirs too.[65] What was needed for the East was an explanation of how this could work, of how one might indeed say that Father and Son are one God, and that this is not a matter of levels, without thereby falling into modalism, that is, how one could hold to Origen's decisive insight that Father, Son, and Spirit are indeed three in God, otherwise than by ranking them ontologically.

Such a theory was finally provided in the 370s by a brilliant new generation of teachers and bishops, again schooled by Origen but using his dialectic to overcome his subordinationism. The most powerful thinkers among these were the Cappadocians: Basil, primate of Cappadocia, his brother, Gregory of Nyssa, and his protégé, Gregory of Nazianzus. Analysis of their thought belongs to the next chapter. Here a rough characterization will suffice. The Cappadocians took Origen's three hypostases and his real distinctions among them, in Origen a ladder reaching vertically from God to time, and tipped it on its side, to make a structure horizontal to time and reaching from point to point in God. Just such a stroke of dialectic was what was needed to enable general acceptance of Nicaea's dogma.

Emperor Theodosius I, determined like his predecessors to reunite the church, summoned yet another council at Constantinople in 381.[66] It was a council of Basil's followers, and it succeeded where all before had failed. It proclaimed the Nicene confession as the official confession of the East by adopting another regional baptismal creed that in Nicene use had been enriched with the Nicene phrases. And it added an affirmation of the full deity of the Spirit, with insertions into the third article: ". . . the Lord, the Giver of life, proceeding from the Father, worshiped and glorified with the Father and the Son. . . ." In this article, the word *homoousios* was itself avoided, so as not to start the struggle about terminology again.

The article on the Spirit completed the trinitarian dogma. Since the Spirit was, on the subordinationist hierarchy, one more step from God than the Logos, affirmation of the full godhead of the Spirit marked final rejection of the whole subordinationist principle. On this affirmation the middle of the road sorted itself into those who entered the reconstituted ecumenical church and those who continued in waning opposition or sectarianism.[67]

One step remains in the story of the Nicene dogma. In 451, long after these battles were over, the Council of Chalcedon formally proclaimed both the creed of Nicaea and the creed of Constantinople as dogma for the whole church, East and West.[68] Since then, the Constantinopolitan creed—incorrectly called the Nicene Creed—has come to dominate liturgical use, since it contains the phrases for the Spirit. Both creeds together are the dogmatic documents. It has since been an ecumenical rule of all talk in the Christian church: In all three temporal directions of our relation to Jesus Christ, we have unsurpassably to do with God, and just by this circumstance our God differs from the culture-God of Western civilization, even in his christianized versions.

NOTES

1. The following depends on the standard histories: Jane Ellen Harrison, *Prolegomena to the Study of Greek Religion* (Cambridge: At the University Press, 1903), chaps. 1, 6, 7; Martin P. Nilsson, *A History of Greek Religion*, trans. F. J. Fielden (Oxford: At the Clarendon Press, 1925); Martin P. Nilsson, "Die Griechen," in *Lehrbuch der Dogmengeschichte*, ed. Chantepie de la Saussaye (Tübingen: J. C. B. Mohr [Paul Siebeck], 1925), 2:281–417; Ulrich von Wilamowitz-Moellendorf, *Der Glaube der Hellenen* (Berlin: Weidmann, 1932). The interpretation is heavily influenced by Ulrich Mann, *Vorspiel des Heils* (Stuttgart: Klett, 1962).

2. Mann, *Vorspiel*, pp. 62ff.

3. Sophocles, *Oedipus the King*, ii,1528–30.

4. Aristotle, *Metaphysics*, 1051b,29–30.

5. Werner Jaeger, *The Theology of the Early Greek Philosophers* (Oxford: At the Clarendon Press, 1947).

6. Aristotle, *Physics*, 4,203b7.

7. See Eberhard Jüngel, *Zum Ursprung der Analogie bei Parmenides und Heraklit* (Berlin: Walter de Gruyter, 1964).

8. K. von Fritz, "The Function of *Nous*," *CP* 38 (1943): 79–93; 40 (1945): 223–42; 41 (1946): 12–34; Werner Marx, *The Meaning of Aristotle's "Ontology"* (The Hague: Nijhoff, 1954), pp. 8–29.

9. See Hans Jonas, *Gnosis und spätantiker Geist* (Göttingen: Vandenhoeck &

2 / THE TRIUNE GOD

Ruprecht, 1954); Hans Jonas, "Gnosis und Moderner Nihilismus," *KuD*, 1960, pp. 155–71. On the *Corpus Hermeticum*, which preserves the best witness of the crisis, see André M. J. Festugière, *La Révélation de l'Hermes Trismégiste* (Paris: Lecattre, 1944–54), vol. 4.

10. E.g., Hal Koch, *Pronoia und Paideusis* (Berlin: Walter de Gruyter, 1932), pp. 180–314; Nilsson, "Die Griechen," pp. 394–417.

11. Plato, *Symposium*, 101A–212B.

12. See Wolfhart Pannenberg, "Die Aufnahme des philosophischen Gottesbegriffs als dogmatisches Problem der frühchristlichen Theologie," *ZKG* 70 (1959): 1–45; Yehoshua Amir, "Die Begegnung des biblischen und des philosophischen Monotheismus," *EvTh* 38 (1978): 2–19.

13. E.g., Theophilus of Antioch, *Apology to Autolycus*, i,2,5; Melito of Sardis, *Address to Antonius Caesar*, 6–8.

14. Jaroslav Pelikan, *The Christian Tradition*, vol. 1, *The Emergence of the Catholic Tradition (100–600)* (Chicago: University of Chicago Press, 1971), pp. 52ff.; René Braun, *Deus Christianorum: Recherches sur le vocabulaire doctrinal de Tertullian* (Paris: Presses Universitaires, 1962), pp. 62ff.

15. Justin Martyr, *Apology*, i,12, 13, 25; Melito of Sardis, *Address to Antonius Caesar*, 2; Theophilus of Antioch, *Apology to Autolycus*, i,3; Athenagoras, *Supplication for the Christians*, 10. On the standard middle-Platonist theology of Justin, see L. W. Barnard, *Justin Martyr: His Life and Thought* (Cambridge: At the University Press, 1967), pp. 79ff.

16. Barnard, *Justin Martyr*, pp. 77ff.; Braun, *Deus Christianorum*, p. 74.

17. On the failure of creative synthesis, see Pannenberg, "Die Aufnahme," pp. 312–46.

18. Pelikan, *Emergence*, pp. 136–82; RGG³, s.v. "Trinität," by F. H. Kettler.

19. The first great antimodalist work was Tertullian's *Against Praxeas*, shortly after A.D. 207. At the theoretical level, another had never been needed.

20. Aloys Grillmeier, *Christ in Christian Tradition*, trans. J. S. Bowden (New York: Sheed & Ward, 1965), 1:190–206.

21. See *TDNT*, s.v. "Word," by H. Kleinknecht.

22. E.g., *Theologia Graeca*, 16; "Hermes is the Logos, whom the gods sent to us from heaven, to make man rational (*logikos*) . . . but even more to save us."

23. Justin Martyr, *Apology*, i,32.

24. Ibid., 13, 62–63; see also Justin Martyr, *Dialogue with Trypho*, 10, 126–28; Theophilus of Antioch, *Apology*, ii,22.

25. Justin Martyr, *Dialogue*, 55–62; *Apology,* ii,6,13.

26. E.g., Athenagoras, *Supplication*, 10; Theophilus, *Apology*, ii,22; Justin Martyr, *Dialogue*, 61.

27. E.g., Justin Martyr, *Apology*, i,5.

28. See Braun, *Deus Christianorum*, pp. 287–91.

29. Justin Martyr, *Dialogue*, 62,128.

30. Georg Kretschmar, *Studien zur frühchristlichen Trinitätstheologie* (Tübingen: J. C. B. Mohr [Paul Siebeck], 1956), pp. 1–15.

31. E.g., Tatian, *Address to the Greeks*, 7. See Kretschmar, *Studien*, pp. 40–61; Pelikan, *Emergence*, pp. 185–86.

32. On the first, see Justin Martyr, *Apology*, i,13; on the second, see J. Armitage Robinson, ed., "Introduction," in Irenaeus, *The Demonstration of the Apostolic Preaching* (London: SPCK, 1920).

33. Novatian, *On the Trinity*, is entirely concerned for the Logos' mediatorial function but appends a piece on the Spirit (xxx–xxxi) because, he says, "the authority of the baptismal confession reminds us . . . that we also believe in the Spirit" (xxix).

34. E.g., Irenaeus, *Against All Heresies*, ii,i–ii; ii,vi; ii,xvii,3; ii,vii,6; ii,xiii,4–6.

35. On this and the following, see Braun, *Deus Christianorum*.

36. Ibid., pp. 71–72.

37. Ibid., pp. 158–67.

38. On the following, see ibid., pp. 207–32.

39. Ibid., pp. 228–32. On the following, see ibid., pp. 235–36.

40. Ibid., pp. 173–94.

41. On Origen, see Robert W. Jenson, *The Knowledge of Things Hoped For* (New York: Oxford University Press, 1969), pp. 26ff.; there further bibliography.

42. The most typical representation of the left was Eusebius of Caesarea, *Demonstration of the Gospel*, iv, v. For the right, we may name the young Athanasius, *Discourse on the Incarnation of the Word*.

43. On Lucian and the Lucianists, see Gustave Bardy, *Recherches sur Saint Lucien d'Antioch et son École* (Paris: Gabriel Beauchesne, 1936); here the remaining Lucianist texts are collected. On the following theological history, see Louis Duchesne, *Early History of the Christian Church* (New York and London: Longmans, Green & Co., 1912), 2:98ff.; Grillmeier, *Christ*, 218ff.; J. N. D. Kelly, *Early Christian Doctrines* (New York: Harper & Row, 1960), pp. 223–71.

44. See, e.g., Kelly, *Doctrines*, p. 231.

45. Arius, *To Eusebius*, in Bardy, *Recherches*, p. 227: "We do not agree with those who daily cry, 'always God, always Son.' "

46. Ibid., p. 227.

47. Asterius the Sophist, chief publicist for the Arians in the ensuing controversy, formulated the principle: "ageneton . . . to me poiethen . . ." (frag. vii, in Bardy, *Recherches*). The great leader of later Arianism, Aetius, made the whole doctrine of God a mere abstract dialectic on *agennetos/gennetos*; *Syntagmata*, in *PG* 42:533–45.

48. Arius, *Thalia*, in Bardy, *Recherches*, p. 286: ". . . he monas en, he duas de ouk en prin hyparxe."

49. Arius, *To Alexander*, in Bardy, *Recherches*, pp. 236–37.

50. Arius, *To Eusebius*, in ibid., p. 228.

51. Arius, cited by Athanasius, *Discourse against the Arians* (in *PG* 26:321–407), iii,28.

52. Arius, *To Alexander*, in Bardy, *Recherches*, p. 237.

53. Arius, *Thalia*, in ibid., p. 261.

54. Ibid., 267: "Nor is the Logos true God. He is, to be sure, called 'God' . . . , but by participation granted by grace."

55. Eunomius, cited by Gregory of Nyssa, *Against Eunomius*, in his *Opera*, vols. 1–2, ed. W. Jaeger (Leiden: E. J. Brill, 1960), iii/viii,14.

56. The text of the relevant part of the second article and of the appended anathemas: "And in one Lord, Jesus Christ, the Son of God; born of the Father (*ek tou patros*)

uniquely, i.e., out of the being of the Father (*ek tes ousias tou patros*); God of God; light of light; true God of true God; born, not made; of one being with the Father (*homoousion to patri*). . . ." "The catholic church condemns those who say, 'There was when he was not' and 'Before he was born he was not' and 'He originated from what is not,' calling him either 'of another hypostasis' or 'of another being' (*ousia*), so that he would be a changeable and mutable 'Son of God.'"

57. Heinz Kraft, "OMOOUSIOS," *ZKG* 66 (1954–55): 1–24; Adolf M. Ritter, *Das Konzil von Konstantinopel und sein Symbol* (Göttingen: Vandenhoeck & Ruprecht, 1965), pp. 270–93.

58. Origen, fragment 540, as collected by M. J. Rouët de Journal, *EnchP*, 1965.

59. Arius, *Thalia*, in Bardy, *Recherches*, p. 256.

60. If Marcellus was not a modalist (as Grillmeier, *Christ*, pp. 275–96, labors to show), he fooled everyone at the time.

61. See Duchesne, *Early History*, pp. 125–200, 218ff. For the best brief account of the theology, see Michel Meslin, *Les Ariens d'Occident* (Paris: Servil, 1967), pp. 253–99.

62. Athanasius, *Discourse I against the Arians*, 18. Athanasius explains that *homoousios* is the logical product of "possessed of identical characteristics (*homoiousios*)" and "from the being (*ek tes physeos*)" (*Epistle on the Councils of Ariminum and Seleucia*, 41–42).

63. See Ritter, *Konzil*, pp. 64–85.

64. Duchesne, *Early History*, pp. 276–77.

65. Ritter, *Konzil*, pp. 68–85.

66. On this paragraph, see ibid., pp. 21–40, 132–204, 293–307.

67. Meslin, *Ariens*, pp. 325–435; Ritter, *Konzil*, pp. 68–85.

68. Ritter, *Konzil*, pp. 133–51, 172–75, 204–8.

4

The One
and the Three

Developed trinitarian dialectics, such as the proposition that God is "three persons of one substance," are metaphysical analysis of the gospel's triune identification of God, and especially of its difference from the Hellenic interpretation of God. The need for such analysis has not passed; indeed, at present it is more urgent than since antiquity.

THE EASTERN
TRINITARIAN TERMINOLOGY

Two centuries of passionate reflection brought the Eastern church back to the rule of faith with which it began. But now there is an agreed conceptuality, provided by the Cappadocians: "one being (*ousia*) of God in three hypostases (*hypostaseis*)." The conceptuality was derived from expressions of Origen[1] and at a second session of Theodosius' council, in 382, was taken into approved ecclesiastical use.[2] In elucidating it, we will both explicate the Cappadocian analysis and continue to some analysis of our own.

At a first level, "one being in three hypostases" was merely a sort of linguistic settlement, stipulating terminology for a perceived need that somehow we be able to refer both to one reality of God and to three realities of God. In most theological use, *ousia* and *hypostasis* had previously been handled as rough equivalents. The decree of Nicaea used both indiscriminately in the singular in asserting the oneness of the triune reality, as did Athanasius all his life.[3] The entire Origenist spectrum used both in the plural in asserting that there really are three somehow different realities in the Trinity.[4] The new terminological regulation, finding two words for "what is real" in trinitarian use, split the difference and took one for the one and the other for the three.

Thereby the East was provided with a trinitarian terminology extensionally equivalent to the West's "one substance (*substantia*) in three persons (*personae*)." But it is vital to understand that the two terminologies are not intentionally equivalent: If a proposition in the one is simply set into the other, its meaning is not necessarily preserved. Failure to observe this has been and is the cause of a great deal of confusion. "Substance" and "person" had never been interchangeable. Just so, their distinction evoked no new insight. Nor did they carry any history of trinitarian controversy.[5]

Ousia and *hypostasis* both came into theology from the philosophical tradition.[6] There they were used almost interchangeably, for *what is*— conformably to Hellenic apprehension, for what is by possession of some specific complex of permanent characteristics. Just so, they are also used for the "being" so possessed, that is, for both this complex of characteristics and for the stability through time their possession bestows.

Between *ousia* and *hypostasis* there were nevertheless slight nuances of difference. *Ousia* tended to be used for the reality that real things have and so to evoke, for example, the humanity Socrates has, but not so much the marks by which he as human differs from other beings, while *hypostasis* sounded more strongly the notes of distinguishability and identifiability. When trinitarian use divided the terms, the division was made along the line of these nuances. *Hypostasis* now meant simply that which can be identified, while *ousia* meant *what* such an identifiable *is*.[7] This necessarily dropped *hypostasis* to the level of individuals and located *ousia* at the level of the being any one kind of individuals are in common—except that *hypostasis* brought with it an aura of metaphysical dignity that previous terms for the individual lacked.

Just this is the starting position of the Cappadocian analysis: Father, Son, and Spirit, they say, are three individuals who share Godhead, as Peter, Paul, and Barnabas are three individuals who share humanity.[8] The one being of God is common to the three hypostases, which are distinguished by the individually identifying characteristics of "being unbegotten," "being begotten," and "proceeding."[9] Clearly this lays them open to this question: "As Peter, Paul, and Barnabas are three men, why are Father, Son, and Spirit not *three gods*?"[10] The Cappadocians' metaphysical creativity appears in their answer to this challenge.

THE THREE HYPOSTASES

The Cappadocians reworked the concepts *ousia* and *hypostasis*. We will consider *hypostasis* first. The plural individuals that share humanity differ from one another by characteristics adventitious to—indeed, in the usual Hellenic view, privative of—the humanity they have in common: by brown hair, moderate intelligence, Athenian ancestry, or whatever. Just so, they are plural humans. But, said the Cappadocians, Godhead can receive no such adventitious or privative characteristics. Therefore there is no way for a plurality of divine hypostases, if their plurality is somehow established, to make a plurality of Gods.[11] Their argument, it should be noted, holds only if the graded adjectival use of "God" has become utterly inconceivable, which is just what Christian theological self-consciousness had achieved.

And there is indeed a way, without characteristics adventitious to or privative of Godhead, for the three to be individually identified. Their individually identifying characteristics are the *relations* they have to each other, precisely with respect to their joint possession of deity. God is the Father as the source of the Son's and the Spirit's Godhead; God is the Son as the recipient of the Father's Godhead; and God is the Spirit as the spirit of the Son's possession of the Father's Godhead.[12] The different way in which each is the one God, for and from the others, is the only difference between them.[13]

We have arrived at a certain completion of the dialectic. We have also arrived at a point where some more than historical interpretation and reflection is needed. There are two matters to consider.

First, we must remind ourselves what all these word games are about. The "hypostases" are Jesus, and the transcendent will he called Father, and the Spirit of their future for us. Just as vital to remember, the hypostases' "relations" are Jesus' historical obedience to and dependence on his Father and the coming of their future into the believing community. "Begetting," "being begotten," "proceeding," and their variants are biblical terms for temporal structures of evangelical history, which theology then uses to evoke relations constitutive of God's life. What happens between Jesus and his Father and our future happens in God—that is the point.

It was the achievement of the Cappadocians to find a conceptualized way to say this, by arranging Origen's hypostases and their *homoousia* horizontally to time rather than vertically to time, making the hypostases' mutual relations structures of the one God's life, rather than steps from God down to us.[14] Then the Trinity as such is the Creator, over against the creature, and the three in God and their relations become the evangelical history's reality on the Creator side of the great biblical divide. Across the Creator/creature distinction, no *mediator* is needed;[15] "Creator"/"creature" names an absolute difference, but no distance at all, for to be the Creator is merely as such to be actively related to the creature. Each of the inner-trinitarian relations is then an affirmation that as God works creatively among us, so he is in himself.

It was time, we said, to remind ourselves of these things. The Nicene dogma and the Cappadocian analysis were victories in the confrontation between the gospel's and Hellenism's interpretations of God. But the confrontation is by no means concluded. One continuous post-Nicene threat has been the temptation to interpret the Trinity as a whole by the Hellenic negative theology, so that the Trinity in its turn disappears into the old distant timelessness, carrying its internal reflection of evangelical history right with it. Already in the Cappadocians there is a danger signal: their tendency to take refuge in mystery when asked what "begetting" and "proceeding" *mean*.[16] Why should there be a problem? There is none about what these words mean as slogans for saving historical events. No more should there be about their trinitarian meanings—unless the understanding of the triune life itself is infiltrated with impassibility, immobility, and so on, with reference to which a word like "proceeding" cannot indeed mean much.

Once the temporal reference of trinitarian language is reaffirmed, we can turn again to the conceptual problem of the three hypostases. As a piece of trinitarian language, *hypostasis* is merely an item of linguistic debris knocked from Hellenic philosophy by collision with Yahweh. Present understanding would be advanced if we replaced it with a word now philosophically active. Readers will not be surprised that we propose "identity," for as is apparent from the history of the adaptation of *hypostasis* to trinitarian use, it is exactly the ontological function now marked by "identity" that the trinitarian *hypostasis*, in its separation from *ousia*, invoked. We explicate this function in two steps.

First, something's identity is the possibility of picking it out from the maelstrom of actuality so as to talk about it. The enumerability of the world, whereby we can say "this, and this, and then this," is one of the world's deepest metaphysical characters. This character, taken of any one such "this," is an identity.

We identify in various ways. We point and say "this." But often we cannot point. Then we have two linguistic resources: proper names and identifying descriptions, as discussed earlier.

Accordingly, that there are three identities in God means that there are three discrete sets of names and descriptions, each sufficient to specify uniquely, yet all identifying the same reality. Among them that which says "God is what happens with Jesus" has the epistemological priority of the present tense, so that in each of the other two, terms will appear which, if interpretation is required, can only be interpreted by reference to Jesus' story. For example, if we say "God is the hope at the beginning of all things" and then are asked "Hope for what?" we must answer, "Hope for Jesus' triumph."

The three identifications can otherwise be performed independently. But the predicates we use of the one identified in any of the three ways can be made unambiguous—should ambiguity threaten—only by running them across all three identities. For example, "God is good in the way that a giver is good; and God is good in the way that a gift is good; and God is good in the way that the outcome of a gift is good."

Second, "identity" is now regularly used to interpret personal existence, as we may say that someone is "seeking identity." This sense is connected to the first; it names the mode of identifiability proper to certain entities, those we currently call "personal" in a sense very different from the trinitarian "person." As person, in this modern sense, I am what I am only in that I remember what I have been and hope for what I will be. If Jones is a person, in this modern sense, the "is" in "Jones is lazy" is not quite a normal copula; It is more like a transitive verb, modifiable by adverbs. It is the word for a specific act of positing oneself in and through time. Existentialist thought has invented words like "existence" or *Dasein* for this act. *Hypostasis* in its pretrinitarian and prechristological uses did not have this sense, but in the often tortured ways in which the theological tradition has used *hypostasis*, just this sense for the peculiar identity of person-realities struggled for expression already in the Cappadocians.

Accordingly, that there is even one identity in God means that God is personal, that he *is* God in that he *does* Godhead, in that he chooses himself as God. That there are three identities in God means that this God's deed of being the one God is three times repeated,[17] and so that each repetition is a being of God; and so that only in this precise self-repetition is God the particular God that he in fact is. God does God, and over again, and yet over again—and only so does the event and decision that is this God occur.

THE ONE BEING

Back to the Cappadocians. They needed also a correlated analysis of the divine *ousia* to show how it could be the being of three individuals without these being three instances of God. They had a variety of arguments; we will follow one by Gregory of Nyssa.

Since there is only one Godhead, the Trinity is somehow individual and must therefore be identifiable if real. And Gregory indeed provides an identifying description of the one *ousia* of God—but this is precisely that God's being is infinite.[18] We can identify God's one being as and only as life that knows no boundary and that therefore will always go on to surpass each— even true—identifying description.[19] This need not mean we cannot at all identify God affirmatively: God is "the one who raised Jesus," but then we are with the three rather than with the one.

Gregory is fully aware of the break he is making with philosophical tradition. He states the view "of the many," which he rejects. According to that view, "God" is, like "human" or "rock," "an unmetaphorical name by nature," "predicated to identify by the nature of the thing" (*To Ablabius*, 121). Such a word evokes some entity's entire set of essential characters all at once, insofar as these make an organic complex so that each character is itself only together with the others. Just so, such a word uniquely displays "the underlying individual subject" (ibid.), that which in any real thing *has* all the characters by which that thing is what it is, and is itself established as the possible possessor of these characters and no others. For God, says Gregory, there is no such word (ibid.).

Thus—and we are finally to the point—Gregory's answer to the question why three individuals sharing God's *ousia* do not make three gods is that "God" and all its equivalents are not predicated of the divine *ousia* at all, singly or trebly. "God" is a predicate, and how many gods are asserted depends on how many logical subjects it is attached to. A plurality of instances of the divine *ousia* is not a plurality of *gods,* for the *ousia* is not the logical subject of "God" to begin with, and neither then are the *ousia's* instances; how many individuals are instances of God's *ousia* is irrelevant to how many gods there are.

What then *is* "God" predicated of? Gregory's revolutionary answer: of the divine *activity* toward us (ibid., 124). And since all divine action is the structuredly mutual work of Father, Son, Spirit, their divine activity is but one logical subject of "God": "All action which comes upon the creature from God . . . begins from the Father and is present through the Son and is perfected in the Holy Spirit. Therefore the name of the action ("God") is not divided among the plurality of the actors" (ibid., 127). Gregory of Nazianzus once revised an old trinitarian illustration in an astonishing way. Instead of comparing Father, Son, and Spirit to the sun and its beams, he compared them to three suns, so focused as to make but one beam: The beam is God (*Oration XXXI*, 14).

The divine *ousia* does not drop out of the picture, for the inner-trinitarian relations, by which there are three to begin with, are defined in terms of it. It is precisely deity as infinity which the Father gives, the Son receives, and the Spirit communicates; by their relations, the action of each is temporally unlimited, to be *God's* action. But it is the *work*, the creative event, done through Jesus' life, death, resurrection, and future advent, done by his Father for their Spirit, that is the one God.

Surely this tendency is biblically right, at least by that understanding of the biblical witness sketched above. Stipulating an event as the subject of "God" imposes a task of ontological revision, to which we must eventually turn, as did Gregory. But leaving that for the moment, and recalling the discussion of "identity," we obtain the following formula: There is one event, God, of three identities. Therewith this essay's proposed basic trinitarian analysis.

THE WESTERN VERSION

The struggle and creation we have narrated in this and the previous chapter took place in the Eastern church. Its results were assimilated into the West from the late fourth century on. The circumstances of the assimilation have been decisive for the thought and life of the Western church. Without attempting to judge relative importance, we may list three such circumstances.

First, the doctrine of the Trinity came to the West as a finished product. Thus it was more something to be explained, than itself an explanation.

Second, in conducting trinitarian analysis and speculation in Latin, the Greek results were pressed into a terminology previously established in the Latin tradition: There is one "substance" of God (or "essence" or "nature"), in three "persons." But these terms had been through none of the Eastern conceptual wars; and when it came to the creative thrusts of such Easterners as Gregory of Nyssa, Western readers invariably missed the point. Augustine himself confessed incomprehension of the key Greek distinction: "I do not know what difference they intend between *ousia* and *hypostasis*"[20]

Third, the work of synthesis between Eastern thought and Western language and need was almost entirely the work of one man, Augustine, one of history's few history-shaping geniuses. Augustine's personal spiritual and intellectual experiences impressed themselves on Western theology in a way unparalleled in Christian history. In much of theology, this has been a blessing, but it has blighted our trinitarianism, for Augustine's particular religious experience led him to understand the triune character of God as one thing, the history of salvation as quite another. Thus the trinitarian formulas completely lost their original function.[21]

All these circumstances promoted a sort of reversion to pre-Nicene thinking. Hellenic interpretation of God had never been fully overcome in the general theology of the Eastern fathers, only within the trinitarian dogma and analyses themselves, and there by subtle and easily lost distinctions. The way thus remained open for Western theology to repristinate the old apologists' additive tactic in a new form. And that is what happened over the long history of Western theology. The inheritance of Hellenic interpretation was received as what the scholastics would come to call "natural" theology, a body of truth about God shared with the heathen and so taken to be resultant, at least in principle, from the merely created circumstances of life and the merely created religious and intellectual capacities of the soul. Such of the biblical discourse about God as was not shared by the heathen was therefore thought not to be thus generally available; it was received as a higher supernatural body of truth about God, given only by revelation. But when the matter is put so, the natural knowledge of God becomes the foundation of the supernatural; Homer and Parmenides get to write the first chapter in the *locus* on God. Consequently, the supposed timelessness and impassibility of God inevitably determine all that follows, including the trinitarian discourse.[22]

Augustine laid down this axiomatic status of divine timelessness for all subsequent Western theology: "Speak of the changes of things, and you find 'was' and 'will be'; think God, and you find 'is' where 'was' and 'will be' cannot enter."[23] God not only does not change, he cannot; just so, "he is rightly said *to be*" (*On the Trinity*, v,2).

This uncritical repristination of Greek assumptions had two consequences directly relevant to our interest. One was the doctrine of divine "simplicity," which became a key technical device of all consequent Western trinitarian analysis. Since it is by having "accidents," that is, characteristics that can come and go, that ordinary realities give hostages to time, God, it was agreed, has none such (ibid., v,3). As Thomas Aquinas argued it, accidents are the mark of potentiality, of capacity for becoming other than one is; this is absent from God (*Summa Theologica*, i,3,6). But so long as there is a real difference between the thing and its characteristics, it must be possible for the substance to remain while at least some characteristics come and go, that is, some must be accidents. Therefore in God there is no such difference; as Augustine puts it: "God is not great by a greatness other than himself . . . ; he is great by that greatness . . . he himself is" (*On the Trinity*, v,11). "God is called 'simple' because he *is* what he *has*" (*City of God*, 1,xi,10,1).

The second consequence was the reintrusion into the heart of trinitarianism of the old late-antique worry about the relation of a supposedly timeless God to his temporal creation, with evil results. Augustinianism forbade any assertion about God's relation to time that could suggest change in God himself. That there is a difficulty here, Augustine himself acknowledged: "To see how God . . . creates temporal things and events without any temporal movement of his substance . . . is hard" (*On the Trinity*, i,3). Nevertheless, he lays down the rule: When we speak of God being "our Lord," which he could not be before we existed, or of God's "becoming our Father at baptism," or of all the like, we must understand that "nothing is added to God, but only to that to which God is said to take up a relation." Thus, for example, "God begins to be our Father when we are reborn. . . . Our substance is changed for the better when we become his children; therewith he also begins to be our Father, but without any such change" (ibid., v,17).

The single most disastrous trinitarian result of this rule is that Western teaching, rigorously sorting out usages that had in the East been beneficially vague, makes the trinitarian "processions" in God (i.e., "begetting" and "breathing") and the divine persons' "missions" in time (i.e., the Son's Incarnation and the Spirit's entry into the church; i.e., again, the whole triune reality as Tertullian or Athanasius evoked it) be two simply different and metaphysically separated things: "'mission' and 'sending' . . . are predicated only temporally, 'generation' and 'breathing' only eternally."[24] That the Son, for example, is "begotten" by the Father, and that he is "sent" to redeem humanity, are now thought of as distinct events, one in eternity and the other in time: "The Son is said to be sent, not . . . in that he is born of the Father, but either in that he appears in this world as the Word made flesh . . . , or in that he is inwardly apprehended by a temporal mind."[25] Indeed, Aquinas' argument why there must be exactly the two processions is that the Son emerges by an act of the Father's mind and the Spirit by an act of his will, and that thinking and willing are the only two personal movements that do not necessarily emerge from the agent, that is, here, from God to a temporal object (*Summa Theologica*, i,27,5). In this theology, there are in effect two distinct sets of trinitarian relations, one constituting an "immanent" Trinity, the triune God himself, and the other the "economic" Trinity, the triune pattern of God's work.

The final consequence of these developments is that the trinitarian language of "persons" and "relations" in God loses its original meaning and indeed threatens to lose all meaning of any sort. That God is "one and three" becomes the sheer mystification Western churchgoers accept—or reject—it as: something we assert because we are supposed to, not knowing even what we are asserting. Augustine provided Western theology with a neat formula to sum up the decades of Eastern trinitarian reflection: The Father is God, and the Son is God, and the Spirit is God; and the Father and the Son and the Spirit are not the same one; and the three are but one God.[26] But the formula no longer represents an activity of analysis to help to understand God. It is instead a paradox formula: Since God is infinite, so that addition and substration do not apply, "one is as much as three are together." (*On the Trinity*, vi,12). And with his invariable clarity Augustine sees very well what then happens to the trinitarian language. He explicitly stipulates that when we say one "substance" or three "persons" we communicate nothing whatever, using the words only to say "somehow one" and "somehow three" and using these particular words only because they are traditional (ibid., v,10; vii,7–11). Later theology then makes pious mystery-mongering of the vacuity; for example, it is standard from Lombard on that the Son's "being begotten" differs from the Spirit's "proceeding" only by a difference that cannot be "known in this life" (*Sentences*, i,13).

That the saving works of God, the "works *ad extra*," are works of the whole Trinity no longer can mean that each work is the joint work of Father, Son, and Spirit, in which each identity plays a distinct role,[27] but that the saving works are *indifferently* the work of each person and all; the "inseparability" of God's works is now identified with a mathematically equal abstract divinity of the triune persons. Creation is undifferentiably the work of the Trinity as one God. And the "sender" of each divine mission is the Trinity, or any of the persons, including the one sent.[28]

So also there is no longer any necessary connection of the trinitarian persons to roles and structures of saving history. According to Augustine, the theophanies of the Hebrew Scriptures could have been appearances of any trinitarian person, or of the Trinity as such; only exegesis decides for each instance, and no theological difference is made by the result (*On the Trinity*, ii; iii,3). Finally, with Lombard it becomes standard for all scholasticism that "just as the Son was made man, so the Father or the Holy Spirit *could* have been and can be now" (*Sentences*, iii,i,3). With this last proposition, the bankruptcy of trinitarian meaning is complete. "The Son" or "the Logos" were originally titles for Jesus in respect of his role in God's saving reality; now they name a pure metaphysical entity, not necessarily related to Jesus at all and—equally with the other divine persons—available for whatever divine duty comes along.

The original meaning of "Father," "Son," "begets," "gift," and so on, as words for the reality of saving history in God, having evaporated, Western theology was compelled to find other ways of sustaining the trinitarian terminology's meaningfulness—unless, of course, the whole doctrine was to be abandoned, which was not thinkable before the sixteenth century. Since the relation between the creature and God is now back to the old Hellenic stand-off between temporality and its abstract negation, also the Hellenic way of giving meaning to talk of timeless deity was inevitably adopted: "Persons" and "relations" are taken to be reality in God describable by *analogy* from temporal reality.[29] The whole pattern of Western theology is already set in the sequence of Augustine's *On the Trinity*. The first seven books analyze inherited trinitarian formulas by the axiom of divine simplicity and end with their reduction to vacuity. This result demands the search for created analogues of triunity that occupies the remaining books.[30] And the chosen created reality is the human soul, where from Socrates on the "image" of timeless deity had been chiefly sought.[31] In that God is triune, and in that temporal being is ontologically dependent on inner analogy to timeless being, and in that for the intrinsically self-conscious soul the grasp of this analogy is its own active reality, we can meaningfully say "Father, Son, and Spirit" about God[32]—according to Augustine and his followers. Therewith the whole relation of God to his work in time reverted to the pre-Nicene conception of the temporal imaging of timeless reality. Arius was the winner after all.

All temporal being, according to Augustine and his Platonist teachers, is dependent on God in respect of its being, of its intelligibility, and of its activity. The triune image of God in the soul is the realization of these dependences in the mode appropriate to consciousness:[33] "We *are*, we *know* that we are, and we *love* this being and this knowing" (*City of God*, xi,26,7–9). And since this self-consciousness is necessarily also God-consciousness (e.g., *On the Trinity*, viii,3–6), the triple structure of consciousness is an image of divine triplicity: "This . . . trinity of the mind is not the image of God only because the mind remembers itself and knows itself and loves itself, but because it can also remember and know and love the one by whom it is created" (ibid., xiv,12).

All Augustine's trinitarian analogies, the stock-in-trade of subsequent Western reflection, are but variant descriptions of this structure of simultaneous self- and God-consciousness. The triple dependence is most directly reflected in this formula: being/knowledge/love.[34] Since in the soul's dependence its being is love, this formula can turn into: the soul as lover/the soul as object of its own love, that is, as known to itself/the soul as love (ibid., viii,ix,1–3). The love trinity in its turn, translated into a description of the soul as a substance, becomes: mind/knowledge/love (ibid., ix,3–4). And translating yet again, to a more functional analysis, we get memory/knowledge/will (ibid., x), for the mind as consciousness is identical with itself as being in that it is memory, and love is the action of will.

Our discussion of Western trinitarianism must alternate between lamentation and admiration of the virtues of its defects. We must now note the first such virtue. In turning to the soul for a meaning-giving analogue of divine triunity, Augustine necessarily exposed his introspection to some pressure from inherited trinitarian language. Thus he discovered the dialectical complexity of the soul's own reality. That the soul is complex, all antiquity knew. But that the complexity is living and dialectical, that in it each factor is what it is only by and for the other factors, Augustine was first to note. "The soul would not seek to know itself . . . , if it did not in some fashion love itself, with a love which again depends on the knowledge given in memory."[35] In effect, Augustine, looking for analogues of triune deity, discovered the ontological difference of conscious from unconscious being, the great theme of all subsequent Western philosophy.[36] And then Augustine does, however grudgingly, reflect all this back again on God: "Or are we indeed to suppose that the consciousness that God is, knows other things and does not know itself . . . ? Behold therefore the Trinity: consciousness, and knowledge of self, and love of self" (ibid., xv,10). Several steps removed from authentic trinitarian insight though this interpretation of God is, it is a great intellectual achievement in itself, and one made under the pressure of Scripture. That God is personal is a deeply Christian notion and an abiding contribution of Western theology.

The second virtue of Western trinitarianism is that precisely the ultimately hopeless task of thinking the plurality of persons within the notion of a temporally undifferentiable God, and within so abstract a notion of God's unity as represented by the simplicity axiom, compelled Western theology to work out the abstract dialectics of tri-identicality to perfection.[37] Lombard, following Augustine, laid down the dialectical boundary conditions: "The Father is not greater than the Son nor the Father or the Son than the Holy Spirit;

nor are two persons together any greater something than one, nor three than two; nor is the divine essence greater in three persons than in two, nor in two than in one." In consequence, "the Father is in the Son and the Son in the Father and the Spirit in both, and each is in each and all" (*Sentences*, i, vix,4–5). The rule acquired conciliar status: "The three persons are one . . . substance, one essence, one nature, one divinity, one immensity, one eternity; all divine reality is one where an opposition of relation does not prevent it."[38]

Distinctions in God are posited by inner divine "processions," of which there are two: the "begetting" of the Son and the "breathing" of the Spirit.[39] A "procession" is a "movement to an other"; the other of generation and spiration in God is God himself; therefore the divine simplicity is supposed not to be violated.[40] Therefore also, since every procession establishes relations, there are relations in God. Moreover, these are "real" relations, that is, not merely external as between two coins possessed by one owner, each of which is the same as if not so related. For since *both* terms of each such relation are God, the relation cannot be external to its terms.[41]

This immediately gives a list of four relations: The Father "begets," the Son "is begotten," the Father and the Son "breathe," and the Spirit "is breathed."[42] And then we have five "notions" applicable to the inner-divine distinctions, the four relations plus "unbegotten" or "unoriginated" of the Father, marking his position as the starting point of all the processions, who himself does not proceed.[43] If now we seek identifying properties for each of the persons, "unoriginated" drops out, since it applies also to the Trinity as such, and so does "breathes," since it applies both to the Father and the Son. Thus, by the sheer geometry of the relational structure, we arrive at exactly three "properties" or "personal notions": "begets," "is begotten," "is breathed."[44] It surely must be said that the mere aesthetic rightness of this analysis somehow commends it. Figure 1 shows a flow chart of deity.

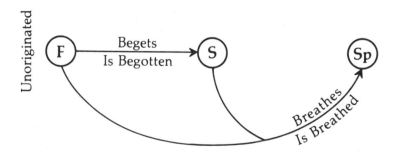

FIGURE 1

Then come the great metaphysical assertions. First, the relations, and so the personal properties, are each identical with the one divine substance, "with respect to the entity," that is, as we would say, "objectively," for "paternity" and "breathing forth" are in themselves divine attributes, and by the simplicity axiom each divine attribute is "with respect to the entity" the divine substance. The relations-properties differ from the divine substance only "with respect to the way we know them," except that "only" is misleading, since this necessity of our knowing is itself founded somehow in the divine reality. The relations and the essence are really the same, but the distinction we cannot help making is necessitated by that one reality.[45]

But if the relations are not merely real in God, but real insofar as and only insofar as they are identical with the divine substance, then they are real in God in the same way the divine substance is real. Thus they "subsist," that is, they are possessors of attributes (here the divine attributes) and doers of deeds (here the divine deeds). That is, again, they are proper "persons" in the regular Latin sense of the word.[46] And now, conversely, we can say what the "persons" truly are: " 'Divine person' . . . means a relation as a subsistent."[47]

Within the metaphysical tradition, the notion of a subsistent relation is of course sheer nonsense. The scholastics labored mightily to mitigate the offense of their definition to what they accepted as natural truth. But so radical a doctrine of the reality of relations cannot be contained by Plato or Aristotle. That some relations, such as paternity, are founded in the related terms, inherited wisdom can accept. But this doctrine identifies the substantiality of the related terms with the internality of the relations between them. Even the classification of the personal properties to which the scholastics are driven—that they are *both* "relative" and yet "eternal and immutable"[48]—is a defiance of all Hellenic common sense.

This assertion of the substantiality of relations, that is, of their ontological independence and possible priority over against the related terms, is the main place at which the metaphysically revolutionary power of the gospel breaks out in Western theology. In the lead of the Greeks, our inherited ways of thinking suppose that there must first be *things* that in the second place may be variously related. But there is nothing intrinsically obvious about it; in fact, by biblical insight, it is the other way around. The general consequences of this reversal of interpretation have long appeared in Western philosophy, most explicitly in some aspects of German idealism, as Hegel's definition of spirit as the relation between self and not-self, which just so is the being of the self.[49] The task of drawing out the more specifically theological consequences has lagged, as it must until the Augustinian doctrine of divine simplicity is discarded. That, indeed, is one purpose of this study, to which we have made various approaches and to which we will return.

THE ATHANASIAN CREED

The extent to which Augustinian trinitarian teaching can be taken as official doctrine of the Western church depends on the extent to which the so-called Athanasian Creed[50] establishes such doctrine. The long first section of this composition is a rhetorically splendid and theologically astute brief statement of Western trinitarian language-rules. The basic principle is that we "are neither to confuse the persons nor divide the substance."

The unity of substance will be preserved if we are careful to attribute all divine attributes equally to each person, but never so as to posit three logical subjects: "Uncreated is the Father, uncreated the Son, uncreated the Holy Spirit . . . ; and yet there are . . . not three Uncreateds . . . but one Uncreated. . . ." Etc. This is hammered home in rolling repetitive periods, choosing just those attributes of God that were decisive over against the Arians: "uncreated," "immense," "eternal," "omnipotent," "infinite." In the straight line from Athanasius, the posit of three kinds of deity is rejected as polytheistic: "For just as we are compelled by Christian truth to confess that each person singly is God and Lord, so we are forbidden by the catholic religion to say that there are three gods or lords."

The distinction of persons is to be achieved by the language of relations, though this technical term does not appear. "The Father is from no one, not made nor created nor begotten. The Son is from the Father only, not made nor created but begotten. The Holy Spirit is from the Father and the Son, not made nor created nor begotten but proceeding." It should be registered that the most unfortunate features of Western analysis do not explicitly appear.

The Athanasian Creed seems to have originated around the turn of the fifth and sixth centuries in Spain or southern France. It became the text for trinitarian instruction in the Carolingian theological institutions, and enjoyed great prestige through the Middle Ages. From the eighth century on, it was sung as a canticle, usually at the first Sunday office. Most Reformation compendiums of official doctrine included it. It does indeed state the unproblematic part of the Western church's trinitarian inheritance.

Yet the text of the Athanasian Creed was never adopted by an ecumenical gathering in the style of Chalcedon. In the modern period, many committed to its doctrine have nevertheless had great difficulty in affirming it, especially in using it liturgically. The problem has been, generally, the creed's identification of "the catholic faith" with a particular theological analysis, and specifically the opening anathema: "which if anyone does not preserve integral and inviolate, he will without doubt perish eternally." That one should be damned for bad, or even merely out-of-date, theology has seemed a bit hard.

Perhaps the difficulty will at least appear in a different light if indeed, as now seems proven,[51] the text was written and initially used neither as a liturgical or personal confession but as a memory piece for seminary instruction. It is one thing for future preachers to understand that salvation hangs on their preaching and that they are to preach thus and so. It is quite another thing for a congregation publicly to proclaim curses on the theologically maladroit or anachronistic. At any rate, the retreat of the Athanasian Creed back into the classroom may be regarded as a return to the proper locus of its authority. There, however, it surely deserves the highest respect.

VICISSITUDES OF
WESTERN TRINITARIANISM

The danger of the West's abstract trinitarian analysis is not only that it is false, but also that it is likely to reflect negatively on the fundamental liturgical and proclamatory levels of trinitarian discourse. It seems plain that this has in fact happened, though tracing the history is beyond the scope of this work. One need only think of such phenomena as popular Catholicism's replacement of the triune structure for prayer with one or another piety of the "Jesus-Mary-Joseph" type, or of denominational Lutheranism's centuries-long affection for forms of prayer and praise with only second-article remembrance-content and no invocation of the Spirit, or of Calvinism's concentration of fear and hope on a pretemporal deity resembling nothing so much as Eunomius' "Unoriginate."

From Augustine on, the doctrine of the Trinity tended to become increasingly a "revealed mystery," taught in the proper place of theological systematics because it was supposed to have been supernaturally revealed that God was in fact triune, but having less and less interpretive force for the actual concerns of believers. As such, it was a setup for destructive critique. The critique has come from both the church and the world.

The doctrine has not easily been seen as functional within religious life. Thus one sort of critique, from within the heart of the church, has been benign neglect. The first Reformation system of theology, Melanchthon's *Loci Communes* of 1521, omitted the developed doctrine altogether, on the grounds that "to know God is to know his benefits," thus clearly supposing that trinitarian discourse is not about God's benefits. Pietists in all branches of the church have regularly taken the same attitude,[52] as did John Locke[53] and other forerunners of the Enlightenment. Another sort of churchly critique has been more explicit. Western Christians have in effect found themselves, so far as experience is concerned, in a pre-Nicene situation. Many, liberated by historical or philosophical critique from affirming inherited doctrine just because it is inherited, have recapitulated pre-Nicene theological history, reinventing apologetic subordinationism and Arianism. It is this phenomenon which appears in such "unitarian" movements as have been explicitly Christian: Servetus, the Socinians,[54] or the English and American Unitarians.[55] It appears again in the "neologians," who in Germany mediated the first impact of the Enlightenment.[56] Since we have been over all that ground once, we need not here investigate any of these theologies, only note their existence and influence.

Such critique has not abated in our century. Currently influential are the arguments of Cyril C. Richardson that inherited trinitarianism is the result of the use of inappropriate biblical and Hellenic language to state necessary theological insight into God's transcendence and immanence,[57] of G. W. H. Lampe, that we need more "personal" language and that the metaphysical problems generated by traditional language are insoluble,[58] and of C. F. D. Moule, that a "binity" would make sense but that there is no need to make a "person" of the Spirit.[59] In general, current objections are not very different from those of the eighteenth and nineteenth centuries and like them are based on the assumption that standard Western teaching is "the doctrine" of the Trinity.

The full Enlightenment, of course, rejected trinitarianism from quite another side.[60] The tradition itself posited two bodies of knowledge of God, "natural" and "supernatural," and stipulated the first as that accessible to "reason" and the second as obtained only by bowing to the authority of some agency of revelation. The Enlightenment was a declaration of reason's freedom over against authority; just so it countenanced only the "natural" part of theology. Thus the Enlightenment affirmed Aristotle's God in its purity, untouched even by such biblical contaminants as maintained by Augustine. Insofar as the Enlightenment was simply unchurchly, as in France, its unitarianism is outside our story. But insofar as it remained inside the church, as often in England or Germany or the United States, it mingled with such currents as described just before, to promote sundry modalisms and subordinationisms, as well as gentlemanly silent compacts to let sleeping "dogmatic" dogs lie. Under all these sorts of critique, the inherited doctrine of the Trinity was by the opening of the nineteenth century nearly defunct in all those parts of the church open to modernity.

The history of nineteenth-century spirituality and theology, at least in such parts of the church, was a series of attempts to overcome the Enlightenment with respect to its evacuation of religious substance, without returning to reliance on supernatural authority. Two great figures dominate the effort: Friedrich Schleiermacher and G. W. F. Hegel. Both are in fact important for current trinitarian thought. Schleiermacher typifies and largely inaugurated the dominant pattern of the nineteenth and twentieth centuries, which continues to get along without much trinitarianism. Hegel deliberately "renewed" the doctrine as a speculative insight, providing the pattern of other such attempts thereafter and much of the impetus and conceptual style for the more churchly twentieth-century renewal by Karl Barth.

Schleiermacher put his exceedingly brief section on the Trinity at the end of his systematics, as a sort of summary. There it cannot function to identify or interpret the God spoken of in the body of the work. Rather, having expounded what is effectively the contents of a three-article creed, Schleiermacher then takes such a creed's "Father . . . , Son . . . , Spirit" as a concluding memory device suggested by tradition. At the level of the immediate expression and critique of piety—which according to Schleiermacher is the only legitimate level for dogmatics—the doctrine's necessary function, he says, is to insist "that nothing less than the divine being was in Christ and inhabits the Christian church as its communal spirit, and that we do not take these expressions in any weakened sense . . . and intend to know nothing of . . . subordinate divinities" (*The Christian Faith*, 170,1).[61] To that we must say, so far so good.

As a doctrine about the "divine being" itself, however, the doctrine of the Trinity is, according to Schleiermacher, a bungle. Such doctrine first results from "eternalizing the distinction between the being of God for itself and the being of God for the unification [with Jesus and the church]" (ibid., 170,3). But just that move is disastrous. Schleiermacher's difficulty, it is vital to note, is precisely Augustine's: uncritical acceptance of the Greek dogma that divinity equals timelessness (ibid., 171,52) and can therefore be spoken of only in analogies. "The divine causality [Schleiermacher's interpretation of God's reality] . . . must be conceived as utterly timeless. This is achieved through expressions which name temporal reality, and is therefore achieved by pictures; . . . one equates the temporal opposites before-and-after, earlier-and-later, and so suspends them" (ibid., 171,1).

But where Augustine struggled to maintain some sense for the inherited trinitarian propositions, Schleiermacher just drops them. He is free to do this because of the new historical situation, but also because, according to him, specifically Christian apprehension does not reach to the basic understanding of God at all; this is borrowed (his word) from universally valid philosophical analysis (*Brief Description of Theological Study*, 43–53). In fact, despite what is usually said of him, Schleiermacher maintains a particularly simpleminded form of the disastrous old distinction of natural from revealed theology.

If, for reasons of purely intellectual harmonization, we still want a doctrine of triunity, Schleiermacher has two recommendations. First, the doctrine should be "Sabellian," a description of successive temporal manifestations of a divine reality itself unaffected thereby. Second, we should take "the Father" as a name for this divine reality, and "the Son" and "the Spirit" as names for the manifestations (*The Christian Faith*, 172,3). Thus Schleiermacher's recommendation is exactly and compendiously Arian after all.

We need not decide whether Schleiermacher's version of the Trinity has greatly influenced nineteenth- and twentieth-century ordinary Christianity, or only marvelously exemplifies it. It is enough to note that most Protestant readers will recognize in the last paragraphs a description of what they gleaned from the catechetics and preaching of the main-line denominations.

Hegel deliberately set out to reinvigorate the inherited doctrine of the Trinity, by releasing its metaphysically revolutionary implications.[62] He made the Augustinian-Western version of the doctrine the center of his philosophy, the West's last universal and perhaps last great system of thought. Augustine, we have insisted, failed to describe a genuinely tri-identical God. But in the attempt he did perceive new truth; he perceived an in the modern sense *personal* God, whose being is constituted in the inner dialectics of consciousness, in the play of—now we will use the language of Hegel's time—immediate self-consciousness ("memory"), objective knowledge of self, and will that unites them. Hegel abandoned Augustine's hesitations, made this interpretation a universal concept of personal being, and then made all reality personal.

It was Hegel's goal to make a true synthesis of the two clashing streams of western thought: the Greek will rationally to grasp reality's sense, and the Bible's grasp of reality as history, with all its contingencies and contradictions. This can be done, said Hegel, if we see that history makes its own kind of sense, which is the sense not of the merely beholding and sense-describing mind, but of the living and sense-creating spirit. The spirited rationality of poets and great statesmen—and of authentic philosophers like Plato—does not abstract from contingency and contradictions, only so to achieve itself; it posits them, to overcome and encompass them and so achieve an expanding, *living* meaning. Napoleon does not abhor enemies; he seeks them, to create a larger European order in the struggle. Goethe does not banish irrationality and conflict from his plots; he invents them, to achieve the meaning of drama rather than of mere chronicle. Abstractly stated: The rational subject posits the object, that which is not itself, not sheer transparent meaning. Then the rational subject achieves itself as the *process*, the *act*, of rediscovering itself in the object, that is, of finding meaning in what is not merely as such meaningful. This reconciliation of reason-as-subject with object-made-reasonable, is living reason, spirit.

Since reality is historical, it is the sort of sense just described that reality has: the eternal creating and overcoming of contradiction in higher harmony. Since reality has this sort of sense, true reason is the mind that fulfills itself as just described, that works out its own reason precisely in contingent and contradiction-laden objective reality. The great metaphysical claim follows of itself: Reality-as-history makes sense only as the object of a Subject that finds itself therein, and so is itself Spirit. God is the Mind that has the world for object; he is the world insofar as Mind indeed finds sense, and so Itself, in the world; and he is the free Spirit that occurs as this event. God is the absolute Poet-Statesman-Philosopher. God is just what Augustine said: Mind and Knowledge and Love that joins them.

Hegel believed Western thought fulfilled itself with him; at least so far as its trinitarianism is concerned, he was right. Augustine's insight can be taken no further. Neither can Augustine's failure: this trinitarianism's distance from the saving history that necessitated it in the first place. In Hegel, Augustine's trinitarianism fulfills its constant tendency by finally explicitly taking the world as God's object, rather than Jesus the Son. From Hegel on, there has been a continuous tradition in which the trinitarian dialectics are exploited for their speculative possibilities, without much direction of the speculation by the dialectics' original object. The most notable recent exponents of this tradition are John Macquarrie and Paul Tillich.[63] From the point of view of this work, such efforts merely perfect ancient error.

In our century, the decisive step in repairing the great flaw of Augustinian-Hegelian trinitarianism has been taken. Karl Barth has reachieved an authentic doctrine of triunity, by what amounts to a christological inversion of Hegel's.[64] Only make *Jesus* God's object in which he finds himself, instead of Hegel's "world" or Augustine's merely metaphysical "Logos," and you have the doctrine of Barth's *Church Dogmatics*, Volume 1 I/1—which observation takes nothing from the extraordinary ingenuity of Barth's move.[65]

Barth perceives the difference between the Hellenic quest for God (he says "natural theology") and the gospel's proclamation that Jesus is God's quest for us (he says "revelation") more rigorously than any but Luther before him and uses this insight as the sole motor of trinitarian discourse. The entire doctrine of the Trinity, he says, is but the specification of which God it is that can so reveal himself as God is in fact revealed in Christ.[66]

The biblical claim of revelation, Barth says, poses three questions: Who is revealed? What does he do to reveal himself? What does revelation accomplish? The answer to each must be God, without qualification.[67] "*God* reveals himself. He reveals himself *through himself.* He reveals *himself.*"[68] And apart from each of these three sentences, the other two remain ambiguous.[69]

The key point is why the answer to all three questions must be simply God. Summarizing drastically, we may state Barth's answer: All three questions must be answered just "God," in order to negate our religious quest conceptually as revelation in Jesus' death and resurrection in fact negates it.[70] If the revelation, Jesus, or the achievement of revelation, the divine presence among us, were not simply God himself, we would by them merely be launched on a religious quest for God himself. But what the cross and resurrection reveal is exactly that such a quest, denying the sufficiency of the word of the gospel, is unbelief. Yet the God who so reveals himself does not thereby become merely identical with historical revelation and accomplished presence; that God is never thus grasped by us is, again, what the cross reveals. Also the one revealed is God utterly. Finally, having thus prevented subordinationism, Barth excludes modalism by the very same considerations. The necessity of giving the same answer to all three of revelation's questions does not amalgamate the questions themselves into one, for then again the real God would remain behind revelation and we would be back on our quest.

Since it is Barth who taught twentieth-century theology—or the living parts of it—the importance and point of trinitarian discourse, his influence has been pervasive through this entire study. That must here be explicitly acknowledged. But his contribution to required new trinitarian analysis is not so great as might be expected. Nor does he carry us to full liberation from a past-determined interpretation of God.

Trinitarian analysis is by no means complete, nor will it be until the struggle between the gospel's and Hellenism's identifications of God is over. It is time to state such of our own proposals as are not yet explicit.

The first step is to free trinitarian doctrine from captivity to antecedent interpretation of deity as timelessness.[71] In part that is already done in this work—as in Barth and some other post-Hegelian treatments—by the mere sequence of topics and by the christological concentration we, again like Barth, have insisted on at every step. In part it must be accomplished in the next chapter, where we will attempt an evangelical concept of deity, the basis of which is already laid throughout the previous chapters.

Within the trinitarian dialectics themselves it is the relation of the "immanent" and "economic" Trinities that must in this connection be reconsidered. The most important contemporary Catholic trinitarian theorist and the most important Protestant, Karl Rahner and Eberhard Jüngel, agree on a rule for the contemporary task: "The 'economic' Trinity *is* the 'immanent' Trinity, and vice versa."[72]

The legitimate theological reason for the "immanent"/"economic" distinction is the freedom of God. It must be that God "in himself" could have been the same God he is, and so triune, had there been no creature, or no saving of fallen creation, and so also not the trinitarian history there has in fact been. Here is a second rule (which is perhaps too little observed by both Rahner and Jüngel). Reconciling it with the other just stated has always been the problem. The two rules are compatible, we propose, only if the identity of the "economic" and "immanent" Trinity is eschatological.

Within theology's captivity to the timelessness axiom, the eternity of Jesus could be conceived only as a reality that always was in God. Thus was posited the "Logos *asarkos*," the "not [yet] incarnate Word," Jesus' metaphysical double, who always was in God and then *became* the one sent in flesh to us. The Logos' relation to the Father was described as a Father-Son relation, and rightly, since it is Jesus' relation to his Father that is to be interpreted. But the begetting and being-begotten of *this* Father and Son had to be timeless; thus this "procession" could not in fact be the same as the temporal relation of Jesus to his Father, that is, as the "mission." The Greek fathers mostly ignored the difficulty, thus permitting authentic trinitarian discourse in which the processions and missions occur together. But when more rigid thinkers came along, the difficulty proved fatal. This whole pattern must be exactly reversed.

Instead of interpreting Christ's deity as a separate entity that always *was*— and proceeding analogously with the Spirit—we should interpret it as a final outcome, and just so as eternal, just so as the bracket around all beginnings and endings. Jesus' historical life was a sending by the Father, the filial relation between this man and the transcendence to whom he turned temporally occurred; and this man is risen from the dead, so that his mission must triumph, so that his filial relation to his Father is unimpeachable. Thus Jesus' obedience to the Father, and their love for us which therein occurs, will prove an unsurpassable event, that is, are a God-event, a "procession" in God. Jesus' Aramaic or Hebrew prayer, and his prophetic apprehension of God's Word, will be the Father's final self-expression, by which he establishes his identity for us and for himself. And the Spirit that is the breath of this future will blow all things before himself into new life. The saving events, whose plot is stated by the doctrine of trinitarian relations, are, in their eschatological finality, God's transcendence of time, God's eternity. Thus we need posit no timelessly antecedent extra entities—Logos *asarkos* or not-yet-given Spirit— to assert the unmitigated eternity of Son and Spirit.

Within trinitarian thought's captivity to an alien definition of deity, we have been unable to say simply that Jesus *is* "the eternal Son," that what happens between the human Jesus and his father and the believing community *is* eternity. Instead, we have had to say that Jesus is the dwelling and manifestation of his own preexistent double—and with that, all the impossibilities we have trudged through are there. It is the need for the "pre-" that causes them; that is, it is the interpretation of eternity as persistence of the first past that causes them. If instead we follow Scripture in understanding eternity as faithfulness to the last future, *these* problems merely disappear.

Truly, the Trinity is simply the Father and the man Jesus and their Spirit as the Spirit of the believing community. This "economic" Trinity is *eschatologically* God "himself," an "immanent" Trinity. And that assertion is no problem, for God *is* himself only eschatologically, since he is Spirit.

As for God's freedom, only our proposal fully asserts it. The immanent Trinity of previous Western interpretation had but the spurious freedom of unaffectedness. Genuine freedom is the reality of possibility, is openness to the future. Genuine freedom is Spirit. And it is only in that we interpret God's eternity as the certainty of his triumph that we are able without qualification to say that God is Spirit. If we so understand God's freedom, we are indeed unable to describe *how* God could have been the selfsame triune God other than as the Trinity now in fact given. But neither have we any call to, so long as God's utter freedom, as Spirit, is acknowledged. In that acknowledgment we are equally commanded to say *that* God could be otherwise God and forbidden to say *how*.

Therewith we are at the next required amendment of inherited teaching. On a traditional diagram of trinitarian relations, the procession of divine being is all one way, from the Father. Son and Spirit derive their deity from the Father, but Father and Son do not derive deity from the Spirit; in Augustine's formula, "The Father is the principle and source of the whole of deity" (*On the Trinity*, iv,29). The places for relations whose arrows would point *to* the Father are vacant.

Pre-Nicene subordinationism had two closely related roots. One was the need for mediation of time and eternity. The other was the apprehension of God as fundamentally located at the beginning rather than the end, so that the trinitarian relations, even when rightly set parallel to time, had as active relations to point only *with* time's arrow. It corresponded to this apprehension that to command, beget, give, and so on, were felt as more appropriate to deity than to be given, obey, and so on.[73] Of these roots of subordinationism, only the first was pulled up by the Cappadocians. Thus it became a fixed axiom that the Father's begetting marked a sole primacy in deity,[74] that the transcendence to whom Jesus looked back was actively deity, while the Spirit he gave to the future was only passively so.

The asymmetry of the trinitarian relations is the more remarkable in that the Bible clearly presses candidates for the missing parts of the diagram. We propose to fill them in. Which biblical language we choose for the future-to-past active relations is at present of secondary importance. Using "witnesses" for the Spirit and "frees" for the Spirit with the Son, we may say the following. The Spirit's witness to the Son is equally God-constituting with the traditional relations. And so is the Son's and the Spirit's joint reality as the openness into which the Father is freed from mere persistence in his pretemporal transcendence. Moreover, since the only biblical approach to a definition of deity is "God is Spirit," the Spirit must at least be recognized as differently but equally "principle and source" with the Father; let us mark this with a "notion," and let that be "unsurpassed." Thus we obtain a new diagram, shown in Figure 2.

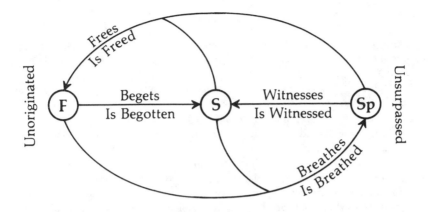

FIGURE 2

The tradition could say how sending and obedience, giving and being given, are realities not merely between God and us, but in God—and so final goods. But it could not say how freeing and being freed, witnessing and being witnessed to, are equally realities in God. Thus the tradition could show that—to use Reformation language—God's *law* is his own true self-expression. But it could not show that the *gospel* is similarly anchored in his being. We do not suggest that the church so persistently slides into legalism because of gaps in a diagram; we do suggest that it does so because of a conception of God accurately represented by the traditional diagram, by which God is indeed God of the law but not of the gospel, defined in his deity as the Father but not as the Spirit. We wish to amend the conception.

This is perhaps also the place where the traditional doctrine of God does indeed reflect male dominance. Whether or not dominance is biologically a male characteristic, it has been culturally. The traditional trinitarian relations, unsupplemented by those we propose, display command as constitutive of deity but not obedience, assertion but not reception. Indeed, the very definition of deity as assertion against time and its chances, which lies behind the asymmetry of relations and against which we have been arguing, bears the same value preference. It has been convincingly argued that these characteristics of traditional trinitarianism are the last outpost of the ancient world's dominance of male solar and sky gods over female earth and lunar gods.[75] Teaching a symmetry of trinitarian relations is not, of course, intended to balance female characteristics with male characteristics, and certainly not to posit obedience or receptivity as inherently female. The point is rather to eliminate altogether the influence of antiquity's sex-role doctrines.

NOTES

1. Origen, *Commentary of Romans*, in *EnchP*, 1965, 502:7, 13: "naturam Trinitatis et substantiam unam." Origen, *Commentary on John*, 2,10,75: "treis hypostaseis . . . tyganein."

2. *COD*, 1973, 28: There is one "deity and power and being (*ousia*) . . . in three perfect hypostases."

3. In Athanasius, e.g., *Discourse III against the Arians*, 65.

4. See, e.g., the "Creed of Lucian," in *Creeds of Christendom*, ed. P. Schaff (New York: Harper, 1889), 2:27.

5. The Greeks occasionally used *prosopon* instead of or with *hypostasis*. *Prosopon* and *persona* should be close translations of each other. But *prosopon* was never of any trinitarian conceptual importance in the East. And the Latins did not adopt *persona* as its translation, but for its own sake. See René Braun, *Deus Christianorum*: *Recherches sur le vocabulaire doctrinal de Tertullian* (Paris: Presses Universitaires, 1962), pp. 240–47.

6. On *ousia*: Joseph Ownes, *The Doctrine of Being in the Aristotelian Metaphysics* (Toronto: Pontifical Institute, 1951); Werner Marx, *The Meaning of Aristotle's "Ontology"* (The Hague: Nijhoff, 1954). On *hypostasis*: *ThWNT*, s.v. "Hypostasis," by H. Koester.

7. Basil the Great, *Letters*, ccxiv,4: "As a common noun is related to a proper name, so is the *ousia* related to the *hypostasis.*"

8. Ibid.

9. E.g., Gregory of Nazianzus, *Oration XXXI*, in *The Five Theological Orations*, ed. A. J. Mason (1899), 9; Gregory of Nyssa, *Against Eunomius*, in his *Opera*, vols. 1–2, ed. W. Jaeger (Leiden: E. J. Brill, 1960), 1:278–80.

10. Posed by Gregory of Nyssa, *To Abablius: That There Are Not Three Gods*, in his *Opera*, vol. 2/1, ed. F. Mueller (Leiden: E. J. Brill, 1958), p. 117.

11. E.g., Gregory of Nazianzus, *Oration XXXI*, 15–16.

12. E.g., Basil the Great, *Against Eunomius*, ii,22; Gregory of Nazianzus, *Oration XXXIV*, 10.

13. According to Gregory of Nyssa, *To Ablabius*, 135, there are three ontological questions: "Whether [it] is," "What [it] is," "How [it] is." The distinction of the three hypostases is relative to the third question only.

14. E.g., Gregory of Nazianzus, *Oration XXIX*, 11: "If it is a great thing for the Father to have no source, it is no less great for the Son to have the Father as source."

15. Or alternatively, the incarnation and not the Logos as such is the mediation. So Gregory of Nyssa, *Refutation of Eunomius' Second Book*, in his *Opera*, 2:144.

16. E.g., Gregory of Nazianzus, *Oration XXXI*, 8.

17. This is Karl Barth's language.

18. This is now so thoroughly researched that there is no point in passage-listing here; Ekkehard Muehlenberg, *Die Unendlichkeit Gottes bei Gregor von Nyssa* (Göttingen: Vandenhoeck & Ruprecht, 1966). For earlier theological use of "infinite," see Werner Elert, *Der Ausgang der altkirchlichen Christologie* (Berlin: Lutherisches Verlagshaus, 1957), pp. 118–32.

19. This too is now thoroughly analyzed; Jean Daniélou, *L'Être et des Temps chez Grégoire de Nysse* (Leiden: E. J. Brill, 1970).

20. Augustine, *On the Trinity*, v,10.

21. So much at least is proven by Olivier du Roy, *L'intelligence de la Foi en la Trinité selon Saint Augustine* (Paris: Études Augustiniennes, 1966); his conclusions are summarized on pp. 413–14, 435–56.

22. Thus in Aquinas, *Summa Theologica*, i,2–26, the existence, simplicity, perfection, goodness, infinity, etc., of God are all discussed before there is any reference to his triunity. And note which of these comes first.

23. Augustine, *Commentary on John*, 38,10.

24. Aquinas, *Summa Theologica*, i,43,2. On Augustine himself, see Alfred Schindler, *Wort und Analogie in Augustin's Trinitätslehre* (Tübingen: J. C. B. Mohr [Paul Siebeck], 1965), pp. 160–62; Jean-Louis Maier, *Les Missions Divines selon Saint Augustin* (Freiburg: Presses Universitaires, 1960), pp. 7–98. Lombard, at the foundation of medieval discussion, develops the distinction at great length in *Sentences*, i,14–16.

25. Augustine, *On the Trinity*, iv,28.

26. Michael Schmaus, *Die psychologische Trinitätslehre des heiligen Augustinus* (Münster, 1927), pp. 125–26, lists the texts.

27. As, e.g., again in Athanasius, *Letter to Serapion*, iv, 3.

28. Augustine, *On the Trinity*, i,12–15; iv,30; i,7–10.

29. Schindler, *Wort*, lays all this out; there is a summary on p. 233.

30. Ibid., e.g., p. 180.

31. Augustine, *On the Trinity*, iv,1: "Let the reader strive to use those things which are made, to know him by whom they are made; so we will arrive at that image that man himself is, in that . . . which is called 'mind' or 'soul.'"

32. Du Roy, *L'intelligence*, esp. pp. 420–28, 447–50. In *On the Trinity*, it is the argument of book 8 that makes this pivot.

33. Ibid., pp. 447ff.; there abundant citations.

34. Pervasive in *City of God*.

35. Maier, *Missions*, p. 187.

36. If we line up Augustine's main soul-analogies in columns, so:

being	knowledge	will
lover	loved	love
mind	knowledge	love
memory	knowledge	will

The posited equivalence of the terms in the first column gives the proposition: the being of mind as subject is immediate self-consciousness. Therewith the whole of Western philosophy to come.

37. On the following technical history, *DThC*, s.v. "Trinité" and "Relations Divines," by A. Michel.

38. Council of Florence, "Decree for the Copts," *COD*, 1973, pp. 57–58.

39. Aquinas, *Summa Theologica*, i,27–28; Bonaventura, *Sentences*, xiii,1.

40. Aquinas, *Summa Theologica*, i,27,1.

41. E.g., ibid., i,28,1.

42. In all these formalities, I will follow Aquinas' version; here, ibid., i,28,4.

43. Ibid., i,32,3.
44. Ibid., i,40.
45. Ibid., i,28,2–4; Bonaventura, *Sentences,* xix/ii,1,2. This is the main medieval line; *DThC,* s.v. "Relations Divine," 2147ff. It was denied by a line of thinkers from Gilbert de la Porrée to Joachim of Flores; see ibid., 2145ff.; *DThC,* s.v. "Trinité," 1715–32.
46. E.g., Bonaventura, *Sentences,* xxiii,1,1; 1,2; xxv,1,1–2.
47. Aquinas, *Summa Theologica,* i,29,4.
48. Lombard, *Sentences,* i,xxvi,2–3.
49. E.g., Georg W. F. Hegel, *Phänomenologie des Geistes,* 1952, ed. in *PhB,* pp. 313ff.
50. The critical text is in J. N. D. Kelly, *The Athanasian Creed* (New York and London: Longmans, Green & Co., 1964), pp. 76ff., which see also on the following.
51. Ibid., pp. 53–69, 109–14.
52. Emanuel Hirsch, *Geschichte der neuern evangelischen Theologie* (Gütersloh: Bertelsmann, 1951), 2:114–20, 186–93.
53. John Locke, *The Reasonableness of Christianity as Delivered in the Scriptures,* 1695.
54. *RGG³,* s.v. "Servet," by H. Bornkamm; and "Sozinianer," by H. R. Guggisberg.
55. Ibid., s.v. "Unitarier," by M. Schmidt.
56. Hirsch, *Geschichte,* 4:1–119.
57. Cyril C. Richardson, *The Doctrine of the Trinity* (Nashville: Abingdon Press, 1958).
58. G. W. H. Lampe, *God as Spirit* (New York and London: Oxford University Press, 1977).
59. C. F. D. Moule, *The Holy Spirit* (Oxford: Mowbray, 1978), pp. 43–51.
60. The classical document of Enlightenment religion is Immanuel Kant's *Religion within the Limits of Reason Alone* (1783). On this, see Hirsch, *Geschichte,* 4:271–76, 320–29.
61. Quotations from Friedrich Schleiermacher's *The Christian Faith* are from the 7th edition (Berlin: Walter De Gruyter, 1960).
62. Hegel, *Phänomenologie* iv,A; vii,C; Georg W. F. Hegel, *Vorlesung über die Philosophie der Religion,* Intro.; pts. 1, 3; *Encyclopädie der philosophischen Wissenschaften,* 1840 ed., vol. 6; Hirsch, *Geschichte,* 5:231–68; Robert W. Jenson, *God after God* (Indianapolis: Bobbs-Merrill, 1969), pp. 33–35.
63. John Macquarrie, *Principles of Christian Theology* (New York: Charles Scribner's Sons, 1966), pp. 94–110, 174–93; Paul Tillich, *Systematic Theology,* 3 vols. (Chicago: University of Chicago Press, 1951–63), 3:283–94.
64. On Barth's trinitarianism, see Eberhard Jüngel, *The Doctrine of the Trinity* (Grand Rapids: Wm. B. Eerdmans, 1976); Colin Gunton, *Becoming and Being* (New York and London: Oxford University Press, 1978), pp. 117–85.
65. For fuller analysis, and on the following, see Jenson, *God after God,* pp. 95–156.
66. Karl Barth, *Church Dogmatics,* vol. 1/1, trans. G. T. Thomson (Edinburgh: T. & T. Clark, 1936), pp. 32, 329.
67. Ibid., pp. 311–52.
68. Ibid., p. 312.

69. Ibid., pp. 321-22.

70. On this and the following, see ibid., pp. 101-8; there also citations.

71. Eberhard Jüngel, "Das Verhältnis von 'ökonomischer' und 'immanenter' Trinität," *ZThK* 72 (1975): 363: "The concept of the divine essence can no longer be thought in abstraction from the event of God's triune existence." This demand, nearly universal in contemporary theology, is variously met, most ambitiously by Karl Barth and "process theology."

72. Karl Rahner, *The Trinity*, trans. J. Donceel (New York: Herder & Herder, 1970), pp. 21-22; Jüngel, "Verhältnis."

73. Bluntly stated, e.g., by Tertullian, *Against Praxeas*, ix,2-3.

74. E.g., Bonaventura, *Sentences*, vii,1,ii.

75. Franz K. Mayr, "Trinitätstheologie und theologische Anthropologie," *ZThK* 68 (1971): 427-77.

5

The Being of God

Specification of the kind of being God is must follow the trinitarian identification. When it does, we will specify God's being as event, person, spirit, and discourse.

THE METAPHYSICAL QUESTIONS

All the creeds begin "I believe in God, the. . . ." It is dogma that God *is*. There can be no such thing as a Christian atheist, except in very special senses of "atheist."[1] But in what sense "is" God? Is God as an idea is? Or as a tree is? Or how? The question needs only to be asked to become desperately puzzling. The question of the being of God is thus dogmatically imposed on the theological enterprise and has in fact been at all times vigorously investigated. With it, we land decisively on the far side of a border we have been crossing through the previous two chapters. We land in the middle of metaphysics.

Metaphysics asks two great questions. First, What sort of being has . . . ? Second, Whatever sorts of being there are, how are they all sorts of "being"? That is, What is being? These are not esoteric questions. We will instantly see that the first is not, if we insert "I" in the blank: What sort of being have I? The sort that vanishes with time? The sort that transcends time? Or some other? That there are several kinds of being is at a common-sense level obvious; there are things, events, ideas, numbers, consciousnesses, and who knows what else. It is against the threat of time that the plurality of being's kinds becomes portentous, as our expansion of the question in the first person assumed. Thus the Greeks' reflection about kinds of being was driven by the fear that all "things" may pass away. Ordinary things clearly are subject to time, they saw; ideas clearly are not; how about consciousnesses?[2] And if the first metaphysical question is lively, so—at one further remove—the second must be.

Theology has asked the first metaphysical question also about God: What kind of being has God? This is clearly a grammatically possible instance of the question, but it is a logically odd one, for the word "God," as we have seen, means "eternal reality." Therefore any actual religion which identifies its God and so specifies how God is eternal thereby answers the metaphysical

163

question in advance. Adherents of an actual religion have no direct need to ask what sort of being God has. For them, the questioning runs the other way around. And it is of course only the adherents of some religion who use the word "God," in such questions or otherwise. Thus, "What kind of being has God?" can be a lively question only *between* religions, as the effort of one religion to understand itself over against another.

In fact, it is in the long confrontation of biblical and Hellenic religion, to which we have already devoted so much attention, that Christianity has necessarily and rightly asked about the being of God. The special character of these two religions has made the confrontation uniquely creative metaphysically, but it has also given the confrontation a treacherous twist. Since Greece needed criteria by which to recognize "real" deity when its quest should reach it, its religious reflection involved an embryonic form of the metaphysical question about God: What are the marks of true timelessness? Because Christian Hellenists had to deal with the demand that Jesus' Father be displayable as *really* God, and so had to deal with the demand for criteria of true deity, it was all too easy for them to be led to pose the question of God's being in a way that begged the question to their own betrayal: What are the other metaphysical characteristics of God, besides timelessness?[3] It is in this very form that we have already encountered the question in Augustine. Insofar as the fathers thus entangled themselves, Christianity was set in the pattern we have been trying to overcome: that Christianity's interpretation of God, properly become metaphysical in discussion with Greece, assumes an initial definition of deity that aborts the discussion and merely recites Hellenic principles.

Method, therefore, is decisive. A doctrine of any putative God's being is a certain abstraction from the reflectively developed form of that God's identification: if, for example, "God is the one who raised Jesus," we have already referred to him as a person, by speaking of him as "the one who" followed by a transitive verb. Thus theology's habit of treating God's being first and his triunity thereafter is a disaster, for if the trinitarian identification of God is not made the basis of the doctrine of God's being, some other identification will too easily be unwittingly presupposed. The right question, which we will try to answer in the following, is: What sort of being must God have, since he is triune?

The second metaphysical question "What is being?" has no special theological form, since it is itself a theological question. Thus Aristotle himself sometimes defined his "first philosophy" as the investigation of deity[4] and sometimes as the investigation of *ousia*,[5] for if there is God—and the denial that there is, is also a theological position—then to be is either to be God or to be dependent on her/him/it to be whatever else. In a religious reflection, therefore, it is the "either . . . or" of the previous sentence that is the key to the question of being. The question will be answered by finding a determinant that can be switched to display the difference between God and other reality and then stating it indifferently to this switch. For example, the standard such move in scholastic Christian thought is: God is the explanation; creatures are that-which-needs-explanation; and therefore to be is to be intelligible—*ens est veritas.*

Our tradition has a standard answer to the first metaphysical-theological question: God has persistent being. And to the second: God is persistent, all else is temporary, and therefore to be is to have a past. We need not here again attack these answers. The entire story of the last two chapters told of Christianity's struggle with them; our rejection is already stated. It is the task of this chapter to display the faith's alternative. We will make four specifications of God's being: that God is event, person, spirit, and discourse.

Since the great confrontation began with the capture of biblical faith by its rival and interlocutor, faith's alternative has always appeared as breakthrough, as Christian thinkers' wrenching disaccord with what they too suppose is obviously true. The full story of the long breakthrough would be a complete history of theology; we will here proceed more systematically, referring at random to a few great figures of the tradition. In what ways our own contribution is also a wrench with deep assumptions of our thinking, we cannot say; others will have to do that.

We will not explicitly investigate the second metaphysical question. That would carry us too far beyond the limits of dogmatics. But an answer to that question will at once guide and emerge from our consideration of God's being. It will be well to state that answer here, that readers may know it as they read: God anticipates; creatures recoil; therefore to be is to have a future.

GOD AS AN EVENT

The entire exposition of God's triunity demands our first proposition: God is an event. The kind of reality God has is like that of a kiss or an automobile accident. The argument for this proposition is the previous three chapters.

In the dominating tradition, God's being has been specified by the notion of "substance," whether understood more according to Plato or more according to Aristotle: for example, John Gerhard, "God is a spiritual substance: utterly simple, infinite. . . ."[6] A substance[7] is *what is* something, maintaining itself in being by possessing some definite complex of attributes answering to "something"; or substance is the reality possessed by and as those attributes; and the word in use shimmers between the two and derives much of its metaphysical power from the ambiguity. A substance is, for example, what is "legged," "with a seat," and so on, so as to *be* a chair, and persists in being as long as it retains possession of "leggedness" and "seatingness."

Thus the metaphysics of substance realize a cluster of existentially-laden notions: of persistence, independence, and possession. To be substantial is to endure, by having reality as "attributes," that is, independently of other substances. It is plain that no immediately experienced reality quite fulfills this vision. All are subject to action by other realities, and thus from time to time gain and lose attributes: The two-legged animal, Jones, may in fact lose a leg. Thus all give hostages to time, and may endure long but not forever: The bipedal, vertebrate Jones may survive the loss of bipedality but not of vertebration. "God" is then posited as the one *true* substance,[8] all of whose attributes are securely possessed, so that times' chances are nothing to him. God has no "accidental" attributes which come and go, and so gives no hostage to time or other realities. God is the *perfect* substance. All the attributes we attribute to God—"simplicity," "infinity," "omnipotence," or whatever— merely explicate God's perfection.

That Christians cannot approve this metaphysics should have been apparent: "For whoever would save his life will lose it" (Matt. 16:25). We have seen how the greatest trinitarians were driven by the dialectics of the trinitarian identification of God to deny that there is any complex of attributes by possessing which God is, and so had to make the subject of "is God" be not a substance at all but an act, an event. We have also seen how thoroughly most theology subsequently relapsed from that insight.

Rejection of the dominant tradition just at this point is endemic in contemporary theology. We may illustrate almost at random. So the Roman Catholic radical Leslie Dewart: We must "de-hellenize" the faith by overcoming the ideals of immortality, stability, and impassibility.[9] But so also the conservative Lutheran Peter Brunner: "In view of God's . . . self-determination to us, we must . . . abandon all pictures of God that with the help of antiquity's mode of thought read into God a fixed, unmovable, and abstract perfection, so that . . . talk of new judgments, new reactions, new deeds, and new words in God . . . appears to be naive anthropomorphism." [10]

But while the demand is general, the fulfilling thereof is less frequent. One great project of twentieth-century theology was devoted to it, Karl Barth's *Church Dogmatics*:[11] "God's deity consists, into its farthest depths, therein—or at least *also* therein—that it is event." Moreover, God's being is not eventhood, or something of the sort, but a particular event, "that event of God's activity in which we are involved in his revelation," [12] the active relation of the triune persons.[13] Barth's doctrine of God's being as love and freedom is then the explication of this being-as-event.[14] To the extent that theology currently tends to ignore the main parts of Barth's work (and in English-speaking territories has never grasped them), it has cut itself off from the only fully-realized attempt thus far to fulfill modern theology's own constant demand.

One other ponderable and very influential contemporary theological project is often thought to specify God's being as event, but in fact does not. Just so, we must devote some attention to "process theology." We will here not denote by this phrase every theology that has learned from Alfred North Whitehead or Charles Hartshorne (that would be almost all English-language theology) but only those theologies that find in their thought "the right philosophy" and so maintain the key doctrines of their interpretation of God.[15] Thus our own analysis will be of Hartshorne himself.[16]

It is true that "process" metaphysics understands all reality as concretely consisting in events, and so also God as so consisting. What there most concretely is, is in no case a substance (e.g., "this man") but the momentary events of the man's life. The enduring human is a series of the events, established as a series by certain kinds of likeness and relation between the events. "This man" is the fact that a unity can be abstracted from some particular sequential events that is more than their mere aggregate.[17]

Thus no enduring entity is, in this metaphysics, an event, but rather an abstraction from some set of events. But whereas each human, or each galaxy or indeed each other enduring entity than God, is an abstraction from its own specifiable set of events—so that it makes sense to say that this human *is* such-and-such events—the events that God concretely is are simply all the events that are the history of the world.[18] Therefore, if our discourse remains at the concrete level, the word "God" has no import of its own; we cannot with it denote any identifiable reality. Concretely (i.e., as *event*) there is only the world. There is God as *God*, as more than the world, only in God's "*abstract* character," in that sort of his reality that is grasped by our abstractions from concrete reality, that is, there is God, not as event but only as an in itself timelessly given structure of relations between all events. Process metaphysics contribute greatly to our understanding of the general character of reality. But they do not expound the assertion "God is an event," since they do not in fact make the assertion. Process metaphysics ontologically demote the notion of substance. But once we do come to speak of the enduring entities to which the notion was traditionally applied—whether "Jones" or "God"—they also apply it, and then do not really modify it at all.

We wish to say that God is an event. We see two necessary explanations.

First, traditional metaphysics are insofar commonsensically right, that an event must happen *to* some enduring entity. What does not follow and what we have denied is that the enduring entity is therefore ontologically prior to the event. What God happens to is Jesus and the world. God is the event of the world's final transformation by Jesus' love. That "all manner of things will be well" and that it is now true that all manner of things will be well is the reality of God. Thus God is not an event in time, nor even an event extended through all time. God is rather the event by which the world has a future, to *be* a world of time. Were there no eschaton, were the world as a whole not thus open to a future, the world would not occur within that unstoppable oncoming of uncertainty which we call time. God is the temporalizing of the world.

But what if no such thing happened to the world, if it were not temporalized? Then *this* world would be no-thing at all. Instead of the world that actually is, there might be another world, of which the great mythic vision of circling time were true, in which all things always returned to their beginning. And for this world there might be its appropriate God, Brahman-Atman. But that is another matter altogether. As to whether the real God could have been God without any world, we can only answer as before: The analysis of God as free event, as spirit, equally compels us to say that he would have been and forbids us to say how.

Second, God, if real, must be a logical subject. It must be possible to make sentences with a verb and "God" as the subject. And if the God is the one we have been speaking of, it must be possible for the verb to be active, indeed transitive. With events in time, it is precisely the awkwardness of making an event a logical subject, especially of active verbs, that has led to the doctrine of the priority of substances to what happens to them. How can an *occurrence* be said, for example, to "speak by the prophets" or to "sustain the universe?"

A logical subject must be not only identifiable but also reidentifiable, as when one calls the service station and says, "This is the man who brought (note the tense) in the Horizon for tuning." For if I say, "John is angry," and you say, "Who is John?" I cannot merely respond with "the one who is angry." A logical subject must indeed be an enduring entity in some sense or other.[19] It is just this point that has traditionally disqualified events as logical subjects: an event happens, and then where is it?

It is, we suggest, in that God is the *triune* event, that God is not over after God happens. It is the tri-identicality of the divine action that makes it a logical subject. What happens to the world with Christ has plural identifiabilities bracketing time and just so reaching through time. Nor are these disconnected, leaving, as it were, gaps of time between them, for their plurality is the same as their relations with each other. Thus we may say that what happens with Christ has a self-repeating identifiability, which we may plausibly treat as the continuing identifiability of a logical subject, without this being the sort of reidentifiability the tradition has taken for the only sort: the persistence of some one set of identifying characteristics, the temporal extension of a "substance."

We will pick up one last suggestion from Gregory of Nyssa. The divine *ousia*, "deity," is, according to him, sheer temporal infinity.[24] For Gregory, the word no longer stands for something that is God; it denotes sheerly the infinity of the act that is God. It is this *ousia* that the three hypostases derive from and with each other, that is, the acts of the Father or the Son or the Spirit, within their joint act that is God, are indeed *within* that act, are *divine* acts, in that they are subject to no temporal limits. The distinction and relation of three identities are a structure of pure triumphant possibility-as-such. They are the structure of the temporally plural ways in which the action that is God overcomes all conditions. The Cappadocians' *"one ousia"* means that whether the conditions that might be imposed on what happens with Christ are the burdens of the past (imposed on the Father, were only he God) or the risks of the future (imposed on the Spirit, were only he God) or the statistics of the present (imposed on the Son, were only he God), they are no hindrance to the action that in fact is God, which just in this utter unhinderedness can be only *one* action.

GOD AS PERSON

The concept of personhood as a particular kind of being seems to be modern and, moreover, a result of Christian theology's influence on Western life and reflection.[20] But once the concept is there, it is obvious that all the Bible's talk about God in fact speaks of him as what we now call personal.[21] Indeed, most practiced religion treats deity as personal, since it addresses deity in hope of response. Yet the personhood of God is also regularly attacked religiously. Thus all actual Vedic religion assumes the personhood of deity, and nearly all sophisticated Vedic reflection denies it.[22] In the history of Christian theology, discomfort with the notion of God's personhood or, prior to the emergence of the notion, with those biblical descriptions of God which we now comprise therein, has greatly depended on the Hellenic interpretation of deity. In that this deity is the timeless ground of temporal reality and can therefore be simultaneously and successively manifested by many different persons, it is natural for Hellenic interpretation to conceive deity itself as impersonal.

There is a problem here that cannot be obviated merely by decrying Hellenic religion. As soon as the confrontation with Hellenism awakens metaphysical reflection in the church, whether in antiquity or now, it becomes clear that it will not do to call God "a person," without qualification. For "a" person is individualized by difference from other persons, and in the case of God who would they be? But if God is not "a person," can it be meaningful to call him "personal"? The problem is not esoteric. Every believer faces it, and it is safe to say that most merely take their choice and either think vaguely of God as rather like electricity or picture God entirely mythically as a mighty but invisible woman or man.

The tendency of our analysis is given in advance. In view of the clear language of the Bible we will maintain God's personhood until driven from it. We have already entered Christianity's deep stream of insight into God's personhood, as represented by Augustine and Hegel, and will not leave it willingly.

Johann Gottlieb Fichte may pose the problem. He imprinted the turn of the eighteenth and nineteenth centuries in Germany with the "atheism controversy" occasioned by his views.[23] A conscious being, said Fichte, with all the thought of his time, and rightly, establishes its individual being by *self-consciousness*. But it is not possible for there to be an object of consciousness that has no boundary distinguishing it from the rest of reality. Therefore the self of self-consciousness must be a bounded, finite self; and therefore, said Fichte, God cannot be a conscious being, since God is infinite and so cannot know himself as finite. And therefore again, God cannot be personal, since "unconscious personhood" is a contradiction.

There are two possible replies to Fichte's sort of worry. One is argument that God can be personal without being *a* person. The other is argument that there can be an infinite person, meeting Fichte head-on. We will pursue the latter.

The object as which God knows himself is Jesus. Thus God's self-consciousness is indeed consciousness of a bounded, particular individual, so that this requirement of personhood is fulfilled. But the decisive question is just *how* the reality of this individual is bounded. The reality of each created person is defined by the event sequence, the plot, of his life, as this sequence is made into a determinate whole, into indeed a plot, by his death. So with Jesus. He is defined by his particular life and particular death as "love," as a life for all other lives. He is the crucified one, whose life was lived in the promise he brought his fellows and who finally gave up his self wholly to that promise. That he is risen does not mean that this death is canceled so that this life is again undefined. It means that *this one*, this defined one, is future and present reality and not merely past, so that he can be the objective self of the living God. But if God's self-consciousness is consciousness of *this* present, bounded individual, God is conscious of his self as the person for all persons, as a particular defined love, and so is not shut in by this bounded self-consciousness, but freed.[24]

It all depends on what sort of infinity, what sort of freedom from limitation, we have in mind when we attribute infinity to God. If we think of simple absence of definition, an infinite being cannot indeed be self-conscious. But if we think of God's infinity as trinitarianism (e.g., Gregory of Nyssa) should teach us to think of it, as freedom to transcend each new definition while never lacking one, or as the Hebrew Scriptures should teach us to think of it, as unconquerable faithfulness, then that the bounded individual Jesus is God's object-self does not hinder God's infinity, it constitutes it.

The "a person" that God is, is the human person Jesus, the Son. The triune event that God is, is by its triunity a person, this one. We need not, therefore, think of the other identities, of the Father or the Spirit, as, with respect to their distinction from one another, individual personal beings in the modern sense. If the Father and the Son were singular persons, they would be metaphysical somethings in the very style of the "Logos *asarkos*" we have just eliminated, about whom we might well have Fichte's qualms. Instead, we will press the scholastic interpretation of the triune identities as "subsisting relations." We will say, All there is to being God the Father is being addressed as "Father" by the Son, Jesus; all there is to being God the Spirit is being the spirit of this exchange.

In that Jesus cries "Father if it be possible . . . ," and in that he will give up his rule at the last, and in that he is not disappointed in these relations, there is the Father. In that Jesus gives his spirit, and in that he will gather all to himself in that spirit, and in that this movement is final, there is the Spirit. This does not mean that the Father and the Spirit are created by Jesus. The relations necessarily posit some individual terms, but this does not mean they are secondary to them. And finally, in that all this is true, Jesus *is* the Son (not: *there is* the Son!). About the Father and the Spirit, Fichte and those who have argued as he did were right. The sort of being possessed by them, and so by the triune God each of them is, *relatively to* each of them, is not that of a something, personal or otherwise. But that is not the entire account. God is not an individual person. But there *is* an individual person who is God. And therefore the Augustinian-Hegelian dialectics of consciousness, which define the very notion of personhood in the modern sense, can indeed in their trinitarian application to God establish the personhood of God.

We now can deal with a difficulty that may bother readers: Can it make any sense to speak of an event as a person, even in the sense just described? We respond: *Only* an event can be a person.

The life of any of us is an event, but it is also made up of many events. To grasp my life as an event, I must therefore grasp the dramatic connection, the faithfulness, of each of its constituent events to all the others. But I, as a creature, do not have this faithfulness in myself. The days of my life do not cohere in anything visible in them but only in the promises of God. And I, as a fallen creature, do not hearken to Gods' promises. My days therefore threaten to fall apart, to become an incoherent sequence that could just as well have members other than those it does, to become "absurd." Yet so long as God does not punish my unbelief by indeed loosing my identity into the flux of events, I cannot avoid recognizing some events as *my* deeds and sufferings and others as not. Thus I am driven either to faith in God or to suppose a mysterious something other than my life and its intrinsic coherence, "whose" life my life is, "whose" deeds and sufferings the events of my life are. And so arises the myth of the "person" I am as something other than the event that I am.

In our fallenness, we may in fact be unable to deal with ourselves without the myth just described. But there is no reason to apply it to God. God is neither creature nor fallen. God is speaker and hearer of the Word by which he lives. And he believes his Word. With God, "person" and "event" are therefore only alternative insights into one reality.

Now we can also deal with the difficulty raised by the Bible's drastically personal language about God: that God changes his mind, reacts to earthly events, and the like.[25] Or rather, we can see that there is no difficulty.

Over against and in the time established and embraced by the occurrence of God, God is an enduring entity by virtue of his triunity. And this enduring entity's objective self, the criterion of its self-identity, is Jesus of Nazareth, in his openness to his fellows. Therefore, that over against time God listens and considers and truly responds is but faithfulness to himself. God's action and reaction over against us through time, in that it is faithful to his self that is Jesus and so is an indefatigable wooing and rescuing, does not compromise God's eternal self-identity, it constitutes it.

That God answers prayer, that God makes threats and "repents" of them when the evil is past, that God makes promises and fulfills them by new and unexpected promises—all this is not "anthropomorphic" or "symbolic" statement. It is the strictest descriptive propositional truth. It is when *we* are said to initiate something new, to be surprising and faithful at once, that language must be stretched a bit. God has no problem here at all. "From eternity the Father sees us in the Son . . . , as determined for fellowship with him. . . . In that God in the totality of his being and from eternity thus enters the covenant of relation he has willed, saving history as real history is possible also for God."[26]

It is in the determinations of God's being as event and person that the main problems arise. "God is spirit" and "God is discourse," to which we now turn, can therefore be more briefly discussed. Nevertheless, they are the religiously decisive determinants.

GOD AS SPIRIT

Western understanding of personhood as a kind of being has classically found two great essential movements of and within personal being: mind and will. Thus Thomas Aquinas, following Aristotle, lists five powers of "the soul," but gives only two theological significance: the "intellectual" and the "appetitive."[27] Schleiermacher based the necessity of religion on the necessity for unity in our life of "thinking" and "acting."[28] Or again, all Kant's thought can be read as an analysis of personhood; his great work was in three volumes, one on knowing, one on willing, and a third on how they work together.[29]

As the examples of Schleiermacher and Kant suggest, the great analytical problem about personhood has been how mind and will are joined. Is the person a mind steering appetites, as Socrates and all his followers have taught (e.g., Plato, *Phaedrus*)? Or is the person a will, using reasoning to think through how to get his way, as Arthur Schopenhauer taught most bluntly?[30] Or are they joined in some other way? We are here not concerned with this problem as a problem about human persons.[31] But in that we see God as person, we see also God as mind and will. Augustinian-Hegelian trinitarianism defines God as consciousness established in knowledge of self—the Son, and love of self—the Spirit. And so the problem is posed also about God.

The great scholastics argued the problem in a particularly sophisticated form. Since God is Creator, what God knows and what God wills are the same. And since God is good, what God wills is the good. So the question: Does God know what is good, and therefore will it; or is the good good because God wills it? Thomas Aquinas was the great proponent of the first option, Duns Scotus and the later nominalists of the second.[32]

The matter at issue is vital for faith, despite its esoteric appearance. We may think of an absolute event and person, and yet not think of *God*—or anyway of the God of the Bible. The God whose primary reality is unmovedly to know us and all things, as what we are, in order then perhaps to make plans for us accordingly, is simply not the one of whom the Bible speaks. The God of the Bible is a storm, blowing us like leaves from what we are to what we will be and only knowing us in this motion. The great Mind's Eye is doubtless a noble conception and may even subsist, but he is much too harmless to be God by an Ezekiel's lights. Yet neither is the Bible's God a sheerly arbitrary force. We must somehow learn to think God as *faithful* will.

One work, from all the history of theology, can be the reality test. Martin Luther's *On the Bondage of the Will*[33] is intemperate, prolix, and sometimes misguided; it is also the book after the Bible that is most inescapably about God. God is the one who "works life, death, and all in all" (*Bondage*, p. 685), who indeed cannot not work all in all (ibid., pp. 709, 712). We know this about God not because of philosophical speculation but because of the gospel. Only in confessing that God is responsible for all that happens are we so humbled before him as to need the gospel. And only in that God rules absolutely can he make unconditional promises, that is, can the gospel be true (ibid., pp. 614, 619, 632). But just so God is hidden, and exactly in his reality as God of the gospel, for the "all" that he works is at best morally ambiguous by the gospel's own lights: "This is . . . faith, to believe that he is merciful who saves so few and condemns so many . . . , so that he seems . . . to delight in the tortures of the wretched and to be more worthy of hate than of love" (ibid., p. 633). Our only hope is to flee from God in this undefined power and naked majesty, to God as he has defined himself in Christ, as redeeming love (ibid., pp. 684–85). Yet this self-definition is not a *mitiga-*

tion of God's unchecked will and majesty, nor therefore our flight to it a flight to a mitigated God, as nearly all other theology understands it. For God's self-definition as love occurs as the crucifixion, as yet another hiding, yet deeper than the first in the world's ambiguity (ibid., pp. 689–90), and so as the final event of that powerful hiddenness which, we have just seen, *is* God's majesty.

With this touchstone, we may not define God either as mere mind or mere will. We must make will the more central to our reflection, but we must posit a will that just *is* also mind. That is, we will think of God as spirit.

Were God the Father God by himself (which is contrary not merely to fact but to logic), there would indeed obtain about him precisely the scholastics' problem: Does he choose what he chooses because he knows what is good, or is what is good good because it is what he chooses? And the problem would be insoluble, given in the very conception of such a "naked majesty."

As it is, God is God the Father and God the Son, and just so God the Spirit. Therefore if we first think of the Father as *mind*, so that he has his self-identity in self-knowing, then the self as which he knows himself is Jesus, and so is a particular love and particular hope, a particular good thing *willed* by the Creator, that is, by God himself. Or if we first think of the Father as *will*, so that he has his self-identity in self-choice, then the self he chooses for himself is Jesus, who as a created person is always determined in his choices by others, that is, by his *knowledge* of them, including of the Father. Thus as God in fact is, the abstract and finally impotent dialectics of mind versus will cannot describe him. His reality is complex and alive; mind and will are given in him only in original structured unity.

That is, God is freedom. God is neither mind using will nor will using mind; God is creativity that is both. God is transforming and faithful liveliness. God is *spirit*.

We must hasten to prevent misunderstanding. The word "spirit" is often now used in a way that has little to do with its use in Scripture or here. That God is spirit does *not* mean that God is disembodied, a "pure spirit" in the vulgar sense. On the contrary, he has a body,[34] and did he not, would in fact not be spirit. That God has a body means, first, that[35] there is an *object* of our intention that is he, and that this same reality is the object of God's own intention of himself. And second, that there is an enduring entity by which God can be identified and by which he identifies himself. This enduring object that is God's body is the Jesus that walked in Palestine and was raised into present eternal life. Had God no body, he could not be spirit, for we have just seen how the freedom and complex temporal urgency of God is given in his having Jesus as his objective self.

The common religious conception of "pure spirit," meaning disembodied personhood, has no application to the triune God, even though nearly the whole theological tradition has tried to apply it, led by confusion between the biblical opposition of "spirit"/"flesh" and the Hellenic opposition of "mind"/"body," and by too hasty identification of "body" with "mass in space." The suppositious mere "God the Father" of three paragraphs back would be such an entity, and just so neither free nor temporally potent. A "pure" spirit would be either an impotent mind or an aimless will. To our salvation, the real God is neither. He is the living union of the Father and the Son. He has a body and therefore can be free creative spirit, the power of the last future.

GOD AS DISCOURSE

"In the beginning was the Word, and the Word was with God, and the Word was God" (John 1:1). It was the first deliberate dogma of Christianity, by which the faith forever defined its difference from other religions, that with Christianity's God there is *no* "silence of eternity," that we do *not* lose our voice and ears as we approach him, that he not only has a word for us—which is eccentric enough in the world of religion—but *is* his word for us: The Word is "of one being with the Father."

God is event, person, and spirit. The three propositions achieve their synthesis, and therewith their final clarity, in the proposition that God is word. Or perhaps we should say that Christianity first knew that God is word and has been engaged in working out the other three determinants.

It is religiously offensive to say that God is word. To be sure, all religions acknowledge that God must initially reveal itself/himself/herself to us if we are to know her/him/it, for if God were simply there for our inspection, she/he/it would not be God. A communication of some sort, a "word" in some kind of sign system, must begin the relation. But then, by normal religious apprehension, we must move on to a deeper or higher grasp of God. And as we move toward God we move beyond the initial communication, for God as such is silence. The God of normal religion is not personally present in address to us; God addresses us only to call us into the distance where God truly dwells.[36]

The word is the medium of life in time. It is because the world is not merely present to us, but present as *interpreted* in signs and symbols of indefinitely many sorts, that time can be the horizon of our life. For the world experienced in and by interpretation is just so the world that could be experienced as interpreted otherwise than it is; and thus *potentiality* is present in our world. Since the word is the medium of life in time, normal gods eschew the word except as a temporary measure.

The word is the medium of our life's commonality. It is in speech about the world, in whatever kinds of signs, that we inhabit a world that is not my world only or yours only but precisely *ours*, so that we can come together in it. Since the word is the medium of mutual determination, normal gods are in themselves silent.

That the Bible's God is different in this respect became so soon apparent that there is on this point no continuing history of theological alienation such as we have traced on other points. The temptation has worked mostly in the mystical tradition, and in the tradition of piety, in hymnody and prayer. Thus an anonymous English mystic counseled: "Forsake as well good thoughts as evil thoughts, and pray not with thy mouth."[37] And we have a considerable number of vehemently anti-Christian poems that by virtue of their pious sound and associated sentimental tunes are favorites of the congregations. We cite only the most brazen: the communion between Jesus and the Father is "the silence of eternity, interpreted by love," to share in which we are exhorted to "let sense be dumb, let flesh retire."[52]

Not only does the *triune* God speak to initiate relation to us, but the initiated relation eternally remains speech, remains communication. This God's eternity is his unconquerable futurity, and it is in the word that the future is present. This God *is* fellowship with us, and it is in the word that we are there for one another. The Christian vision of the end is not of a great silence but of a great liturgy, of preaching and our eternal response of praise and acclamation (Rev. 4—5).

Nor is the triune God speech only over against *us*. The second identity is "the Word," is God's address to us. The third identity is the Spirit of this address, the Word's power to open us to the last future. It is precisely the relation between these three in which God lives. God *is* each of the identities, so he *is* the Word. And by the triune reality of whatever God is, the word that God is is an exchange, not a lecture. Thus the final characterization of God's reality must be: God is a conversation. Or choosing a more dignified word: God is discourse.

The conversation that is God is not a conversation in heaven—at least, if heaven is some other *place* than earth. The conversation that is God is the proclamation of the law and the gospel. Where human discourse occurs which opens human life to the last future, there is the occurrence of God. It is precisely as the exalted Lord, as what trinitarian theology has come to call the second hypostasis of God, that Matthew quotes Jesus: "Where two or three are gathered in my name, there am I in the midst of them" (Matt. 18:20). And it is as God-*present* that the second identity *is* God. God is indeed present to every quark or every galaxy, but he is present to all things at and from the verbal event of the law and the gospel.

Thus the body of God, the object that is God and by virtue of which he indeed has a location, is "the body of Christ," the body-side of the law-and-gospel event. Every communication event has a body-side, an object-reality, as which those who address each other are there for each other.[38] If the preaching of the gospel is indeed the occurrence of God's word, then the body-side of the preaching of the gospel—the sights and sounds, the bread, the cup, the bath, the gestures of fellow believers—is the body-side of God's presence. Christ, we said earlier, is the body of God. It is into the embodiment of the gospel, that is, into the objective life of the church, that Christ is bodily risen. It is the embodiment of the gospel that is the "body of Christ" and so the body of God.

This matter has some dogmatic significance. We confess in the Lord's Prayer that God the Father is in "heaven," and in the three-article creeds that Christ is risen as a body and is at the Father's "right hand" there. But where is that?

The location of heaven, or rather the nature of heaven as a location for God, became confessionally divisive between Calvinists and Lutherans. Calvinists have maintained that heaven is a metaphysical *part* of creation, created by God as his own place within creation, so that it makes sense to speak of going and coming between heaven and the rest of creation, and of Christ's risen body being located there and therefore not located elsewhere in creation, for example, in the assemblies for the Supper. This tradition is still maintained by Karl Barth. Lutherans have, with some waverings, followed Luther's own view: that God has no *particular* space within creation, and that just so his place in creation, that is, his object-presence for us, is wherever the gospel sounds, to let us apprehend him there. Heaven is the "space" of the Word and the sacraments, the space of the Supper and baptism and however many other such events there are.[40] Readers will perceive this work's adherence to the Lutheran position, indeed, the determining force of that decision for the whole understanding of God. At the same time, we will hardly now wish to judge any continuing division on the matter itself as legitimately church-divisive.

NOTES

1. As in Altizer's use; Thomas J. J. Altizer, *The Gospel of Christian Atheism* (Philadelphia: Westminster Press, 1966).
2. E.g., Plato, *Phaedo.*
3. Wolfhart Pannenberg, "Die Aufnahme des philosophischen Gottesbegriffs als dogmatisches Problem der frühchristlichen Theologie," *ZThK* 70 (1959): 1–45.
4. E.g., Aristotle, *Metaphysics*, 1028a,13–15.
5. E.g., ibid., 1026a,15–19.
6. John Gerhard, *Loci communes theologici*, ii,93. Aquinas, *Summa Theologica*, i,3,3. Since Boethius, *essentia* was the standard theological equivalent for *ousia*, instead of *substantia*, which is more natural and used elsewhere. To compound confusion, translating *essentia*, where it stands for *ousia*, into English, we are compelled to revert to the anglicization of *substantia.*

7. See, e.g., Werner Marx, *The Meaning of Aristotle's "Ontology"* (The Hague: Nijhoff, 1954).

8. In Aristotle, see *Metaphysics*, bk. lambda.

9. Leslie Dewart, *The Future of Belief* (New York: Herder & Herder, 1966), pp. 134–43.

10. Peter Brunner, "Die Freiheit des Menschen in Gottes Heilsgeschichte," in *Pro Ecclesia*, vol. 1 (Berlin: Lutherisches Verlagshaus, 1962), p. 110.

11. Karl Barth, *Kirchliche Dogmatik* (Zürich: Zollikon, 1932–69), 2/1:288–305.

12. Ibid., p. 284.

13. Ibid., p. 300.

14. Ibid., pp. 306–61. On this, see Colin Gunton, *Becoming and Being* (New York and London: Oxford University Press, 1978), pp. 17–214; Robert W. Jenson, *God after God* (Indianapolis: Bobbs-Merrill, 1969).

15. E.g., John Cobb, *A Christian Natural Theology* (Philadelphia: Westminster Press; London: Lutterworth Press, 1965); Ralph E. James, *The Concrete God* (Indianapolis: Bobbs-Merrill, 1967); Schubert Ogden, *The Reality of God* (New York: Harper & Row, 1966).

16. I will be heavily dependent on Gunton, *Becoming and Being*, pp. 11–114.

17. E.g., Charles Hartshorne, *The Logic of Perfection* (LaSalle, Ill.: Open Court Publishing Co., 1962), pp. 216ff.

18. On this paragraph, see, e.g., Charles Hartshorne, *A Natural Theology for Our Time* (LaSalle, Ill.: Open Court Publishing Co., 1967), pp. 6–28; Charles Hartshorne, *The Divine Relativity: A Social Conception of God* (New Haven: Yale University Press, 1948), pp. 30–47, 67–75, 88–94.

19. P. F. Strawson, *Individuals: An Essay in Descriptive Metaphysics* (Garden City, N.Y.: Doubleday & Co.; London: Methuen, 1959).

20. *RGG*³, s.v. "Person," by Wolfhart Pannenberg.

21. *RGG*³, s.v. "Gott," by E. Würthwein.

22. Sten Konow, "Die Inder," in *Lehrbuch der Religionsgeschichte*, ed. Chantepie de la Saussaye (Tübingen: J. C. B. Mohr [Paul Siebeck], 1925), 2:1–88; Radakrishnan, *Indian Philosophy* (New York: Macmillan Co., 1923–27), 1:63–267; and vol. 2.

23. On the following, Emanuel Hirsch, *Geschichte der neuern evangelischen Theologie* (Gütersloh: Bertelsmann, 1949–54), 4:345–75. Also *RGG*³, s.v. "Person," 232.

24. It is worth noting that this is the same dialectic by which Paul Tillich argued Jesus' qualification to be "final revelation": *Systematic Theology*, 3 vols. (Chicago: University of Chicago Press, 1951–63), 2:135–37.

25. For a change of reference, Johannes Pedersen, *Israel*, trans. A. J. Fausboll (London: Oxford University Press, 1926–40), 2:611–69.

26. Brunner, "Freiheit," pp. 109–10. This article is the best single investigation of the matter here at issue.

27. Aquinas, *Summa Theologica*, i,78,introd.

28. Friedrich Schleiermacher, *Speeches on Religion to Its Cultured Despisers*, ii.

29. *Critique of Pure Reason* (1781), *Critique of Practical Reason* (1788), *Critique of Judgment* (1790).

30. Arthur Schopenhauer, *The World as Will and Idea*, ii,19.

31. The first Protestant systematic theologian, Philip Melanchthon, built his entire

systematics around the disconnection of mind and will in the fallen creature; *Loci communes* (1521), (T. Koldeed, 1890), pp. 68ff.

32. Neatly summarized in RGG³, s.v. "Voluntarismus," by H. Blankhertz.

33. Martin Luther, *On the Bondage of the Will* (1525), hereafter cited in the text by pagination of *WA* 18. See Gerhard Forde, "Bound to Be Free: Luther on the Gospel and Human Freedom," *Bulletin of the Lutheran Theological Seminary, Gettysburg* 57 (Winter 1977): 3–16; Eberhard Jüngel, "Quae supra nos, nihil ad nos," *EvTh* 32 (1972): 197–240.

34. For more extensive analysis, especially on soteriological import, see Robert W. Jenson, *Visible Words* (Philadelphia: Fortress Press, 1978), pp. 120–39.

35. Ibid., pp. 34ff.

36. On this paragraph, see, e.g., G. van der Leeuv, *Religion in Essence and Manifestation*, trans. J. E. Turner (London: George Allen & Unwin, 1938), p. 21.

37. Cited from Evelyn Underhill, *Mysticism* (1910; New York: Noonday, 1955), p. 320.

38. For further analysis, see Jenson, *Visible Words*.

39. Read Martin Luther's *Confession Concerning Christ's Supper* (1528), *LW* 37:151–372.

40. Ibid. One great Lutheran thinker, Johannes Brenz, developed a profound speculative understanding of space from this position of Luther; e.g., *Von der Majestät unsers lieben Herrn und einigen Heilands Jesu Christi* (1562).

6

The Attributes of God

Since God is, we can make factual statements about God. The method of obtaining such statements is decisive for their truth. True attributions to God are then forms of the gospel.

THE NECESSITY OF THE DOCTRINE

If there is God, it must be possible to form subject-attribute sentences (such as "God is loving" or "God is a nuisance") that are and can be judged to be true or false. The traditional doctrine of God's attributes is the attempt to make a list of the important true attributes and to work out the method of their derivation. Given the initial meaning of the word "God," and given a previous specification of God's sort of being (so that we are not concerned, e.g., with whether God is liquid), the words in question as predicates will be those that name some value.

The attempt now easily assumes a comic air. There was no problem so long as certain assumptions of classical philosophy could be made: that there just are a definite number of desirable attributes, each in any given natural language with its appropriate word. But we now tend to think of language as a creative activity, and so of the good as a pie that can be divided by words indefinitely many ways. Thus the possible number of value words is infinite. On these assumptions, it is absurd to ask What are God's (six? seven? or one hundred?) perfections? Shall we put "gentle" on the list? Or hold the slot for "humorous"?

What can be retained from the traditional doctrine is the attempt to state the method of deriving predicates for use with "God" and the discussion of a sampling of cases. But so much must be retained, for if we cannot say, for example, "God is loving" and know that we speak truth, God is not real. It is dogma in the three-article creeds that God is in fact Father, Almighty, Creator, Lord, Judge, and Giver of life, and so also that such statements can be factual. It will probably also be desirable to take our cases mostly from the traditional lists since these have shaped the language of the church.

THE METHOD OF DERIVATION

Our first concern is method. Unfortunately we have a quarrel also with the traditional method of derivation. It is an immediate consequence of everything in the previous chapters, that Martin Luther was correct when in 1518 he presented the thesis "The true theologian is not the one who comes to see the invisible things of God by thinking about what is created; the true theologian is the one who thinks about the visible and hinder parts of God, having seen them in sufferings and the cross."[1] The key to the thesis is the chiasmus on "see" and "think about," which readers should note before proceeding.

Luther's first clause exactly captures the standard method,[2] at least since Augustine. God, in his timeless glory, is "invisible." Our initial object is therefore the created, "visible," world. About this world, thought reveals that it contains within itself no sufficient reason for its own existence or character. Unless the world is reasonless—an unthinkable possibility until recently, and perhaps in fact not capable of consistent assertion—there must be a reason of the world that is not part of the world.

This reason can be reached only by the method of negative analogy. To the world's reason can be attributed those characters which it must have to *be* the world's reason. But all our words for causation and purpose are modeled on causes and outcomes that belong to the created world. We can fit them to the world's reason only by striking their reference to the world: so, for example, "God is a loving Father—only not as created fathers love, unreliably . . . [etc.]." And we will perform this operation only on such of our words as, in their worldly use, name what is good in creation, for it is the reason, the value, of the world for which we are reaching. The end of this path cannot be thought in the normal sense; the logic of our words has been disrupted on the way by the striking of temporal reference. The end is rather a vision, a seeing with the mind's eye[3] "of the invisible things of God." It should also be noted that there is no fundamental difference of method here between "natural" and "revealed" knowledge. The revelation in Christ simply adds special items to the total of the effects in the world from which God's character as its reason in intuited.

Luther's second clause proposes a very different method. The starting point is not our reflection on the world but particular events *in* the world, summed up as "the cross." These are directly presented to our experience, our "seeing." Nor do these exemplify the perfections of the world; they are rather "sufferings." The vision of God is then not the end of our cognitive path; it is the same act as this—cognitively normal—experience of the cross, and so the beginning. The events summarized "cross" simply *are* God insofar as God becomes our object, what we can see. This does not mean that there is no mystery in our experience of God, but the mystery is not the mystic shimmer of distance; it is that God presents himself in sufferings. What we see as God is correspondingly God's "visible" and inglorious reality, God's participation in sin and death and ignominy. And the work of the theologian is now to think hard about all this, in itself a normal rational exercise rather than a seeing at great distance. Just so, the world by no means drops out as an object of theological reflection. On the contrary, it is in at the beginning *and* at the end.

One step must be added to Luther's description, a step he either assumed or perhaps inadequately noted. That on the cross we see God is not our arbitrary choice. It is the crucified one's resurrection, which presents him and his sufferings as God-for-us, in which alone, indeed, he *is* God-for-us.[4] Whether we thereby quite follow Luther or not, we must say that the worldly object as which we have God for our object is the historic Jesus *as* the body of the risen Lord.

With the foregoing demands in mind, we propose a method of attribution to God, which can be summarized: Every true proposition of the form, "God is . . ." is a *slogan* either for the gospel's pivotal claim or for some true version of actual gospel proclamation. In this summary, "the gospel's pivotal claim" denotes one pole of all actual gospel proclamation: the assertion that "Jesus is risen," where "Jesus" can at need be backed up by such descriptions as "the one who preached the kingdom's imminence and was crucified for it." The other pole is the hopes and fears by which those of a time and place have a future, for example, hope for freedom or heaven or food. "Actual gospel proclamation" occurs as the mutual interpretation of these poles.

We should give an example of this interpretation. Large areas of the world are now swept by the hope of "liberation," of escape from conditions of institutionalized economic and political exploitation. The claim of Jesus' resurrection can interpret this hope and interpret itself by it. In the one direction, the interpretation gives an eschatological vision: Jesus, whose life and death defined him as life for others, lives in spite of the death such selflessness had to bring, so that there is now one human who need not exploit others, and so that his relation to others must finally shape all their lives. Therefore, we *will* be liberated. In the other direction, the interpretation gives ethics: Our hope for liberation is a realistic hope in that it is finally hope for Jesus' triumph; and therefore also we need not become ourselves exploiters in order to pursue it. "God liberates" is a slogan for this entire gospel interpretation.[5]

There are, we have proposed, two classes of divine attributes: slogans for the gospel's claim merely as such, and slogans for actual versions of gospel proclamation. In this dualism, we follow the tradition, in which the habit of bipartite classification is universal and deeply rooted. Thus John Gerhard lists nine possible classification systems, all bipartite (*Loci communes theologici*, ii,105). This dualistic propensity is doubtless finally rooted in the dualism of God and creature and the correlated dualism (following Luther's scheme) of God in his naked majesty and God in his defined majesty.

But while we may approve the deep reason for bipartite classification, we cannot approve the particular bipartite classification that in fact dominates the tradition. Continuing with Gerhard: "Some [attributes] are predicated of God *absolutely*, i.e., without any relation to creatures, as when God is called 'eternal' or 'immense'; and some are predicated *relatively*, as when God is called 'creator,' 'being,' or 'judge' " (ibid.). This division betrays all too clearly the definition of God himself by abstraction from his relations, against which we have been struggling. We therefore have proposed a different classification, to serve the legitimate part of the same purpose.

Some true subject-attribute sentences about God are slogans simply for "Someone (Jesus) is *risen*." They stipulate, over against some religious concern, what is involved in saying that he is "risen." Thus, for example, over against the question whether Jesus, this figure of historic antiquity, can mean anything to us in our so very different world, we may reply that since he is risen, his life is not in fact distant in time but brackets our time, defining all our possibilities. As a slogan: "God [always the *triune* God, of whom Jesus is the second identity] is eternal."

Other true subject-attribute sentences about God are slogans for actual proclamations of the gospel, for what is said when "Jesus is risen" and some community's or individual's penultimate hopes and fears so interpret one another as to give eschatological vision and founded ethics. We have already given an example, and will give others later. Such slogans are intrinsically historic in their validity. For the hopes and fears of humankind are not constant; their change and succession are indeed the very substance of history. Thus that because Jesus lives we will yet be free of exploitation would not have been a gospel-proclamation to, say, Paul's Corinth, and "God liberates" therefore would not have been a meaningful predication to God. Herein these attributes differ from those of the first class, which always have point.

The true God occurs as Jesus' resurrection. With some oversimplification, we may say that the two classes of God's attributes are those posited in saying that anyone is risen, and those posited in saying that it is Jesus who is risen. Had Nero risen instead of Christ, there would still be an eternal something, but it would be an eternal malignity. That there is instead an eternal benignity is what is said by attributions of the second class. And it is the actual content of Jesus' human life that interprets penultimate hopes and fears to give such content to eschatological vision. That Jesus' humanity and ours interpret each other at all depends on his resurrection, but the matter of the interpretation depends on the specificity of his humanity.

"JESUS IS RISEN":
ATTRIBUTES FOR THE PREDICATE

The first class of attributes, then, are those that explicate the notion of resurrection, bearing always in mind that this notion is itself derived not from general considerations but from the apostles' attempts to describe a particular event that happened to them and Jesus the Nazarene after his death. That stipulated, we may say that the first class of attributes are those which explicate the notion of deity as such, that deity which Father, Son, and Spirit have together in that they derive it from each other. We already have our primary explication of this deity, and so our first attribute: *temporal infinity*.

God is *infinite*. That is, God can be limited by no temporal conditions. Rules of the form "If X happens/has happened, Y must/cannot therefore happen" do not apply to God. God can accept and approve not only the godly but also the ungodly. He can use in his final fulfillment not only the virtues and successes of history, but also its sins and disasters. God can give life not merely to the not-yet born but also to the already dead. He is not predictable by the probabilities. God transcends what has happened and now is, creating what cannot but must yet be. Allowing for the skew introduced by the majority tradition's presumption of divine timelessness, we thus state the legitimate content of a traditionally listed attribute of the "absolute" class, *eternity*.[6]

Since this infinity occurs as the resurrection of Jesus, God's creative transcending is not arbitrary. It has a character: faithfulness to the historical Jesus. A second attribute: God is *faithful*. With this, we replace a second traditional "absolute" attribute, changelessness,[7] and we replace it with a fundamental apprehension of the Hebrew Scriptures. God's continuity as an enduring entity is that of a successful personal life, the very truth of which is to unite unpredictability and reliability. Aristotle defined a successful drama as one in which each event is a surprise when it happens, but makes us afterward say it was just what had to happen.[8] It is this sort of continuity that we attribute to God's temporal infinity by calling him *faithful*.

Following the lead of the traditional listing of "absolute" attributes, we next come to *omnipresence*, or as the Protestant scholastics were accustomed to say, "immensity." Here we have less quarrel with the tradition. According to Aquinas,[9] God "is everywhere by essence, presence and power" (*Summa Theologica*, i,8,3). He is everywhere "by essence," that is, in his own selfhood, in that he is the creator, the giver of being. Both any place and what is located in it exist only by the direct action of God, who just so is at that place (ibid., i,8,2). God is everywhere "by presence" as anyone is present to those things that are in the scope of his intention, that he "sees" (ibid., i,4,3, resp.). God is everywhere "by power," as a ruler is present to all those subject to him (ibid.). It will be seen how, partly in spite of the language, this concept of omni-presence is that of a *personal presence* to all creation: God is present to the world as I am to one I meet and effectively and creatively address.

In the Christian tradition, there has been a long rethinking of the notion of space—beginning decisively with the Greek fathers,[10] and achieving a fulfill-ment in the work of the seventeenth-century Lutheran metaphysicians—that has moved from the notion of a universal container to the notion of a coordi-nate system for mutual presence. Thus later scholastics distinguished three modes of spatial presence: an entity may be somewhere "locally," in that the entity has spatial boundaries; an entity may be somewhere "definitively," in that a bounded space can be indicated as the entity's location, even though the entity has itself no spatial boundaries, as a thought is in the brain; or an entity may be somewhere "repletively," by "containing" the space. Only in the third mode is God anywhere, and in it he is everywhere: "God, con-tained in no space, contains all spaces by the immensity of his being."[11]

We have only one amendment to this general tradition but that is sizable. The traditional doctrine, subtly and distinctively Christian though it is, assumes the essential disembodiment of God. Against this (but continuing in the scholastic terminology) we will want to assert the "definitive" presence of God at certain places in created space. Just so, Martin Luther made "definitive" presence the mode of Christ's presence in the Eucharist.[12] God, he argues, is "repletively" present everywhere, and so therefore is Christ, "at his right hand." But if God in Christ is to be present *for us* as conscious beings, we must be able to direct ourselves toward him, to *intend* him. Though this is not Luther's language, God's subjective "repletive" omnipresence must have an objective side, constituted by his "definitive" presence at certain places to which his word calls us. If we direct ourselves to the space occupied by, for example, the eucharistic loaf, we thereby are spatially related to God, even though God has no spatial boundaries.

God's infinity, in our view, is basically his temporal infinity, the unhindered-ness of his transcendence through time. God's *spatial* infinity is merely an expression thereof. He "contains" all spaces not by being a larger space but by temporally bracketing the spatial world. The subtly interrelated meanings of the word "present" are no accident and may guide our thinking. Space, the horizon of presence, is simply the experienced reality of the temporal pres-ent. God's spatial infinity is his ability to be *now there* for, to be present to, every creature. God's spatial infinity is the present tense of his faithful-ness: God is wherever Jesus' self-giving reaches.

We could continue indefinitely with such absolute attributes, but perhaps infinity, faithfulness, and omnipresence are enough and sufficiently basic cases. Taking Gerhard's list as typical of the tradition, he had also spiritual, uncorporeal, invisible, simple, immortal;[13] all these have in fact been considered at some place in this *locus*. We turn to the second class of attributes.

"JESUS IS RISEN": ATTRIBUTES FOR THE SUBJECT

The second class of attributes are those that state what it means that it is *Jesus* who is risen. They explicate what it means that it is the particular event that happens between *him* and *his* Father and *their* Spirit, and not some other, to which "deity"—temporal infinity—pertains. Despite the skew of which we constantly complain in this part of traditional doctrine, this logic can easily be seen also in the traditional lists. Thus Gerhard had as his second class: omnipotence, goodness, mercy, justice, omniscience, freedom of will, and truth, all of which explicate the gospel. The assertion of God's attributes of this sort, for example, "God is good," is therefore itself a mode of gospel proclamation.

It must be admitted that some traditional relative attributes seem but distantly related to the gospel, for example, omnipotence and omniscience. Yet why must God be, for example, omnipotent? Many putative Gods are not, and it would even seem possible to speak of someone as risen and yet not attribute omnipotence to that being. It is the specific character of the promises to be made because *Jesus* is the risen one that requires believers in those promises to think of God as omnipotent. These are promises of the triumph of the *unconditionally* loving one and therefore of a good so encompassing as to be realizable only by a will that encompasses all events, and so contrary to probability as to be expectable only from a will that recognizes no other mode of impossibility than self-contradiction. It must be admitted that in many scholarly deductions of God's omnipotence this evangelical derivation is not very apparent; yet even in the most abstract it can be detected in the warrants and biases of the argument. Luther goes straight to principle: "It is the one and highest *consolation* of Christians in all their adversities, to know that God . . . does all things immutably, that his will cannot be resisted nor yet changed or impeded."[14]

We will therefore not be surprised that also the creedal "almighty" had its matrix of a particular era's hopes and anxieties.[15] The great fear of late antiquity was meaninglessness: that the gap between this temporal world and eternity might be unbridgeable, or, expressed in terms of the divine, that the God who is fully divine, who is unqualifiedly eternal, may not function as God of this world. That would mean that no divine being was all-ruling. To those so tormented, the gospel speakers said: Jesus' Father and ours is in spite of everything *all*-ruler, Lord both of this world and the next.

Once current in the church's language (and in this case even taken into the creed) a word like "almighty" tends to acquire a life of its own. "God is almighty" becomes a theological axiom, from which can be deduced soteriology for situations very different from that in which it had its own soteriological meaning. And the word itself lies in the language, ready for life when the gospel again meets fear of debility at the heart of being, as decidedly in our present time. Both these continuing histories can go well or badly for the gospel.

We continue to a second attribute of this sort, this one untraditional. If we adhere to Luther's methodological rule and then examine traditional lists of attributes, we find them radically incomplete. All the traditional "relative" attributes are characteristics that are good also in this world. That we see God in sufferings and the cross would never be guessed from them. Of possible attributes that are *not* good in this world, we will discuss the most offensive and decisive: God is mortal. God has in fact suffered death and therefore is somehow or other qualified and qualifiable by dying.

Jesus died, indeed, was executed. According to trinitarian apprehension of God, he is an identity of God. What he does and suffers, God does and suffers. Nor can his significance for us be abstracted from his death. The crucifixion cannot be made an incident irrelevant to Jesus' being as God for us, however our otherwise derived suppositions about God may make us wish it could: "but we preach Christ crucified, a stumbling block to Jews and folly to Gentiles" (1 Cor. 1:23). It is therefore an unavoidable item of Christian proclamation and reflection: "God the Son died." And such language was from the first deeply anchored in the liturgy and piety; so, for example, Melito of Sardis: "The Invisible is seen . . . , the Impassible suffers . . . , the Death-less dies. . . . God was killed."[16]

Despite the proposition's obvious gospel-necessity, it has been resisted through the whole history of the church. Arianism was at heart one long attempt to evade it: The Logos could not be God straight out precisely because he is one person with Jesus and so a sufferer of death. Indeed, the whole agony of trinitarian development was, as we have seen, occasioned by second-century acceptance of the impassibility axiom, of which "God died" is the extreme contradiction.

In the christological controversies leading to and following the Council of Chalcedon, the continuing attempt by those most committed to the impassibility axiom to evade attributing death and suffering to the Logos, and the insistence by those most committed to the biblical image of Christ that this must *somehow* be done, was perhaps the chief problem.[17] These controversies generally belong in another *locus*, but we must here note the "theopaschite" controversy at the turn of the fifth and sixth centuries, where the matter was put explicitly to the test.[18] In the first phase of the controversy, liturgical enthusiasm and theological scruples clashed directly. A new and instantly beloved version of the *Trisagion* "Holy God, Holy Almighty, Holy Immortal," enriched with "who were crucified for us," was suppressed by church authorities committed to standard theology, lest the Trinity be taken for the subject of suffering. In the second, a compromise explanation of such liturgy was proposed, phrased to make clear that the Trinity as such was not crucified: "*One of* the Trinity suffered in the flesh." But even this was resisted, by the pope among others, despite its manifest biblical authenticity and perfect agreement with orthodox tradition. It took the Emperor Justinian, whose motives were mixed, to compel official churchly acceptance, sealed at a general council in 553.[19] And even though theopaschite language has thereafter had dogmatic status, it has continued to be rare in systematic theology and has remained unreckoned with in standard lists of divine attributes.

The understanding of God's mortality must indeed be trinitarian. "*One of the Trinity*" died; and when patripassionists have extended the suffering of Jesus' death to the Father, this has rightly promptly been rejected.[20] Let us set up the dialectics by posing a naive but inescapable question: What about the time between Jesus' death and his resurrection? If the second identity died on Friday and rose on Sunday, was God meanwhile a binity?

If we have grasped the point of trinitarianism, the question answers itself. Jesus' death was not an interruption of his deity; as the conclusion of his obedience to the Father, as part of what the Father intends in intending Jesus as his self, Jesus' death is *constitutive* for his relation to the Father and so for both his deity and the Father's. Jesus is not God despite his death; he is God in that he died.

This answer will still seem puzzling if we continue to understand being as persistence, if we think that something really *is* whatever it was and persists in being. Then the three days of death must be an interruption of Jesus' being and so of his godhood. But just that understanding of being is what Christian interpretation of God contradicts. Something really *is* what it will be and now is open to being.

Jesus' death is part of his eventful relation to the Father and the Spirit. In that he is risen, this relation is future and present reality. And just this event is God's eternity, in which Jesus is always God. Jesus' death and resurrection are the way the particular Christian God goes about to be eternal, to be temporally infinite. For it is what happens between the identities, of which event Jesus' death is a main constituent, that *is* the eternal God.

Participation in our finitude, alienation, and consequent disaster thus belongs to the event that in fact God is. Exegeting "belongs"; it essentially characterizes the true God that, *if* there are creatures and fallen creatures, he is able and apt so to participate in their life. It is appropriate to what it means to be this God that in his second identity he died with and for us. God is not subject *to* death, but he conquers death only by undergoing it. In this way God is indeed mortal.

Finally, one other of the traditional attributes must be discussed: *goodness*.[21] Given the creeds and the liturgy, it is dogma that God is good. It is the simplest and most encompassing interpretation of the resurrection: History will have a good outcome; goodness is the heart of events.

Yet there are two traps in the notion of divine goodness. The first is that "God is good" is construable as gospel-proclamation in any and all situations, and just so tends to become general and then empty. Second, since the traditional derivation of divine attributes by analogy from features of creation necessarily used the *"good"* features of creation, it has been easy to confuse the divine goodness proclaimed by the gospel with an abstractly necessary character of the prime reason, and so again to empty it of its gospel import. Either way, the outcome is the familiar conception of "the good God," whose goodness is unquestionable and mostly irrelevant.

"God is good" is a Christian sentence only insofar as it is used precisely equivalently for "Jesus of Nazareth will triumph." The difference between the two sentences is only that between rhetorical or metaphysical contexts in which one or the other is more convenient: One sentence is in the present tense, the other in the future.

There is no way to round off our discussion of the attributes of the second class, since in principle we can invent new ones forever. We will instead round off our entire *locus* on God by harking far back. God is the universally transforming event between Jesus the Israelite, and the transcendence he called to as "Father," and their Spirit among us. Given who Jesus is, this event is good. So we conclude the doctrine of God.

NOTES

1. Martin Luther, *Theses for the Heidelberg Disputation*, WA 1:350–74, theses 19–20. English translations of these theses have not successfully dealt with the ingenious chiasmus of *conspicere* and *intelligere* and therefore miss most of the point.

2. The following is modeled on Aquinas, on whom see Ralph McInerny, *The Logic of Analogy* (The Hague: Nijhoff, 1961); George P. Klubertanz, *St. Thomas Aquinas on Analogy* (Chicago: Loyola University Press, 1960); Robert W. Jenson, *The Knowledge of Things Hoped For* (New York: Oxford University Press, 1969), pp. 67–85. That classic Protestantism followed the same general method can be seen from, e.g., John William Baier, *Compendium theologiae positivae* (1686–94), i,i,4ff.

3. This "intellectual perception," *nous*, is the deepest and most original ideal of Greek theology; here it dominates the methodology of theology as elsewhere it

dominates the matter. See Werner Marx, *The Meaning of Aristotle's "Ontology"* (The Hague: Nijhoff, 1954), pp. 11–16.

4. Behind this amendment lies that broad methodological movement in recent theology that can be represented in one of its aspects by Wolfhart Pannenberg, ed., *Revelation as History*, trans. D. Granskou (New York: Macmillan Co., 1968); and in another by Jenson, *Knowledge.*

5. For the intellectually most vigorous instance of this interpretation, see the work of James Cone, e.g., *A Black Theology of Liberation* (Philadelphia: J. B. Lippincott Co., 1970).

6. Aquinas, *Summa Theologica*, x; John Gerhard, *Loci communes theologici*, i,137; and for an example from the Calvinist tradition, the textbook of colonial American theology, William Ames, *The Marrow of Theology*, i,iv.

7. Aquinas, *Summa Theologica*, ix; Gerhard, *Loci communes theologici*, ii,150; Ames, *Marrow of Theology*, i,iv.

8. Aristotle, *On Poesy*, 1452a,1–11; 1554a,33–36.

9. Standard Protestantism is materially identical; e.g., Gerhard, *Loci communes theologici*, ii,171ff.

10. Pioneeringly analyzed by Thomas F. Torrance, *Time, Space, and Incarnation* (New York and London: Oxford University Press, 1969).

11. Gerhard, *Loci communes theologici*, ii,172.

12. Martin Luther, *Confession Concerning Christ's Supper* (1528), *WA* 26:327ff.

13. Gerhard, *Loci communes theologici*, ii,113.

14. *On the Bondage of the Will*, *WA* 18:619.

15. On this paragraph, J. N. D. Kelly, *Early Christian Creeds* (New York and London: Longmans, Green & Co., 1950), pp. 136ff.

16. Melito of Sardis, fragments xxxi, xvi.

17. On this, see Werner Elert, *Der Ausgang der altkirchlichen Christologie* (Berlin: Lutherisches Verlagshaus, 1957), pp. 71–169.

18. Ibid., pp. 105–9.

19. Ibid., pp. 165ff. The council's decree reads: "If someone does not confess that the one crucified in the flesh, the Lord Jesus Christ, is the true God and the Lord of Glory, and one of the Holy Trinity, let him be condemned" (*Sacrorum counciliorum nova et amplissima collectio*, ed. J. D. Mansi [Firenze, 1759–1827], 9:375).

20. Jaroslav Pelikan, *The Emergence of the Catholic Tradition* (Chicago: University of Chicago Press, 1971), pp. 176–82.

21. Aquinas, *Summa Theologica*, vi; Gerhard, *Loci communes theologici*, ii, 208–15.

THIRD LOCUS

The Knowledge of God

PAUL R. SPONHEIM

THE KNOWLEDGE OF GOD

Introduction

Introduction

One who in the late twentieth century sets about to write dogmatically of the knowledge of God faces two kinds of difficulties. The first difficulty is *textual.* What will the text be? The church has not produced a clear dogmatic statement on this matter. Yet the teaching of the church does entail a claim that God is known. Moreover, there is an ample body of Christian reflection concerning the knowledge of God. That body is characterized by a bewildering diversity; it is ample in range as well as in extent. Hence the difficulty: A dogmatic statement calls for some clear and definitive formal teaching, but we look for such in vain, finding instead a buzzing multiplicity of individual Christian opinion.

The second difficulty is *contextual.* To speak convincingly of knowing God now seems too hard, or too hard to be worth the effort. It is difficult, for example, to speak of knowing a present ontological ground for the universe, when such unlikely colleagues as the rule of law (even statistical law) and respect for raw historical particularity combine to resist such speech. The battle for explanatory control seems to be between these two: my stubborn sense of subjectivity and the ineluctable web of objective causality which natural and social scientists monitor. That standoff hardly hints at a "wholly other" explanatory principle. On the contrary, the Christian is regularly offered explanations of the thinking and speaking that were once supposed to be about God. It is no easier today to enter the realm of historical contingency in order to elevate a single instance to the status of the norm by which I am to be judged and from which I am to take my bearings in life. That seems against the grain, if we are dealing with something that is, after all, precisely a part of an historical series.

Is it worth the effort to attempt such speech concerning the knowledge of God? Why bother to stake out intelligibly in the public arena such knowledge claims regarding God, if the splendor of private ecstasies is available? These difficulties must be addressed if Christian faith in God is to be clearly distinguished from mystical union with who-knows-what. The stakes are high. If God is not known, our claims elsewhere in these volumes are altered in devastating fashion. If God is known but we know not how, at least we can be asked to say how we understand our possession of and confidence in such knowledge.

3 / THE KNOWLEDGE OF GOD

There seems to be a sort of reciprocal dependence in these matters. We have just stressed the importance of our task for the content-claims that occur elsewhere in this dogmatics. Yet the Christian understanding of that and how we know God cannot be developed adequately in purely formal terms. Some attention must be given to *what* is claimed to be known about God, as the reference to a ground and a goal for the world suggests. We shall draw on that content as it bears on the questions concerned with the knowledge of God. We shall also need to consider the reflective significance for this topic of other *loci*, such as those on sin and the person of Christ. Thus the textual problem will be addressed, as the faith's claims about God can and must be probed to speak of how God is known.

To speak of the knowledge of God is to speak of aspects of the relationship between God and humankind. Thus this *locus* cannot be comprehended without clarity about how human beings come to know accurately and then to speak clearly about that which they know. To speak of human beings in their knowledge of God is to speak of them widely. In that breadth of speech the occasion is given for responding to the contextual difficulties.

Indeed, breadth is needed materially as well as formally. We shall argue that to speak of the knowledge of God is to speak of much more than religion. Without trying to argue that Christianity is not a religion, or that there is no truth in any other religion, one may well contend that God is not to be known merely in matters religious—Christian or otherwise. It is, after all, God of whom we speak in this matter. God is not merely the beneficiary of our ritual, but the benefactor who is ceaselessly at work to bless in all that is real. But may God, *is* God, to be known that widely? That question and the others put so far drive us to the *locus* itself.

1

The Reality
and Revelation of God

God is known because in creation and in redemption God's will
and action to bless reveal God to humankind as the world's ground
and goal. In the mission of Jesus, what God intended and intends
in creation is firm and therefore clear, though it is grasped as the
word of promise to a pilgrim whose question and quest can only
be answered by one who is qualitatively other.

THE SELF-REVELATION OF GOD

Christians understand their claim to know God to be dependent on the will
and action of the one who is known. While our knowledge of God is emphatically human in its condition, its origin lies in the revelation of God.

Three further claims are involved in this assertion. The first is of the reality
of God. While, for the believer, faith and God may belong together, the
believer is clear that faith does not create God and does not elect God. While
theologians like Paul Tillich may doubt that it is appropriate to formulate
the reality of God in terms of existence, that doubt does not hint at unreality,
but is rooted precisely in the conviction of God's superiority. It may seem
offensively obvious to begin thus with a repudiation of all fictionalist
understandings, but popular appeals to the power of positive thinking and
scholarly references to religion as the "entertaining" of a story make it
necessary.[1]

The second claim is of the categorical supremacy of God. Charles Hartshorne
makes the point well:

God is a name for the uniquely good, admirable, great, worship-eliciting being.
Worship, moreover, is not just an unusually high degree of respect or admiration; and the excellence of deity is not just an unusually high degree of merit.
There is a difference in kind. God is "Perfect," and between the perfect and
anything as little imperfect as you please is no merely finite, but an infinite step.
The superiority of deity to all others cannot (in accordance with established word
usage) be expressed by indefinite descriptions, such as "immensely good," "very

powerful," or even "best" or "most powerful," but must be a superiority of principle, a definite conceptual divergence from every other being, actual or so much
as possible. We may call this divergence "categorical supremacy." [2]

It is this truth that leads some theologians to suggest that "existence" is in-
appropriately applied to God. I disagree, as I shall try to make clear later.
It is this truth, moreover, which has (unfortunately, I believe) encouraged many
theologians—particularly when the lure of Platonism was strong—to
distinguish God's reality from God's actions in the world of time and space.
Many contemporary theologians, from otherwise differing perspectives, insist
that the categorical transcendence of God is to be found and so known not
apart from but precisely in the divine action in history.[3]

The third claim is of the initiative of God. God is not merely *there*—even
eminently there—as an object to be known. It is God who acts to reveal. We
know God because of God, who is categorically superior. Both God's action
generally and God's revelation specifically are marked by the decisiveness
available to a will that is fully free. Thus the writer to the Ephesians speaks
of God blessing us "in the heavenly places," choosing us "before the foundation of the world." Action that is so emphatic leads toward revelation that
is sure: "For he has made known to us in all wisdom and insight the mystery
of his will, according to his purpose which he set forth in Christ as a plan
for the fulness of time, to unite all things in him, things in heaven and things
on earth." (Eph. 1:9–10).

Revelation by God and so knowledge of God occur because God's living
will is for relationship. The Christian teaching about the Trinity reminds us
that to speak of God's relatedness is to speak first about God. But faith also
confesses that God wills to relate to that which is not God. Again we speak
of all of God: the works of the Trinity may be *internally* divisible, but when
we are related to God we are related to all of God, to the only God. This
God wills to relate to that which is not God. So do Christians speak of God's
will in terms of creation, of covenant, of presence.[4]

God wills, then, to reveal. That is the basis for Christian confidence in claiming the knowledge of God. But what does the reality of the God known suggest about the nature of the knowing? Let it first be said that it does not
undercut the reality and reliability of the knowledge. Christians find their
clearest access to the knowledge of God in the gospel concerning what God
has done in the person and work of Jesus for the salvation of all. Knowledge
is claimed emphatically, as when Lutherans and Catholics in dialogue agree:

This gospel (a) was proclaimed by witnesses—apostles and others in the early
Church; (b) was recorded in the New Testament Scriptures, which have a "normative role for the entire later tradition of the Church"; (c) has been made living
in the hearts of believers by the Holy Spirit; (d) has been reflected in the "rule

of faith" (*regula fidei*) and in the forms and exercise of church leadership; (e) has been served by Ministers.[5]

Clearly there is here a claim to content and to confidence. The categorical uniqueness of God undergirds rather than undercuts that claim. That which is known here is the sure will of God. The testimony of the Scriptures is clear: "Do not be deceived, my beloved brethren. Every good endowment and every perfect gift is from above, coming down from the Father of lights with whom there is no variation or shadow due to change. Of his own will he brought us forth by the word of truth that we should be a kind of first fruits of his creatures" (James 1:16–18). And "If we are faithless, he remains faithful—for he cannot deny himself." (2 Tim. 2:13). May we not say that Paul is sure that "nothing can separate" from the love of God in Christ Jesus not merely because there is no adequate external threat, but also because there is no internal challenge at all? It is God's role to justify, Paul knows. He is confident that God will not turn against what none other than God has done in Christ.

What God has so surely done can be stated intelligibly. It can be communicated to those who do not share the faith; it is not a word whose meaning can be understood only by initiates. Moreover, the one who believes does not fall prey to blind credulity, precisely because there is in this relationship clear content which can be possessed competently and with integrity. Wolfhart Pannenberg has made this point forcefully: "Every act of trust reaches backwards (or forwards) to a ground of trustworthiness in the object being relied on. . . . Knowledge of the content of faith (*notitia* with *assensus*) remains the logical presupposition of the trust which is based upon it."[6] It also follows that the content of the faith can be formulated, that faith may seek understanding. Clarity can be sought in the statement of the gospel and in the formulation of its implications, because the word here is that the one who is categorically supreme has willed to bless. Toward that end light is given, and so sermons are preached and dogmatics are written.

But perhaps we have made things too easy for ourselves. Søren Kierkegaard appropriately reminds us that as soon as we speak of revelation everything becomes dialectical.[7] It is after all *God* of whom we speak: the categorically supreme one who is radically unlike us. This God is the one who creates out of nothing and whose revelation seems discontinuous with what precedes it. So Paul can claim that he did not receive the gospel from some human source, "nor was I taught it, but it came through a revelation of Jesus Christ. . . . When he who had set me apart before I was born, and had called me through his grace, was pleased to reveal his Son to me . . . I did not confer with flesh and blood" (Gal. 1:12, 15–16). Moreover, even when God is revealed, that revelation hardly makes perfect sense. We are told that God's revelation is always in the form of the opposite, indeed, that God remains hidden even in self-revelation.[8]

This dialectical emphasis does not contradict what we have said of the sure will of the God who reveals. It is will and life with which we deal here. God is not a principle or a mechanism droning on through the ages. When we speak of a personal will, we speak of that which has newness about it. The freshness and spontaneity of living will may so surprise the knower as to yield cognitive dissonance. Nor should we underestimate the distortions due to finitude and sinfulness in our reading of God's acts.

Similarly, the categorical supremacy of God complicates any attempt to respond simply to the question. "Is God's revelation direct *or* indirect?" Revelation is indirect in the sense that God works through means: persons, words, water, bread, and wine. While mysticism will require attention, Christian knowledge must be distinguished from unmediated knowledge. Even the clearest revelation of God is "dialectical," if the humanity of Jesus is not to be denied. Yet we need also to say that it is God's own self who is at work in and through these means. God is not off in some more interesting corner of the universe; the one who works here is none other than God. Again, the categorical supremacy of God is such that the one who brings reality into being is able to be potently at work in that being, directly but mediately. It is thus fitting that the church has steadfastly insisted that the content of revelation includes both a *who* and a *what*, a someone as well as a something. Through God's work and word we do in fact know God.

GOD AS THE
WORLD'S GROUND AND GOAL

The God whom Christians know is "maker of heaven and earth." The categorical supremacy of God cannot be stated simply in moral terms. Indeed, in moral terms it may be that the more than moral superiority of God is that the will of God grounds the meaning of "the good" and "the right," even if one goes on to affirm that God's will is so sure and clear that the good can be known apart from God. Thus Christian thinkers have been drawn to ponder the connection between moral and metaphysical supremacy, as when Kierkegaard develops the theme that purity of heart is to will one thing. Anyway, it is clear that Christian faith attributes to God a metaphysical or ontological uniqueness. At times this uniqueness seems even to threaten the moral character of God, as when Second Isaiah writes: "I form light and create darkness, I make weal and create woe, I am the Lord, who do all these things" (Isa. 45:7).

A prevailing traditional dogmatic focus for this ontological supremacy is the doctrine of creation *ex nihilo* (from nothing). The focus has usually been formulated in terms of the absolute temporal origin of all that is not God, as expressed in the notion of original creation. That formulation is currently the subject of considerable debate on both exegetical and contextual grounds. The matter is of intrinsic importance and is directly discussed in the *locus* on creation. It is not necessary here to enter that debate, since the bearing of the *ex nihilo* doctrine on the subject of the knowledge of God can be discussed independently. In such a way Langdon Gilkey, for example, affirms the formula "from nothing" as an apt statement of God's present relationship to us; in that relationship God is "the deep, transcendent, and yet immanent ground of our passage; the power that gives us our past and preserves it, that creates and recreates our freedom, and that lures and calls us with new possibilities." [9] Even those who affirm a distinction between original creation and continuing creation or preservation claim also under the latter categories such a special ontological role for God as Gilkey has described.

It seems helpful to gather these associations together in the metaphor of God as the world's *ground*, letting logical and ontological priority mingle in this metaphor. Without following Tillich at every point, one may well speak with him of God as the originating, sustaining, and directing ground of the world.[10]

The church has steadily affirmed that it is possible for human beings to know that they are so grounded. Indeed, it may be that those Christian thinkers are right who have spoken of human being as precisely freedom that asks even about its own basis, that asks the question of God. Is life sound and fury only, signifying nothing, or is there a ground, a purpose, on which freedom can build, a call to which freedom can respond? Humankind naturally—precisely *naturally* as created by God—asks this question of the ground and can find an answer that is affirmative. Perhaps that is why atheism did not become a major problem before the modern period. It is only the fool who supposes there is no God. If the question is disallowed or distorted, can the answer be expected to fare any better? It is not our task at this point to ask what is different about the modern context. Here we seek only to clarify what it means to speak of God as foundation for *knowledge*.

It is striking that perhaps the major motif carrying this meaning, the *logos* tradition, links *life* and *light* so intimately (John 1). It would be a mistake completely to identify these themes, since God's *creative* work is the more encompassing. Yet the word that orders does reveal. Thus the church does speak of God as there to be known, whether by appeal to an original creation or to a more present grounding.

Even the least optimistic of the church's voices affirm such a "natural" knowledge of God. Thus Luther spoke of a "general knowledge" of God to be had in reflection on creation, reason and philosophy, and conscience.[11] John Calvin affirmed a universal "sense of divinity." [12] Even Tertullian spoke of a "natural knowledge" of God deriving from the order and beauty of the visible cosmos and from the immediate testimony of the soul, though he found that philosophy confuses this knowledge (*Apologeticus*, 17.6). Christians agree that God may be known as the ground for the project that is the world, for the venture that is humankind.

Christians also agree that to know God as the world's ground is not sufficient. To know the world's ground is not yet to know the world's goal, the *telos* of the striving that is human life. On the reading of matters represented by the faith, to ask about the goal is to ask about God. The God who is alpha will be omega as well. Where does the world go? It goes to God. Humankind particularly is not merely made *by* God—as is everything that is; we are made *for* God. Perhaps we ask the question of God as ground precisely because we are in quest of God as goal. To know God as the world's ground is to know that life is well begun. But humankind is haunted by its dream of a goal out ahead. The dream is not of the last item in a series, so that the world ends in stultifying sameness, but of a new reality of unending life and light. Christians call it "heaven" and believe that then we shall know God "face to face."

Meanwhile, we do not know so. It is, after all, a venture of freedom upon which we are embarked. Freedom as we now know it is characterized by risk, by contingency. It is a good and noble thing to know God as the ground of life, for in knowing that one knows the gift of freedom and its concomitant, responsibility. Thus one may speak of knowing God, the world's ground, not only as *logos*, but as *nomos* as well. So Clement spoke of philosophy as the "torah" of the Greeks, and Tertullian explained the good elements in pagan philosophy on the basis of natural law.[13] The law is given for life; God acts here to bless.[14]

Can one know anything about God as goal in one's knowledge of God as ground? God's claim as ground does call toward God as goal. It suggests that the meaning of life is somehow to be found in the relationship to God. But it does not reveal what that meaning is. Inference might well lead to an association of God with the moral good—we shall ponder that process of inference later. But this would not seem to yield any decisive resolution to the multifarious project which any human life— and a fortiori all human life— represents. Just as the good of being called by God does not yield the goal of sure consummation, so these indicators in the area of knowledge remain indecisive. Such ambiguity may well be the epistemic correlate to the ontological reality of freedom.[15]

Moreover, given the reality of sin and our sense of sin, it is not strange at all that the knowledge of God as *logos* and *nomos* would in fact terrify. This is the particular contribution of Luther's understanding. Regin Prenter points out that the God of creation's purpose is blessing and life. But this purpose is hidden to the sinner, because sin's curse opposes God's work and hides its purpose.[16] The wisdom the law brings thus accuses and kills. One does not blame the law for this, as Luther says in the twenty-fourth Heidelberg thesis:

"Nevertheless, this wisdom is not bad nor is the law to be fled. But without a theology of the cross man misuses the best things in the worst way."

But of course the Christian need not be without a theology of the cross, for the world is not in fact without a cross. It is not the task of this *locus* to develop a soteriology, to ponder what was wrought in Jesus. Christians have spoken differently about Jesus, but it is he about whom they all speak when they reflect on God as the world's goal. Pannenberg says: "God's revelation in Jesus Christ is indeed only an anticipation of the final event, which will be the actual revelatory event. And yet, we have the well-founded confidence that the final event will not bring anything decisively new that was not already anticipated in the resurrection of Jesus."[17] Thus Luther, pondering the God hidden in predestination, can appeal to the way in which the light of grace resolves the questions of the light of nature to sustain the hope that the light of glory "will one day reveal God, to whom alone belongs a judgment whose justice is incomprehensible, as God whose justice is most righteous and evident."[18]

This Jesus is kairotic for the *reality* of the relationship between God and humankind. That point is developed elsewhere in this dogmatic. Here we merely note that the church's recognition of Jesus also has kairotic significance for the *knowledge* of God. The author of the prologue to John's Gospel, that poet of the Word of God active as the light to bless in all that has life, declares: "For the law was given through Moses; grace and truth came through Jesus Christ. No one has ever seen God; the only Son who is in the bosom of the Father, he has made him known" (John 1:17–18).

So, then, God is known as ground and goal, as *logos* (*nomos*) and in *kairos* (*eschatos*). God acts to reveal. How shall the relationship between the two be formulated? Two major tendencies are apparent in the history of Christian thought. The first thinks that the kairotic, the special, supplements and fulfills the natural or general knowledge available through God as *logos*. This view has been developed in strikingly different ways. In general it may be said that special and general knowledge of God are here regarded as logically comparable and materially congruent. One way in which this is done is to say that the philosophers have systematized the natural knowledge of God and then call Christianity a philosophy as well. That early Christian thinkers such as Justin Martyr and Clement of Alexandria tended so to speak may not surprise if one recalls that the philosophies of the early Christian era were highly religious and were, as opposed to the cults, monotheistic.[19]

In the writings of the theologians of the golden age of scholasticism, especially Bonaventura and Aquinas, there is the confidence that philosophy, if rightly understood, is on the side of theology and that reason is in fundamental harmony with revelation. Bonaventura, following Augustine's epistemology, traces an ascent from finding God's vestiges in the visible world, through seeking his image in our soul, to mystical knowledge of God. Aquinas, reflecting a more Aristotelian epistemology, argues to God from features of the existence of the sensible world, applying the *via negativa*, analogy, and eminence and then adds truths to be known only through revelation. Thus reason can show that God created the world, but revelation informs us that God willed it in time rather than in eternity.[20]

The relationship of supplementation in Aquinas is not a simple one. Many things which can be known naturally can also be known by scriptural revelation. Indeed, all knowledge necessary for salvation has been specially revealed. Moreover, reason is not excluded from the realm of faith, for revealed doctrines can be shown to have a certain fit with reason. Yet the two spheres do not simply converge. The closest classical Christian thought comes to an argument for complete convergence may be Anselm, whose "faith seeking understanding" led him to try to prove the necessity of the Trinity and the incarnation.[21] We exclude here those thinkers, such as the extreme deists, who really did not think of two realities that converge, but spoke instead simply of the gospel as the "republication of the religion of nature."[22] Insofar as theological liberalism stopped short of such identification, it represents the position of supplementation, as when Friedrich Schleiermacher located the decisiveness of Jesus' redemption in the strengthening of a universally present consciousness of absolute dependence on God.[23]

If the tendency in this first group of thinkers is synthesis, diastasis prevails in the second tendency. The general and the special, the natural and the revealed, do not come together but are driven apart.

The opposition may be thought of as a logical opposition. John Duns Scotus declined to be troubled by logical contradiction, when the subject at hand is the action of infinite will. Clearly nothing that can be derived philosophically can bind the operation of an absolutely free will. The best that philosophers can muster is the notion *that* there is an infinite will. William of Ockham carried this tendency further. While Scotus spoke of God choosing the essences to be created, Ockham suppressed universals altogether and stressed instead the ultimate reality of singulars. No intrinsically necessary relation of causality can be recognized between singulars, and—a fortiori—between the realm of the finite and the infinite. To speak of a conflict between faith and reason is really beside the point. Nicholas of Cusa made the point still more emphatically, speaking of the infinite as the absolute and perfect coincidence of contraries, thus rejecting Aristotelian reliance on the principle of contradiction.[24]

The opposition between *logos* and *kairos* can be cast in more existential terms. Tertullian represents this emphasis. Athens and Jerusalem do not converge, not because there is no accurate natural knowledge of God, but because only Jerusalem heeds the call of true religion to obey the supreme and active will of God known in the rule of faith.[25] More clearly still, Luther and Calvin denied that natural revelation can be a foundation for the proper knowledge of God. In Calvin, natural revelation serves to leave the human person without excuse. In Luther it condemns and terrifies. This view prevailed in the mid-twentieth century's so-called neo-Reformation or neo-orthodox reaction to theological liberalism's custodial distribution of the heritage of the Enlightenment. At times the reaction seemed so sharp as to say that natural knowledge of God does not avail because it does not exist.

Since dogma does not decide between these tendencies, how may the contemporary Christian understand the church's voices as a common witness to the knowledge of God? The range of opinion reflected in these tendencies may be integrated into the argument begun earlier—and so that argument may be advanced—in two summary comments:

1. The Christian faith confesses the epistemic priority of the kairotic event of Jesus for the knowledge of God. The faith utters a resounding "yes" to Kierkegaard's questions: "Is an historical point of departure possible for an eternal consciousness; . . . is it possible to base an eternal happiness upon historical knowledge?"[26] Here the human person knows what beings questing after the *telos* of life need to know, for here the word of justification is spoken. This knowledge is distinctive and decisive because God who is living will has acted decisively toward the world in Jesus.

2. Yet the authority of this kairotic word depends on its being the word of the one who is maker of heaven and earth. It is precisely the *logos* that becomes flesh in this *kairos*. Thus continuity must be affirmed. The faith understands that the continuity is the constancy of the personal will of God who is active for us also in creation. Thus some measure of continuity also in knowledge is to be affirmed. In some measure this is an inverted continuity. Thus Calvin can speak of how the regenerate again see God in the world.[27] Or one may speak of how the *nomos* is sharpened in the ministry of Jesus.[28] But the continuity is not altogether inverse. Perhaps that is the point to the law-gospel dialectic's order. It is the question about God that gives rise to the quest for God. However sinful we may be, it remains true, as Luther said, that God did not make heaven for geese.[29]

THE LEGITIMATION AND
LIMITATION OF THE KNOWLEDGE OF GOD

We have spoken of God's active will to reveal himself. This is the foundation for Christian claims to know God. God's activity does in principle legitimate such human claims. The genitive in the phrase "the knowledge of God" is objective; it is human beings who know God. Therefore Christian talk on this theme should avoid such easy disjunctions as "divine disclosure, not human discovery." Rather, is it the case that because God discloses, humans do discover.

This understanding of the situation of knowing is appropriate to the content claimed to be known concerning a categorically supreme will seeking a relationship of trust and obedience with finite freedom. We have spoken of God as the world's ground and the world's goal, as the one answering the human question and the human quest. Those metaphors do just that: they answer. What Christians say about God represents a response to human reality, a word that supports and receives human striving. In turn it is fitting that when Christians reflect on *how* it is *that* they know *what* they know, an affirmation of the human is heard. Revelation, address, word—and so knowledge— fit a God who creates and woos freedom.

In this understanding, knowledge is affirmed but is not absolutized. Along with legitimation there is limitation. Once again the order of knowing reflects the order of being. We are speaking of the being and becoming, of the relationship between God and the human person. Let us begin with ourselves and ask the counterquestion: What view of the human would undercut the assertion of a revelation by God to humankind? Abraham Heschel has pointed out that two anthropological conceptions have militated against the notion of revelation: "One maintained that man was too great to be in need of divine guidance, and the other maintained that man was too small to be worthy of divine guidance. The first conception came from social science, and the second from natural science."[30] The human person, on the Christian view, is one for whom revelation is "right."

The conception of God and of humankind also qualifies the conception of revelation/knowledge which it has introduced. We have already spoken of certain limits to human knowledge of God which divine revelation entails. Some of those limits derive from human finitude over against the categorically supreme. In this relationship the persons are not ontological equals.[31] We have sought to cast this divine transcendence in dynamic and relational terms. God is one; we are not. God's will is sure; our wills are not. God's becoming is not subject to contingency in the way that ours is. Christian thinkers have struggled to express the notion of transcendence in relationship.[32]

To finitude must be added sin and its effect on the human capacity to know God. We have already argued that faith in the categorically supreme God entails the confidence that God can accomplish revelation. This applies to both *logos* and *kairos*, in differing measure perhaps. Nonetheless, the sin which turns us in on ourselves does impede God's revelation. Perhaps it cannot destroy revelation, but it does seem to distort it. Here it would be difficult to disentangle the factors. How are ignorance and defiance related? When is ignorance culpable?

One of the ways in which human sin may distort divine revelation is precisely in reading the relationship between the knowledge of God given in *logos* and the knowledge of God given in *kairos*. In what sense is God hidden? One may think of God as hidden apart from the kairotic word. But one may also think of God as hidden *in* the kairotic word, which speaks of God's "opposite," of suffering and death. While both sin and finitude may contribute to a certain element of distortion euphemistically hiding under "hiddenness," it is particularly instructive to consider the relationship between the two kinds. Thus one may well suppose that an original misreading of *logos* contributed to the identification of suffering as "opposite" to God. Conversely, appropriate confidence in the kairotic word may mistakenly lead one to diminish God's revelation as *logos*, classifying it simply as ignorance. Perhaps Luther's thought runs this risk. Or, worse yet, one may suppose that kairotic advance can be won only at the price of actual opposition between *kairos* and *logos*. Brian Gerrish worries about this tendency in Calvin: "Perhaps Calvin went further than Luther toward a resolution of the theoretical problem of the 'two wills,' although at the fearful cost of reducing the universal benevolence of the revealed will to a mere appearance."[33]

It seems better to follow Luther's insistence that predestination is intended as gospel for the anguished conscience. That God is for us already as *logos* is not to deny that in the mystery of freedom sin can be against God and as such real for God. A will is a living reality that can be sure and yet know struggle and advance. In *kairos*, God's rule also over sin is shown. That kairotic word does not merely confirm the creative logos. Yet part of its decisive advance may precisely be to correct our distorted reading of *logos*.

How, then, is our knowledge of God here both legitimated and limited? For the most part Christians have legitimated faith's content, the "faith that is believed," but have not sought to claim a direct relationship for faith's passion, the "faith that believes." In faith, God's will and work are known, but God is not possessed. Claims for infallible teaching seem to stretch this legitimation beyond the breaking point; though it is encouraging to note the economy that characterizes the identification of such infallible pronouncements.[34]

But what may be said of the act of knowing that takes place in faith, of the "faith that believes"? Clearly here the limitation applies. This was made clear when the church rejected the gnostic heresy that makes gnosis itself perfect redemption.[35] This limitation corresponds with the fact that knowledge is not the height of the human condition, since it merely though significantly "raises the bid." So pagans also know of God, Luther noted, and Kierkegaard reluctantly raised his voice against Socrates, since sin lies not in the understanding but in the will.[36]

Yet legitimation applies as well. Just as some knowledge of God is given in the call of God to salvation, so there is knowing of God in the relationship of faith. The distortions represented by gnosticism and mysticism do not invalidate this truth.

What, then, of the condition of knowing, however limited the significance? In what sense is the finite "capable" of the infinite, or even the infinite of the finite? What account may be given of the condition of knowing God? How far is an epistemology of the knowledge of God possible? We must next consider what may be legitimately said of this matter.

NOTES

1. I have in mind that awesome spectrum running from Hans Vaihinger, *The Philosophy of "As If," a System of the Theoretical, Practical, and Religious Fictions of Mankind* (London: Routledge & Kegan Paul, 1965), through R. B. Braithwaite, *An Empiricist's View of the Nature of Religious Belief* (Cambridge: At the University Press, 1965), to the "positive thinking seminars" held in sports stadiums.

2. Charles Hartshorne and William L. Reese, eds., *Philosophers Speak of God* (Chicago: University of Chicago Press, 1953), p. 7.

3. That insistence may be found in Barth's handling of the doctrine of the Trinity in the terms of revealer, revelation, and revealedness, in Pannenberg's theme of the prolepsis in Jesus of the absolute future, and in process thought's attempt to understand God within the metaphysics of creativity. It is not, however, universal; a prominent exception would be Tillich's preference for "being-itself" as a term descriptive of God, despite the dynamic aspects present in his own analysis of the ontological polarities.

4. Cf. Walther Eichrodt, *Theology of the Old Testament*, trans. J. A. Baker, 2 vols. (Philadelphia: Westminster Press, 1961–67); Samuel Terrien, *The Elusive Presence: Toward a New Biblical Theology* (New York: Harper & Row, 1978).

5. Paul C. Empie, T. Austin Murphy, and Joseph A. Burgess, eds., *Teaching Authority and Infallibility in the Church: Lutherans and Catholics in Dialogue VI*, "Common Statement" (Minneapolis: Augsburg Publishing House, 1980), p. 15.

6. Wolfhart Pannenberg, *Basic Questions in Theology*, vol. 2, trans. George H. Kehm (Philadelphia: Fortress Press, 1971), p. 30.

7. Perhaps Kierkegaard's most thoroughgoing statement of this point is *The Concluding Unscientific Postscript to the Philosophical Fragments*, trans. David F. Swenson and Walter Lowrie (Princeton: Princeton University Press, 1944), where the dialectical is discerned in appeals to the Holy Scriptures, the church, and "the proof of the centuries."

8. One thinks of Luther's theses for the Heidelberg Disputation. See B. A. Gerrish, "To the Unknown God: Luther and Calvin on the Hiddenness of God," *JR* 53 (July 1973): 263–93.

9. Langdon Gilkey, *Message and Existence: An Introduction to Christian Theology* (New York: Seabury Press, 1979), p. 84. For a fuller discussion see his *Maker of Heaven and Earth* (Garden City, N.Y.: Doubleday & Co., 1959).

10. Paul Tillich, *Systematic Theology*, 3 vols. (Chicago: University of Chicago Press, 1951–63), 1:252–71.

11. See B. A. Gerrish, *Grace and Reason* (Oxford: At the Clarendon Press, 1962); and Roland Zimany, "Enduring Values of Luther's Approach to Knowing God," *LuthQ* 27 (Fall 1975): 6–26.

12. Edward A. Dowey, Jr., *The Knowledge of God in Calvin's Theology* (New York: Columbia University Press, 1952), pp. 50–56, distinguishes this sense from a special organ or faculty of soul, from the formality of a "religious a priori," and from the products of ratiocination (as Calvin grants in his notion of *semen divinitatis*). He speaks of it as an "intensely numinous awareness" and links it with the universality of religion, the servile fear of God, and the troubled conscience.

13. See John Ferguson, "The Achievement of Clement of Alexandria," *RelSt* 12 (1976): 59–80. Jaroslav Pelikan in *The Emergence of the Catholic Tradition (100-600)* (Chicago: University of Chicago Press, 1971), p. 32, notes: "Tertullian's explanation of the presence of noble and good elements in paganism employed the idea of natural law rather than that of seminal Logos. For him these elements included knowledge of the existence, the goodness, and the justice of God, but especially the moral precepts flowing from that knowledge."

14. Claus Westermann, *Creation*, trans. John J. Scullion (Philadelphia: Fortress Press, 1974), pp. 90–91, relates and distinguishes taboo (prepersonal), command (personal), and law (postpersonal). But the intent of command would seem to apply here: "The command therefore opens up the possibility of a relationship to him who commands. . . . Something is entrusted to man in the command. The command introduces him to freedom. . . ."

15. Cf. John Hick, *Evil and the God of Love* (New York: Harper & Row; London: Macmillan & Co., 1966), p. 317, on "epistemic distance."

16. Regin Prenter, *Creation and Redemption*, trans. Theodore I. Jensen (Philadelphia: Fortress Press, 1967), p. 207.

17. Pannenberg, *Basic Questions*, 2:44.

18. Quoting John Dillenberger's edition of *The Bondage of the Will*, in *Martin Luther: Selections from His Writings* (Garden City, N.Y.: Doubleday & Co., 1961), p. 202.

19. See A. D. Nock, *Conversion* (Oxford: At the Clarendon Press, 1933), chap. 11.

20. E. Gilson, *History of Christian Philosophy in the Middle Ages* (New York: Random House, 1955), pp. 325–79.

21. Ibid., p. 129.

22. I take this phrase from the subtitle of Matthew Tindal's *Christianity as Old as Creation* (London, 1732). Other such authors are John Toland and Thomas Chubb.

23. Friedrich Schleiermacher, *The Christian Faith*, trans. and ed. H. R. Mackintosh and J. S. Stewart (New York: Harper & Row, Harper Torchbooks, 1963), par. 100. For a general discussion of these tendencies in recent thought, see my *Contemporary Forms of Faith* (Minneapolis: Augsburg Publishing House, 1967), chaps. 4, 5.

24. Gilson, *History*, pp. 454–539.

25. R. A. Norris, Jr., *God and World in Early Christian Theology* (New York: Seabury Press, 1965), chap. 4.

26. The sources in Kierkegaard are *Philosophical Fragments* and the *Postscript*. It is this theme in Kierkegaard that Gordon Kaufman takes as the key for his *Systematic Theology: A Historicist Perspective* (New York: Charles Scribner's Sons, 1968).

27. François Wendel, *Calvin: The Origins and Development of His Religious Thought*, trans. Philip Mairet (New York: Harper & Row, 1950), p. 165.

28. Gustaf Wingren, *Creation and Law*, trans. Ross Mackenzie (Philadelphia: Fortress [Muhlenberg] Press, 1961), pp. 42–43.

29. Luther, *Bondage of the Will*, Dillenberger ed., p. 188.

30. Abraham J. Heschel, *God in Search of Man: A Philosophy of Judaism* (New York: Farrar, Straus & Cudahy, 1955), p. 169.

31. Michael Polanyi even broadens this question to ask of the nature of scientific knowledge in particular in *Personal Knowledge: Towards a Post-Critical Philosophy* (Chicago: University of Chicago Press, 1958).

32. G. L. Prestige, *God in Patristic Thought* (London: SPCK, 1964), pp. 25, 57.

33. Gerrish, "To the Unknown God," p. 285.

34. Thus "Roman Catholic Reflections," in *Lutherans and Catholics in Dialogue VI*, p. 52, note three undoubted instances in which infallibility has been invoked: the conciliar dogma of papal infallibility itself (1870) and the two papal dogmas of the Immaculate Conception (1854) and the Assumption (1950).

35. R. M. Grant, *Gnosticism and Early Christianity*, 2d ed. (New York: Columbia University Press, 1966).

36. Walther von Loewenich, *Luther's Theology of the Cross*, trans. H. Bouman (Minneapolis: Augsburg Publishing House, 1976), p. 48, argues against T. Harnack and Seeberg that Luther's theology of the cross is the native soil of his concept of the hidden God. For an anthropological limitation, see Kierkegaard's *The Sickness unto Death*, trans. W. Lowrie (Princeton: Princeton University Press, 1941).

2

The Reception and
Recognition of Revelation

Human beings know the categorically supreme God in the purposive
receiving of the world as the self is created and claimed. In knowing
God as ground and goal, it is the one will for human good that
is known. While the human experience of this knowing varies
significantly, there is given here the reality and commonality needed
for intelligible speech about God.

THE EXPERIENCE OF
WORLD, SELF, AND GOD

The concern of this chapter is to discuss the state of knowing God. Wherever
God is known, *how* is he known? Our task is confessional: it is to overhear,
albeit somewhat analytically, Christians speaking of their knowledge of God.
It is not essentially apologetic. We are not trying to persuade non-Christians
that they can or do know God.

If knowing God is truly a human act, the accounts of it will likely reflect
the diversity that characterizes us. We may begin with a famous passage from
Paul Tillich in which he points to one such apparently basic difference:

> One can distinguish two ways of approaching God: the way of overcoming
> estrangement and the way of meeting a stranger. In the first way man discovers
> *himself* when he discovers God; he discovers something that is identical with
> himself although it transcends him infinitely, something from which he is
> estranged, but from which he never has been and never can be separated. In
> the second way man meets a *stranger* when he meets God. The meeting is acci-
> dental. Essentially they do not belong to each other. They may become friends
> on a tentative and conjectural basis. But there is no certainty about the stranger
> man has met. He may disappear, and only *probable* statements can be made
> about his nature.[1]

It is clear, in this instance at least, that when one overhears Christians speaking
about knowing God, one hears talk of the God whom they know. That is

fortunate, and it would be a mistake to try to develop the discussion in this chapter apart from content claimed to be known about God. Again our work is shown to be reflective. But when one attends to the difference to which Tillich points, one suspects that it is human diversity with which one is occupied. Or at least it is clear that a Christian is called to consider how varying human accounts of knowing God, as they develop within the church catholic, may in truth speak of the same God.

In any case the difference is there. The names of Augustine and Aquinas leap to mind as one reads Tillich's sentences. Tillich set his stage in the thirteenth century, when the roles were well defined. Let us examine first the second and less favored of Tillich's options: the cosmological approach. Thomas Aquinas, as Tillich says, rejected claims to immediate knowledge of God. We do not know God as one with the knowing self, for in knowing a human concept or a human drive, we do not yet have God. Moreover the ideal reality of concepts must not be confused with extraideal reality. Statements about extraideal reality must be derived from sense-experience. Here the Aristotelian heritage is clear.[2] But given divine effects, we can reason to God.

Bonaventura, on the other hand, held that "God is most truly present to the very soul and immediately knowable; He is knowable in Himself without media as the one which is common to all. For He is the principle of knowledge, the first truth, in the light of which everything else is known."[3] God's image in our soul is the midpoint in the ascent from the visible world to the mystical knowledge of God. In this ontological approach one does sense a kinship to Plato's sustaining unity of being in which, even though the natural mind does not possess vision, a sudden illumination may overwhelm the self from its own depth. Just as the sun, supremely visible in its own right, renders other things visible to the eye, so the Good, supremely intelligible in itself, renders the other forms intelligible to the mind. This analogy had a long future ahead of it.[4]

So there does seem to be a difference between the two traditions to which Tillich points, the empiricist and the illuminationist. Leaving aside for the moment the matter of the knowledge of God available in special revelation, it becomes clear that we must move with care in describing this difference. One familiar characterization employs the contrast between faith and reason, as far as priority in knowing is concerned. If we use the word "reason" to refer to reflection on a publicly accessible reality, then the Thomistic approach stresses reason, to be sure. On the other hand, what could be more public than the bare logic of the notion of perfection, which the ontologically superior being authorizes in the Anselmian version of the Augustinian tradition? We seem in either case to say that knowledge of God is readily available, though the means are different.

One wonders how dominant even this difference is, once one considers the actual history of theological reflection. Can the data be organized by the familiar appeal to Plato versus Aristotle? It is true that in both the *Summa Theologica* and the *Contra Gentiles*, Thomas places great stress on the Aristotelian "prime mover," which provides an unchangeable "pure act." But Thomas knows that Aristotle's prime mover is not the *efficient* cause of anything (*Metaphysics*, xii,1072,a and b). Aquinas in fact appeals to other arguments, indeed to other sources. Thus he argues from degrees of being to a highest being, as Anselm does, and appeals with John of Damascus to the governance of the world.[5] Moreover, his empiricism is checked otherwise by an aprioristic element, in that knowledge occurs as principles present in the intellect are applied to the data of experience. When Thomas repeatedly says, "And this all understand to be God," the point is that the arguments help us find the God we already have.[6]

It is not far to the appeal to supernatural truths of faith which step into place of the natural principles of knowledge (*Summa Theologica*, i,12,5). So too the Augustinian-Anselmian tradition appeals to both faith and reason. While Augustine is not prepared to begin otherwise than with faith, the most significant ground for that insistence is not the reality of the inner self's quest, but the historical actuality of the divine response in the raw particularity of Jesus. Moreover, there is movement here toward intelligibility precisely as the things of God become clearer through the employment of human knowledge and experience. Augustine is no fideist; understanding is affirmed. The human hearing of the word occurs by the mind, not by the body (*City of God*, xi,2). Thus, true to their master, the Augustinians always resented the Thomistic notion of the soul as the form of the body, because it entailed an empirical intellectualism, eliminating the illumining supplement which was to be affirmed even in natural cognition. Nevertheless, similitudes drawn from human experience are helpful to the mind, as is clearly illustrated by Augustine's sustained evocation of the several trinities of the human soul as intelligible likenesses of the triune God.

Thus we find significant unity in classic Christian accounts of the knowledge of God. In both streams which Tillich identifies, there is a strong sense that the God known is—knowledge notwithstanding—transcendent. Hence both traditions emphasize negation, if not estrangement, in the knowing of God. The *via negativa* is suggested early, in the works of Clement of Alexandria and Origen. The issue is first focused directly, however, in the controversy between the Cappadocians and Eunomius. To Eunomius' assertion, "I know God as God knows himself," the Cappadocians replied that God is fundamentally incomprehensible and that all human knowledge of God is remotely analogical. In the East this led to the development of a highly apophatic theology, which served a Christianized Plotinean mysticism. In the West Aquinas also used Plotinus' threefold method of negation, analogy, and eminence—but with more pronounced noetic concerns.[7]

Perhaps, then, Gilson is right in arguing that the East and the West do not differ because the East was more Platonic but because the West from Augustine on was concerned for the relationship of nature to grace, while the East was concerned for the relationship of the image of God to the process of deification.[8] In turn this theological difference yields, on the Western side, a still deeper epistemological divide, when we introduce the distinctive emphases of Reformation thought. In the theocentric stress of the Reformation, there is a tendency to juxtapose faith either to experience as universally accessible as one's own self or to the shared experience of a world. Given human obduracy, the knowledge of God must be God's doing. Writing in this tradition, Helmut Thielicke says:

> God's true presence, then, is to be sought in the incarnate Word, in the manifestation of Jesus Christ. Here is the mirror of the fatherly heart (Luther) and hence the Father himself. Even under the cover of the cross, even in the alien form of the suffering, death, and lowliness of the Son of God, even under apparent concealment, God is present in the directness of his form as the Word. For the lowliness of this manifestation is the form of his self-emptying love. This is his very nature. It is God himself.[9]

Is this really a *third* view? Is faith—or even God—to take its place alongside world and self in our sketch? Is fideism to be placed in a list of epistemological options? It is apparent that any answer cannot be an unqualified one. Just as the other two views intermingle historically and conceptually, the Reformation emphasis retains some of their elements. One might well argue that its strong emphasis on the historical revelation in Jesus is more Aristotelian than Platonic, at least in the sense that when one is looking outside the self one is facing in the right direction. Similarly, Luther placed great stress on those "visible words," the sacraments. Indeed an argument has been made that Luther follows Aquinas' course of correction of Aristotle, by which revealed truths both check any simple empiricism and replace Platonic apriorism.[10]

Yet sharp differences remain between Luther and Aquinas. For Luther, the knowledge of God given in Jesus is not a particular item of doctrine, which supplements a general knowledge of God, but is the beginning of all true knowledge. This is fundamentally a theological difference. It is linked with a philosophical difference in that Luther represents the nominalist rejection of realism's structure of necessary essences.

Nominalism's purpose was to show the deficiencies of the natural knowledge of God.[11] The notion of will came to be crucial. Nothing that depends on the free decision of an absolutely free God is philosophically deducible. Both the Thomistic *analogia entis* and the Anselmian *necessitas* are eliminated. Reason is reduced to probabilities, not simply in the encounter with empirical reality—as Thomas would readily grant—but in the process of inference from such particulars.

When God cannot reliably be known metaphysically, revelation takes on crucial importance. Nominalism lifted up the historical particularity affirmed also in the other traditions. There seems to be the more reason for this in Luther; and the reason is theological, even anthropological, rather than merely metaphysical. After all, on issues of nature and grace Luther stood even further from nominalism than he did from Thomism. Thomas, at least, granted that no person could turn to God unless God turned to that person first and offered assisting grace. In nominalist thought, on the other hand, a person without God's aid can perform works worthy of merit.[12] Luther reached back behind both realism and nominalism to the anti-Pelagian side of Augustine.

We are in effect asking what epistemological theory is to be associated with the view that opposes *logos* and *kairos*. Both the empiricist and the illuminationist traditions can be viewed as translations into epistemology of the view that *logos* and *kairos* supplement each other. Does Luther have a distinct epistemology, derived from the stress on historical revelation?[13] One can argue that on epistemological issues, as often otherwise, the reformers stand with Augustine. John Smith has written of the appeal to experience in the work of Luther and Calvin:

> The appeal to experience meant a *trying out*, an actual attempt to live through the cycle of contrition and penance, so that each could truthfully say, "the traditional way of understanding justification before God has been *tried* and found wanting." The important point is that, while all experience must remain subject to the interpreting word, it nevertheless exercises a *critical* function, since the individual makes a discovery for himself.[14]

Thus Luther could declare that "only experience makes a theologian," and Calvin made a determined appeal to the inner witness of the Holy Spirit, both in service of the revelation in history.[15]

Yet it must be said that Augustine's sense for the unity of being—which remains in restless tension with his writing on sin and grace and which informs *his* appeal to experience—is missing in the reformers. Thus in them the explicit theological stress on history stands out the more. While there may be in the reformers an appeal to experience as against late medieval Aristotelianism's analytical detachment, there is not a developed cosmological or metaphysical position that could prevent Protestantism from being regarded as, and indeed from becoming, merely "subjective." When that danger threatened in "enthusiasm," the mainstream figures became understandably restive. The opposite danger then threatened: new scholasticism. This

217

epistemological vacillation seems to suggest that the striking directness of the historical appeal requires some fuller conceptual framework if its gains are not to be lost.

Christian thought has faced many of the same pressures in the modern period. Would Christianity be best linked with the line from Descartes through Leibniz and Spinoza, with its emphasis on the self and the *a priori* knowledge available to the self? Or would empiricism in the British tradition be a resource with which the faith could make alliance? How shall one identify and appraise such influential appeals as that made by Schleiermacher to the consciousness of absolute dependence, or by Kant to moral experience? These appeals do seem reminiscent of the Platonic turn within, and suggest the difficulty facing any attempt to reclaim a shared world of experience once reductionistic empiricism has swept it clean of spirits, divine or human. But is there a genuine third way? Is God to be known apart from self and world?

We shall address some of these issues when the context of the knowledge of God is discussed. Our contention will be that we must claim a knowledge of God "in, with, and under" the knowledge of self and world. Regrettably, contemporary thought seems to represent the dynamic of diastasis, by which the realities of the self and the world are so pulled apart in perception that one is nearly persuaded that God can slip through the chasm unscathed and indeed unclothed. We need to think of self and world together in such a way that the God who is truly other than either can be understood to be known without requiring the repudiation of self and/or world, as if their presence and service in the knowing of God were a threat.

In Chapter 1, speaking of God as the world's ground, we spoke of the giving of the past, the creating of freedom, the lure to the future. Without relationships a person is not a self. As the temporal passage is gathered into the focus of the self, a world is given to the self. God is at work in that. As the reality of a world is gathered to be given, a self comes to be, a fresh synthesis of necessity and possibility held together in freedom.[16] And God is at work in that.

We can transgress no further on the anthropological *loci*; but it does seem that, having said only this much, it is already apparent how the differences chronicled in this section come about. Some Christians attend particularly to the giving of the world, others to the fresh coming-to-be of selfhood. As the categorically superior one, God is at work in precisely their connection. Both the empiricist and the illuminationist emphases have a place, it would seem. Also, the more specific approaches can be understood to develop aspects of God's reality as ground. The gift of the world, a cosmological association, is received as bearing purpose, a teleological association. God does act; God does will. That purpose bears in on the self with its claim, a moral association. The differences are fitting, and the commonality is no less so, for the God who does all this is eminently one.

And the "ontological" approach? Perhaps it not only suggests the creation of selfhood, but the reality of categorical supremacy which underlies all the approaches. In a sense, then, it does abstract from specific associations, as if it were indeed an argument or approach from concept alone. But if matters are as we have portrayed them, it is not strange that this most rationalistic of approaches at the same time keeps company with mysticism. Perhaps Tillich is right, after all, that *"Deus est esse*, and the certainty of God is identical with the certainty of Being itself: God is the presupposition of the question of God."[17] This is, it must be affirmed, an existential presupposition and not merely an activity alluring to people with a penchant for abstractions.

The kairotic knowledge of *telos*, while bearing priority, does fit within this framework. I have argued that how we know depends on what we know. Inasmuch as this Jesus reveals to us none other than God, the ground and goal of the world, our knowing that fact must at least cohere with the patterns applying in the knowledge of God as Logos. Our discussion has distinguished strands stressing world and self. The claim to know God in this Jesus does essentially involve that which is neither God nor the self; but in this knowing the self understands its world and indeed itself in a way that is decisively new. One must come to hear from without the story of this one from Galilee. In that sense at least it is a "worldly" story. But one may well say more. A God who wills so to be known will be at work within the hearer to make the occasioning word an enabling word, even an efficacious one. It is to be hoped that the theologians who have worked so hard to make clear the decisive newness of the historical word of revelation will apply themselves to showing how that word becomes concretely decisive by being known in relation to self and world.

We turn now to a specific part of that task. If what has been said in this section is true, then we must face the question of the cognitive status of our knowledge. If God is known, then the intelligibility and truthfulness of the claims made about God need to be discussed and even defended. However much it may be God who reveals, it is we who know; and we must give account of what it is so to know as to speak as we do.

KNOWLEDGE AS PARADIGM, PARABLE, AND PROPHECY

Our task is to reflect on the cognitive claims involved in the knowledge of God. The question is not what they are but of what sort they are. How is language being used when Christians speak of God? We ask about *Christian* speech; therefore again in this section our discussion must be conducted precisely in the light of what the faith says of God. If God is as the faith declares, how does language work in this instance? But, of course, it is *our* language and *our* meaning and speaking, so we need to ask as well how such God-talk finds a place within the range of human speech-acts. How is it like and how is it unlike other uses of language?

Obviously the discussion of this topic in our time will reflect the concerns raised by the philosophers of language. We cannot avoid the familiar issues raised about the meaningfulness of religious language by the likes of Alfred Jules Ayer and Anthony Flew. A brief review may be in order. Crucial in this regard was insistence on the criterion of verifiability to test the genuineness of apparent statements of fact. In Ayer's words, "We say that a sentence is factually significant to any given person, if, and only if, he knows how to verify the proposition which it purports to express—that is, if he knows what observations would lead him, under certain conditions, to accept the proposition as being true, or reject it as being false."[18] Metaphysical statements were found by this criterion to be "pseudo-propositions," since one could not conceive of an observation which would verify or falsify such statements. Claims about the existence of a transcendent god or an immortal soul were stripped of literal significance because of their metaphysical involvement. Flew shifted the issue to that of falsifiability, and voiced his skepticism in these terms: "Now it often seems to people who are not religious as if there was no conceivable event or series of events the occurrence of which would be admitted by sophisticated religious people to be a sufficient reason for conceding 'there wasn't a God after all' or 'God does not really love us then. . . . '"[19] He went on to speak of religious assertions' death "by a thousand qualifications."

How shall one respond to this challenge? On balance, if offered a multiple-choice question concerning the nature of their statements, Christians would have to pass by "analytic or definitional" and "emotive" and select "synthetic" or "empirical" in *some* sense. While Christians make statements of different logical types, the game is up unless among those types is speech about real states of affairs. We have just been speaking of the *experience* of revelation in world, self, and God. "God is the world's ground and goal" belongs with "There is a tiger in this room" (to take a notorious example), more than with mathematical formulae or moans and groans.

Is the Christian then subjected to the tyranny of the verification principle? Already at the early stage of the discussion two points were clear: that it would not do to say that Christian claims were empirical yet nonfalsifiable in principle, and yet that the standards of verification/falsification by sense perception left Christian theologians puzzled about how even to formulate the conditions for meeting the challenge. Of course it soon became evident that those standards tended to undercut the verification principle itself, as Ayer seemed to acknowledge already in the second edition of *Language, Truth, and Logic*. Christian theologians were then tempted to take comfort in the afflictions of the enemy, and to mask their own difficulties by appealing to faith, as when Basil Mitchell wrote: "So the theologian *does* recognize the fact of pain as counting against Christian doctrine. But it is true that he will not allow it—or anything—to count decisively against it; for he is committed by his faith to trust in God."[20] Such papering over the problem could not settle the matter for long.

There followed the enthusiastic discovery of the later Wittgenstein with his fine sense for the concreteness and specificity of particular language usages. One may even wonder whether the theologians did not invent rather than discover the master, for the alacrity and even abandon with which apologists pleaded the distinctiveness of the religious "language game" was impressive. At the very least, insufficient attention was given to formulating the distinctive rules (but rules nonetheless) which were to be understood to apply in this game—not to mention engaging in discussion of how this game was related to other games, why anyone would want to play this game, and the like.

Where is the discussion now? A major movement attaches itself to the category of "paradigm," rejecting the positivist model of scientific understanding. We are thinking of such writers as Thomas Kuhn, N. R. Hanson, and Stephen Toulmin. Briefly, this movement has argued that there are large-scale models, assumed in every era of science, and that these are never able to be verified because it is in terms of them that verification is carried out. The practice of science refutes the positivist model of scientific thinking. Moreover, the history of science shows that there is a class of propositions which are not capable of verification but are clearly meaningful—and meaningful in a nontrivial and nonpathological sense.[21]

It is understandable that this view has won many adherents. Yet the points cited in its favor actually count against it, not least because they reveal that the view does not accommodate the historical reality of the Christian religion. The view seems to take us beyond the verification/falsification disputes; issues of theodicy become mere methodological anomalies.[22] Commitment can be described as inheritance. But the history of the Christian church contains arguments *for* God, not merely from God. Christians and adherents of other religions do in fact converse with each other and change their views. True, we speak of "conversion" in such a case, but the change does not take place without attending to the data. Formal criteria—simplicity, scope, coherence, and the like—are not sufficient in such matters. Christians claim something about the world, about the self—indeed, about God.

There is the rub: the Christian faith is about God. The solution in terms of "paradigms" suggests that religious statements be treated not as statements about particulars but as statements functioning at the level of theoretical entities in complex, multileveled systems. Patrick Sherry puts the point in these terms:

Now the comparison between theology and theoretical concepts or explanations
in science is trying to meet these problems, by suggesting that a system of religious
belief is like a scientific theory in that it only needs to "touch down" at some
points in our experience (though unlike it in that we do not seek to test religious
beliefs through experiments).[23]

But surely it is crucial that the faith touches down by reference to alleged
states of affairs in reality in such a way that control is exercised in the process
of stating the faith. While difficulties abound in identifying those states, the
debate is about the data, not merely about how best to organize the data
conceptually. Data and theory must be held together. Christians speak their
language not because, or not merely because, it serves well to organize the
state of affairs in which they find themselves, but because they consider it
to be the truest account of what is there to be confronted by any inquirer.
They might well find themselves more naturally linked with those philosophers
of science who suggest that while all data are theory-laden, rival theories are
not incommensurable as if walled off from each other. Such contend that
while comprehensive theories are highly resistant to falsification, observation
does exert control over theory construction and maintenance.[24]

The faith, then, would seem to suggest that in principle questions of verification and falsification are appropriate to it. Obviously recent understanding
of how to proceed in arbitrating these questions coheres more easily with the
empiricist tradition of theology than with the illuminationist. Perhaps that
understanding works better with certain types of statements. One might, for
example, specify with Sherry three categories of statements: first, those about
the unique (miracles, prophets and their statements, events in the lives of
believers), second, those about the recurrent (the beauty of nature, love and
holiness, stages of human life), and third, those about the world as a whole
(the universe as such, being as such).[25] Sherry suggests that Christian speech's
difficulties are with the first and the third categories of statement and the
relationships between them.

Comment is possible, even with the so far minimal sketch of content. To
start with the last point, Christians do speak about the whole. But it is important to note that what is said is not that God is the whole, but that God
works in the whole, that God is the ground and goal of the whole. That is,
Christian talk is discriminate talk about the whole: the world is not God,
though it is *by*—and for—God; we are not God, though we are *for*—and
by—God; most emphatically, sin is not God's doing, though it is *against* God.
Everything has to do with God; we do talk of the whole in that sense.

Clearly Christians talk as well about a unique person and event, and assign
epistemic priority to that talk. Speech about the unique is difficult enough,
but here we are called on to speak of this one precisely in relation to the whole.
This is *kairos*, but it is the *kairos* of the *logos*. Perhaps we may catch up this

connection with the term "parable." In such a way Austin Farrer says: "If Christ is called Word or Logos, it is not meant that he is the lucid instance of general ideas, but that he is the self-enacted human parable of Godhead."[26] Above all we must recall that in a unique and normative way we are linking this particular one with the one who is categorically supreme. *That* is the infamous "scandal of particularity." That is what lies behind appeals to an analogy of proportionality which includes negation—"As a father pities his children, so the Lord pities those who fear him" (Ps. 103:13).[27] Perhaps this is why some Christians speak of the *kairos* "sub contrario" as reflecting back even on the cognitive status of statements made about God.[28] Such talk does seem very fuzzy and soft—almost in principle, as it were. But there is a cognitive claim here. As Robert King puts it, "The story of Jesus has become for Christians the master-image by which God's action is identified. This master-image functions in at least two ways: it focuses the action of God in relation to man, and it particularizes God's intention for man."[29] King's statement is helpful, though it may still understate the reality of the new in the historical particularity of Jesus.

We have at best barely managed to hold the cry for verification at bay. What may we say of this? It may be possible by the art of imaginative generalization to formulate meaningful propositions about the whole, which have a significant empirical anchorage.[30] Of course, if the one at work in the whole is categorically supreme, if God works precisely in giving a world that is creative of self, then ordinary ostensive reference will fail. There will be an indirectness, a "parabolic" character to the data which can be introduced.

We have neglected to mention another major impediment facing an attempt to respond to the verification challenge. How shall one verify empirical claims about the *whole*, given the "open texture" character of reality? How shall we know about the truth of such claims, *in medias res*? Does this make the matter of verification an essentially eschatological matter, as people as different as John Hick and Wolfhart Pannenberg have suggested?[31] We think not, though we have of course already alluded to the Christian recognition that only "then" will we see "face to face."

We appropriate the multisignificance of the word "prophecy" to address this issue. The prophets were at once "forth-tellers" and "fore-tellers"; that point is not really in dispute. What we underline, however, is that they could be both precisely because of the character of the God whose word came to them. It is precisely the prophets with whom we associate a so-called "moral" interpretation of holiness, as distinguished from a ritualistic view. It is clear what God will do, because it is clear what God is doing. In the parable of God we have the prophecy of God. Christians can attend to the developing reality of the whole in the light of the parable of God.

This is why Christians speak of the *living* character of the word of God.

Luther, for example, spoke of the church as a "mouth house," rather than a "book house," and the Reformation tradition speaks of how the Scriptures *function*, of what they *do* to the hearer. This seems to fit with such approaches to language as Wittgenstein's emphasis on *use* and Austin's stress on the performative character of speech. If this faith claim is true, if the whole is a developing reality, it is not strange that such a fundamental matter as language reveals that characteristic.

Where, then, does that leave us, in the unfriendly present, in understanding the cognitive status of the statements we make concerning God? We list a series of points.

First. We should claim no more than what fits the relationship between two free and personal wills. Philosophers have worked hard—perhaps too hard, reflecting excessively dualistic premises—to explain how we know that other minds exist. Some ambiguity is appropriate and perhaps even inevitable in such a matter. We are in contact, sharing a common world; but we do not inhabit each other as centered selves. As we join together in common cause, we seem to know the other more significantly as we know the other's will. But significant clarity is possible for the message's intention without commitment in advance. Obviously there may be nuances in a lived relationship of trust which are not available apart from the relationship.[32]

Second. The faith declares that the will and activity of God are essentially clear. Moreover, they are true, for reality will come to correspond to them. The prophetic word will prove true. It *is* proving true. The kingdom grows now, albeit secretly.

Third. Given the emphasis on time and the developing reality of God's intention, it is helpful to speak in terms of the "story" character of reality, and our language may appropriately reflect that character. This, of course, does not compromise the truth claims involved. In particular, it does not diminish the importance of affirmation of, and critical study into, the historical event which created the story the Scriptures tell.

Fourth. Given the constancy of God, the Christian is not a Lone Ranger on some frontier of spirituality. We find ourselves together in the faith; we write confessions and subscribe to them, though we may hesitate when infallibility is claimed for such statements.[33]

Fifth. The direction in which God is working is clear. God is *for* us; and the promise is that what God intends in creation and has made sure and clear in Jesus will come to pass.

Sixth. Given the continuity of God's creative-redemptive intention for us, faith fulfills the structure of human personhood, while transcending it; it does not destroy it.[34] While it is notoriously difficult to attach specific empirical reference to such a phrase as "true personhood," it is clear that plastic smiles do not adorn the altar of God.

So we claim to know God in the giving of world creative of self. We claim to have more than a paradigm; we confess a parable and claim a prophecy. It remains to be seen how wisely and how well such knowing may be said to occur in the reality of the human context.

NOTES

1. Paul Tillich, *Theology of Culture*, ed. Robert C. Kimball (New York: Oxford University Press, 1959), p. 10. (Italics his.)

2. Gustave Weigel and Arthur Madden in *Religion and the Knowledge of God* (Englewood Cliffs, N.J.: Prentice-Hall, 1961), pp. 123–24, apply this position in Aquinas' rejection in *Contra Gentiles* of Anselm's argument for the immediate knowledge of the existence of God: "Even if we wish to define God as the being than which nothing greater can be conceived, we are confronted by a double possibility: either that we have conceived a merely ideal reality which does not necessarily imply extra-mental existence or we are supposing without guarantee that there is a being than which nothing greater can be conceived."

3. Tillich, *Theology of Culture*, p. 13. For a recent influential statement in this tradition, see John Baillie, *The Sense of the Presence of God* (New York: Charles Scribner's Sons, 1962). In these Gifford lectures Baillie notes of such Christian "God-talk" as eternal, unchanging, omniscient, holy: "It is quite impossible to believe that such characters as these are suggested to us by anything we find in ourselves or elsewhere in the created world. To say that we gain the conception of perfect being by arranging our feeble human approaches towards perfection in an ascending series, and then imagining the indefinite prolongation of this series, is to forget that such an arrangement could not have been made by us save by the aid of a standard of perfection already present to our minds. . . . What is false is the assumption that the comparison moves from man to God instead of from God to man" (pp. 116–17).

4. A. H. Armstrong and R. A. Markus, *Christian Faith and Greek Philosophy* (London: Darton, Longman & Todd, 1960), pp. 59–77, note particularly that the Platonic understanding includes the dependence of the forms on the Good not only in the order of knowledge, but also in that of being. Wolfhart Pannenberg, *Basic Questions in Theology*, vol. 2, trans. George H. Kehm (Philadelphia: Fortress Press, 1971), pp. 119–83, provides a useful account of that history, noting, e.g., of Origen that even though the Platonic doctrine of illumination presupposed divine assistance for knowledge of God, Origen argued that this doctrine was independently available in Hosea and John.

5. *Contra Gentiles*, i,13. Weigel and Madden, *Religion and the Knowledge of God*, pp. 126–27, suggest that the argument from the degrees of being is already insinuated in Augustine in *City of God*, viii,6; *Of True Religion*, xviii,35–36; and *Confessions*, vii,11,17.

6. Weigel and Madden, *Religion and the Knowledge of God*, p. 128.

7. For a discussion of "the Eunomian problem," see John Murray, *The Problem of God* (New Haven: Yale University Press, 1964), pp. 53–62. On the uniqueness of the Byzantine form of this theology, see John Meyendorff, *Byzantine Theology:*

3 / THE KNOWLEDGE OF GOD

Historical Trends and Doctrinal Themes (New York: Fordham University Press, 1974), pp. 11ff. Jaroslav Pelikan, *The Spirit of Eastern Christendom* (Chicago: University of Chicago Press, 1974), p. 34, comments: "It was the consensus of the theologians that God was not to be worshipped on the basis of his essence, which is supremely unknowable, but on the basis of his procession 'outward,' that is, his providence and foreknowledge."

8. E. Gilson, *History of Christian Philosophy in the Middle Ages* (New York: Random House, 1955), p. 94. Gilson is arguing that Plato heavily influenced *both* East and West.

9. Helmut Thielicke, *The Evangelical Faith*, 2 vols., trans. and ed. G. W. Bromiley (Grand Rapids: Wm. B. Eerdmans, 1967), 2:13.

10. Pannenberg, *Basic Questions*, 2:56–57, expanding on the works of Bernard Lohse, *Ratio und Fides: Eine Untersuchung über die ratio in der Theologie Luthers* (Göttingen, 1958).

11. Heiko Oberman, "Headwaters of the Reformation," in *Luther and the Dawn of the Modern Era* (Leipzig: E. J. Brill, 1974), p. 57. In his *The Harvest of Medieval Theology: Gabriel Biel and Late Medieval Nominalism* (Cambridge, Mass.: Harvard University Press, 1963), p. 41, Oberman notes that the nominalist epistemology granted experimental, intuitive, and indirect knowledge of the world but not of God.

12. B. A. Gerrish, *Grace and Reason* (Oxford: At the Clarendon Press, 1962), pp. 68–69. Cf. my discussion of this point in the *locus* on sin.

13. See Pannenberg, *Basic Questions*, 2:63–64, on the difference that remains between faith and reason even when reason is itself conceived historically: "Faith is directed to this future which constitutes reality as a whole and thereby brings everything individual to its essential perfection. However, because this future is not alien to reason, but is rather its origin from which it implicitly always derives, faith cannot stand in opposition to reason. Much more does it remind reason of its own absolute presupposition by speaking about the eschatological future and its pre-appearance in the history of the resurrection of Jesus, from which faith derives."

14. John E. Smith, *The Analogy of Experience: An Approach to Understanding Religious Truth* (New York: Harper & Row, 1973), p. 28. (Italics his.)

15. In *The Bondage of the Will* (in *Martin Luther: Selections from his Writings*, ed. John Dillenberger [Garden City, N.Y.: Doubleday & Co., 1961], p. 171), Luther makes a very specific statement of this sort: "The Holy Spirit is no Sceptic, and the things He has written in our hearts are not doubts or opinions, but assertions—surer and more certain than sense and life itself." François Wendel in *Calvin: The Origins and Development of His Religious Thought*, trans. Philip Mairet (New York: Harper & Row, 1950), p. 157, summarizes Calvin's emphasis: "The Spirit inspired the authors of the books of Scripture, and it is he also who inspires us when we read their writings so that we may have tangible proof of the identity of that inspiration. . . . For Calvin, the interior witness of the Holy Spirit is the supreme criterion upon which the authority of the Scriptures is founded."

16. While I do not believe this formulation is particularly idiosyncratic, I take it from Kierkegaard's *Sickness unto Death* (Princeton: Princeton University Press, 1941).

17. Tillich, *Theology of Culture*, pp. 15–16.

18. Alfred Jules Ayer, *Language, Truth, and Logic*, 2d ed. (New York: Dover Publications, 1946), p. 35.

19. Anthony Flew and Alisdair MacIntyre, eds., *New Essays in Philosophical Theology* (London: SCM Press, 1955), p. 98.

20. Basil Mitchell, in ibid., p. 104.

21. Thomas Kuhn, *The Structure of Scientific Revolutions*, 2d ed. (Chicago: University of Chicago Press, 1970); cf. his "Second Thoughts on Paradigms," in *The Structure of Scientific Theories*, ed. Frederick Suppe (Champaign: University of Illinois Press, 1973). N. R. Hanson, *Patterns of Discovery* (Cambridge: At the University Press, 1958); and Stephen Toulmin, *Foresight and Understanding* (New York: Harper & Row, 1961).

22. L. Hughes Cox, "Why Not Drop the Theological-Falsification Issue Altogether?" *Pers.* 58, no. 1 (January 1977): 18–27.

23. Patrick Sherry, *Religion, Truth, and Language Games* (New York: Barnes & Noble, 1977), p. 108.

24. Ian Barbour, *Myths, Models, and Paradigms* (New York: Harper & Row, 1974).

25. Sherry, *Religion, Truth, and Language Games*, pp. 71–73.

26. Austin Farrer, "Revelation," in *Faith and Logic*, ed. Basil Mitchell (Boston: Beacon Press, 1957), p. 98.

27. For a defense of Aquinas' use of the analogy of proportionality, see Henri Bouillard's *The Knowledge of God*, trans. Samuel D. Femiano (New York: Herder & Herder, 1968). According to Bouillard, the attack is from Karl Barth, who "supposes that there is a supreme concept . . . embracing at the same time God and his creature. . . ." Bouillard contends that "when Barth reproaches the 'Thomistic *analogia entis*' for placing God and creature under the common denominator of being, it is not St. Thomas himself whom he is thinking of, but the theologians who claim to take their inspiration from Thomas. . . . Several of the theologians in question seem to have let the Thomistic notion of analogy slip away from the order of judgment toward that of concept (as representation). In doing so they have followed the interpretation of Cajetan, or sometimes that of Suarez. In their writings, analogy seems to us to designate the *partial resemblance* of the creature to the Creator, or the imperfect representation of God in human speech, rather than the *mode* in which one affirms the first and validates the second. The process of negation is less radical than in St. Thomas" (italics his). The suggestion made in Chapter 1 that divine transcendence be formulated in qualitative and relational terms may caution against casting the debate in the terms of negation, though distinction is essential.

28. Gerhard O. Forde, "Infallibility Language and the Early Lutheran Tradition," in *Teaching Authority and Infallibility in the Church: Lutherans and Catholics in Dialogue VI*, ed. Paul C. Empie, T. Austin Murphy, and Joseph A. Burgess (Minneapolis: Augsburg Publishing House, 1980), pp. 120–37.

29. Robert H. King, *The Meaning of God* (Philadelphia: Fortress Press, 1973), p. 112.

30. A related case may be metaphysical propositions formulated by such a method; see Alfred North Whitehead's *Process and Reality*, ed. David Ray Griffin and Donald W. Sherburne (New York: Free Press, 1978), chap. 1.

31. John Hick, *Faith and Knowledge* (Ithaca, N.Y.: Cornell University Press, 1957); Pannenberg, *Basic Questions*, 2:27, e.g.: "Since the emergence of historical con-

sciousness, the unity of all reality is conceivable only as a history. The unity of truth is still possible only as a historical process, and can be known only from the end of this process."

32. See Alvin Plantinga, *God and Other Minds* (Ithaca, N.Y.: Cornell University Press, 1967). Plantinga's "tentative conclusion" is: "If my belief in other minds is rational, so is my belief in God. But obviously the former is rational; so, therefore, is the latter" (p. 271). On the critique of dualistic tendencies in this regard, see P. F. Strawson, *Individuals: An Essay in Descriptive Metaphysics* (Garden City, N.Y.: Doubleday & Co.; London: Methuen, 1959).

33. Thus in *Lutherans and Catholics in Dialogue VI*, pp. 13–14, Lutherans worry about usurpation of what is conferred on Jesus Christ alone.

34. Paul Tillich, *Systematic Theology*, 3 vols. (Chicago: University of Chicago Press, 1951–63), 1:111–15.

3

God's Call and the Human Question about the Ground of Life

As Logos, God blesses by calling into life. In varying degrees and forms that life asks of and knows its ground in both its gift and its task. The call is sure as the response is not, so that the question of life may seem to be most certainly answered apart from life.

THE DIVINE INCOGNITO: THE REAL, THE BEAUTIFUL, AND THE GOOD

This *locus* is about the knowledge of God. We began in Chapter 1 by asking *why* God is known and found the answer in God's will and action to reveal. We continued in Chapter 2 by asking *how* God is known, and spoke of the human condition of knowing and speaking of God. Taking a leaf from Aristotle, we might say that Chapter 1 treated the efficient cause and Chapter 2 the material cause of the knowledge of God. In this chapter and the next we shall ask how widely God is known. Perhaps this chapter is about Aristotle's formal cause, the forms or structures in and through which God is known. *Where* is God known? That is our theme.

How well is God known? That question is also our concern in these chapters. We have two matters in mind: First: With what degree of awareness is God known? One may perhaps "know" without recognizing the true identity or full significance of what one knows. Does one know that one knows *God*? Second: What is the effect of this knowing? Is the knowledge of God received as the answer that it is to the human question?

These matters are, of course, more than we can manage. To address these questions is to risk both offense and ridicule, quite apart from the answers one offers. I make no claim to command the phenomenological amplitude of data, as would be necessary if one were to somehow evoke the categorial scheme from the context. It is, after all, still context. That is, it is still a theological inquiry which I conduct. Thus it is the theological understanding of God as ground which identifies what we are looking for in this chapter, though it is to be hoped that orientation does not tell us what we see. Context, then, is not trivialized. We do look about, albeit selectively and with text in mind.

That text speaks of God as the world's ground. If human beings ask about their ground, what form(s) will the question take? The question will be *about* us, that frail synthesis of necessity and possibility thrown ahead in freedom.[1] It will be about how a world is given, how a self created, how that self is claimed. The question will be *after* a word that fits us, that grounds us. Such a word must be sure and it must be universally applicable. Life is and life intends. It knows the dialectic of being and becoming; it is gift and task. As such, life finds its ground in order to move toward its goal. Ground may support life's movement toward goal by directing in bestowing. God calls into life and calls in life—toward the goal. It is that kind of word for which we are looking. How widely and how well is it heard?

We begin with words like "the real," "the beautiful," "the true." These words are good words, but not clearly God-words. Precisely so! They are not *clearly* God-words. But here humankind asks about and knows of God as the world's ground. Bernard Lonergan speaks about such asking:

> The question of God is epistemological, when we ask how the universe can be intelligible. It is philosophic when we ask why we should bow to the principle of sufficient reason, when there is no sufficient reason for the existence of contingent things. It is moral when we ask whether the universe has a moral ground and so a moral goal. It finally is religious when we ask whether there is anyone for us to love with all our heart and all our soul and all our mind and all our strength.[2]

The faith assures us that God is the world's *present* ground, for that is a matter of God's action. God wills to be known and can be known. It remains to look about to see how widely and how well question and ground fit each other.

One may ask how we are called into life, by asking what is most fundamental in reality. *Metaphysics*, in identifying indispensable explanatory principles, seems to provide a word that is sure and universal. We seek the pervasive and primitive in reality. The real, so understood, becomes God's incognito. Perhaps it was this incognito that prevailed in the ancient world. Werner Jaeger has argued so about the pre-Socratics, saying that we meet here not rudimentary natural science, but rather natural theology bent on identifying the God who does not depend on convention.[3] It is clear that the Socratic-Platonic literature contains occasional explicitly religious references alongside the quest for wisdom deriving from knowledge of the most real. But it is in Aristotle that metaphysics and divinity come together most clearly. He is looking for "a cause which will move things and bring them together" (*Metaphysics*, i.4.984b30), and reasons that "if there is an immovable substance, the science of this must be prior and must be first philosophy, and universal in this way, because it is first" (ibid., vi.1.1026a23–30). Thus Aristotle reaches the first mover which "exists by necessity" (ibid., xii.7.1072b10–29) and "produces motion by being loved, whereas all other things move by being moved" (ibid., xii.7.1072b1–4).

With Aristotle, we do seem to be on the ground of religion, but it may be doubted that the project of life is well grounded in his answers to the metaphysical question. How does one whose categorical supremacy lies precisely in being unmoved sustain the striving that is life? One can understand the suspicion with which such God-talk will be greeted by those who are dedicated to affirmation of the human venture. Aristotle pulls ethics back into metaphysics; the good life is the life that comes closest to the divine life in self-sufficiency. Philosophic wisdom is the higher virtue (*Nicomachean Ethics*, x.7.1177a24), for its pleasures are pure and enduring and the philosopher needs no one besides himself to exercise his virtue. A just man, on the other hand, needs others to be just.

There is clearly something right about the metaphysical question about God. We should not be troubled by the emphasis on reality in incognito, or by the certainty claimed here. It is not strange that Christians like Clement of Alexandria speak of philosophy as having a divine origin and of Christianity as the true philosophy. Yet the fit here is not as fine as one might wish. The fundamental difficulty is not the specific one examined in the previous paragraph, that the Greek tradition happens to regard what is unmoved as having a higher reality than what is moved. It would hardly remove the difficulty if we were to make no such distinction. It is precisely a distinction between God and all else that is needed; and reality merely as such hardly seems supple enough to yield it. We need to state God's ontological superiority, but the sense of reality merely as such is too blunt an instrument to convey that superiority. The identification of God's incognito requires some specificity; God's creature is not only called into life, but called in life. That is hard to come by in an appeal to "the real," particularly in the modern situation, where distinctions between degrees of being lack persuasive power.

But perhaps the *beautiful* can serve as God's incognito. After all, is there not here a combination of givenness and specificity?

Clearly a kind of transcendence is claimed in art. At least that is the testimony of many who write about art. John Dewey argued that in aesthetic experience the factors determining any experience "are lifted high above the threshold of perception and are made manifest for their own sake."[4] R. G. Collingwood makes apparently salvific claims for the healing power of art. What is healed?

Consciousness can never attend to more than a part of the total sensuous-emotional field; but either it may recognize this as belonging to itself, or it may refuse so to recognize it. In the latter case, certain feelings are not ignored, they are disowned; the conscious self disclaims responsibility for them, and thus tries to escape being dominated by them without the trouble of dominating them. This is the "corrupt conciousness" which is the source of what psychologists call repression.[5]

If art is to be more than entertainment, and yet not heal by magic,

It must be prophetic. . . . But what he has to utter is not, as the individualistic theory of art would have us think, his own secrets. As spokesman of his community, the secrets he must utter are theirs. The reason why they need him is that no community altogether knows its own heart. . . .[6]

There is a kind of revelatory completeness about the clarity art bestows; it is a joy to experience it. But if the disease is more than ignorance, what then? Does art offer any sense of the efficacy of the new? Or perhaps art is exercised precisely to call us back to the beginning? Schiller puts it well:

It is neither charm, nor is it dignity, which speaks from the glorious face of Juno Ludovici; it is neither of these, for it is both at once. While the female god challenges our veneration, the godlike woman at the same time kindles our love. But while in ecstasy we give ourselves up to the heavenly beauty, the heavenly self-repose awes us back. *The whole form rests and dwells in itself—a fully complete creation in itself*—and as if she were out of space, without advance or resistance; it shows no force contending with force, *no opening through which time could break in.*[7]

No wonder, then, that we find ourselves "in the state of greatest repose." Things were (are) clearer at the beginning—a beginning in which creativity has reached its end. Matthew Arnold, stricken with skepticism and despair, reaches for that kind of salvation in his "Memorial Verses" on the death of Wordsworth. This long passage is not too long to repeat:

He too upon a wintry clime
Had fallen—on this iron time
Of doubts, disputes, distractions, fears.
He found us when the age had bound
our souls in its benumbing round;
He spoke, and loosed our heart in tears
He laid us *as we lay at birth*
on the cool flowery lap of earth,
Smiles broke from us and we had ease;
The hills were round us, and the breeze
Went o'er the sun-lit fields again;
Our foreheads felt the wind and rain,

Our youth return'd; for there was shed
On spirits that had long been dead,
Spirits dried up and closely furl'd
The freshness of the early world.[8]

How can one achieve a salvation that is other than romantic reverie or ironic perception? Or, short of salvation, how can we understand the ground sensed in art as one which supports and informs human striving, and so points toward a goal which is not simply the "freshness of the early world"? Hegel sought to do so by linking art with the movement of the "idea," by which movement the sensuous is spiritualized in the "concrete universal." But this emphasis on concreteness is still linked with stress on the independence of the object of art, so that the interest of art is purged of desire.[9] Indeed, this difficulty about human freedom may reveal that art in this reading still suffers from the more general deficiency in specificity noted above in the Greek metaphysical vision. How may the gift of beauty preserve its independence and universality and yet engage the task of the individual life?

Kant may provide a transition. Here there is no attempt to make understanding of the efficacy of art dependent on acceptance of a metaphysical vision, for such visions always reach beyond what our senses can tell us. *The Critique of Judgment* opens in art a kind of spiritual vista closed to empirical reason, by identifying an objective purposefulness in nature. Here there is the ecstasy of self-discovery, which is yet purged of particularity through the universality of aesthetic judgment.[10]

Yet on Kant's view we must proceed cautiously in speaking of transcendence. If God is known here as ground, it is certainly through an incognito: "*Beauty* is the form of the *purposiveness* of an object, so far as this is perceived in it *without any representation of a purpose*."[11] Kant does try to muster a kind of religious passion for his "philosophy of as-if," despite the subjectivity of all purpose-language:

We can regard it as a favor which nature has felt for us that, in addition to what is useful, it has so profusely dispensed beauty and charm, and we can therefore love it, as well as regard it with respect on account of its immensity, and feel ennobled ourselves by such regard, just as if nature had established and adorned its splendid theatre precisely with this view.[12]

This is followed by explicit rejection of any religious inference:

If then we introduce into the context of natural science the concept of God, in order to explain the purposiveness in nature, and subsequently use this purposiveness to prove that there is a God, there is no internal consistency in either science [i.e., either in natural science or theology]; and a delusive circle brings them both into uncertainty, because they have allowed their boundaries to overlap.[13]

Kant's reading of art attempts to link the ground with freedom, by way of the category of purposiveness. The self is engaged here in relation to the world outside the self. Nature is extolled, as is evident in the view that art is to copy nature. Yet Kant's skepticism prevents him from making any direct connection with religious talk at this point. What "physico-theology" (the endeavor of reason to infer the supreme cause of nature from the purposes of nature) *does* appropriately do is to open another door, in that "it discloses to us an outlook over nature by which perhaps we may be able to determine more closely the otherwise so unfruitful concept of an Original Being."[14] Aesthetic judgment has brought us across the great divide separating the barren world of pure reason from the richer fields of moral reason. While Kant's distinctions may be tidier than we would like, it is clear that in pointing to *moral* reason he directs us to another pseudonymous witness to the reality of God as ground. Perhaps "the good, the right" may represent an incognito which may convey the sense of personal will missing in metaphysical and aesthetic approaches.

We delay further consideration of Kant to the next section, where we attend to explicit appeals to God. The incognito may be vanishing there. But people do make moral claims without such a theological appeal. We are not thinking of people who make such claims precisely *against* religious appeals (as Kai Nielsen from a Wittgensteinian perspective and S. DeBeauvoir from an existentialist perspective).[15] Rather, we are thinking of the way in which Erich Fromm could commend "the art of loving," or of how Walter Kaufmann can argue that "humbition" (the synthesis of humility and ambition, of course) is "intrinsically admirable."[16] Such people seem to hear a word that is universal and sure. Moreover, that word is specific and instructive; these people hear a call in life. Do they have a sense for the ground of that call?

If ancient Greek wisdom seemed a good place to sample the *metaphysical* incognito, and the idealistic-romantic writers served such a function for the *aesthetic* approach to the question about the ground, is there some such natural locus also in the moral good? We ask, "How does one get an ought from an is?" and the contemporary Anglo-Saxon discussion invites attention. Granting the presence of moral claims, how are we to understand their origin and justification? Hume and others in the empiricist tradition caution against arguing for the empirical character of ethical claims. A matter's "oughtness" does not seem to reside in its "isness." The theologian who insists on the full reality of evil would seem to agree. But then what ground(s) may be found for moral claims?

John Searle's famous article, boldly entitled "How to Derive Ought from Is," exploits a form of language—the performative, e.g., "I promise"—which is neither descriptive nor evaluative. But it seems clear that Searle's derivation is dependent on existing "institutions," that is, public standards or systems of rules within which obligations are defined, and on commitment to those institutions. Here we seem at best to have hypothetical imperatives, for he gives us no convincing reason for uttering the performative.[17]

It would seem more promising if we could identify some form of discourse or activity which every rational person engages in, and then show that this requires a certain presupposition. Thus R. S. Peters argues that public discourse presupposes that one ought to consider the interests of others, and Alan Gewirth claims that the very concept of action entails the securing of respect for the freedom and well-being of all agents.[18] Here we do seem to have sufficient scope to ground human life as such. One finds oneself asking, however, "What do the presuppositions this transcendental approach uncovers themselves presuppose?"

As one follows out that question, one encounters a large group of writers who appeal not to logical presuppositions but to particular aspects of the human condition. We are, of course, near the natural law argument. At the level of argument, the incognito is being removed. But the approach can be quite restrained, as when H. L. A. Hart develops a limited concept of teleology (e.g., survival) and appeals to some broad constants of human nature (e.g., vulnerability). Similarly, Karl Rahner seeks to find not a moral law-code, but simply a constant reference point, the creative self, from which to interrogate experience.[19] This is not an appeal to prudence, or if it is, it is a very fundamental prudence indeed. One is saying that injustice, immorality, and amorality destroy or obliterate a dimension of reality in the self.

This last group of moral theorists hints at something very fundamental in the human condition. Can human reality stand alone and still provide a sense of its own ground? The Anglo-Saxon discussion seeks to provide an affirmative answer, since it disavows any metaphysical or theological consideration. But this does leave the discussion rather circular. One wants to ask, May something itself ground this (only apparently) self-authenticating spiritual dimension of human existence?

In all these visions—metaphysical, moral, and aesthetic—there is talk that sounds like faith's speech about *logos* and *nomos*, albeit in an altered tongue. Faith will be interested in the task of translation. Faith may find an ally in that task, for explicit God-talk is clearly not exclusively Christian property. Having followed the putting and answering of the question of a ground, in what do seem to be divine incognitos—the real, the beautiful, the good—we turn to consider this question in explicit connection with the notion of *God*. If human beings ask of and know God this widely without knowing well what they are about, may we not be hopeful in turning to human speaking of God, even outside the Christian community?

HUMAN AWARENESS:
ARGUMENT AND ADORATION

We consider here human speech that makes explicit reference to the notion of a God. One large body of such thought is the attempted "proofs"—we shall make clear that it seems better to consider them "arguments"—for the existence of God. Specifically, we are asking: How is the God declared in the Christian faith known in these arguments? How widely and how well? I take "How widely?" to ask "How accessibly?" I understand "How well?" to mean "How certainly?" "How accurately?" "How completely?" From within the dogmatic orientation, two preliminary observations direct our discussion. In arguing for the *existence* of God, the "proofs" are "about" an appropriate subject: the reality of the God who does intend and does act. And the focus for our discussion will be the understanding of God as the world's ground, though the notion of God as the world's goal will be in view as well.

We have suggested that if we are looking for a ground for the world, we are looking for a word that is sure and universal, for something that will not be found inapplicable because of internal discord or external limitation. If it is certainty that we seek, it would seem that it would be the ontological argument which would interest us most strongly. Here, after all, is an argument which proceeds *a priori* from analysis of a concept, so that we are not nervously collecting instances while watching over our shoulders for falsifying counterinstances. Moreover, if the argument is from a concept only, it ought to be accessible to anyone who can think. It is accordingly not surprising that the ontological argument has been and is the object of a great deal of interest.

The historically most influential form of the argument is that presented by Anselm in *Proslogion* II. Here is offered the famous definition of God as "that than which nothing greater can be thought." Does this concept, which even the atheist can entertain, exist only in the mind, or does it also exist in external reality? If it existed only in the mind, it would be lesser than that which existed in the external reality as well. Therefore it must exist in external reality as well.[20]

Does the argument work? Kant has a great deal of company in contending that "existence is not a predicate" that can form part of the concept of perfection, but something that must always be asserted (or denied) on synthetic grounds. Does it help to offer a "second form" of the argument depending on the notion of *necessary* existence, the existence of something which is such that it cannot be thought not to exist?

Can, on the contrary, God's nonexistence be shown to be necessary? Is the notion of God self-contradictory? Charles Hartshorne has argued that a classical concept of divine perfection which effectively denied the divine relativity would be self-contradictory. But if the perfect God is defined as the "self-surpassing surpasser of all," self-contradiction is avoided and the necessity of existence for the divine essence is shown. Other philosophers continue to grumble that Hartshorne has reached his conclusion by sleight of hand, moving equivocally from logical necessity to factual or ontological necessity.[21]

The difficulties and dissent cited suggest that the "ontological" proof functions as an argument rather than a proof. Apart from the issue of the validity of the argument, how accurately is God known in this approach? We find here the theme of God's aseity, an important element in Christian tradition. John Hick elaborates what is at stake:

> From God's *aseity* his eternity, indestructibility and incorruptibility can be seen to follow. A self-existent being must be eternal, i.e., without temporal limitation. For if he had begun to exist or should cease to exist, he must have been caused to exist or to go out of existence by some power other than himself; and this would be inconsistent with his *aseity*. By the same token, he must be indestructible, for to say that he exists in total independence is to say that there is and could be no reality able to constitute or to destroy him; and likewise he must be incorruptible, for otherwise his *aseity* would be qualified as regards its duration.[22]

The difficulty, however, is that once again a God so conceived hardly seems to ground human freedom. Spinoza, following out the logic of the notion of aseity, must finally simply locate within God the reality of everything. Ground and goal, as different as they are for us, coincide in God's "total independence." What is expressed in this approach is what we have earlier called the categorical supremacy of God. But if God is to be known as the authorizing ground of human freedom, God's supremacy must be stated in such a way that it relates to what is not God. By definition the ontological argument declines to do that.

Perhaps we may group the cosmological and the teleological arguments together in that both try to think of God's superiority in "worldly" terms. Indeed, unlike the ontological argument, both depend on empirical premises, which might roughly be identified as causality and design (adaptation toward an end) respectively. As such, they will inevitably offer less certainty, since they remain forever open to empirical counterattack, as David Hume so remorselessly observes.[23] Yet presumably most people will grant such empirical premises.

In the famous Thomistic presentation of the cosmological argument (*Summa Theologica* la,2,3), those premises were motion, causation, and contingent existence. What will suffice as a reason explaining those premises? Perhaps the second form is most representative:

> In the world of sensible things we find there is an order of efficient causes. There is no case known (neither is it, indeed, possible) in which a thing is found to

be the efficient cause of itself; for so it would be prior to itself, which is impossible. Now in efficient causes it is not possible to go on to infinity, because in all efficient causes following in order, the first is the cause of the intermediate cause, and the intermediate is the cause of the ultimate cause, whether the intermediate cause be several, or one only. Now to take away the cause is to take away the effect. Therefore, if there be no first cause among efficient causes, there will be no ultimate, nor any intermediate, cause. But if in efficient causes it is possible to go on to infinity, there will be no first efficient cause, neither will there be any ultimate effect, nor any intermediate efficient causes; all of which is plainly false. Therefore it is necessary to admit a first efficient cause, to which everyone gives the name of God.[24]

It may be possible to restate this argument in terms of logical, not temporal, priority. That might make the argument more attractive to many moderns, who find the notion of an infinite temporal regress more plausible than the idea of an absolute beginning. Is the complex *present* hierarchy of causes infinite, or is there a higher cause which does not itself depend on the existence of another cause? If some are inclined to appeal to the existence of the universe as no less arbitrary than the existence of God, they will be rejecting the priority of mind over matter as an explanatory principle. John Hick writes of that priority:

> We can readily conceive of superior minds to ourselves; but not of kinds of reality superior to mind. Thus there is for us an explanatory ultimacy about mind which we do not find in the existence or the laws of matter. As minds we do not ask why there should be any such thing as mind, although we do ask why there should be any such thing as matter obeying the particular laws which we find matter to obey.[25]

Here the cosmological argument's link with the teleological appeal to design becomes apparent. The latter provided the last of Aquinas' five ways, but was most prominently displayed in the seventeenth and eighteenth centuries. Once again one explains what is experienced, now order in nature, by tracing it back to something mental, divine purpose in the creator. As with the cosmological argument, contemporary restatements are available, such as Alfred North Whitehead's appeal to a single "primordial" decision responsible for the novel yet relevant order characterizing the beginning of *every* particular actual occasion of reality.[26]

How well is God known here? How accurately? How certainly? In each case the argument's reach seems to exceed its grasp, though something valuable is indeed possessed. The difficulties are particularly apparent in the unqualified forms of the argument that proceed on large scale, appealing to the origin and design of the cosmos as a whole, and command much popular attention.

I have mentioned the matter of an infinite regress. Similarly, the logic of design hardly reaches to creation "from nothing"—a destination which is further troubled by the apparent presence in the universe of considerable disorder. In both instances philosophers may well hesitate over what seems to be a probability argument for an absolutely unique case.[27] In the revised forms of the arguments available in current discussion, the reach is reduced so that the grasp seems surer if not larger. Perhaps we no longer find ourselves brought to shudder under what Tillich called the shock of nonbeing. Rather we find ourselves pondering at best why there is *such* a world as there is. Why this? Why that?

But in putting that question and in answering it, these arguments have something valuable in hand. They do not speak convincingly of an absolute beginning or of an invincible purpose, but they speak appropriately of a being who does intend and who does act. They invite us to broaden talk about a first time to talk about every time. Moreover, that talk will be undertaken by faith in relationship to action and purpose which is not God's. The reality of evil (which was, so to speak, lying in wait for the ontological argument— how good can a perfect God be in this world?) points to the nondivine, as the sense of human agency and responsibility already does. The hesitancy about the principle of sufficient reason ("Why can't the world be self-regulating, self-generating?" "Why does a fact—*especially* the fact of freedom—need an explanation?" "Is God *as fact* any different from, any more explanatory than, other facts as facts?") does so as well. That is, here the categorical supremacy of God is expressed in gift and claim, so that the venture of human freedom can be supported.

Of course not every kind of supremacy is available within relationship, as Hume's Cleanthes knew:

> I scruple not to allow, said Cleanthes, that I have been apt to suspect the frequent repetition of the word *infinite*, which we meet with in all theological writers, to savour more of panegyric than of philosophy, and that any purposes of reasoning, and even of religion, would be better served were we to rest contented with more accurate and more moderate expressions. The terms, *admirable, excellent, superlatively great, wise*, and *holy*—these sufficiently fill out the imaginations of men. . . . If we preserve human analogy, we must forever find it impossible to reconcile any mixture of evil in the universe with infinite attributes; much less can we ever prove the latter from the former. But supposing the Author of nature to be finitely perfect, though far exceeding mankind, a satisfactory account may then be given of natural and moral evil. . . .[28]

It seems unwise to ask a philosopher limited to empirical reason to give us any fuller statement of God as the world's ground.

What, finally, may be said of the moral argument for the existence of God? Can we take any comfort from the fact that Kant, who was so critical of the other arguments, actually offered this one, almost as if in their place? For us, I suspect, the moral argument will seem more like the cosmological-teleological argument than it did to Kant. That is, this argument also appeals to an empirical premise, the moral sense.

The argument in the *Critique of Practical Reason* proceeds by pleading that "ought" implies "can" and that "can" requires the postulate of a God who can bring about the coincidence of moral virtue and happiness. Other forms of the moral argument contend that if there were no God, the moral "ought" could not even be known. The "ought" can be known because it can be justified, by appeal to the will of God. As one justifies the "ought," one reaches for its ground in God.

How certainly does this argument begin? Does the world, as we know it, offer the enabling premise? A moral sense, formally considered at least, does seem a remarkably stubborn survivor. The formulation of this argument's premise will today emphasize more the quantitative extension than the qualitative sureness of the moral sense. Those philosophers who argue eloquently for the widespread existence of moral conviction without association with religion should not be permitted suddenly to withdraw the data at this point. Furthermore, there are those, such as anthropologist Clyde Kluckhohn, who will argue for a remarkable cross-cultural material unity in that moral sense.[29] Of course, the argument remains empirical, and in its modern setting it is particularly vulnerable to the open-textured character of an empirical approach. One wishes to avoid trying to persuade individuals and/or cultures that *really* deep down they too have a moral sense.

Also, the movement from the premise may not be wholly untroubled. Is "God" needed to sustain commitment to the moral ideal, if that ideal is of a will devoid of (self?) interest and as such presumably indifferent to result or reward? Perhaps for many moral moderns the notion of God is simply not readily available as a "regulative idea" functioning in the unifying work of pure reason's realm, and thus will not be appropriated as easily by them as by Kant.

Nonetheless also this argument does grasp something essential in the Christian understanding of God as the world's ground. In the giving of the world, as the self is created the self is claimed, for the right and good of humankind. For the Christian the "ought" is from God—that is what the moral argument sees clearly. But it is also for us and indeed for our good. That is what nontheistic ethicists see so clearly. They see less clearly, though, when they go on to argue that a claim that is *for* us cannot be *from* someone who is other than us. Simone de Beauvoir seems to fall into that disjunction:

When a man projects into an ideal heaven that impossible synthesis he wishes the regard of this existing Being to change his existence into being; but if he agrees not to be in order to exist genuinely, he will abandon the dream of an inhuman objectivity. He will understand that it is not a matter of being right in the eyes of a God, but of being right in his own eyes.[30]

That the claim is for us humans is no embarrassment to the faith. That nontheists, non-Christians, can know what is right and, so far as any of us can judge, give their energy to that right is no objection to faith in God.[31] Rather, the Christian finds here precisely the grounding and directing of the human venture of freedom. It is God's good pleasure to make the claim known, and God's will is sure. God's will *will* be known, even if its origin and its issue remain in doubt. That is why a humanistic ethic does not collapse into absurdity and values do not collapse into tastes. The Christian faith does not contradict human convergence and competence at this point, but precisely comprehends them. It takes them within a more inclusive and far-reaching perspective which roots the human good in the one sure divine will for all. God is the world's ground. The argument will "click" for those who seek such comprehensiveness. But the Christian will have a moral commonality also with those who choose instead to cling to the integrity which seems imperiled by a theistic grounding.

What we have been examining thus far in this chapter may not be "proofs," as if their recital could lock in the mind's assent by logical entailment. But they are arguments, for they do appeal to something that may be had in common, and seek to guide us from there toward an understanding of reality in which the notion of God is essential. How well that journey will go will depend on one's material reading of the other components of reality, one's methodological judgment concerning what kind of perspective is desirable, and one's existential judgment as to whether the theistic conclusion supports or undermines the human locale of the starting point(s). Christians will recognize the arguments as approaches to God, the world's *ground.*

God is the world's *goal* as well—so the faith confesses. Is anything known about that in these arguments? Not very much. The ontological argument might suggest certainty of destination, *if* it could more easily accommodate a significant divine mission in the world. The cosmological argument does suggest that the theme of consequence rhymes with talk of God, but a contemporary setting stressing action with and in the world does not yield a sense of an ultimate goal. The sense of a goal is in the teleological argument's stress on purpose, but only of a goal *sought.* That is true of the moral argument as well, particularly if our contemporary sense for the ineluctability of human failure seems to challenge the Kantian postulate, "I ought . . . therefore I can."[32]

Thus, without being ungrateful for the knowledge of the ground, there is reason to look for more. That will be particularly true if God is, as faith declares, personal and active will. Will can instruct, but it can respond as well; it can judge. Whatever God may be formally or metaphysically, what has God decided about us? What is God's heart, so far as we are concerned? Is the universe and its churning course related to a personal will? Does life not only come from something, as a "ground," but matter to someone? The moral and teleological arguments move in this direction, but there may be less abstract materials to consider in this connection. I refer, of course, to religion. What may be known of God there?

When human people act to adore, what do they know? My response to this question occurs within a Christian dogmatics. It does not claim to be disinterested and notes that such claims to objectivity are made today less often and less loudly than in the burgeoning early years of the history of religions. In making this response we are grateful that there are available expository and analytical accounts of the religions. The competence of those accounts does not depend on disinterested objectivity.[33]

We have already argued in Chapter 1 that God as the world's ground can be—indeed *is*—known, apart from the specific Christian *kairos*. It was, after all, the apostle Paul who spoke about the natural knowledge of God's "invisible nature, namely, his eternal power and deity" and of the law written on the heart (Rom. 1 and 2). We continue to ask "how widely and how well" is God known, now applying that question to the dizzying plentitude of things religious. Thus the Christian faith itself prepares us to consider other faiths with the expectation that there is knowledge of God in those faiths. Moreover, since the Christian faith dwells in human houses and hearts, the Christian needs to be self-critical about the Christian religion. One way of doing that is to try to hear the word that comes from other faiths. One still hears the word as a Christian, of course, though one also does so as a human being to whom the faith may seem a restless guest. As a human being, however "secular," when one faces the reality of religion, one is struck by the power, the intensity, the persistence of what is there. Something real is at work. Is not God, the world's ground, known here? Knowledge may not be joined by trust and true worship, as Paul says in Romans 1 and 2. That is a more advanced question. Our question is: Can the Christian recognize in the other religions knowledge of God?

Very apparently the venture of living is caught up in the religious. Some call is heard here; life is engaged. Perhaps no religion illustrates this as well as Islam, which for its adherents is clearly not part of life but a way of life, steadfastly resisting any cordoning off in "religion." "Islam" is "submission," and not just in literal translation; for the orthopraxy of the five pillars orders all existence. And what of the many faiths not sharing Islam's formal similarities with Christianity? Hinduism has not the same emphasis on the moral, but the self is claimed for meditation, while the caste system continues to order life. Indeed, the tolerance stressed in Hinduism itself doubles back to affect life: The individual must choose his or her God.

Life is engaged here, but is it grounded? Is life's Other known? Again, one could make things easy for oneself by referring to Islam, for the Quran makes the point directly in regarding Adam as Allah's vice-regent. As Annemarie Schimmel puts it: "When the Quran says 'He taught Adam the names' (2/31) it means that he gave him power over the things, since to know the name of something means to possess power over it."[34] But there appear to be non-theistic religions, Hinayana Buddhism and some forms of Zen, for example. It will not do to ask simply about a specific notion of God. Is life engaged in relationship to a reality which is categorically supreme, whose call can be sure?

Clearly, the religious person has a sense of something absolute, something ultimate. On this the records agree.[35] In some instances this sense is stated theistically. I have argued that if God's call is to be sure, it cannot be subject to internal division. Islam has such monotheistic sureness in spades. First against Arabic pagan polytheism, then against the Christian doctrine of the Trinity, Sura 112, the logical end of the Quran, proclaims: "Say: He is Allah, the One; Allah, the Eternal; He brought not forth nor hath He been brought forth; Co-equal with Him there hath never been anyone." But matters are not as clear elsewhere. Hinduism is notoriously polytheistic. The Confucianist absolute, "heaven," is probably best conceived as impersonal, though subordinate gods are recognized.

How, then, does the absolute or ultimate known in religion engage life? It is in that connection that the notion of God as ground roots. There seem to be dynamics at work in religion which divert or distort the sense of grounding. It may be useful to list those dynamics:

First, an emphasis on the magical, whether by direct divine action or through human intermediaries, seems to compromise the clarity of the ground's authorization of the human venture. This emphasis is not found only in primitive religions. One thinks of the incantations of the early Hindu Atharvaveda and of the Tantras from the fifth century A.D. One may think as well of magical tendencies elsewhere, not the least within Christian history.

Second, at times the categorically supreme One seems to be the only actor. Schimmel identifies such a tendency within Islam:

God has created the world once from nothing and does not cease creating it every moment—this idea of atomism was developed in ash'arite circles: secondary causes are eliminated, and whatever happens happens through the direct action of God: fire does not burn by its inherent quality but because it is God's custom to connect burning with fire. This *sumnat Allah*, "God's custom" is visible both in nature and in the course of history. . . .[36]

This emphasis does not seem actually to cancel the place of human effort, but such striving is set within a fatalistic perspective, as the phenomena of Christian religion also reveal.

Third, the sense of efficacy toward the new which seems essential to the reality of freedom may be compromised if the ultimate truth about reality is cast in terms of being rather than becoming. The idea of harmony can be stated in such terms, as may be suggested in the statement by J. R. Fox concerning "the essence of the religions of the aboriginal Americans":

> Harmony between nature, Man and the supernatural, means fertility of men and crops, and success in hunting, war and personal achievement. Disharmony— often caused by witchcraft—leads to tribal, personal and even cosmic disaster. Ritual therefore is a means of either maintaining or restoring this basic harmony.[37]

But one need not speak only of the aboriginal, if one recalls the Taoist emphasis on the balance between the Ying and the Yang, or the Confucianist casting of this theme in the metaphysical basis for ethics, Ch'eng.[38] While dynamic balance as in stable advance would seem possible, the religious employment of this theme seems regularly to draw this theme back into the association of rest and original order.

Fourth, in Buddhism the ultimate is so understood as to yield precisely an escape from the world of striving. Obviously the point must be delicately put; after all, we do seem called toward, we even *desire*, escape into nirvana. Yet here we seem near the core of the Buddhist understanding, as Alex Wayman recounts:

> When ancient Buddhism divided into eighteen sects, naturally there arose discussion of what the basic Buddhist doctrinal position is, upon which all sects can agree, however disagreeing on other points. The solution to this problem came to be called the four "aphorisms" or "seals" of the Doctrine: (1) All constructed things are impermanent; (2) All constructed things are suffering; (3) All natures are devoid of self; (4) Nirvana is calm.[39]

Perhaps we may break off this tally of trends to risk a more general question: Does religion tend to answer the question of God by referring the questioner to a realm more real than and competitive with the sphere in which human beings struggle to survive and create? This seems to be Mircea Eliade's understanding of preliterary religion.[40] Moreover, many literary religions find a "golden age" in the past and can speak of creation as merely the "sport" of a self-sufficient deity. R. N. Dandekar speaks thus of Hinduism:

The theory which seems to have been found generally acceptable by various schools of thought is that the world-process is but the sport—*lila*—of God. This *lila*, which provides an outlet for the exuberant spirit of God, is to be thought of just as play for the sake of play. . . . Actually to impute any motive to god's activity would mean denying his very god-head.[41]

Eric Voegelin offers comparisons at this point:

In the culture of Hinduism, historical consciousness is muted by the dominance of late-cosmological speculations on the cosmos as a "thing" that is born and reborn in infinite sequence. The hypostasis of the cosmos, and the fallacious infinite of cosmological speculation, can be identified as the stratum in the Hinduist experience of reality that has not been broken by epochal events comparable to the noetic and pneumatic theophanies in Hellas and Israel.[42]

One may find in these dynamics something like what was noted in discussing the divine incognitos: The call is back to the "freshness of the early world." Perhaps that attraction is not hard to comprehend. On Christian faith's account, God's call is sure, but the response is not. Are we not constantly tempted to find the answer to the question of life apart from life? Then a call is still heard, but its content calms us by suggesting that the beginning is what really matters—now in the middle and at the end. It does seem to be so in the world of religion, and Christian religion may at times illustrate the same dynamic. Of course, one must make the point carefully.[43]

At least it seems clear that there is also life and striving in the world of the religious. Religion may at times identify the categorically supreme in such a way that the venture of life is undercut, but that threat of formal contradiction does not seem much to bother the submissive devotee of Islam or the capitalistic Calvinist. At its best, religion does affirm the significance of the human venture in responsible freedom. The adherent of Islam with its high doctrine of God does stand with father Abraham looking toward the future. Human deeds do matter; the Muslim will not fast beyond the month of Ramadan lest the body be weakened. Even Hinduism, in which the Vedic sacrifice establishes a magical rapport with cosmic order, adapts and shows itself in fact to be a "growing" religion. As Radhakrishnan points out: "Hinduism is a movement, not a position; a process, not a result; a growing tradition, not a fixed revelation."[44] In its practice, if not as clearly in its theory, religion asks after and knows about the ground for life, for living.

Perhaps the difficulties noted here remind us that more is needed for life than a ground. That may be clearly seen precisely where the ground's connection with life seems clearest: the moral, ground as *nomos*. That God wills something for the world honors temporality in that it does not call us back from the project of existence. To give my life to the case of God *is* deeply

245

meaningful. But what of the end? Even if matters were to go well, and especially as they go quite other than well, humankind quests after God as the goal.

NOTES

1. Søren Kierkegaard, *The Sickness unto Death*, trans. W. Lowrie (Princeton: Princeton University Press, 1941).

2. Bernard Lonergan, *Philosophy of God and Theology* (London: Darton, Longman & Todd, 1973), pp. 54–55.

3. Werner Jaeger, *The Theology of the Early Greek Philosophers* (Oxford: At the Clarendon Press, 1947), pp. 2ff.

4. John Dewey, *Art as Experience* (New York: G. P. Putnam's Sons, Capricorn Books, 1958), p. 57. Dewey is notable for his emphasis on imaginative purpose in art: "Art has been the means of keeping alive the sense of purposes that outrun evidence and of meanings that transcend indurated habit" (ibid., p. 348).

5. R. G. Collingwood, *The Principles of Art* (New York: Oxford University Press, Galaxy Books, 1958), p. 224.

6. Ibid., p. 335.

7. F. Schiller, "Letters on the Aesthetic Education of Man," in *Modern Continental Literary Criticism*, ed. O. B. Hardison, Jr. (New York: Appleton-Century-Crofts, 1962), p. 38. (Emphasis added.)

8. "Memorial Verses," April 1850, from *Poetry and Criticism of Matthew Arnold*, ed. A. Dwight Culler (Boston: Houghton Mifflin, 1961). (Emphasis added.)

9. Consider this passage as one which catches up these themes: "Thus, the element of art distinguishes itself from the practical interest of desire by the fact that it permits its object to subsist freely and in independence, while desire utilizes it in its own service by its destruction. On the other hand, artistic contemplation differs from theoretical consideration by the scientific intelligence, in cherishing interest for the object as an individual existence and not setting to work to transmute it into its universal thought and notion." Georg W. F. Hegel, *On Art, Religion, and Philosophy*, ed. J. Glen Gray (New York: Harper Torchbook, 1970), p. 66.

10. Immanuel Kant, *The Critique of Judgment*, trans. J. H. Bernard (New York: Hafner Publishing Co., 1968), p. 28.

11. Ibid., p. 73. (Emphasis added.)

12. Ibid., p. 227.

13. Ibid., p. 228.

14. Ibid., p. 287. Again: "For if the contemplation of the world only afforded a representation of things without any final purpose, no worth could accrue to its being from the mere fact that it is known; we must presuppose for it a final purpose, in reference to which its contemplation itself has worth. . . . That is, a good will is that whereby alone his being can have an absolute worth and in reference to which the being of the world can have a final purpose" (p. 293).

15. Kai Nielsen, *Contemporary Critiques of Religion* (New York: Macmillan Co., 1971), chap. 6; Simone de Beauvoir, *The Ethics of Ambiguity*, trans. Bernard Frechtman (New York: Philosophical Library, 1948).

16. Erich Fromm, *The Art of Loving* (New York: Harper & Row, 1956); Walter Kaufmann, *Without Guilt and Justice* (New York: Dell Publishing Co., 1973).

17. John R. Searle, "How to Derive 'Ought' from 'Is,'" in *Theories of Ethics*, ed. Philippa Foot (New York and London: Oxford University Press, 1967), pp. 101–14. In a footnote (p. 113n) Searle argues as follows from—or beyond—the concept of institution: "Standing on the back of some institutions one can tinker with constitutive rules and even throw some other institutions overboard. But could one throw all institutions overboard (in order perhaps to avoid ever having to derive an 'ought' from an 'is')? One could not and still engage in those forms of behaviour we consider characteristically human."

18. Alan Gewirth, *Reason and Morality* (Chicago: University of Chicago Press, 1978). See the discussion by E. M. Adams in *RMet* (March 1980): 579–92. A. J. Watt, "Transcendental Arguments and Moral Principles," *PhQ* 25 (January 1975): 40–57, contains a helpful discussion of R. S. Peter's argument that public discourse presupposes that one ought to consider the interests of others.

19. H. L. A. Hart, *The Concept of Law* (Oxford: At the Clarendon Press, 1961). D. J. O'Connor, *Aquinas and Natural Law* (New York: Macmillan Co., 1967), offers a contemporary attack, stressing the variability of natural law faced with a society changed by education and technology. James F. Bresnahan, "Rahner's Ethics: Critical Natural Law in Relation to Contemporary Ethical Methodology," *JR* 56 (January 1976): 36–60, notes that Rahner's approach is grounded in an ontology of freedom which requires a critical response to an instrumentalist view of human activity.

20. In addition to Anselm's treatment, see Descartes, *Meditations*, v, and Spinoza's *Ethics*, pt.1, props. 7–11. For Kant's famous criticism, see *Critique of Pure Reason: Transcendental Dialectic*: II, chap. iii, sec. 4.

21. Charles Hartshorne, *The Divine Relativity: A Social Conception of God* (New Haven: Yale University Press, 1948), pp. 20–21. For a good sample of the debate, see John Hick and Arthur C. McGill, *The Many-Faced Argument: Recent Studies on the Ontological Argument for the Existence of God* (New York: Macmillan Co., 1967).

22. John Hick, *Arguments for the Existence of God* (New York: Herder & Herder, 1971), pp. 86–87. (Italics his.)

23. David Hume, *Dialogues Concerning Natural Religion*, ed. with intro. by Henry D. Aiken (New York: Hafner Publishing Co., 1948).

24. I am quoting the translation in Anton C. Pegis, *Basic Writings of Saint Thomas Aquinas*, 2 vols. (New York: Random House, 1945), 1:22.

25. Hick, *Arguments for the Existence of God*, pp. 49–50. (Hick moderates the discussion between such contemporary defenders as Eric Mascall, *He Who Is* (New York and London: Longmans, Green & Co., 1948), and critics as Anthony Kenny, *The Five Ways* (London: Routledge & Kegan Paul, 1969).

26. See Alfred North Whitehead, *Process and Reality*, ed. David Ray Griffin and Donald W. Sherburne (New York: Free Press, 1978), pp. 32–33. Cf. Lewis S. Ford, "Process Philosophy and Our Knowledge of God," in *Traces of God in a Secular Culture*, ed. G. F. McLean (New York: Alba House, 1973), pp. 85–115, esp. pp. 108ff.

27. F. R. Tennant's *Philosophical Theology*, 2 vols. (Cambridge: At the University Press, 1935–37), 2:245ff., provides a statement of the probability argument. See John Hick's *Arguments for the Existence of God*, pp. 28–33, for a discussion of the objections.

28. Hume, *Dialogues*, p. 71. (Italics his.)

29. David Little cites numerous publications of Kluckhohn (and others) in constructing his argument in "Calvin and the Prospects for a Christian Theory of Natural Law," in *Norm and Context in Christian Ethics*, ed. Gene Outka and Paul Ramsey (New York: Charles Scribner's Sons, 1968), pp. 175–98.

30. De Beauvoir, *Ethics of Ambiguity*, p. 14.

31. Kai Nielsen has argued against theism by pointing out the devastating consequences that follow on any attempt to deny independence of access to ethical judgment. See his *Ethics without God* (Buffalo, N.Y.: Prometheus Books, 1973).

32. It should be noted that Kant did deal specifically with the "propensity to evil in human nature" in *Religion within the Limits of Reason Alone*, trans. Theodore M. Greene and Hoyt H. Hudson (New York: Harper & Row, 1960), pp. 23–40.

33. For a bibliographic survey at this point, see Hans H. Penner, "Fall and Rise of Methodology," *Religious Studies Review* 2 (January 1976): 11–16. In "Method in the History of Religions," *ThTo* 32 (January 1976): 382–94, Paul Ingram contrasts a Whiteadian model with a Cartesian model in such studies. Robert Baird, *Category Formation and the History of Religions* (The Hague: Mouton, 1971), asserts the possibility of objective historical knowledge, and accepts the qualification that such historical statements can only be very probable at best (pp. 38, 51).

34. Annemarie Schimmel, "Islam," in *Historia Religionum*, ed. C. Jouco Bleeker and G. Widengren, 2 vols. (Leiden: E. J. Brill, 1969, 1971), 2:179.

35. See the survey by Reinhard Pummer, "Recent Publications on the Methodology of the Science of Religion," *Numen* 22 (December 1975): 161–82.

36. Schimmel, "Islam," p. 144.

37. J. R. Fox, "Religions of Illiterate People: North America," in *Historia Religionum*, 2:593.

38. Hans Steininger, "Religions of China," in *Historia Religionum*, 2:488.

39. Alex Wayman, "Buddhism," in *Historia Religionum*, 2:420.

40. E. g., consider Mircea Eliade's discussion of the "abolition of time" in *Cosmos and History*, trans. W. R. Trask (New York: Harper & Row, 1959), pp. 49–92. As an instance of the Jungian psychology (and ontology) presupposed here, see Eliade's *Rites and Symbols of Initiation: The Mysteries of Birth and Rebirth*, trans. W. R. Trask (New York: Harper & Row, 1965), p. 128, where "modern man" is in view: "The imaginative activity and the dream experiences of modern man continue to be pervaded by religious symbols, figures, themes. As some psychologists delight in repeating, the unconscious is religious. From one point of view it could be said that in the man of desacralized societies, religion has become 'unconscious'; it lies buried in the deepest strata of his being; but this by no means implies that it does not continue to perform an essential function in the economy of the psyche."

41. R. N. Dandekar, "Hinduism," in *Historia Religionum*, 2:298. (Italics his.)

42. Eric Voegelin, *The Ecumenic Age*, vol. 4 of his *Order and History* (Baton Rouge: Louisiana State University Press, 1974), p. 321.

43. Ibid., p. 327.

44. Dandekar, "Hinduism," p. 341.

4

The Human Quest
and God's Free Answer

Human life is so grounded that it is intended toward a goal. In varying degrees and forms, human life seeks that goal and so knows that
it is made for God. In the *kairos* of Jesus, God has acted freely to
answer the quest of all by giving a sure word about the end which
honors and intensifies life.

HUMAN INTENTIONALITY
AND HISTORICAL AMBIGUITY

Human beings sense that their reality is tied up with their eventuality. In
what will the events of life eventuate—finally? The question cannot be
answered abstractly, as if life did not exist. It is not a question about the presuppositions for life and thus a question about something intelligible apart from
life. In this way, the question about the goal is logically asymmetrical with
the question about the ground. Indeed, perhaps it is better not to speak of
this matter as a question. What we speak of here is the human quest for God
as the one in whom life can well end.

What is required if life is to end well? Three elements cluster together in
the notion of a goal: First, life must end here; that is, all of life must be caught
up in this reality. Universality is needed. Second, life must end here; that
is, the end must comprehend, cohere with, fit, receive that which here ends.
Affirmation is needed. Third, life must end here; that is, the end must be
sure, not subject to overturning. Finality is needed. That God is the world's
goal in these senses we have already claimed in Chapter 1. Does the world
know about this? Does the world know its goal?

It is clear that human beings know that the meaning and worth of life must
be won within life, and that the odds often seem to be against us. While
it is to be won within life, the goal is recognized to be not simply another
state of life—a piece of the process arrogantly reified and absolutized.[1]

The quest for the goal seems to be against great odds. That is true already
analytically in that the very certainty and finality we seek seem incompatible

with the contingency essential to the quest that we are. One can well under-stand Sartre's sentiment that the human project is a useless passion. It is more than analytically true in that the diagnosis of the human venture materially may speak of something much darker than the mere incompleteness of our progress. With such odds at hand it is not strange that one witnesses a tendency to isolate the quest from the goal.

That tendency may be found in the many-splendored wonder of "humanism." At work in such thinkers as Bertrand Russell, the early Sartre, and Camus in the *Myth of Sisyphus* is an affirmation of the human venture for efficacy, together with a strong suspicion of any more-than-human ap-peals. Still, the quest itself seems in jeopardy, and not because of any appeal to a goal. At one point the problem may appear to be that of incompleteness due to the inexorable reality of the death of the individual. Classical humanism could handle this difficulty easily enough, as George Steiner notes:

> The thrust of will which engenders art and disinterested thought, the engaged response which alone can ensure its transmission to other human beings, to the future, are rooted in a gamble on transcendence. The writer or thinker means the words of the poem, the sinews of the argument, the personae of the drama, to outlast his own life, to take on the mystery of autonomous presence and present-ness. The sculptor commits to the stone the vitalities against and across time which will soon drain from his own living hand.[2]

But now the difficulty within the quest comes to be seen as more qualitative and hence as more far-reaching. Again Steiner:

> The time-death copula of a classic structure of personal and philosophic values is, in many respects, syntactic, and is inherent to a fabric of life in which language holds a sovereign, almost magically validated role. Diminish that role, subvert that eminence, and you will have begun to demolish the hierarchies and transcendence-values of a classic civilization. Even death can be made mute.[3]

If faith in the humanities' core curriculum is beset by failing vision in the future and failed health in the present, to what may the humanistic quest repair? We have each other, one might reply—and then hurry to try to make that good news. Thus on the matter of meaning in history Karl Popper insists,

> We should refuse to speak of the meaning of history in the sense of something concealed in it, or of a moral hidden in the divine tragedy of history, or in the sense of some other meaning which might perhaps be discovered by some great historian or philosopher or religious leader.[4]

Yet he insists that we can give meanings to history that are "feasible for and worthy of human beings." The appeal is to the free competition of thought, not a singular scientific method but precisely the public testing of ideas. That process is to make possible a piecemeal social engineering.

There is a quest here, but it seems to amount to "keeping on keeping on." One finds the same sense of resignation to historical destiny cast in aesthetic terms in George Steiner:

> We cannot turn back. We cannot choose the dreams of unknowing. We shall, I expect, open the last door in the castle even if it leads, perhaps *because* it leads, onto realities which are beyond the reach of human comprehension and control. We shall do so with that desolate clairvoyance, so miraculously rendered in Bartok's music, because opening doors is the tragic merit of our identity.[5]

This sort of appeal is deliberately antitheistic, as a kindred statement by novelist Brigid Brophy makes clear:

> I suspect the correct answer to "What have we put in the place of religion?" is "What have we put in the place of belief in fairies?"—not by way of a rhetorical debating point but because, if you anatomize the answer, it indicates what we *ought* to put in the place of belief in God. One branch of the answer implies that we have used our scientific imaginations. . . . The other branch of the answer refers to the other branch of our imagination, with its faculty for lending aesthetic belief. . . . Shakespeare's poetry bears witness to more and to something of greater constancy than literal-minded belief. It performs the psychological, non-supernatural miracle of creating in us poetic faith. We have replaced belief in fairies by A Midsummer Night's Dream.[6]

More than that, it gives up any appeal to a more than human agency and an other than historical destiny. For all that such thinkers acknowledge difficulty (Popper even dedicates *The Poverty of Historicism* to those who "fell victim to the fascist and communist belief in Inexorable Laws of a Historical Destiny"), or perhaps precisely because of the difficulties they can only "acknowledge," these humanists seem almost romantically optimistic. It remains to consider a casting of human hope which seems to speak of something other than more of the same, while still stopping short of theism.

The vision of Karl Marx qualifies. Here something is known about the quest for the goal of human life. Human essence is human quest, as surely as that essence "is not abstraction inhering in each single individual [but is] in its actuality . . . the ensemble of social relationships."[7] With this social understanding the individual is called to and constituted in relationships. Of course not every relationship is appropriate. Marx attacked religion as the externalizing of the self-consciousness: "And indeed religion is the self-consciousness and self-regard of man who has either not yet found or has already lost himself. But *man* is not an abstract being squatting outside the world."[8] But while the criticism of religion may be the premise of all criticism, religion is the *sigh* of the oppressed before it is their opiate. To address the conditions which cause human suffering human effort is needed, of course. The scope of Marx's vision is impressive. He looks as well to the emergence of the proletariat, the class that is not a class and which can redeem itself only "through the total redemption of humanity."[9]

Marx's vision was historical. How do matters stand now? What do his visionary disciples see? In a figure like Georg Lukacs one still senses the grasp for totality and the commitment to historical dialectic. But the vision seems to be fossilizing. Even if one successfully resists the tendency toward positivism and its predictive laws of the evolution of human society, one may still let the dialectic lose its genuine historical expectancy. It seems to have become a matter of a standpoint or perspective:

> The task of orthodox Marxism, its victory over Revisionism and Utopianism can never mean the defeat, once and for all, of false tendencies. It is an ever-renewed struggle against the insidious effects of bourgeois ideology on the thought of the proletariat. Marxist orthodoxy is no guardian of traditions, it is the eternally vigilant prophet proclaiming the relation between the tasks of the immediate present and the totality of the historical process.[10]

In other Marxists reactions to this *via media* may be found. Adorno's negative dialectics retains the struggle, though it is not as clear that we may here speak of quest:

> Negation or negativity did not designate a spiritual haven or retreat but rather the scene of an incessant struggle or hand-to-hand combat between thought and reality—a struggle which ultimately was an outgrowth of man's involvement in nature and his concrete sufferings as an embodied creature.[11]

On the other hand in the statements of Antonio Negri, of the Italian Communist party, the eschatological vision does seem within reach; though one may struggle to find here the affirmation (goal) of all life:

> I immediately feel the warmth of the worker-proletarian community every time I pull the ski mask over my face.

> Our sabotage organizes the proletarian assault on heaven so that finally that damned heaven may be no more.[12]

Maurice Merleau-Ponty has argued that the essential task of Marxism is to find a violence which recedes with the approach of the human future. But he recognizes the difficulties at this point:

> Marxism does not offer us a Utopia, a future known ahead of time, nor any philosophy of history. However, it deciphers events, discovers in them a common

meaning and thereby grasps a leading thread which, without dispensing us from fresh analysis at every stage, allows us to orient ourselves toward events. Marxism is as foreign to a dogmatic philosophy of history which seeks to impose by fire and sword a visionary future of mankind as it is to a terrorism lacking all perspective. It seeks, rather, to offer men a perception of history which would continuously clarify the lines of force and vectors of the present.[13]

The obvious difficulty is that one is left without any sure brake against terrorism when the contingency in history seems to prevail over the rationality.

Faced with this difficulty, one may of course simply renounce closure and affirm the essential and radical incompleteness of the human quest, as Sartre's rendition of the Marxist vision suggests.[14] Or one might settle for an aesthetic resolution of the dilemma, as Georg Lukacs seems to do:

> This principle [of art] is the creation of a concrete totality that springs from a conception of form oriented toward the concrete content of its material substratum. In this view form is therefore able to demolish the "contingent" relation of the parts to the whole and to resolve the merely apparent opposition between chance and necessity.[15]

But we have already suggested (in Chapter 3) that an aesthetic reading of transcendence hardly seems to honor the reality of the human quest. Some clear expression of transcendence as goal seems needed, something that so speaks of the end as to yield the clear and sure resolution sought. Marx had that in principle in the notion of the proletariat. But as the proletariat fails to develop, the Marxist movement threatens to come apart, yielding the disparate versions we have briefly sampled.

In the instances just cited we do find an authentic human sense for life's intentionality. There is a recognition of the significance of history, that a goal lies ahead of humankind. But there appears no clear and convincing word about the shape of that goal. There seems to be an erosion of hope occurring within the movement itself. That history will end, or at least that life is always ending, that at the end and the endings it will matter what we have made of life, all this is clear. But the clarity still seems formal and pales before the material ambiguity of history. Is more known? Perhaps the best place to look may be to the stuff of explicit appeal to transcendence, the religious quest of humankind.

TELEOLOGICAL RELIGION
AND DIVINE DECISIVENESS

In *The Christian Faith*, Friedrich Schleiermacher argued that the widest diversity between forms of piety is that which exists, with respect to the religious affections, between those forms which subordinate the natural in human conditions to the moral and those which, on the contrary, subordinate the moral to the natural.[16] In the former class, which he designates "teleological,"

> the passive states (whether pleasant or unpleasant, whether occasioned by external Nature or by social relationships) only arouse the feeling of absolute dependence in so far as they are referred to the spontaneous activity, i.e. in so far as we know that some particular thing (just because we stand in that relation to the totality of existence which is expressed in our passive state) has to be done by us, so that the action which depends on and proceeds from that state has thus precisely this God-consciousness as its impulse.[17]

The notion of absolute dependence is not the most felicitous formulation of our relationship to the One who is categorically supreme. God's honor is secured by robbing human reality. But what is striking about Schleiermacher's work at this point is that despite the strong pressure toward passivity which the notion of absolute dependence exerts, he appraises teleological religion, rather than "aesthetic," as the higher form. Schleiermacher thus identifies a concept of religion, if not a clear concept of deity, which supports the human venture with its concern for efficacy.

Teleological religion does exist, or at least teleological elements are to be found within the world of the religious. It is apparent that the religious self may know not only that its mission is from God but also that it is for God and to God, that, as Schleiermacher puts it, "the action which is pre-figured in the religious emotion is a practical contribution to the advancement of the Kingdom of God." We are concerned in this section to ascertain "how widely and how well" this knowledge may be at hand, and we have a particular interest in how the concept of God functions in this connection.

Schleiermacher classifies Islam with Christianity and Judaism as teleological religions. There is indeed a very direct teleology in the notion of Allah, who will punish those who treat their slaves badly and do not care for orphans, widows, and the poor, and will reward those who do good. But there are teleological elements also elsewhere. These elements bear witness to the human sense for God as the world's goal, but they seem subject to distortion in their respective contexts. Thus Hans Steininger finds such elements even in the East, as in Taoism:

> In contrast to Buddhism which sees life as suffering and demands that, when he attains the ideal stage of ultimate reality, man ought to be "dead" to the things of this world, Taoism holds that life is valuable and ought to be enjoyed in the right way, and prolonged. The World and the individual's Ego are not illusions but are very agreeable realities. He who has understood the teaching of *Yang* and *Ying* and their interaction in the Five Elements and in the all-embracing (Taoist) *Tao*, is able to procure for himself a glorified body so that he may enjoy immortality or at least longevity. . . .[18]

"Immortality or at least longevity"—precisely so! One finds conceptions of the next life that are so much like this one as to constitute a merely quantitative supplement. In a sense the Hindu teaching about *karma* represents this, since a person's doings in the course of one life inexorably govern the nature and conditions of that person's next life. Any religious formula by which God functions as a direct instrument of judgment would seem to do so as well. Tellingly, deliverance (*moksa*) entails freedom from involvement in this chain of causality, precisely by realization of one's essential identity with the one absolute reality.[19]

Eric Voegelin has stressed the linkages between the questions human beings ask when they act religiously. He identifies six structures that raise questions:

1. The existence of the cosmos
2. The hierarchy and diversification of being
3. The experience of questioning as the constituent of humanity
4. The leap in existential truth through noetic and pneumatic illuminations of consciousness
5. The process of history in which the differentiations of questioning consciousness and the leaps in truth occur
6. The eschatological movement in the process beyond its structure

Despite his concern to find continuity in the questioning, Voegelin acknowledges that "the questions concerning the existence of the cosmos and the essence of its order (1 and 2) differentiate earlier than the questions concerning the process of consciousness (5 and 6)."[20] If the process of life does not get "beyond the structure," we do precisely have immortality as longevity, or resurrection as immortality, one might even say. Here the given hardly seems to hold a hint of anything qualitatively other, unless by opposition.

Is there any way out of this bind? Can the categorical supremacy characterizing God as goal be so cast as to get humankind surely beyond a "more of the same" future, while yet receiving the efficacy of the historically contingent present? Such a goal would warrant precisely the preposition "beyond," rather than "before," "with," or even "against" to formulate the relationship between that God and us. If there were such a God, could we know about that? Do we?

There is and we do. At least that is the claim of the Christian faith: God *has acted* decisively within time and because of that a sure word is clear about the end. The Christian understanding of "the work of Christ" is that the God who is at the end has acted decisively in the chaotic middle and that this can be surely known. This decisive action does not undercut human efficacy. But it does make clear that we do not need to be in doubt about the will and work of the categorically supreme one who is the world's goal.

Christians claim to know this. Is knowledge like this claimed elsewhere?

3 / THE KNOWLEDGE OF GOD

Here we must proceed carefully. One would like to avoid adding to the list of those who have claimed unique doctrines for Christianity only to suffer the embarrassment of encountering empirical disconfirmation. Thus the idea of a God of love is hardly the private property of Christians. For example, Dandekar writes of Hinduism:

> Divine grace is a frequently occurring religious motif. God is said to have assumed finite forms for the sake of love for his worshippers and in order to free them from the shackles of this worldly existence. . . . Ramanuja, who seeks to give a philosophical foundation to the theistic ideology, has to encounter the problem of the coordination of the two concepts, namely, the grace of god and the law of Karma. . . . God is the source and substratum of both grace and law of Karma. There is, therefore, no question of one of these two being subservient to the other. God often employs the law of Karma as a kind of testing exercise for one to whom grace is to be ultimately shown.[21]

Similarly, the notion of incarnation has not been successfully patented by Christianity. Moreover, this notion is present precisely in linkage with human freedom, as when the Hindu *avataras* are understood to present a person with a norm for orienting that person's spiritual quest. God comes to us that we might come to God.[22]

Here we have human responsibility, human hope, divine initiative—all familiar themes. What may not be present is a conception of incarnation which entails a free and sure resolution of the human quest for a goal. There is some sense for the sure: the incarnation of the Hindu *avataras* is held to be unmistakable, and in Islam the person of the prophet is considered the expression of God's greatest mercy since in the exemplary pilgrimage Allah's will is *finally* revealed. There is as well some sense in the world of the religious for the divine freedom. Confucianism, for example, resists classification as moralistic, because the believer here knows that good conduct cannot force Heaven to be benevolent and distribute blessings and benefits. Islam's variegated history includes a debate between those who held that God, comprehending all qualities of possibility and impossibility, can do anything whatsoever and those who held that God's justice was such that God must bring the pious to paradise and condemn the sinner to hell.[23]

What Christian faith does is draw these dynamics together into a center that deserves to be designated kairotic on formal terms, if for no other reason. Christian faith claims that the sure word about the end is now known in the free action of God in history in Jesus. Because of this one, "nothing can separate" and none can condemn. Here the free and the sure come together in the good. This good is not unrelated to the good of the call into life and the call in life; *kairos* does come in the context of *logos* and *nomos*. But this

256

good is not won out of nothing; it is won against something. In this *kairos* God proves to be Lord even over sin. God does this precisely by accepting what is human. The one who took human flesh into his person takes human sin into his mission.

Here we do not speak as does the Hindu of Kalki, who is yet to come at the end of ages when he will put an end to all evil powers and reestablish moral order. We speak of the goal as present, not of the ground as future. Christian faith does not share Islam's appeal to the unicity of God, which although it permits Jesus a special place in the Quran does not allow him a special place in God. The God of the Christian knows relationships within— and without. Thus Christians do not share the Quran's denial of Jesus' cruci- fixion; their Jesus was not replaced by someone "made in his likeness" and taken up immediately into heaven to return shortly before doomsday (43/61).[24] For the Christians' Jesus, humankind seems to have been looking; the elements are there. They come together in the confession of the decisive act of God in Jesus, so that Christians find themselves saying to others, "This one we declare to you."

Just how scandalous is this particularity? We have risked analytical com- parisons lest it be supposed that one may settle the status of "the religions" without looking at them. More—much more—of that needs to be done by Christians. But at the same time it is important to render some judgment which reflects the faith centered in this particular. Thus we make five responses:

First. All *life* is grounded in the gracious will and activity of God, the world's ground. Humankind can hear and respond to the call of God in life, quite apart from the kairotic word.

Second. What God has done decisively in Jesus, God has done *for all*. When the time was full, God acted once for all time; that is the scope of the divine decisiveness. Jesus, then, does not belong to the Christians in his efficacy; he is the Son of the One in whom all life is grounded.

Third. The knowledge of this kairos does matter, so surely as it is we in our knowing and willing who are to be saved. It makes a difference to us, to what and whom we can become, that we know of this kairos. The God who acted decisively in Jesus is a God who cares that humankind know this good news and rejoice in it. There is joy in heaven over every sinner who repents.

Fourth. Our knowledge of this *kairos* is particular and confessional. We know a gospel which tells of this divine decisiveness and which has claimed us in the telling. We are instructed by this word that comes to us from beyond ourselves. We do not deduce it analytically; we do not derive it experientially; we confess it because we have been told of it.[25] This gospel does win us; we do believe it; the *logos* in this *kairos* is one that we can recognize. But there remains a certain stubborn idiosyncrasy about the particularity. We would not have guessed the ending, much less the name. We are glad to know now and to tell.

Fifth. We do not know as surely about others who do not know of the *kairos*. That fits the particularity of our knowledge. We do know that God is their goal and that God is surely for them. Whatever the next life is for them, it will be *their* life. Who they are as they come to God will depend on what is given to them and on what the given has come to be in their lives.

In these last remarks stress has been placed on the time between *kairos*— and knowledge of *kairos*—and *eschatos*. The word about the end of the quest is not *at* the end. We are to continue. Without the "in-between" ground and goal coincide. They do not in the Christian reading of reality. So we must speak of how the knowledge of the *kairos* honors and even intensifies the reality of human life.

GOD'S JUSTIFICATION
AND HUMAN RESPONSIBILITY

The Christian knows a God whose act in Jesus for all humankind is so sure and free and good that it answers the world's quest for a goal. Nothing beyond this one is asked or expected. In the bargaining logic of the marketplace, to reveal the goal so surely might be to encourage slackness, even embezzlement, in the use of the gift given. But that logic does not apply. It is not merely that the goal is known only "in principle" in this *kairos*, that this one must still come again "in glory." Such a tactical delay would not suffice to nerve our effort, so long as the end was already clear. Rather, it is intrinsically the case that to know this God as ground and goal is to have one's life honored and even intensified.

This follows from the specific nature of God's act in Jesus. What has been made firm and clear in Jesus is God's will to love, even in the teeth of our sin. Thus Kierkegaard writes;

> Seriousness lies precisely in this: that loving and being loved is God's passion, almost as if—infinite love—he were himself bound in this passion, in the power of the passion so that he could not cease loving, almost as if it were a weakness, while it is indeed his strength, his omnipotent love, in such a degree is his love not subject to change.[26]

God has acted for our justification in Jesus, and this justification is not a ledger entry but a living commitment, which works toward and in the beloved. Love creates freedom and responsibility. This does not undo what God has done; it empowers and directs our doing.

In effect I have pointed out in the preceding paragraph that our "continuance" is called for *from God*. That call takes effect *in us*. That God's justifying *kairos* is a living will to love us, no matter what, "changes the values" in our own situation. To know of this is to be unable to go on unchanged. Knowing this may not create response, but it clearly entails responsibility. In the rhythm of Kierkegaard, we might speak of the bid, which is human life, being raised:

> But what an infinite accent falls upon the self by getting God as a measure! The measure for the self always is that in the face of which it is a self; . . . so each thing is qualitatively that by which it is measured; and that which is qualitatively its measure is ethically its goal. . . . And now for Christianity! Christianity teaches that this particular individual, and so every individual, whatever in other respects this individual may be . . . this individual exists *before* God, . . . can talk with God any moment he will, sure to be heard by Him; in short, this man is invited to live on the most intimate terms with God! Furthermore, for this man's sake God came to the world, let himself be born, suffers and dies; and this suffering God almost begs and entreats this man to accept the help which is offered to him! Verily, if there is anything that would make a man lose his understanding, it is surely this!

The Christian understands this and knows life to be intensified!

One might add that life is intensified by the knowledge that it is *for God*. The Christian knows a goal which is not an unmoved mover, but a loving will, not merely something we can desire, but someone who can desire and receive, and so honor and intensify, our life. That our lives matter so calls us, precisely as justified, to continue.

The task of these final pages is not to write of the Christian life in general, but to speak of the Christian life with respect to what follows specifically from and for our knowing God. In doing so, we add the "final" cause to our earlier discussion of "efficient," "material," and "formal" causes in the knowing of God. In a sense, of course, we need give no final cause for the knowledge of God. Why know God? Know God to worship God—simply that is the final cause, after all. But in knowing and trusting God we are caught up in a relationship which carries us into a number of activities. The joy of God and the service of God come together as one continues in these activities. As we consider them we shall find the *logos/kairos* relationship and distinction serviceable again. And one last time we may enumerate.

First. We continue as we respond to the task of dogmatics. Our knowledge of God makes us responsible to do this. In every age the church is called to state faithfully and winsomely what it knows. There is a gracious familiarity about this task because the "old, old story of Jesus and his love" does not change. It is this story and its telling which have given birth to the church, again and again; and the church neither dares nor desires to give it up.

But the telling is ours and so emphatically human. It is a story about which we must think, for it speaks of a world, of persons, of time. Understandings of such matters do change, and have changed dramatically since the classic statements of Christendom were cast. Thus two Christian groups who agree in valuing tradition, Catholics and Lutherans, also appropriately agree that "as cultures evolve, new emphases in the proclamation of the gospel may be needed, new conceptualizations may take shape, new formulations may become urgent."[27] So the church struggles to find the best categories, the most illuminating perspective in which to tell the story. Christians who so struggle know that the reality they study to develop these conceptual tools is in fact grounded in the God of their salvation, as surely as it was the *logos* who came to be flesh in this *kairos*. So too in their thinking, Christians may find the understanding of the *kairos* revealed freshly to them in their probing of the *logos*, of the order or structure of reality.

Thus responsible continuance in the statement of the faith calls for both continuity and novelty. Just so, the church has reached dogmatic consensus on some points of doctrine, but not on others.

Second. We continue as we respond to the task of the mission. To know and trust this story is to be responsible to tell it. We have tried to consider how God may be known in the other religions. That consideration is appropriate precisely on Christian grounds, given the recognition that God is known beyond the boundaries of the Christian church. How well and how widely, are empirical questions. The Christian will find those questions answered in specific contact with persons of other faiths. In that contact the Christian aims to tell the story. Thus the Christian is not open in that contact, if to be open is to be without an identity. But in order to tell the story the Christian need not believe that the person of the other faith knows nothing of God.

The Christian knows that this precious *kairos* is held in earthen vessels. Indeed, the very specificity of the *kairos* makes it especially vulnerable to cultural accommodation as one seeks to make it bear flesh freshly in each time. To know Jesus is not necessarily to know what it means to do everything in the name of the Lord Jesus. Moreover, this *kairos* is only to be understood within the structure of the *logos* in whom all things hold together, even now. Surely that has some application to something as powerful and pervasive as a religion! So one comes to the contact with persons of other faiths pledged to tell, expecting to teach, prepared to learn.

Third. We continue as we respond to the task of apologetics. Since we know God, we are prepared to give a reason for the hope that is in us (1 Pet. 3:15). In the apologetic task we respond to the questions, the concerns, indeed the objections, of those who are outside the household of faith. In doing that we render a responsible service to God who wills to be known by all. God may need no defense, but our formulations and understandings surely do. Indeed, such a defense may itself provoke revisions—so human is our grasp of the truth and thus so fundamental is the apologetic task.

Again our knowledge of God as *logos* and in *kairos* informs us. To one who knows God as *logos*, all convincing statements about reality are pertinent, even if they seem to undergird objections to the faith. The Christian accepts God-questions generated by those understandings of reality, for the Christian recognizes that what is at stake in these exchanges serves the specific kairotic confession of Jesus. What the faithful apologist may do is plead for the richest understanding of reality, as those convincing nontheistic statements about reality are indeed comprehended within a perspective in which reality is grounded in God and claimed by God. Moreover, the apologist may find that knowledge of the *kairos* serves to focus and direct what is otherwise quite properly known in particular terms.

Fourth. We continue to the task of ethics. In this *locus*, of course, our reference is not so much to our doing as to the thinking we must do for that doing. Here the Christian happily makes common cause with all those who respond to the call of God in the good and the right. Their insights are honored, as the world's Ground is known as *nomos*. But the ethical call is also intensified, and so Christian ethicists come to speak of an "accentuation, newness, and heightening" of the law, as the Christian is "filled with a new willingness to suffer for the good of the neighbor and to do so with joy."[28] One may speak here of specific motivations, such as a sense of dependence, gratitude, repentance, obligation, and possibility.[29] Beneath them all is the recognition that God is the world's goal in the sense that what we do does go to God, does matter to God. Thus Wolfhart Pannenberg can draw such an allegedly abstract doctrine as the Trinity into ethical relevance. As Jesus refers us to the Father, so we serve in the Spirit:

> Thus the doctrine of the Trinity is the seal of the pure futurity of God, which does not harden into an impotent diastasis, a mere beyond contrasting with man's present, but which instead draws it into itself and through enduring the pain of the negative reconciles it with itself.[30]

Again one detects the relationship between *logos* and *kairos*. The Logos may well teach that relatedness is given with creatureliness, but it hardly reveals sacrifice and suffering as that to which we are called. But the Logos may well help one to understand that the kairotic call is not to masochism, so that self-sacrifice becomes the means to the end of neighbor-regard rather than an end in itself.[31] Or again, the Logos teaches well enough about the eventful character of life, but the Kairos focuses that character materially. Thus Kierkegaard writes, "a man's eternal worth lies precisely in this, that he can get a history; the divine in him lies in this, that he himself, if he will, can give that history continuity."[32] So wrote Kierkegaard as a philosophical ethicist; but Kierkegaard the Christian also knew of a "second ethics":

> The new science then begins with dogmatics, in the same sense that the imma-
> nent science begins with metaphysics. . . . The first ethic foundered upon the
> sinfulness of the individual . . . for the fact that the sin of the individual widens
> out and becomes the sin of the whole race. At this juncture came dogmatics
> and helped by the doctrine of original sin. The new ethics presupposes dogmatics
> and along with that original sin, and by this it now explains the sin of the in-
> dividual, while at the same time it presents ideality as a task, not however by
> a movement from above down, but from below up.[33]

So, knowing God, we continue in dogmatics, missions, apologetics, and ethics. We know of our Ground and of our Goal. Our knowledge is of one who justifies us, who honors our life by undergoing it, and intensifies it by calling us freshly into the mission for which we were created. We know this and so we continue, but there is much we do not know. We believe this contin-uance will itself come to an end and then all ambiguity and error will cease in the most blessed vision of God:

> For now we see in a mirror dimly, but then face to face. Now I know in part;
> then I shall understand fully, even as I have been fully understood (1 Cor. 13:12).

NOTES

1. Wolfhart Pannenberg, *What Is Man?* trans. Duane A. Priebe (Philadelphia: Fortress Press, 1970), p. 8.

2. George Steiner, *In Bluebeard's Castle* (New Haven: Yale University Press, 1971), p. 89.

3. Ibid., p. 114.

4. Karl Popper, "Emancipation through Knowledge," in *The Humanist Outlook*, ed. A. J. Ayer (London: Pemberton Publishing Co., 1968), p. 283.

5. Steiner, *In Bluebeard's Castle*, p. 140. (Italics his.)

6. Brigid Brophy, "Faith Lost—Imagination Enriched," in *The Humanist Outlook*, p. 197.

7. Karl Marx, "Theses on Feuerbach," in *Writings of the Young Marx on Philosophy and Society*, ed. and trans. Loyd D. Easton and Kurt H. Guddat (Garden City, N.Y.: Doubleday & Co., 1967), p. 402.

8. Karl Marx, "Toward the Critique of Hegel's Philosophy of Law: Introduction," in *Writings of the Young Marx*, p. 250. (Italics his.)

9. Ibid., p. 263.

10. George Lukacs, *History and Class Consciousness: Studies in Marxist Dialectics*, trans. Rodney Livingstone (Cambridge, Mass.: M.I.T. Press, 1971), p. 24.

11. This summary is by Fred R. Dallmayr in "Phenomenology and Critical Theory: Adorno," *Cultural Hermeneutics* (July 1976): 393.

12. I have these quotes of Negri's by way of Thomas Sheehan, "Italy: Behind the Ski Mask," *New York Review of Books*, August 16, 1979, p. 26. The first is from Negri's *Domination and Sabotage: On the Marxist Method of Social Transformation*; the second is not documented.

13. Maurice Merleau-Ponty, *Humanism and Terror, an Essay on the Communist Problem*, trans. John O'Neill (Boston: Beacon Press, 1969), pp. 98 and xviii.

14. In "Sartre's Constriction of the Marxist Dialectic," *RMet* 33 (September 1979). George Allan provides a useful summary (p. 87): "Jean Paul Sartre, in the *Critique de la raison dialectique*, develops a theory of praxis which extends the anthropology of *L'être et le néant*, while simultaneously claiming to correct and complete Marxism. Central to Sartre's argument are two assertions: (1) that dialectic is fundamental to human action, and (2) that all historical development is rooted in the *praxis* of individual persons. These twin assertions, by insisting upon the existential element in social change, do not merely correct Marxism. They fundamentally alter it. In affirming the dialectical structure of *praxis*, Sartrean Marxism is compelled to deny a dialectic of history. It modifies the Marxian dialectic by radically constricting its scope, denying a becoming of the dialectic by insisting upon a dialectic of becoming."

15. Lukacs, *History and Class Consciousness*, p. 137. Agnes Heller makes the juxtaposition even more explicit in "The Philosophy of the Late Lukacs," *Philosophy and Social Criticism* (Summer 1979): 161: "Works of art—as unities of the individual and the species—have always represented the immanence of humankind, and are in fact objectivations of this immanence. Myths and religions, because they are expressions of transcendence, have always been enemies of art, even in times when art made use of mythical and religious subjects. Only in a free world, a world without myths and religions, will art be 'homebound' again, returning to the everyday life of man. Lukacs still insists on his absolute, but this absolute is no longer identical with a movement, a class, or a party. The absolute is simply the proclamation of Karl Marx—since that proclamation the world of freedom is open to us. . . . The philosophy of history inherent in this aesthetics is conceived in the spirit of hope, in the sense of a *guaranteed* hope." (Italics hers.)

16. Friedrich Schleiermacher, *The Christian Faith*, trans. and ed. H. R. Mackintosh and J. S. Stewart (New York: Harper & Row, Harper Torchbooks, 1963), 1:39–40.

17. Ibid., p. 41.

18. Hans Steininger, "Religions of China," in *Historia Religionum*, ed. C. Jouco Bleeker and G. Widengren, 2 vols. (Leiden: E. J. Brill, 1969, 1971), 2:497. (Italics his.)

19. R. N. Dandekar, "Hinduism," in *Historia Religionum*, 2:241.

20. Eric Voegelin, *The Ecumenic Age*, vol. 4 of his *Order and History* (Baton Rouge: Louisiana State University Press, 1974), pp. 326–27.

21. Dandekar, "Hinduism," pp. 307–8.

22. Ibid., p. 303.

23. Annemarie Schimmel, "Islam," in *Historia Religionum*, 2:143, 145.

24. Ibid., p. 175.

25. One might find this emphasis reflected in Paul Ricoeur's shift to language as

the encompassing category (rather than the voluntary/involuntary) for understanding the human. Gary B. Madison has stated one view of the consequences: "If systematic metaphysics is something more or something other than poetry, something more than the pure imaginative use of metaphorical language, as Ricoeur wants to say, it would seem that it would have to be the *abuse* of metaphor, in which case it would be a form of myth, and the truths of metaphysics would be believed-in dead metaphors." "Reflections on Paul Ricoeur's Philosophy of Metaphor," *Philosophy Today* 21 (supp) (Winter 1977): 429. For responses see Mary Gerhart, "The Extent and Limits of Metaphor: Reply to Gary Madison," ibid., pp. 431–36; and David Pellauer, "A Response to Gary Madison's 'Reflections on Paul Ricoeur's Philosophy of Metaphor,'" ibid., pp. 437–45.

26. Søren Kierkegaard, *Papirer*, ed. P. A. Heiberg and Victor Kuhr, 11 vols. (Copenhagen: Gyldendals, 1909–48), XI 2 A 54 (translation mine). The quotation which follows on page 259 is from Kierkegaard's *The Sickness Unto Death*, trans. W. Lowrie (Princeton: Princeton University Press, 1941), pp. 210, 216. (Italics his.)

27. Paul C. Empie, T. Austin Murphy, and Joseph A. Burgess, eds., *Teaching Authority and Infallibility in the Church: Lutherans and Catholics in Dialogue VI*, "Common Statement" (Minneapolis: Augsburg Publishing House, 1980), p. 24.

28. Gustaf Wingren, *Gospel and Church*, trans. Ross Mackenzie (Edinburgh: Oliver & Boyd, 1964), p. 181.

29. James Gustafson, *Can Ethics Be Christian?* (Chicago: University of Chicago Press, 1975), pp. 92–93.

30. Wolfhart Pannenberg, *Basic Questions in Theology*, vol. 2, trans. George H. Kehm (Philadelphia: Fortress Press, 1971), p. 249.

31. Gene Outka in *Agape: An Ethical Analysis* (New Haven: Yale University Press, 1972), pp. 276–78, points out how self-sacrifice leads to self-contradictory circumstances if everyone were so to act, and that this theme can at best be incorporated as a subordinate feature in neighbor-regarding considerations.

32. Søren Kierkegaard, *Either/Or*, trans. David F. Swenson, Lillian M. Swenson, and Walter Lowrie, 2 vols (Princeton: Princeton University Press, 1944), 2:209–10.

33. Søren Kierkegaard, *The Concept of Dread*, trans. Walter Lowrie (Princeton: Princeton University Press, 1944), pp. 18–19.

FOURTH LOCUS

The Creation

PHILIP J. HEFNER

THE CREATION

Introduction

1. The Biblical Witness to Creation
   The Form of the Biblical Witness
   The Substance of the Biblical Witness: The Old Testament
   The Substance of the Biblical Witness: The New Testament

2. The Creation of the World
   The Nature of the Claim
   God and the World: Issues for Creation Arising from God's Nature
   Creation Out of Nothing ("*ex nihilo*")
   Contemporary Challenges and Contributions to the Doctrine

3. The Human Being
   The Question of Human Destiny
   The Human Being as Created Co-Creator
   The Primeval Condition ("*status integritatis*")
   The Imago Dei
   Spirit and Matter in the Human Creature
   The Fall and Original Sin ("*status corruptionis*")
   Restoration
   Challenges to Christian Anthropology

4. The Continuing Work of Creation
   Historical Survey
   Perennial Concerns of the Doctrine of Providence

5. Challenges to the Ongoing Doctrinal Task
   Credible Doctrine in Every Situation
   Creation and the Concept of Evolution
   Evil and the Reliability of the Created Processes

Introduction

In asserting the doctrine of creation, the Christian community affirms a relationship between God and the world. In spelling out what the doctrine involves, the community gives conceptuality to the relationship and thinks through its meaning. When we grasp fully what the affirmation and the concept of creation are about, we understand at the same time the scope of the doctrine. We understand its significance and the challenges it faces.

As our reflection on creation will make clear, even though our understanding and affirmation of creation does not precede the doctrines of grace and redemption, the creation doctrine does decisively affect the framework in which those latter beliefs occur. Langdon Gilkey's statement is still true:

> Thus without the idea of God's creation of the world, of history, and of man, the Gospel of redemption of man's life from sin becomes meaningless, self-contradictory, and vain. The idea of creation expresses that fundamental relation between God and the world within which the Gospel of redemption is both important and viable, and so this conception provides the indispensable framework within which the Christian faith speaks its message of love.[1]

Several examples reinforce the sense that the doctrine of creation is decisive for other doctrines. Our conception of creation is correlated directly to our concept of the way God encounters us. If, for example, we consider the creation activity of God to be of a piece with the evolutionary process of the world's development and of life within that world, our "natural" development itself becomes the arena for meeting God. But, on the contrary, a kind of sovereignty over the processes of nature may be ascribed to the creation work of God, such that they are made to appear so inferior as to be only indirectly related to God's action. It would then appear blasphemous to assert that any particularities of our natural constitution are correlated with the mighty acts of God.

Neither of these views separates God from the created world. Nor does either deny the divine freedom and sovereignty over God's creation. But one will veer more toward God's immanence, while the other will move toward God's transcendence. There is a substantial difference between these two positions for our understanding of the way God encounters us. The creation concept is not less immediately relevant than issues about redemption and revelation, because unless those issues are correlated consistently with creation, they will appear absurd or incredible.

As the doctrine of creation conceives the relationship of God and the world, it also lays the groundwork for understanding the relationship of faith and the community of faith to the world. This may be illustrated by referring to four sets of faith/world polarities: reason and revelation, nature and grace, world and church, creation and redemption. A firm understanding of God's action as Creator out of nothing of all that is builds bridges between the two terms in each set. As such, this understanding makes a decisive difference in how one understands the pairs.

If, for example, the creative power of God is the source and continuing ground of reason, Christian faith need not struggle to discover a basis or occasion for relating revelation and reason. Rather, faith can proceed directly to the task of setting forth the benefits that accrue if reason and revelation take each other seriously. Or, if God has created the world according to plan, then the church, as a community within the world, need not wrestle with the questions whether it ought to address the world, or whether it is possible for it to address the world. On the contrary, as a coexistent with the world in the larger framework of creation, it can speak immediately to the world about the life both share. It can speak also about the meaning of the church's gospel for the world. The church can proceed as Paul did in his letter to the Romans: "Ever since the creation of the world . . . [God's] eternal power and deity have been clearly perceived in the things that have been made" (Rom. 1:20). From there Paul went on to state the implications of Christ's gospel.

As the doctrine of creation unfolds, it will be clear that one very fundamental challenge faces it. This challenge raises the question whether any of the foregoing is meaningful. Philosopher Ronald Hepburn has written correctly:

> The doctrine of creation is remarkably rich in the evaluative and evocative overtones characteristic of religious doctrines. If God, as Christianity conceives him, is the author and sustainer of the world, then the world is a planned and purposed enterprise. It will not do to speak of life as "absurd," as the atheist existentialists do. It will make sense to ask "Why am I here? What is the purpose God has for my life?" The questions may not be readily answerable, but they will at least be meaningful and proper.[2]

The challenge that confronts faith today is the widespread skepticism whether the world is a "planned and purposed enterprise." This challenge may take a number of forms. The scientist, who will certainly not wish to cast doubt on the orderliness of the world, will nevertheless often feel uneasy at the Christian's talk about plan and purpose. The absurdist—to whom Hepburn refers—

and the Marxist will reject plan and purpose. The absurdist rejects these categories altogether, while the Marxist insists that the only plan and purpose that exist are those that enlightened human agents themselves conceive and actualize.

Behind the dilemma the Christian faces is the fundamental implication of the creation doctrine: not only that the world is "a planned and purposed enterprise," but also that its processes are so reliable and trustworthy that we can say the created world is a home for humans and other forms of life, rather than an uncaring or even hostile environment.

The ultimate sources of the challenge must be noted. One criterion for judging the adequacy of a doctrine of creation will be its ability to hold its own in the face of these counterproposals. Science is a source of the challenge to the extent that it propounds a view of nature's laws proceeding inexorably, impersonally, and by chance. Some hold, for example, that the evolutionary development of stars is inexorable and by chance, and further that our own sun's evolution will take it to the stage of a "red giant," during which phase it will expand in size and engulf planet earth in its fiery mass. If such claims are accepted, it becomes difficult to assert the postulate of creation: that the world is planned, purposeful, and a congenial home for life. Even if the possible hostility of nature is dealt with, the challenge is not disposed of. The breathtaking new vision of what nature is, both physical and human nature, challenges Christian theological reflection on creation. The challenge calls for a religious vision that is both intelligible and persuasive when facing current views of the created world.

The appearance of evil in all its forms is a source of challenge to the doctrine of creation. "The theologian must admit to the thoughtful inquirer that the existence of evil poses no such intellectual problems for other points of view as it does for the Christian faith." This statement is Gilkey's, and he has shown how such secular philosophies as the dualisms, monisms, and naturalisms seem to be confirmed by the presence of evil.[3] As our subsequent discussion will elaborate, the presence of evil is baffling for those who affirm that the good God has created the world out of nothing, and that therefore all unfolding of the world and all purpose are dependent on God.

Neither the facts of science nor the appearances of evil can be ignored or gainsaid by Christian theologians. The doctrine of creation may be understood and interpreted, however, in the light of these realities. When it is, it will naturally assume a form that seeks to take such realities into account and speak to them. Just how the doctrine of creation is to be explicated in the face of these challenging forces today is a matter of much attention and some controversy. Still, the outlook is not altogether bleak for theological reconstruction that takes the challenges seriously.

The present situation in theology has been made difficult for our understanding of the doctrine of creation by the response of theologians to science over the past two centuries. When it became clear, under Immanuel Kant's sharp gaze, that religion could not validate its concerns and its truths in the same manner that science did, many theologians followed Kant's lead into a "special realm" in which religion could be free. Religion and theology were restricted to the realm of values, separated sharply from the realm of everyday life and of the physical world. These were the realms where scientists carried out their work and dazzled populations with their insights and technical accomplishments.

The consequence of this restriction was a short-term benefit: that faith gained a "storm-free area," where it could speak its word in peace. The long-term cost of such a restriction is, however, now clear to us. Theology is cut off from the world of "facts," the world at issue in the developments of science and technology and in the ecological crisis. Theology is alienated from our efforts to alter radically the pathological relationships that have developed between the human species and the environing world.

Since Kant's "fact" versus "value" distinction is now widely accepted, the Christian finds great difficulty in affirming the doctrine of creation. That doctrine, after all, involves the repossession of the physical world and the physical aspect of human existence for theological discourse. When we wish to emphasize the doctrine of creation, we find that we must overcome a considerable intellectual tradition at least two centuries old, one asserted by some very prestigious figures in modern Western thought.[4]

The doctrine of creation not only serves as an essential framework on which the soteriological statements of faith depend for their credibility and meaning. It is also one of the chief resources for overcoming what has come to be known, perhaps exaggeratedly, as the "unitarianism of the second article." The object of concern in this phrase is a reduction of Christian theology to soteriology, which falsifies the Christian faith because it cuts off the larger connectedness between redemption in Christ and the panorama of God's intentions and actions from creation to consummation. Such a reduction also thereby cuts the link between redemption and the physical world, society, and world history. If theology does not overcome this tendency, it finds it difficult to relate the faith to such issues as ecological concerns, our vocation in society, and the manifestations of God's Spirit in the world's history.

We take as the scope of the doctrine of creation those matters that pertain: (1) to the constitution of the world and the picture that has emerged in the Christian faith of God as the Creator of the world; (2) to God's provision of modalities of grace within the created world and the relations of those modes to the creation; (3) to the creation of humankind in particular.

These themes are prefaced by a discussion of the biblical understanding of creation, since that understanding has figured so prominently in the Christian doctrinal tradition.

NOTES

1. Langdon Gilkey, *Maker of Heaven and Earth* (Garden City, N.Y.: Doubleday & Co., 1959), p. 17.

2. Ronald Hepburn, "Creation, Religious Doctrine of," in *The Encyclopedia of Philosophy*, ed. Paul Edwards (New York: Macmillan Co., 1967), 2:252.

3. Gilkey, *Maker of Heaven and Earth*, pp. 178-82.

4. Gustaf Wingren, *Creation and Gospel*, trans. Henry Vander Goot (New York and Toronto: Edwin Mellen Press, 1979), pp. 57ff. See Ole Jensen, *Theologie zwischen Illusion und Restriktion* (Munich: Chr. Kaiser, 1975), pp. 267-77.

1

The Biblical
Witness to Creation

Christians confess their faith when they praise God as Creator, who has made the world and human beings. God has created humans in the divine image, thereby giving them a special place in that world and special responsibility for it. The creation has taken place through Christ. God's work as Creator is originating, continuing, and consummating. Human beings are the recipients of this creative power of God, not only in their origination but also in the availability of God's creative power to redeem them, to make them "new creatures," to make them participants in the reality of Christ, and thereby to enable them to work God's will in a transforming manner in the world.

THE FORM OF
THE BIBLICAL WITNESS

Two aspects of the biblical witness to creation make it significant for our theological understanding. Both the *content* of its witness and what its *form* tells us about the style or method of Christian testimony to creation are important. We will first consider method.

John Reumann writes: "More than fifteen different 'creation theologies' in the Old and New Testaments can be identified, to say nothing of variations which appear in the literature of the Intertestamental Period outside the usual canon." [1] This statement may be an exaggeration, but it does pose a problem for those who insist that theology should be able to propound "*the* biblical doctrine of creation." The diversity of the biblical materials does not, however, destroy the unity of witness to creation. Rather, it points to the wide range of situations in which the creation witness was forged and to the impressive flexibility and versatility with which biblical traditions responded to those situations. The biblical witness to creation, like the witness to many other themes of faith, did not appear full-blown. On the contrary, it emerged from the testimony of believers in different situations.

No fixed way of presenting the belief in creation can be found in the Bible. Instead, "a number of different presentations, which have arisen at different times and with different philosophical presuppositions, have been allowed to stand side by side." [2] This is particularly evident in the traditions concerning the creation of man and woman, as we shall note in more detail. The fundamental affirmations in the creation traditions remain remarkably unified, however.

Most commonly, the biblical understanding of creation is identified with the first three chapters of Genesis. This is unfortunate and even misleading on several counts. For one, chapters 1–3 do not convey fully what the Yahwistic and Priestly traditions intended to say about origins. Genesis 4 is essential, in order to assert that the fall includes crime against fellow humans as well as disobedience toward God. The subsequent chapters in Genesis are essential if we are to understand that creation includes culture and civilization as well as nature (Gen. 4:17–22) and that the growth and development of culture, including the diversification of labor, are part of the creation account of origins. Chapters 6–9 in Genesis are parallel to the first chapters and relate the motifs of destruction and creative preservation to primeval creation. As God has created life in the world, so God can also destroy it—but God has promised to sustain creation (Gen. 9:8–17).

Beyond Genesis, however, we find that other parts of the Old Testament are rich in creation traditions. The period after the exile was especially rich in such traditions. We refer to the Psalms (e.g., 8, 19, 24, 46, 74, 77, 89, 93, 97, 99, 104), First Isaiah (27, 30, 17, 34), Second Isaiah (40–55), and Third Isaiah (65–66). Further, there are Habakkuk 3; Ezekiel 29; Nahum 1; Jeremiah 4, Amos 4, 5, and 9; Hosea 8; Malachi 2; Proverbs 3 and 8; Ecclesiastes 3 and 12; and Job 3, 22, 37, and 38.

Theologians have often suggested that the Hebrew Scriptures should be read from the viewpoint of the New Testament. Such a starting point radically challenges the view that Genesis 1–3 constitutes the essential creation testimony. Emil Brunner speaks so forcefully for this position that we cite him at length:

Unfortunately the uniqueness of this Christian doctrine of Creation and the Creator is continually being obscured by the fact that theologians are so reluctant to begin their work with the New Testament; when they want to deal with the Creation they tend to begin with the Old Testament, although they never do this when they are speaking of the Redeemer. The emphasis on the story of Creation at the beginning of the Bible has constantly led theologians to forsake the rule which they would otherwise follow, namely, that the basis of *all* Christian articles of faith is the Incarnate Word, Jesus Christ. So when we begin to study the subject of Creation in the Bible we ought to start with the first chapter of the Gospel of John, and some other passages of the *New* Testament, and not with the first chapter of Genesis. If we can make up our minds to stick to this rule, we shall be saved from many difficulties, which will inevitably occur if we begin with the story of Creation in the Old Testament.[3]

Brunner's position raises a host of questions. In his insistence on the priority of the New Testament, is he suggesting that the Old Testament is so alien to the Christian faith that if one began theological reflection in the former, that reflection would not be consonant with Christian faith? Does Brunner's position blend into Marcion's, that the God of creation in the Old Testament is another God from the Redeemer-Father of the New Testament?

The Christian confidence in God's providence lets us accept Old Testament traditions as reliable, yet also affirm the New Testament as the fulfillment of Israel's religious pilgrimage. Such a position grows out of our faith as much as our reasoned scholarship.

More often, theologians who agree with Brunner's essential thrust use a christological interpretation of the Old Testament to make their point. Karl Barth's discussion in the third volume of his *Church Dogmatics* is one such approach. Our approach shall be a dialectical one, in which the faith and affirmations of Israel are accepted as our own faith, as well as that of Jesus, but in which that faith will finally be interpreted christologically.

The most nearly adequate way to handle the diversity of creation witnesses in the Bible is to incorporate, within our Christ-centered faith, the traditions-history approach so prominent among biblical scholars. Such an approach puts the biblical testimonies in the sequence in which they emerged, to the extent that such a sequence can be established. "The biblical doctrine thus becomes a series of statements of faith in differing situations over the centuries, about which we must make decisions concerning what is normative and what is useful today."[4] John Reumann has produced two traditions-history studies of the biblical doctrine of creation that serve as models of such presentation.[5] In the discussion of biblical content that follows in the next section, we shall follow Reumann's organization of the traditions.

The relations between the biblical witnesses to creation and the various cultural situations from which they emerged is a much discussed, disputed, and thorny issue. Scholarly opinions have tended to insist on the distinctiveness of the biblical traditions, even though the past two centuries have seen a growing appreciation of their borrowing from other cultures.

Studies of the history and structure of world religions shows their universal concern for creation. These studies remind us that, although biblical reflections on creation may be distinctive, there is nothing distinctive about their preoccupation with the issue.

A number of scholars have classified the myths of creation in the world's religions. Charles Long, for example, has provided five different categories of such myths: emergence myths, world-parent myths, myths of creation from chaos and from the cosmic egg, creation from nothing, and earth-diver myths.[6] Within the creation-from-nothing classification, he gathers the following: the Australian myth of the Great Father, Hesiod, Rig Veda, the ancient Maya myth from the Popol Vuh, and myths from Polynesia, the Maori, the Tuamotua, the Egyptians, and the Zuni—in addition to the Hebrew myth from Genesis.

Although there is no suggestion that all the myths are related or that they exerted influence on one another, it is instructive to place the Hebrew/Christian primal myth of creation within the context of the universal human mythic reflection upon origins. We find that all the creation-from-nothing myths share four characteristics:

> First of all, the Creator deity is all-powerful. He does not share his power with any other deity or structure of reality. Secondly, . . . the deity exists by himself, alone, in a void, or space. There is no material or reality prior to him in time or power. . . . Thirdly, the mode of ceation is conscious, ordered, and deliberate; it reveals a plan of action. Finally, the Creator is free since he is not bound by the inertia of a prior reality.[7]

It is important to keep such universal characteristics in mind, so that we can understand more adequately just what our own traditions share with humanity and where they differ. Each of these four shared characteristics has at one time or another been mistakenly heralded by theologians as unique to Judaism and Christianity. As we shall see, however, there are other genuinely distinctive marks of our creation traditions. They have mainly to do with the elevation of history as the medium of revelation and creation.

Claus Westermann has properly said that it is misleading to dwell exclusively on the distinctiveness of biblical creation traditions. Since we now know that the various myths have arisen independently over the whole of the earth and its history, "the conclusion is unavoidable that mankind possessed something common in the stories about primeval time."[8]

This broad common basis of thought and understanding suggests to Westermann that the Old Testament traditions were first of all part of this universal human reflection. He finds that whatever is distinctive in the traditions can thus be seen as a contribution to the larger human quest for understanding. Among the shared motifs, Westermann counts the creation of man out of clay, the flood, the first offense, the origins of death, of civilization, of fratricide, and the building of a tower.

Westermann distinguishes four types of creation myths: creation through making, through generation or birth, through conflict, and through the word. He finds all four of these types reflected in Genesis, not discounting that the Hebrews interpreted the shared material in their own way.[9] The motif of making is seen clearly in the creation of man from clay and of woman from Adam's rib (Gen. 2); generation is the motif of the seven days of creation, which form a segment of the *toledot* ("generations"); conflict is not accepted as a motif in the Old Testament view of creation, but it echoes in Isa. 51:9–10, where the myth of Rahab the dragon is recalled, and in Gen. 1:2, where the word for "deep" is a "distant reminder" of Tiamat (the dragon in the Babylonian epic *Enuma Elish*), conquered in battle at the time of creation.

Westermann has made another significant contribution to our understanding of the Old Testament traditions' relationship to the larger human quest for understanding of origins. He notes four basic stages "in the reflection on Creation in the overall history" of humankind: the primitive stage, the stage of great religious cosmogonies, the philosophical-theological stage, and the scientific stage.[10] The primitive and the religious cosmogonic eras are marked by the fact that only in reflecting on the world's coming into being could humans grasp the world as a whole. Philosophical-theological reflection moved into an abstract manner of reflection, away from personal categories to those of causality. Or, in the case of Christian theology, they combined the personal and the philosophical concepts of causality. The final era, the mathematical-scientific, is marked by the empirical approach to the whole of the world, with experiment and calculation as its hallmarks.

Westermann's point is that the Old Testament traditions fall in the middle of these periods, toward the end of the religious cosmogonic era. Since the first two periods are much longer than the latter two, the Old Testament actually represents a huge segment of human reflection. It absorbed essential elements of early humankind's reflection on creation and preserved them for our benefit today. This is the great significance of the obvious Babylonian, Egyptian, and other influences on the Old Testament accounts of creation. The distinctiveness of the Old Testament must be viewed in this greater context of the history of human reflection. Furthermore, the advances made in the New Testament and in later Christian theology are to be understood as proceeding out of this grand historical sweep, of which the Old Testament is a part.

THE SUBSTANCE OF
BIBLICAL WITNESS: THE OLD TESTAMENT

Given the diversity of the biblical witness and its complex relation to the cultural settings in which it emerged and developed, let us survey what has been bequeathed to us in the many-layered repository of biblical tradition. What follows illustrates how the traditions-history method may bear fruit in uncovering scriptural materials. It is also a brief compendium of the essential, primal testimony to the creation affirmation to which Christians hold themselves accountable. What we encounter in this primal testimony is itself rich, complex, and intellectually challenging. It grew, after all, out of a wide variety of circumstances in which it was necessary, first for the Hebrew community and then later for the Christians, to raise their witness to the creator God and the work of that God.

We will devote much of our discussion to the biblical materials—there is so much there! Perhaps more than any other doctrine, creation is central to much of the biblical witness. It is not only central, but so richly developed that theological reflection can preoccupy itself with Scripture and become engrossed with the themes, complexities, and ramifications of the biblical legacy. It is not enough to be so preoccupied, but one finds a great deal in the ancient sources that is immediately relevant for theological reflection.

Certainly no theological presentation can be thought adequate if it overlooks Scripture and the five basic biblical propositions outlined at the end of this section. What follows should be considered the irreducible minimum to be retrieved from the biblical witnesses for the current theological exposition of the creation affirmation.

We have already discussed the first chapters of Genesis, commonly thought to be not only normative but also exhaustive of the biblical witness. Scholars are nearly unanimous that Genesis 1–11 is put together from several literary accounts. The one called "J" (designated by the Germans "Jahwist"—English spelling, "Yahwist"—from its habit of calling God "Jahweh") begins with Gen. 2:4 and continues off and on through chapter 11. The other called "P" (from "Priestly" writing) begins with the first chapter. J emerged in the tenth or ninth century B.C., probably under the reign of King Solomon, while P is from the fifth century B.C., as Israel was trying to reestablish Jerusalem after its destruction and the exile in Babylon. We shall not have occasion to discuss Genesis 1–11 as a whole; in accord with the traditions-history method, we will divide its parts, noting each in the context of its period.

It is not surprising that Israel should begin in a major way to put its traditions into more permanent and ordered form during the time of its first great king. We keep in mind that a multitude of traditions—stories, hymns, cultic materials, brief historical sketches, and the like—existed before the ordering process. The process of reflection, writing down, editing, and creative rewriting required a certain sophistication. It required education and leisure for reflecting and learning. The process had to await the right conditions. It became possible only when the society had achieved the affluence and "high" civilization that emerged with the Israelites' monarchy. Israelite kings moved to Jerusalem, a Jebusite city. There began the trend toward centralization of all aspects of life. This was a genuinely new phenomenon for Israel, and much had to be borrowed or created from scratch, including the characteristics of a temple religion and a cult—all largely borrowed from existing forms. The collecting of traditions and the putting together of a sacred tradition and a "theology" in a usable form were part of this new phase of the community's life.

Some scholars have suggested that "Yahweh" itself is a name that refers to the Creator, while others have said that the new Jerusalem priesthood (Jebusites) of David applied the creator name to Yahweh, in accordance with Canaanite usage. In any event, the significant development is that this rising monarchy and high civilization sought to relate the God of the cosmos, of creation, and of the very foundations of the world to its own particular history. The Israelite people and their exodus from Egypt, their wilderness journey and their conquest of the land, their nation-building phase and their burgeoning monarchy—all this was to be brought into relationship with the God of the cosmos. All was to be given the kind of affirmation and reinforcement that such a linkage could bring. Here we see the process that Jaroslav Pelikan has described: "The story or stories of creation in Genesis are not chiefly cosmogony but the preface to the history that begins with the calling of Abraham." [11] It was important for the monarchy of David to make this connection. Gen. 14:19, 22 is probably the earliest reference to God as Creator in the Old Testament.

The formation of the creation traditions, in the context we have just described, is part of what the scholars call the development of a "Zion theology." It aimed at legitimizing the monarchy and the whole culture centralized in David's city. Creation themes were important in this theology (see Psalms 24, 74, 77, 89, 93, 97, 99). Psalm 89 is particularly revealing of this theological tendency; verses 5–13 set forth the power and glory of the creator God, while the succeeding verses 19–37 relate that God to the reign of David. These psalms speak of creation as originating the world, but also as continuing to sustain the world and to redeem it. As Helmer Ringgren writes,

> The doctrine of creation is not primarily a theoretical statement about the origin of the world, about something that has happened long ago. It is rather a proclamation of a present reality; creation means that the evil powers are defeated, and that the order of the world is established for ever. . . . Creation, therefore, is also a redemptive act. . . . [12]

The Zion theology borrowed from the traditions of other cultures, as we see in Psalm 104, with its reworking of Egyptian sources. Developments of the time were shaping an alternative interpretation of Israel's identity, an alternative to the almost exclusive emphasis on the exodus. Israel's identity was now said to be rooted not only in God's mighty acts in history but also in the very origins of the cosmos itself. The witness from this source is almost exclusively from the cultic life of the people—hymns and prayers as found in the Psalms.

Turning to the preexilic prophets, we find scanty evidence of creation-themes, and what we do find has been inserted in places to underscore the prophets' judgments. For example, Amos (4:13; 5:8–9; 9:5–6), in contrast to the "Zion theology," invokes the creator God against the immorality and injustice of his society. First Isaiah appears to invoke the creator God against the nations (Isa. 17:12–14; 27:1; 34:11). As we read these sections, it is easy to understand why some scholars argue that they could be insertions from a later period when creation theology was more in vogue. A verse like Jer. 4:23, with its view of the "world without form and void," makes us wonder whether the prophet borrowed from earlier traditions that later became Genesis 1, or whether later writers were influenced by the prophet.

Some of the grandest expressions of the creation witness come from the wisdom traditions. This material is not distinctive to Israel; it is part of an international movement. Generally, these traditions speak in universal human terms, with fewer references to Israel's particular history. Proverbs (3:19–20; 8:22–31) and Ecclesiastes (3:11; 12:1, 7) invoke creation themes to reinforce their ethical reflections. This amounts to the assertion that human patterns of living are rooted in the foundations of the created world itself, and that they are of concern to the Creator.

Job intensifies this affirmation in what may be the most stunning witness to creation in the entire Bible (Job 3:1–10; 22:12–14; 37; 38:22—39:30). These passages also imply what Christians later called creation "out of nothing." He relates the life of the individual directly to the creator God, with virtually no references to Israel and its history with God. The individual stands naked before God with no mediator whatsoever. In this position, Job reflects on the grandeur of God:

> Hearken to the thunder of [God's] voice and the rumbling that comes from his mouth. Under the whole heaven he lets it go, and his lightning to the corners of the earth. . . . God thunders wondrously with his voice; he does great things which we cannot comprehend. For to the snow he says, "Fall on the earth"; and to the shower and the rain, "Be strong."

This meditation on grandeur turns to amazement at God's ways, and then to perplexity and resentment. The creator God is the God who speaks from the whirlwind: "Where were you when I laid the foundation of the earth?" The man is reduced to silence; adoration and awe are the only appropriate responses before the creator God; God's ways are beyond understanding and not to be questioned. Nevertheless, the implication is that this God will redeem humanity, not destroy it. This literature is a profound reflection on the relationship between human affairs and the God of creation. A holy agnosticism as to God's plans is encouraged, with an undertone of confidence in the final outcome as one that will be a blessing for the world.

Genesis 2—4:26 is considered to be part of the Yahwist's history of Israel, designated by scholars as the "J" document. Written between 950 and 900 B.C., during the movement of "Solomonic humanism," the J document was an attempt to show that God has indeed worked through history from the time of creation through David's reign. J might be considered a counterpoint to the Zion theology of the same period. The Yahwist seems to have been a layperson, in contrast to the cultic, priestly setting of the authors of the Zion theology. The centralizing developments that we discussed earlier did indeed bring together a "critical mass" of educated, capable people committed to the cultural enterprises of the Davidic monarchy. At the same time, the age was marked by several contrasting trends of considerable moment.

There was an enormous amount of borrowing from other cultural sources, for example, the new capital city, Jerusalem, the Jebusite priesthood, and a new cultus. There was an incredible attempt to bridge the disjunctions between the nomadic-tribal social and religious traditions that emerged from the exodus period and the subsequent generations of wandering, of conquering Canaan, and of settling the land, on the one hand, and the new, highly civilized society centered in Jerusalem, on the other. There was also a secularizing thrust brought about by the combination of two dynamic elements. One was a group of highly gifted people capable of thinking for themselves quite apart from the ancient traditions. The other was the influx of much cultural borrowing not readily assimilated into older Israelite patterns of thought and action.

In this situation, it is not surprising that a crisis of meaning developed in some quarters. In the midst of great change, where was God to be found? Where was God at work? The Zion theology gave one response, the Yahwist another. The Yahwist was a product of the Solomonic humanism that emerged in the new cultural context. He sought to show how Yahweh had worked in Israelite history up to his own time. He did so by recasting older traditions, by relating Yahweh to the everyday life of his age, by utilizing traditions borrowed from other peoples (like the creation out of clay) or which (like other creation motifs) were previously not much used, and by trying to cut through the jargon and cult which was losing its credibility in some quarters.

The achievement of J, when seen in the light of the times, is very attractive. J's story of creation is not stylized or abstract, as is the Genesis 1 account. Rather, it is a bit irreverent, earthy, vivid, perhaps even tongue in cheek. The account is rich with provocative meanings. Humans are totally dependent on God for their life—their very breath comes from God. The man at first was given the animals for companionship but could be at peace only with a companion that was free and personal like himself. The fact that woman came from Adam's rib could mean that she is his subordinate, but it could also mean that she is the only one who is "like" man so as to be a genuine companion, a genuine mate.

Evil is not a cosmic, ontological phenomenon so much as it is the product of human will and disobedience. If we read Genesis 3 as if it were an eye-witness account, written on the very day of the fall, it is misleading, because then it seems that humans were from the very beginning sinful. But when we keep in mind that the account is put together in the tenth century B.C. as an explanation of how God works in history, then it becomes not an etiology or even a protology but rather a way of expressing far greater optimism, of saying that evil is not written in the very law of things, but is located discretely in human will. As such it can be dealt with and guarded against. The writer is saying, "Humans are like this. If you keep this in mind, it is possible to deal with sin and evil constructively."

In light of the Canaanite fertility and nature-religion of the Yahwist's time, both the creation account in Genesis 2 and the story of the fall in Genesis 3 may be viewed as polemics against those who would encourage the Israelites to ape their neighbors. Yahweh is Lord over nature. Sinning is not a cosmic principle inherent in the structure of the world. God is able and willing to work the divine will and forgiveness through ordinary history.

We have surveyed the three chief traditions that witness to the creation affirmation in Israel before the exile—Zion theology, Wisdom, and the Yahwist. That they are relatively scanty reminds us that creation was not a dominant motif in Israel's self-understanding prior to the exile. Exodus, Sinai and the law, and the patriarchs figured more prominently than creation in the traditions and beliefs of Israel. Nevertheless, the witness to creation is clear and significant. Both the Yahwist and the Zion theology make creation the prologue to the more extensively elaborated historical narratives. Israel's history, particularly as it reaches a climax in the Jerusalem monarchy, is rooted in the very foundations of the cosmos, in God's activity as Creator. The Creator is all-powerful; the creation is essentially good; there is ground for hope.

We follow the scholars who put the Wisdom literature, including chapters 38 and 39 of Job, into the period before the sixth century B.C. These Wisdom pieces contain an internationally widespread type of reflection which Israel accepted and harmonized with other traditions. Even though it could equally well be placed after the exile, this literature, too, may have its origins in the Solomonic court of the tenth century; its appeal is a universal human one, with little reference to the particularity of Israel. It makes a statement that is of a piece with the other traditions, namely, that human existence transpires in the hand of the creator God. Beyond this, however, the testimonies to that God are grander than those found in the Yahwistic account in Genesis 2—4 and at the same time less overtly confident of God's mercy than either the Zion theology or the Yahwist.

After 586 B.C. we find a much more developed witness to creation. Although it is only speculation, we can imagine why the emphasis on creation emerges more extensively at this time. Perhaps the invocation of the historical traditions—of exodus, Sinai, and the patriarchs—was no longer persuasive precisely because that strand of historical development had been interrupted. Interrupted, the promise lost credibility, because it had been one of fulfillment and blessing, not of devastation, dispersion, and exile. Something beyond those historical traditions was needed. Furthermore, in the dispersion in Babylon, the Hebrews were brought into intimate contact with a people who interpreted themselves by means of a powerful creation theology—the theology of Marduk, the victor in the struggle with the chaos monster at creation, and the annual representation of this battle at the New Year festival.

Chapters 40–55 of Isaiah (Second Isaiah) present to us the work of a prophet who dramatically recast Israel's story, in an attempt to renew his people's sense of identity and purpose and to restore that people's *esprit de corps*. No element of his effort is more striking than his extensive use of creation themes. He introduces creation as a sign of God's power and merciful plan, as well as an image for God's future work. A typical example is chapter 42, where, in the context of an oracle about the servant of Yahweh, we find this:

Thus says God, the Lord,
   who created the heavens and stretched them out,
   who spread forth the earth and what comes from it,
who gives breath to the people upon it
   and spirit to those who walk in it:
"I am the Lord, I have called you in righteousness,
   I have taken you by the hand and kept you;
I have given you as a covenant to the people,
   a light to the nations,
   to open the eyes that are blind,
to bring out the prisoners from the dungeon,
   from the prison those who sit in darkness."

The juxtaposition of creation images and redemptive—for the Christian, messianic—motifs makes clear why one scholar has termed this Isaiah's "creative redemption" or "redemptive creation."[13] The point is that God's creation work is continuing now and will constitute the future as well. Chapter 40 concludes with this exalted imagery after a long affirmation of God as the Creator, almost reminiscent of Job:

The Lord is the everlasting God,
   the Creator of the ends of the earth.
He does not faint or grow weary. . . .
He gives power to the faint. . . .
They who wait for the Lord shall renew their strength,
   they shall mount up with wings like eagles. . . .

Whether this prophet borrowed heavily from the Babylonians is finally not certain (even though plausible), but his development of a vision of Israel that incorporated creation motifs in a central fashion is unmistakable. He has not forgotten the preexilic ways of telling Israel's story, but he has recast the story in a dramatic new way. He has taken creation from protology—in which he is not much interested—to continuing creation and new creation.

It will seem strange to many that "the" basic text for the doctrine of creation, Genesis 1, is discussed late in this survey of biblical traditions. As with all the bodies of tradition, this one contains very early material, but the Genesis 1 account was put in its present form rather late, in the sixth or fifth centuries B.C., by the person or group known as the Priestly writer. P is a long segment of historical narrative, stretching throughout Genesis, Exodus, Leviticus, and Deuteronomy. Since this compilation contains a great deal of cultic material, including most of the liturgical rubrics of the book of Leviticus, it has been said that it was politically motivated to legitimate the postexilic cult. Others have said that it was theologically intended, to affirm that God is present in the postexilic community of the chosen people, and that the inclusion of cultic and other detailed materials are part of this intention to speak of God's concrete presence.

Whatever the circumstances of P's composition, P has taken in a wide range of sources, including ancient Near Eastern ones. It has purified them of pagan notions and woven them into the powerful, stylized account that Jews and Christians look on as normative. A detailed exegesis of the first chapter of Genesis is not essential here, but it should be noted that this witness to creation is a doxology whose intention is to praise God and honor the mystery of creation, not to "explain" the world's origins in a modern sense. At the same time, the account is not a stumbling block to those who want to relate creation to modern ways of thinking.

Whether there is a creation out of nothing implied in the first verses is debatable; some interpreters even use those verses to substantiate a view of preexistent chaos on which God worked as a demiurge. It is probably safer to rest the *ex nihilo* on other texts. The progressive unfolding of God's work of creation in Genesis 1 renders it congenial to modern notions of evolution or development. The creation of humans is given special emphasis, with the introduction of the concept of the "image of God." This term will occupy us at some length at another point, but its mention in this creation account is the basis for the church's preoccupation with it. The conjunction of being created in God's image with multiplying and filling the earth, with subduing the earth and having dominion over it, has been at the root of much later thought and practice, even as it has been the source of much difficulty in recent decades. Genesis 1 places the creation work of God in a large, symmetrical framework; its conclusion is the sabbath, the perfect wholeness of God's work.

The prophet responsible for Isaiah 56—66 (so-called "Third Isaiah") introduces a new element into the creation witness—that of the "new heavens and a new earth" (Isa. 65:17; 66:22). This writer lived in the restored Jerusalem of the Second Temple of Zerubbabel. The times were hard and disappointing for those who had expectations of a grand rebuilding of Jerusalem and a restoration of former glories. Some scholars interpret Third Isaiah as a harbinger of apocalypticism. This writer does not look for the continuation of previous grand historical developments that hark back to the exodus and to David. Nor does he simply affirm that God has led the people to their present state. He does not take the stance of the Priestly writer (who wrote at the same time), that God's hand is discernible in the times. Rather, Third Isaiah speaks in tones that are desperate in one sense, that are not corollary to the experience of this world, but are in radical contrast to it.

The oracle in 65:17–25 bears this out. The new heavens and the new earth will include a Jerusalem in which there is no weeping or crying; the wolf and the lamb will feed together, the lion will eat straw like the ox. There is a definite intent to glorify the "new Israel," a sort of eschatological Zion theology, but the dimensions of universality are also present in 66:23—'all flesh shall come to worship before me, says the Lord.' The same creative work of God is lifted up at this point, but the arena of that work is different from what was spoken of in earlier traditions. God's creative work is not to legitimate Zion-Jerusalem, nor is it to sustain human existence, as in Job. It does not even point to a future restoration of Jerusalem. Rather, God's creative work builds a new world that is related to this world only in the sense that earthly metaphors are used to describe it in a most un-earthly fashion.

From this survey, it is clear that the Old Testament traditions of the Hebrews possessed a deep conviction in God as Creator and ruler of all things. As several scholars have suggested, creation was not really a creedal matter with the Hebrews; rather it was a presupposition that the Hebrews would not think even of questioning. This they shared with their Near Eastern neighbors. From very early times, they demonstrated the desire to forge links between their earthly existence and the power and purpose of the creator God. They were distinctive among their neighbors in that they did not forge these links through the immediacy of the nature and fertility cults, but rather rooted them in their concrete historical pilgrimage. In so doing, they inevitably spoke of creation in three nuances: originating, continuing/sustaining, and consummating. The creator God thus, in the creating activity, was redeemer and final perfecter.

THE SUBSTANCE OF
THE BIBLICAL WITNESS: THE NEW TESTAMENT

The New Testament stands in continuity with the Old Testament traditions in that Christians believed that their existence was just as surely linked to the creator God as Israel's had been. They were convinced that the God of the Hebrew traditions was the God who had drawn near to them in Jesus Christ. When once we understand these twin affirmations—which are really one—as the basis of continuity between the two Testaments on the theme of creation, the New Testament materials take on naturally their role as the extension of Israel's belief for Christians.

The traditions of the synoptic Gospels do not include reference to the doctrine of creation as such. At the same time, it is clear that the intimate relationship they describe between Jesus and the Father implies an affirmation of the creation-belief. Jesus is pictured as a person "in touch" with the creator God and God's activity. As such he is himself an agent of the Creator's power. The nature miracles portray this vividly. Jesus stills the storm in a quiet and matter-of-fact manner; the swine serve his purposes with the demoniac; he knows where the fish are to be found even when the master fishermen are confounded. "The so-called 'nature miracles,' whatever their exact background, are really creation stories reflecting Jesus' basic trust in the creator."[14] Matthew 6:26–34 is another example of Jesus being portrayed as one who was close to the basic rhythms of nature and to their purposes—hence also to their Creator.

If we view Jesus through the apocalyptic traditions, as we surely must, the creation-motifs are also implied. It was of the essence of the apocalyptic vision that the dramatic events of judgment and messianic redemption which it proclaimed were the work of the cosmic God, who was Creator of the world and Lord over history. The apocalyptic world view was preoccupied with history, it is true, but history is guided by the God who controls all things, including cosmic realities. The very power of the apocalyptic interpretation of history lies in the assumption that all cosmic powers are focused in the historical unfolding that the apocalyptist describes. Consequently, there is an irresistible character to the movement of history that is analogous to the movements of the cosmos.[15] Therefore, the widely attested apocalyptic background of the synoptic presentation of Jesus assumes for its credibility that this man is the agent of the cosmic God who is Creator of the world and the controller of its history. In the events of history in which the messianic agent figures, "God will create a new world, a new heaven will appear, and the whole creation will be renewed."[16]

One of the most striking and significant contributions of the New Testament to the creation-affirmation is the effort of Paul and other writers to place Christ in the position of preexistent agent of creation. 1 Cor. 8:6, Heb. 1:2–3, Phil. 2:6–11, Col. 1:15–20, and John 1:1ff. are the passages that deal with this theme. First Corinthians 8:6 is perhaps the most significant: "Yet for us there is one God, the Father, from whom are all things and for whom we exist, and one Lord, Jesus Christ, through whom are all things and through whom we exist." This creedal statement, complex and polished in its literary form, dates from not later than A.D. 50, finding its way into Paul's letter by the year 54 or 55. To find a passage such as this at such an early time is impressive: a creed in a polished form, whose substance is such "high" christology, so metaphysically demanding, no later than twenty-five years after Jesus' earthly ministry. The complexity must be noted. The four lines contain high Hebrew-Jewish tradition ("One God, the Father"), Stoic borrowing ("from whom are all things and for whom we exist"), allusion to the wisdom tradition ("through whom are all things and through whom we exist"—this could also be Stoic), and a breathtaking leap of creative imagination in placing Jesus Christ in this context. Christ is explicitly paralleled to Yahweh, "the One God," as well as to the Jewish Wisdom (cf. Prov. 8:22ff.).

When we consider how early this piece is, that it is in the letter of a writer who is thoroughly Jewish in upbringing, and that it has a history of creedal use before Paul appropriated it, we are impressed by the audacity with which the early Christians "upped the ante" of belief claims for their contemporaries and for us. The passage poses nearly insuperable difficulties for those theories that hold that Christian belief evolved from the simpler to the complex, from low christology to high, and that the apostolic generation was blissfully unburdened by developed beliefs in contrast to later generations of theologians who allegedly dogmatized the simpler beginnings.

Theologically, two items must be considered. On the one hand, we see in this affirmation of Christ as agent of creation a profound intensification of the Old Testament effort to link present historical and personal experience to the creator God, thereby providing legitimation for such experience. The Christian affirmation is that not only is the apostolic experience rooted in the creator God, it is the experience *of* that God in a form that is very nearly univocally related to the Creator. Hebrews 1:2 (which dates from the generation after 1 Corinthians, A.D. 80–90) accentuates this: "In these last days he has spoken to us by a Son, whom he appointed the heir of all things, through whom also he created the world." We see here another way in which the *skandalon* of Christianity to the Jews may be stated, that Yahweh-Creator is identified with Jesus. Some scholars have observed that, in the New Testament, Jesus' person replaces the Jewish temple; Jesus' presence is the successor to Zion. If this be so, then we might suggest that we have in the passages from 1 Corinthians and Hebrews a radically recast "Zion theology."

Also to be noted, however, is the great difficulty these New Testament affirmations pose to *us*. It simply staggers the mind to attempt to explain conceptually how Jesus Christ could be declared to be the agent of creation, "through whom are all things and through whom we exist." One is finally moved to recognize that only a very nearly full-blown trinitarian theology can explain these affirmations which date from the late 40s and early 80s A.D. Such a conclusion is not popular, nor is it one that settles easily on the theologian, because it seems to impose too much on an early time of Christian faith. The conclusion brings with it intellectual and historical difficulties, but it appears to be inescapable. J. N. D. Kelly provides us some support when he writes, in the context of his discussion of 1 Cor. 8:6 and other binitarian creedal statements that occur in the New Testament:

> A host of other passages stamped with the same lineaments might be quoted. In all of them there is no trace of fixity so far as their wording is concerned, and none of them constitutes a creed in any ordinary sense of the term. Nevertheless the Trinitarian ground-plan obtrudes itself obstinately throughout, and its presence is all the more striking because more often than not there is nothing in the context to necessitate it. The impression inevitably conveyed is that the conception of the threefold manifestation of the Godhead was embedded deeply in Christian thinking from the start, and provided a ready-to-hand mould in which the ideas of the apostolic writers took shape. If Trinitarian creeds are rare, the Trinitarian pattern which was to dominate all later creeds was already part and parcel of the Christian tradition of doctrine.[17]

It has been said that these hymnic pieces, including the sections from Philippians, Colossians, and John, are expressions of the early Christian's immediate experience of redemption through Christ, not of ontological claims. There is no doubt much truth in such a claim. At the same time, it is difficult to believe that the apostolic generation was unaware of the implications of bringing the creation-motifs into conjunction with their affirmations about Jesus, particularly in light of Judaism's long tradition of such motifs. In any case, the substantial thrust of this Christian contribution to the creation-belief stands: What transpired in the life and work of Jesus Christ is a direct expression of the Creator; what Jesus did and said points to the underlying meaning and purpose of the creation.

Paul's writings are immensely significant for at least two reasons. He laid the foundations for relating Christ to the Old Testament as well as to intertestamental and Hellenistic reflection upon creation. And he also developed the concept of new creation to the point where it becomes a prime source for thinking about God's providential work in the world as an extension of the creation-work.

Paul's reflection on Christ as the Second Adam is a substantial contribution to the creation-affirmation (1 Cor. 15:45–49; Rom. 5:14, 4:17), because he is one of the few biblical writers, and the most important, to pick up the themes of Genesis 1—3 and develop their meaning. The Second or New Adam reflection is a way of saying that what was done at creation is Christ-shaped and fulfilled in Christ. Geoffrey Lampe has written:

> The Pauline parallel between Christ and Adam implies that God's design for Adam has been effectively realized in Christ. Adam was intended to be son of God; he was created in the image of God. Christ is God's Son; he is the image of God; he is "in the form of God"; he is truly Adam, which means that he is truly and completely human. The sonship to God which was fully realized in Christ belongs to the nature of all men; it characterizes humanity as the Creator intends it to be.[18]

When Lampe's comments have added to them the nuance that Christ is not only affirmed to be the true Adam but also is the one who was the agent of Adam's creation, then the richness and complexity of the New Testament propositions about Christ and creation begin to unveil themselves. Conceptually, nothing less than a doctrine of the Trinity could give coherence to such a proposition. In Rom. 4:17, Paul gives the earliest New Testament witness to creation out of nothing. This term originated in 2 Macc. 7:28 and also appears in Heb. 11:3. It is worth noting that in this passage Paul parallels the resurrection of Jesus with the creation out of nothing: "the God in whom [Abraham] believed, who gives life to the dead and calls into existence the things that do not exist." The Second Adam discourse in 1 Corinthians 15 also parallels that creation-motif to the resurrection.

Such insights lead naturally to Paul's thought about the new creation. Romans 5—8, as well as Gal. 6:15 and 2 Cor. 5:17, show this motif. In the Romans passages, we see Paul moving from the parallelism of 4:17 between resurrection and creation out of nothing to the discussion in chapter 5 of Christ as the Second Adam overcoming sin and restoring the original creation of humans. There follows the reflection on baptism as dying with Christ, so that we might rise with him. This new life is related to the law/grace duality, culminating in chapter 8 with commentary on our redemption as the new creation which liberates the rest of creation (8:19), "the creation waits with eager longing for the revealing of the sons of God." This redemption is our participation in God's predestination (8:20), which leads to the final victory, in which neither death, life, angels, heights, depths, "nor anything else in all creation will be able to separate us from the love of God in Christ Jesus our Lord."

Paul here rises to unrivaled heights of intensity as he pictures our redemption as a participation in God's ongoing creation work. When this motif is added to those discussed earlier, of Christ as Creator, Second Adam, whose resurrection parallels creation out of nothing, then it becomes clearer how fully Paul has integrated his christology with the creation affirmation. This is a concept of new creation that differs from the Old Testament concepts, in that the desired outcome is in no sense tied to the self-interest of the religious community and its reestablishment and vindication. Rather, the end that is sought is participation in God's work for its own sake. Paul interprets his own individual experience as "new creation" (Gal. 6:15), and he attaches the image to the life of all Christians. "New creation" is a description of what happens when we are united with Christ, and it is the goal of such union. "Therefore, if any one is in Christ, he is a new creation; the old has passed away, behold, the new has come" (2 Cor. 5:17).

Ephesians 1 and Colossians 1 have in recent decades been lifted up, particularly by Teilhard de Chardin, Allan Galloway, and Joseph Sittler, to set Christ clearly at the center of God's creator-activity and of the whole created world which Christ redeems.[19] Some exegetes have now sought to discredit such an emphasis, on several grounds. Even allowing for their objections, the cosmic christology of these passages is significant. It amounts to the assertion of Christ's preexistence; ". . . even as he chose us in him before the foundation of the world" (Eph. 1:3–4). It joins together our history with Christ and God's eternal creative will; "For he has made known to us in all wisdom and insight the mystery of his will, according to his purpose which he set forth in Christ, as a plan for the fulness of time, to unite all things in him, things in heaven and things on earth" (Eph. 1:9–10). In light of our survey of the biblical literature, these affirmations appear to be fully consistent with what the Old Testament and the other New Testament traditions set out to do.

Revelation 21 and 2 Pet. 3:13 speak of God's "new heaven and a new earth." The content of Revelation 21, as well as the language, is reminiscent of Third Isaiah. The intent is to encourage persecuted Christians with visions of hope. The New Testament image of the New Jerusalem, however, is a heavenly city "from above," rather than the earthly restoration of Zion. Second Peter puts apocalyptic creation imagery in the service of a just city where the righteous can live in peace.

As we observed at the outset, this lengthy survey of the biblical materials was undertaken not so much because theology must in every time reiterate the Bible, but because the Bible has such a rich and complex witness to creation. Even if subsequent history had contributed nothing, theology would be fully occupied with elaborating and seeking to understand more fully what the Bible has bequeathed to us. The following summary statements may serve as the transition to the next part of our theological reflection.

First. The scriptural witness evidences a basic assumption that God is creator of all that is. This is, even when it is doubted (as in some Wisdom sections), so basic an assumption that it may be termed preconceptual and predecisional. To recall Ronald Hepburn's phrase, the biblical witnesses seem scarcely ever to have doubted that God "is the author and sustainer of the world" and that consequently "the world is a planned and purposed enterprise."

Second. Despite this nearly unanimous affirmation, there is genuine and ineradicable diversity in the biblical witness. The Zion theology of David's and Solomon's court is not the same as the Yahwist's humanism or the Wisdom reflection of Job. And none of these is the same as Third Isaiah's eschatological vision. Paul's profound, sometimes involuted, probings are still different. This diversity has produced richness, which in turn provides for us an almost illimitable resource for speculation and edification. The diversity stems largely from the fact that creation was affirmed by groups and individuals with integrity in the situation in which they found themselves, with admirable freedom from simply reiterating what previous generations said. Note, for example, how little explicit reverberation Genesis 1 and 2 make in subsequent sections of Scripture.

Third. There is a persistent effort in each biblical witness to forge links between the situation of the witnesses and the activity of the creator God. This has often been explained as a subsuming of the interest in origins under existential need or soteriology. No doubt the judgment is profoundly true, but it also runs the danger of making the creation-witness seem to be an afterthought, whose legitimation must be sought in a sort of perennial ritual. It may be preferable to say that for most people the current existential situation does not make full sense unless it is related to origins and to the power of creation. Many peoples forged links between their present and their origins through nature and fertility cults. Israel (both old and new) eschewed such a strategy. The linkage for our biblical and Christian traditions has been made by relating to the creator God through our history, as well as through our reflective capacities (as in Job), our wills, and our introspection, rather than through "natural unification," such as might come through liaison with ritual prostitutes, worship of the seasons, and the like.

Fourth. When the links are forged between the present and the original creation and its God, creation becomes as much a present and a future reality as a present one. From this circumstance it develops that creation becomes what Paul Tillich has called originating, sustaining, and directing creativity.[20] The tradition has called these protology, continuing creation, and new creation or Providence. From our survey, it should be very clear that such terms grow quite naturally from the biblical witnesses; they are not "new creations" of the theologians.

Fifth. It is unmistakably clear that the Christian traditions in the apostolic period placed Christ in a revelational and ontological center position with respect to the creation affirmation. They did not work out the conceptual details of this position, but they left us no option but to confess Christ's centrality as the agent of creation, the goal of creation, and the power of creation's fulfillment in the new creation. This central position is intimately tied to the later doctrine of the Trinity.

Each of these five elements becomes a given for subsequent theological reflection, including our own theological efforts. How they are spelled out shapes the task of the next chapters of this locus.

NOTES

1. John Reumann, *Creation and New Creation* (Minneapolis: Augsburg Publishing House, 1973), p. 20.
2. Claus Westermann, *Creation*, trans. John J. Scullion (Philadelphia: Fortress Press, 1974), p. 48.
3. Emil Brunner, *The Christian Doctrine of Creation and Redemption*, trans. Olive Wyon (Philadelphia: Westminster Press, 1952), p. 6.
4. Reumann, *Creation and New Creation*, p. 21.
5. The more scholarly study is John Reumann, "Creatio, Continua et Nova," in *The Gospel as History*, ed. Vilmos Vajta (Philadelphia: Fortress Press, 1975), pp. 79–110. *Creation and New Creation* is longer and more popular. Neither, as Reumann points out, is a complete treatment.
6. Charles H. Long, *Alpha, the Myths of Creation* (New York: George Braziller, 1963).
7. Ibid., p. 149.
8. Westermann, *Creation*, p. 10.
9. Ibid., pp. 39–41.
10. Ibid., pp. 36–39.
11. Jaroslav Pelikan, "Creation and Causality in the History of Christian Thought," in *Issues in Evolution*, ed. Sol Tax (Chicago: University of Chicago Press, 1960), p. 31.
12. Helmer Ringgren, *The Faith of the Psalmists* (Philadelphia: Fortress Press, 1963), p. 96.
13. Carroll Stuhlmueller, "Creative Redemption in Deutero-Isaiah," *AnBib* 43 (1970): 9, 233.
14. Reumann, "Creatio, Continua et Nova," p. 91.
15. Walter Schmithals, *The Apocalyptic Movement*, trans. John E. Steely (Nashville: Abingdon Press, 1973), chaps. 1–2.
16. Ibid., p. 22.
17. J. N. D. Kelly, *Early Christian Creeds* (New York and London: Longmans, Green & Co., 1960), p. 23. See also G. B. Caird, "The Development of the Doctrine of Christ in the New Testament," in *Christ for Us Today*, ed. Norman Pittenger (London: SCM Press, 1968), pp. 4–80.
18. Geoffrey Lampe, *God as Spirit* (New York and London: Oxford University Press, 1977), p. 178.

19. See Joseph Sittler, "Called to Unity," *ER* 14 (1961–62): 177–87; Joseph Sittler, "The Scope of Christological Reflection," *Inter.* 26 (1972): 328–37; Allan Galloway, *The Cosmic Christ* (New York: Harper & Brothers, 1951); Pierre Teilhard de Chardin, *Science and Christ*, trans. Rene Hague (New York: Harper & Row, 1969), pp. 37–86, 151–73.

20. Paul Tillich, *Systematic Theology*, 3 vols. (Chicago: University of Chicago Press, 1951–63), 1:252–70.

2

The Creation
of the World

The Christian doctrine of creation is above all a statement of how Christians regard the world in a manner commensurate with what they believe about God. This linkage between God and the world must be respected if we are to comprehend this Christian doctrine fully and adequately. The idea of creation "out of nothing" is integral to the doctrine, because it is a powerful way of asserting the total dependence of the world on its Creator. Elaborating how this dependence is to be conceived is at the heart of theological reflection.

THE NATURE OF THE CLAIM

To begin with, we must be clear about what sort of statement the Christian affirmation of creation is. Arguments about this point are endless, and probably no other theological issue has caused more misunderstanding. In a notable dialogue entitled "Creation," Donald MacKinnon and Antony Flew point out that most of the laity believe the doctrine of creation deals with the beginning of the world and its details. As such, the creation-doctrine is a matter for preaching, but also one to which "the latest news from the science front" is also relevant.[1] The average theologian, on the contrary, insists on quite a different understanding of the doctrine, one to which scientific discoveries are simply irrelevant, because the doctrine intends to affirm something that science is not competent to assess. Such a division of the church according to theological expertise cannot go without close scrutiny. The issue is all the more pressing for Americans because of the "creationist" challenge, which insists on understanding the doctrine of creation as a parallel to scientific cosmology. The problem strikes modern Christians with particular force, since before the rise of modern science and secularization, nearly all Christians, including sophisticated theologians, took for granted that the doctrine of creation addresses both the question of the world's origins and other theological questions.

The doctrine of creation is thoroughly and completely a religious-theological affirmation. We must probe more deeply just what this means before we can go on to clarify the relationship between the doctrine and modern knowledge about the world and its origins. The affirmation of creation is the form in which the community of faith sets forth its understanding of the world. As it does so, its goal is to permit its understanding of the world to be fully congruous with its belief in God. This point must be appreciated in depth. Theology, when it speaks of creation, does not seek to obfuscate or avoid certain embarrassing questions, or stake out an esoteric realm beyond common language where only the initiated can enter. Rather, it insists that Christian belief in God has consequences, consequences to which we are accountable and consequences that must be observed if the coherence of Christian faith is to be respected. "Creation" is a word that refers to the whole of the world when viewed as belonging to God, and the doctrine of creation is an elaboration of how we understand the world when we permit our understanding of God to permeate and dominate our thinking.

The doctrine of creation is from the outset, therefore, shaped by powerful presuppositions, the most important of which concern God. It presupposes a conviction both that God is related to the world and that this relationship makes a difference that is determinative of all else. Because it does rest on such presuppositions, the affirmation of creation is an article of faith.[2] It is not the case that our affirmation of creation rests partly on our belief in God and partly on our natural knowledge. On the contrary, no matter what role natural knowledge plays in our affirmation, the belief in God plays the decisive role. It is belief in God that makes our statements about the world a doctrine of creation, rather than cosmology plain and simple. Our affirmation of creation is consequently not "more or less" influenced by our belief in God; it is decisively influenced by such a belief or else it is not an affirmation of *creation.*

From such considerations, the following axiom derives: There is a correlation between the nature of the world and the nature of its source or creator. In this axiom is to be found the power and the unsettling pointedness of the Christian affirmation of creation. When the Christian faith takes this axiom seriously, its proclamation of the creation-witness becomes a vital advocacy that allows neither the church nor the world to treat it as if it were a bland utterance of thoughtless piety. It demands attention, even if that attention is hostile, because what it says about the world does make a difference.

GOD AND THE WORLD:
ISSUES FOR CREATION
ARISING FROM GOD'S NATURE

The creation-affirmation requires a relationship between God and the world that is complex, difficult to conceptualize, and sometimes more significant for what it hints at or denies than for what it explicitly asserts. We may say of the Christian view of the God/world relationship what Langdon Gilkey has said of the Christian concept of God's transcendence, that it "is a baffling mixture of ontology and religious faith."[3] We may summarize the issues here as they pertain, first, to the way in which the creation came into being and, second, to the way in which God and the creation coexist after God's creative work.

There are two basic Christian doctrinal assertions about the beginning. The world came into being as a result of a free act of God. And God *created* the world, as opposed to generating it, or putting its parts together as a carpenter might, or being the origin of the world as the source of its emanations.

That God creates freely, by God's own volition, is a universal theological assertion in the Christian tradition. The assertion is put in a representative way by Irenaeus:

> I . . . begin with God the Creator, who made the heaven and the earth, and all things that are therein . . . and demonstrate that there is nothing either above him or after him; nor that, influenced by any one, but of his own free will, he created all things, since he is the only God, the only Lord, the only creator, the only Father.[4]

Irenaeus instructively places the assertion of God's freedom in the context of a recital of God's greatness and uniqueness. The assertion of God's freedom is not an attempt to preserve God's right to be arbitrary or God's distance from the creation. Rather, if God did not create freely, God would not be God. If God created by some necessity, it would imply some antecedent, determining power.[5] It is sometimes asserted that insistence on power and uniqueness is rooted in archaic notions of imperial power or place God beyond meaningful relationship with the created world.[6] While such arguments are not without grounds, they miss the point: creation by an entity that does not have the character of genuine deity is religiously and theologically unsatisfying.

There has been much debate over the centuries concerning the nuances of the words "create," "make," "generate," and the like when applied to God's activity. Athanasius and Arius debated this point at length during the fourth century. Athanasius' argument was that the verb carries overtones as to whether the outcome of the activity was like God, identical, equal, or dissimilar to God. In the Arian controversy, he insisted on a verb that expressed the unity and equality of Father and Son, so he argued that "beget" was the proper word, whereas Arius, with contrary interests, argued for "make."[7] There is a comparable problem with respect to describing God's creative activity. Thomistic theology has recognized the parallels between the persons of the Trinity emerging from one another (*processio*) and the emergence of the creation from God (*emanatio*).[8] The chief difference between the two kinds of emergence is that the inner-trinitarian process is necessary and results in co-equal entities, whereas the process of creation is a freely willed action of God's, and it produces an entity that is qualitatively different from God the Creator.

The narratives of Genesis 1—3 were able to use a term for "create" (*bara*) that was used exclusively for God's activity. It is not so simple for us. "Emanate" and "generate" may seem to be satisfying concepts for describing God's creating activity because they point to the intimacy between God and the world. We may even be influenced by the fact that Thomas Aquinas used the term *emanatio* to designate creation activity. These terms are to be rejected, however, because they suggest that the world is "of the same substance" with the Creator. Such terms suggest the bizarre notion that the created world is a "piece" of God, a child of God, or even God's body. Such suggestions are manifestations of the age-old option of pantheism or extreme monism, which the theological tradition has repudiated time and again. An example of pantheism is found in the Hindu Upanishads: "That which is the finest essence—this whole world has that as its soul. That is Reality. That is Atman."[9] Besides Hinduism, other Eastern religions could be called pantheistic. So can Neo-Platonism, Stoicism, and Spinozism. Pantheists hold that the world is a tightly unified whole whose parts perfectly intertwine and that this system is divine, made of the same substance as God. The power of pantheism lies in its ability to speak of the intimate relationship between God and the world and to give high value to the created order. It also provides the basis for a thoroughly ordered and reliable world.

Pantheism, while it does make certain appealing affirmations, violates what Christians deeply believe about God and God's relationship to the world. Christians have opposed pantheism because they perceive that it takes away God's freedom, so essential to the Christian concept of deity. For the world to be of the same substance with the Creator bespeaks a process whereby creation has "oozed" from God or broken off from God in some sort of mitosis. The Christian understanding of creation rests on a conviction that the world is the product of God's intentional activity; it did not just happen, nor is it a "natural" process. This free intentionality is essential to the Christian understanding of God. Gordon Kaufman has put it accurately: pantheism "maintains in its own way that the world is not God's deliberate creation, the purposive and meaningful expression of his will."[10]

The carpentering image of God's activity is also unsatisfactory from a Christian point of view. This image is essentially that of Plato's Demiurge, who found preexistent material at hand and imposed order upon it, thereby creating the world. Such an image is once again being proposed by some theologians as fully consonant with Christian faith.[11] The difficulty with the Demiurge image of the creator is that it violates the Christian conception of God as the originator of *all* that is. Preexistent material suggests a pre-God source.

Demiurge theories often are employed to provide a source for evil other than God. God is absolved of responsibility for evil, because, after all, God is not responsible for the tendencies to be found in the preexistent material before God began to work on it. Often these tendencies are those associated with chaos.[12] This sets up a dualism that not only deprives God of being the Creator of all things but also resolves the problem of evil by introducing material thrusts beyond God's power to control. This would postulate a source and process of evil that God cannot overcome. Such an image of God is foreign to the biblical traditions we have observed in Job ("Where were you when I laid the foundation of the earth?") or in the Psalms (e.g., Ps. 104) or in Second Isaiah. It is not in accord with the christological contributions the New Testament makes to our understanding of creation. These traditions bespeak a God who is the origin of all that is.

The nature of God, in the Christian conception, also makes demands on our concept of how God and the creation coexist after creation has come into existence. On this point the basic Christian affirmations are that the world is qualitatively different from God, that God maintains a caring concern for the world, that the world is totally dependent on its Creator from whom it has received order and unity, purpose, and goodness, and that the world has its own freedom and value. These elements are not readily brought into conceptual harmony. One might argue that they have never been adequately conceptualized, despite vigorous effort today to do so.

Emil Brunner has stated the qualitative difference between God and creation correctly:

> As the One who alone is Creator, God stands "over against" His creation, because it does not participate in his Being as Creator—the "Wholly Other." The fact that God is the Wholly Other refers to that which distinguishes Him as Creator from the creature. He alone is Lord, He alone is the Source of all life; He alone is the giver of every good and perfect gift. He alone is *"a se, non ab alio."* Thus there is no "way" between the creaturely and the divine; between both there lies the absolute gulf: that outside of God there is only that which has been created, outside Him who is *"a se,"* only that which is *"ab alio"*; thus outside the One who is entirely independent, there is only dependent being, the creature. This difference is greater than all other differences of any kind; this is the absolute transcendence of essence of Him who alone is God.[13]

This is the famous "wholly other," the *totaliter aliter* of the so-called "neo-orthodox" theology of the mid-twentieth century. Whatever the ramifications of this school of thought, it is important to see that the quality of "wholly otherness" in this citation is focused on one point: the distinction between Creator and created, source and sourced. This is not a statement about distance, uncaring, or otherness as such; rather, it is an assertion about the infinite qualitative difference between source of all that is and that which is sourced, which receives its being from the source of all being.

Conjoined with the assertion of God's freedom in creation, the assertion of God's otherness is not made to distance God from the world, nor is it an attempt to preserve for God some glory or status that protects God from the world's contamination. Rather the affirmation is this: This world is the creation of a God who created the world freely and who is the source of all that is. The governing considerations are that God can in no way be considered a created being and that God's creating activity is not coerced. There are no limits on our conceptions of the closeness, reciprocity, or intimacy between God and the world, so long as these essential elements are preserved intact. On the contrary, we are pressed to probe deeply the nature and quality of the intimacy that exists between God and the world. Theologically and religiously, however, we cannot be satisfied until our concepts take into account that such relationships are really with as the God whom Christians have worshiped in Jesus Christ. If this genuine godhood of God is not maintained in our theological concepts, then the closeness between God and the world that may be illumined will prove meaningless and intolerable.

Emphasis on the nature of God as free and qualitatively different from the world, in that God is its source, should not inhibit our reflection on the closeness of God and the world. The character of this closeness or intimacy is best described as *caring*. The Lutheran tradition has emphasized this caring quality of God vis-à-vis the creation by referring to the Creator as "Father." In his Large Catechism, Luther conveys the intimacy of God's caring both in the form and in the content of his explanation of the creed:

> The Creed is nothing else than a response and confession of Christians based on the First Commandment. If you were to ask a young child, "My boy, what kind of God have you? What do you know about him?" he could say, "First, my God is the Father, who made heaven and earth. Apart from him alone I have no other God, for there is no one else who could create heaven and earth."[14]

And when we turn to Luther's explanation of the first commandment, we find:

> A god is that to which we look for all good and in which we find refuge in every time of need. To have a god is nothing else than to trust and believe him with our whole heart. . . . The purpose of this commandment, therefore, is to require true faith and confidence of the heart. . . . The meaning is: "Whatever good thing you lack, look to me for it and seek it from me, and whenever you suffer misfortune and distress, come and cling to me. I am the one who will satisfy you and help you out of every need."[15]

The caring motif is elaborated at great length in the theological concepts of continuing creation (*creatio continua*) and providence (*conservatio*, *concursus*, and *gubernatio*), which receive extended discussion below. A number of recent theologians have insisted that this caring dimension of the creator God may be rendered more vivid if we keep in mind Christ's role in creation. Brunner suggests that the purpose of the creation is the will of God, and God's will is love. God's will is the "sufficient reason" (*ratio sufficiens*), whereas the love of God is the "final cause" (*causa finalis*) of creation. "In Jesus Christ this ideal reason for the Creation is revealed."[16] Gustaf Aulén and his successor as the Lundensian dogmatician, Gustaf Wingren, assert strongly what has come to be a hallmark of contemporary Swedish interpretations of creation:

> The doctrine of creation implies that God's loving and sovereign will is the matrix of creation. The purpose of creation is that God's will should rule and control all things. In other words, God's loving will is the law of creation. . . . It must be strongly emphasized again that this law of love which Christ has revealed and fulfilled is in principle nothing else than the law of creation.[17]

The Danish theologian, Regin Prenter, varies this general emphasis by suggesting that creation is proclaimed both as law and gospel; the caring emphasis is asserted under "The Gospel of Creation."[18]

The coexistence of the creator God and creation is characterized by the world's utter dependence on the Creator and yet also by its genuine freedom and autonomy. Dependence on God is an inescapable consequence of the qualitative difference we have mentioned. God alone is source, and therefore everything that is must be dependent on God in the most significant way: It has received its being from God. Thomas Aquinas asserted this point in scholastic terms: "Therefore all beings other than God are not their own being, but are beings by participation . . . caused by one First Being, who possesses being most perfectly."[19] The psalmist uses poetry in Psalm 104:

> When thou hidest thy face, they are dismayed;
>   when thou takest away their breath, they die
>   and return to their dust.
> When thou sendest forth thy Spirit, they are created;
>   and thou renewest the face of the ground.

Dependence on God is the chief thrust of the idea of creation "out of nothing." All that is is contingent on a cause, a source, a creator.[20] Again, this is not an insistence on coercive or imperial power for God, but rather an acknowledgment that the source of all that is exercises the power appropriate to being that source, namely, the activity of sourcing, on which all else depends. Friedrich Schleiermacher, in his dogmatic work *The Christian Faith*, which first appeared in 1821, made dependence the heart of Christian faith. His dogmatic theses concerning creation and preservation are worth repeating here.

In Thesis 36, Schleiermacher states the issue: "The original expression of this relation, i.e., that the world exists only in absolute dependence upon God, is divided in Church doctrine into the two propositions—that the world was created by God, and that God sustains the world."[21] Of creation, he wrote: "The religious consciousness which is here our basis contradicts every representation of the origin of the world which excludes anything whatever from origination by God."[22] Of preservation: "The religious self-consciousness, by means of which we place all that affects or influences us in absolute dependence on God, coincides entirely with the view that all such things are conditioned and determined by the interdependence of Nature."[23] The assertion of dependence as made by Aquinas—and as discussed by such contemporary theologians as Robert Neville, Thomas Torrance, and Wolfhart Pannenberg—is an ontological statement, whereas Schleiermacher is reporting on what the religious self-consciousness perceives in its experience. While it is impossible to move from the consciousness of experience to ontological statements, the combined testimony of an Aquinas and a Schleiermacher expresses what the Christian tradition has asserted.

The affirmation of the world's total dependence on the Creator as its source provides an opportunity to reflect on the inadequacy of all dualistic modes of relating God and the world. Dualism holds a special significance for Christian faith, because in the first two and a half centuries, the church was threatened both within and without by a dualism of massive proportions: gnosticism. The onslaught lasted over a century and involved church government, liturgy, and the understanding of Christ and his redemption, as well as the interpretation of the obedient life and doctrine. In the early centuries, the church faced other dualisms besides gnosticism, such as Manicheism. One can hardly overemphasize the importance of the fact that the church, out of this turmoil, came down decisively against dualism.

For our purposes, it is enough to characterize gnosticism as positing the essential inferiority and evil of the world, separating the God of creation (in the Old Testament) from the God of redemption (in the New Testament), and as exhorting people to flee the earthly and bodily realm. Tertullian and Irenaeus stand as the formative and normative theologians in responding to the gnostics. Irenaeus deserves preeminent consideration because of his nonlegalistic, creative theological responses. Tertullian, although he defended the church's authority against the gnostics, was himself prone to dualisms; hence his eventual submission to Montanism.

In their elaborate theosophical systems, the gnostics saw the origin of the created world in a liaison between a feminine divine figure (an "Aeon") with a nondivine male figure. The result is that, in their terminology, the world is "the fruit of a defect." With the inferiority of the earthly realm thus onto-logically grounded, the earth-renouncing of gnosticism came "naturally." The "spiritual" realm and the more "spiritual" persons took preeminence over "physical" counterparts. The goal was to free the spirit from its prisonhouse of matter. This might lead to world-renouncing through asceticism or through scornful antinomianism. The bifurcation of the Old and New Testaments was initiated by Marcion, the gifted mid-second-century schismatic and heterodox organizer. With it came the corresponding separation of the God of creation, the God of law, purported to be cruel and arbitrary, from the God of redemp-tion, the God of love.

The church's struggle with the gnostics should not be construed as a case of "orthodoxy" confronting and successfully vanquishing "heresy." The issue was more ambiguous than that. Even though the gnostics were part of a larger intellectual and religious movement existing also outside the church, the strug-gle was between two groups within the church, each of whom could claim some "orthodox" antecedents. Orthodoxy was defined in the conflict. The definition included the formation of a canon of Scripture that included both Old and New Testaments, and a creed that affirmed one Creator and Redeemer God, an affirmation of the goodness of the created world and a confession of God's intentions to bring it to consummation. Irenaeus developed his celebrated christology of "recapitulation" (*anakephalaiosis*), which spoke of the created world as being incomplete in the beginning but possessing the capacity to grow into its fullness. Christ was affirmed by Irenaeus as the proto-type of what creation should become. Christ recapitulated, incorporated all things and their destiny in himself. To be created in the image of God meant to be created in Christ's image and to grow into the Christ-destiny for which God has prepared creation.

Irenaeus thus effectively counters the view that would set God against the world, that would put a part of the created world outside God's sphere of responsibility, and that would abandon a part of the world to remain outside God's redemption. These two elements, pitting God against the world (or a part of it), and removing a part of the world from both God's creating and consummating activity—these are at the core of dualism, ontologically speak-ing. Irenaeus repudiated both these core elements by insisting that the world was created in Christ, that Christ is the prototype of its development or growth, and that at the end it will grow into its Christ-perfection. We have already observed the roots of creation-through-Christ in early traditions. *Apokatastasis*, or "universalism," as it is sometimes called (often tendentiously), has been affirmed by theologians from Origen to Barth as a way of asserting that there is no evil that God cannot overcome, that God is intent on bringing the whole of creation to its perfection at the end.

Irenaeus' specific resolutions of the problems posed by dualism are distinctive and not reiterated universally throughout the tradition. Nevertheless, the points he made have become the Christian faith's perennial response to dualisms that threaten the fundamental assertion that God is the God on whom all creation is dependent for its being.

This discussion of dualism has focused on its ontological aspect. Moral dualism is a different matter; this aspect has been prominent in Christian faith. Paul Tillich has said that Christian faith grants evil only moral, not ontological, foundation.[24] The Christian recognizes that the struggle between good and evil is an inescapable characteristic of earthly existence, but that it is not written into the very nature of things. It is not at the foundation of the creation. Tillich thereby laid bare the limits to the Christian faith's tolerance of dualism.

Christians are sensitive to the ongoing conflict within each person's existence and within history between good and evil in many different forms. Precisely, however, because they believe that evil has no ontological foundation, Christians can believe in the redemption of existence and history. As we shall discuss in detail later, this firm belief is rooted in the character of the creator God and God's creation activity.

Thus far, we have noted only the general dependence of the created world on the Creator for its being. This being is specified in Christian belief to include the order and unity, purposiveness, and goodness of creation. These characteristics of the created world derive from the character of God. The nature of God as one and good, together with the conviction that God has created the world intentionally and freely, leads inescapably to the assertion that the created world is a unity, that it is good, and that it has a purpose and meaning. These characteristics are reinforced by the assertion of Christ's role in the creation.

We have observed the intimate relation between the biblical assertion of Christ's role in creating and the doctrine of the Trinity. In recognizing Christ as the second person or hypostasis of the triune Godhead, the Christian faith emphasized his position as Logos and Wisdom, as *ordo intellegendi*. In locating Christ so, the theologians demonstrated their dependence both on stoic and Platonist philosophy and on the Hebrew wisdom tradition. They also demonstrated the creative imagination that put together a new intellectual and religious synthesis the exact like of which had not been seen before.

So to place Christ and to link him with the agency and the goal of creation is to put meaning and purpose "deep-down in things," precisely because the second person of the Trinity *is* meaning and purpose, thematized within the Godhead and revealed in all reality. The same must be said about goodness.

God the Creator is good, and that goodness is revealed, actualized, and incarnate in Christ.

Finally, in recounting the manner in which the Christian understanding of God influences our understanding of the God/world relationship, we turn to the question of the world's independent reality, its autonomous worthwhileness. God gives creation a genuine reality, not a docetic pseudoreality. As Gilkey writes, "Christians believed that the finite world was the product of the will as well as of the divine wisdom. Nature was, therefore, a creature and not an appearance of God, a distinct and relatively independent reality posited into being by God's will."[25] Erich Frank has made a similar point:

> The concept of creation . . . acknowledges both the rational and irrational elements in the world. For creation means that free individual beings are brought forth, or, from the point of view of the creator, it signifies that he has infused his own being into another thing which thereby has taken on an independent existence of its own and may later on itself become productive. Thus the idea of creation, although transcending human experience, serves to explain the world as it really is in its twofold character of individual autonomy and universal dependence.[26]

This concept of a certain autonomy belonging to the created order has been judged by historians to be distinctive of the Judeo-Christian tradition. There is no concept of "nature" in the Bible, writes the Dutch historian, R. Hooykaas, but only the concept of creatures. "Nature" had the ring of a deified order that was of the same substance as God, whereas the biblical view of nature is "de-deified."[27] Not only the nature and fertility cults of Canaan, which surrounded the Israelites, but also the views of Plato, Aristotle, and the other Greek philosophers, bestowed a divinity on nature, though the philosophers' reasoning was different from that of the Near Eastern religions.

Among the consequences of this view of creation was an antipathy to pantheism in any form. Earlier we observed that pantheistic views violate the basic concept of how God was originally related to the world. It contravenes the assertion of God's free creative act. Pantheism also violates the integrity of the created order. This requires some spelling out.

We might think that pantheism would not downgrade the earthly order but rather would glorify it, since this monistic world view asserts that at its most essential all matter is divine. However, pantheism has always resulted in a depreciation of matter—as in the cases of the Neo-Platonists, the stoics, Indian pantheisms, and the like. The clue to this depreciation lies in the essential idea "that the reality and value of finite things consist in the degree to which they are identical to or united with God. What is not God, then, is neither real nor good."[28] Finite things, insofar as they are finite, possessing the characteristics of materiality, partialness, changeableness, relativity, limitedness, and the like, are certainly not God. What results is a degradation of the material order. Matter becomes illusory; docetism enters in. The claim is that "at the core" or "in their essence," finite things are divine, so what is required is a strategy of sloughing off all that is not of the essence or at the core. This poses at least two problems for the Christian. In the first place, we are impressed that the quantity of what must be sloughed off is rather great, including a good deal that we consider central to our humanity. Further, we know that at the core we are sinners, capable of considerable evil.

A strong argument could be made that what must be sloughed off as unessential is so central to the earthly realm that without this "unessential" element there would be no identifiable material realm left. For people, such "unessentials" would include changeable emotions, physicality, and dependence upon others. We could also argue that the reality of evil in the heart of every person, with the enormous harm that those evil hearts can accomplish, is a testimony not to the unreal, illusory quality of finite selves but on the contrary to the very much undeniable, concrete reality of those same selves.

The distinctive Christian affirmation of the independent reality of the created order has had other important consequences. Chief among them is the influence this affirmation may have had on the emergence of modern science and on the development of secularization. A substantial number of historians argue that in both cases—science and secularization—Christianity's de-deification of nature has triggered significant historical trends.[29] The change from a deification of nature to the assessment that nature is creation brought with it an interest in nature for its own sake, as well as an affirmative attitude free from inordinate fear of nature. The conviction that God had bestowed orderliness, intelligibility, and unity upon creation (especially strong among the medieval theologians) encouraged confidence that scientific study of nature would produce results. If the Christian theological tradition as a whole contributed significantly to the intellectual foundations of the rising science, the "Protestant ethic," particularly the zeal of English Puritans in the seventeenth century, provided practical energy and (through the rise of capitalism) a financial base for science.

Secularization is the development of the attitude that nature is its own realm, that it does not need to be decoded like a cipher in order to be understood. Weather can be understood by terrestrial principles, without consulting oracles and divinities. So can illness, nutrition, sexuality, and warfare, to mention just a few aspects of life affected in important ways by secularizing trends. Some theologians—Friedrich Gogarten, Schubert Ogden, J. A. T. Robinson—would distinguish between "secularization" and "secularism." The former is the wholesome recognition that nature, including human and social nature, is not divine, that it has its own rationale and orderliness. Secularism, in contrast, is a destructive elevation of this insight of secularization into an all-encompassing philosophical position. Secularization recognizes that the natural world is not itself a system of reality that is ontologically self-sufficient, and as such is reconcilable with the Christian view of God and creation. Secularism denies both God and creation, and as such is antithetical to the Christian faith.

CREATION OUT OF NOTHING
("EX NIHILO")

Although we have scarcely mentioned it explicitly, we have been skirting the classical doctrine of *creatio ex nihilo*, creation out of nothing. Because of linguistic difficulties with the formulation, which may lead to confusion, we have deliberately made our way to the doctrine through these other reflections, so that it might be clear just what kinds of considerations the *ex nihilo* tries to comprehend. Augustine, in his *Confessions*, gives us one of the most vivid formulations of the doctrine:

> But *how* didst thou make the heaven and the earth, and what was the tool of such a mighty work as thine? For it was not like a human worker fashioning body from body, according to the fancy of his mind, able somehow or other to impose on it a form which the mind perceived in itself by its inner eye (yet how should even he be able to do this, if thou hadst not made that mind?). He imposes the form on something already existing and having some sort of being, such as clay, or stone or wood or gold or such like (and where would these things come from if thou hadst not furnished them?). . . . But how didst thou make them? How, O God, didst thou make the heaven and earth? For truly, neither in heaven nor on earth didst thou make heaven and earth—nor in the air nor in the waters, since all of these also belong to the heaven and the earth. Nowhere in the whole world didst thou make the whole world, because there was no place where it could be made before it was made. And thou didst not hold anything in thy hand from which to fashion the heaven and the earth, for where couldst thou have gotten what thou hadst not made in order to make something with it? Is there, indeed, anything at all except because thou art? Thus thou didst speak and they were made, and by thy Word thou didst make them all. But how didst thou speak? . . . Whatever it was out of which such a voice was made simply did not exist at all until it was made by thee."[30]

Augustine wrote his *Confessions* between A.D. 395 and 398. He was by no means the first to assert *creatio ex nihilo*. There is some question among scholars as to whether already the Old Testament asserts this proposition. A recent "process" theologian, David Griffin, has argued that Plato's theory of creation out of chaos, with God as Demiurge, is consistent with Genesis 1 and is philosophically preferable to the *ex nihilo*.[31] The contention of our discussion has been that the traditions in Job, Second Isaiah, and the Psalms do indeed imply the *ex nihilo* and that the New Testament traditions, particularly in their christocentric dimension, are consistent only with the *ex nihilo*. The first explicit reference to the idea as such is in Macc. 7:28 (which dates from the period between 100 B.C. and A.D. 70), which in the Vulgate is translated *"ex nihilo fecit illa Deus"* (God made them out of nothing). Romans 4:17 and Heb. 11:3 express the idea. In the mid-second century A.D., the term is found in Hermas, *Visio*, 1,1,6, and in the latter half of the century, it is argued by a number of theologians, including Clement of Alexandria, Theophilus of Antioch, Tertullian, and Irenaeus.

We have already rehearsed the principal contents of the doctrine of creation out-of-nothing. We do not properly understand the doctrine, however, unless we recognize that it is not only a material assertion. The *ex nihilo* is just as importantly a proposition of method or strategy. In this respect, it teaches: Unless the formula "out of nothing" is emphasized, the basic affirmations Christians want to make about God the Creator and God's relationship to the world cannot be maintained. This recognition prompted Paul Tillich to observe: "The formula *creatio ex nihilo* is not the title of a story. It is the classical formula which expresses the relation between God and the world."[32] The doctrine does not assert that God created all things out of the prior reality called "nothing," "nonbeing," the Greek *ouk ōn*. It is rather insisting that everything that is depends for its being on God the Creator. *Creatio ex nihilo* is first and foremost a statement about who God is and what kind of a God that God is. It is because of their experience of God that the Hebrews, the Jews, and the Christians have asserted the Creator of the *creatio ex nihilo*. Writers as diverse as Augustine and Schleiermacher have described the existential correlate of the doctrine, namely, the sense that one's existence is totally dependent, that it is itself a created entity. Philosophers have also expended great effort to make intellectual and conceptual sense of the assertion.[33]

It is only through this assertion of the total dependence of all things on the creator God that the axiom can be maintained that there is a correlation between the nature of the world and the nature of the God who created the world. This correlation is essential for genuinely religious and theological statements; without the axiom, it is not possible for Christians to state what difference their understanding of God makes for their understanding of the world. On this ground the theologian is bound to say that beyond the historical witnesses to the *ex nihilo* in Scripture and in the tradition, there is a theological rationale which renders the concept necessary for Christian faith. As we have already discussed, the affirmations about the goodness of the created order, its unity, and its meaningfulness are all consistent with the axiom of the correlation between the nature of the Creator and that of the world. Conversely, the rejection of dualisms, pantheism, and monisms also follows from the axiom. These affirmations and rejections would be compromised without the "out of nothing." In this sense, we can speak of the Christian proclamation of the good news about nothingness. Every religion and philosophy of life requires the axiom of correlation, but not every one of them requires the *ex nihilo* in order to sustain the axiom. For this reason, we conclude that the *ex nihilo* formula is essential to Christian belief.

There are several objections to the *ex nihilo* in current theological thought.

First. The *ex nihilo* diverts attention away from creation as a statement about the dependence of the world on God.[34] This point of view argues that theologians have allowed themselves to be preoccupied by the arguments of the Hellenistic philosophers who opposed Christianity. It argues that, in defense of the faith, they fell into the trap of arguing that creation has to do with *origins* rather than *dependence*. Aquinas is criticized in particular, because he allowed dependence to be a matter of public debate by reason, whereas *ex nihilo* was a matter of faith in his system, discernible only with the help of revelation.

Our discussion to this point should have demonstrated that the *ex nihilo* is a statement about dependence as much as it is about origins. The wisdom of the "out-of-nothing" formula holds that dependence cannot otherwise be persuasively set forth. This fact tells us something about the interrelationship of the concern for origins with the more existentially vivid themes associated with the creation-affirmation. The question of origins is a matter of logic and speculation, rather than of existential consolation. Augustine's reflections demonstrate, however, that the existential raises the logical/speculative considerations and that it cannot be at peace unless it finds an existentially satisfying and reasonable speculative resolution of its concerns. Furthermore, it is clear that in this matter not all speculative resolutions are equally adequate. Our discussion has insisted that the criterion of satisfaction and adequacy is the concept of God. The *ex nihilo* is the only explanation of origins that meets the criterion of consistency with the Christian concept of God.

Second. The *ex nihilo* renders it difficult, if not impossible to deal with the problem of evil. In his history of Christian theology, Jaroslav Pelikan writes that the second century theologians accepted the *ex nihilo* "in spite of the difficulties [it] raised for any attempts to cope with the problem of evil."[35] What was apparent in the second century has proved true ever since. If we could say earlier that its effective grounding of the basic Christian affirmations about God's relationship to the world makes the *ex nihilo* formula our good news about nothingness, we are forced now to say that the problems it raises for Christian reflection on evil very nearly turn it into bad news.

The problem is that the "out-of-nothing" idea makes God responsible for everything, including evil. Christian theology seems to be faced with the alternatives of asserting that God is ultimately responsible for evil or that there

311

are some things over which God has no control, one of which is evil and the matrix out of which it comes. The *ex nihilo* doctrine disposes the theologian to the first of these alternatives. There is scarcely a more offensive idea for the Christian than one that holds God in some way responsible for evil. Perhaps the only idea more repugnant is the alternative we mentioned—that God is limited in power over anything, including evil. We face here, in an inescapable manner, the limitations of human thought.

We realize that the *ex nihilo* doctrine is itself a speculation that is always a matter of faith, not of observation and demonstration. As such it leaves origins in a secondary position. A comparable statement must be made about evil: its origins are a matter of speculation. The primary affirmation in the creation-doctrine is that we are dependent on the Creator for our being; the primary affirmation with respect to evil is that we are dependent on God for victory over evil, whatever form that victory takes.

We should, however, not consider that the *ex nihilo* concept is without value for the discussion of evil. If the concept renders evil a particular bafflement because it seems to root the ultimate ground of evil in God, it also provides a source of high motivation for engaging in the struggle against evil. And it adds hope that the struggle will finally succeed.

The rationale of the creation-affirmation's support for this motivation and hope is a bit involved, but it should be grasped clearly. The hope for victory over evil stems ultimately from the conviction that God is directly responsible for the creation, "out of nothing." The essential goodness and purposiveness of the world, assertions that are rooted in the *ex nihilo*, give hope that evil cannot ultimately hold out against God's creative purpose.

The ground for motivation to enter the struggle against evil lies in the basic Christian notion that humans live in a realm that includes nothing else but this created order and the will and power of God who has created the world and whose intention is to bring it to consummation. The historian of religions G. van der Leeuw has written about the Hebrew understanding of creation: "The God who sustains the world is not a static source, but one who is active from *olam* to *olam*. The source is nothingness; *God's act of creation is the only reality*. God is not contingent on the world; the world is only and always contingent on God. This is expressed in the *theologoumenon* of *creatio ex nihilo*."[36] "God's act of creation is the only reality"—in these words, van der Leeuw has rightly emphasized the important matter. Contrary to most of the world's other myths of creation, the Hebrew creation-traditions give no more than a hint at any significant events in primordial time. There are no stories of gods and goddesses whose behavior in heaven influences what happens on earth, as, for example, in Virgil's *Aeneid*, where Aeneas' fortunes hang on the events taking place "in heaven above." There is no Hebrew hint at such heavenly history, whether before the world began or contemporaneous with world history. Consequently, Christians and Jews have not looked for an escape hatch out of history and nature. Rather, they look for their hope in the future of the created continuum, its consummation at the hands of the creator God. This being the case, the Christian has a vested interest in the betterment and perfection of this created world, regardless of how Christians at any given time and place have defined the terms "betterment" and "perfection." Since evil is a definite obstacle to the purposes of God and God's will to consummate the world, the Christian should be mightily motivated to participate in God's struggle against evil.

The emphasis on God's act of creation as the only reality and on the historical character of this reality that moves toward consummation has received renewed interest in the "eschatological" theologies, as well as in the "liberation" theologies of Latin America. Jürgen Moltmann, an exponent of eschatological theology, calls for an "eschatological understanding of creation," to replace a predominant "protological understanding of creation." The latter view sees redemption as "nothing other than the restoration of original creation. . . . History . . . is primarily the history of the Fall. It cannot bring anything new."[37] Such a "protological" understanding betrays what van der Leeuw rightly lifts up as the distinctive heart of the Christian view of creation. This view is also emphasized at many points in the tradition, beginning with the growth and development-oriented theology of Irenaeus. "Liberation" theology makes the same point as, for example, when Juan Luis Segundo links creation and Providence, with the power of God directed to the remaking of history.[38] Paul Tillich emphasized Christianity's distinctive interpretation of history, one which opposes the "nonhistorical" interpretations of Chinese, Indian, and Greek philosophies. At one point he underscores the biblical roots of this historical interpretation and contrasts the biblical-traditional view of creation with the Greek concept of the Demiurge, who does not create, but rather "fashions." Tillich writes:

> The *demiourgos* has shaped the world by forming and ordering the matter according to the picture of the idea of the good. In doing so, he elevates the matter which is controlled by necessity to the greatest possible similarity with the idea. But he can succeed only in a limited way. He cannot overcome the evils which are rooted in the resistance of matter. The Septuagint and the New Testament use the word *ktizein* for the creative activity of God, emphasizing the idea of a new foundation and dropping entirely the connotation of something "given" by the idea of a creation out of nothing. The world is *ktisis*, it is created, not shaped; therefore it is good in itself; the evil has no ontological, but only moral, foundation, *and thus a history of salvation is possible*.[39]

Elsewhere Tillich suggests that the *ex nihilo* formula has two truths inherent in it: that tragedy is possible in the created order, but that it is not rooted in the essence of that order.[40]

CONTEMPORARY CHALLENGES AND
CONTRIBUTIONS TO THE DOCTRINE

For many Americans the most energetic discussions of creation may arise from the efforts of "creationists" to revise public school textbooks. Parallel to scientific accounts of the world, its origin, and its development, they seek a presentation of divine special creation as set forth—in their opinion—in Genesis 1—3. This creationist effort is earnestly intended to reshape the teaching of natural science in the schools. After a creationist victory in California in 1972, the prestigious National Academy of Sciences passed a resolution taking note of the California controversy and closing with the strong plea "that textbooks of the sciences utilized in the public schools of the nation be limited to the exposition of scientific matters."[41]

The substance of the creationist position seems to consist of the following tenets. First, the biblical accounts of creation in Genesis 1—3 and other biblical statements about the natural world are factual accounts. "We insist that God is communicating history to us here."[42] Second, evolution-based views of the world's origins and processes are antithetical to a belief in God and to the Bible. A "theistic evolutionism" is unacceptable, because it is a contradiction in terms. Third, the essence of the biblical position on creation is belief in God's special creation, involving catastrophic interventions at times, belief that God has created everything with a purpose and that this purposiveness continues up until the present, and belief that God's continuing creation is efficacious today. Fourth, evolutionary theory is not able to explain all that science has discovered about the world. The scientific establishment imposes evolutionary theory ideologically, until it has attained the status of a de facto religious belief-system.

Creationism can be applauded for its opposition to *scientism*—the improper elevation of certain hypotheses to ideologically oppressive positions. Similarly, creationists are not to be faulted for calling attention to the biblical witness as a relevant body of tradition for contemporary people, a witness that contains an intellectual challenge for current culture, as well as a religious and a moral challenge. Beyond this, however, there are few points where we can agree with them or join forces with them. We mention three chief areas of critique.

First. The creationists misuse the biblical literature by setting it over against scientific treatises, as if there were a one-to-one correlation between them. It is asserted, for example, that there is "absolute Bible accuracy on the subject of plant physiology," among the proofs for which is that Deut. 33:14 ("Precious fruits brought forth by the sun" [KJV]) correctly "indicates that sunlight plays a role in plant food synthesis."[43] Our studies show, however, that the Old Testament combines many types of literature, most of which is doxological in one way or another, and that much of it is poetic, symbolic, often borrowed from other cultures, and certainly not intended as "science" or "history" in our sense of those terms. Furthermore, and very significant, creationists utilize only a small portion of the biblical witness to creation.

Second. The creationist position is so simplistic in relating the Bible to scientific discoveries and so unwilling to accept dynamic change in natural processes through natural development that it actually betrays the Christian affirmation that God relates to the world as it is, in all its plural forms. The creationists do not relate the biblical affirmations to contemporary science or to our contemporary experience of the world. Rather, they relate contemporary scientific understandings to the understandings of the world that prevailed in biblical times, then proceed further to insist that such a matching of epochs is what is required for faith. To believe in God the Creator is supposedly to relate photosynthesis to biblical statements about the sun and plants, and then to affirm that God has created it all, and so marvelously! The result is that the classical creation witness is proclaimed with little relevance to the world that people today actually experience.

Third. The creationist strategy does not relate biblical faith to the ongoing activity of scientific research and discovery; it only tries to verify biblical statements about the natural world. The task for the creationist scientist is to lift out hypotheses from Scripture and show that they fit the facts. When this is done, "it is conceivable that theoretical frameworks in this whole discipline can be brought back to reality while being brought back to God the Creator."[44] There is no two-way traffic between faith and science. The creationist, from the descriptions that proceed from creationists themselves, is not interested in contributing to scientific discovery so much as in verifying the Bible with scientific means. If this is an accurate picture, they do not enter vigorously into the pursuit of knowledge as scientists.

The greatest harm done by the creationists is certainly their energetic pressing of a simplistic understanding of the creation-affirmation and its significance. They thereby deprive both their adherents and the secular society of a forceful presentation of the power and the problematic of the claim that this world is dependent on God the Creator for its being, with all that entails.

No school of twentieth-century theology has devoted more attention to the themes of which this essay is comprised than the so-called "process theology," the theologians who have taken the metaphysical constructions of Alfred North Whitehead and Charles Hartshorne as their basis for theological work. This school is so substantial and extensive in its achievement that it cannot be discussed in detail here. However, precisely because of its importance, some mention must be made of the significant and problematic contributions it has made to the understanding of creation.

Succinctly put, process theologians deny the *ex nihilo* doctrine and challenge the interpretation of evil associated with it. However, before any response can be given to their challenge, some analysis must be made of how their position came to be what it is.

Proceeding as it does from the base of Whitehead's philosophy, process theology restricts itself to the realm of "actual entities," to what we would popularly call *this world*. Whitehead called this a "descriptive" metaphysics, and he intended that it should interpret "every element of our experience . . . everything of which we are conscious."[45] As such, Whitehead stands in the long tradition of philosophers who do not presume to discuss ultimate origins or endings. In this, Whitehead stands in the same position as the whole body of natural, physical, and social sciences to which he intentionally conformed his philosophy. We do not fully comprehend the process theological opposition to the *ex nihilo* if we do not understand this methodological feature of restriction to the interpretation of experience, a restriction which is the result of a conscious intention on Whitehead's part and on the part of those who follow him.[46]

Beyond this important methodological characteristic, which proceeds from their starting point, process theologians tend to limit their discussions of the natural world to the area in which theology and philosophy share perspectives. In this they resemble Thomas Aquinas, who distinguished clearly between knowledge gained by reason and knowledge gained by revelation. The former knowledge constituted the area in which theology did not go beyond philosophy, whereas in the latter area it left philosophy behind. Process theologians do not actually leave philosophy behind when they discuss items of Christian belief that plainly exceed the natural realm—for example, christology—but they do follow a strategy similar to Aquinas in the area of the natural world.[47] One such theologian terms the *ex nihilo* "exceptional talk," which should not be appealed to when theology is in the same arena of conversation as philosophy.[48] This might be viewed as an apologetic strategy.

The most important aspect of the process theological restriction is its effect on the concept of God. The process theologians, by and large, present the concept of a God who does not *create* in the *ex nihilo* sense. A passage from a leading process theologian, John Cobb, illustrates this point:

> In Whitehead's analysis, God's role in creation centers in the provision to each actual occasion of its initial aim. This role is of such importance that Whitehead on occasion acknowledges that God may properly be conceived in his philosophy as the creator of all temporal entities. Yet, more frequently, he opposes the various connotations of the term "creator," as applied to God, and prefers to speak of *God and the temporal world as jointly qualifying or conditioning creativity*, which then seems to play the ultimate role in creation.[49]

Cobb testifies clearly that "Whitehead envisions no beginning of the world, hence no first temporal creation out of nothing."[50]

This concept of God is clearly not the same as the one that we have elaborated in our survey of biblical and later traditional sources. We have portrayed a God who is Creator *ex nihilo*, a God on whom all things depend for their being, as well as for meaning and purpose, goodness, and order. Process theologians object that such a picture of God is autocratic, "imperial," and conceptually impossible, since a being who has the power to control and determine other beings is not even thinkable to our minds. Our discussion has put the matter in such a way as to suggest that the process-theological objection is not precisely on target. The Christian concept of God intends to break away from an autocratic God and an imperial image of deity. It wishes to speak of the freedom and self-determination that the entities of this world possess. It insists, however, that all this must be done without overlooking or dismissing the fact that God is Creator and source, while the entities of this world are created and sourced by God.

What sorts of relationship of reciprocity, interaction, and the like are possible between source and sourced? And how can they be conceptualized so as to maintain the source/sourced distinction, yet be faithful to the insistence that God is loving Father, good shepherd, as tender and sensitive as Hosea depicts? The process theological concept of God has tended to dismiss one side of this bifocal view of God, the source/sourced, to focus only on the caring, sensitive, intimate side. This is understandable in light of their restriction to the realm of actual entities and their experience, since the *ex nihilo* is an item not of experience but of faith. Schleiermacher came as close as possible to the experience of the *ex nihilo*, namely, the experience of being *fully caused* in certain areas of life. But that is still not truly an experience of the "creation out of nothing."

The challenge *to* process theology must focus on its concept of God. Philosophical alternatives have been suggested,[51] perhaps the most important of which is a form of Hegelianism, which builds upon the datum of christology. The challenge *of* process theology is its insistence that its conceptualities are more adequate to contemporary experience, as described and analyzed in the give-and-take of public discussion, providing corrections to the traditional ways of conceiving of God and the world.

It will not do, in the final analysis, simply to rule against process theology because its God is not the God of the tradition, although that is an important point too seldom argued clearly. Rather, one must ask whether the process-theological concept of a God who creates jointly with the cooperation of the rest of the world is a more adequate interpretation of our experience of creativity.

On the question of evil, one must ask whether the process-theological view that evil is rooted in the primordial chaos, which God was confronted with and put into some sort of order, but over which God had no control, is more consonant with what we experience. These questions cannot be argued here. One can suggest, however, that our experience does include the never-satisfied quest to discover the ultimate beginning, the beginning-point for both the Demiurge and the preexistent chaos on which he worked. This raises the question whether the process-theological position has yet truly found the God to which the Hebrew-Christian tradition witnesses. This question cuts through to the process-theodicy, as well. If there is a defect in the concept of God, then the theodicy based on that concept must be reworked too.

The most adequate conclusion to be drawn at this point is that the dialogue between process theology and the classical Christian tradition is not yet finished. The continuation of the dialogue is an item high on the Christian theological agenda; until it is carried out with thoroughness, dogmatics today has not finished its work.

The challenges and contributions of *modern science* to our theme of creation are enormous. Since these challenges are relevant to subsequent sections as well, the examination of science will be placed later in the discussion. It is useful, however, to keep in mind the specific areas of challenge posed by science.

Scientific discovery in the past 150 years has opened up breathtaking vistas for a new understanding of nature (physical, biological, and social). The concepts of the creator God and of creation must be related to this new understanding of nature if they are to be credible. Scientific concepts provide the most persuasive interpretations of the natural world for the majority of people today. Those interpretations, however, cannot undergird the Christian affirmations that the world is dependent on God for its being and that it is a purposive order. But neither do scientific concepts, properly understood, disprove the ideas of dependency and purpose. Nevertheless, considerable effort is required to relate the Christian affirmations to the scientifically described earthly realm.

NOTES

1. Antony Flew and Donald M. MacKinnon, "Creation," in *New Essays in Philosophical Theology*, ed. Antony Flew and Alisdair MacIntyre (London: SCM Press, 1963), p. 174.

2. Emil Brunner, *The Christian Doctrine of Creation and Redemption*, trans. Olive Wyon (Philadelphia: Westminster Press, 1952), pp. 7–9. Karl Barth, *Church Dogmatics*, vol. 3/1, trans. G. T. Thomson (Edinburgh: T. & T. Clark, 1936), pp. 3–4.

3. Langdon Gilkey, *Maker of Heaven and Earth* (Garden City, N.Y.: Doubleday & Co., 1959), p. 94.

4. Irenaeus, *Against Heresies*, ii,1,1, *ANFa* 1.

5. See Robert Neville, *God the Creator* (Chicago: University of Chicago Press, 1968), pp. 80–81.

6. Such charges are made by some of the process theologians. See Schubert Ogden, *The Reality of God* (New York: Harper & Row, 1966), pp. 16–18; Bernard Loomer, "Two Kinds of Power," *Crit.* 15 (Winter 1976): 11–29. The source of this tendency may be found in Alfred North Whitehead, *Process and Reality* (New York: Free Press, 1978), p. 520.

7. See Athanasius' *Discourses against the Arians*.

8. *Summa Theologica*, qu. 45. See also the discussion in Johannes Brinktrine, *Die Lehre von der Schöpfung* (Paderborn: Ferdinand Schoeningh, 1956), pp. 16–19.

9. From the Chandogya Upanishad, in R. E. Hume, *The Thirteen Principal Upanishads* (London: Oxford University Press, 1949), p. 246.

10. Gordon Kaufman, *Systematic Theology: A Historicist Perspective* (New York: Charles Scribner's Sons, 1968), p. 293.

11. David Griffin, *God, Power, and Evil: A Process Theodicy* (Philadelphia: Westminster Press, 1976), p. 39.

12. Ibid., pp. 286–91. Pierre Teilhard de Chardin, "Reflections on Original Sin," in his *Christianity and Evolution*, trans. René Hague (New York: Harcourt Brace Jovanovich, 1969), pp. 187–98.

13. Emil Brunner, *The Christian Doctrine of God*, trans. Olive Wyon (Philadelphia: Westminster Press, 1950), p. 176.

14. *BC* 412.

15. Ibid., p. 365.

16. Brunner, *Christian Doctrine of Creation and Redemption*, p. 13.

17. Gustaf Aulén, *The Faith of the Christian Church*, 2d ed., trans. Eric. E. Wahlstrom and G. Everett Arden (Philadelphia: Fortress Press, 1960), pp. 162–66. Gustaf Wingren, *Creation and Law*, trans. Ross Mackenzie (Philadelphia: Fortress [Muhlenberg] Press, 1961), pp. 42–45.

18. Regin Prenter, *Creation and Redemption*, trans. Theodore I. Jensen (Philadelphia: Fortress Press, 1967), chaps. 16, 17.

19. *Summa Theologica*, qu. 44, 1st art.

20. See three important recent discussions of contingency and creation: Neville, *God the Creator*; Wolfhart Pannenberg, "Theological Questions to Scientists," in *The Sciences and Theology in the 20th Century*, ed. Arthur Peacocke (London: Routledge & Kegan Paul, 1981); Thomas F. Torrance, "God and the Contingent World," in ibid.

21. Friedrich Schleiermacher, *The Christian Faith*, trans. H. R. MacKintosh and J. S. Stewart (Edinburgh: T. & T. Clark, 1928), thesis 36.

22. Ibid., thesis 39.

23. Ibid., thesis 46.

24. Paul Tillich, *The Protestant Era* (Chicago: University of Chicago Press, 1948), p. 2.

25. Gilkey, *Maker of Heaven and Earth*, p. 117.

26. Erich Frank, *Philosophical Understanding and Religious Truth* (London: Oxford University Press, 1956), p. 62.

27. R. Hooykaas, *Religion and the Rise of Modern Science* (Edinburgh: Scottish Academic Press, 1977), pp. 1–28.

28. Gilkey, *Maker of Heaven and Earth*, p. 60.

29. See Friederich Gogarten, *Verhängnis und Hoffnung der Neuzeit, die Säkularisierung als theologisches Problem* (Stuttgart: Friedrich Vorweg, 1958); Hooykaas, *Religion and the Rise of Modern Science*; H. van Leeuwen, *Christianity in World History*, trans. H. H. Hoskins (London: Edinburgh House, 1964); Michael Foster, "The Christian Doctrine of Creation and the Rise of Modern Natural Science," *Mind* 43 (1934): 446–68; Herbert Butterfield, *The Origins of Modern Science*, rev. ed. (New York: Free Press, 1965). For a brief summary, Ian Barbour, *Issues in Science and Religion* (Englewood Cliffs, N.J.: Prentice-Hall, 1966), pp. 44–50.

30. *Confessions*, bk. 11, chaps 5, 6.

31. Griffin, *God, Power, and Evil*, p. 39.

32. Paul Tillich, *Systematic Theology*, 3 vols. (Chicago: University of Chicago Press, 1951–63), 1:254.

33. Neville, *God the Creator*, pp. 64–81.

34. Pelikan, "Creation and Causality." Also L. Charles Birch, *Nature and God* (Philadelphia: Westminster Press, 1965), pp. 85–90.

34. Jaroslav Pelikan, *The Christian Tradition: A History of the Development of Doctrine*, vol. 1, *The Emergence of the Catholic Tradition (100–600)* (Chicago: University of Chicago Press, 1971), p. 36.

35. G. van der Leeuw, "Primordial Time and Final Time," in *Man and Time*, ed. J. Campbell, vol. 3 of *Papers from the Eranos Yearbooks* (New York: Pantheon Books, 1957), p. 346.

37. Jürgen Moltmann, "Creation as an Open System," in his *The Future of Creation*, trans. Margaret Kohl (Philadelphia: Fortress Press, 1979), p. 116.

38. Juan Luis Segundo, *Our Idea of God* (Maryknoll, N.Y.: Orbis Books, 1974), pp. 196–99.

39. Tillich, *Protestant Era*, p. 29. Emphasis added.

40. Tillich, *Systematic Theology*, 1:253–54. This is basically the position of the Lutheran tradition, as enunciated in Article I of the Formula of Concord.

41. October 1972. Quoted in Arthur Peacocke, *Creation and the World of Science* (Oxford: At the Clarendon Press, 1979), p. 2.

42. John W. Klotz, "Creationist Viewpoints," in Henry Morris et al., *A Symposium on Creation* (Grand Rapids: Baker Book House, 1968), p. 49.

43. George F. Howe, "Creationist Botany Today: A Progress Report," in *Symposium on Creation IV*, ed. Donald Patten (Grand Rapids: Baker Book House, 1972), p. 62.

44. Ibid., p. 79.

45. Whitehead, *Process and Reality*, p. 4.

46. See Robert Neville, *Creativity and God: A Challenge to Process Theology* (New York: Seabury Press, 1980), p. 139.

47. See important hints in Paul Sponheim, *Faith and Process* (Minneapolis: Augsburg Publishing House, 1980), pp. 47, 261.

48. Ibid., p. 47.

49. John Cobb, *A Christian Natural Theology* (Philadelphia: Westminster Press,

6

CREATION OF THE WORLD

1965), pp. 203–4 (emphasis added). See also Charles Hartshorne and William L. Reese, *Philosophers Speak of God* (Chicago: University of Chicago Press, 1953), pp. 23, 270–71, 274.

50. Cobb, *Christian Natural Theology*, p. 205. See also Griffin, *God, Power, and Evil*, pp. 37, 50. Also John Cobb and David Griffin, *Process Theology: An Introductory Exposition* (Philadelphia: Westminster Press, 1977), chap. 4.

51. See the comments of Richard Swinburne, *The Coherence of Theism* (Oxford: At the Clarendon Press, 1977), chap. 8, p. 139, for a philosophical view that is not inhibited in its talk about the *ex nihilo*. See also Neville, *Creativity and God*, pp. 139–40, for a trenchant statement of how the denial of the *ex nihilo* weakens the process-theological case.

3
The Human Being

The important thing to say about human being, from a Christian perspective, is that it is created with a destiny, the unfolding of which comprises the human adventure. This understanding must now be cast in new terms if it is to convey Christian faith adequately. We choose the term "created co-creator" to articulate what humanity under God's will is about. This term speaks of dependence, of God-given power and authority, and of freedom within finitude.

THE QUESTION OF HUMAN DESTINY

Nathan Scott ended his 1965 essay on the Christian understanding of the human being with these words:

> So now we have come full circle: created in the "image of God"; "fallen"; restored to God by Christ's reconciling work, for life in the Blessed Community of *diakonia*, of "deputyship," of service "for others"—this, in short, is the story that Christianity tells about humankind. And though it is a story that on one ground or another may be rejected by a generation eager to congratulate itself on having arrived at the threshold of what is trippingly spoken of in the Sunday supplements as our "post-Christian" age, there is at least one ground on which it is gloriously secure against all attack. For, amidst all the isms and ologies of our time which willy-nilly have worked to impugn or to reduce the fullness of man's human stature, at least it cannot be said of the Christian faith that it is in any way *against* man.[1]

Scott strikes the appropriate note in considering the human factor within the framework of the doctrine of creation. He calls attention to a drama of the human: created in the image of God, fallen, restored to God in Christ for service to others. This drama will occupy us in what follows. Scott also points correctly to the intention of the Christian story of humankind: to tell us who the human being really is and to remind us that the whole creation and God the Creator support human beings in their efforts to become more fully what they are created to be. Christian anthropology sets forth a distinct understanding of who and what the human is. The force of its interpretation of the human experiment is definitely for humans, not against them.

323

In the present context, our purpose in discussing the human being is to set forth the created roots and the created destiny of humankind. This is Christian anthropology in its broadest sense. Since there are other *loci* on sin and evil and the Christian life, a good deal of Christian anthropology is left for discussion in those places.

The human being is created with a destiny. We use the term "destiny" to include the connotations of "vocation" or "calling" as well as to point to an intrinsic character that is a dimension of the human's created "nature." Therefore, "destiny" has the nuances of gift, determinism, purpose, and goal. The first task of the distinctively Christian view of the human being is to make this clear: that *Homo sapiens* has a destiny, and a high one at that. One need not subscribe to Nicolas Berdyaev's philosophical presuppositions to affirm his statement of this essential point: "Christian anthropology should unfold the conception of man as a creator who bears the image and likeness of the Creator of the world. . . . Man has sprung from God and the dust."[2] Christian anthropology does not isolate itself from any other source of knowledge about the human being—from the sciences, experience of all sorts, literature, or art. What the Christian view has to say about human being is in the context of the knowledge gleaned from these other sources.

Nevertheless, no knowledge from other sources can be allowed to hide or weaken this fundamental assertion of Christian faith: As people created by God, we are beings whose origin and destiny are linked with that God. Everything that was said earlier about the implications of the doctrine of creation *ex nihilo* applies here, to be sure: that human being is caused, not self-generating, and is *creature*, not *creator*. Despite the truth in the often-repeated assertion that humans are proud creatures whose arrogance is their undoing, the affirmation of God-given destiny takes priority over all other elements in Christian anthropology. The basis for this priority is simply stated: Unless we perceive the human being's divinely ordained destiny, we have failed, from the outset, to comprehend who and what *Homo sapiens* is. It is not even possible to assert human pride, sin, or fallenness, if we overlook human destiny. Without a sense for that destiny, it would be as meaningless to describe humans as "sinners" and "evil" as it would be to describe a pet dog in such terms. Only the presupposition of high destiny gives point to the discernment of sin and evil in humans.

The theological tradition has spoken of this destiny in two important sets of symbols: paradise or the Garden of Eden, and creation in the image of God. As we survey these two sets of symbolic statements, we shall note that they are difficult to accept at several points because of a present cultural awareness that shies away from the concept of "destiny." On the one hand, the idea of "human destiny" seems too grandiose for the contemporary spirit to comprehend. Despite many opinions to the effect that humans suffer from the disease of pride, a hubris that presses them on to storm the gates of heaven and make themselves equal with the gods, we find impressive contrary voices that point to the contemporary human loss of nerve.

Preston Roberts's analysis of the contemporary human situation as one of all-encompassing pathos has an accurate ring.[3] The pathetic hero, or antihero, of contemporary drama epitomizes this contemporary loss of morale. The antihero is not an Oedipus engaged in an Olympian struggle with his fate. Nor is he a Macbeth, consumed with a primal power of greed. Rather, today's man or woman is like Camus's nameless stranger, who is sentenced to die in a trial he does not understand, because he has committed a crime of absurdity that he does not recognize. Or, perhaps even more vividly, as Arthur Miller portrays in *Death of a Salesman*, our current hero is a nondescript traveling salesman, sitting in a cheap hotel room, depressed and sentimental at the same time, contemplating his inability to buy love on the road and his unwillingness to cultivate love in his home.

To speak to a pathetic antihero about human "destiny," about an origin that links this earthly species with the foundations of the universe, is to lay on a burden which pathos simply has not the strength to carry. We cannot go into a detailed discussion here of the historical and cultural roots of this condition of pathos. We must note, however, that even though the Christian view of human being as founded in a high destiny is essentially a message that is *for* humanity, it comes across to the condition of pathos as a hard word of obligation. Because it portrays what is perceived in the current malaise as an impossibility, it appears as a threatening pronouncement of a law that can be neither obeyed nor escaped.

It is not clear just how this condition of pathos is related to a second element of the current cultural condition. This is the element that finds anthropocentrism and the thought of human superiority over other species so repugnant that it forecloses the possibility of intelligible speech about humanity's obvious distinctiveness and preeminence within its earthly ecosystem.[4] We shall have occasion to note how such a concern can, when subjected to the pathetic modulation, become antihuman in itself, and thus destructive of life's wholeness within creation.

THE HUMAN BEING AS CREATED CO-CREATOR

The motif by which we gather together the various affirmations of the Christian tradition about the human creature, and that expresses their meaning, is that of *created co-creator*. This motif is novel in its formulation. We are driven to novelty at this point because of a basic characteristic of the Christian view of human being. The primary dramatic description of the human adventure—that we are created in the image of God, fallen, and restored for service—is universally asserted as a formal framework, but it allows for a number of material elaborations. Formally, human destiny is to bring to fulfillment the position the human was given at creation—placed by God the Creator in the preeminent position in the ecosystem. The material elaborations of this formal status of the human species have included rather rapacious anthropocentric justifications of human manipulations of the world about us. But they have also included sensitive interpretations of how humans are the responsible stewards of the "garden" in which they are placed.

The human species is clearly distinguished from all other species, even as it is intimately related to the rest of creation. This relation is in part external; *Homo sapiens* is dependent on all the other elements in the ecosystem, just as the species contributes reciprocally to the same ecosystem. But it is internal as well. The elements of the world, focusing in that "primordial soup" from which all living creatures emerged, are the elements of the human; every atom in the human body has been elsewhere in the universe before it came to rest in *Homo sapiens*; the evolution of hydrogen and DNA—for just two examples—has reached the point where it shapes the human's internal constitution.

Homo sapiens is distinctive in terms of six important characteristics: consciousness, self-consciousness, the ability to make assessments, the ability to make decisions on the basis of those assessments, the ability to act freely on those decisions, and the ability to take responsibility for such action. Such self-aware, free action becomes a kind of creating activity, a co-creating, with God. Humans can claim no arrogant credit for being co-creators; they *were created co-creators*. Even put in materialistic terms, humans did not evolve themselves; the evolutionary process—under God's rule, we would argue—*evolved them as co-creators*.

To be co-creator means that *Homo sapiens* shares self-consciously and responsibly in the formation of the world and its unfolding toward its final consummation under God. Teilhard de Chardin has put this evocatively in his maxim that "man is evolution become aware of itself."[5] Whatever range we give to human creative activity, the destiny of that activity is to participate in and perfect the substance and goal of God's creative activity. God's creating is the norm for human co-creating, not in the sense that *Homo sapiens* is to equate its activity with God's, but rather in the sense that human activity is perverse if it does not finally qualify as participation in and extension of God's primordial will of creation. Put in this way, the created status of the human is thoroughly eschatological; that is, it is an *unleashing*, not a full-blown given that has simply to be reiterated and replicated throughout time. The primordial *humanum* that emerges from God's creation is constituted by the calling (destiny) and the capacity to participate as an ordained co-creator in the creative thrust of God. That thrust consists of sharing as a free, self-aware creature in shaping the passage forward toward God's own *telos* of the consummation and perfection of the creation.

Thus construed, the motif of created co-creator points clearly to the distinctiveness of humans as creatures with a high destiny, a destiny that is essential to the world if it is to bear the mark of its creator God. The characteristics of being co-creator are in continuity, within the evolutionary scheme, with previous forms of life, but at the same time unique in their precise and highly sophisticated configuration in the human species. We suggest that this co-creatorhood is what it means to be "in the *image of God*." The characteristics of being able to make self-aware, self-critical decisions, to act on those decisions, and to take responsibility for them—these are the characteristics which comprise the image of God in us. However, it is not just these characteristics that comprise this image. In addition, the human reflection on its unique abilities unveils a deep mystery that, if profoundly probed, clarifies to the human creature the sense in which they are grounded in a basic relationship to God. Without such grounding, the abilities themselves would mean little.

When humans ponder their co-creator status, they recognize that it includes the freedom to conceive of actions and to carry them out. This is a pleasant, even delicious, freedom; it undergirds human aggressiveness as *homo faber*, even to the large-scale technological results now around us. Beyond this freedom, however, lies the freedom in which the human agent must take responsibility for judging whether the conceived action is desirable. Then there is the responsibility for living with the consequences of the action, even if they prove undesirable.

Human agents always seek to determine whether their plans and actions are good or bad, desirable or undesirable. The tendency is to seek legitimation for carrying out the intended action or for prohibiting it, and to rest content if either the carrying out or the prohibiting conform to persuasive laws or motives.

Thus, for example, we ask whether we should in fact proceed with the capabilities we possess for production of nuclear energy, and we tend to take comfort in mandates or motives that count either for or against. The tendency to take such comfort is, however, a retreat from our real freedom as co-creators. That freedom presses us to the point where we recognize that finally it is neither an absolute mandate nor pure motivation that legitimates the action, but rather only our own free decision. Furthermore, to be co-creator means that we must continue to live with the decision and exercise our responsible co-creatorhood, whether the decision proves to be desirable or undesirable or, as is more likely, to have both undesirable and desirable consequences.

When we ponder our co-creatorhood at this depth, we discover our likeness to God and our origin and destiny in God, but we also come face to face with our own finitude, with our createdness. We do so when we recognize that, even though there is no legitimation for our action beyond our own free and responsible decision, such free and responsible decision is limited. We cannot foresee adequately the outcomes of our most important actions, nor can we mitigate all the undesirable consequences of our free but finite decisions and actions. In the exercise of the *imago dei*, in carrying out our co-creatorhood, we come hard upon the fact of our createdness. This is the fact that our mandate to co-create has come to us as creatures, at the behest of the creator God *ex nihilo*, and not from our own self-generating will.

Furthermore, when we ponder such considerations, we come to know that our sin is both our understandable unwillingness to accept our status as co-creator—even our fear of that status—and our faulty execution of our co-creatorhood, once we are forced to accept it. This sin is both original and actual. With this contemporary motif in mind, we proceed to unfold the traditional materials that inform all thinking on Christian anthropology.

THE PRIMEVAL CONDITION
("STATUS INTEGRITATIS")

It is now almost universally held among theologians that the stories and concepts we have of Adam and Eve in paradise are legends and myths. The idea of humans living in a blessed primeval stage before the fall is looked on as poetical speculation, not history. It is sometimes argued that faithfulness requires our belief in a primeval condition of blessedness. Such an argument confuses faithfulness with the imposition of a mythical speculation on a modern historical outlook on human life. To hold to the primeval condition in Eden as a matter of history would be an intellectual impossibility and to misunderstand faith. Emil Brunner states the problem for theology:

> Thus we are confronted by the very difficult theological task of formulating the distinction between the nature of man in accordance with Creation and as sinner, and the idea which this involves of the Fall of Man, *without using the thought-form of an historical "Adam in Paradise" and of the Primitive State.*[6]

Having said this about the myths of primeval conditions in Paradise, we must immediately add that these myths tell us a great deal that is essential to Christian anthropology. No one has probed the meaning of these myths more profoundly than Paul Tillich. His thesis is that these myths of the primeval time point to the *essential rootage* of human existence. He shares with Nicolas Berdyaev the insight that "the fall" speaks not so much of the degradation of the human as it does of the glory of the human, that it could fall so low.[7] Only a creature of very great stature would be described as "fallen." As Tillich says:

The possibility of the Fall is dependent on all the qualities of human freedom taken in their unity. Symbolically speaking, it is the image of God in man which gives the possibility of the Fall. Only he who is the image of God has the power of separating himself from God. His greatness and his weakness are identical. Even God could not remove the one without removing the other. And if man had not received this possibility, he would have been a thing among other things, unable to serve the divine glory, either in salvation or in condemnation.[8]

In short, the myths of our primeval conditions are important affirmations of the ultimate destiny of the human being, which is grounded in the origins of the human in ultimacy. Another citation from Tillich lays out the argument:

We must have an image of the state of essential being in which the motifs [of the primeval myths] are working. The difficulty is that the state of essential [i.e., primeval] being is not an actual stage of human development which can be known directly or indirectly. The essential nature of man is present in all stages of his development, although in existential distortion. In myth and dogma man's essential nature has been projected into the past as a history before history, symbolized as a golden age or paradise.[9]

What we have called the "ultimate destiny" of the human being is what Tillich calls the "essential nature." This essential or primeval nature and destiny are attested to by the myths of creation and the image of God. Gregory of Nyssa (fourth century) was one of the most brilliant and influential theologians in Christian history. His treatise *On the Making of Man* is a pivotal document for our theme. He underscores the exalted origins of the human being by describing the beauty of the prehuman creation—the stars, the sea, the air, and the earth: "The gentle motion of the waves vied in beauty with the meadows, rippling delicately with light and harmless breezes that skimmed the surface; and all the wealth of creation by land and sea was ready, and *none was there to share it.*"[10] When all this natural beauty was fashioned, then and only then was it appropriate for the human being to enter on the scene. Gregory proceeds immediately to say:

For not as yet had that great and precious thing, man, come into the world of being; it was not to be looked for that the ruler should appear before the subjects of his rule; but when his dominion was prepared, the next step was that the king should be manifested. When, then, the Maker of all had prepared beforehand, as it were, a royal lodging for the future king, . . . and when all kinds of wealth had been stored in this palace, . . . he thus manifests man in the world. . . . For this reason man was brought into the world last after the creation, not being rejected to the last as worthless, but as one whom it behoved to be king over his subjects at his very birth.[11]

We observed above the difficulties that such talk poses for our cultural condition of pathos today. It is not popular nowadays to speak of "man, the crown of creation," because it seems to invite a manipulation of the created world by humans, a manipulation deemed dangerous today. These concerns are certainly laudable and not to be ignored, but they do not exhaust the meaning of the Christian emphasis on the high calling of the human being. This emphasis, far from intending to insulate humans in their superiority, is much more concerned with reminding them of their lofty origins. The conclusion to be drawn is that they are gifted with a noble destiny, even as they are charged with great responsibility.

THE "IMAGO DEI"

Genesis 1:27 has provided one of the key building blocks for Christian anthropology since the first century: "So God created man in his own image, in the image of God he created him; male and female he created them." The image of God (*imago dei*) presents a fundamental image of human being as being-with-a-destiny. "The image of God" has been one of the most discussed and ambiguous phrases in the history of Christian theological reflection. It has been used to mean a number of different things over the centuries and within each century. Some theologians have even suggested that the term be excised from the theological vocabulary, so frustrating is its interpretation. Accordingly, we provide here a brief survey of the concept; given the historical ambiguities, we shall be content with a few hints as to its possible meaning for us today.

The exegesis of Genesis is itself the battleground of varying interpretations of the *imago dei*. As Claus Westermann indicates in his own survey of the exegesis of Gen. 1:27, even though the topic has been of enormous interest in the history of theology, it played little role in the Old Testament itself, and the discussion among specialists in Old Testament studies did not really begin until the end of the nineteenth century.[12] He lists the following groups of opinions in the history of interpretation: (1) those who distinguish between natural and supernatural likeness to God; (2) those who define the likeness in spiritual capacities or abilities; (3) those who interpret it as external form; (4) those who differ sharply with 3; (5) those who interpret the term as denoting that the human being is God's *counterpart*, one who corresponds to God; (6) those who interpret the *imago* as the human's status as representative of God on earth.[13]

Although Westermann himself favors the fifth option, he is quite skeptical about the history of exegesis: "One is deeply convinced that Biblical exegesis is very time-conditioned."[14] The Old Testament, one must conclude, asserts that the human is indeed created in God's image, without much specification of what that means. Nevertheless, representing God, exercising dominion over the earth and other living things, and being God's "co-responding creature" seem to be the chief contenders as interpretations of the term. New Testament exegetes have done very little on the term, but the chief conclusion is that *Christ* is the image of God (*eikon tou theou*) and therefore the image into which humans are formed.[15]

In the history of the concept, James Childs suggests four categories: (1) the *imago* as ideal humanity (Gregory of Nyssa, Aquinas, Schleiermacher); (2) dualistic interpretations (Irenaeus, Aquinas); (3) ontological monism, that is, the *imago* indicates an "ontological communion between God and man that is constitutive of man's being"[16] (Augustine, Tillich, Reinhold Niebuhr); and (4) theological monism, that is, a relationship of the total human person to God, described in theological terms (Luther, Calvin, Barth, Brunner).[17]

These categories are useful, but for the purposes of a brief survey, it may be just as well to speak of two categories: those interpretations of the *imago dei* which speak of it in terms of specific human attributes, and those which speak of it as a fundamental relationship between God and the human. In the first group, which is by far the largest, we can place the second-century apologists, who identified the *imago* with freedom of the will, capacity for goodness, moral responsibility, and reason. Basil the Great also fits in this group, defining the *imago* as human dominion over the earth.[18] Gregory of Nyssa writes:

> I would have you understand that our Maker also, painting the portrait to resemble his own beauty, by the addition of virtues, as it were with colours, shows in us his own sovereignty: and manifold and varied are the tints, so to say, by which his true form is portrayed . . . *purity, freedom from passion, blessedness, aliena-tion from all evil*, and all those attributes of the like kind which help to form in men the likeness of God.[19]

He goes on to say that the *imago* includes love as Christ has loved us, wisdom, and possession of the word.

The second group of interpreters consider the image of God to refer to the fact of relationship to God, of co-responding to God, of being God's counter-part, as Westermann says. Augustine is the monumental representative of this position. To be created in God's image brings with it the capacity to know God and, more profound, a human nature correlative to God's, so that within the human self the knowledge of God is to be found. Augustine points to the trinitarian character of human psychic life as a great *analogy* (*analogia entis*) of God's triune life; and the exposition of this triune psychic life forms his great treatise, *On the Trinity*. In his *Confessions*, he pursues the same line of thinking, linking the *imago dei* to the transformation of the human spirit into God's likeness, quoting Rom. 12:2, "Do not be conformed to this world but be transformed by the renewal of your mind." The human was not, like the other animals, "created after their kind," but rather created in the image and likeness of God.

> Therefore thou didst not say, "Let man be made," but rather, "Let us make man." And Thou didst not say, "After his kind," but after "our image" and "likeness." Indeed, it is only when man has been renewed in his mind, and comes to behold and apprehend thy truth, that he does not need another man as his director, to show him how to imitate human examples. Instead, by thy guidance, he proves what is thy good and acceptable and perfect will. . . . Man is thus transformed in the knowledge of God, according to the image of Him who created him. And now, having been made spiritual, he judges all things—that is, all things that are appropriate to be judged—and he himself is judged of no man.[20]

Luther, too, emphasizes the relationship between God and the human as the *imago*, although he is critical of Augustine's way of speculating.[21] In his lectures on Genesis, Luther describes the image of God in Adam thus:

> . . . that Adam had it [the image] in his being and that he not only knew God and believed that He was good, but that he also lived a life that was wholly godly; that is, he was without fear of death or of any other danger, and was content with God's favor. In this form it reveals itself in the instance of Eve, who speaks with the serpent without any fear.[22]

This statement is striking in that it is a direct corollary to Luther's understanding of original sin, as stated in Article II of the Augsburg Confession, that "since the fall of Adam all men who are propagated according to nature are born in sin. That is to say, they are without fear of God, are without trust in God, and are concupiscent." Fear and trust in God are the criteria of the *imago dei* by their presence, and of original sin by their absence.

Luther is critical of Augustine and other early theologians because their descriptions of the image of God foster "works." Westermann is critical of much of the tradition because it speaks of attributes or qualities of human nature as the *imago* rather than of the relationship with God. Such criticisms do indeed point to some real differences in interpreting the image of God in humans. Aquinas, for example, included in the *imago* the "superadded gift" (*donum superadditum*) granted to humans before the fall so that they could achieve the good. This gift was lost in the fall and therefore needs to be infused by grace after the fall. For Aquinas, the *imago* functions at both levels: It is the superadded gift that enables the attainment of the good, and it is also the constant (pre- and post-fall) human nature that enables us to know and love God. Such speculations lose the point that Luther and Gregory and Westermann wish to make, that the image of God refers to a total orientation of the human toward God, a total relationship. As such it cannot be divided or parceled out, as Aquinas was wont to do. On the other hand, Westermann's polemic against equating the image of God with attributes may be misguided, since the attributes generally associated with the *imago* are so profound that they are not separable from the human's basic orientation to God.

SPIRIT AND MATTER
IN THE HUMAN CREATURE

The composition of the human being has been a matter of great concern for the Christian theological tradition. This tradition of thought has been closely tied to secular philosophical and scientific understandings of the human creature, no doubt because of the deep-seated conviction that even though human being possessed marvelous spiritual capabilities, it emerged from the earth (Gen. 2). Gregory of Nyssa expresses the thought of many early theologians in speaking of the human as a middle factor between the earthy, animal realm and the spiritual realm of God. In every age, the theologians have been alert to what secular knowledge could say about the physical structure of *Homo sapiens*.

Consequently, the elements of "body," "soul," and "spirit" have figured prominently in Christian anthropology over the centuries. These concepts serve to make the theological view of the human quite complicated and at times beyond easy interpretation. The terms grow out of Greek thought, particularly the body-soul dualism of Plato and the revision of that dualism by Aristotle, called "hylomorphism," whereby he insisted that the human is indivisible.

We can summarize a voluminous body of historical material by saying that "spirit" (*pneuma, ruach*) refers generally to life itself, in distinction from "body," whereas "soul" (*psyche, nephesh*) refers to life as it occurs in a particular, concrete organism, the organism being the medium of the soul's action. All human bodies possess spirit, and the spirit manifests itself within the soul of the individual. "Spirit is the condition, soul the manifestation, of life."[23] The soul includes the spirit within itself, but it is the spirit that enables the soul and the body to be integrated into a *personal* existence and to be oriented on God.

We speak of a "trichotomous" view when we speak of body, soul, and spirit, whereas a "dichotomous" view knows only body and soul. The dichotomous view has been more prevalent in Christian theology for two reasons. First, it recognizes that the spirit is a reality that has caught up the entire person, body and psyche, and it does not exist as a third entity alongside physical (somatic) and psychical aspects of the human. Further, the dichotomous interpretation is not so susceptible to the Platonizing, dualistic tendency to speak of the spirit as a detachable part of human being that can have a special relationship to God, just as gnosticizing views such as Origen's considered that souls could leave the body to join God, apart from the body.

Since the soul is such a precious dimension of human existence, that aspect of human being that orients it to God and makes it possible to know about the destiny and origin of the human, it was important for earlier theologians to explain how humans receive their souls. "Traducianism" is the theory, held, for example, by Tertullian and the reformers, that the soul comes into being with the normal generative process, through sexual intercourse. "Creationism" (not to be confused with the cosmological theory of fundamentalist Christians), holds that God creates each person's soul in a special act. This view is affirmed by Arnobius, Lactantius, and the Thomist tradition. "Preexistence"—a minority Platonizing tradition, represented by Origen—holds that souls come into this world from some preexistent soul-material.

There is a serious question whether any of these categories is useful or even intelligible to us today. Luther, for example, already challenged them because he believed that the human creature was a unitary being before God, a person wholly the creation of God, wholly sinful, and wholly redeemed. In the phrase, *"simul justus ac peccator"* (justified and sinner at the same time), the creature is wholly *"justus"* and wholly *"peccator."* As Emil Brunner puts it, for Luther, "man's relationship to God is not something added to his human nature; it is the core and the ground of his *humanitas.*"[24]

In addition to this theological consideration, contemporary understanding of the human being and the human personality structure do not allow of either a dichotomous or a trichotomous view, except metaphorically. A modern evolutionary perspective is called for. Within this perspective, there is still considerable ambiguity, uncertainty, and disagreement about the relationship between body and spirit or mind. There is not even total agreement on how the mind should be described. Nevertheless, spirit or mind and body or matter are seen to be part of the same process, rather than separate entities. The unification of the human organization into a centered self, governed by spirit or mind, is a process in which the organizing spirit is understood as matter, but matter that has become complex enough to become an ordering force. Put physiologically, the spirit is a function of the brain that is neither immaterial nor nonmaterial but that is matter in the form that can become spirit, that can conceive of God and one's personal relationship to God, that can write poetry, conceive of and build a space ship, compose music, organize and govern a city, and engage in altruistic love for others.

Robert Francoeur has pursued this contemporary thrust with respect to the doctrine of the human being more thoroughly than most theologians. He describes it as a sort of "evolutionary monism."[25] This term may be objectionable, but it does point up the problem of all types of dualistic thought that seek to avoid evolutionary modes of thought. He writes:

Instead of picturing man as the fixed, though active unity of prime matter and substantial form, of body and soul, would it not be more appropriate to our modern understanding to look at man as a whole, an inner consciousness or spiritual (personal) aspect emerging out of our materiality, our outer aspect seen in the relationships and dependence on persons and things outside which form the background of being for our emerging selfhood. . . . As Teilhard noted so emphatically, the two aspects of man, personality and materiality, are dynamically and *genetically* related in a life-long process. Thus, man's personality gradually emerges from the universe in which he is conceived, from our necessary dependence on others, on the structured complexity of human society and the world in general.[26]

For theologians in the Reformation tradition, the contemporary categories of thought are liberating, because they allow lucid expression of a unitary perspective on the human creature. The human is one creature, a creature of nature, created with a special relationship to God the Creator, and with the capacity to perceive that relationship and to live a life of responsiveness to God. The human is one unitary creature in terms of origin and destiny, in terms of sin and error, and in terms of redemption.

THE FALL AND ORIGINAL SIN ("STATUS CORRUPTIONIS")

According to the myth of the fall, the *imago dei* is partially intact but grievously damaged, so that restoration is necessary. Here we wish simply to indicate how these realities fit into the general Christian anthropological scheme. The Christian traditions are not at one on these issues. The Eastern churches were inclined to put greater emphasis on the grace inherent in creation, to speak less stringently about original sin. Thus they conceived of Christ's restoration differently. These conflicts in viewpoint were central to the controversies between Augustine and Pelagius. Although Pelagius has in the West been considered unambiguously defective and in error, the East never did canonize Augustine and did not accept his theology. Robert Evans has termed Pelagius "one of the most maligned figures in the history of Christianity."[27] Some important Eastern traditions, such as those of the Syriac church, considered sin a cause of the fall, not its consequence. Arthur Vööbus has written of these traditions,

Sin cannot be located inherently in nature. Therefore one cannot say that human nature has been fundamentally affected by sin or transformed into evil. . . . Man's moral power and ethical strength may have received a blow from Adam's example; in themselves, however, they have not been seriously endangered. The reason is that man's freedom has not been affected.[28]

335

Such views are strange to the Western tradition and to Reformation theology in particular. These views do not violate the formal structure of the Christian drama concerning the human adventure, but they do place an uncomfortable material content into the phases of that drama.

These Eastern views remind us, however, that the basic Christian insight into the human wishes to preserve the integrity of humanity over against sin. Sin and evil are not to be equated with humanity, even after the fall. For Lutherans, this is stated in the first article of the Formula of Concord:

> We believe, teach, and confess that there is a distinction between man's nature and original sin, not only in the beginning when God created man pure and holy and without sin, but also as we now have our nature after the Fall. Even after the fall, our nature is and remains a creature of God. The distinction between our nature and original sin is as great as the difference between God's work and the devil's work.[29]

John Gerhard, in dealing with the *imago dei*, listed five ways in which the *imago* might be said to be lost in the fall.[30] He judged that in four of these ways, the image was *not* lost, namely, insofar as the *imago* (1) refers to the very essence of the human soul; (2) refers to the general similarities to divinity, intelligence, etc.; (3) refers to human dominion over other creatures; and (4) refers to some moral principles. It is in the fifth sense, when the *imago* refers to righteousness and holiness, that the image of God is lost in the fall. Our very need for regeneration proves that the *imago* in this last sense is lost.

It is exceedingly difficult to conceptualize persuasively the sinfulness of human beings and their actions while at the same time asserting the goodness of human nature as such, since that nature is "a creature of God." However, it is a perennial trait of the Christian theological and homiletical tradition that it has attempted to do so.

RESTORATION

God, in Jesus Christ, has restored humanity to reconciliation with its Creator. This has been said in many ways, but it is the climactic assertion of Christian faith. The recovery of the dimension of eschatology in the Christian faith, which has taken place since 1900, has reminded us that the restoration of humanity is not a return to Eden. It is not a return to the primeval state. Much of the tradition is defective in this respect: It has viewed the reinstitution of the primeval *status integritatis* as the goal and consequence of God's restorative work. Such a view fundamentally contradicts the basic understanding of the human as participating in the divine work of bringing the creation to its consummation, a work that is always eschatological.

Jürgen Moltmann has called for a view of "creation as an open system," which calls for a revision of the understanding of creation as a *restitutio in integrum*. He argues that only in this way can we envision creation as a process of God's genuine creativity, rather than a spelling out of the fall, endlessly.[31]

CHALLENGES TO
CHRISTIAN ANTHROPOLOGY

The Christian view of the human is beset on all sides. One of the most perverse and potentially devastating challenges comes from the widespread inability to accept the high view of *human destiny* as Christian theology sets it forth. We mention here two sources of this challenge: emerging scientific knowledge and the view that evil is intrinsic to human nature.

In its most straightforward manifestation, each scientific discipline threatens our view of human destiny, because it tends to perform one type of reductionism or another on the human being. Life of all sorts is reduced to processes that operate by pure chance. Or, it is reduced to genetic processes, or to psychosocial trends, or to unfathomable psychic or physical drives, depending on the discipline in question. All these reductionisms do indeed *reduce* the human to something much less than is set forth in the myths of creation in the image of God, as co-responding, co-creating creature of God who shares in the dynamic unfolding of the universe.

There is an even more devastating threat from scientific knowledge, one that is more subtle than the reductionisms. Our emerging knowledge of ourselves challenges our ability to accept ourselves as creatures in the *imago dei*. Traditionally, certain attributes of the human were clear testimonies to the *imago*. We think of Gregory of Nyssa's descriptions: purity, freedom from passion, love, intellect. Can human beings look at themselves today and read the image of God off the script of these attributes? Our knowledge of love, for example, now includes deep insights into its physical and psychic components, how it serves our sexuality, how it is intermingled with lust, self-interest, masochism, and the like. How does one go about sorting out these elements and pointing to the purity of love in oneself that is genuinely the *imago dei*? Of course, we are no more sensitive to this dilemma than the great Christians of the past—Paul, Augustine, Luther, Ignatius. But we are undoubtedly much more keenly aware of how all our actions, even at their purest, serve our needs, whether physical, sexual, or emotional.

To say, with the Lutherans and with Westermann, that an introspective look into ourselves will never reveal *imago* attributes, that we must instead look to our total relationship to God as co-responding creatures, depending on God and yet rebelling against the dependence—this is not much help in our dilemma either. We are only too aware of the ways in which our total stance toward the world and our fellow humans is shot through with the same complex set of survival demands. So long as we see ourselves in all our complexity serving proximate mechanisms of survival, at several levels, it will not be possible to see ourselves as created in the *imago dei*. That is, it will not be possible unless we can reconceive our self's dynamic processes or unless we can bring all those processes, survival-oriented as they are, under God's providential will. This challenge will occupy our theological efforts, because we know the centrality of the Christian affirmation of high human destiny at God's hands.

Many critics have charged Christianity with an essential *ecological* irresponsibility, whether with respect to the natural and physical ecosystem or with respect to the intrapersonal network of relationships. Christian anthropology has been charged with anthropocentrism, with a concern to dominate ("Have dominion over the fish of the sea and over the birds of the air and over every living thing that moves upon the earth"), and with a sense that nothing has value outside the human.

Efforts are well under way to recast certain aspects of the Christian view in the direction of ecological responsibility, toward the physical world and the world of humans around us. This ecological understanding of anthropology will be incomplete, however, until it also fully recognizes how the ecosystem has made us what we are and continues to do so. The challenge is clear, whether we think of the Feuerbachian *"Man ist, was er isst"* (Man is what he eats), of more complex interrelationships between our selves and the entire evolutionary process, or of complex social and cultural interactions—language, for example—that have "created us." On the one hand, we dare not separate ourselves from the ecosystems in which we live and move and have our being. On the other hand, we have the task of re-forming our vision of how God creates us in, with, and under these ecosystem processes. For many Christians, it is not an easy thing to retain God's glory as Creator, while at the same time giving credit to the proximate processes of creation. We shall deal with this question at greater length in the next section.

One of the sorriest thickets in the Christian tradition of thought is that of *sexuality* and the relationships between the sexes. There is little question that too often sexuality and the man/woman relation are described in ways demeaning of the body, the physical element of human life, and of woman. Gregory of Nyssa wrote that, since Paul tells us that in Christ there is no male or female, original creation must not have included sexual differentiation. Since the prototype of the human, Christ, did not allow of sexuality, sexual differentiation must be subsequent to the fall, along with sexual propagation. Gregory was a rigorous ascetic, Augustine was less so, yet Augustine fell into similar errors. He writes that sexuality existed in Eden, but was governed by will, not by desire or passion. Sexual desire in marriage was not sin, but it was the transmitter of sin. Martin Chemnitz paraphrases Augustine in the following passage, and accepts Augustine's ideas as normative: "In matrimony there are two things which are good and of divine ordination and institution, but *there is also a desire in marriage* without which there is no propagation, and *because of that desire infants are born in sin.*"[32] We have other ways of explaining sin's transmission, but much work remains to develop a theological understanding of sexuality that can be a persuasive substitute for such a discussion as Chemnitz's.

The problems our tradition has had in interpreting men/women relationships are well known. Luther's lectures on Genesis are humorous and painful reminders of how even Luther's basically wholesome understanding of marriage and of the earthy aspects of life was not unambiguously clear about the worth of women and could not separate women from their role as objects of masculine sexual desire. Over and above the development of genuinely humane theological interpretations of sexuality and women in their relationship to men, there is the question of how our increasing insight into the male/female character of all people and of all aspects of personhood can be translated into our anthropology. This task awaits a great deal more work.[33]

The sexual dimension of life raises, more generally, the appreciation of the material, earthy aspect of human creaturehood. As our discussion has suggested, the human was created material, and this material has evolved spirit. To denigrate the earthy is to undercut the material foundations of spirit. This insight is yet to be incorporated in a lucid manner which can enable Christian doctrine to conceive the spirit-matter unity of creation.

NOTES

1. Nathan A. Scott, Jr., "The Christian Understanding of Man," in *Conflicting Images of Man*, ed. William Nicholls (New York: Seabury Press, 1966), pp. 7–30.

2. Nicholas Berdyaev, *The Destiny of Man* (London: Geoffrey Bles, 1948), pp. 49, 54.

3. Preston Roberts, "A Christian Theory of Dramatic Tragedy," *JR* 31 (1951): 1–20.

4. See the classic essay by Lynn White, "The Historical Roots of Our Ecologic Crisis," in *The Subversive Science: Essays Toward an Ecology of Man*, ed. Paul Shepard and Daniel McKinley (Boston: Houghton Mifflin, 1969), pp. 341–50.

5. Pierre Teilhard de Chardin, *The Phenomenon of Man*, 2d ed., trans. Bernard Wall (New York: Harper & Row, 1965).

6. Emil Brunner, *The Christian Doctrine of Creation and Redemption*, trans. Olive Wyon (Philadelphia: Westminster Press, 1952), p. 52. Emphasis added.

7. Berdyaev, *Destiny of Man*, chaps. 2, 3.

8. Paul Tillich, *Systematic Theology*, 3 vols. (Chicago: University of Chicago Press, 1951–63), 1:32–33.

9. Ibid., p. 33.

10. Gregory of Nyssa, *On the Making of Man*, i,5, *Nicene and Post-Nicene Fathers*, vol. 5 (Grand Rapids: Wm. B. Eerdmans, 1954), pp. 389–90.

11. Ibid., ii,1,2.

12. Claus Westermann, *Genesis*, vol. 1, Biblischer Kommentar, Altes Testament (Neukirchen: Neukirchener Verlag, 1980), pp. 204–5.

13. Ibid., pp. 205–14.

14. Ibid., p. 57.

15. See the discussion by James M. Childs, "The *Imago dei* and Eschatology" (Th.D. diss., Lutheran School of Theology, 1974), esp. pp. 253ff.

16. Ibid., p. 66.

17. Ibid., chap. 3.

18. Basil, *The Hexaemeron*, ix,5.

19. Gregory, *On the Making of Man*, v,1. Emphasis added.

20. *Confessions*, chap. xxii,32.

21. *LW* 1:60.

22. Ibid., pp. 26–32.

23. *NSHE* 11:12.

24. Emil Brunner, *Man in Revolt*, trans. Olive Wyon (Philadelphia: Westminster Press, 1947), p. 94.

25. Robert Francoeur, *Evolving World, Converging Man* (Englewood Cliffs, N.J.: Prentice-Hall, 1970), p. 101.

26. Ibid.

27. Robert Evans, *Pelagius: Inquiries and Reappraisals* (New York: Seabury Press, 1968).

28. Arthus Vööbus, "Human Nature in Ancient Syrian Traditions," in *The Scope of Grace*, ed. Philip Hefner (Philadelphia: Fortress Press, 1964), p. 109.

29. *BC*, p. 466.

30. John Gerhard, *Loci Theologici*, Locus IV, 9, in *The Doctrine of Man in Classical Lutheran Theology*, ed. Herman Preus and Edmund Smits (Minneapolis: Augsburg Publishing House, 1962), pp. 61ff.

31. Jürgen Moltmann, *The Future of Creation*, trans. Margaret Kohl (Philadelphia: Fortress Press, 1979), pp. 119–20.

32. Chemnitz, *Loci Theologici*, Locus VII in *Doctrine of Man*, p. 171. Emphasis added.

33. For new and relevant insights to many items discussed in this chapter, from a position that is open to feminist views, see Phyllis Trible, *God and the Rhetoric of Sexuality* (Philadelphia: Fortress Press, 1978).

4

The Continuing
Work of Creation

The creation-affirmation has never been solely a statement of protology, of how things were at the beginning. It has also confessed
God's active presence throughout history, leading to divine consummation of the world at the end. That the term "creation" or "new
creation" is used to describe this presence is an important witness
to the Christian sense that the One God deals with the world in
a manner that is consistent with God's original creative and benefi-
cent intention. We ordinarily use the term "providence" to express
this confession. The great challenge to faith and theology today is
to comprehend how this world's history can be said to be unfolding
within God's will and guidance.

HISTORICAL SURVEY

The creation is in its very essence historical; that is, it is always *in transit*.
It develops, unfolds, builds cumulatively on the past, and yet begets novelty
throughout its course. Consequently, the question of God's ongoing relation
to the creation is a perennial concern for religious traditions in general and
for Christian faith in particular. There is no theme in the Christian tradition
that has received more attention than this one, unless it is that of the saving
work of Jesus Christ.

A rich and complex vocabulary has grown up in the theological tradition
to express what Christians have believed and hoped for in God's work in the
world. Much of this vocabulary has been developed to link God's ongoing
work to the original creating work. This vocabulary has, furthermore, developed
in the dual attempt to describe the ongoingness of the created world and
to testify to the character of God, as God relates to the world. "Redemption"
and "new creation" are two of the most obvious terms that relate to God's
continuing work. They certainly are not unrelated to creation.

Johannes Brinktrine, the contemporary Thomist, writes that the creation-
act of God is "the foundation and the necessary presupposition, the *condicio*

sine qua non of all God's redemptive works,"[1] and as such it is the transitional doctrine between our teachings about God and about redemption. Redemption, however, receives fuller treatment in other sections of this work, and therefore we let it pass unmentioned. "New creation" has figured prominently in our discussion of the biblical traditions about creation. As we observed, the biblical writers, in both the Old Testament and the New, used the terminology "new" or "renewed" creation to describe God's continuing presence in the lives of individuals and in the life of the nation and the church. They also used such terminology to refer to what God would do at the end of history to bless humanity. These issues are also given detailed attention elsewhere in this work. They cannot, however, be far out of mind when we reflect on creation if we remember the forceful presentations of such theologians as Gustaf Aulén and Karl Barth. Aulén's emphasis we have already noted, in his statement that the *lex creationis* (law of creation) is finally identical with God's loving will, the *lex redemptionis* (law of redemption). Barth puts the point even more strikingly: "The ordaining of salvation for man and of man for salvation is the original and basic will of God, the ground and purpose of His will as Creator."[2]

Traditionally, however, a substantial body of reflection has developed that speaks of God's involvement with creation in terms other than of redemption as such. This reflection has spoken of "continuing creation" (*creatio continua*), "preservation," and "providence." In the Middle Ages, in the Reformation, and in Protestant orthodoxy, these terms became quite complex, with many adjunct phrases that related them to Aristotelian philosophy.

Much has been written about the biblical breakthrough in understanding nature and history in linear, temporal terms. As a consequence, the Old Testament vision perceived both the created order as dynamic and unfolding teleologically and God as the One who called this dynamic movement into being and guided it. At times this sensibility related to nature, as dependent on the processes of God's own free direction of creation. At other times and more often, it focused on human history, with varying perspectives that ranged from the confidence that God was building the Hebrew nation in specific regimes (e.g., David and Solomon), to a hope for a new and reformed existence (Amos, Hosea), and to brilliantly eschatological and apocalyptic visions (Second Isaiah, Third Isaiah, Revelation). This understanding conceives of God *guiding* the course of the world and also being *involved in it*. God's guidance furnishes confidence and hope in history, whereas God's involvement gives rise to central, pivotal events, which provide structure and meaning.[3]

Although the Bible focuses upon the history of human beings in its witness to God's providential guidance of creation, the natural order also figures. Furthermore, there is no perceived conflict between nature and history, in respect to their both being under God's guidance. Some theologians of our time suggest that nature and history are discontinuous, that they are two different orders of existence. Our contemporary understanding of nature, however, shows it to be a dynamic, unfolding constellation of processes, marked by the same contingency, relativity, and event-character as history, so that history appears to be in nature in one sense, while nature is also one of history's substrates.[4] Collingwood has suggested that the concept of nature that proceeds from modern science draws on analogies from the historical continuum, so that a thorough reflection upon the idea of nature leads directly to the idea of history.[5] This is quite in line with our growing awareness of the interrelatedness of spirit and matter, *psyche* and *soma*. From the evolutionary perspective, God created history through the instrumentality of a nature that is itself a process, one that becomes increasingly complex until it reaches the sphere of human being.[6] In the light of this realization, we must comprehend both physical and social "nature" under the concepts of creation and providence.

Origen (185–254) and Augustine (354–430) provided the two most important and influential discussions of providence in the ancient church. Both of them related providence directly to God's activity as Creator. Origen's work stands in the context of Hellenistic philosophy, which spoke forcefully of fate, *pronoia*. Pelikan describes the situation of Origen's predecessors:

> In the period of the empire, this consciousness of fate grew even more dominant, as the Stoic doctrine of necessity coincided with the incursion of the Chaldean astrologers. . . . Stoicism identified fate with divine will, but in the process had to surrender the freedom of the human will. . . . In the conflict of Christian theology with classicism it was chiefly this sense of fate and necessity that impressed itself upon the interpreters of the gospel as the alternative to their message.[7]

Origen shared this context of philosophical pressure toward fate as determinism, and he considered it to be antithetical to the Christian teaching. He did not reject destiny or providence, but he linked it to free human will, which emphasized the need for humans to take responsibility under God. For Origen, the central theme of Christianity was "the idea of the pedagogy of free rational beings through Providence."[8] Origen painted a broad picture of this "pedagogy" of God's, through creation, Judaism, the Logos, the church, and future fulfillment. He acknowledged the universal immanent Logos of the philosophers, but protested that it had not succeeded in carrying out the proper pedagogy that would bring humankind from sin into blessedness. It was only in the incarnation of the Logos in Jesus Christ that a change occurred; only Christ the Logos can be teacher and leader of all.

Augustine, in his *Confessions* and in his *City of God*, gives us a grand vision of both creation and providence. In the former work, he relates providence to his own individual life, his pilgrimage from unbelief among the pagans to Christian faith. The latter work relates God's guidance to universal history. In book 5, chapter 11, he writes:

> Therefore God supreme and true, with His Word and Holy Spirit (which three are one), one God, omnipotent, creator and maker of every soul and of every body; . . . who made man a rational animal consisting of soul and body, who when he sinned, neither permitted him to go unpunished, nor left him without mercy; . . . who has not left, not to speak of heaven and earth, angels and men, but not even the entrails of the smallest and most contemptible animal, or the feather of a bird, or the little flower of a plant, or the leaf of a tree, without an harmony . . .—that God can never be believed to have left the kingdoms of men, their dominations and servitudes, outside of the laws of His Providence.[9]

Augustine preserved the emphasis on human freedom, just as Origen had done, within the framework of God's providence. His *City of God* literally moves from the original creation to his own time and beyond, showing how God has raised up the church, even as the Roman Empire collapses.

The Lutheran tradition has taken on a complex set of categories to speak of continuing creation and providence, categories which it received from the medieval tradition. Thomas Aquinas had spoken of Providence and of its constituent actions: preservation (*conservatio*), divine cooperation (*concursus*), and divine control (*gubernatio*).[10]

Luther himself had a vivid sense of God's continuing creative work. In his study of Luther's theology of creation, David Löfgren believes that he has found the key to the Reformer's entire thought.[11] *Creatio continua* encompasses all of human life for Luther:

> For Luther, the world is not a ship which is built in order to sail by itself; the "nihil" of the world from which it has come, therefore, does not lie somewhere in the past but is that from which each new creature, each new person appears at his birth; in fact, every moment and every hour are constantly newly created by God.[12]

Luther apparently held to a view that emphasized God's continual interventions for the sustaining of creation, even though created things participate and cooperate in their conservation. God's personal relationship to the world, not its own immanent powers, sustains creation. This sense of God's creative presence made it difficult for Luther to hold much stock in miracles, because God is so much at work in creation that it is difficult to distinguish between what is natural and what is supernatural.

The dogmatic development of post-Reformation Lutheranism used the medieval scholastic terms to speak of this closeness of Creator and creation. The vigor of Luther's sensibility was thereby dampened, but the emphasis on the closeness of God and the role of continuing creation is still expressed.

Technically, *creatio continua* was included under "preservation" (*conservatio*), which Hollaz describes as "the act of Divine Providence whereby God sustains all things created by Him, so that they continue in being with the properties implanted in their nature and the powers received in creation." The dogmaticians believed that without God's sustaining activity created things could not maintain themselves. Gerhard wrote, "God the Creator of all, did not desert the work which He framed; but, by His omnipotence, up to the present time preserves it."[13]

Concursus, or divine cooperation with the processes of creation, is defined by Hollaz as the activity "whereby God, by a general and immediate influence, proportioned to the need and capacity of every creature, graciously takes part with second causes in their actions and effects."[14] This introduces us to the concepts of "first and second creation" or "matter" (*creatio* or *materia prima* and *secunda*), as well as "first and second causes" (*causa prima* and *causa secunda*). The broad consensus of the earlier theologians, which Aquinas and Luther shared, was that *ex nihilo* God created *prima materia*, an as yet shapeless matter. In his lectures on Genesis, Luther calls it "crude and formless masses. . . . This primary matter, so to speak, for His later work God, according to the plain words of the Decalog (Exod. 20:11), did not create outside the six days but at the beginning of the first day."[15] This primary matter, the result of the *creatio prima*, was directly dependent on the *causa prima*, God the Creator. Subsequent to this, however, God undertook the *creatio secunda*, in which secondary matter, that is, specific, determinate things, was created. These determinate things possessed their own *causae secunda*; that is, species could continue to propagate themselves. They are dependent on God, but not at first hand. As the First Cause, he moves the secondary causes.[16] In both the medieval and Reformation theologies, this concept of *concursus* bespeaks God's intimate involvement in the created processes. The concept lent itself to many fine distinctions. John Andrew Quenstedt conveys the general tone in this passage:

> With second causes, God concurs according to the need and requirement of each, i.e., when, as often as, and in the manner that, the cause, according to the condition of its nature, demands this concurrence. For God does not change the nature of the agents or the manner and order of their action, but He permits natural agents to act naturally, free agents to act freely.[17]

This intimacy of relationship and divine cooperation is set forth meticulously. One could argue that it is no more intimately conceived than the conception of the court theologian in David's and Solomon's times, who saw the hand of God working in the details of political intrigue and nation-building. It is this notion of *concursus* which enables us to give scholastic foundation to the possibility of God working in and through the evolutionary process—

whether it be biological evolution or the psychosocial evolution we call *history*.

Abraham Calov described God's "government" (*gubernatio*) as "the act of divine providence by which God most excellently orders, regulates, and directs the affairs and actions of creatures according to His own wisdom, justice, and goodness, for the glory of His name and the welfare of men."[18] Whereas *conservatio* pertains to the continuation of created things, *gubernatio* speaks of the divine ordering of those actions which creatures carry out. As Heinrich Schmid puts it, "God inclines and leads them according to His will so as to accomplish His designs."[19] Further specifications are possible, partially in order to preserve freedom of the creation, such as "permitting," "hindering," "directing," and "determining" providence.

The so-called "orders of creation" terminology was originated in the nineteenth century, probably by Adolf von Harless, but it does carry on a genuine interest of the Reformation. These are structures within the creation, structures that provide order and governance for human life. The orders consist of *status politicus*, *status ecclesiasticus*, and *status economicus*—corresponding, in some renditions, to heads of state, clergy, and all other people, whereas others say that every person, in Luther's view, exists in all three orders.[20]

Regin Prenter separates the orders of creation from providence under the rubrics "The Law of Creation" and "The Gospel of Creation" respectively. His argument is that the historical orders are the covenants of creation, in which "the Creator forces his law of creation into external realization, this law being known in the world of man as the commandment of love to God and the neighbor. Through a struggle against death and damnation God thus promotes among men the life and blessing of creation."[21] However, this divine "forcing" also brings human rebellion, and to this rebellion, the divine action seems to be wrath. Prenter is surely correct in this insight. The most oppressive law, as Tillich rightly observes, is the law of our own being, the law formed by the shape of what we are created to be.[22] "The Gospel of Creation" is the proclamation that through God's grace creation is indeed "working for good," that is, that it is governed by providence. Prenter writes:

> But the gospel of creation proclaims that all tribulation, suffering, and anxiety which God allows to come upon man, serve to restore man and to impart life to him. Tribulation can destroy only the old Adam, without whose death man cannot arise to eternal life. When this gospel is heard, the will rejoices and thankfully accepts even suffering, because it clings to the hope for resurrection. . . . *All* things work for the good of those who love God. It is therefore impossible for anyone who believes the gospel of creation to hold life in contempt.[23]

The purpose and value of this concept of the "orders" can be readily appreciated. It has come under critique for its possible distortions, the chief of which is that the dynamic and change of "orders" may be overlooked. This can have

the result that the societal structures of a given time are elevated to norma-
tiveness. Or the orders may be defined according to the vested interests of
the one who is defining, and thus be made oppressive.

What has just been said of the "orders of creation" could be said about
all the scholastic categories as well, categories that have become a part of
theological reflection on providence. They bear a general evangelical thrust
that can scarcely be faulted. But when taken with philosophical overtones that
may or may not have been intended, they may lead to perversions. For example, the "primary/secondary causes" scheme may be helpful in speaking about
how God works in this world without violating the inherent laws and energies
of the orders that God created. As Brunner suggests, however, if one were
to take the laws of causality with precise seriousness, the question arises whether
it is not a perversion to subject God to those laws. Or, even if one may do
so, can one do so intelligibly?

The concern for providence has continued strong to our day. The traditions of pietism emphasized the doctrine, personalizing it with great force.
The nineteenth-century liberal theologians, Friedrich Schleiermacher and
Albrecht Ritschl, made significant contributions. Schleiermacher collapsed
the distinction between creation and preservation; thus providence became
the whole of creation. So conceived, providence becomes progressive. It works
immanently to perfect human potentiality in the processes triggered by Jesus
Christ's God-consciousness. Those processes manifest the efficacy of Jesus' consciousness in subsequent history. Ritschl was of great importance, because he
introduced in a significant manner the concept of the kingdom of God. He
believed that the kingdom was a this-worldly, social reality. It was a kingdom
of ends, in which God worked to bring about a harmony between the *sum-
mum bonum* of humans, for which they strove, and God's own *telos* for the
creation. This too resulted in a progressivist concept. Ritschl's ethicized
kingdom of God now appears somewhat out of touch with biblical witness,
but he made a salutary contribution because he brought the concept into
the center of theological reflection.

Twentieth-century theology, under the aegis of Barth, Brunner, and
Bultmann, corrected Schleiermacher and Ritschl. They elevated the kingdom
of God and other categories of providence, but they also took them out of
the realm of concrete history into that of salvation history (*Heilsgeschichte*).
Barth emphasized providence as intensively as did the Protestant orthodox
theologians. He outlines a "radically contingent, relativized and transient
history preserved and ruled by God's will."[24] The providential will of God
serves the covenant community above all, which idea is the source of Barth's
celebrated notion that creation is the "external basis" for the covenant, whereas
the covenant is the "internal basis" for creation.[25]

The early Paul Tillich[26] and the so-called "eschatological" and "liberation" theologians have introduced a new and constructive element into the discussion of providence. They are thoroughly eschatological, which means that they preserve the forward-looking emphasis which the generation of Barth and Bultmann lost. For these older theologians, "eschatological" had tended to mean "eternal," whereas for the newer group it refers to the horizontal unfolding of God's final goal for history. The final end of God's creation is what determines every moment of the preceding continuum. Further, these newer theologians tend to see definite social and political consequences emerging from the providential activity of God. These consequences lie in the realm of universal history; they do not restrict themselves to the history of the covenant community. Providence is in the public realm, where it can be discussed, debated, and demonstrated. As such, it enters into dialogue with other, non-Christian proposals for interpreting human history.

The liberation theologians of Latin America have provided indications that they may make a decisive new contribution to theology precisely on the ground of the doctrine of providence. The Latin Americans have fashioned their thought in reflection on their sociocultural situation and the relation of God's work of creation and redemption to that situation. Their thinking is therefore thoroughly social from the very beginning.

It has been observed that these thinkers are constructing a natural theology that takes into account and criticizes the exclusively revelational theologies of the mid-twentieth-century neo-orthodox period. This new natural theology takes as its reference point, however, not so much the realm of physical nature as that of social nature and history.[27] Obviously, even though the term may not appear explicitly throughout their works, if this interpretation of the liberation theologians is correct, theirs is inherently a theology of providence.

From this perspective, it is understandable why a concept such as that of *liberation* surfaces as central, since in a context of sociocultural bondage God's providential work may well be described as liberation. Providence is distinguished from pure human passivity, however, since it incorporates human effort to share in the liberating and building up of the creation. These assertions have been hotly debated by European and North American critics, but it is fair to say that the measure of the Latin American proposals has not yet been taken.[28]

Two citations may give the flavor of the Latin American theologians' contribution to this doctrine. Hugo Assmann writes: "The Kingdom of God does not ever identify itself with the structures of the world, but it inserts itself into and unfolds itself in them as a process. The notion of process is perhaps one of the categories to introduce into the theological vocabulary in order to talk about the Kingdom of God."[29] From Juan Luis Segundo:

We can see that the *divine providence*, in the Christian view, is not and cannot be a doctrine, propounding some sort of divine interference that dislocates man's affairs and efforts. Nor can it be the inaccessible start of a world that goes on from there to operate under its own laws. In the concrete, temporal history of his love for us, God gives us a world that functions in accord with its own proper laws. But he does not give it to us as some sort of alien and inert material. He fashions this world into a system of signs and revelation which culminates with his total insertion of himself into this world. Thus he leads us to shoulder the task of freeing all its dimensions for the service of love and the construction of the world.

In its definitive form, this world will be not only the *new earth* of man, but also the new heaven of God. "Providentialism" and "passivity," which were so often tied together in customary usage, are in reality contradictory.[30]

PERENNIAL CONCERNS OF THE DOCTRINE OF PROVIDENCE

In a recent study of providence, Langdon Gilkey summarizes the classical concept as it has developed and persisted over the centuries:

(1) Representing the sovereignty of God over history, the activity of God's providence was controlled, directed and defined by God's eschatological goal. (2) The work of providence concerned itself with the external realm of "objective" events, both natural and historical, cosmological and social, amidst which men and women lived in time. (3) Because of providence there was no fate in historical experience; rather, the purpose of providence, and so the ultimate goal of history, was the establishment and so the freeing of freedom—the transformation for all men and women of fate into destiny. (4) God does not work in history as an external cause but in and through the creaturely forces and dynamic factors of history. (5) Thus providence works through, not against, human freedom; it is, therefore, not contradicted by man's sin but made necessary because of sin—if the eschatological goal is to be reached.[31]

Gilkey's statement corresponds to the brief survey we have presented here.

The doctrine of providence has been set within the context of the doctrine of creation by the theological tradition, and that setting is instructive for us as we look at the perennial concerns and problems of the doctrine. First, it presses to our attention that creation and redemption cannot ultimately be separated. God's work is the expression of God's will, wherever it takes place. As the Swedish theologians remind us, God's redemptive love is the rationale of whatever God does, whether in original creation, in the governance of history, or in redemption. What occurs under the rubric "creation," however— whether it be originating, sustaining-continuing, or guiding-governing—is not appropriated as redemptive grace except in faith, because unless one has accepted the action of God as grace, set forth in Christ, the activities of creation come across with the force of demand, of law, as imperative rather than indicative.

It is part of the dialectic of creation that since the fall, and perhaps even before it, we have not yet become what we were created to be. We must heed the dictum of Goethe's *"Sei was Du bist!"* (Become what you are). Under grace, the created order and its processes do not alter outwardly, but are perceived as friendly, fulfilling, under God's eschatological activity. These are processes to which we are reconciled in grace, rather than being oppressive demands to which we can never live up. Ritschl was correct in observing that the gift of grace did not change the world-system of nature and history, except at two points: It enabled people to see the rationale of that system as God's system rather than as an inexorable, natural, cause-and-effect machine; and it revealed the proper human response within that system.

Two errors are of great concern in this context. On the one hand, the oppressive appearance of the created order apart from grace must not lead us to separate creation from redemption, as if creation could never be subsumed under redemption or as if redemption would lead us out of creation rather than into it. On the other hand, creation and redemption must not be collapsed into equivalence, as if redemption has nothing to add to creation. Redemption, properly perceived, is the fulfillment of creation. It is indeed true that "grace does not destroy nature, but perfects it" (Aquinas).

Thus, the necessity for creation to be linked with faith is even more vividly brought home to us when we consider providence. Only faith could look on this world and call it "creation." Similarly, only such a faithful reflection could look on the ongoing processes of nature and history and call them *"creatio continua, concursus, gubernatio—*providence." The issues raised by this set of insights lead us to a consideration of the great problem facing the doctrine of creation in all its manifestations—original, continuing, and eschatological.

This great problem stems from the fact that the affirmation of creation, original and continuing, is an affirmation that the processes of nature and history are basically friend and not foe, ultimately fulfilling under God and not destructive. To perceive the world as creation is to understand that its processes are finally reliable and trustworthy, because they do proceed from our God, *ex nihilo*. This judgment about the world of nature and history is precisely what is called into question, particularly in our own time.

This calling into question of basic assumptions underlying the Christian doctrine of providence brings us to what Gilkey and others term the foremost challenge of the contemporary world to that doctrine: modern historical consciousness. As Gilkey analyzes it, this consciousness includes several basic elements: the relativity of historical life, a new insight into the role of human creativity and freedom in history (note our emphasis on "created co-creator"), the temporalizing of all being, and a new sense of progress in history. Gilkey is certainly correct in his assessment that the concept of providence must take these issues into account if it is to be credible in our time.

In one form, this challenge is another instance of the problem of evil, and it is because evil manifests itself in this context that theodicy is often discussed within the doctrines of creation and providence. Creation affirms that the processes of this world are God's instrumentalities for initiating, maintaining, and perfecting God's handiwork, creation itself. Evil appears on every hand, because those processes of nature and history seem to disrupt, pervert, and ultimately to destroy that divine handiwork, specifically the human sector but in general all nature. Consequently, one cannot accept the affirmation of creation in any of its forms unless one has come to terms with evil.

Furthermore, the logic of this set of insights underscores that creation, faith, and evil cannot be considered for long apart from the action of redemption from and over evil. The Christ who is the Logos of creation is the Christ who redeems. His creative work illumines the meaning and scope of his redemptive work, as his redemptive work clarifies the purposes and the underlying principles governing his creative work. The perennial concern of the doctrine of creation in all its forms is to lift up with crystal clarity this Christian affirmation: Despite all appearances, in the face of all apparent signals to the contrary, this world of nature and history *is* creation!

NOTES

1. Johannes Brinktrine, *Die Lehre von der Schöpfung* (Paderborn: Ferdinand Schoeningh, 1956), p. 16.

2. Karl Barth, *Church Dogmatics*, vol. 4/1, trans. G. T. Thomson (Edinburgh: T. & T. Clark, 1936), p. 9.

3. Karl Löwith, *Meaning in History* (Chicago: University of Chicago Press, 1957), pp. 182ff. R. G. Collingwood, *The Idea of History* (New York: Oxford University Press, 1957), pp. 49ff.

4. See C. F. von Weizsäcker, *The History of Nature*, trans. Fred D. Wieck (Chicago: University of Chicago Press, 1947); S. C. Alexander, "The Historicity of Things," in *Philosophy and History*, ed. R. Klibansky and H. J. Paton (Oxford: At the Clarendon Press, 1936).

5. R. G. Collingwood, *The Idea of Nature* (New Haven: Yale University Press, 1945), pt. 3, esp. pp. 174–77.

6. It was Teilhard's significance to have emphasized and explained this fact with great detail and force. See his *Phenomenon of Man*, 2d ed., trans. Bernard Wall (New York: Harper & Row, 1965). See also Charles E. Raven, *Natural Religion and Christian Theology* (Cambridge: At the University Press, 1953).

7. Jaroslav Pelikan, *The Emergence of the Catholic Tradition (100–600)* (Chicago: University of Chicago Press, 1971), p. 281.

8. Hal Koch, *Pronoia und Paideusis* (Berlin: Walter de Gruyter, 1932), p. 159.

9. *Nicene and Post-Nicene Fathers*, vol. 2 (Grand Rapids: Wm. B. Eerdmans, 1956), p. 93.

10. *Summa Theologica* i, qu. 97, 103–19; i–ii, qu. 109–14. *Summa contra Gentiles*, bk. iii, chaps. 64–113.

11. David Löfgren, *Die Theologie der Schöpfung bei Luther* (Göttingen: Vandenhoeck & Ruprecht, 1960), p. 7.

12. Ibid., p. 25.

13. Hollaz and Gerhard quoted in Heinrich Schmid, *The Doctrinal Theology of the Evangelical Lutheran Church*, trans. Charles A. Hay and Henry E. Jacobs, 3d ed. rev. (Minneapolis: Augsburg Publishing House, 1875), pp. 170–71.

14. Quoted in ibid., pp. 171–72.

15. *LW* 1:6.

16. Brinktrine, *Die Lehre von der Schöpfung*, pp. 76–84.

17. See the selections in Schmid, *The Doctrinal Theology of the Evangelical Lutheran Church*, p. 185.

18. Ibid., p. 172.

19. Ibid.

20. Werner Elert, *The Christian Ethos*, trans. Carl S. Schindler (Philadelphia: Fortress [Muhlenberg] Press, 1957), pp. 77–81.

21. Regin Prenter, *Creation and Redemption*, trans. Theodore I. Jensen (Philadelphia: Fortress Press, 1967), p. 202; see also pp. 202–16.

22. Paul Tillich, *Morality and Beyond* (New York: Harper & Row, 1963), chap. 1.

23. Prenter, *Creation and Redemption*, p. 211.

24. Langdon Gilkey, *Reaping the Whirlwind: A Christian Interpretation of History* (New York: Seabury Press, 1976), pp. 219–20.

25. Barth, *Church Dogmatics*, 3/1:231.

26. See esp. Paul Tillich, *Systematic Theology*, 3 vols. (Chicago: University of Chicago Press, 1951–63), vol. 3, pt. 5.

27. This insight is elaborated by Vitor Westhelle, in his "Representation and Method: The Element of *Vorstellung* in the Hegelian-Marxist Tradition and the Locus of Theology" (Th.D. diss., Lutheran School of Theology, 1984).

28. E.g., Gustavo Gutierrez, *A Theology of Liberation*, trans. Sister Caridad Inda and John Eagelson (Maryknoll, N.Y.: Orbis Books, 1973), pp. 154, 159–60.

29. Hugo Assmann, *Teología desde la praxis de la liberación: Ensayo teológico desde la América dependiente*, 2d ed. (Salamanca: Sgueme, 1976), p. 154.

30. Juan Luis Segundo, "Intelecto y salvación," in G. Gutierrez, J. L. Segundo, et al., *Salvación y Construcción del Mundo* (Santiago/Barcelona: Dilapsa-Nova Terra, 1968), pp. 163–64.

31. Gilkey, *Reaping the Whirlwind*, p. 240.

5

Challenges to the
Ongoing Doctrinal Task

We turn to a recapitulation of some challenges that face anyone intending to carry theological thinking forward, so as to render it relevant to new situations and epochs. Some of these challenges have
already been discussed; others appear briefly here for the first time.
In this catalog of challenges lies the ongoing excitement of theology.
Even though the theologian may bring reflection to an end before
these challenges are thoroughly dispatched, there can be no final
satisfaction that the task has been completed until such issues as
we shall here face have been confronted.

CREDIBLE DOCTRINE
IN EVERY SITUATION

The mandate for theological reflection on creation was clear from the survey
of biblical materials—a deep attachment to the creation-affirmation was evident at the same time we noted a refreshing freedom to let that affirmation
take whatever form the situation demanded. The ground of this freedom lies
in the overriding concern that doctrine be *credible* in whatever circumstance
it finds itself. Since the creation-affirmation stands in an especially intimate
interface with the ordinary, secular, nontheologically conceived realities of life,
the demand for credibility impinges on it with particular poignancy.

The various themes in which the discussion here has been divided indicate
the points at which the nontheological conceptions engage the reflection on
creation: beginnings of the world and life; the process of history; the nature
of the human being and the processes underlying human development; endings, whether that be thought of as extinction of the species, the death of
the planet and the universe, or individual death; and the question of final
perfection whether in this life or in some other. The information and conceptualities rush in on the theologian when the attention is turned to any of
these issues, and a doctrine of creation fails of credibility to whatever extent
it ignores these data or fails to deal with them adequately. When one con-

353

siders that each of these interfaces represents an area on the forefront of scientific discovery and interpretation, and at the same time an area in which common experience is undergoing great change, the task that faces the theologian becomes almost overpowering.

We can recite only a few of the pertinent questions raised in scientific study and common experience: Did the universe have a beginning, or is it without beginning or end, the so-called "Big Bang" being only an episode in its oscillation? How can a *telos* be ascribed to history when its processes appear to be free and blind? What sort of divine fulfillment can we conceive in light of the seemingly assured demise of our planet in two and a half billion years by the evolution of our sun into a huge fireball (a so-called "red giant") that will burn the earth to a cinder?[1]

CREATION AND THE
CONCEPT OF EVOLUTION

The Christian church and its theologians have found the concept of evolution difficult to handle, especially since Charles Darwin elaborated it in 1859. Consequently, some Christians have rejected it altogether. Even among those who have accepted the concept, there has been relatively little done toward a thoroughly reformulated doctrine commensurate with evolutionary theory yet faithful to the tradition. A summary of the key issues may help to set the agenda.

According to R. G. Collingwood, the concept of nature is a changing one, and our own epoch is one that has moved from a relatively static view of nature, which compared nature and its elements to a machine and its parts, to a dynamic view, which operates with the analogy of history for interpreting nature. The sciences, ranging from physics and astronomy to biology and psychology, have opened for us a view that recognizes change, mystery, and unexpected potential in nature. That the marvelous creature we call human being could evolve in its entirety from the explosion of the Big Bang or, more immediately, from the "primordial soup" of perhaps three billion years ago, suggests vividly that this "nature" that could traverse the space and time those billions of years encompass is in its own right marvelous.

The first chapter of Genesis speaks of creation as a process of six days. Reflection on those days, whether twenty-four hours in length or simply symbols denoting indeterminate periods, has proliferated over the centuries. The enormous time-scale of evolutionary thinking has seldom been carefully considered, however. A few simple observations will make the point. The universe may have come into existence through the Big Bang some 18 billion years ago; the earth's crust congealed 4 billion years ago; dinosaurs flourished 180 million to 63 million years ago; *Homo erectus*, an important ancestor of our species, flourished 600,000 to 350,000 years ago.

If we were to put the history of planet earth on a calendar division, with one "day" equaling 14 million years and one "hour" equaling a half million years, the facts just recounted would appear thus: The earth's crust congealed on January 1; dinosaurs appeared on December 21; Neanderthal man, after 11:50 P.M. on New Year's Eve. If we change the time equivalence to one "day" equaling 6,000 years, Neanderthal appears in mid-November, agriculture begins during the evening of December 29, Greece flourished in the afternoon of December 31, and Columbus discovered America shortly after 10 P.M. on New Year's Eve.

Human creatures, whom we consider to be created in the image of God and whose history is the arena of divine providence, fill a very small portion of the history of the universe. This does not detract from the marvel that attaches to human being or from the significance of history, but it does add an important dimension of mystery and complexity to our consideration of the creation of human beings and the providential guiding of human history. Why was *Homo sapiens* created in this manner? What is the significance of the eons of nonhuman history? Why did God do it this way?

It is impossible today to conceptualize how God might have control over every item and event in nature and history. The best of current scientific thought also renders inadequate the picture of the evolutionary process proceeding by pure chance, as Jacques Monod forcefully insisted some years ago in his celebrated book, *Chance and Necessity*. It now appears that chance plays a role in evolution at its most primitive condition, but order and patterning also play a role alongside chance. The interrelation of the two factors is complex and beyond our scope here. Arthur Peacocke has suggested that the most adequate picture of the creator God is that of the composer of intricate fugues, who builds on original elements while employing an almost infinite number of variations of those elements.[2] Others have suggested the Hindu God of the dance, Shiva. In any case, it appears that the transcendence of God the Creator may now be conceived more adequately as being "in there," in the very stuff and possibility of creation, rather than "out there."

The most recent advances in biological evolutionary theory point to the complex and unexpectedly rich role played by genes. Genetic materials can no longer be thought of as only "crass material" in the customary sense of the term. Some basic and refined human values, such as altruism, honesty, mother-love, truthfulness, and curiosity, are understood to be correlated to genetic bases, even though that base is too complex to identify precisely. What does such an insight do to the traditional assertion that God's revelation presents the purest form of love and other such values? Or that Christ is the

Logos of all truth? We might suggest that such scientific insights into the relative autonomy of genetic evolution need not be considered antithetical to Christian faith. Is the place of Christ, the promulgator and embodiment of sacrificial love, as Logos of all truth, not enhanced when that truth is seen to be written into the genetic structure of life itself?[3]

Our new appreciation for the complexity of matter and the versatility of the evolutionary processes points to the possibility that spirit and matter may have the same point of origin and that it may indeed be true to say that the terms "matter" and "spirit" refer to two configurations of the same reality, not to two different realities.

Traditional doctrine has predicated that humans were perfect in paradise, that they possessed the maximum of their abilities and their goodness at the beginning of their career on this earth. Evolutionary theory suggests that humans were primitive at their origins, particularly if those origins include humanoid forms prior to *Homo sapiens*. Consequently, the career of the human being is an ascent toward fulfillment rather than a descent from greatness. For this reason, we have emphasized the concept of "destiny," namely, that human being was created with a high destiny, toward which it is tending. The reinterpretation of the fall and original sin as universally valid myth enables this line of thought.

EVIL AND THE RELIABILITY
OF THE CREATED PROCESSES

As we conclude this essay, it is appropriate once again to describe what is surely the most serious challenge to the doctrine of creation and the issue that provokes our deepest reflection. We are confronted with the question whether this world intends us good or ill. We ask about participation in the processes of creation, whether those processes be within us or external to us (the evolution of DNA illustrating the former; the progress of our technology, the latter). We ask whether participation will bring us to fulfillment, to destruction, or to a natural end that deserves to be thought of as neutral, neither a fulfillment nor a destruction, not a bang but a whimper. This is the setting in which the God-question engages us today, perhaps with more force than in any other realm. The question of evil enters here dramatically because it is the force that appears to destroy whatever reliability the world processes have, that appears to undercut our sense of the trustworthiness of the creation and to devastate our thought of fulfillment.

The creation-doctrine is an item of faith, because in the absence of any final demonstration or disproof, faith affirms that the created world, including ourselves, *is* God's creation—that it is finally friend, not foe; cosmos, not chaos; consummation, not dissolution. If this is the doctrine's character, the recognition of that fact illuminates both the substance and the task of proclamation, namely, to make actual in our time the sense that we are creation and that we live in a creation that will ultimately unite us with the creator God.

NOTES

1. Robert Jastrow, *God and the Astronomers* (New York: Warner Books, 1978).

2. Arthur Peacocke, *Creation and the World of Science* (Oxford: At the Clarendon Press, 1979), chap. 3.

3. For suggestive hypotheses that give a lead to further theological thinking, see Ralph Wendell Burhoe, "Religion's Role in Human Evolution: The Missing Link between Ape-man's Selfish Genes and Civilized Altruism," *Zygon: Journal of Religion and Science* 14 (1979): 135–62. Also Donald T. Campbell, "On the Conflicts between Biological and Social Evolution and between Psychology and Moral Tradition," *Zygon* 11 (1976): 167–208.

FIFTH LOCUS

Sin and Evil

PAUL R. SPONHEIM

SIN AND EVIL

Introduction

1. The Nature of Sin
   The Object of Sin
   The Agent of Sin
   The Efficacy of Sin

2. The Origin of Sin
   Creation and Fall
   The Goodness and Integrity of Creation
   The Possibility and Actuality of Sin

3. The Effect of Sin
   Sinner and Creature
   Bondage and Responsibility

4. Metaphysical and Natural Evil
   Finitude
   Suffering

5. The Work of God against Evil
   The Continuity of God
   The Decisiveness of God
   The Directivity of God

Introduction

Christian dogmatics has no independent interest in sin and evil, for it seeks to follow the order of faith which claims and confesses God, who is Lord whether there is evil or not. But the reality of sin and evil is in fact of crucial importance to dogmatics, for faith clings to a God who forgives sin and delivers from evil. The Christian theologian will find reason to speak of sin and evil in connection with nearly every rubric of the faith. Thus all three articles of the Apostles' Creed raise questions for one who knows sin: Does sin or evil undercut the meaningfulness of Christian claims about creation? How is God's work in Jesus of Nazareth to be understood in relation to sin and evil? What hope may the Christian have that sin and evil may be combated and indeed overcome?

Talk about sin and evil does not stand at the same level as talk about God; it is derivative. Yet the reality embodied in these words is so thoroughgoing in extent and so critical in quality that the Christian's talk of God is in fact always in the face of that which stands against God.[1] While the concept of God can be adequately defined in principle apart from any reference to sin, the converse is not true. Sin is, precisely, "before God." More explicitly, sin is a person's volition, action, or condition which is against the will of God. In speaking so of sin, the emphasis is on personal activity or on a condition issuing from and sustained by such personal activity. "Evil," on the other hand, is not so much action as passion; it is the undergoing or suffering of something. We may link the two theologically by speaking of both sin and evil as being against the will of God. Thus we may speak of sin as moral evil, issuing from volition and issuing in experience that is against God, as distinguished from metaphysical evil which seems to follow from the very structure of existence, or natural evil that comes from subpersonal causes.

The action of sin against God may not require that the sinner be conscious of God. Clearly the sensing of an experience as evil does not require explicit reference to God. Rather, evil may be experienced and described simply as that which thwarts such purposes as seem intrinsic to the human condition. The Christian accepts such an account as formally appropriate, but seeks to transcend purely subjective material definitions of human nature by reference to a doctrine of creation. We cannot assume that the knowledge of that for which we were made is consciously intact in us. Yet the criteria needed to mark and measure evil lie in our creaturehood.

While the experience of evil may not include conscious reference to God, it does provide a large part of the basis for a formidable contemporary case against belief in God. In the face of evil the goodness of an omnipotent creator and/or the sovereignty of a suffering divine victim are in jeopardy. In a time when the experience of evil is indisputable but the sense for God flickers faintly, Christian attention to this rubric must accept an apologetic as well as a dogmatic agenda. While the issue of theodicy, "the justification of God," conventionally ranges broadly through the experience of evil, from the indiscriminate destructiveness of the tornado to the obscene selectivity of terminal illness in children, the reality of sin already serves in its own right to focus the issue of the goodness and power of God.

Even the mere task of *stating* the Christian understanding of God intelligibly faces considerable difficulties today. How will the category "against God" be clear if the meaning of God is muddled? If there is no sense for God, sin-talk will have to settle down uncomfortably in psychological and sociological categories.[2] If God stands more for a principle than for a person, the framework will be intrinsically juristic, potentially legalistic. Or the difficulty may be precisely in what we think of the nondivine self; our view may be too high or too low to let speech about the sin of such a self make sense. Sin is only possible for a self set in the ambiguous "middle distance" constituted by God's gift and task of freedom with responsibility. Finally, Christian speech about sin reaches for some understanding of the connectedness of human selves, for some notion of involvement in a being-against-God which goes well beyond individual volition. Such speech is problematic in a time when atomistic or episodic accounts of reality prevail, at least to the extent that responsibility does not reach beyond individual agents. Even if there were no problem about the meaning of "God," how shall talk of sin make sense without will, without self, without race, without Satan? How shall we proceed?

First, the *scope* of our work must be rather broad, because sin is not an eternal reality that can generate its own tidy dogmatic discussion regardless of what history may bring. This is so also because sin, while derivative, is so experientially and systematically pervasive that an extraordinarily rich set of resources exists for our work. Neither the control of personal speculation nor the clarity of determinative dogmatic subordination is available here. Both authoritative word and experiential world call for attention in this locus in a more complete way than can be said to be a commonplace in dogmatics.

Second, crucial to the direction of the argument is the matter of the *order* in which the several facets of our topic are to be considered. The Christian faith entails an essentially historical perspective as the key to find the invariant structure of what is real. Accordingly, our consideration begins with moral evil, rather than with metaphysical or natural evil. The interest in concreteness characterizing an historical approach further suggests that we begin our consideration of moral evil by confronting its nature, rather than by inquiring after its cause. Starting with moral evil suggests that we focus on God's action in Jesus of Nazareth. Christian faith may appropriately be said to be clearer about the remedy than the disease. Of course, one cannot fully possess the confession *that* in Jesus God has decisively addressed the human predicament, if one cannot state *what* that predicament was/is. But one can let that which is more clear guide one in probing what is less clear. Thus it may be appropriate for the faith to permit clear convictions concerning the "second Adam" to lend firmness to the shadowy figure of the first Adam. That process would be inappropriate only if it violated the sense of what, apart from Christ, commends itself as true about either the specific reality of evil or the broader drama in which God and humankind are involved.

Third, the *status* of what we seek is a "second-order" understanding of the "first-order" reality of confession and faith. We do not seek to replace faith with understanding, but to serve it. For example, with respect to sin, two distortions of this relationship must be resisted. The first-order must not rule out the second-order, as when the fact that we cannot understand *why* we sin is taken to mean that we cannot describe whence sin comes and whither it goes, or even locate that which is inexplicable in relation to that which is explicable.[3] And the second-order must not rule out the first-order, as when one supposes that the dogmatician's act of identifying the world of sin somehow discharges the sinner's responsibility for the confession and the commission of sin.

NOTES

1. This point has been made recently and emphatically by Douglas John Hall in *Lighten Our Darkness* (Philadelphia: Westminster Press, 1976).

2. See, e.g., Karl Menninger, *Whatever Became of Sin?* (New York: Hawthorn Books, 1973).

3. Another form of this error suggests that reflection about sin is impossible because sin has cast the reason into darkness. This claim seems at once to overestimate the connection of reason and will (dismissing clear-eyed defiance, for example) and—granting *some* connection between reason and will—underestimate the illumination available within the Christian community. Presumably the call to sanctification somehow includes the reason as well as the will. One wonders, then, if it is not the power of piety which seems to suppose that to understand the depth of one's predicament is somehow to resolve that predicament—in which case, understanding must be resisted as arrogance.

1

The Nature of Sin

Sin is an act and state of personal will against God and the will of God. Sin arises from the total person rooted in and related to that which is beyond the person, expresses itself in the complexity of the person's strength and weakness, and issues in distortion in all the person's relationships.

THE OBJECT OF SIN

Sin has to do with God; it is against God. Were there no God and no relationship to God, there could be no sin. The biblical writings come together to make this point. While there are traces in the Old Testament of a dynamistic system of thought, in which the objectivity of the offense is so extreme that an unwitting ritual offense involves punishable guilt, the main development of thought is otherwise.[1] The ritual gives way to the moral. Assessment in moral terms points toward the God who stands behind the commandment. One may still speak of law, but no longer in a purely formal or juristic sense. By a sheerly objective understanding the emphasis is placed on factual failure in performance, and so on an equivalent reparation. The moral understanding anchors the appeal to the law in the unconditional authority of the covenant God, from whom in principle no sphere of life can be isolated.[2]

The sense of the presence of God as personal transcendent will lay behind the constant struggle of the prophets to resist the erosion of the concept of sin in dynamistic and moralistic understandings. Similarly, in the New Testament sin is understood as against the kingdom of God, against Christ (Matt. 10:33; 11:20, 24; 12:28-32; John 15:18, 23-25) and against the Holy Spirit (Mark 3:28-29). Most fundamentally sin is *asebia*: the sinner acts and wills as though there were no God. Sin as sin "against God" is not a simple unity; it encompasses a great diversity of human dynamics. Sin may be described as denying God the fear and trust God deserves.[3] Thus Paul describes both the root of sin and its flowering in Rom. 14:23: "Whatever does not proceed from faith is sin."

The sinner is against God, but what is the sinner *for*? In turning from God the sinner turns toward something. That something may be something outside the self, yielding the phenomenon of idolatry, which receives the condemnation of both Testaments. Indeed, Gerhard von Rad finds in Israel's "awareness of the barrier which men erect between themselves and God by means of images" nothing other than "Israel's greatest achievement."[4] This dynamic can also be described as adultery (Hosea); it means seizing something tangible as directly representing God. That must be diagnosed as sin, despite the elements of world affirmation in the biblical witness. To affirm the world as created and therefore good is not to divinize it, despite the temptation of the nature-religions.[5] Perhaps that temptation is especially difficult to resist because it sets the sinner's quest for security within the control of the self. While the natural object possesses a kind of illusory transcendence in its externality, the self can largely manipulate the relationship to that object.[6]

Or one may speak of the sinner turning from God so as to turn more directly toward the sinner's own self. This is what Reinhold Niebuhr means by sin as pride.[7] Paul Tillich prefers the term "hubris," which is universally human and can appear in acts of humility as well as pride.[8] Hubris amounts to an attempt to deny the limits of finitude. Thus in the Genesis account the temptation to sin is the temptation to claim "knowledge of all things and the mastery over all things and secrets, for here good and evil is not to be understood one-sidedly in a moral sense, but as meaning 'all things.'"[9]

A self seeking to be without limits is a concupiscent self, one that would draw the whole of reality into itself.[10] But such self-expansion does not create self-fulfillment. Sin against God, whose commandment is "for life," becomes sin against the self as well.[11] Nor can the reality of sin be isolated within a God-self relationship insulated from the rest of humankind. The decalogue invokes God in forbidding sins against the neighbor, and the prophets' denunciation of injustice must not be forgotten. The claim on the self is at once a claim for God and neighbor. Sin is lawlessness.[12] Nathan's word from the Lord to the murderous David links these two: ". . . because you have despised me, and have taken the wife of Uriah the Hittite to be your wife" (2 Sam. 12:10).

The persistent tendency to lose this linkage and so to spiritualize sin— which, of course, is precisely to misunderstand the extent of the disrelationship between self and God in sin—has recently called forth a sharp protest from the theologians of liberation. In their view the interior, personal dimension of sin derives from its social and historical character.[13] These theologians certainly identify an important component in emphasizing what José Maria Gonzalez Ruiz has called the "Hamartiosphere," referring to objective oppressive structures which transcend individual agency. We discuss this component in Chapter 3, relating agency and efficacy in the continuity of sin. At this point we are describing the nature of the agency, and on this point a derivative status for the personal is not the clear testimony of Christian theology. But that the social and the historical dimension requires treatment in any adequate understanding of sin has been made indisputably clear by the theologians of liberation.

Sin is *against* God and the will of God. It is, accordingly, not *from* God. Whence does it come? To that question we must turn, but we pause to draw two inferences from this opening discussion. First, Christian faith is incompatible with *monism*; sin is against God and thus not from God. To speak of sin—as already to speak of creation—is to speak of a relationship or disrelationship between God and an other.[14] In the next chapter, in articulating the bearing of the theme of creation on our topic, we shall grant that in wishing to resist eternal or metaphysical dualisms, Christian reflection may acknowledge or even insist that God bears some responsibility for the origin and issue of all that is real. But such reflection should not lose sight of this: that sin, while emphatically real, is against God and not from God.

Second, Christian faith is incompatible with *moralism*. Sin is against *God*. The objection here is not to the necessary attempt to include other humans in the God-self relationship, but rather to all views that exclude God in the conception of sin. Both friends and foes of Christianity represent this misunderstanding.[15] Indeed, the very tendency to objectify matters in such a way that the Lord is lost in the commandment becomes the target of the Pauline critique of any justification by the works of the law.[16]

In all this it is assumed that humankind, the sinner, knows God. The knowledge of God is discussed elsewhere in this dogmatics, but the understanding of sin as being against God has a contribution to make to that discussion. Briefly, we may note the following components of that contribution.

The biblical materials, classically represented in Paul's indictments in Romans 1—3, do assume sufficient universal knowledge of God to sustain an appeal to responsibility. Yet the problem of cognitive atheism warrants serious consideration in its own terms, without simple reduction to volitional atheism. The will is not to be reduced to the reason, nor fully isolated from it. That sin may take the form of self-deception in culpable ignorance (*agnoema*) does not require us to deny the ambiguity of claims for God. Such ambiguity in the relationship of knowledge may appropriately reflect the character of the participants in the relationship as the epistemological correlate to the ontological character of both divine and human freedom. Accordingly, a simplistically moralistic assessment of cognitive atheism must be resisted. Clearly "the bid is raised," when we consider the revelation of God in Jesus of Nazareth, though the dialectical cautions mentioned above may reappear, if Pascal's sense of the "divine incognito" did not overstate matters too strongly when he wrote, "God is hidden more decisively in the incarnation than in the creation."[17]

THE AGENT OF SIN

To recognize that sin rises up against God *from an other* is to distinguish Christian reflection from certain historically influential interpretations. Thus we cannot say that sin is nonbeing or privation, since we are not prepared to say the person is unreal. Any confidence in divine victory which so underestimates evil is purchased with inflated currency.

How shall one account for the prevalence of the privation theme? It seems best to view this tradition as entailing an understandable confusion between the formal and the material analysis of sin. As surely as God deserves worship and trust, sin·may be described as having the *form* of "missing" (Gk., *hamartia*) or "twisting" (Heb., *awon*). One may even say, though less satisfactorily, that the *material* effect of sin is disruptive, destructive. The negative reference of those adjectives begs for a positive definition of the truly human good. Surely in our time, when the formal notion of varying degrees of being seems counterintuitive and when the holocaust is our mentor materially, it should not be difficult for the reality of sin to warn us against the seductive assurances of the interpretation of sin as privation.

A more subtle form of the same error might be to accede to an anthropological dualism by which the reality of sin is ostensibly acknowledged, but promptly relegated to something less than the essential center of the person. We need to reclaim the biblical meaning of *sarx* as referring to the *whole* earthly person: "We all once lived in the passions of our flesh, following the desires of body and mind" (Eph. 2:3).[18] Perhaps to hold the two together a third is needed: will. That was the point of Kierkegaard's attack on the "Socratic" position of sin as ignorance.[19] Kierkegaard saw this point very clearly—and it needs to be seen, for the gnostic virus in the religious body does not die easily. Yet ironically Kierkegaard may have been so preoccupied with the relationship between reason and will that his own anthropology may lack balance. He aligned the notion of will so closely with that of consciousness that his own notion of a sinful alternative to sinful defiance is somewhat underdeveloped.[20] We shall want to examine that option in a moment. But his desire to locate sin in the self's very center faithfully seeks to resist any tendency toward an anthropological dualism. Our task here is not to develop a full-scale anthropology, though in this and the next chapter we sketch a view that is much in debt to Kierkegaard's voluntarism. What is required of any Christian theologian is to indicate that the entire person is involved in the reality of sin. Such scope is suggested by the biblical emphasis on the unity of the person.[21] An adequate doctrine of sin will, then, be no less complex than a truly descriptive anthropology.

In fact, the biblical writings not only incorporate many different shades of meaning in their portrayal of sin; they also offer an explicit awareness of these differences and their relationships, as in Job 34:37: "For he adds rebellion (*pesha*) to his sin (*hatta'th*)." [22] Cutting across the richly nuanced understanding of sin in the tradition is a fundamental distinction between what we may call—following Kierkegaard—sins of "weakness" and sins of "strength."

By sins of "strength" we have in mind the classic action of unmitigated conscious defiance. It is clear-eyed rebellion of which we speak—*pesha* or *asebia*. Here the self is assertive with a fist clenched in the face of God. It was this of which Luther wrote, "Man cannot of his nature desire that God should be God; on the contrary, he desires that he himself might be God and that God might not be God." [23] In such sin there is an element of consciousness; the next short step is direct knowledge, and then direct defiance. If one *knows* God, does one not know (have) what it takes to *be* God? Thus in his theses for the Heidelberg Disputation Luther warns that the wisdom which beholds "the invisible things of God as perceived from works—puffs up, blinds, and hardens man altogether." [24] Paul Ricoeur warns against premature syntheses, violent totalizations as the birth of "idols, substituted for the 'Name,' who should remain faceless." [25] While one may demur if the suggestion is made that conscious knowledge of God *entails* conscious defiance, it may be granted that such knowledge seems at least a condition for what Reinhold Niebuhr analyzes as pride or what Tillich describes as "hubris."

This is the understanding of sin that stands out most starkly in Western Christendom. That is not strange, for here the positive "being" of sin, or perhaps even more clearly its "becoming," is most sharply displayed. Indeed, the power of sin in this dynamic has been so dramatically apparent in Western history that sin easily comes to be seen as involving something more and other than the self. There arises a tendency toward a *theological* dualism in which the sinner is no longer personally responsible but is seen rather as the helpless victim of an alien power. Thus the Kittel article on sin in the New Testament traces the development of sin as an individual act through sin as a determination of human nature to sin as a personal power, as in Rom. 7:14-20:

> We know that the law is spiritual; but I am carnal, sold under sin. I do not understand my actions. For I do not do what I want, but I do the very thing I hate. Now if I do what I do not want, I agree that the law is good. So then it is no longer I that do it, but sin which dwells in me. For I know that nothing good dwells within me, that is, in my flesh. I can will what is right, but I cannot do it. For I do not do the good I want, but the evil I do not want is what I do. Now if I do what I do not want, it is no longer I that do it, but sin which dwells within me. [26]

Clearly some account of the bondage of sin is required of us. It will not do to regard such talk as a fanciful extension of the self's capacity to objectify itself. [27] Fuller consideration of the demonic in itself will be deferred to a discussion of the origin of sin. Here we are concerned with the demonic in relation to the human experience of sin. In this context the demonic must be considered as far as the temptation to sin and the results of sin are concerned. The agency intervening between temptation and result is our immediate topic in this subsection; here the consensus of Christian reflection resists any reference to the demonic that would compromise the reality of human responsibility. Even the bondage of which we must speak below must be understood to affirm human responsibility.

Hans Conzelmann has collected the "hints" regarding the satanic as the tempter (as 1 Thess. 3:5), the seducer (Acts 5:3), the hinderer (2 Thess. 2:18), the unleasher of persecution (1 Pet. 5:8–9), as the one who has the power of death (Heb. 2:14), who holds the kingdoms of this world (Luke 4:5–6), and who can change himself into an angel of light (2 Cor. 11:14). He concludes:

> There is no question of reconstructing a "New Testament doctrine of Satan" from these hints. They are simply fragments. For example, the devil acts in the passion, but his work there has no significance for theological understanding. No account is taken of him in the description of God's rule. Paul outlines man's position before God, the nature of sin, judgment and salvation, without using the idea of Satan (Rom. 5; cf. on the other hand the account in the Wisdom of Solomon). In the New Testament, Satan is not a being with whom one can explain, e.g., sin and death. He is the evil one against whom precautions must be taken, and who is driven away by the confession of faith.[28]

Whatever we shall make of the tempter's role in the origin of sin, in the primeval account the human pair come to bear the consequences of their own deeds. At best one might speak of the demonic and the human as conjunctive causes in the evil that comes into God's good world. The Lutheran confessions, for example, use such a construction, as when Article XI of the Epitome of the Formula of Concord speaks of the source of sin as "the devil and man's wicked and perverse will."

In any case, Christian reflection concerning the demonic does not challenge, but rather supports and strengthens, our understanding of sin as will against will. It is will *against* God, as Article XI of the Formula puts it: "Everything which prepares and fits man for damnation emanates from the devil and man through sin, and in no way from God" (*BC* 629). And it is *created* will against the Creator. The Fourth Lateran Council (1215) put the point in these terms in confessing that the true God is one alone and eternal: "For the devil and other demons were created by God good in nature, but they themselves through themselves have become wicked."[29]

Of course, human freedom is not without its social, historical, and natural roots. Freedom could not be efficacious if it were not related precisely to that which is other than itself. But in this very rootedness, in this relatedness, resides the possibility of temptation of the self by that which is outside the self.[30] This can be put very strongly in some Christian circles, as when the explanation to the second article in Luther's Large Catechism says: "When we were created by God the Father, and had received from him all kinds of good things, the devil came and led us into disobedience, sin, death, and all evil" (*BC* 414). Yet the explanation continues by immediately claiming that it is *we* who accordingly "lay under God's wrath and displeasure, doomed to eternal damnation, as we had deserved." Human responsibility is here intact. Human sin occurs through external temptation, but not through external coercion.

The sheer reality of defiant human will is such a challenge to understanding that it is not strange that the "clearer" position of an eternal dualism seems attractive, as in the rabbinic speculation on Gen. 6:5, which excuses humankind because of the evil imagination implanted in human hearts after the "sons of God" took to themselves "the daughters of man."[31] But Paul Ricoeur seems right in contending that Christian symbolism of evil represents a choice of the Adamic myth, though it may incorporate "tragic" elements. Regin Prenter summarizes the dynamic that drives Christian thought to such incorporation of the tragic: "Because sin, understood as man's rebellion against creation, is the absolutely unexplainable reality, it is without any presupposition (original sin). Original sin, understood as the unexplainable and all embracing reality, is itself the indispensable presupposition for the Christian message concerning creation and redemption."[32]

We agree: the very experience of our "actual" sin requires that we repair to the topic of original sin; that movement is no heteronomous dogmatism. It is the logic of this chapter which leads to the next chapter's discussion of original sin. But it may be questioned whether our description of that experience of actual sin is not incomplete even in its own terms as yet. That is, the difficulty with the notion of sin as defiant will, as the sin of strength, may not be so much its conceptual dissonance as its empirical deficiency. Who sins so, after all? Apart from the brooding existentialist in the dark garret, who musters so mighty a charge on the gates of heaven? One may suspect the answer is that *we* do, we *all* do. The stress on defiance is not unempirical. Yet much of our failing seems less flamboyant. We need to recognize what may be called sins of weakness.

The largest amount of biblical material referring to sin does not support a strict identification with consciously willed defiance. The most frequently used words are the Hebrew *hatta'th* and the Greek *harmartia*, with which the Septuagint usually translates *hatta'th*. Of *hatta'th* Gottfried Quell writes: "This word conveyed a clear objective picture to the mind, with no reference to the inner quality of sinful behavior."[33] Eichrodt has noted that in the preprophetic period "the Israelite concept of sin was primarily concerned with establishing an objective offence. . . . *All the emphasis falls on the objective offence*, while the sinful will of the person involved manifestly plays no part." [34] Eichrodt seems to devalue this material in speaking in this connection of "the after-effects of a dynamistic system of thought," but he does not dispute its presence and prevalence. Ricoeur takes these materials more seriously in noting "the decisive fact that those archaic modes of behavior were *resumed* after the ethical stage represented by propheticism":

> It seems to me that this resumption, this resurgence of a postethical ritualism, so to speak, cannot be understood unless we take as our point of departure the project of a consistent and voluntary heteronomy. The esotericism of the rite bears witness to conscience that conscience is not the source of the Law, since the Law is not transparent to conscience. [35]

May it be that this Old Testament material, despite its tendency toward prepersonal tragic defilement talk, is not so recessive, formal, and pictorial after all?

The New Testament material may shift the emphasis, if Gustav Stählin is right that it follows the Septuagint usage of *hamartia*, where the term "first came to have the moral and religious quality which it lacked, both in the rapidly changing Greek of common speech and in the 'tragic' language of Aristotle, and to indicate guilt as the outcome of an evil will, an evil purpose, i.e., of a conscious rebellion against God and contradiction of him (equals *adikia*)." [36] Yet Stählin notes that aside from John and Paul the word is always used in the plural and that the emphasis is on single acts, and he cites considerable Johannine material which seems more like the synoptic stress on *sins* than on the Pauline understanding of sin as a positive force alienating from God. Such usage does not readily suggest the unified inwardness of defiance. Must this biblical material be understood simply as the underdeveloped raw material of the prophetic and Pauline emphasis on consciously defiant will, or does it deserve consideration as an alternative dynamic within the complex reality of sin?

Kierkegaard's discussion of "sins of weakness" depends on his notion of the self as a synthesis of necessity and possibility that relates itself to itself in freedom. God's will for that self is not only that God be trusted, as if that could be done almost impersonally and passively, but that "by relating itself to its own self and by willing to be itself the self is grounded transparently in the Power which posited it." [37] Thus it becomes possible to discern a twofold structure to sin. As Wanda Warren Berry has put it, "One can lose the relationship either by negating God in defiant 'strength' or by negating the self in weakly refusing to constitute a gathered will." [38]

This latter notion seems to fit the conventional idea of sins of omission, just as defiant strength is a matter of commission. Moreover, this category seems helpful in evaluating the contemporary human predicament. Omission will be a particularly crucial category in a time when a more static conception of reality and of God's claim within reality gives way to a recognition of the thoroughly temporal character of life. Without endorsing every rebellion or designating every development divine, one may in such a time be more sensitive to the sinfulness of clinging to past formulations of thought and life.[39] The crucial determiners of contemporary life seem beyond the control of any individual. One's sin in such a state seems to be collaboration in anonymous injustice, as the theologians of liberation have not failed to point out.[40]

Even in an apparently impersonal age the sense of innocent helplessness may depend on a capacity for self-deception. But the self's very exercise of that self-deception seems to yield a weakened self.[41] This is the sin of weakness. This may make some sense of the interpretation of sin as privation or nonbeing, beyond the formal sense of nonconformity, of which we spoke earlier.

There is will in such sin. But if God's call is to become a particular synthesis of givenness and possibility, to acquire continuity by "making a decision and renewing it," [42] then the will to decline God's call will manifest itself in the diffuse swamp of immediacy of which we have been speaking. The synoptic emphasis on the plurality of sins fits this category. The self does not gather itself, even defiantly. One might even consider the biblical emphasis on lack of consciousness, even on unwitting defilement—which seems both post- and preprophetic—as fitting the decision to decline the call to a particular synthesis. There is motion here, but not gathered movement toward that to which God calls.[43]

Indeed, perhaps the will that acts in such weakness and the will more starkly on display in defiance are not unrelated to each other. Clinical psychoanalysis suggests that pride and self-contempt are often mutually fortifying companions.[44] At least they are together in being the pathological agency that is sin.

THE EFFICACY OF SIN

Whither, then, sin? As a "positive" act of will, as something totally other than "nonbeing," sin is "effective"; it brings about effects. It is against God, and it affects God. Here the categories of guilt and wrath apply. The psalmist finds the one blessed "unto whom the Lord imputes not iniquity" and the Pauline speech about God's judgment of human guilt echoes the psalmist's cry (Ps. 32:1–4; 51:1–4; Rom. 1:20, 2:2, 3:19–20). Guilt belongs to humankind; indeed, it belongs to the individual sinner, for here the symbolism of evil reaches a deeply personal level. But this is no mere subjective intrapsychic reality to be banished by the analyst's wand—though such there surely are.[45] The sinner is guilty before God, and God is wrathful toward the sinner. Yahweh refuses to go in the midst of Israel because they are a stiff-necked people who would be consumed at once (Exod. 33:3–5). When God shines the light of the divine presence on hidden human faults, sinners are consumed in God's anger (Ps. 90:7–8).

Is this biblical reference to the wrath of God to be set aside as a hopelessly anthropomorphic category, because God is purely and simply Love? That God's love is pure is central to Christian faith, but it does not follow that it is a simple thing to love sinners. Sin does create something in God: wrath.[46] But sin does not create God; it cannot make God over in its own image. Indeed, perhaps it is best to think of God's wrath as letting sin be precisely what it is. The act of sin in its reality and so its efficaciousness produces a destiny. Particularly in the Old Testament this sense of correspondence between crime and punishment plays a role, though not an unchallenged one.[47] This sense of nemesis in history, of divine judgment active in life, depends on the theme of God's continuing activity in the world. Our task here is to recognize that the biblical witness calls for such a notion in understanding God's reaction to sin. As the persistent Pauline theme has it: "For the wrath of God is revealed from heaven against all ungodliness and wickedness of men. . . . Therefore God gave them up in the lusts of their hearts to impurity . . . to dishonorable passions . . . to a base mind and to improper conduct" (Rom. 1:18–32). Two statements seem required here: sin produces its own effect, *and* that producing passes not only into God but through God back into the world.[48]

But God's reaction to sin is not to be likened to the mechanical functioning of a pipeline for sin's self-destructive tendencies. The fuller biblical witness speaks of God's action in freedom toward what God receives from the world. Thus Hosea:

> How can I give you up, O Ephraim! . . .
> My heart recoils within me,
>   my compassion grows warm and tender,
> I will not execute my fierce anger,
>   I will not again destroy Ephraim;
> for I am God and not man,
>   the Holy One in your midst,
>   and I will not come to destroy.
>
> (Hos. 11:8–9)

Judgments following disobedience are no mechanical system. Gerhard von Rad makes that clear:

Certainly, the Old Testament tells of many judgments which overtook the disobedient nation. But who was their author? Was it the Law? It was God himself acting on Israel, and not a legal system of salvation which worked out according to a prearranged plan. In particular, it was God himself who always remained

Lord even over Israel's sin, and whose judgments even the pre-exilic prophets—
and their successors even more clearly than they—represented as being at the
same time evidence of his faithfulness to his chosen people.[49]

That God is Lord even over sin does indeed anticipate the witness in the New
Testament to the decisive divine response to the human predicament.

Whatever one may say soteriologically regarding God's lordship over sin,
it cannot be denied that sin is efficacious. One might even say that through
sin a world is made. We have been speaking of how sin yields effects in the
sinner. A completely episodic account of this reality is manifestly inadequate.
At least the cumulative character of action must be recognized. In the words
of John: "Every one who commits sin is a slave to sin" (John 8:34). Kierkegaard
can hardly be charged with ignoring the event-character of human existence
but he recognizes that precisely the positive character of the act of sin yields
something more:

> Is not sin precisely the discontinuous? Lo, here we have again the notion that
> sin is merely a negation to which one can acquire no title, as one can acquire
> no title to stolen property, a negation, an impotent attempt to give itself con-
> sistency, which nevertheless, suffering as it does from the torture of impotence
> in the defiance of despair, it is not able to do. Yes, so it is speculatively; but
> Christianly . . . sin is a position which out of itself develops a more and more
> positive continuity. And the law for the growth of this continuity is moreover
> different from the law which applies to a debt or to a negation. For a debt does
> not grow because it is not paid, it grows every time it is added to. But sin grows
> every instant one does not get out of it.[50]

Our contemporary sense for the particularity of events may be so keen that
it is difficult for us to grasp the coming-to-be of a state or a condition. Yet
this is what is required of us to locate rightly the depth of sin. Perhaps one
might say that in the case of sins of strength the state grows precisely because
it does yield defiant acts, while in the case of sins of weakness the state grows
because the call of God to becoming a self is not heeded. In neither case
does the will to commit or to omit sin begin with a clean slate. In any case
the biblical writers do recognize a "continuity in sin," particularly in Paul,
whose advance on the synoptic stress on individual sins and even on the Johannine stress on the condition of sin yields a personification of sin as a power,
as Gustav Stählin notes:

> Thus, dwelling in man (Rom. 7:17, 20) and bringing forth passions (7:5) and
> lust (7:8), sin obtains mastery over him, as a demonic power. Man is under sin
> (Rom. 3:9; Gal. 3:22; cf. Rom. 11:32), as a slave (Rom. 6:16, 20; John 8:34; cf.
> Gal. 2:17), sold to it (Rom. 7:14), in bondage to it (Rom. 6:6), under its law
> (7:23, 25; 8:3), presenting parts of his body to it as instruments of unrighteousness
> (6:13).[51]

The sinful act of will yields cumulatively a sinful state of willing; sin yields sin which yields sins. Sin, then, makes a world *in* the *sinner.* But surely sin also makes a world *for* the *creature.* The effects of sin do not rest tidily with their individual makers. Selves do not exist in insulated tubes of becoming; they exist in relationships, and it is those relationships which make up the world. Whither sin? The sin and sins of selves enter the world to yield a solidarity in sin. No self begins with a clean slate; it is born into this world with its racism, sexism, profit-oriented economy, consumerism, and so forth.

But the biblical authors seem to speak of solidarity in sin in a still stronger sense. Eichrodt notes:

> [The prophets] bring not only their own contemporaries before God's judgment, and denounce them for their rebellion, but also see them linked with all previous generations in a unitary entity, for which the sins of the fathers are also the sins of those now alive, and will be required of them, while at the same time the fact that the sinful condition of the present generation has resulted from the perverted direction of an earlier one in no sense does away with the responsibility of the former group.[52]

Here we seem to move through a solidarity of effect to a solidarity of agency. The "whither" of sin seems to yield a "whence" for sin. In Chapter 3 we will discuss more fully the very considerable reflections of the church on the subject of such connectedness in agency. Obviously there we must consider the relationship between "original sin originated and original sin originating" and varying theories as to how humankind stands together before God in sin. But even in this chapter in considering "actual" sin as act and state, we come to issues which drive us to anticipate that later discussion. Beyond what has already been discussed, two points may be mentioned: the universality of actual sin and the inevitability of actual sin.

A familiar biblical refrain is "There is no man who does not sin" (1 Kings 8:46; 2 Chron. 6:36), "None is righteous, no, not one" (Rom. 3:10). Even those who may be said to be righteous (as Noah and Job) are such not because they are without sin but because they are in relationship with God. This judgment of universality seems more than a striking statistical consensus. The sense of inevitability builds in the prophetic materials of the Old Testament. Thus von Rad points out that Ezekiel is concerned to demonstrate the "total dominion" of sin: "It is not a matter of separate transgressions, nor simply of the failure of one generation, but of a deepseated inability to obey, indeed of a resistance to God which made itself manifest on the very day that Israel came into being."[53] At times this inevitability seems to be associated with active willing, which we have spoken of as sins of strength.

Yet there may be a sense in which those reformers who minimized the role of active will were right in their view of original sin. Without our consent,

sin ineluctably separates us from God.[54] Still, the "I" is other than an innocent victim in some mechanical march of sin. One may exorcise the will too
readily, particularly if will does not entail contingency. Perhaps the will at
work in what we have called the sin of weakness may help us approach the
notion of truly personal yet noncontingent will. In any case, in speaking of
inevitability Christians do not intend to give up responsibility, as Reinhold
Niebuhr makes clear.[55] Hans Conzelmann finds that concern to be faithful
to the theology of the New Testament: "I am not relieved of responsibility
for myself through the *servitude* of my *arbitrium*. I may be subjected to an
alien power and incapable of freeing myself, but the seat of my actions is
still myself. It is I who bring about the compulsion of sin." [56]

What we have brought together here is clearly an unstable mixture. We
seem to have arrived at something like Augustine's "I had willingly come to
be what I unwillingly found myself to be"—though even that formulation
may permit an easing of the tension through a temporal parceling out of the
dynamics.[57] While we may not be able to resolve the tension, clearly more
must be said. Paul Ricoeur is right in claiming that the concept of the servile
will is not directly accessible and depends on other symbolism for the filling
out of its content.[58]

Niebuhr found the clue to responsibility-despite-inevitability in the situation of the creature as finite freedom.[59] We turn in the next chapter to the
discussion of the absolute origin of sin, the first sin, in order to isolate the
essential components and dynamics in the coming-to-be of sin over against
that which is not sin. But for us sin does not come to be as an interruption
of a course well begun. Indeed, many of the biblical references and much
of the church's reflection concerning the inevitability of sin refer to some kind
of givenness at birth: "that which is born of the flesh is flesh" (John 3:6;
cf., of course, Ps. 51:7).

Where does sin end? Christian faith wishes to say that it ends in the broken
and risen body of our Lord. This is hardly the place to develop this point,
but it needs to be sounded, however abruptly. We do not speak here of the
whence of sin. While sin ends in the Christ, it does not begin there. It ends
well, there—at least that is the confidence of the blessed who cry out on Easter
Eve: "O happy crime which merited such and so great a redeemer." But in
this saying one's temporal location does matter. Sin does not begin well, for
its being is against God. But in our "second-order" reflection about sin, we
may indeed take our bearings by the decisive divine response to sin. This is
true most fundamentally of the act of God in Christ in its emphatic quality
and universality of scope. It is true as well of such subordinate "divine
response" themes as the virgin birth and infant baptism which have assumed
a kind of primacy in the life of Christian people.[60]

It is not strange that sin should be understood most clearly through the remedy made available by divine faithfulness. This is not a challenge to the anti-monistic emphasis which has prevailed in this chapter's discussion of the nature of sin. Sin is *against* God. But it turns out that *God is against sin* and has contrived to deal with it. Sin is most clearly understood when viewed from the perspective the divine response provides.

NOTES

1. Walther Eichrodt, *Theology of the Old Testament*, trans. J. A. Baker, 2 vols. (Philadelphia: Westminster Press, 1961–67), 2:382. Cf. Paul Ricoeur, *The Symbolism of Evil*, trans. Emerson Buchanan (Boston: Beacon Press, 1967), p. 48.

2. Eichrodt, *Theology of the O. T.*, 2:383.

3. Article II, The Augsburg Confession. Cf. Luther's famous explanation of the first commandment in his Large Catechism.

4. Gerhard von Rad, *Old Testament Theology*, trans. D. M. G. Stalker, 2 vols. (New York: Harper & Row, 1962–65), 2:340.

5. Ibid., p. 339.

6. Wolfhart Pannenberg, *What Is Man?* trans. Duane A. Priebe (Philadelphia: Fortress Press, 1970), p. 35.

7. Reinhold Niebuhr, *The Nature and Destiny of Man*, 2 vols. (New York: Charles Scribner's Sons, 1941–43).

8. Paul Tillich, *Systematic Theology*, 3 vols. (Chicago: University of Chicago Press, 1951–63), 2:50. Luther also emphasized the sins of the pious. See Albrecht Peters, *Glaube und Werk: Luthers Rechtfertigungslehre im Lichte der Heiligen Schrift* (Berlin: Lutherisches Verlagshaus, 1962), pp. 147–51.

9. Von Rad, *Old Testament Theology*, 1:155. Cf. Dietrich Bonhoeffer's reference to the prohibition showing Adam his limit in his creatureliness, *Creation and Fall*, trans. John Fletcher (New York: Macmillan Co.; London: SCM Press, 1959), p. 52. In *Images of Good and Evil*, trans. Michael Bullock (London: Routledge & Kegan Paul, 1952), pp. 17–19, Martin Buber criticizes this "favorite" interpretation (and others) and settles for this: " 'Knowledge of good and evil' means nothing else than cognizance of the opposites which the early literature of mankind designated . . . the opposites latent in creation."

10. Tillich, *Systematic Theology*, 2:52.

11. Rudolf Bultmann, *Theology of the New Testament*, trans. Kendrick Grobel, 2 vols. (New York: Charles Scribner's Sons, 1954–55), 1:232.

12. For a development of this Johannine theme (1 John 3:4), see Werner Elert, *The Structure of Lutheranism*, trans. W. A. Hansen 2 vols. (St. Louis: Concordia Publishing House, 1962), 1:33.

13. Gustavo Gutierrez, *A Theology of Liberation*, trans. and ed. Sister Caridad Inda and John Eagelson (Maryknoll, N.Y.: Orbis Books, 1973), p. 175. Cf. Dorothee Soelle, *Political Theology*, trans. John Shelley (Philadelphia: Fortress Press, 1974), p. 90.

14. Ricoeur, *Symbolism of Evil*, p. 143.

THE NATURE OF SIN

15. Søren Kierkegaard, *The Sickness unto Death*, trans. W. Lowrie (Princeton: Princeton University Press, 1941; Anchor Books), p. 213 (emphasis his). Cf. Ricoeur, *Symbolism of Evil*, p. 52.

16. Ricoeur, *Symbolism of Evil*, p. 143: ". . . that in it [scrupulousness] which had not been felt as fault, becomes fault; the attempt to reduce sin by observance becomes sin. That is the real meaning of the curse of the law."

17. Kierkegaard cites Pascal to this effect in *Papirer*, ed. P. A. Heiberg and Victor Kuhr, 11 vols. (Copenhagen: Gyldendals, 1909–48), X 3 A 626, and adds his own development of the theme.

18. See Werner Georg Kümmel in *Man in the New Testament*, trans. John J. Vincent (London: Epworth Press, 1963), p. 84. Bultmann (*Theology of the N. T.*, 1:209) has argued against any attempt to split up the self by appeal to the various Greek terms Paul uses.

19. Kierkegaard, *Sickness unto Death*, pp. 220–21.

20. Ibid., p. 162: "Generally speaking, consciousness, i.e., consciousness of self, is the decisive criterion of the self. The more consciousness, the more self; the more consciousness, the more will, and the more will, the more self." For a correction of this tendency from within Kierkegaard, see Wanda Warren Berry, "Images of Sin and Salvation in Feminist Theology," *AThR* 60 (January 1978): 25–54.

21. As Eichrodt, *Theology of the O. T.*, 2:147.

22. Cf. Jer. 33:8; Lev. 16:21.

23. *Disputatio contra scholasticam* (1517), *WA* 1:225. See also Gerhard Ebeling, *Luther*, trans. R. A. Wilson (Philadelphia: Fortress Press, 1970), chap. 13; and Peters, *Glaube und Werk*, pp. 142, 146.

24. Heidelberg Thesis 22. See also theses 19 and 21.

25. Paul Ricoeur, "Guilt, Ethics, and Religion," in *Talk of God*, Royal Institute of Philosophy Lectures (London: Macmillan & Co., 1969), vol. 2 (1967–68), pp. 115–16. Ricoeur is developing Kant's critique (in *Religion within the Limits of Reason Alone* [New York: Harper & Row, 1960]) of the reconciliation of virtue and happiness.

26. Walter Grundmann, "Sin in the New Testament," in Gerhard Kittel, *Sin*, in *Bible Key Words*, trans. and ed. J. R. Coates (New York: Harper & Brothers, 1951), pp. 64–87.

27. As Bultmann does, *Theology of the N. T.*, 1:195.

28. Hans Conzelmann, *An Outline of the Theology of the New Testament*, trans. John Bowden (New York: Harper & Row, 1969), p. 18.

29. Cf. Denzinger, 427, 237. See also C. K. Barrett, *From First Adam to Last* (New York: Charles Scribner's Sons, 1962), pp. 12–13.

30. Gordon Kaufman, *Systematic Theology: A Historicist Perspective* (New York: Charles Scribner's Sons, 1968), pp. 355–56.

31. N. P. Williams, *The Ideas of the Fall and of Original Sin* (New York and London: Longmans, Green & Co., 1927), chap. 2.

32. Regin Prenter, *Creation and Redemption*, trans. Theodore I. Jensen (Philadelphia: Fortress Press, 1967), p. 284. For Ricoeur's distinction, see *Symbolism of Evil*, chap. 5.

33. Gottfried Quell, "Sin in the Old Testament," in Kittel, *Sin*, pp. 1–32.

5 / SIN AND EVIL

34. Eichrodt, *Theology of the O. T.*, 2:381 (emphasis his). Cf. von Rad's discussion of subjectively guiltless sin in *Old Testament Theology*, 1:267.

35. Ricoeur, *Symbolism of Evil*, p. 135. Cf. in *Talk of God*, p. 104: "Stain was still external contagion, sin already the rupture of a relation; but this rupture exists even if I do not know it; sin is a real condition, an objective situation."

36. Gustav Stählin, "Greek Usage," in Kittel, *Sin*, pp. 46–52.

37. Kierkegaard, *Sickness unto Death*, pp. 146–47.

38. Berry, "Images of Sin and Salvation," p. 46.

39. Bernard Häring, *Sin in the Secular Age* (Garden City, N.Y.: Doubleday & Co., 1974), p. 18.

40. Soelle, *Political Theology*, p. 89.

41. Berry, "Images of Sin and Salvation," p. 46.

42. This formulation is from Kierkegaard's *Concluding Unscientific Postscript to the Philosophical Fragments*, trans. David F. Swenson and Walter Lowrie (Princeton: Princeton University Press, 1944), p. 277, although the theme is already suggested in his earlier work, *Repetition*.

43. See F. R. Tennant, *The Concept of Sin* (Cambridge: At the University Press, 1912), chaps. 5 and 6; and Friedrich Schleiermacher, *The Christian Faith*, trans. H. R. Mackintosh and J. S. Stewart (New York: Harper & Row, Harper Torchbooks, 1963), pp. 291–304.

44. See, e.g., Karen Horney, *Neurosis and Human Growth* (New York: W. W. Norton & Co., 1950), p. 341.

45. See Ricoeur's masterful discussion of guilt, *Symbolism of Evil*, chap. 3, in which Greek, Judaic, and Christian conceptions are distinguished and related. Cf. Grundmann, "Sin in the N. T.," p. 79.

46. Jürgen Moltmann, *The Crucified God*, trans. R. A. Wilson and John Bowden (London: SCM Press, 1974), p. 272, drawing on the thought of Abraham Heschel, writes: "His wrath is injured love and therefore a mode of his reaction to men. Love is the source and basis of the possibility of the wrath of God. . . . As injured love, the wrath of God is not something that is inflicted, but a divine suffering of evil. It is a sorrow which goes through his opened heart."

47. Von Rad, *Old Testament Theology*, 2:73–74. For a discussion of this theme from a more systematic standpoint, see Langdon Gilkey's *Reaping the Whirlwind: A Christian Interpretation of History* (New York: Seabury Press, 1976), pp. 253–65. Cf. Klaus Koch, "Gibt es ein Vergeltungsdogma in Alten Testament?" *ZThK* 3 (1955): 1–42. For a brief discussion of Koch's view, see W. Sibley Towner, *How God Deals with Evil* (Philadelphia: Westminster Press, 1976), pp. 48–50.

48. There is also the sense in which divine wrath not only reveals sin as what it is but makes it more what it is—the hatred of God. For this strand in Luther's thought, see Peters, *Glaube und Werk*, p. 154.

49. Von Rad, *Old Testament Theology*, 2:405–6. Thus the Priestly writer has God giving Noah and his sons a new blessing (Gen. 9:1ff.) and the Yahwist suggests a divine resolution of grief (6:5ff.) in mercy (8:21–22).

50. Kierkegaard, *Sickness unto Death*, pp. 236–37.

51. Stählin, "Greek Usage," p. 51.

382

52. Eichrodt, *Theology of the O. T.*, 2:407. See A. M. Dubarle, *The Biblical Doctrine of Original Sin*, trans. E. M. Stewart (London: Geoffrey Chapman, 1964), pp. 34ff., for an application of connectedness to contemporaries.

53. Von Rad, *Old Testament Theology*, 2:229. Cf. Eichrodt, *Theology of the O. T.*, 2:394.

54. Holsten Fagerberg, *A New Look at the Lutheran Confessions*, trans. Gene J. Lund (St. Louis: Concordia Publishing House, 1972), p. 143: "According to Catholic theologians sin was not sin unless carried out with the consent of the will. To speak meaningfully of sin requires that man can be held responsible for his actions. . . . The reformers, on the other hand, saw in sin something which ineluctably separates man from God. . . . To speak of will and the freedom of the will in this context is evidently meaningless."

55. Niebuhr, *Nature and Destiny of Man*, 1:255–60.

56. Conzelmann, *Outline of the Theology of the N. T.*, p. 255 (emphasis his). Elert, *Structure of Lutheranism*, pp. 34–35, traces suggestions of the "tragic synthesis of destiny and guilt" "even in Kant and Schiller."

57. *Confessions*, bk. 8, chap. 5.

58. Ricoeur, *Symbolism of Evil*, p. 151.

59. Niebuhr, *Nature and Destiny of Man*, p. 251.

60. Jaroslav Pelikan, *The Emergence of the Catholic Tradition (100–600)* (Chicago: University of Chicago Press, 1971), p. 286, and Denzinger, 102 (Carthage, 418) on virgin birth and infant baptism; L. Sabourin, "Original Sin Reappraised," *Biblical Theology Bulletin* 3 (1973): 51–81, and Fagerberg, *A New Look*, p. 143, on redemption/justification.

2
The Origin of Sin

The nature of sin points to the origin of sin in a fall, a human reality disrupting the integral goodness of the creature. As the object of God's special creative endowment, the creature is good; as one called in finite freedom to God's special intention, the creature is not yet perfect, but able to be tempted and able to sin; and in the mystery of freedom, the creature originates sin.

CREATION AND FALL

The Christian struggle to diagnose, if not understand, the nature of sin has led the faithful to speak of the origin of sin. There are two steps in such speech: (1) the absolute origin of sin in the "fall"; (2) the proximate origin of sin in the connectedness of humankind. Thus one speaks of the distinction between "original sin originating" and "original sin originated." Or less abstractly, both themes are held together in single sentences, as when the fathers at the Council of Carthage in 418 reject the opponents of infant baptism who suppose that infants "draw nothing of the original sin from Adam" and the confessors at Augsburg teach that "since the fall of Adam all men who are born according to the course of nature are conceived and born in sin."[1] Or more concretely still, in the *locus classicus* of Rom. 5:12 Paul writes: "Therefore as sin came into the world through one man and death through sin, and so death spread to all men because all men sinned."

Sin comes into the world . . . death spreads . . . all sin. In this chapter we pose the question of the absolute origin of sin. Why must Christians raise this question? Sin is so pervasive a reality that the issue of origin, though latent in this as in any phenomenon, might be set aside. To ask, "Why sin?" seems almost like asking, "Why anything at all?" Why not recognize that sin presents its credentials simply by its omnipresence and then get on with the warfare against sin? It is because of God that Christians must speak of the origin of sin.

Faith in God yields the distinction between creation and fall. The intentionality of the distinction represents a choice of what Paul Ricoeur has called the Adamic myth that roots sin in human freedom over against the tragic myth that roots sin in divine decree and the theogonic myth that roots sin in an eternal dualism.[2] We shall follow out this intentionality in three respects: (1) the distinction between creation and *falling* with respect to the *reality* of evil, (2) the distinction between creation and *fallenness* with respect to the *continuity* of evil, and (3) the distinction between creation and the *fall* with respect to the *negativity* of evil.

The intention of Christian faith in God requires us to move fully through this series of distinctions—though the three are not on the same level of immediacy. The commitment of the Christian tradition is clear on this point. It is also clear that this commitment is an exceedingly difficult one for modern people to make, since it seems to fly in the face of much of what contemporary science tells us of the history of the race. Since the contemporary Christian can hardly relinquish either the contemporary pole or the Christian pole, reflection on this matter is mandatory if we are not to be split in two by appeal to a double truth theory. Here we turn to the tradition to analyze the intentionality of the three distinctions showing *why* in each case the distinction matters and *that* it drives us toward an absolute origin of evil in "the fall." Next we will show *how* the distinctions can be stated intelligibly for the contemporary sensibility without sacrificing the concerns of the tradition.

Faith in God leads the Christian to the distinction between creation and fall. Christians claim superiority for this God, not superiority to other gods, there being none, but to other life, there being some. God is not only other than we and all else that is not God, but God is superior. It is not moral superiority to which we refer. To compare God to us by appeal to a moral standard is to insult God. Charles Hartshorne has seen the point clearly:

> The superiority of deity to all others cannot (in accordance with established word usage) be expressed by indefinite descriptions, such as "immensely good," "very powerful," or even "best" or "most powerful," but must be a superiority of principle, a definite conceptual divergence from every other being, actual or so much as possible. We may call this divergence "categorical supremacy."[3]

One of the ways in which Christians appeal to such categorical supremacy is in speaking of God as Creator. Because of God, Christians refuse any ultimate dualism, even if that refusal drives them to such awkward abstractions as *creatio ex nihilo.* Nothing at all comes into being without God. Christian reflection assigns as *ontological* superiority to God, the Creator.

This theme is essential, but an obvious question interrupts the hymn to the Creator. If God is the maker of heaven and earth, how can anything as real as sin slip past God's creative hand? Must not this too come from God? Yet two considerations weigh heavily against such a conclusion: The superiority of God is sensed as carrying *moral* as well as ontological meaning. Faith cries out: "Give thanks unto the Lord, for he is *good*; his steadfast love endures for ever" (Ps. 107:1). This does not imply that there is some eternal principle of goodness to which both God and humankind are subservient. But while it is God's creative will that determines what "good" means materially for God's creatures, this God does work for that good. God is for us, but sin is not. Moreover, sin is against God, not just indirectly by being against the creatures God loves, but with violent directness. Sin is an assault on the goodness of God. Perhaps that character is most clear to faith in what sin does to the Anointed One of God and in what God does to sin through that One.

Somehow, thus, a distinction is required of faith. God is Creator, but clearly sin is not from God, but against God and the creatures of God. One must grant that the tradition does not always make this distinction. Even the soteriological center in which the distinction seems so clear does not always control the work of theologians. Thus one may find that a more dualistic tendency in atonement thinking and a more monistic one in matters of theodicy exist side by side.[4] As to theodicy, it is as if the fathers of the church followed the attractive note of God's ontological superiority and, somehow swallowing all the objections welling up within, appealed to none other than God as the ultimate author of what we call evil. Thus for the writer of Isa. 45:7 the God who can say, "I am the Lord and there is no other, besides me there is no God" is the God who has to say: "I form the light and create darkness, I make weal and create woe, I am the Lord, who do all these things."[5]

There is more than one way in which this can be done. One can opt for monism stridently with Augustine and Calvin by arguing for a doctrine of double predestination, a move which the Second Council of Orange (529) rebuffs in violent terms: "We not only do not believe that some have been truly predestined to evil by divine power, but also with every execration we pronounce anathema upon those, if there are any such, who wish to believe so great an evil."[6] Perhaps a subtler form of this same dynamic can be seen in a theological concept of the human person, such that sin—whether or not it is to be regarded as particularly grievous—*must* occur sooner or later. Or one may try for a more obscure connection with God by linking sin with Satan, who not only tempts but seduces humankind but who must himself be none other than "God's devil."[7] Of Satan there must indeed be speech in this discussion, but it is clear already from Chapter 1 that such speech is of one who is against God.

Despite the presence of this monistic strand which would collapse the distinction between creation and fall, faith remembers the two themes just mentioned: the moral superiority of God who is for us, as sin is not, and the against-Godness of sin. Faith knows a third thing as well. Sin is against me, but it is also *by me*. The stubborn sense of responsibility points the way toward some kind of free-will defense. God's love for human creatures entails the risks the gift of creaturely freedom bears. This, in turn, permits the quest for a cause for sin to appeal to the free "falling" of creatures, if not to *a* race-shackling fall. In this appeal the distinction between sin and God's good work of creation is intact, as Langdon Gilkey makes clear:

> Because sin is an estrangement of our essential structure, an alienation from our nature, a misuse of freedom in which freedom is itself bound, it is not possible to describe it in ontological terms—for ontology knows only structure and not its misuse. Among the most important things a Christian interpretation says of history is that that which is fated or evil in experience, while an undoubted part of the concrete reality of history, is not the result of its ontological and so its necessitating structure. Rather, this strange, "fallen" aspect of concreteness is the creation of sin, of a warped human freedom, and not of God, of time, of the structure of our finitude or of inexorable natural and social forces.[8]

Could one leave it at that, saying simply that "each of us is the Adam of his or her own soul"?[9] After all, whatever we say must not defy the reality of personal will which we know to be sin's nature. Whatever we say of Paul's Adam (original sin originating) and of the psalmist's (Ps. 51) mother (original sin originated), it will not do to put either "outside the race," so that they no longer relate to that which I know as my personal will to sin.[10]

It is the nature of sin itself which brings faith to say more of sin's origin. We have already referred to the empirical and confessional witness to the universality of sin. This is a remarkable and troubling coincidence. But an episodic account of this universality fails on another score as well. We refer to the experience of the *continuity* of sin. Sin represents a state or condition in the individual. This state carries a sense of the ineluctability, the inevitability of sin. We find ourselves not just falling freely but *already fallen*, and so falling. Heinrich Ott has tried to describe this by appealing to the Kantian notion of a "transcendental act":

> The fall, the primal guilt, the turning away from God, the loss of freedom, is no doubt an act; but it is not an act which, historically or biographically demonstrable, has taken place once for all (when in fact could it have taken place?), but an act which has always already taken place, in short, a "transcendental act." . . . For each sinful deed takes place in a state of bondage because the sinner has already and always lost his freedom; and that is so, not through one particular action which initiates the series of all other acts of effective sin, but through one transcendental act which lies behind and governs the whole series of particular acts, and which does not take place at some time or other but which always takes place, or rather, which has always already taken place.[11]

We are always already fallen. We seem to be saying here that sin is the sort of thing that simply goes with being human. Paul Tillich does that, for example, when he speaks of the tragic-universal character of existence as the motif of the myth of the transcendent fall: "The meaning of the myth is that the very constitution of existence implies the transition from essence to existence." [12]

But if we are speaking of "the very constitution of existence," we would seem to be back to speaking of the work of the Creator. If sin is something that is given with existence, is not its giver God? That seems to be the logic which controls the tortuous history of Gen. 6:5's reference to the evil imagination of humankind.[13] While the immediate context might suggest a dualistic origin in the marriages of the "sons of God" to the "daughters of men," the evil imagination has also been regarded as something implanted in the person, presumably then a matter for which the ultimate responsibility is to be assigned to the Creator. Thus in Gen. 8:21 the presence in humankind of an evil imagination "from youth" brings God to promise never again to curse the ground.

The sense of the fallenness of human existence does tend to lead reflection away from the theme of individual responsibility. It can lead faith toward the "tragic" assignment of responsibility for evil to God. It can lead as well toward the theogonic myth where evil roots in an eternal dualism. The heritage of paganism and the persistence of dualism might well have inclined early Christians to a simplistic distortion of the Johannine "You are of your father the devil, and your will is to do your father's desires" (John 8:44).[14] But the dualistic lure was resisted. Even those biblical passages where the demonic is stressed stop short of metaphysical dualism. It is in the postcanonical writings that we detect the movement toward a complete absolutizing of Satan over against God.[15] John's dualism, while it may exceed Paul's, still remains an ethical dualism, and so stops short of gnosticism. Similarly, Reformation and neo-Reformation critiques of optimism have not been made by appeal to the pessimism of dualism, though that continues to attract occasional representatives.[16]

Christian faith is called back from the tragic and the theogonic by the sense that fallenness somehow must derive from falling. While Satan may be goodness fallen par excellence, that figure explains human fallenness only by illustration and not by causation. Temptation is not coercion. But it is difficult to resist the tragic lure, given the universal sense of fallenness, for is it not precisely the universals of life, including death, which we wish to assign to God? Again, further reflection is required of faith.

The continuity of sin reveals itself to be temporal, an organic continuity. Sin spreads not only within but between people. We refer to this aspect of the nature of sin to indicate how Christian faith follows the distinction between creation and fall into a third range to speak of the *negativity* of evil. Kant suggests that the "already fallen" cannot be limited to the individual:

> Since, therefore, we are unable to derive this disposition, or rather its ultimate ground, from any original act of the will in time, we call it a property of the will which belongs to it by nature (although actually the disposition is grounded in freedom). Further, the man of whom we say "He is by nature good or evil" is to be understood not as the single individual (for then one man could be considered good, by nature, another as evil), but as the entire race.[17]

Yet Kant's application of fallenness to the race seems more a summary statement of individual findings than a recognition that the continuity of sin points to something at work not merely within all individuals but *between* and therefore within them. Such a recognition would support the sense of the inevitability of sin. But this recognition seems once again to acquit human beings and convict God, for what would fall under God's continuing creation and preservation if not care for the continuities of life? Of course one can extend the free-will defense to include the point that in the gift of freedom God gives freedom such efficacy that its misuse results in the spreading of sin remorselessly through the structures that sustain human life. Freedom even in its misuse has access to those very structures. Ultimately, then, responsibility and bondage are not discrete themes to be kept on parallel tracks. Rather, I am responsible in my bondage, and humankind is responsible for its bondage.

Still the question troubles: Whence this falling and this fallenness? If sin is granted reality and continuity, does it not compete with God on fully equal terms? Presumably the point that sin is against and so not from God has been made by now. But is it not eternally against God, given its reality and its continuity? If sin comes from freedom, and yet freedom-become-sin is no work of God, is freedom perhaps not so much given by an ontologically superior God as given *for* God, so that it is some kind of eternal other as the theogonic myth supposes? If it is not so, then one must be able to distinguish freedom and sin temporally. Paul Ricoeur does recognize the temporal echo in the Adamic myth's emphasis on contingency:

> In telling of the fall as an event, springing up from an unknown source, it furnishes anthropology with a key concept: the *contingency* of that radical evil which the penitent is always on the point of calling his evil nature. Thereby the myth proclaims the purely "historical" character of that radical evil; it prevents it from being regarded as primordial evil. Sin may be "older" than sins, but innocence is still "older." [18]

What is at stake here is making clear the *negativity* of sin. Faith confesses the ontological ultimacy of God and exposes the nullity of sin's claims. The fall shows that sin has no fair title to the lordship it claims. It is a usurper, real and efficacious, but an intruder and pretender for all that. Were it not so, humankind would elect "God" and evil's bid to be good would become a matter for determination by popular mandate. Faith resists this not because it supposes evil to be unreal or inefficacious. Evil is neither, but it is parasitic. Moreover, the claim that God's creativity is *ex nihilo* is not merely retrospective. Here faith finds the ontological conditions required for God to act decisively with respect to sin within what we now know as time and beyond it as well.

Clearly it is a difficult task to think of the fall. Thus Ricoeur for all his phenomenological "distance" grumbles that "the myth puts in succession that which is contemporaneous and cannot not be contemporaneous," though he acknowledges that this "is how it attains its depth." Similarly Tillich assigns to "biblical literalism" any who cannot join him in the indentification of actualized creation and estranged existence. Several difficulties may be distinguished. We may prove too much, so that what begins with the first fall has a mechanistic efficacy that denies the responsibility of later individuals. Or we may wonder how the structure of life can serve the spread of sin so efficaciously without God being implicated or evacuated from the universe. Our present difficulties concern the matter of absolute origin itself: they are, as it were, ontological and epistemological. The ontological: How shall one conceive of an absolute beginning to sin? How may that be supposed to occur? Is God implicated? The epistemological: How shall one recover the vanishing moment? Or, if that is not to be expected, can one intelligently speak of the history of humankind as such that a "fall" could have occurred?

THE GOODNESS AND
INTEGRITY OF CREATION

What, then, may be said of the human creature apart from—before—sin? What do the sources of our faith lead us to say? We speak of the existence in relationship of one who in finite freedom is the object of God's special endowment, relationship, and intention.

The human creature is finite: limited and dependent. This one is not God. This one is of the earth and belongs to the earth. Despite occasional diversions, such as with Origen's notion of a premundane fall of souls into the earthly realm, Christian faith has insisted that the fact that humans are physical, earthly beings who belong to nature is due to the creative work of God, not to sin against God. Any discontinuity with nature in the coming-to-be of the human is within continuity—though there is reason to talk of such discontinuity. Given that continuity, if an evolutionary account of origins is convincing in general, that account will also have its contribution to make to Christian anthropology. It may be that the Lutheran traducianist position expresses the continuity more consistently and more emphatically than the Calvinist and Roman Catholic preference for the "creationist" view by which a special act of God is posited to account for the human soul. But no Christian theologian claims that our finite participation in the web of physical nature is in itself alien to our identity as God's creatures.[19]

Yet we must speak of discontinuity in such continuity. Even nontheistic writers have rightly observed that the human person stands out from nature, although such writers tend to speak of this as a "fall upward." [20] Christian faith welcomes the comment of the descriptive sciences on the differences that seem to mark the emergence of the human: walking upright, social organization, the use of tools, the development of language and of religion.[21] Teilhard de Chardin links the whole spectrum with "the threshold of reflection":

> In man, considered as a zoological group, everything is extended simultaneously—sexual attraction, with the laws of reproduction; the inclination to struggle for survival with the competitions it involves; the need for nourishment, with the accompanying taste for seizing and devouring; curiosity, to see, with its delight in investigation; the attraction of joining others to live in society. Each of these fibres traverses each one of us . . . and each one of them has its story to tell of the whole course of evolution—evolution of love, evolution of war, evolution of research, evolution of the social sense. But each one, just because it is evolutionary, undergoes a metamorphosis as it crosses the threshold of reflection.[22]

Chardin emphasizes that in the augmentation of consciousness there is the enrichment of new possibilities. The movement from external dependence to inner autonomy may be traced in the movement from stimuli to signals to symbols.[23]

If our physical nature confirms our finitude and dependence, does reason—that novel level of consciousness reached, as Chardin suggests, when some further calories were added to the anthropoid already mentally at the "boiling point"—promise freedom? At the least one might speak with Paul Tillich of reason as "the structure of freedom" in that in the movement from "environment" to "world" one reaches what Pannenberg has called "openness to the world." Here at least is qualitatively distinct possibility, if not yet freedom. Possibility waits on will to become realized freedom.

The distinctively human, then, is a dynamic reality. Any unique possession is but a presupposition for purpose, function, and becoming. One can make that case concerning human existence apart from the issue of origin. As Pannenberg writes: "Openness to the world must mean that man is completely directed into the open. He is always open further, beyond every experience and beyond every given situation."[24] But the dynamic character of human existence is rooted in God's cosmic creative work of origin, as in Genesis the Priestly writer incorporates creation into a great genealogical framework, the plan of *Toledoth* (Gen. 2:4).[25]

What is to be made of these dynamic elements of human existence? That which gives meaning to the functional forward thrust of human being is the reality of relationships. Moreover, this relatedness is not to be regarded as merely the raw material for a solitary advance into autonomy. Rather, freedom itself, the dynamic core of selfhood, is to be construed in relational terms. Thus Dietrich Bonhoeffer has caught the biblical sense of freedom well:

> In the language of the Bible, freedom is not something man has for himself but something he has for others. No man is free "as such," that is, in a vacuum, in the way that he may be musical, intelligent or blind as such. Freedom is not a quality of man, nor is it an ability, a capacity, a kind of being that somehow flares up in him. . . . Why? because freedom is not a quality which can be revealed—it is not a possession, a presence, an object, nor is it a form for existence—but a relationship and nothing else.[26]

Perhaps this is the point in the contrast Brunner stresses: that other creatures come to be *through* the word, but humankind comes to be only *in* the word, and thus summoned to responsibility.[27] Clearly something was meant to come from the human: The divine blessing yields imperatives: "Be fruitful . . . multiply . . . fill the earth . . . subdue it . . . have dominion." Something is supposed to happen in response to God who visits and holds converse with the human creature (Ps. 8:4).

We have been speaking of God's work of creation, seeking to disassociate that work from the evil associated with the fall. It is God's verdict that creation is good. What would good mean in this dynamic context? Westermann writes:

> "Good" in this context does not mean some sort of objective judgement, a judgement given according to already fixed and objective standards. It is rather this: it is good or suited for the purpose for which it is being prepared; it corresponds to its goal. But for what or for whom can creation be good? . . . The Creation story with its goal as the rest on the seventh day shows that Creation introduces a self-contained history—history in the broadest sense that can be given to the word—a history of the cosmos and in the midst of it a history of the human race which, as it has grown out of God's Creation, will also have a goal, which has been set for it by God. Looking then at the history both of the cosmos and of mankind, "All is very good."[28]

That, then, is the context for speaking of the goodness of the human creature. This creature can respond to the word heard; this creature is "able not to sin." Many voices in the tradition have not stopped with this strong but simple statement, but have gone on to speak of an "original righteousness" by which Adam is the more emphatically separated from us as each excellence is added. Ambrose is a representative of the strong theme in the fathers in speaking of Adam's life before the fall as "heavenly," "most blessed," and "like the angels." [29]

For Thomas Aquinas the original *rectitudo* entailed that a right relationship to God was formed on the basis of a person's inner harmony. Perhaps the reformers placed the emphasis on the relationship rather than on the internal psychological harmony, but the Apology resists too simple a distinction at this point:

> But what is righteousness? Here the scholastics quibble about philosophical questions and do not explain what original righteousness is. In the Scriptures righteousness contains not merely the second table of the Decalogue, but also the first, commanding fear of God, faith and love toward him. So original righteousness was intended to involve not only a balanced physical constitution, but these gifts as well: a surer knowledge of God, fear of God, trust in God, or at least the inclination and power to do these things.[30]

Indeed, the German variant can claim for Adam "perfect health and, in all respects, pure blood, unimpaired powers of the body."

Difficulties abound. Descriptive claims are here made which fly in the face of contemporary scientific opinion concerning the earliest stages of human life. Prescriptive claims are so extravagant that writers so dissimilar as Schleiermacher and Kierkegaard must agree that a "fall" for such beings becomes inconceivable.[31] One may respond to that difficulty by collapsing the distinction between creation and fall either in an evolutionary (Schleiermacher) perspective or an existentialist (Kierkegaard) perspective.

But are not those alternatives chosen too readily? For the reasons identified in the first section of this chapter, Christian faith has much at stake in the assertion of the ontological and temporal priority of God's good creative work in the coming-to-be of the human. Let us follow the suggestion implicit in the stress on the dynamic and functional character of the human creature. This will prevent us from supposing that the human creature was perfect in the sense of being complete. With Adam, God's adventure with humankind was not perfected, but begun and well begun.

Unfallen humanity was not perfect, then. Perhaps the first step in constructing a rehabilitated notion of the state of integrity is to remove the descriptive extravagances, which tend to draw attention away from what matters: the relationship to God. While still drawn to the idealistic notion of "complete consciousness," C. S. Lewis points the way:

> Judged by his artefacts, or perhaps even by his language, this blessed creature

was, no doubt, a savage. All that experience and practice can teach he had still to learn. We do not know how many of these creatures God made, nor how long they continued in the Paradisal state. But sooner or later they fell.[32]

Such a correction of the description is not a product of intimidation by the scientific community. Attention to our own story suggests no evidence of an exceptionally developed original knowledge or culture. These creatures could name animals and appreciate one another. They may be supposed to have had a kind of confidence and mutual esteem—"naked and not ashamed," despite the fact that otherwise nakedness suggests the loss of human and social dignity. They were, in Westermann's word, "adequate" for that to which they were called.[33]

But what of the relationship to the One who calls prescriptively? The distinction between creation and fall requires that we begin with a negative determination: as created the human is not fallen. Adam is indeed innocent. But surely this relationship is not perfected either. In such a case God's call would be merely an echo in Eden. It seems better to speak of a kind of childlike innocence which provides the necessary presupposition for will. Thus Augustine writes:

> No one is so foolish as to call an infant foolish, though it would be even more absurd to call it wise. An infant can be called neither foolish nor wise though it is already a human being. So it appears that human nature receives an intermediate condition which cannot be rightly called either folly or wisdom. . . . There is a transitional state between sleeping and waking as between folly and wisdom. But there is this difference. In the former case there is no intervention of will; in the latter the transition never takes place except by the action of the will. That is why the consequence is just retribution.[34]

Thus it seems important to draw the notion of original righteousness toward the theme of integrity rather than that of perfection. Integrity is to be understood in dynamic and relational terms. In this creature of God there is together what is needed for what God seeks with this being. Adam is able not to sin. But will becomes real through alternatives, and clearly Adam is also able to sin. What does this require regarding the creature's relationship to God, not as goal but as given? That depends on how we conceive the relationship between will and reason. John Hick draws the two close together:

> In creating finite persons to love and be loved by Him God must endow them with a certain relative autonomy over against Himself. But how can a finite creature, dependent upon the infinite Creator for its very existence and for every power and quality of its being, possess any significant autonomy in relation to that Creator? The only way we can conceive is that suggested by our actual situation. God must set man at a distance from Himself, from which he can then voluntarily come to God. But how can anything be set at a distance from One

who is infinite and omnipresent? Clearly spatial distance means nothing in this case. The kind of distance between God and man that would make room for a degree of human autonomy is epistemic distance. In other words, the reality and presence of God must not be borne in upon man in the coercive way in which their natural environment forces itself upon their attention. The world must be to men, to some extent at least, etsi deus non daretur, "as if there were no God." God must be a hidden deity, veiled by his creation. He must be knowable, but only by a mode of knowledge that involves free response on man's part, this response consisting in an uncompelled interpretive activity whereby we experience the world as mediating the divine presence.[35]

In some ways this is an attractive speculation, though one may wonder whether Hick underestimates the present experience of conscious defiance and extrapolates too much from our experience of sin as weakness. Different Christian anthropological emphasis will yield parallel differences in what it takes to have sin as a real possibility.

We have studiously avoided introducing the concept of the creation of humankind in the image of God. We have wanted to stay closer to the particulars, before they come to be assembled in such a concept. But the biblical witness and the massive historical tradition at this point cry out for some attention which may provide an occasion to collect and summarize the discussion in this section.

In identifying the "image" the sources of our faith hardly speak with a single voice. The notions emerging from the tradition seem to be strict alternatives, yet their negations may not be strictly tied to their affirmations. That is, without being hopelessly eclectic, it seems possible and desirable to fashion a formulation which encompasses most of the traditional themes—albeit in a different conceptual environment. Our lead sentence for this chapter speaks of the human creature as the object of God's special endowment, relationship, and intention. The "image of God" (*imago dei*) concept draws on the relational and functional emphases already offered in this section in order to speak of endowment in and for relationship as serving the divine intention.

Emil Brunner argues that to speak of the image of God in the human person is to speak at once of a gift and a task, and it may be helpful to follow Brunner in speaking of the gift as formal and the task as material. Such a distinction permits us to accommodate both the Old Testament sense for the human universality of the image (*tselem* and *demuth*) and the New Testament sense for the Christian specificity of the image (as Rom. 8:29). Unfruitful efforts to distinguish between image and likeness should not obscure a valid distinction by which each term refers distinctively to the full unified person.[36] The Western church has tended to stress the divine endowment, and the East the divine intention. The notion of relationship, set in a dynamic, functional context, permits us to hold the two emphases together. The relationship is both gift and task. What is needed for the task is given, given for the task.

What, then, is this given in the human person? Whatever we say at this point dogmatically must not put asunder the almost complete consensus of biblical scholars concerning the unity of the human person.[37] Such putting asunder of the consensus and, more important, of the person has tended to deny any place for the physical. Thus the medieval church tended to identify the *imago* (*tselem*) with human reason to which the supernatural likeness of the *similitudo* (*demuth*) had been added. Or one may hear the same tendency in Tillich's linking human *logos* with divine Logos.[38] But Gerhard von Rad helpfully responds that if one must accept the physical versus spiritual set of alternatives as the terms for the discussion, "we should have to decide in favour of a predominantly physical likeness," although he declines to speculate on God's form or corporeality.[39] Moreover, one's bodiliness may be said to be the primary vehicle through which one responds to the divine call to relate to other creatures as God's representative. As surely as our bodies bear the traffic of our becoming through and in each other, so surely does a wholly non-physical image concept contribute to an individualistic piety.

In turn, mind may be understood as the custodian of possibility, of planning by which direction is given to the human person's physically anchored stewardship. So Irenaeus alternately identifies reason and body as the image.[40] Neither body nor mind moves from given to goal effectively without the agency of will. We stress again that in speaking of "body," "mind," and "will," we distinguish conceptually what is always together existentially, although in particular instances there will be variety in the manifestation of this unity.

We are suggesting that an adequate understanding of the *imago dei* concept requires incorporation of both the Roman Catholic anthropological emphasis and the Reformation theological emphasis. With the former we need to speak of a togetherness—even a balance—of the constituent elements in the human person, but without deferring the God-relationship to a separate superadded gift. With the latter we need to stress the relationship to God, but ward off any spiritualizing tendency to deny anthropological, even psychological, participation in this relationship.[41] It seems important not to freeze this understanding in some momentarily fashionable anthropology. Perhaps Augustine's thought recognizes this dialectic, even if he did not offer a unified synthesizing formulation. On the one hand, Augustine sought for a trinity immanent in the human individual, of self-memory, self-knowledge, and self-love; on the other hand, he prayed: "Thou hast made us for Thyself and our hearts are restless until they find their rest in Thee."[42]

The endowment of which the *imago* concept speaks is, then, precisely the relationship to God. As Westermann remarks: "The creation of man in God's image is directed to something happening between God and man. The Creator created a creature that corresponds to him, to whom he can speak, and who can hear him."[43] The Eastern church has tended to cast this dynamic relationship in mystical terms. One is human only as one "participates" in God. Indeed, that is already the human's particular privilege as created in God's image. But one is to *grow* toward the divine likeness. The Western church draws back from the idea of divinization, responding to the fact that of the two creation stories the *imago dei* concept is to be found in P with its emphasis on divine transcendence. Following this line, one will preserve the distinction in the relationship and stress that as made in the divine image the human creature is *for* God.

The one made in God's image acts for God toward the world; "have dominion" immediately follows "let us make." This one acts for God toward the human other as well: "In the image of God created he them, male and female he created them." If the sexual relationship symbolizes the relatedness which is the goal for humankind—both a parable and an earnest of the relation of the church to God in Christ—it is also a primordial gift in which the self is created in relationship. As such it does mirror the God who is eternally in relationship within God and who creates and makes covenant in order to be in relationship with that which as free is fully other than God's self. The one made in God's image is made for God; gift and goal are to serve God's purpose, ultimately to share and reflect the divine glory (Rom. 5:2; 1 Pet. 5:4), to bring God delight. The purpose clauses continue to carry the note of contingency needed for the free-will defense. If one is to fault God for the human freedom by which sin springs up, one must deny God love for the creature—a love meant to be a joy to both parties in the relationship.[44]

Our discussion of the distinction between image as formal endowment and material goal has itself been quite formal, especially with respect to that goal. May something more be said of that? One may at least suggest that the indicative and the imperative are to be held together. As surely as God's creation praises God by being what it is made to be—witness Job's hymn of praise sung by the creatures and the psalmist's reference to the praise rendered by sun and moon and the shining stars—so must the human goal be rooted in the human given. One has dominion over the earth only by listening to, even obeying, the earth of which one is, after all, a part.[45] Perhaps, too, one seeks so to relate to other creatures as to serve and prosper what is in them. So act, one might say, as to maximize the other's harmonious participation in the structures of creation.[46] These structures are corruptible in the sense that they may also carry the efficacy of sin. Similarly, one's response to God is rooted in what God is, the being truly worthy of worship, but sin may reject God precisely for what God is.

Our discussion of the *imago* has spoken only of creation and not of fall.

How much shall we claim for creation apart from and before the fall? Again we seek to hold together the formal and the material. There is given here what is needed to move toward the goal. There is here such endowment in relationship as is needed to move toward the destiny God has intended. That much must be claimed, though no more, if Adam was created good but not perfect. Was that movement toward destiny also begun? Was there a focusing of endowment in will to respond to the divine call? To speak of that would be to speak of human will, not of divine will, to speak of creaturely life, not of divine creating. Our distinction between creation and fall does not require such a claim, although it permits it.

We said that we would seek to show how the distinction between creation and fall could be stated intelligibly for the contemporary sensibility without sacrificing the concerns of the tradition. Our immediate task has been to respond to questions we termed ontological: to suggest a conception of the human person such that an absolute beginning to sin, a "fall," is conceivable. The issue really is the intelligibility of our link with that creature of God who originates sin absolutely. We can imagine creatures who do not sin, but they have no link with us, for they cannot sin, and we, it seems, cannot not sin. Can we see ourselves linked with a creature in whom sin makes a contingent but absolute start? The issue here has not been sin's continuance. But can we, who continue to sin, identify with one in whom sin begins absolutely? By definition the point of identification cannot be that sin *continues* in this one, for it is sin's *start* of which we are asking. We have spoken here of what is not (yet) sin, arguing that even in this respect we can somehow identify with this one, for even we are not simply sin. Moreover, this creature is such that sin can start with this one. Such a start of sin is a fall, though we are eager to insist that the *degree* of the fall is reduced for one for whom perfection represents only a goal and not a given.

THE POSSIBILITY
AND ACTUALITY OF SIN

What is required if the fall is to be into that very condition of sin in which we can recognize our bondage? What cannot be required is that the fall is itself bound to happen before it happens. Were that the case, we would no longer be speaking of a start of sin, but of how sin presupposes itself endlessly. That surely would reflect against God's good and efficacious work in creation.

If sin roots in freedom, it cannot be finally explained. This is true if the task of explanation is to identify conditioning factors, causal connections, and the accumulation of ingredients out of which the act naturally emerges. Such an understanding may serve us fairly well in many circumstances—as in the chemistry laboratory—but it will fail before the origin of sin. The Adamic myth, with its emphasis on human responsibility, pleads that all such explanatory talk regarding the origin of sin is necessary but not sufficient. Such talk is relevant. It does explain *that* and *how* sin is *possible.* Yet finally one must say that the actual fall occurs in freedom. The *start* of sin is that emphatic. But the theologians of the church have been restless with this idea.

Some would find the cause of sin to reside in the imperfection which necessarily characterizes a creature made for a freely chosen relationship with God. Irenaeus seems to stop just short of saying this:

> For it was necessary, that at first, that nature should be exhibited; then, after that, that what was mortal should be conquered and swallowed up by immortality, and the corruptible by incorruptibility, and that man should be made after the image and likeness of God, having received the knowledge of good and evil. (*Against Heresies*, iv,38,4)

Much depends on whether one takes "mortality" and "the receiving of the knowledge of good and evil" as consistent with the human creature's status as good though not perfect. But it is clear that Irenaeus has been the inspiration to others who more resolutely draw the cause of sin back into the immaturity of humankind. This may be done in various ways. One may speak of one's abiding immaturity, or traces of it, as representing that which impedes intended human development, that is, of immaturity as itself sin. Thus Williams writes of the "arrested development of the herd instinct" and Schleiermacher of the "head-start" by which the sensuous consciousness hinders the development of the God-consciousness.[47] In this handling of the immaturity theme the guilty component is usually regarded as human physicality. Thus Clement of Alexandria writes:

> The first man, when in Paradise, sported free, because he was the child of God; but when he succumbed to pleasure (for the serpent allegorically signifies pleasure crawling on its belly, earthly wickedness nourished for fuel to the flames), was as a child seduced by lusts, and grew old in disobedience by disobeying his Father, dishonoured God. Such was the influence of pleasure, man, that had been free by reason of simplicity, was found fettered to sin. (*Protrept.*, xi)

Or, more broadly and more starkly, one may identify human immaturity as sin by speaking of the inevitability of both positive and negative factors in evolution, appealing to entropy and the proclivity of the human person to settle for simple syntheses against the evolutionary call to complexity.[48] Perhaps one may find something here that is analogous to the manifestation of the sin of weakness.

On the other hand, one may more brazenly identify human incompleteness with human immaturity. To move ahead from this "given" is to "fall."[49] All that is needed is to regard sin as that which emerges naturally from the unstable synthesis. Development becomes defiance. What, after all, is more natural than the acquisition of knowledge? Does the prohibition concerning the tree of knowledge invite, perhaps even require, this interpretation by which one can remain innocent only by remaining ignorant? How could such an interpretation be aligned with other biblical materials, as, for example, the emphasis in the Wisdom literature on the human person "summoned and wooed by the mystery of the world itself and responding to that wooing with an intellectual love"?[50]

Claus Westermann gives an alternative interpretation of the prohibition which does not violate the boundaries of the "good, not perfect" theme. Of the temptation to be like God, he writes:

> This is a temptation not because the drive towards knowledge, towards all-embracing knowledge, was of itself opposed to God; it is not, because man is created with it. But the possibility is there of a disturbance and a destruction of the proper relationship between God and man, when man in his drive after knowledge oversteps or tries to overstep his limits.[51]

To grow in knowledge is indeed God's intention for the human creature, but that is to occur in relationship with God. The growth intended is for a self who is in its development to come to trust God the more fully. Bonhoeffer has caught well this intended combination of dependence and development:

> In the prohibition Adam is addressed in his freedom and in his creatureliness, and by the prohibition his being is confirmed in its kind. . . . *Man's limit is in the middle of his existence*, not on the edge. The limit which we look for on the edge is the limit of his condition, of his technology, of his possibilities. The limit in the middle is the limit of his reality, of his true existence. Adam knows that. . . . The limit is grace because it is the basis of creatureliness and freedom; the limit is the middle. . . . The prohibition of paradise is *grace* of the Creator towards the creature. God tempts no man.[52]

To resist identifying the cause of sin as human immaturity in either of these senses is not to deny the relevance of such immaturity for the understanding of the origin of sin. To reject a physicalist understanding of sin is not to opt for a disembodied will, as most dramatically represented by Origen's speculation concerning a premundane fall of souls.[53] As immature we are able to sin—formally. But more than that, the very stuff through which sin comes to be draws on the volatile mixture underlying the immature self. That which is given in creation is not merely the abstract possibility of sin, but sin's real potential as well. But while in our created givenness we must, in Kierkegaard's image, be dizzy, that is not yet to fall.

What of the fact that the given is there only as given toward a goal? As immature the human person is called to become. Indeed, this being has the peculiarity that only by becoming can it continue to be. In speaking of the gift of freedom, we recognize again that sin is more than abstract possibility; rather, the possibility attaches itself to the dynamism that centers the person. Thus Kierkegaard speaks of the dreadful sense of "being able" which the prohibition awakens:

> What it is he is able to do, of that he has no conception; to suppose that he had some conception is to presuppose, as commonly is done, what came later, the distinction between good and evil. There is only the possibility of being able, as a higher form of ignorance, as a heightened expression of dread.[54]

Similarly, the Genesis story underlines the momentousness of freedom with the sense of consequence: "Thou shalt surely die."

Yet this development is still dread, not sin. It resides in the sphere of creation, not the fall. To move from "being able" to the act itself is not in principle sin. Thus to stress that sinning will be more than the "given," more than the body (sin does not lie in the instincts), and more than the mind (sin does not lie in the acquisition of knowledge) is not to suggest that freedom in its very mutability must sin. Perhaps in this "more" there is a kind of *ex nihilo* quality to will, but that does not entail holding that the nonderivable choice must be to sin. Thus Christians reject the privation view in which the cause of freedom's incompleteness issuing in sin is sought precisely in the *nihil* out of which the human person is created. That which starts—from nothing even—need not be sin. But in rejecting such an easy explanation, they deny themselves as well the confidence which would seem to follow for the future. To be able to sin is not yet to sin. But in the more that is needed lies the fuller possibility of ultimate defiance.

The various forms of the sin/immaturity correlation all amount to placing sin within the divine creative work and thus either compromise the goodness of God or the radicality of sin—and commonly do both. The other non-Adamic option has been to move toward some kind of eternal dualism. This option is incompatible with Christian faith. The most vigorous proponents of dualism within Christianity have recognized this and proceeded to a counterproposal: an angel created good but fallen in freedom does not in principle violate the monotheistic character of the faith. Indeed, one might argue that this notion simply advances the free-will defense to its ultimate level. In this instance there is no mitigating tempter whom the fallen can cite as at least an accessory before the fact.

Yet the unrestrained development of this dualistic theme compromises the responsibility of the human creature for sin. Some compromise may indeed be required of faith. The figure of Satan speaks powerfully of such realities as the clarity (Kierkegaard), the ineluctability (Ricoeur), and the perversity (Kant) of the evil will. But one still struggles to retain the reality of human responsibility.

The argument of this chapter has been that Christian faith, following the distinction between creation, the good work from God's hand, and sin, that which is against God, locates the absolute origin of sin in a fall from created goodness. Yet ironically this third section in which the actual agency of the fall formed our topic has been the briefest part of the chapter. Perhaps that must be so, if we speak of a "free fall." True origin by hypothesis is the nonderivable, and Kierkegaard applies the point to the origin of sin:

> That human nature must be such that it makes sin possible, is, psychologically speaking, perfectly true; but to want to let this possibility of sin become its reality is shocking to ethics and sounds to dogmatics like blasphemy; for freedom is never possible; as soon as it is, it is actual. . . .[55]

"Sin presupposes itself" when we say glibly that a good Adam fell into sin because of pride, of wanting to be like God. Just when we may think we are halfway to an explanation, we discover we have slipped in an appeal to sin in speaking of the path to sin.

Have we by some sleight of hand banished what we earlier called the epistemological question? Need we no longer seek to recover the moment of the fall in our store of the memory of the race? If freedom is as we have described it, perhaps the act of the fall itself does not itself reside somewhere to be unearthed with the other relics in a cave. It is not only that despite the scientific consensus that humankind roots in a single stem (monophyletism), the scale on which science works requires one to say with Chardin that "man came silently into the world" and also fell as silently.[56] In order to have a start, sin must come from the center of the person, and that defies the most avid paleontologist. But what of the effects? While our appeal to the fall is by way of consistency with the tradition and coherence with the requirements of the doctrine of creation, we accept the point that one must be able to speak intelligibly of the history of humankind as being such that the "fall" could have occurred. We have tried to show that a creature with whom we sense some linkage apart from sin could bring sin to start. That start becomes fully *the* fall as sin proves itself to continue in those after Adam. How certainly, how massively, how at all does sin continue? It is to those questions we now must turn.

NOTES

1. Denzinger, 102; Augsburg Confession, Article II, *BC* 29.

2. Paul Ricoeur, *The Symbolism of Evil*, trans. Emerson Buchanan (Boston: Beacon Press, 1967), pp. 171–74.

3. Charles Hartshorne and William L. Reese, eds., *Philosophers Speak of God* (Chicago: University of Chicago Press, 1953), p. 7.

4. Frances Young, "Insight or Incoherence? The Greek Fathers on God and Evil," *JEH* 24 (1973): 113–26.

5. Cf. Deut. 32:39; 1 Sam. 2:6; Amos 3:6; and Job 2:10.

6. Denzinger, 200.

7. See Karl Heim, *Jesus the Lord*, trans. D. H. van Daalen (Edinburgh: Oliver & Boyd, 1959), pp. 99–102. Cf. a "softer" tension in Walther Eichrodt's *Theology of the Old Testament*, trans. J. A. Baker, 2 vols. (Philadelphia: Westminster Press, 1961–67), 2:406, where "two essential statements" are: "Evil does not come from God, and it is subject to God's power."

8. Langdon Gilkey, *Reaping the Whirlwind: A Christian Interpretation of History* (New York: Seabury Press, 1976), p. 256.

9. As Martin J. Heinecken, *Christian Teachings* (Philadelphia: Fortress Press, 1967), p. 88.

10. Søren Kierkegaard, *The Concept of Dread*, trans. Walter Lowrie (Princeton: Princeton University Press, 1944), chap. 1.

11. Heinrich Ott, *Theology and Preaching*, trans. Harold Knight (Philadelphia: Westminster Press, 1965), p. 104.

12. Paul Tillich, *Systematic Theology*, 3 vols. (Chicago: University of Chicago Press, 1951–63), 2:38.

13. N. P. Williams, *The Ideas of the Fall and of Original Sin* (New York and London: Longmans, Green & Co., 1927), chap. 2. Cf. J. Daniélou, *The Theology of Jewish Christianity*, trans. J. A. Baker (Chicago: Henry Regnery, Co.; London: Darton, Longman & Todd, 1964).

14. In his *A History of the Christian Church* (New York: Charles Scribner's Sons, 1959), p. 39, Williston Walker suggests that since it was hard for ex-pagans to deny the existence of the old gods, those gods persisted for them as demons. On the struggle with dualistic gnosticism, see R. M. Grant, *Gnosticism and Early Christianity*, 2d ed. (New York: Columbia University Press, 1966), pp. 174–75. Grant sums up the rejection of gnosticism (against Harnack's thesis that the gnostics were the first Christian theologians) in these terms: "The triumph of orthodoxy meant the triumph of the created world over the aeons, of collective experience over individual freedom, of history over the freely creative imagination, of objectivity over subjectivity. Something was lost. . . . Yet something was certainly gained. The rule of God over history and nature could be asserted by the Church as by no Gnostic group. The goodness, actual and potential, of the creation and of human existence could be affirmed. The reality and meaningfulness of historical events could be proclaimed. In other words, orthodox Christians could hold, as Gnostics could not, that this world is neither heaven nor hell."

15. The Kittel article on *diabolos* makes this clear (*Theological Dictionary of the Bible*, ed. Gerhard Kittel, trans. G. W. Bromiley [Grand Rapids: Wm. B. Eerdmans,

1964]). Gerhard von Rad, *Wisdom in Israel*, trans. James D. Martin (Nashville: Abingdon Press, 1972), p. 305, argues that no dualism is to be found, even in Job, until the appearance of the Wisdom of Solomon.

16. For Reformation writers the favored formulation is a conjunctive one in which sin is caused by "the will of the devil and of all ungodly men" (Augsburg Confession, Art. XIX, *BC* 41), though subjection to the devil may be spoken of in connection with the *consequences* of sin (as in the Smalcald Articles, I, 1). More recent writers inclining toward dualism are Edwin Lewis, *The Creator and the Adversary* (New York: Abingdon-Cokesbury, 1948); and Kenneth Cauthen, *Science, Secularization, and God* (Nashville: Abingdon Press, 1969). On the role of nature as a "third" in the relationship between God and humankind, see Gordon Kaufman, *Systematic Theology: A Historicist Perspective* (New York: Charles Scribner's Sons, 1968), p. 355.

17. Immanuel Kant, *Religion within the Limits of Reason Alone*, trans. Theodore M. Greene and Hoyt H. Hudson (New York: Harper & Row, 1960), p.21.

18. Ricoeur, *Symbolism of Evil*, p. 251. (Emphasis his.)

19. For a Lutheran statement of the traducianist view, see Heinrich Schmid, *The Doctrinal Theology of the Evangelical Lutheran Church*, ed., trans. Charles A. Hay and Henry E. Jacobs (Minneapolis: Augsburg Publishing House, 1875), pp. 166, 248. For a Calvinist statement of the creationist position, see G. C. Berkouwer, *Man: The Image of God*, trans. Dirk W. Jellema (Grand Rapids: Wm. B. Eerdmans, 1962), pp. 279–309.

20. Erich Fromm, *Man for Himself* (New York: Holt, Rinehart & Winston, 1947), pp. 47ff.

21. See, e.g., C. Loring Brace and Ashley Montagu, *Human Evolution: An Introduction to Biological Anthropology*, 2d. ed. (New York: Macmillan Co., 1977).

22. Pierre Teilhard de Chardin, *The Phenomenon of Man*, trans. Bernard Wall (New York: Harper & Row, 1959), p. 179.

23. John B. Cobb, Jr., *The Structure of Christian Existence* (Philadelphia: Westminster Press, 1967), pp. 36–40.

24. Wolfhart Pannenberg, *What Is Man?* trans. Duane A. Priebe (Philadelphia: Fortress Press, 1970), pp. 3–8. Tillich, *Systematic Theology*, 1:71–105.

25. Gerhard von Rad, *Old Testament Theology*, trans. D. M. G. Stalker, 2 vols. (New York: Harper & Row, 1962–65), 1:139. It is not surprising that the Yahwist's account is not as clear at this point if Humbert is right in finding a struggle here between a creation myth (2:4b–7, 9a, 18–24; 3:20–21, 23; and 4:1) and a paradise and fall myth (2:8, 9b, 16–17, 25; 3:1–19, 22, 24).

26. Dietrich Bonhoeffer, *Creation and Fall*, trans. John C. Fletcher (New York: Macmillan Co.; London: SCM Press, 1959), p. 37.

27. Emil Brunner, *Man in Revolt*, trans. Olive Wyon (Philadelphia: Westminster Press, 1947), pp. 96–99.

28. Claus Westermann, *Creation*, trans. John J. Scullion (Philadelphia: Fortress Press, 1974), p. 61.

29. See Ambrose's sermons on the Psalms, *PL* 15:1422.

30. Apology of the Augsburg Confession, Article II, 15–17, in *BC* 102.

31. Friedrich Schleiermacher, *The Christian Faith*, trans. and ed. H. R. Mackintosh

and J. S. Stewart (New York: Harper & Row, Harper Torchbooks, 1963), par. 72. Kierkegaard, *The Concept of Dread*, chap. 1.

32. C. S. Lewis, *The Problem of Pain* (New York: Macmillan Co., 1948), p. 65.

33. Westermann, *Creation*, p. 72.

34. Augustine, *On Free Will*, iii, 71, 73; translated by John H. S. Burleigh (*Augustine: Earlier Writings*, LCC [Philadelphia: Westminster Press, 1953]).

35. John Hick, *Evil and the God of Love* (New York: Harper & Row; London: Macmillan & Co., 1966), p. 317.

36. Brunner, *Man in Revolt*, p. 98. See David Cairns, *The Image of God in Man* (London: SCM Press, 1953). It is this distinction Barth employs in drawing on the ambiguity of the German *Bestimmung* to speak of the image as "determination" and as "destiny."

37. See Gerhard von Rad, *Genesis*, trans. John Marks (Philadelphia: Westminster Press, 1961), p. 58; and W. D. Davies, *Paul and Rabbinic Judaism* (London: SPCK, 1948), p. 54.

38. Tillich, *Systematic Theology*, 1:156–59.

39. Gerhard von Rad, "The Divine Likeness in the Old Testament," in *Theological Dictionary of the Bible*, 2:391.

40. Cairns, *Image of God in Man*, p. 76.

41. Robert C. Schultz, "Original Sin: Accident or Substance: The Paradoxical Significance of F.C.I., 53–62 in Historical Context," in *Discord, Dialogue, and Concord*, ed. Lewis W. Spitz and Wenzel Lohff (Philadelphia: Fortress Press, 1977), pp. 38–57, seems to stress the distinction: "Luther could describe both sin and salvation in terms of people's relationship to God without needing to describe the interior structure of human personality" (p. 44).

42. For the grounding of this Augustinian theme, see *On the Trinity*, xiv,8.

43. Westermann, *Creation*, p. 56.

44. See Karl Barth, *Church Dogmatics*, 5 vols. in 14 (Edinburgh: T. & T. Clark, 1936–77), 3/1. Cf. John Meyendorff, *Byzantine Theology: Historical Trends and Doctrinal Themes* (New York: Fordham University Press, 1974), pp. 139ff.

45. H. Paul Santmire, *Brother Earth* (Toronto: Thomas Nelson, 1970).

46. Tillich, *Systematic Theology*, 1:156–59.

47. N. P. Williams, *The Ideas of the Fall and of Original Sin* (New York and London: Longmans, Green & Co., 1927), pp. 477–88; Schleiermacher, *The Christian Faith*, pars. 67, 68.

48. F. R. Tennant, *The Concept of Sin* (Cambridge: At the University Press, 1912), p. 122; Juan Luis Segundo, *Evolution and Guilt* (Maryknoll, N. Y.: Orbis Books, 1974), p. 129.

49. Reinhold Niebuhr's notion of the instability of the human synthesis of the finite and the infinite (*The Nature and Destiny of Man*, 2 vols. [New York: Charles Scribner's Sons, 1941–43]), Paul Ricoeur's finding that synthesis to constitute a "fault" cutting across the human terrain (*Fallible Man*, trans. Charles Kegley [Chicago: Henry Regnery Co., 1965]), and Ernst Becker's rooting evil in the temptation to Titanism (*The Denial of Death* [New York: Macmillan Co., 1973]) all permit such an interpretation.

50. Gerhard Von Rad, *Wisdom in Israel*, trans. J. D. Martin (Nashville: Abingdon Press, 1972), p. 309.

51. Westermann, *Creation*, p. 93; cf. p. 106.

52. Bonhoeffer, *Creation and Fall*, pp. 52–53 (emphasis his). Cf. von Rad, *Old Testament Theology*, 1:155, on the knowledge of all things suggesting the mastery of all things.

53. Origen, *On First Principles*, I, v, vi, vii; II, viii, 3; III, v, 4.

54. Kierkegaard, *Concept of Dread*, p. 40.

55. Ibid., p. 20.

56. Teilhard de Chardin, *Phenomenon of Man*, p. 185.

3

The Effect of Sin

The effect of sin is to work against the Creator within creation. Sin works against the Creator by misappropriating the endowment, distorting the relationship, and frustrating the intention, though the person still remains the creature of God. Sin works within creation by spreading inexorably through the structure of reality represented by the responsible self in tragic relationship.

SINNER AND CREATURE

When we spoke in Chapter 1 of the "whither" of sin, we briefly described a "continuity" in sin which seems to make acts of sin inevitable. We now return to address that topic in the light of Chapter 2's discussion of creation and fall. Here we are asking two questions. First, What does sin effect in the one who is God's special creature? Here the question is not Chapter 1's more abstract question regarding any and all effects, but rather that of what effects previous sin has on the individual at any present state of existence. And second, How do such effects of past sins come to bear on the present?

We are pursuing these questions in the light of the distinction between creation and fall, following our contention in Chapter 2 that the fall must not be identified with creation logically or even temporally. Yet these questions must be faced also by those who grant no temporal distinction between creation and fall. All Christian theologians make the logical or theological distinction and so accept the terms of our first question. This question presses, since no Christian theologian asserts that the individual starts from scratch, with respect to sin or otherwise. What then, in the individual's legacy, derives from God's creativity and what from sin? Similarly, our second question of the "how" of the continuity of effect does not depend on arguing for the notion of an absolute beginning for sin. Even if one does not wish to speak of original sin "originating" somewhere, some*time*, it is clear that it is *originated*, though the difference in the degree of continuity granted indicates that there is no clear consensus about how and whether to speak of "sin" in this human connectedness. In any case, what we seek to understand is how the sin that is before me comes to yield so surely the sin that is in me.

As Christian faith probes these questions, it is aware of others as well, touching the "God and self" structure that underlies Christian experience and understanding. If faith must ask "*What* does the sin of one creature create in others?" must we not wonder if a fulsome answer will usurp God's role in the coming-to-be of these creatures? We speak to that in the first section. Perhaps some distinction can still be managed in what is given, but what of the giv*ing*? If faith asks *how* the continuity in sin is constituted, must we not wonder whether God will be implicated in the answer? Of course these questions are such that the answers we intend to give seem to cancel each other out. Can God still be significantly Creator for one thoroughly in sin without assigning to God responsibility for the sin itself? In addressing both questions we remain concerned to show that the responsibility of the individual is not lost. Here the threat is not only from God. Perhaps God can somehow show omnipotence precisely by creating freedom.[1] But will not sin's power to originate effects in and then through the individual proportionately reduce that individual's responsibility for sin?

We begin with the reflection of the church. It is clear that the biblical witness claims that sin is efficacious. In the Genesis material one may see how, in Ricoeur's words, sin "pervades all the registers of human life"—naming, communication, the relationship to nature, procreation, death.[2] The Pauline litany of effects in Romans 1 may lie behind the pondering of the principle of connection in Romans 5. It seems best to begin with the church's very considerable and very developed reflection and let the material lead us back to and through the biblical understanding, and then on to the interpretation of our contemporary experience.

Rhythms may be detected in the historical material. An overarching issue deals with the degree of gravity assigned to the ongoing consequences of sin. Frederick Tennent says that the earliest patristic thought on this subject falls far short of Augustine's dark appraisal of the human condition. His argument is helped because it is set in terms of the role of "absolute origin," of the effects of Adam's sin on his descendants. While we accept that setting, we should not ignore the negative appraisals which do not appeal to an absolutely original fall as cause. In any case, Tennant surveys the material:

> Polycarp speaks of the universality of sin, but not of the cause thereof. Ignatius, after S. John, conceives of the world as lying in wickedness, in the might of Satan and under the rule of death, or in a state of *phthora*, but this state is not ascribed to the fall of mankind in its first parent. . . . Justin speaks strongly of the universality of sin, and of our need of grace; and he alludes to an evil inclination which is in the nature of every man. These things, however, are not deduced from, or connected with, the Fall.[3]

Putting the issue in these terms, linking "original sin originating" and "original sin originated" so strictly, Tennant may be right in stressing the gap between Augustine and the earlier fathers. It does seem that the corruption traced to Adam was at first largely limited to our mortality. Moreover, even leaving aside the issue of the link with the absolute origin, the earliest fathers do not anticipate Augustine's pessimism.

Jaroslav Pelikan stresses the effects of the context: the church provided what is needed in the polemical situation. What was needed?

> While both responsibility and inevitability had been prominent in the classical understanding of man, [it was] chiefly this sense of fate and necessity that impressed itself upon the interpreters of the gospel as the alternative to their message, rather than, for example the Socratic teaching that with proper knowledge and adequate motivation a man could, by the exercise of his free will, overcome the tendency of his appetites toward sin.

Moreover: "Not only the Greco-Roman critics of the faith, but also its heretical opponents seemed to err chiefly on the side of emphasizing the inevitability of sin at the expense of the responsibility for sin." Pelikan is alluding to the way in which "the theories of cosmic redemption in the gnostic systems were based on an understanding of the human predicament in which humanity's inability to avoid sin or to evade destiny was fundamental."[4]

Perhaps one might qualify this optimistic pattern in the pre-Augustinian fathers by appeal to Irenaeus and Origen. Irenaeus, after all, does develop a recapitulation soteriology and so needs to appeal to some kind of unity of condition brought about by the first Adam. Yet Irenaeus not only places the emphasis on unity in mortality—not in sin—but seems to qualify even this by suggesting that the "likeness" was present only in a germinal way before sin (*Against Heresies*, iv,38,1). While the "likeness" may be lost, the "image" remains with its reality of freedom:

> And to as many as continue in their love towards God does He grant communion with Him. But communion with God is life and light, and the enjoyment of all the benefits which He has in store. But on as many as, according *to their own choice*, depart from God, He inflicts that separation from Himself which they have chosen of *their own accord*. But separation from God is death, and separation from light is darkness; and separation from God consists in the loss of all the benefits which He has in store.[5]

Origen represents a more significant qualification of the prevailing optimism. While his earlier writings place a strong emphasis on human freedom, two later elements change this emphasis. The one is the infamous appeal to premundane fall, which Origen develops in dependence on Platonic sources. Yet this theme is still cast in individualistic terms, where concupiscence is not regarded as sin until voluntary consent has carried the natural desire into action (*On First Principles*, iii,2,2–3). More significant is Origen's appeal to a "stain of sin," which he makes after coming in contact with the practice of infant baptism in Caesarea. In this appeal the physical (mortality) and the moral (guilt) merge, without great precision, but we do seem significantly on the way to Augustine.

But the way is not any sort of broad path. Thus the Antiochenes stress free will more than Origen, insisting that sin is always personal sin, though mortality can be inherited. The Cappadocians resemble Origen, in appealing to a fall from a celestial, though not premundane, paradise to account for the division of the sexes, and for mortality, desire, and darkened understanding. But they insist that the image of God remains, so that free will may be exercised in progress toward the likeness of God. This is the position that wins out in the East in the person of Maximus the Confessor.

One pattern, then, that suggests itself is relatively optimistic. We shall see this reasserting itself, after Augustine, in the work of medieval theologians and after the Reformation, in the Tridentine formulations. It is helpful to understand this pattern in the light of the contextual elements Pelikan identifies. Yet the context calls forth what is in the faith already, as other responses to such contextual elements, including other readings of the context, were indeed possible. This relatively optimistic reading of the human condition does retain something essential to Christian faith: the sense of human responsibility. Moreover, even in doing that this pattern does not fail to make a significant judgment against unqualified optimism. Even later, when this pattern casts itself in only negative terms, without positing a continuity in a positive potency to sin, it is still significant that to speak thus of the privation of the human is to speak of a genuine existential loss, not merely of the logic of negation.

But the church did come to speak more strongly of sin's continuity in effect. Augustine represents the classical foundation for such speech, but we may do well to begin with his antecedents in Tertullian and Ambrose. Tertullian represents an important third-century parallel in the West to Origen's anticipation in the East of Augustinian thought. In *On the Soul*, 41, he writes:

> There is, then, besides the evil which supervenes on the soul from the intervention of the evil spirit, an antecedent and in a certain sense natural, evil, which arises from its corrupt origin. For, as we have said before, the corruption of our nature is another nature having god and father of its own, namely the author of that corruption.

Clearly we are dealing here with an active sinfulness, not merely with a negative effect.

Tertullian's most famous contribution to the doctrine of original sin is no doubt his traducianist theory of the derivation of the soul's reality from the parents and ultimately from Adam's soul. That theory bears most directly on the concerns of the next section, where we ask how the effects of the sins of the past reach us. But it is worth noting here that the traducianist theory supports the emphasis on active sinfulness and may even have functioned to suggest that theme to Tertullian. Tennant has presented Tertullian in that light, with the additional speculation that the notion of a corrupted nature, once that action has been so derived, continues to have a life of its own, cut off from its foundation in a theory of traducianism.[6] While there may be something to Tennant's scenario, we would argue that the notion of a corrupted nature has a more direct empirical source in Christian experience.

In any case, Augustine seems to have been more directly influenced by Ambrose. Ambrose speaks of the fall as involving the loss of the divine image and is cited by Augustine as an upholder of the doctrine of hereditary corruption. Clearly sin for Ambrose is fully a state, not merely individual acts. Yet he appears to stop short of regarding concupiscence as itself sin. As with Tertullian, his most significant contribution may be to the issue of the "how" of our connectedness in sin, for Ambrose was the first to draw a definite connection between Christ's sinlessness and his virginal conception. While we have argued that the issue of the "how" of continuity in effect is not only separable from but also secondary to the issue of the "what," it does seem probable that at times in the church's reflection formative influence also flowed in the other direction.

Several threads of Christian reflection on original sin are woven together by Augustine in a complex pattern that puts these materials at the church's disposal in a distinctively new way. His defenders and detractors agree that matters were not the same after Augustine. The originality of his synthesizing work should not be minimized. He draws on Cyprian's connection between infant baptism and original sin, though Tertullian had affirmed original sin but not infant baptism. Indeed, whereas Cyprian had taught that the sins remitted in the baptism of infants are not properly their own sins, Augustine draws from original sin the strict conclusion that unbaptized infants are condemned. He drew on Ambrose's connection between Christ's sinlessness and his virginal conception. This led him toward a conclusion regarding the mode of transmission—the topic of our next section in this chapter—though he did not embrace Tertullian's traducianism as the foundation for that conception. We have been taught that he reacted to Pelagius, but Augustine's originality is suggested by the fact that his main positions on this matter were developed well before the Pelagian controversy.

What were those positions? What is the human condition "after Adam"? Augustine argues that our condition is one of guilt (*reatus*) and corruption (*vitium*). We defer the topic of guilt to the next section and consider here only corruption. To speak of this with Augustine is to deal with his elusive concept of "concupiscence," which stands for everything that makes us turn from God to find satisfaction in material things. While Augustine's emphasis at times seems to be on unbridled sexual passion, this concept of concupiscence is broad enough to include pride (*cupiditas*). Concupiscence is both a consequence and a cause of sin. Most basic of all distinctions bearing on this concept is that between liberty (*libertas*) and free will (*liberum arbitrium*). While we retain psychological free will, we have no actual liberty. There is in fact a "cruel necessity of sinning" upon us, for the race is after Adam "a universal mass of perdition." [7]

Original sin, then, is in Augustine's view clearly something more positive, more virulent than a mere privation. No informed reader will charge him with optimism about the human condition. As if to leave no doubt about that, Augustine placed this doctrine of original sin in the framework of absolute predestination, reading the "all" of 1 Tim. 2:4 as "all the predestined." This teaching—together with Augustine's attack on human liberty after Adam—provoked the criticism of a number of churchmen (Prosper of Aquitaine, Hilary, John Cassian) who have been identified since the seventeenth century as "semi-Pelagians." While the Council of Orange (529) reaffirmed the emphasis of the Council of Carthage (418) on original sin inherited from Adam and present as a taint of sin in every person, it did specifically drop the predestinarian casting of the doctrine. [8]

Can Augustine's thought be accommodated within the dialectic suggested by this section's title, "Sinner and Creature"? That each person after Adam is sinner is surely clear to him, but is each one still God's special creature? In some ways against the grain of his thought, Augustine clings to this theme:

> For man has such excellence even after the fall in comparison with the brute that what is a fault in man is nature in the brute. Still man's nature is not changed into the nature of the brute. God, therefore, condemns man because of the fault by which his nature is disgraced, not because of his nature, which is not abolished through its fault. (*On Original Sin*, 40, 46). [9]

Similarly, even in his late writing on predestination Augustine distinguishes the "grace by which we are distinguished from cattle" as a natural endowment from that grace "which pertains to a holy life." Thus he writes: "The capacity to have faith, as the capacity to have love, belongs to man's nature; but to have faith, even as to have love, belongs to the grace of believers" (*On the Predestination of the Saints*, 5, 10).

The affirmation of the Augustinian theology at Carthage and Orange and the explicit condemnation of Pelagianism at Ephesus (431) would seem clear. But development in the church's thinking on original sin does not stop at this point. Jaroslav Pelikan finds the seeds of such continuing development in the resolution of Orange itself:

The official Augustinianism of Gregory also contained the possibility for subtle shifts from the doctrine of the sovereignty and necessity of grace, to a reintroduction of the notions of merit and human initiative; on the other hand, the thought of Augustine always contained the possibility for a shift back in the direction of predestinarianism.[10]

In an historical tracing of the oscillating "footnotes to Augustine" the first direction to be noted would be toward a weakening of Augustine's emphasis on the positive character of concupiscence as sin. Medieval reflection on the human condition after Adam has in common this more optimistic view, though nuances abound. In the earlier scholastics a comparison of Anselm and Abelard at the turn of the twelfth century can serve to make this point. Anselm defines sin negatively as the privation or absence of "owed justice," through the loss of a special gift of a right directedness of the human will. Yet Anselm's realism yields a concept of race that retains a more active conception of original sin. Thus the sin of infants is not personal, but it is voluntary, carrying with it condemnation, albeit the lightest sort. Abelard concurs in Anselm's judgment, but he lacks the philosophical realism needed to support it. Since the sin of infants does not pass the criterion of a free and voluntary act of an incommunicable person, Abelard's vague appeal to "carnal concupiscence" finally settles for saying: God's justice is not our justice.[11]

Thomas Aquinas appears to offer a synthesis of Augustine and Anselm, for he speaks of concupiscence as the matter and privation of original justice as the form of original sin. But this places the matter within the form of a disorder of human nature—rather than, say, the defiance of personal will in relationship to God. Adam's rebellion brings the loss of God's sanctifying grace, so that the interior harmony of human nature is lost and natural drives are no longer under the control of reasoned will. Accordingly, despite the reference to "material" concupiscence, Aquinas seems to regard the human condition less gravely than even Anselm does and *a fortiori* than Augustine—at least that may be suggested by the fact that he assigns unbaptized infants who die to a state of natural bliss. Moreover, despite the loss involved in original sin, the natural human inclination to virtue is in no way diminished by sin, though without special grace it will fall short of its goal. Human nature, though wounded, remains intact.[12]

In Anselm and Aquinas, Irenaeus' distinction between "image" and "likeness" returns, but now cut off from the view that Adam was created immature. "Likeness" becomes "superadded gifts" which can be lost without a radical corruption of human nature itself, made in God's image. In Scotus and the Franciscans this affirmation of human nature is the more emphatic and once again is aligned with the notion of human immaturity. If Adam had preserved the "supernatural gift," he would have acquired a confirmation in grace. The same rule would have applied to every other human being.

5 / SIN AND EVIL

In the fallen state concupiscence is seen as fully natural, as the necessary reaction of the sensitive part of the soul to intrinsically desirable objects. Though weakened by the loss of the supernatural harmony, we are not in sin. Yet we are in guilt, for we participate forensically in the debt represented in the lost original righteousness. While Scotus himself could still stretch toward this unity in guilt by appeal to philosophical realism, more nominalistic later Franciscans settled for a bare appeal to the independence from criticism of the truths of faith. In any case the creature after Adam, though weakened, remains free both psychologically and metaphysically. As Heiko Oberman puts it:

> Man after the fall is prone to all evil, through an error of judgment; the will, weak in its fights against the lower powers, is tempted to disobey the command of reason; spirit and flesh are in constant struggle, and the will is unstable and weak because of the physical impact of original sin. . . . All these obstacles, due partly to man's created condition, partly to the consequences of his initial disobedience, do not, however, diminish the liberty of the will to choose freely between good and evil; they only diminish the ease with which the good acts are elicited.[13]

Good can, then, be done and done efficaciously. God is obligated to infuse divine grace in all people who have done their very best ("facere quod in se est").

This way of conceiving the human person "after Adam" is essentially optimistic. That is not so obvious in Aquinas, who insists that no person can turn to God unless God turns to that person first and throughout offers "assisting grace." But there is a place for merit in his thought, as Brian Gerrish points out:

> Justification is not enough, not even when interpreted as itself a "making righteous." It is merely the first step towards ultimate salvation, and eternal life is only to be obtained by the justified man who goes on, in the power of habitual grace, to perform meritorious works . . . and from this it follows of necessity that salvation is given as a reward, indeed a reward "de condigno."[14]

Gerrish's reference becomes clearer when set over against nominalist theology with its still more optimistic slant:

> First, acting upon his own native powers a man may perform acts worthy of merit "de congruo." Now, strictly speaking, God is not obliged to reward such imperfect merit; God is not thereby made a debtor. . . . Still, provided only that a man has done his best ("quod in se est"), it is at least fitting ("decet") that God, being both just and good, should crown human endeavor with divine grace. Thereupon, the second stage in man's attainment of eternal life begins: equipped with the inpouring of divine charity, he is enabled to perform works meritorious

416

in the strictest sense, that is "de condigno." God now becomes, quite precisely, a debtor, and He is obliged ("cogitur") to grant eternal life as a well-earned reward.[15]

These summaries serve to set the stage for the Reformation corrective to this optimism, whether in its more subtle form or its more blatant form. This seems the more important context in which to regard Luther's attack against optimism—rather than, say, that of his argument with Erasmus. Long before the dispute with Erasmus, Luther had been asserting the bondage of the will. Thus in the Heidelberg Theses (13) of 1518 he asserts: " 'Free Will' after the fall is nothing but a word, as long as it is doing what is within it, it is committing deadly sin." Here the foundation is already laid for his response in 1525 to Erasmus: "Hence it follows that free choice without the grace of God is not free at all, but immutably the captive and slave of evil, since it cannot of itself turn to the good." [16] John Calvin also defines himself directly over against the medieval Catholic optimism:

> Those who have defined original sin as a lack of original justice which ought to be in men, although in these words they have comprehended all the substance, still they have not sufficiently expressed the force of it. For our nature is not merely empty and destitute, but it is so fecund of every kind of evil that it cannot be inactive. (*Institutes*, ii,1,9)

Here Luther and Calvin must be distinguished from the so-called "radical" reformers, whose more individualistic concept of sin yielded the Anabaptist refusal to baptize children, since Christ took away original sin from the whole world.[17]

Can this pessimism about the human condition speak of the person as still God's special creature? Luther's inclination is to identify the image of God so strongly with the "material image" that he will not be apt to speak of the continuing creaturely status in terms of the "image." Yet we can find a trace of a "relic" theory, evident in our continuing dominion over the animals.[18] In any case, Luther continues to recognize human competence in reason and morals regarding "the things that are below us." Gerrish argues for a threefold distinction in Luther's understanding and evaluation of reason:

> (1) natural reason, ruling within its proper domain (the Earthly Kingdom); (2) arrogant reason, trespassing upon the domain of faith (the Heavenly Kingdom); (3) regenerate reason, serving humbly in the household of faith, but always subject to the Word of God. Within the first context, reason is an excellent gift of God; within the second, it is Frau Hulda, the Devil's Whore; within the third, it is the handmaiden of faith.[19]

But what of the relationship to God? Has this endowment been so misappropriated that the relationship no longer exists? Is it necessary to assert a complete loss of relationship to God in order to correct the medieval optimism? It is not, for Luther's critique asserts that humankind is against, but not without, God.[20] Indeed, *The Bondage of the Will* (ix) seems to suggest that only one who is especially meant for God can truly sin against God, and that the later point does not eliminate the former:

> But if the power of free choice were said to mean that by which a man is capable of being taken hold of by the Spirit and imbued with the grace of God, as a being created for eternal life or death, no objection could be taken. For this power or aptitude, or as the Sophists say, this disposing quality or passive aptitude, we also admit; and who does not know that it is not found in trees or animals? For heaven, as the saying is, was not made for geese.

Calvin follows Luther in these matters. The "natural gifts" bestowed on the human creature have undergone a loss in efficacy but have not been wholly obliterated. Even in the God-relationship sin means that we are deprived not of will but of a healthy will. Calvin cites Bernard as follows: "Simply to will, is human; to will the bad belongs to corrupted nature; to will the good is of grace" (*Institutes*, ii,3,5). This leads him to a formulation reminiscent of Luther's distinction between necessity and constraint:

> We must observe this distinction: that man, after having been corrupted by the Fall, sins voluntarily, not against his heart nor by constraint; that he sins, I say, by liking and strong inclination, not by constraint or violence; . . . and nevertheless that his nature is so perverse that he cannot be moved, driven or led except to evil. (Ibid.)

In Calvin's assertion that "every part of man, from the understanding to the will, from the soul to the flesh, is defiled and altogether filled with that concupiscence"[21] we hear a hint of the anthropological interest which dominated medieval discussion of this topic. On the Lutheran side this interest is represented by Melanchthon. At least in his *Loci Communes* of 1543 (if not earlier) he implies a distinction and cooperation between the Holy Spirit, who effects and generates new spiritual affections through the reading or hearing of the word of God, and the human will that follows the affections, namely, the love of God and the knowledge of God's mercy. Ekkehard Muehlenberg comments:

> Human will does not materially add anything to the process, because object and objective are given in reason's knowledge and the movement or locomotion in the affection. Nevertheless, human will has to turn to the new affection and has to follow it against other affections in man.[22]

In the debate between Strigel and Flacius that led to the Formula of Concord's decisions, Strigel wanted to defend the Lutheran doctrine of original sin against the Catholic assertion that it denied the goodness of creation by making the created human appetite the cause of sin. Strigel argued that God indeed creates the appetites, but whether they fasten on good or bad ways of fulfillment is contingent. Thereby Strigel returned to the basic medieval frame of reference. It was to precisely this that Flacius objected. But he too did not fully escape the medieval frame, and so was trapped into describing sin as the substance of human nature.[23]

The Formula of Concord, leaning to Flacius' insight but not accepting his conclusion, stated the issue, but hardly resolved it. What we seek to understand is how "that which is accident and not substance" can be

> inexpressible impairment and such a corruption of human nature that nothing pure nor good has remained in itself and in all its internal and external powers, but that it is altogether corrupted, so that through original sin man is in God's sight spiritually lifeless and with all his powers dead indeed to that which is good. (BC 519)

What is it to say that the fallen person retains the capacity for salvation, though this is not an active capacity but a passive one? Muehlenberg argues that the Formula impales itself by arguing on the one hand that the unregenerated person is "a stone, a block, or a lump of clay," "a wild unbroken animal" and on the other hand that "the Lord God draws the person whom he wills to convert, and draws him in such a way that man's darkened reason becomes an enlightened one and his resisting will becomes an obedient will." Muehlenberg comments:

> Either the Holy Spirit effects and accomplishes an initial turn and change of sinful man against the thoroughly sinful will of man, or unregenerated man is capable of responding to the offer of grace. . . . The Formula of Concord wants it both ways, that is, it rejects forceful conversion but does not admit the Philippist alternative either.[24]

Is this the self-contradiction Muehlenberg finds it to be? An adequate response to that question forces us to focus the dialectic of this section (sinner/creature) in that of the next: tragic/Adamic. But before doing that we need to close the historical discussion pertinent to this section and offer some assessment of the historical development from a constructive theological vantage point.

The rival currents of optimism and pessimism may be identified once again as we complete our sampling of the reflection the church has made available for contemporary faith. For a post-Reformation Roman Catholic response, the decree promulgated on June 17, 1546, at the fifth session of the Council of Trent is the most important document. The ambiguity in the formulation probably reflects the fact that the participants were split between Augustinian, Anselmian, and Thomistic emphases. But the ambiguity does not obscure a clear weakening of the gravity of the effects of original sin, when these formulations are measured against those of Orange.

Thus the Tridentine decree on original sin specifies that Adam "lost his holiness and the justice in which he had been established" and proceeds to cite Orange to the effect "that through that offense of prevarication the entire Adam was transformed in body and soul for the worse" (Denzinger, 788). What is more striking is that the formulation at Orange adds that the freedom of the soul does not remain uninjured. This is omitted at Trent, despite the fact that a preliminary text of this canon did have a weakened version of the formulation at Orange. Consistently, Trent's decree on justification makes the point explicitly that the free will "was not extinguished in them, however weakened and debased in its powers" (Denzinger, 793). Other canons speak more directly to the questions we defer to later: How do the effects reach us, and how may they be overcome? But one may say that in none of them is the more optimistic "privation" emphasis significantly challenged.

On the other hand, a challenge to this optimism may be heard in the formulations found in the Thirty-Nine Articles of the Church of England (1571) and the Westminster Confession of Faith (1647). The text of the ninth article of the former hardly requires comment:

> Man is very far gone from original righteousness, and is of his own nature inclined to evil, so that the flesh lusteth always contrary to the spirit; and therefore in every person born into this world, it deserveth God's wrath and damnation . . . the Apostle doth confess, that concupiscence and lust hath of itself the nature of sin.

Accordingly, the tenth article ("Of Free Will") stresses that "we have no power to do good works pleasant and acceptable to God without the grace of God" and the thirteenth article ("Of Works before Justification") adds:

> Works done before the grace of Christ . . . are not pleasant to God, forasmuch as they spring not of faith in Jesus Christ; neither do they make men meet to receive grace, or (as the School-authors say) deserve grace of congruity . . . we doubt not but they have the nature of sin.

The Westminster Confession also rejects any human preparation for salvation and speaks of our share in the "original corruption" by which we are "dead in sin, and wholly defiled in all the faculties and parts of soul and body" (Westminster Confession of Faith, VI, II).

The most interesting differences in the formulations concern not the human condition after Adam, but God's role in all of this. The Thirty-Nine Articles affirm simply selective "predestination to life," while the Westminster Confession has God permitting the sin of "our first parents," "having purposed to order it to his own glory," and among those hearing the word specifies an "effectual calling" only to the predestined, who can never fall from the state of justification. Of the others, it is said:

> The rest of mankind God was pleased, according to the unsearchable counsel of his own will, whereby he extendeth or withholdeth mercy as he pleaseth, for the glory of his sovereign power over his creatures, to pass by, and to ordain them to dishonour and wrath for their sin, to the praise of his glorious justice. (Ibid., III, VII.)

We mention these differences not because we intend to treat them as they bear on the issues of earlier chapters (the agency in sin) or of later ones (the remedy for sin). We do so because it is apparent that a doctrine of God may in effect bracket one of two apparently essentially identical formulations of original sin and so significantly qualify any comparative assessment of its optimism or pessimism. Nonetheless, both formulations—each in its distinctive systematic context—still stand as challenges to optimism in the church's teaching on original sin.

From this brief discussion of the massive material that represents the church's reflection on the effects of original sin, we draw a few statements in relation to considerations that are other than historical:

First, despite Luther and Calvin, it will not do to speak of the image of God as being entirely lost. Already the Priestly writer of the Pentateuch has God blessing humankind after the flood of judgment in nearly the same terms as the initial blessing and making specific appeal to the image of God (Gen. 9:1–2). Ernst Käsemann's statement is simply too strong: "Adam is a different person before and after the fall. The apostle therefore does not adhere to the Jewish view which . . . maintained a divine likeness still remained. For him, only Christ has an *imago dei*, an image which is only given back to us with faith."[25] Emil Brunner serves both empirical and biblical sense better—and grants the status the reformers' own statements about the "non-brutish" character of the human creature after Adam seem to require.

> We make a distinction of category; formally the image is not infringed upon even in the least degree—whether he sins or not, man is a subject, and responsible. Materially, the image is completely lost, man is a sinner through and through, and there is nothing in him which is not stained by sin.[26]

The strain of optimism in the tradition appropriately raises the question whether Brunner's complete pessimism concerning the material is warranted. What material reality, if any, is given in order to retain formal responsibility?

Second, biblical faith and contemporary experience witness to the universality and inevitability of sin. The "positive pessimism" strand within the tradition accords with this witness better than the privational understanding does.

421

Third, the unity of the human person is such that the affirmation and the critique of that person after Adam cannot be isolated from each other. Edmund Schlink makes this point well in commenting on the Lutheran Confessions: "There is no doubt that the same features of man recur whether we view him in his creatureliness *or* in his corruption. No part of man is mentioned which, subtracting corruption from his creatureliness, could remain as a positive residue."[27]

Fourth, the unity of the human person, together with the recognition that that person is fully a sinner and fully a creature, suggests that Luther's distinction between freedom toward that which is "below us" and bondage toward that which is "above us" is too facile. At this point fresh constructive work is needed. Perhaps the recognition in Lutheran circles that "civil righteousness" is possible can point the way, if one asks how such righteousness matters to God without displacing the more direct relationship to God.

Fifth, the unity of the person in sin and creatureliness forbids only the isolation of elements, not the empirical description of this dialectic. Against Schlink's characteristically Lutheran claim that "it is evident that this is merely a conceptual distinction, in no case an empirical one,[28] the Augustinian, medieval, and Melanchthonian anthropological interest is to be affirmed.

How is all this to be held together? While one may appropriately distrust simplicity and finality about a topic over which Christians have differed so strenuously, some further word of orientation within the maelstrom of opinion is clearly desirable. We attempt that now by asking about the "how" of this "what" of sin that reaches us after Adam.

BONDAGE AND RESPONSIBILITY

Let us look back to see where the momentum of our argument may be tending. In the Christian view of things the human project is not what it should be, given the divine intention denoted by the "image of God." This is not a matter of some few depraved or deprived types. Christian witness and human experience come together to speak of the universal human predicament. For Christians the chief (though not the only) word to describe this state is "sin." We shall speak later of other forms of evil. What matters now is to ponder further the Christian conviction that all come to be sinners—all, save one, at least. There is essential Christian agreement on the universality of sin, despite the disagreements reported in the previous section. But what shall one make of this universality? If all come to sin, are all bound to sin? Many Christians will grant that the sin they know in themselves has the quality of inevitability to it. But *how* does it begin with us? Surely in some sense what we come to be is rooted in how we begin to be, in what we are as we begin.

Thus sin's quantity and sin's quality drive Christian reflection to ask of the beginning of each of us, to ask how it is that we are such when we begin that we all come to be sinners. Do we all end bound in sin because we are bound to sin as we begin? It clearly makes sense to relate the sad tale of what we come to be to the ominous suggestion that there is something radically wrong with us even as we begin to be.

Yet we wish whatever we say of how we are bound at the beginning to be coherent with what we said in earlier chapters about the Adamic character of the agency at work in sin. Both Christian witness and human experience bring us to speak of human responsibility for the human predicament. To speak of human responsibility may well be to speak of more than individual responsibility, but it is surely not to speak of less. When we speak of what is given as we begin, we speak of the "bound." But we must ask as well how that which is given for us can become fully and responsibly our own. This suggests that we should speak of guilt only as and after we speak of sin. Sin is that *in* me which constitutes something *about* me: guilt. Thus juridical understandings which assign guilt without recognizing sin are inadequate. The formulations of fathers like Ambrose, who declined to speak of con- cupiscence as sin but who spoke of guilt through our involvement with Adam, or of Augustine, who spoke occasionally of concupiscence as the punishment for Adam's sin, depend on some clarification of a more than legal or forensic relationship to Adam. Just ahead we turn to that. Further ahead, in the next chapter, we attempt to state how the dying which inevitably comes on us is related to this chief reality of sin.

At times human connectedness in sin has been thought of as a kind of mystical unity. Thus Nygren can comment on Rom. 5:12, "Adam is signifi- cant as the head of the 'old' humanity, as the head of the present aeon. That which happened to the head involves the body also."[29] Old Testament scholars speak of the reality of a common spiritual world, by which the proph- ets can condemn later generations for the sins of earlier ones, for the later generations are still responsible.[30] Perhaps this is more a rejection of the ques- tion of "how" it is that we are bound than it is an answer to it. Yet at times this conception is clarified by appeal to definite conceptual structures, as when theologians appeal to what H. Wheeler Robinson has called the notion of "corporate personality" in ancient Israel. Robinson identified four aspects to this notion: the "vertical" extension into past and future, the "realism" by which the concept is distinguished from fictitious or poetic personifications, the "oscillation" between more individual and more group reference, and the persistence of the concept despite developing emphasis on the individual.[31]

Does this concept adequately clarify how we are bound but still responsi- ble? A sense of corporate responsibility cut off from the reality of some kind of psychical unity will be hard put to sustain itself. Thus in 1 Samuel 14 the people suffer the consequences of Jonathan's sin but are not responsible for the sin itself. An individual's responsibility for his or her sins is not denied, but one does need to recognize that an individual affects others to the point, as it were, of possessing or defiling them.[32]

What, then, of psychical unity? Robinson's appeal to Levy-Bruhl's hypotheses about the primitive mind has been weakened by the work and writing of field anthropologists.[33] The effect of these responses to Robinson is not to deny a sense of corporateness but to cast doubt on a supraindividual agency at work within the individual. Even without such specific responses, the theme of corporate personality may be said to have been in considerable difficulty in its implicit appeal to philosophical realism in a pervasively pluralistic context.

But perhaps "corporate personality" is a premature speculative synthesis of elements which require further attention. I refer particularly to the realism and extension into past and future of which Robinson speaks. These, taken together with the symbols of defilement, may suggest a way forward. Paul Ricoeur may be right that the symbolism of defilement resists reflection, because it is pre-ethical and quasi-material.[34] Yet it should be noted that the notion of defilement does accept the event structure sustaining individuals as the context in which the human predicament spreads. It is thus implicitly closer to our experience (which surely includes being acted upon) than the notion of a psychical unity which somehow acts in us. Perhaps some clue to the universality of sin can be found by attending to the structures through which sin spreads. After all, that structure at once sustains and binds the self. That structure applies both in the beginning-to-be and the coming-to-be of the self. As that structure reaches back behind the self, it may well carry the deeper continuity of sin to the self.

The sense for this more empirical connectedness has been prominent in the church's reflection. Such connectedness is not a matter of choice. Thus it was seen to be clearly inadequate to speak merely of sin spreading by the force of example, as did Pelagius, who held that sin "is carried on by imitation, committed by the will, denounced by the reason, manifested by the law, punished by justice."[35] To this the church was moved to insist that sin is carried "not by imitation, but by propagation" at Carthage in 418 and at Trent in 1546, for example.[36] Here the church's teacher has been Augustine, whose conviction was that it is "by the begetting of the flesh . . . that sin is contracted which is original."[37] This biological emphasis may have been first suggested by Ambrosiaster and was brought to bear on Augustine through Ambrose's linking the sinlessness of Jesus and his virginal conception. The passage in Ps. 51:5 ("Behold, I was brought forth in iniquity, and in sin did my mother conceive me") seemed to point this way. And Augustine's Latin

Bible translated Rom. 5:12: "Sin came into the world, and death through sin, and so death spread to all men, through one man, in whom [*in quo*] all sinned."

This formulation of the "how" of connectedness faces insuperable difficulties. Exegetically there are compelling arguments to translate Rom. 5:12 "because all men sinned," at least weakening the note of presence in Adam. More significant, this view seems to attribute too great and too negative a role to our biological givenness. Tertullian's traducianism—while not clearly held by Augustine—is the logical basis for this understanding of original sin. Drawing on Stoic sources, Tertullian wrote: "Everything that is, is body." He drew what seemed to be the necessary conclusion for our theme:

> Our first parent contained within himself the undeveloped germ of all mankind, and his soul was the fountain-head of all souls: all varieties of individual human nature are but different modifications of that one spiritual substance. Therefore the whole of nature became corrupt in the original father of the race, and sinfulness is propagated together with souls.[38]

The difficulty here is that what is claimed is claimed on an insufficiently ample basis: Biological connection lacks the tensile strength to support such a prison house of personal bondage. The way ahead is not to appeal to a "creationist" theory of God's special role in the coming-to-be of souls, for that— apart from its inherent conceptual two-world difficulties—threatens to make sin trivial or God evil. Nor is it helpful to pull back to a vague mystical connectedness or to settle for a clear but shallow individualism, which in compromising the corporateness must always puzzle over the universality of sin. Rather, it seems better to recognize that the alternatives "imitation or propagation" are too simple. A growing stream of reflection about sin draws on material in the middle distance between the logical extremes of propagation and imitation. That others inevitably play a constitutive role in relation to our very selfhood is increasingly recognized, even by someone as attracted to individualism as J. P. Sartre, who closes his autobiography with these words: "What remains? A whole man, composed of all men and as good as all of them and no better than any."[39] To move in this direction is not to jettison talk of corporateness but to extend the move implied in the shift from mystical identity to biological propagation. By that shift such talk is placed in the context of empirical, temporal connectedness.

Piet Schoonenberg has shown that this doctrine of "social heredity" can speak of far more than bad example. Writing of "the sin of the world" he speaks of how certain values may be totally obscured for a child, so that freedom cannot realize itself in that sphere.[40] Rosemary Ruether has made the same claim on a broader scale:

The breakup of the communal life of earlier tribal society coincided historically with the patriarchal systems of the formative period of Western civilization. Psychologically, this means that the emerging individual ego did not have its negative projections challenged by the independent self-definition of the "other." Therefore the ego became fixated in immature adjustments, habitually dealing with threats to its rule through strategies of separation, denial, devaluation, and oppressive domination.[41]

Perhaps it may be objected that this way of speaking seems to claim too much, that it fits better with the privation theme than with the view of original sin as positive concupiscence. No act of individual will seems needed to sustain the human predicament. It may be difficult to see how guilt could be claimed in this situation, unless one says with some current Roman Catholic thought that original sin, as the historical privation of that to which the self is transcendentally oriented, is a condition of guilt because it exists in contradiction to that to which we are called.[42]

But perhaps the sociality of our existence can illumine also the positive character of our predicament after Adam. Schoonenberg tries to cling to both the individual and the sociality of existence for that individual: "As a free person, I cannot be deprived of my freedom by the free decisions of others, but they may well place me in a situation which may determine me inwardly even in my freedom. Another can, for instance, disclose a value which makes an appeal to my freedom."[43]

Let us pause to assess the argument. There is will in this conditioning by social heredity. It does pass through the center of my person. There is, to be sure, a givenness here which seems not to possess the sense of contingency we normally require for will. But must personhood and personal will be linked with contingency?

The possible responses to the last question are not many. If one responds in the affirmative, one may then emphasize the sense in which no contingent act of will is required for sin to emerge.[44] Or if one holds that sin must be "personal," one may then decline to speak of this condition itself as sin, bearing guilt, though one may still grant that out of it does culpable sin invariably proceed.[45] In this view, linking the person so strongly with contingency, the reality of sin's universality proves puzzling. Perhaps this position need not collapse before the question just when a freely personal will to sin joins the difficulties given at the self's beginning; for that question is not harder than the broader one about when the freely personal will can be said to be "there." But one would need to ask *how* the one yields the other. That which is free cannot derive necessarily from that which is unfree. Here, then, we seem near affirming responsibility so simply that the sense in which we are bound is lost.

If, on the other hand, we grant that personal will may be present without contingency, we will likely call this condition at the beginning personal sin.[46]

426

Where there is sin without contingency there can surely be guilt of the same sort. But if sin begins in a free fall, must it not somehow continue still in freedom and so with responsibility? Otherwise I join Adam only as victim and not as co-perpetrator after all. But when and how does individual responsibility come to be associated with sin—through contingency or otherwise? Here we seem near affirming bondage so simply that the sense in which we are responsible is lost. These difficulties drive a Catholic theologian like Charles Baumgartner to say: "This state, antecedent in choice, is real but analogous guilt, thus lying midway between personal guilt and natural defect."[47] Perhaps such Catholic anthropological ambiguity states in simpler fashion the principled ambiguity characterizing many Protestant theologians in the existentialist tradition. Kierkegaard stressed that sin roots in individual will, but he could add: "and this corruption of the will goes well beyond the consciousness of the individual. This is a perfectly consistent declaration, for otherwise the question how sin began must arise with respect to each individual."[48]

While such Protestant writers may not share the anthropological interest in specific distinctions which characterize the Catholic approach to hamartiology, they too seem to recognize that it is difficult to know where to locate the self so that its responsibility can be properly assessed. The problem is not merely postcanonical. Consider Paul's plight in Romans 7. To say with Conzelmann that I am necessarily concerned for the good and necessarily fail, or with Bultmann that "man has always already missed the existence that at heart he seeks, his intent is basically perverse, evil," is in principle to share the difficulty afflicting the Catholic discussions.[49]

Perhaps current reflection concerning the nature of human selfhood, which recognizes the plenitude of competing centers of organization within the self, can provide an empirical context for the discussion of these difficulties. Similarly, the contemporary sense for the temporality of the self might help us understand that what is given is given for a self freshly constituting itself precisely in the terms of what is given to it. While in many respects the given poses more possibilities, there are in principle always some nonnegotiable realities *there* for the self. Part of what is there is the structure, given by God, which leads the self to seek someone to worship, to trust, to seek some God. Thus Augustine could say that the health in us expresses itself in our desire to relate by using and enjoying, but that our disease twists the relationships so that we enjoy things and use people. *How* do we do so? Faith is only prepared to say that we do so as persons bound but still responsible. Thus one can well say that Paul in Romans attempts no explanation of the physical or historical relations between Adam's sin and those who followed and "became sinners." Can one simply leave it at that?

There is an agenda here for constructive theology— precisely this dialectical dogmatic conviction that in sin we are bound, but responsible still. That

427

claim can be responsibly made on material grounds. We have argued that it fits faithfully the witness of the tradition. It is anchored as well in our own experience. Blaise Pascal makes the point well:

> Nothing, to be sure, is more of a shock to us than such a doctrine, and yet without this mystery, which is the most incomprehensible of all, we should be incomprehensible to ourselves. The tangled knot of our condition acquired its twists and turns in that abyss; so that man is more inconceivable without the mystery than the mystery to man.[50]

We cannot let the formal criterion of coherence intimidate such material testimonies. Yet we accept that criterion, but recognize the direction in which further progress may be sought: the empirical connectedness of selves. This difficulty would only become intolerable if it were to immobilize Christian thought and life. We have at least indicated a direction in which to think.

NOTES

1. Søren Kierkegaard, *Christian Discourses,* trans. Walter Lowrie (London: Oxford University Press, 1939), pp. 132–33.

2. Paul Ricoeur, *The Symbolism of Evil,* trans. Emerson Buchanan (Boston: Beacon Press, 1967), pp. 246–47.

3. F. R. Tennant, *The Sources of the Doctrines of the Fall and Original Sin* (Cambridge: At the University Press, 1903), p. 275.

4. Jaroslav Pelikan, *The Emergence of the Catholic Tradition (100-600)* (Chicago: University of Chicago Press, 1971), pp. 281–83.

5. *Against Heresies,* v,27,2 (emphasis added). See Adolf von Harnack, *History of Dogma,* trans. Neil Buchanan, 7 vols. (Boston: Little, Brown & Co., 1961), 2:270–71; and John Hick, *Evil and the God of Love* (New York: Harper & Row; London: Macmillan & Co., 1966), chap. 9. For such an emphasis in contemporary work, see Alfred Vanneste, *The Dogma of Original Sin* (Brussels: Vander, 1975); and Maurizio Flick and Zoltan Alszeghy, *Il peccato originale* (Brescia: Queriniana, 1972). See also Brian O. McDermott, "The Theology of Original Sin: Recent Developments," *TS* 38 (September 1977): 478–512.

6. Tennant, *Sources,* pp. 332–36.

7. See J. N. D. Kelly, *Early Christian Doctrines* (New York: Harper & Brothers, 1958), pp. 365–66.

8. Ibid., pp. 369–72. Cf. Pelikan, *Emergence,* pp. 318–29.

9. Cf. Kelly, *Early Christian Doctrines,* p. 364: "Augustine does not inculcate a doctrine of 'total depravity,' according to which the image of God has been utterly obliterated in us. Even though grievously altered, fallen man remains noble, 'the spark, as it were, of reason in virtue of which he was made in God's likeness has not been completely extinguished.' "

10. Pelikan, *Emergence,* p. 330.

11. See G. Vandervelde, *Original Sin: Two Major Trends in Contemporary Roman Catholic Interpretation* (Amsterdam: Rodopi N.V., 1975), pp. 26–28; and Henri Rondet, *Original Sin: The Patristic and Theological Background,* trans. Cajetan Finegan (New York: Alba House, 1969), pp. 143–45.

12. Vandervelde, *Original Sin,* pp. 28–32.

13. Heiko Oberman, *The Harvest of Medieval Theology* (Cambridge, Mass.: Harvard University Press, 1963), p. 49.

14. Brian A. Gerrish, *Grace and Reason* (Oxford: At the Clarendon Press, 1962), p. 132.

15. Ibid., p. 122.

16. This passage and the one cited below on p. 417 are taken from Luther's *The Bondage of the Will;* see *Luther and Erasmus: Free Will and Salvation,* trans. Philip S. Watson, LCC 17 (Philadelphia: Westminster Press, 1969), p. 141, for both passages.

17. George Hunston Williams, *The Radical Reformation* (Philadelphia: Westminster Press, 1962), p. 799.

18. As in Luther's comment on Gen. 1:26 ("Let them have dominion over the fish of the sea. . . .") in his lectures on Genesis.

19. Gerrish, *Grace and Reason,* p. 26.

20. Robert C. Schultz puts the point nicely in "Original Sin: Accident or Substance: The Paradoxical Significance of F.C. I, 53–62 in Historical Context," *in Discord, Dialogue, and Concord,* ed. Lewis W. Spitz and Wenzel Lohff (Philadelphia: Fortress Press, 1977), p. 44: "Unbelief—not fearing, not loving, not trusting God—does not mean that relationship has been lost. The personal relationship to God remains, but it has been converted into its opposite. Mistrust is not the absence of trust but an active relationship which not only results in the commission of sins but is the essence of sin itself."

21. *Institutes* ii,1,8. See also François Wendel, *Calvin: The Origins and Development of His Religious Thought,* trans. Philip Mairet (New York: Harper & Row, 1950), pp. 188ff.

22. Ekkehard Muehlenberg, "Synergia and Justification by Faith," in *Discord, Dialogue, and Concord,* p. 34.

23. Schultz, "Original Sin," pp. 47–50.

24. Muehlenberg, "Synergia and Justification by Faith," pp. 21–23.

25. Ernst Käsemann, *Perspectives on Paul,* trans. Margaret Kohl (Philadelphia: Fortress Press, 1971), pp. 58–59.

26. This passage is from Emil Brunner's *Natural Theology* (1935), trans. Peter Fraenkel (London: Geoffrey Bles, 1946). For a discussion of this widespread emphasis in Brunner, see David Cairns, *The Image of God in Man* (London: SCM Press, 1953), pp. 146–63.

27. Edmund Schlink, *Theology of the Lutheran Confessions,* trans. Paul F. Koehneke and Herbert J. A. Bouman (Philadelphia: Fortress [Muhlenberg] Press, 1961), p. 45.

28. Ibid., p. 46.

29. Anders Nygren, *Commentary on Romans,* trans. Carl C. Rasmussen (Philadelphia: Fortress [Muhlenberg] Press, 1949), p. 312.

30. Walther Eichrodt, *Theology of the Old Testament,* trans. J. A. Baker, 2 vols. (Philadelphia: Westminster Press, 1961–67), 2:407.

31. H. Wheeler Robinson, *Corporate Personality in Ancient Israel* (Philadelphia: Fortress Press, 1964).

32. Cf. J. R. Porter, "The Legal Aspects of the Concept of Corporate Personality in the Old Testament," VT 25 (1965): 379: "The Hebrew realized as well as we do that, if a particular person commits a crime, he is responsible and guilty for it, in a way that even those closest to him, his wife and his son, really cannot be. But his basic recognition is qualified, as far as the operation of the law was concerned, not so much by ideas of 'corporate personality' as by the notion that a man can possess persons in much the same way that he possesses property and by early religious beliefs about the contagious nature of blood, holiness, sin, and uncleanness."

33. J. W. Rodgerson, "The Hebrew Conception of Corporate Personality: A Re-examination," *JThS* 21 (April 1970): 1–16.

34. Ricoeur, *Symbolism of Evil,* pp. 25–28.

35. Pelikan, *Emergence of the Catholic Tradition,* p. 315.

36. At Carthage the formulation stresses baptism for infants "so that that which they have contracted from generation may be cleansed in them by regeneration." (Denzinger, 102). For Trent, see Denzinger, 790.

37. Pelikan, *Emergence of the Catholic Tradition,* p. 300.

38. This is the paraphrase of Augustus Neander in *General History of the Christian Religion and Church,* vol.2, trans. Joseph Torrey (London: Henry G. Bohn, 1851), pp. 346–47.

39. Jean-Paul Sartre, *The Words,* trans. Bernard Frechtman (New York: George Braziller, 1964), p. 255.

40. Piet Schoonenberg, *Man and Sin,* trans. Joseph Donceel (Notre Dame, Ind.: University of Notre Dame Press, 1965), pp. 115–18.

41. Rosemary Radford Ruether, *Liberation Theology* (New York: Paulist Press, 1972), as paraphrased by Wanda Warren Berry, "Images of Sin and Salvation in Feminist Theology," *AThR* 60 (January 1978): 25–54.

42. For a full statement of this theme drawn from Karl Rahner, see K. H. Weger, *Theologie der Erbsünde* (Freiburg: Herder Verlag, 1970).

43. Piet Schoonenberg, "Sin," *SM(E)* 6, p. 90.

44. Holsten Fagerberg, *A New Look at the Lutheran Confessions,* trans. Gene J. Lund (St. Louis: Concordia Publishing House, 1972), p. 143, with special reference to Apology II.

45. See Brian O. McDermott, "The Theology of Original Sin: Recent Developments," *TS* 38 (September 1977): 478–512, for a summary of such thinking in Alfred Vanneste and Domiciano Fernandez.

46. Ernst Kinder, *Die Erbsünde* (Stuttgart: Schwabenverlag, 1959).

47. I have the paraphrase from McDermott, "Theology of Original Sin," p. 485. Cf. Ricoeur, *Symbolism of Evil,* p. 100.

48. Søren Kierkegaard, *Sickness unto Death,* trans. W. Lowrie (Princeton: Princeton University Press, 1941), p. 226.

49. Hans Conzelmann, *An Outline of the Theology of the New Testament*, trans. John Bowden (New York: Harper & Row, 1969), p. 234; Rudolf Bultmann, *Theology of the New Testament*, trans. Kendrick Grobel, 2 vols. (New York: Charles Scribner's Sons, 1954–55), 1:227.

50. Blaise Pascal, *Pensées* (New York: E. P. Dutton, 1958), p. 121, no. 434.

4

Metaphysical and Natural Evil

As finite freedom the creature suffers. The creature is called to a life which transcends this life but depends on it, is set within a structure impartially bestowing connection and consequence, and undergoes the distortion—objectively and subjectively—of that structure due to sin.

FINITUDE

After three chapters devoted to the treatment of moral evil, we turn to consideration of metaphysical and natural evil. We have found ourselves speaking of the universality of sin; we begin here with another universal: finitude. That we are finite in understanding, in ability to communicate, above all in span of years, is this not evil? Christians have not agreed about this matter, and we shall have to chronicle that division. But we can begin by identifying two convictions that are held in common and that bear on this issue.

The first is the conviction that God is categorically supreme. In Chapter 2 we considered this theme in speaking of God as Creator. Now it becomes the basis for constructing a perspective on finitude, especially on death. First, God's supremacy strips death of the sacral or numinous qualities so commonly associated with it. Death possesses no independent power, as if to rival the sovereignty of Yahweh. Second, somehow God must be related to death, if God is the Creator, if there are not two Gods.

But how is God related to death? Close at hand lies the inference that part of God's categorical supremacy is that God alone is infinite, so that our finitude, our death, is given with creation as a "natural" state. Yet this reflection must face the second common Christian conviction in this matter: that our death, our dying, is evil. The Scriptures do not deny the hideousness of death.[1]

How shall these two convictions—God's supremacy, death's evilness—be held together? At times the sense of the evil character of death seems to get its very content from its relationship to the categorically supreme God. Von Rad comments on Psalm 88: "The dead were cut off from praising Jahweh and from hearing him proclaimed, and above all, they were cut off from him himself."[2] But what follows from this for our understanding of the cause of death? Perhaps the clearest line in Christian reflection moves back from the universality of death to the universality of sin, with the connecting link being provided by the experience of death as evil. God's supremacy, then, finds expression in the notion that death is the fruit of sin. Perhaps Paul is often too simply identified with this view, which fits Romans 5 better than it does 1 Corinthians 15.[3] In any case, by the time of the Council of Carthage (418) it was clear to the church that

> whoever says that Adam, the first man, was made mortal, so that, whether he sinned or whether he did not sin, he would die in body, that is he would go out of the body not because of the merit of sin but by reason of the necessity of nature, let him be anathema. (Denzinger, 101)

This understanding prevailed at the Council of Orange as well and has been the most prominent view in the teaching of the church to our day.

This position can recognize the implication of God's categorical supremacy. To be sure, one might say, only God is naturally immortal, but the possibility of indefinite life in dependence on the living God is given as promise until sin severs the connection with God, rendering death effective.[4] What shall be said of God's role in this? While the simplest view is to see the deed of sin as bringing its own destiny, there is a persistent biblical witness to God's own involvement in human death. It is possible, of course, to conceive of that involvement as direct and particular causation, entailing specific, albeit apparently universal, intervention. The problems concerning such divine involvement are part of more general difficulties afflicting this view.

While this view does coherently combine the two orienting convictions, two objections occur: First, there is the ecological or evolutionary point, as made by R. Troisfontaines:

> Evolution as an incontrovertible fact . . . is unthinkable without death, for immortality would by its very nature undo evolution because of a surplus of people. Indeed, life—and certainly its progressive development—is unthinkable, unless by the grace of the death of individuals. Hence human nature must be necessarily mortal in its very essence.[5]

This objection is strengthened the more we grant humankind's membership in the animal kingdom, where death presumably occurred well before the advent of sin with humankind. We may seem here to be on too secular ground. But the second major objection to an absolute causal link between sin and death is an exegetical one. Claus Westermann puts the point directly enough: "Man, just because he has been created, carries within him limitation by death as an essential element of the human state."[6] The curse applies until we die; we die because we were created out of dust and shall return to dust. On the edge of death one knows this: "I am about to go the way of all the earth" (Josh. 23:14; 1 Kings 2:2).

The force of these objections has led nearly all contemporary theologians to regard physical death as something given with creation.[7] It does not follow from this that such natural death would have been simply a peaceful transition, "the highest, definitive, personal self-consummation," in the words of one of the more enthusiastic exponents of this view.[8] Rather, Barth seems more right in speaking of this death, though natural, as yet belonging to the "shadowside of creation."[9] That fits with the recognition that humankind was created "good, not perfect" and that if the human creature's relationship to God knew the tension of "epistemic distance," surely the reality of death would not be unaffected.

Perhaps this contemporary emphasis is not without some continuity with the church's traditional reflection. Canon 1 of the Council of Carthage, which we have cited above, was not specifically approved by Pope Zosimus in the letter he addressed to the whole church on the subject of original sin. The Council of Trent did not reproduce this canon, and a draft condemnation which said, "If anyone says that Adam was bound to die in any way, even if he had not sinned, let him be anathema," was left in the archives.[10] Within the Lutheran tradition, similarly, there has been a recognition that the *most* one could claim for the creature was "a freedom from the proximate power of dying and the natural tendency to death," not an absolute freedom from death which belongs only to God.[11]

More important, the contemporary understanding surely agrees with the traditional view that there is a connection between sin and death, though it does not conceive that connection in simple and absolute causality. In sin death is exacerbated. It is changed objectively. Thus von Rad notes that Israel's wisdom teachers spoke of "having to die" and by this meant "the premature death which the fool, the lascivious and the lazy bring upon themselves" by ignoring the proper limits involved in the relationships of created goodness.[12] Death is also changed subjectively—it takes on a new quality. Bonhoeffer writes:

> Death as transitoriness is not the death that comes from God. What does "to be dead" mean? It does not mean the abolition of created being; it means no longer being able to live—and yet having to live—in the presence of God . . . outlawed, lost and damned, but not nonexisting . . . to have life not as a gift but as a commandment.[13]

Thus death is not exhausted in the physical process of dying. In the qualitative experience of dying one knows the distortion of the relationship to God. While at the immediate level of causality it may seem sensible to follow an organic rather than a juridical link between sin and death,[14] it re-

mains doubly true that our dying cannot be fully separated from God. Helmut
Thielicke writes of Luther's understanding:

> The terrifying quality of man's death consists thus not merely in his loss of physical
> life, but in his forfeit of the living fellowship with God . . . death is not merely
> a quantitative boundary, but the imposition of qualitative limits; it is a fateful
> event in the personal relationship between God and man . . . death still carries
> the poison of wrath and thus remains a living reality focused on us, a power
> holding us spellbound.[15]

While reflection will resist substituting such theological considerations for
the organic connections by which sin hurries us toward our death quantitatively,
the sinner's qualitative experience of dying does include the painful awareness
of that which is terribly wrong in the relationship with God. Even abstracting
from sin to the death given with creatureliness, one must say that God does
not stand related to the death-bearing organism of life merely deistically, but
as living will. The "wrath of God" refers to something real within the sinner,
within God, and between God and the sinner. Our dying is also caught up
in the reality. Also, God has acted in Christ to show that God is Lord over
sin, Lord even over God's own wrath.

Given these quantitative and qualitative links between sin and death,
perhaps the contemporary emphasis can even find itself in significant continuity with conciliar statements which seem to take the other tack. Pelagius
said that Adam would have died even if he had not sinned, and the church
rejected his assertion. But Pelagius was speaking of the only death he and
we in fact know: death as punishment for sin.[16]

Perhaps contemporary reflection can also understand itself in continuity
with that tradition in the Eastern church which stresses that after the sin of
Adam we "fell sick of corruption" and that "by becoming mortal, we acquired
greater urge to sin." [17] Ernest Becker has argued persuasively that one of the
things that follows from death is a will to deny it. The denial of death yields
many aberrations, including the sacrifice of the lives of others, whether literally
or through scapegoating: "The death fear of the ego is lessened by the kill-
ing, the sacrifice of the other; through the death of the other, one buys oneself
free from the penalty of dying, of being killed." [18]

God's faithful have managed to live with death, because they lived with
God. In the Old Testament fear of death is overcome, not by appeal to the
particularity of another life but by calm reliance on the One whose faithfulness
cannot be destroyed.[19] Later the believer's confidence became more specific:

> What you sow does not come to life unless it dies. And what you sow is not
> the body which is to be, but a bare kernel, perhaps of wheat or of some other
> grain. . . . So is it with the resurrection of the dead. What is sown is perishable,

what is raised is imperishable. . . . The first man was from the earth, a man of dust; the second man is from heaven. . . . Just as we have borne the image of the man of dust, we shall also bear the image of the man of heaven (1 Cor. 15:36–37, 42, 47, 49).

Again we return to the theme of the divine intention in creation. Humankind is meant for God and is given what is needed to that end. Freedom is such a gift, and a precious one, though from that gift comes the reality of moral evil. But trust does not mature without risk. Moral perfection cannot be created "from nothing," if mature trust is intrinsic to the conception itself. Now Paul seems to suggest that while we are meant for unending life, that too cannot be given as inherent possession but only as something to which one passes trusting the promise of God. Just as sin can disrupt the gift of freedom, so it can sorely trouble the passage from finitude.

There is as well a third face of evil which troubles the human pilgrimage and we must now turn to that reality, suffering, and its relationship to our status as creatures and sinners.

SUFFERING

How does a child dying of inoperable cancer of the brain serve humankind? Must not the Creator who establishes the criteria by which such an event could count as service be regarded as simply evil? With a God like that who needs a devil? Perhaps it is in face of the stark reality of suffering that the issue of the justification of God comes before us most unavoidably. Perhaps moral evil (sin) and metaphysical evil (finitude, death) do not pronounce the verdict of guilty with unambiguous finality, though the indictments are hardly silenced. But before the face of suffering, will one not respond with Dostoevski's Ivan?

> Too high a price is asked for harmony; it is beyond our means to pay so much. And so I give back my entrance ticket, and if I am an honest man I give it back as soon as possible. And that I am doing. It's not God that I don't accept, Alyosha, only I most repectfully return the ticket to Him.[20]

Alyosha's response, "That's rebellion," and his appeal to the One who, having given "His innocent blood for all and everything," has a right to forgive and does forgive does not satisfy us. That response fits better the context Dostoevski has chosen: the suffering we inflict on each other in sin. We have commented on that by speaking of God's commitment to the venture of human freedom. But what, now, of that suffering which comes on us from sources that are not human? What of that evil we call "natural"? How can human freedom intercept the verdict against God in this case? If God has made us such that this suffering serves us, is not such a God to be rejected? Some familiar responses must be resisted.

It will not do to say that suffering does not exist. Although there may be a basis for distinguishing between the physiology of pain and the psychology of suffering,[21] and although we can create suffering subjectively which has no basis in reality outside ourselves, the sheer reality of pain and suffering still stands out as precisely that violence against our being which comes on us against our will and without our receptivity.

Nor may we say that suffering serves us by its sheer testimony to the splendor of existence. This way of thinking, loosely called the principle of plenitude, amounts to the sheer evocation of existence; what could be, should be—suffering included. Christian theology has at times drunk from this metaphysical wisdom, as when Augustine writes: "From things earthly to things heavenly, from the visible to the invisible, there are some things better than others; and for this purpose are they unequal, in order that they might all exist." (*City of God, xi*,22). But to argue so is finally to reduce goodness to being, which is to solve our difficulty by giving up what we are seeking to defend, that the Creator of being is not marred by the evil which is so real in the world of creatures.

We must also deny that suffering serves by introducing contrast into the universe. This response can be put in an aesthetic and static way, as when one argues that one would not appreciate the good without the experience of its opposite. Or it can be cast in an ethical and active way, as when one argues that suffering is needed as challenge to the human project. Both responses seem to cling still to the distinction between good and evil, and thus do not represent a simple appeal to some self-justifying transcendence of aesthetic contrast. Against both responses arguments converge from two sides. The inner life of the Trinity does not depend on contrast or challenge for its goodness. Why must we, made in God's image, need such? The argument is in difficulty on theological grounds. And in any case, there is far too much suffering for these purposes, and it is far too unevenly distributed. The argument fails on empirical grounds.

We have given cursory treatment to these historically influential responses because they do not represent genuinely theological responses. They are metaphysical, aesthetic, or at best moral arguments. But there are as well three theological responses which are commonly made but which need to be emphatically resisted.

First, whatever God does is right, and thus suffering is to be accepted without complaint. This response has something right: that no independent standard exists to which God's conduct must be held accountable. To grant the existence of such a standard would be to jettison the moral absoluteness of God. But it has at least two things badly muddled. God is committed to

438

a venture with creation. Indeed, in the covenant and in Christ God has willed that all the peoples of the earth will be blessed. God's own intention, then, does become a basis on which the faithful accept the question of the justice of God, as that question is put outside and inside the walls of the sanctuary. Nor does mere acceptance of suffering follow from the claim that whatever God does is right, unless it can be shown either that God does all things or that God does the particular things that cause suffering. God's responsibility must be assessed with respect to the framework, its creation and preservation, within which specific events occur, but this is vastly different from contending that God "does" the specific events.

A second inadequate theological response argues that the devil causes the specific events of suffering. We have already repelled an appeal to the devil as the direct explanation for sin, for two reasons. One of these reasons, that stressing human responsibility, would seem by definition not to apply in speaking of natural evil. Perhaps it is not surprising, then, that theologians should seem to move the demonic into the vacuum.[22] We have accepted Paul Ricoeur's suggestion that the demonic be incorporated into the Adamic myth as a complicating factor, because such a move is suggested by the logic of temptation, the experience of the pervasiveness of evil, and the biblical witness particularly to the liberating work of Jesus. Here too there may well be a subordinate place for such incorporation. But that is all. The second reason holds also for natural evil. What is at stake is responsibility for the framework in creation by which natural evil comes upon us. Any simple appeal to the devil as an explanatory factor would once again jettison the absoluteness of God—in this case saving God's goodness at the expense of sacrificing God's power.

A third inadequate theological response suggests that specific sufferings are "sent" by God to particular individuals for specific purposes: punishment, education, and the like. Again, this view raises the issue of how God acts in the world. In raising this issue the view moves near the difficult territory of prayer for the sick and gratitude for those who recover. That God wills health and is at work against the forces of destruction in an ultimate sense is something we strongly affirm. But our attempt to recognize death as given within human finitude should give us pause even in our grateful praise. More pointed still, the excruciating differentiations ("Why me, O Lord?") baffle, if we are assuming that God sends specific sufferings directly. What is needed is a retreat to the general framework in order to ask the basic question of how God can be said to be good inasmuch as God made a world which is turning out no better than this one.

We have been saying that God willed human freedom as a necessary means toward a greater end. We believe the best approach—and it is surely none too splendid—is to seek to understand natural evil within what is required for a metaphysics of freedom. The structure of reality, whence natural evil comes, is made by God in the service of human freedom. Let us take the argument apart.

God gives what freedom needs to be freedom, and part of what is needed is consequence. In saying this we do not rush ahead to the commonsense truth that we must suffer the consequences of our folly or to the tragic one that in our defiance we bind ourselves. It is natural evil of which we would speak. C. S. Lewis makes the point that human beings need nature, if human freedom is to have consequence:

> What we need for human society is exactly what we have—a neutral something, neither you nor I, which we can both manipulate so as to make signs to each other. I can talk to you because we can both set up sound-waves in the common air between us. Matter, which keeps souls apart, also brings them together.[23]

Lewis's idealism shows through in his ghostly view of human identity, but he is quite right about the human necessity for that which is not human. Moreover, he is right about the required stability of that which sustains the human:

> But if matter is to serve as a neutral field it must have a fixed nature of its own. . . . If you were introduced into a world which thus varied at my every whim, you would be quite unable to act in it and would thus lose the exercise of your free will.[24]

Given the needed neutrality of the natural field, this reality can oppress and destroy us as well as serve us. As Frederick Tennant puts it:

> If water is to have the various properties in virtue of which it plays its beneficial part in the economy of the physical world and the life of mankind, it cannot at the same time lack its obnoxious capacity to drown us. The specific gravity of water is as much a necessary outcome of its ultimate constitution as its freezing point, or its thirst-quenching and cleansing functions.[25]

This seems particularly the case if it is the identical capacity within a natural system which in one instance blesses and in another destroys. Would we trade such a system for a world of instant miracle in which the deity would act to intercept the deleterious consequences of a natural system before they could occur? Two responses are possible:

We might say that the possibility of suffering—even its actuality—is not too high a price to pay for the moral benefits of stability of structure. Thus Tennant writes: "Without such regularity in physical phenomena there could be no probability to guide us: no prediction, no prudence, no accumulation of ordered experience, no pursuit of premediated ends, no formation of habit, no possibility of character or of culture."[26] It seems important to note that this does not claim that suffering is directly useful, as providing a stimulus to the development of certain human virtues. That tack seems to amount to one or the other of the errors we have said should be avoided. But it is not always avoided. Thus John Hick writes of what is required for human love:

> It is, in particular, difficult to see how it could ever grow to any extent in a paradise that excluded all suffering. For such love presupposes a "real life" in which there are obstacles to be overcome, tasks to be performed, goals to be achieved, setbacks to be endured, problems to be solved, dangers to be met.[27]

It seems better not to be so optimistic about actual suffering, though at least Hick stops short of sanctifying specific sufferings as sent by God.

Or we might say that God's commitment to human freedom, including as it does what freedom needs to be freedom, is so complete that God cannot intervene to prevent suffering. We seem prepared to say this about the direct exercise of freedom yielding consequence: What is sown shall be reaped. Again C. S. Lewis put it well:

> His omnipotence means power to do all that is intrinsically possible, not to do the intrinsically impossible. You may attribute miracles to Him, but not nonsense. This is no limit to His power. If you choose to say "God can give a creature free-will and at the same time withhold free-will from it" you have not succeeded in saying *anything* about God: meaningless combinations of words do not suddenly acquire meaning simply because we prefix to them the two other words "God can."[28]

Lewis seems to have understood that freedom's reality is in its efficacy. Now should we not say as much of the natural structure which is required in God's gift of freedom? God's commitment to freedom is so absolute that God cannot intervene in the workings of the world where freedom flourishes and flounders.

We hasten to add that this is not to say that God does not work *within* the structure; a limited God is not a deistic God. Nor is what we have said to suggest that God does not have in store for this world a reality which is qualitatively other than this, one where every tear of suffering too shall be wiped away.

Before hastening to a summary, two important though secondary matters must at least be mentioned. First, that suffering oppresses as well as serves us is surely due in large part to sin. That has not been our emphasis in these remarks, because we find the common correlation between suffering and sin to be sorely incomplete. But we do bring suffering on others and ourselves, objectively, in our sin, and we do experience suffering more intensely subjectively because of our unfaith. Here too the exacerbating and perduring character of the demonic is apparent.

Second, we have not spoken of pain and suffering below the human level in the evolutionary cycle. While humankind must be held responsible for a great amount of such suffering, clearly we did not cause such suffering before we came into being, and presumably we do not cause all of it even now. Two responses seem to be appropriate: (1) Suffering below the human realm is to be understood in relation to the structure needed for human freedom. That structure out of which human nature evolved and which now oppresses as well as serves possesses in its very neutrality the same dialectical capacities in relation to all life. (2) God intends a new heaven and a new *earth*. Whether or not there is something analogous to human freedom in the "lower" levels of life, the suffering as oppression experienced at those levels constitutes a groaning in travail to which God will not fail to respond.

To what, then, have we come? We have tried to understand suffering within the creative intention of God, since the connection between suffering and sin seems inadequate in scope and in principle. In this area we do not have available the kind of gathered dogmatic resolution to which we have been able to refer in our consideration of moral evil and, to a lesser extent, of metaphysical evil. Lacking that, we have tried to offer a line of argument which is congruent with what we take the faith to have asserted dogmatically regarding the relationship between God and humankind in creation. But we are conscious that in doing this we appear to move against a strand of piety which would place at least much greater emphasis on suffering as directly willed by God. Some brief recognition of this strand and response to it are needed.

One way in which the direct connection between suffering and God is made is to interpose the reality of sin. One could do this softly by simply tracing suffering back to sin, while recognizing that whether we suffer as victims or as perpetrators, God can heal.[29]

Or, one may take a harder stand and introduce a notion of retribution, a theme that has probably prevailed in the thinking of many of the faithful who have undergone suffering of an unusual degree or kind. W. Sibley Towner has shown that the biblical writings do have a cycle of retribution in such materials as the Wisdom psalms, where God rewards the righteous and destroys the wicked. But he notes too the softening of this theme within the very texts themselves, appealing to the relative late date of the suzerainty treaty pattern of curse and blessing, for example. Or he looks at the vehicle that carries the texts:

Finally, the very literary form of the book of Deuteronomy seemed to me suggestive of a way of giving a softening nuance to the obvious retributional understanding of history contained in the book. Israel is left at the brink of the Jordan not yet foresworn to a course that will lead to certain disaster. . . . The people wait eternally at the bank of the Jordan. In the open-ended literary structure of the book, the people still have the option to obey. In its form and in its hortatory style, the book emerges as an evangelical appeal to obedience rather than an announcement of doom.[30]

Towner then proceeds to a second cycle:

Over against the lex talionis and Deuteronomy . . . the J creation story in Genesis. In contrast to the prophetic oracles of judgment . . . the prophetic promise. Job and Ecclesiastes countered the language of the Psalms of the Two Ways. Christological materials and parables of the Kingdom . . . as alternatives to the apocalyptic world judgment by God and the Son of Man.[31]

Among the conclusions emerging within this second cycle is what Towner calls the affirmation of the place and the integrity of the secular world: "There are events in the world which happen by chance or because some chain of causes made them inevitable, and over which God exercises sovereignty only in the remote sense of allowing them to take place within his created world."[32]

Some Christian theology has linked God with specific suffering without interposing talk of sin, consequence, retribution, and the like, by speaking of God's testing or trying the believer. The book of Job would seem to be the *locus classicus* for this theme. What shall one make of the conclusion of Job in which the power of the Creator seems to strip humankind of all significance? Dorothee Soelle states what may seem to be God's case against Job: "What is man, compared to oceans and galaxies, to impressive meteorological displays, to the permanency of nature! A nonentity, a grain of sand, a being that simply because of his insignificance, his cosmic triviality, has no rights whatsoever."[33] She then vents the reaction that wells up within us:

This God is a nature demon, who bears no relation to the God of the exodus and of the prophets. What once revealed God to the prophets was not the depths of the sea but justice which flows like water. . . . That Job at the conclusion of the book submits himself to this power-being who dwells beyond good and evil, is incredible because it is intolerable.

Soelle goes on to point to the interpretation of the atheist Ernst Bloch, who focuses on Job's quest for an advocate (19:25, 16:18–19):

This helper, this true friend, goes beyond all the roles for God offered in the book of Job. He is neither the arbitrary tester, nor the avenger who establishes his absolute purity by dirtying his own hands with blood, nor the Lord of stars, seas and clouds, "the mere *Tremendum* of nature."

Bloch finds Job appealing to the God who led the chosen people out of suffering in Egypt, while the God Job encounters seems merely another pharaoh. So Bloch must conclude: "Job is pious precisely because he does *not* believe." Soelle's conclusion, in turn, is:

> But then Job's call for the advocate, the redeemer, the blood-avenger and blood-satisfier is to be understood only as the unanswered cry of the pre-Christian world which finds its answer in Christ. Job is stronger than the old God. Not the one who causes suffering but only the one who suffers can answer Job.

Soelle's simplicity is misleading but instructive. It is misleading because it grants too easily the severity of Bloch's judgment about Job, and especially because it ignores so much else in the "pre-Christian" world, such as the steel in Hosea's eloquence about a God who will not come to destroy. But her simplicity is also instructive. Though God did not come to destroy, God did come. It is time to turn to the divine response to evil—whether moral, metaphysical, or natural—and to the subject of how we are to live in the light of that response.

NOTES

1. On the first conviction, see Hans Walter Wolff, *Anthropology of the Old Testament*, trans. Margaret Kohl (Philadelphia: Fortress Press, 1974), p. 107; and Gerhard von Rad, *Old Testament Theology*, trans. D. M. G. Stalker, 2 vols. (New York: Harper & Row, 1962–65), 2:349. On the second conviction, see Wolff, p. 102.

2. Von Rad, *Old Testament Theology*, 2:349.

3. Robin Scroggs, *The Last Adam* (Philadelphia: Fortress Press, 1966), p. 73; Rudolf Bultmann, *Theology of the New Testament*, trans. Kendrick Grobel, 2 vols. (New York: Charles Scribner's Sons, 1954–55), 1:246–49.

4. As Robert Martin-Achard, *From Death to Life*, trans. John Penny Smith (Edinburgh: Oliver & Boyd, 1960), p. 19: "Before the Fall, between Adam and death, which is part of his natural lot as an element in his human heritage, there stands the Living God; His presence is sufficient to ward death off, to conceal it. . . . But when God withdraws, nothing is left to Adam, but the presence of death. . . . Man, then is born mortal, but by his sin he renders death effective; it enters as a reality into his existence."

5. As paraphrased by S. Trooster, *Evolution and the Doctrine of Original Sin*, trans. John A. Ter Haar (New York: Newman Press, 1968), p. 22.

6. Claus Westermann, *Creation*, trans. John J. Scullion (Philadelphia: Fortress Press, 1974), p. 22.

7. E.g., John Macquarrie, *Principles of Christian Theology*, 2d ed. (New York: Charles Scribner's Sons, 1977), p. 264: "Apart altogether from sin, death belongs to finitude." For a statement of the consensus in recent theology on this point, see H. Paul Santmire, *Brother Earth* (Toronto: Thomas Nelson, 1970), chap. 6.

8. Trooster, *Evolution and the Doctrine of Original Sin*, p. 23.

9. Karl Barth, *Church Dogmatics,* 5 vols. in 14 (Edinburgh: T. & T. Clark, 1936–77), 3/3: 296.

10. W. J. Rewak, "Adam, Immortality, and Human Death," *ScEc* 19 (1967): 67–79.

11. Heinrich Schmid, *The Doctrinal Theology of the Evangelical Lutheran Church,* trans. from the 5th ed. by Charles A. Hay and Henry E. Jacobs (Philadelphia: Lutheran Bookstore, 1876), p. 249.

12. Gerhard von Rad, *Wisdom in Israel,* trans. James D. Martin (Nashville: Abingdon Press, 1972), pp. 304–5. Cf. Santmire, *Brother Earth,* pp. 125–26.

13. Dietrich Bonhoeffer, *Creation and Fall,* trans. John Fletcher (New York: Macmillan Co.; London: SCM Press, 1959), p. 55; cf. p. 86.

14. Hans Conzelmann, *An Outline of the Theology of the New Testament,* trans. John Bowden (New York: Harper & Row, 1969), p. 197. Paul Ricoeur, *The Symbolism of Evil,* trans. Emerson Buchanan (Boston: Beacon Press, 1967), pp. 141–42. Bultmann, *Theology of the N.T.,* 1:246.

15. Helmut Thielicke, *Death and Life,* trans. Edward H. Schroeder (Philadelphia: Fortress Press, 1970), p. 153. Cf. Walther Eichrodt, *Theology of the Old Testament,* trans. J. A. Baker, 2 vols. (Philadelphia: Westminster Press, 1961–67), 2:406.

16. Rewak, "Adam, Immortality, and Human Death," p. 78.

17. John Meyendorff, *Byzantine Theology: Historical Trends and Doctrinal Themes* (New York: Fordham University Press, 1974), p. 145: "There is indeed a consensus in Greek patristic and Byzantine traditions in identifying the inheritance of the Fall as one essentially of mortality rather than sinfulness, sinfulness being merely a consequence of mortality."

18. Ernest Becker, *Escape from Evil* (New York: Free Press, 1975), p. 108, quoting Otto Rank.

19. E.g., Wolff, *Anthropology of the O.T.,* pp. 108–9.

20. Feodor Dostoevski, *The Brothers Karamazov,* trans. Constance Garnett (New York: New American Library, 1957), p. 226.

21. John Hick, *Evil and the God of Love,* rev. ed. (New York: Harper & Row; London: Macmillan & Co., 1975), pp. 328–30.

22. See, e.g., Arthur C. McGill, *Suffering: A Test of Theological Method* (Philadelphia: Geneva Press, 1968), pp. 41ff.

23. C. S. Lewis, *The Problem of Pain* (New York: Macmillan Co., 1948), p. 19. Cf. F. R. Tennant, *Philosophical Theology,* 2 vols. (Cambridge: At the University Press, 1935–37), 2:199.

24. Lewis, *Problem of Pain,* p. 19.

25. Tennant, *Philosophical Theology,* p. 201.

26. Ibid., pp. 199–200.

27. Hick, *Evil and the God of Love,* p. 362.

28. Lewis, *Problem of Pain,* p. 16. (Emphasis his.)

29. Von Rad, *Old Testament Theology,* 1:274–75: On the theology of the hexateuch: "all serious illnesses were subject to a . . . sacral assessment. . . . Such disturbances of the vital basis of human existence brought a man into a *status confessionis.* Only God could heal. . . . It was of course from Jahweh that bodily sickness came . . . there was a very close connection between sin and physical disease."

30. W. Sibley Towner, *How God Deals with Evil* (Philadelphia: Westminster Press, 1976), p. 145.

31. Ibid., p. 147.

32. Ibid., p. 149.

33. This and the following quotations are from Dorothee Soelle, *Suffering,* trans. Everett R. Kalin (Philadelphia: Fortress Press, 1975), pp. 117-19.

5

The Work
of God Against Evil

God continues to work for life and order through people and institutions with and without the knowledge of God. God responds decisively to sin in Jesus and the sacramental life of the church, and God draws human beings to faith, obedience, and hope in a kingdom which is beyond Eden.

THE CONTINUITY OF GOD

In the beginning we emphasized that our topic was a derivative one, logically and theologically. Throughout we have argued for a distinction between creation and fall, between finitude and sin. Our focus has been on sin and fall. Now, in this last chapter, we reenter the broader dogmatic terrain, for we look here at what has been done, what is being done, and what is to be done—in the light of evil. It is the work of God of which we write. While it may have been right in principle to claim that the concept of God can be adequately defined apart from any reference to sin, the Christian claim is that the work of God, in actuality, is against evil—moral, metaphysical, and natural. God works against sin. God leads us through suffering. God summons us beyond death.

Sin is not so strong that it can overrule the creative intention of God. While Western Christendom—particularly in its Pauline-Augustinian-Lutheran form—has done its theology in the form of a drama in the three acts of creation/fall/redemption, this theology should not be read as denying a unity of the entire plot, or action beyond the third act. Of course those theologians who tend not to distinguish chronologically between creation and fall will be able to speak more emphatically of unity, of continuity, in the divine intention and action. Continuity then would be found simply in this: that our talk of God's work, even of the work of creation, is always in the face of evil.[1]

This is correct as far as the situation of the speaker is concerned. But we have argued that the threatened human being is best served by a faith in a God whose categorical supremacy is such that even a chronological distinc-

447

tion between creation and fall is to be affirmed. For such a position, ironically, both creation and fall in their distinctness assume heightened significance. Yet the "new" act of the fall is not so significant that the curtain must be rung down on what God was about in creation. Despite sin, God continues to will and to work in continuity with the divine creative intention. Perhaps one will be more inclined to speak of this as "preservation," distinguishing it from both creation and redemption. There are differences between the three. God acts to constitute and preserve the human project, despite the difficulties due to sin; and God acts to redeem that project even in the defiance that is sin. But underlying the differences, there is the unity of the divine will.[2]

Despite the abstractness of our prose, it is biblical faith of which we speak. Moreover it is not merely the highly theological faith of Paul's Epistle to the Romans. Von Rad notes that the priestly writer in Genesis holds that when sin broke in the earth was corrupted in God's sight and filled with violence (Gen. 6:11, 13), so that "all that Jahweh had 'separated out' at creation was falling together in collapse. . . . The natural relationships between created beings are in desperate disorder." To check the *hatta'th*, the violence,

> Jahweh promulgated certain dispositions. He allowed the killing and slaughter of animals. But the life of man he put under his own absolute protection— though he did so in terms of putting the onus of avenging murder on men themselves. Jahweh even guaranteed the preservation of the continued physical existence of the universe by the making of a covenant (Gen. 9:8ff.). It is within the stability thus established by the grace of Jahweh that the saving history is in due time to operate.[3]

What is it that God does in the face of sin? The Yahwist's Adam names his wife Eve (a variant of the word for "living") *again* (Gen. 3:20; cf. 2:23). His faith is that God will still bless. Perhaps we can still make something of that, saying that in sexuality humankind is creative even in the midst of destruction.[4] What is to be resisted is a reductionist reading of this "order of creation," which makes human identity essentially a matter of biology. Without propagation there is no real life, to be sure, but real life is far more than biological life. In the recognition that despite sin God is still the God of the living, one may hear a call to development, for the human being is created with a vocation—something we have suggested throughout in our evocation of the "good, not perfect" theme. We were not perfected in creation, but called ahead. We are clearly not perfect in our fallenness, but we are to be perfected. We are still called ahead.

It is in this dynamic sense that the notion of "orders" is to be understood. Gustav Wingren warns against a view in which creation is

> assigned to some past time, and the ordinances regarded as a surviving product

of the past act of Creation. In such a case, however, we lose all idea of God's continuing Creation and reforming of the world. And since we have completely lost the "dynamic aspect" of Creation, we also lose *the* dynamic aspect which is the transformation by the Gospel of human life in the attitude to one's neighbor.[5]

Certainly marriage, work, and the economy suggest this dynamic sense easily, though they do remain vulnerable to a rigidifying interpretation. Government, though, seems to retain its developmental character only with the greatest difficulty. Here particularly there is need to stress the possibility of abuse, of forfeiting the mandate, lest the faith become an ideological accessory to oppression.

The "orders," then, are there for life, for the living. Life does require ordering. Even that metaphysical student of novelty, Alfred North Whitehead, wrote, "Novelty may promote or destroy order; it may be good or bad."[6] Order is needed not to balance life but to serve it, indeed to constitute it qualitatively. We are created for relationship; in the gift of life there is the call to the sociality of being. The qualitative value of human order is anticipated in the aesthetic reality of interrelationships and the biological imperative against inbreeding.[7] But on the human level, qualitative life through order is a particularly temporal reality. Thus James Gustafson writes: "To be human is to have a vocation, a calling; that is it is to become what we now are not; it calls for a surpassing of what we are; . . . apart from a telos, a vision . . . we will flounder and die."[8]

The call ahead is a call through the structures of creaturely life, rather than a call to withdraw from those under the inspiration of redemption, although the distinction is often muddled. That distinction seems to be the sense of the Augsburg Confession's rebuff to those who teach that "Christian perfection requires the forsaking of house and home":

> Actually true perfection consists alone of proper fear of God and real faith in God, for the Gospel does not teach an outward and temporal but an inward and eternal mode of existence and righteousness of the heart. The Gospel does not overthrow civil authority, the state, and marriage but requires that all these be kept as true orders of God and that everyone, each according to his own calling, manifest Christian love and genuine good works in his station of life. (Augsburg Confession, XVI, *BC* 37–38)

Moreover, one might suggest that this positive endorsement of civil orders is certainly not required by the emphasis on the spiritual character of the life rooted in God's redemption. Rather, it seems to derive from an implied doctrine of creation which attributes independent value to such social order. Of course such social order may also possess an instrumental value in the service of the gospel.

It should be emphasized that the work of God for ordered life, for living order, does not depend on any conscious awareness in human agents of that work. Indeed, human will may even be at cross-purposes with divine will. Yet it should also be said that despite sin humankind can know the creative will of God for the world. Nor does such knowledge depend on some peculiarly spiritual revelation. At least that is true in the biblical writings. The Old Testament Wisdom literature carries this message strongly, as von Rad notes:

> For Israel there was only one world of experience and . . . this was apperceived by means of a perceptive apparatus in which rational perceptions and religious perceptions were not differentiated. Nor was this any different in the case of the prophets. . . . The experiences of the world were for her [Israel] always divine experiences as well and the experiences of God were for her experiences of the world.[9]

Moving across centuries and literary genera with some abandon, we note the same stress on concreteness in Paul's anthropology.[10]

Biblical faith and human experience come together to suggest that human beings can not only know God's creative will but also can perform it. Again this is open to alternative theological formulations. We have noted the strain of optimism in the medieval interpretation of the human condition after Adam. But even the Lutheran protest against this strain did not fail to grant that "civil righteousness" was possible, despite the bondage of the will toward that which is above humankind. We have wondered whether that concession would not lead to a broader range of significance for the human pole in the relationship to God.

Does this warrant a fundamental optimism about the human project?[11] Optimism seems to depend on an understanding of evil as privation and on a context in which evil's positively defiant character is obscured; such a view is not acceptable to us. We have stressed the efficacy of sin: within God, within humankind, and between God and humankind. As helpful as the theme of the continuity of divine action may be, it does not adequately address the human predicament. Given the extensiveness and efficacy of evil, we need precisely a divine response which is somehow more than the basis upon which we can try and fail again. In a sense we find ourselves with the book of Genesis, where the story of the Tower of Babel concludes without any note of grace. Von Rad comments:

> The whole primeval history, therefore, seems to break off in shrill dissonance, and the question . . . arises even more urgently: Is God's relationship to the nations now finally broken? That is the burdensome question which no thoughtful reader of ch. 11 can avoid; indeed, one can say that our narrator intended by means of the whole plan of his primeval history to raise precisely this question

and to pose it in all its severity. Only then is the reader properly prepared to take up the strangely new thing that now follows the comfortless story about the building of the tower: the election and blessing of Abraham.[12]

We do not now leave behind the continuity of the work of God, but we do advance to a new theme: the decisiveness of God.

THE DECISIVENESS OF GOD

We write here of what was done in Jesus. But our purpose is not to attempt an analysis of the various soteriological theories which have been put forward, or to offer our own. We wish only to speak of the intersection between hamartiology and soteriology in order to show how the analysis of evil with which we have been concerned reenters the dogmatic system. The connection can be suggested by a single phrase: God's decisive response.

The Christian faith understands the work of Christ as a response to the human predicament. While this is not obvious in the Scotist emphasis that Christ would have come even had there been no sin, even in this understanding a significant element of response is recognized. Whatever the formulation, what is done with Jesus carries a heightened sense of newness in comparison with what we have spoken of as God's continuing work of preservation. A new word is needed; the continuing work of preservation will not suffice.[13]

The gravity and efficacy of evil threaten to trivialize the continuing work of God, unless some decisive resolution can be managed. God continues to work, but so does sin, after all. Who is to say that all this does not add up to a cosmic standoff? Or perhaps sin will even wear down the divine determination itself. There is needed something that indicates—more clearly than the "more of the same" of God's preserving work—what the disposition of evil is or is to be, as far as God is concerned.

The church has claimed that a divine response to evil is at hand and that it is so decisive, so clear in its message, that the predicament itself is only first fully understood in light of this response. The shadowy first Adam and we who are of him become clear against the sharper focus of the Second Adam. The decisiveness is not merely an epistemological matter. Repeatedly Paul drives home the point: "For if many died through one man's trespass, *much more* have the grace of God and the free gift in the grace of that one man Jesus Christ abounded for many" (Rom. 5:15; cf. 5:17). "Where sin increased, grace abounded *all the more*" (Rom. 5:20). We have used strong words about sin: inevitable, bound, and the like. Paul and the basic Christian intuition of the normative particularity of Jesus will not let us use weaker ones of the divine response.

One might argue that the alternative formulations concerning this Jesus are so disparate that the sense of decisiveness is altogether eroded. Perhaps one must grant that no single material insight prevails in the welter of soteriological theories. But it is most significant that widely differing theories come together to affirm the decisiveness of Jesus, and then—appropriately, one might argue—specify that decisiveness variously, depending on what humankind, on each view, needs.

Thus even the so-called "subjective" theories of atonement, in which the newness of the response is drawn very far back into God's continuing work, still reach for such decisiveness as is needed to meet the human predicament understood as weakness or ignorance. Thus Schleiermacher's reading of the need as residing in a weak or obscured God-consciousness specified the decisiveness of the Christ to be not that of an example (*Vorbild*), but that of the generative archetype (*Urbild*) from whom redeeming impulses irresistibly arise. Indeed, one might quietly respond to criticisms of the "small Christ" of figures like Schleiermacher and Tillich by noting that even if the soteriological categories employed seem merely epistemological ("realize," "consciousness," "revelation"), they do yield a universal salvation.[14]

If such soteriologies are to be faulted, it must be because they have underestimated the gravity of the human predicament, so that the apparently decisive Christ they provide in fact fails to resolve what we know to be in us. That would be the direction of our own criticism. Ironically, one may purchase one's optimism by selling the reality of humankind too cheaply. One may then understate the gravity of the venture with freedom in which God is engaged. If one fails to recognize the full reality of the nondivine will, one may fail to reckon with our efficacy for ourselves and for God. If we cannot "be" for God (Schleiermacher declines to call God "Lord," inasmuch as that implies too much over-againstness for God), God can hardly be wrathful toward us. If God has not let us out of the divine hand in freedom, we can hardly bind ourselves. It should not then surprise us that God can bring the project to completion without resorting to radically novel means, for God remains clearly in control.

Other main directions in soteriological thinking also cling to the fact that it is God who is at work in the decisive Christ, but formulate the need differently—reflecting a self and a race granted more awful freedom. We spoke in Chapter 1 of the wrath of God as a category supported by the understanding of the divine will and human sin. Perhaps the "objective" soteriological theory—purporting to understand none other than God to be the object of the work of Jesus—permits the most emphatic resolution at this point. Our problem is out of our hands, for it is within God: Our guilt calls forth God's wrath. God must somehow deal with divine wrath, and this God does in the one called Jesus. Thus in Romans, Paul begins his statement of the gospel of which he is "not ashamed" by referring to the "wrath of God . . . revealed from heaven against all ungodliness and wickedness" (Rom. 1:18). He aims to make clear that since we are justified by Christ's blood, we shall "be saved by him from the wrath of God" (Rom. 5:9).

It is no doubt often the case that in theological formulations of this theme it is no longer God who is in control, but some juridical or ritual dynamic. Paul Ricoeur sees the interplay of purification and pardon themes as a hazardous process, but one that ultimately yields rich results:

> It is because the foreign vegetation of ceremonial expiation grew like an excrescence on the tree of "repentance" and "pardon" that the symbolism of expiation could, in return, enrich that of "pardon," and so one sees God invoked in the Psalms as the subject of expiation (78:38; 65:3; 79:9). To say that God "expiates" is to say that he "pardons." The symbolism of expiation, then, gives back to the symbolism of pardon what the latter had lent it.[15]

God is in charge of deciding who will be pardoned; this theory can provide a decisive response precisely because it places the response within God.

The church's belief in the incarnation contends that God takes the venture with human freedom so seriously that this act of pardoning cannot occur "above our heads." Only in God's complete identification with human flesh and human sin can sin find its decisive disposition in God. If wrath is injured love, then surely the resolution will be through suffering.[16] Perhaps love finally does refuse to let its suffering be a passive matter to be undergone. Ricoeur anticipates the merger in one person of what appear to be two quite distinct lines:

> On the one hand, the evil that is *committed* leads to a just exile; that is what the figure of Adam represents. On the other hand, the evil that is *suffered* leads to an unjust deprivation; that is what the figure of Job represents. The first figure calls for the second; the second corrects the first. Only a third figure could announce the transcending of the contradiction, and that would be the figure of the "suffering Servant," who would make of suffering, of the evil that is undergone, an *action* capable of redeeming the evil that is committed. This enigmatic figure is the one celebrated by the Second Isaiah in the four "songs of the Servant of Yahweh" (Isa. 42:1–10, 49:1–6; 50:4–11; 52:13—53:12), and it opens up a perspective radically different from that of "wisdom." It is not contemplation of creation and its immense measure that consoles; it is suffering itself. Suffering has become a gift that expiates the sins of the people.[17]

The logic of Christian faith requires that all of God be involved in this suffering, though this does not require the confusions represented by the patripassianist heresy.[18]

We have not made a gathered statement of the objective tendency in soteriological thought. We have simply remarked that the very objectivity of the theory—its "within-God-ness"—permits a singularly unconditional decisiveness for the work of Christ, though that work must pass through the realm of sin and guilt which is "for God." Since sin is paradigmatically against God, it is God's response to sin which ultimately matters as far as the question of sin's efficacy is concerned. If God is such that a decisive response is available (as we have argued), that is what matters. As Paul says, "It is God who judges." Yet inasmuch as sin is at least as much ours as wrath is God's, there remains open here the issue of the future of human sin. We seek to comment on that in the final section of this chapter, but note even now that some formulations draw such comment back into the very decisiveness of the work of Christ itself. At least that seems to be what is claimed in the "Christus Victor" theory.

In this view sin is seen as an objective power standing behind humankind, and the atonement is seen as the triumph of God over sin, death, and the devil. There is admittedly a dualistic tendency in this view, but Aulén defends the view despite the difficulties:

> The work of Atonement is accomplished by God Himself in Christ, yet at the same time the passive form also is used: God is reconciled with the world. The alternation is not accidental: He is reconciled only because He Himself reconciles the world with Himself and Himself with the world. The safeguard of the continuity of God's operation is the dualistic outlook, the Divine warfare against the evil that holds mankind in bondage and the triumph of Christ.[19]

Again we attempt no full analysis, but we do wish to show that the content of Christ's work and the degree of decisiveness available for that work is directly correlated to the perception of the human predicament. While the "victory" theory overlaps somewhat with the "objective" tendency in what Aulén calls the "Latin" form (cf. the appeal to the law and the wrath of God as enemies), the emphasis in understanding the predicament of humanity shifts somewhat from the Adamic toward the theogonic. Just as in the "objective" view the unity of God and the particularity of Jesus permit a truly decisive disposition to sin in the resolution of wrath, so here the added unity of sin, as an "objective" power, permits an apparently emphatic victory.

Here too, however, there remains the question of the future of *my* sinning, if the Adamic emphasis on responsibility is not to be rejected altogether. Indeed, that question seems to press the more painfully in this understanding, since the formulation of God's decisiveness is cast directly in relation to the occurrence of sin itself, not in relation to the significance of the occurrence to and in God. Yet the more we seem in our sin to be victims before we are perpetrators, even if victims only of our own identity in the race, so much the more does vindication seem to meet our need more truly than forgiveness.

That has been Krister Stendahl's reading of Paul against the distortion represented in the Lutheran "introspective conscience of the West":

> Paul's thoughts about justification were triggered by the issues of divisions and identities in a pluralistic and torn world, not primarily by the inner tensions of individual souls and consciences. His searching eyes focused on the unity and the God-willed diversity of humankind, yes of the whole creation.[20]

The scope of Stendahl's reading of the solution reveals the narrowness of our traditional focus. In this chapter also we have still been focusing mainly on moral evil, on sin. Does the work of God in Jesus represent a response to metaphysical and natural evil as well? The category of "response" seems less appropriate if suffering and death are given with creation rather than being the result of sin. Of course the benefits Christ brings will respond to the exacerbating detriment sin adds to our experience of suffering and dying. But in relation to metaphysical and natural evil there will be greater stress on the coming and activity of Jesus in *continuity with* the creative intention of God. Here Jesus—and in Jesus, God—will be perceived as partners in the pilgrimage of suffering toward perfection. Perhaps Jürgen Moltmann has caught that note in recording the insistence that God must suffer along with the Jews in the holocaust: "To speak of a God who could not suffer would make God a demon. To speak here of an absolute God would make God an annihilating nothingness. To speak here of an indifferent God, would condemn men to indifference."[21] If this is right about that suffering that issues from the sin that is against God, it is *a fortiori* so regarding the suffering that comes through the conditions that are from the Creator's hand.

The resurrection of Christ surely "responds to" our experience of dying. Paul's focus on the link with sin is familiar: If Christ is not raised, we are still in our sins (1 Cor. 15:17). A God who cannot do anything about death provides only a futile basis for any faith in forgiveness. But what of death itself? If one regards death as given with finitude, one will still find in the resurrection a powerful witness to what lies in store for humankind, and indeed for all creation. As Karl Schmitz-Moormann puts it:

> Christ's redemption affects the universe, not just the human race, and it affects the universe at a level deeper and wider than that of factual sin. For the deepest threat to evolution is death—death which is not the fruit of "Adam's" sin but is natural to creation as much as it is a threat to it. Christ's death and resurrection answers the question, does evolution have an issue? Is extinction the ultimate fruit of the human hunger for unconditional meaning? The paschal mystery tells us that all creatures have a definite, consummating goal, thanks to God's creative union in Christ with his developing world. Physical death of the universe through the victory of entropy, and spiritual death through the victory of sin, are both overcome in the identification of Omega with the Lord.[22]

5 / SIN AND EVIL

We are again pressed to return to the issue of God's creative intention, in order to ask how it goes with and in that human partner to whom God is committed. God continues to work for life and order and God responds decisively to sin. But what of the future of my sin and of my sinning? The way to Christian reflection on this troublesome matter leads through the sacramental life of the church, with particular attention to the sacrament of baptism.

The sacrament of baptism represents the decisive response of God to the human predicament of sin. This is clearest in infant baptism. While the practice of infant baptism was not always linked with the teaching of original sin by its supporters or by its opponents, there was an increasing tendency to move in that direction. That baptism is not the act of the baptized is not in doubt in infant baptism, despite occasional attempts to speak of infant faith. Since it is God's act, the faith and character of the officiant are not required for the validity of baptism, as the church decided during the Donatist controversy in the fourth century. Indeed, by the time of the Council of Trent in the sixteenth century, the objectivity of the efficacy of baptism could be put in still stronger terms: rightly administered, baptism is always valid, for it takes effect not as a mere sign of faith, but *ex opere operato.*[23] Many Christians who reject this Roman Catholic formulation still place a strong objective emphasis in their understanding of baptism. Thus, for example, Lutherans stress that it is the Word of God active in baptism which secures its validity. In the words of Luther's Large Catechism, God is bound to the water of baptism by the saving Word, which "contains and conveys all the fullness of God."

Whether one tends toward a Roman substantial emphasis or toward a Protestant dynamic emphasis, baptism is understood as decisive. What God does here need not to be repeated: we do not rebaptize those who fall away and return or who come to us from other Christian flocks. Thus the sacrament of baptism seems to represent the objective decisiveness of God's response to the human predicament in a way quite like the objectivity of God's work in Christ. Indeed, one may sense a certain superfluity here, as did the Anabaptists who refused to baptize their children on the grounds that Christ in effect had already done so.[24] But if God's decisiveness is not completed act but sure and living will, then that will renews itself in the reality of baptism, as God relates the divine self freshly to the one who is baptized. What God has resolved in Christ is now renewed for us.

In saying this we are moving the locus of God's decisiveness into a slightly more relational field. Thus Lutherans argue that baptism is efficacious not merely because it was instituted by Christ in his historical decisiveness, but also because there is attached to baptism the word of promise. The promise is for this one, the one now baptized. The promise thus becomes effective as it is received in faith. If one declines to say this, one seems to exempt baptism from the general truth that in God's will to bless humankind God creates freedom. Roman Catholics agree that response matters, distinguishing between objective validity and a fruitfulness which depends on right dispositions in the baptized. This matter of human response to the divine decisiveness lies ahead of us in the final section. It can surely be overrated, as for example in the tendency in the ancient church to delay baptism until just before death, lest sin after baptism destroy its benefits. Here it will suffice to note that baptism represents the divine decisiveness, but that it calls for the response of faith and obedience.

What, then, are the blessings of God's decisive act in baptism? Just as "justification" seemed most clearly to state the decisiveness of Jesus' works, so the forgiveness of the guilt of original sin stands out as common Christian teaching concerning the benefits of baptism. The Council of Carthage in 418 could assert, "Infants fresh from their mothers' wombs . . . are indeed baptized unto the remission of sins." Original sin is specified in these words: "Even infants, who in themselves thus far have not been able to commit any sin, are therefore truly baptized unto the remission of sins, so that that which they have contracted from generation may be cleansed in them by regeneration" (Denzinger, 102).

This theme is strengthened in later Catholic teaching, as when the Tridentine decree on original sin specifically adds that such baptism is needed for newly born infants "even though they be born of baptized parents" (Denzinger, 791). This strong stand on the forgiveness of the guilt of original sin may rest a little uneasily with those Roman Catholic figures who are not inclined to speak of the infant's condition as truly sin, but it links Roman Christendom with Reformation Christendom in the doctrine of baptism. Reformation Christians may in turn move closer to their Roman colleagues in declining to follow Augustine's robust logic: that unbaptized infants who die are condemned. The sense of baptism as promise suggests not a magical transformation, but a gracious adoption by which God calls the developing person to God. Hence the emphasis on incorporation into a living community of faith.

A harder question is whether a second decisive soteriological theme—that of liberation or healing—is to be found in baptism. With striking differences of degree, Christians of many stripes wish to incorporate this theme. A very ambitious formulation is that of the Council of Orange (529): "Freedom of will weakened in the first man cannot be repaired except through the grace of Baptism" (Denzinger, 186). Of course at issue in this is how to regard the infant before baptism. Liberation will be rather easily purchased if our reading of the human condition sets the price low enough. On the other hand, someone like Luther, with a very strong claim for the sinfulness of concupiscence, will not be inclined to speak as readily of liberation. Despite the new birth in baptism, "our human flesh and blood have not lost their old skin" (Large

Catechism, *BC* 449). Thus the Christian is ever *simul justus et peccator.* Over against this the Council of Trent follows Pope Leo X who had condemned Luther's thesis, "To deny that sin remains in a child after baptism is to despise both Paul and Christ alike."[25] Thus Trent's decree reads:

> But his holy Synod confesses and perceives that there remains in the baptized concupiscence of an inclination, although this is left to be wrestled with, it cannot harm those who do not consent, but manfully resist by the grace of Jesus Christ. . . . This concupiscence, which at times the Apostle calls *sin* (Rom. 6:12ff.) the holy Synod declares that the Catholic Church has never understood to be called sin, as truly and properly sin in those born again, but because it is from sin and inclined to sin. (Denzinger, 792)

Here the more optimistic and more pessimistic strains of our historical survey in Chapter 3 return. Trent is following Thomas, but whether Trent or Luther is nearer Augustine is not clear.[26] But even Lutherans have wished to stress that baptism is to aid the Christian in the struggle against sin, death, and the devil. Perhaps, then, it is best to continue this discussion in the context toward which we have been tending: the Christian's response to the continuing and decisive work of God.

THE DIRECTIVITY OF GOD

Christians are to work against evil. God is committed to a covenant venture with humankind. In the face of evil, God still works for ordered life. God has responded decisively to human sin in the person of Jesus. In baptism God graciously brings human beings directly into the covenant community. God did not do all of this that we might remain in evil. There is not only the sacrament of initiation, there is the supper of continuance. God blesses people through means of grace, that they might move toward the calling God intended even before the cosmic seas were brought into being. The Scripture builds an imperative on the divine indicative: "Work out your own salvation with fear and trembling; for God is at work in you, both to will and to work for his good pleasure" (Phil. 2:12–13). While this dogmatics has an entire locus on "the Christian life," in this final section we need to indicate briefly how the locus on sin and evil reenters the broader system also at this point. If stylistic inelegance be permitted, we may gather our remarks around the theme, the directivity of God.

The struggle against sin is a struggle to believe, to have faith. In that sense the struggle is directed *to* God, for God is the object of faith. In Chapter 1 we spoke of how the opposite of sin is not virtue but faith. While there may be some sense in which one simply does not, indeed cannot, *choose* to believe, one can choose to live out one's life in a way congruent with trust and praise of God. In that sense one is called to discipleship, indeed to obedience.

In this matter we wish to stress the Christian's continuity with God's creative intention and the continuing work of God, as discussed in the first section of this chapter. In Chapter 2 we indicated that to say that humankind is made in the image of God is to say that we are made incomplete. We are directed toward a destiny. That we might reach that destiny, directions are given. This is the point of "Torah," however much this gift of God may be twisted. For the Christian those directions still apply. That is, we have been graciously restored to the pilgrimage toward our destiny, and we stand in need of directions. I am speaking of what Paul Althaus has called the divine *Gebot*, or command, following Article VI of the Formula of Concord. William Lazareth provides a succinct statement:

> As the "command" of the Creator to all creatures in his holy image, it is ultimately love. It is the reverse side of God's Angebot—the offer with which the eternal love of God originally encounters persons. God's Gebot of love corresponds to man's original righteousness. It is supralapsarian, depicting the proper relation between the Creator and his human creatures before their fall into sin. It is the human's ethical expression of the image of God.[27]

Althaus is pleading that this wholistic sense of God's "command" be distinguished from the "law," the Mosaic and Judaic laws by which God punishes crime and reveals sin. While as sinners Christians still need the "law," in their new life they are called to obey the "command" of God. This seems a useful way to lead beyond the strife-torn debates about the "third use" of the law. Moreover, it brings us to a matter of ecumenical consensus: that we are called to obedience.

What, if anything, is the distinctive Christian contribution to this obedience? Does the Christian have a new insight into the command of God? Both the witness of experience and that of faith would seem to deny this. In the first section of this chapter we argued that the human being is able to know the requirements of God. Indeed, we even claimed that as human we are able to perform in some measure what God requires for life on this planet. Yet is there not some kind of ethical "gain" within the Christian community? Gustaf Wingren ponders this matter:

> The connection and the distinction between natural law and the commandment of Jesus is from one point of view a reflection of another connection and another distinction. . . . Redemption gives more than creation when it restores creation. We are dealing here with a connection and distinction between natural and Christian, and both are reflected on the level of law or commandment. . . . This is what is meant by the accentuation, newness, and heightening of the law. The Christian attitude is that of a natural love for the neighbor which is thoroughly

"of this world" and conveyed in the rough forms of man's daily vocations, but it is filled with a new willingness to *suffer* for the good of the neighbor and to do so with *joy*.[28]

Perhaps there is some sharpening of insight here, as suffering and death—though quite natural—are not easily seen as imperatives. Similarly, with respect to the doing of what is seen to be good, the Christian faith can provide a direction for ethical life, and with that such "reasons" or motivations as a sense of dependence, gratitude, repentance, obligation, and possibility.[29] There are, after all, some things that do distinguish the Christian. The Christian knows of God's continuing work and of God's decisive response. This knowledge will make a difference in one's life. To mention only one point here: Christian prayer is directed to and through God against the reality of evil in all its forms.

Our topic happily does not require us to argue for the ethical superiority of Christians. But it does require us to recognize that Christian growth is to be sought in the struggle against evil. That is the word of the Scriptures which should not be relativized by appeal to the idea of an "interim" ethic.[30] Even the Paul of Romans, who can hardly be accused of underestimating sin, could exhort: "Let not sin therefore reign in your mortal bodies. . . . For sin will have no dominion over you, since you are not under law but under grace" (Rom 6:12, 14). It is this kind of Pauline material which suggests that the "righteousness of God" is more than a subjective genitive, for God's gift is with power.[31]

Does the Lutheran Christian have to see in this the specter of Christian perfection? While we should perhaps not worry over much about that, we do need to understand what is involved in Luther's and Calvin's insistence that never in this life do we get beyond sin. We are called in the new life to a direction other than the "curved-in-ness" of sin. But the cumulative power of the past and the complexity of the self's life argue against any expectation of a score of 100 on the quantitative scale of opportunity. Even for John Wesley perfection was seen to be compatible with "involuntary transgression."[32]

That vexing adjective "involuntary" raises the issue of Chapter 3: How fully must contingency be in place in order to speak of personal responsibility for sin? This is still not clear. What is clear is that we are called to a direction other than that of sin. Thus the author of 1 John knows that "if we say we have no sin, we deceive ourselves" (1:8), but knows as well that "no one born of God commits sin; for God's nature abides in him, and he cannot sin because he is born of God" (3:9). The verb in the latter passage is the Greek imperfect: No one born of God keeps on sinning, that is, no one born of God makes sin the direction of life. Or in Paul's language, sin may be present, but it is not to reign, not to have dominion. Christians are called to work against evil. Thus at Ephesus (431) the church condemns anyone who says: "that the grace of God, by which we are justified through Jesus Christ our Lord, has power only for the remission of sins which have already been committed, and not also for help, that they may not be committed" (Denzinger, 136). Similarly, the Formula of Concord (I) rejects the Flacian position as Manichaean: It would deny the scriptural teaching on sanctification and in effect baptize original sin.

To reject the call to sanctification is to open the church to the criticism that ideological diversion is at work here. To accept the call is not to claim the possibility of perfection. Thus Dorothee Soelle notes that a "political theology" need only assume that by making specific changes in social structures "the number of forces compelling us to sin today can be decreased."[33] In this struggle against evil there will be suffering for the Christian. This was seen with particular keenness in the tradition represented by Thomas Münzer, who offers a sharp critique of the "honey-sweet Christ": "This faith, 'that suffering is put on Christ alone, as though we are not permitted to suffer,' corresponds politically to the two kingdoms doctrine, ecclesiastically to infant baptism."[34] We should want to claim that Münzer is right in what he affirms but mistaken in his negative inferences. Baptism admits us to the fellowship of Christ's sufferings and intensifies the suffering to which we are called already as God's creatures. Soelle is right that it is a false faith which would escape suffering, for it represents "a narcissistic desire of the ego to settle down in God, immortal and almighty." In rebuffing this thirst for immediacy, one will recognize that "if it is true that a person's riches consist in the riches of his human relationships, then the pain that grows out of these relationships belongs necessarily to our riches. The more we love . . . the more likely it is that we . . . experience pain."[35]

If natural evil (suffering) and moral evil (sin) persist despite our struggle, what of that third face of evil: death? That this abides seems the most clear of all. But within the struggle the Christian lives in hope for another reality even beyond that third evil, death. It has always been so that God's people have lived in hope. Von Rad writes: "In one way or another (the specific tradition determines the way) Israel was always placed in the vacuum between an election made manifest in her history, and which had a definite promise attached to it, and a fulfillment of this promise which was looked for in the future."[36] For the Christian this becomes confidence, anchored in the resurrection of Jesus, in life beyond the grave. Only then and there will the struggle against evil end.

How does it end? Of that we will say only three things: First, it will be a time of consequence; the direction of our pilgrimage will reach its consummation in a new ontological state in which identity will no longer be linked with contingency. God's faithful will be clearly beyond Eden, for they will be "not able to sin."

Second, in the main Christians have held that God does indeed will that all be saved and come to the knowledge of the truth. Does our confidence in the continuing, decisive, and directing work of God lead us to believe that God's will will prevail? It requires us so to hope, that is clear. It provides us with suggestions that in that life all ambiguity will be removed, so that final clarity will lead all to acknowledge that Jesus Christ is Lord to the glory of God the Father (Phil. 2:11). But the question remains whether God's commitment to creaturely freedom does not leave the possibility that the tongue, the knee, the will—now stripped of any rational basis for resistance—may move only grudgingly, even defiantly.

Third, that new life perfects the pilgrimage which is our present life. But it does not destroy it. Too often static conceptions of heaven have represented a virtual destruction of what we know to be human life in its activity, in its becoming. Surely that new condition will entail an intensification of life, of living. But all that hinders us in our relationship to God will not remain. Ford Madox Ford wrote a poem "to V. H. who asked for a working Heaven." In our life against evil it is as much as we need

> . . . in this beloved place,
> There shall be never a grief but passes; no, not any;
> There shall be such bright light and no blindness;
> There shall be so little awe and so much loving-kindness;
> There shall be a little longing and enough care,
> There shall be a little labour and enough of toil
> To bring back the lost flavour of our human coil;
> Not enough to stain it;
> And all that we desire shall prove as fair as we can paint it.
> For, though that may be the very hardest trick of all
> God set Himself, who fashioned this goodly hall.
> Thus He has made Heaven;
> Even Heaven.

NOTES

1. Claus Westermann, *Creation*, trans. John J. Scullion (Philadelphia: Fortress Press, 1974), p.11, writes that the Old Testament reflection on creation "was the reflection of threatened man in a threatened world. The creation myths then had the function of preserving the world and of giving security to life."

2. Dietrich Bonhoeffer, *Creation and Fall*, trans. John Fletcher (New York: Macmillan Co.; London: SCM Press, 1959), p. 88.

3. Gerhard von Rad, *Old Testament Theology*, trans. D. M. G. Stalker, 2 vols. (New York: Harper & Row, 1962–65), 1:157.

4. Westermann, *Creation*, p. 46: "The act of creation, by directing itself to the living being, includes the capacity to propagate one's kind. That is the basic meaning of the word *bless*: the power to be fertile. The life of the living being, whether man or beast, clearly includes the capacity to propagate." (Emphasis his.) Cf. Bonhoeffer, *Creation and Fall*, p. 78, on the situation in destruction.

5. Gustaf Wingren, *Creation and Law*, trans. Ross Mackenzie (Philadelphia: Fortress [Muhlenberg] Press, 1961), p. 125.

6. Alfred North Whitehead, *Process and Reality*, ed. David Ray Griffin and Donald W. Sherburne (New York: Free Press, 1978), p. 187.

7. William Gallagher, "Whitehead's Theory of the Human Person" (Ph.D. diss., New School for Social Research, 1974), p. 45: "Inbreeding reduces the effectiveness of exploratory behavior, appetitive and aversive learning, and motility. Thus a decline in appetitive initiative on the reproduction level has a 'snowball' effect, which might be described as follows: the second generation suffers from decreased ability to face a novel environment, a low tolerance for challenging situations, a low level of adventuring on several levels."

8. James Gustafson, *Theology and Christian Ethics* (Philadelphia: United Church Press, 1974), p. 244.

9. Gerhard von Rad, *Wisdom in Israel*, trans. James D. Martin (Nashville: Abingdon Press, 1972), p. 61.

10. Cf. Hans Conzelmann, *An Outline of the Theology of the New Testament*, trans. John Bowden (New York: Harper & Row, 1969), pp. 182ff., on Paul's understanding of conscience.

11. F. R. Tennant, *Philosophical Theology*, 2 vols. (Cambridge: At the University Press, 1935–37), 2:194.

12. Gerhard von Rad, *Genesis*, trans. John Marks (Philadelphia: Westminster Press, 1961), p. 149.

13. Langdon Gilkey, *Reaping the Whirlwind: A Christian Interpretation of History* (New York: Seabury Press, 1976), p. 276.

14. Paul Tillich, *Systematic Theology*, 3 vols. (Chicago: University of Chicago Press, 1951–63), 1:147; Friedrich Schleiermacher, *The Christian Faith*, ed. H. R. Mackintosh and J. S. Stewart, 2 vols. (New York: Harper & Row, Harper Torchbooks, 1963), 2:425–38, 720–22.

15. Paul Ricoeur, *The Symbolism of Evil*, trans. Emerson Buchanan (Boston: Beacon Press, 1967), p. 98.

16. Abraham Heschel, *The Prophets* (New York: Harper & Row, 1962), p. 277. Cf. Jürgen Moltmann, *The Crucified God*, trans. R. A. Wilson and John Bowden (London: SCM Press, 1974), p. 272.

17. Ricoeur, *Symbolism of Evil*, p. 324. (Emphasis his.)

18. Moltmann, *The Crucified God*, p. 243.

19. Gustaf Aulén, *Christus Victor*, trans. A. G. Hebert (New York: Macmillan Co., 1931), pp. 162–63.

20. Krister Stendahl, *Paul among Jews and Gentiles* (Philadelphia: Fortress Press, 1976), p. 40.

21. Moltmann, *The Crucified God*, p. 274, drawing on Elie Wiesel's *Night*.

22. Karl Schmitz-Moormann, *Die Erbsünde: Überholte Vorstellung-Bleibende Glaube* (Freiburg: Walter, 1969), as paraphrased by Brian O. McDermott, "The Theology of Original Sin: Recent Developments," *TS* 38 (September 1977): 497–98.

23. So Burkhard Neunheuser, "The Sacrament of Baptism," in *Encyclopedia of Theology*, ed. Karl Rahner (New York: Seabury Press, 1975), p. 72: "Rightly administered in accordance with the intention of the Church, baptism is always valid; it is not a mere sign of faith but takes effect *ex opere operato*, that is, by the power of God that is at work in the sacrament. . . ."

24. George Hunston Williams, *The Radical Reformation* (Philadelphia: Westminster Press, 1962), p. 799.

25. See G. Vandervelde, *Original Sin: Two Major Trends in Contemporary Roman Catholic Interpretation* (Amsterdam: Rodopi N. V., 1975), p. 39.

26. Ibid., pp. 37–42; Holsten Fagerberg, *A New Look at the Lutheran Confessions*, trans. Gene J. Lund (St. Louis: Concordia Publishing House, 1972), pp. 139–43.

27. William H. Lazareth, "Love and Law in Christian Life," *The Seminary Bulletin* (Lutheran Theological Seminary) 12 (Summer 1978): 32.

28. Gustaf Wingren, *Gospel and Church*, trans. Ross Mackenzie (Edinburgh: Oliver & Boyd, 1964), pp. 180–81. (Emphasis his.)

29. James Gustafson, *Can Ethics Be Christian?* (Chicago: University of Chicago Press, 1975), pp. 92–93.

30. Conzelmann, *Outline of the Theology of the N.T.*, p. 125: "The content of the demand—loving one's enemy, etc., is not derived from the nearness of the kingdom of God, nor is its validity restricted to a last, brief period. On the contrary, in ethics, as in the doctrine of God, there is no limit to the duration of the world. Jesus believes that the demand of God is understandable and possible in itself, not only by way of apocalyptic expectation."

31. Ernst Käsemann, *Perspectives on Paul*, trans. Margaret Kohl (Philadelphia: Fortress Press, 1971), p. 77.

32. Van A. Harvey, *A Handbook of Theological Terms* (New York: Macmillan Co., 1964), p. 178.

33. Dorothee Soelle, *Political Theology*, trans. John Shelley (Philadelphia: Fortress Press, 1974), p. 84.

34. This is Dorothee Soelle's paraphrase of Münzer's critique in *Suffering*, trans. Everett R. Kalin (Philadelphia: Fortress Press, 1975), p. 129.

35. Ibid., p. 165.

36. Von Rad, *Old Testament Theology*, 2:414.

SIXTH LOCUS

The Person
of Jesus Christ

CARL E. BRAATEN

THE PERSON OF JESUS CHRIST

Introduction

1. The Nature and Method of Christology
   What Is Christology?
   History, Dogmatics, and Faith
   The Starting Point of Christology

2. The Historical Jesus and the Kingdom of God
   Jesus' Expectation of the Kingdom of God
   The Genesis of Christology in the New Testament

3. Classical Christology and Its Subsequent Criticism
   The Identification of Jesus with God
   Christological Heresies
   From the Creed of Chalcedon to the Formula of Concord
   Criticism of the Dogma

4. The True Humanity of Jesus Christ
   The Historicity of Jesus Christ
   The Humanity of Jesus Christ
   The Identity of the Earthly Jesus and the Risen Christ
   Jesus Christ as the Eschatological One

5. The True Divinity of Jesus Christ
   The Story of God Incarnate
   The Historicity of God
   The Divinity of Christ
   An Ontological Interpretation of the Incarnation

6. The Humiliation and Exaltation of Jesus Christ
   The Preexistence of Christ
   The Virgin Birth
   The Crucifixion of Jesus

CONTENTS

Introduction

Christology is the church's doctrine of the person of Jesus as the Christ. It is always central in a system of dogmatics that claims to be Christian. Every attempt to remove christology from its place of centrality threatens the heart of Christian faith. The christocentric principle of theology does not compete with a theocentric point of view. Whoever looks to Jesus the Christ from the New Testament perspective will inevitably stand within a theocentric frame of reference. The more deeply theology probes the meaning of Jesus as the Christ of God, the more directly is it drawn to the very God of Christ. Jesus' way was to point not to himself but to his Father who sent him. He did not preach his own identity as such. Rather, he announced the coming of God's kingdom; he lived and died to make the kingdom a reality "on earth, as it is in heaven." The entire ministry of Jesus was radically theocentric.

Christian dogmatics is christocentric insofar as no doctrine can be called Christian at all if it bears no significant connection with the definitive revelation of God in the person of Jesus the Christ. The centrality of Christ is not limited to a particular part of theology, for example, the doctrine of the church or the sacraments. Christ is central both in the order of creation and in the realm of redemption. He is central in a Christian theological interpretation of nature, history, and existence. Even our knowledge of God is finally determined by the way in which God is revealed in the person of Jesus. No matter what may be known about God apart from christological revelation, a subject that still remains in controversy, Christian faith looks to the apostolic witness to Jesus the Christ as the final criterion of the truth concerning the nature and identity of God.

In recent times the principle of christocentricity in theology has come under attack. Speaking of Karl Barth's theology, H. Richard Niebuhr coined the phrase "unitarianism of the second article." [1] Others have described Barth's position as christomonist or mono-christological.[2] Christocentricity is allegedly incompatible with the "radical monotheism" of biblical faith. It makes of Christ a "second God" alongside the One God of Israel, thus falsely putting him into the place of Yahweh as the sole object of faith and worship. Theologians who debunk christocentricity maintain that the status of Christ in Christian faith scarcely warrants a central role for christology in shaping and ordering all other doctrines.[3] The christocentric pattern in modern Protestant theology from Friedrich Schleiermacher and Albrecht Ritschl in the nineteenth century to Karl Barth and Paul Tillich in the twentieth century is regarded by the critics of christocentricity as a mark of failure. The mandate to view all theological doctrines in the light of Christ is no longer binding. In dramatic fashion, John Hick has called for a "Copernican revolution in theology."[4] This revolution would place *God* at the center of the universe of all the religions, thus dislodging Christ from the central position he has held in the old "Ptolemaic" scheme of things. The traditional claim of seeing all things *sub specie Christi* and of viewing Christ as the source of our knowledge of God as well as the ultimate standard by which all teachings are to be judged, as the focal point of faith itself, can thus presumably be explained as a habit of mind that could thrive in that age of Christendom when Christianity regarded itself as the one and only saving religion in the world. But now Christendom is dying, and along with it the narrow parochialism which it bred. Christocentricity allegedly becomes anachronistic in an age characterized by ecumenical openness, theological pluralism, and interreligious dialogue.[5]

What is at stake in the principle of christocentricity? The type of christocentricity that accompanied the "death of God" theology has proved to be false.[6] Here Jesus of Nazareth as a figure of history was treated as a substitute for the God who allegedly died with the rise of secular and scientific consciousness and with the demise of myth and metaphysics. For Christian theology the principle of christocentricity is not a mechanism of compensation for loss of belief or lack of meaning in the idea of God. Jesus is no substitute for God! Rather, the principle of christocentricity underscores the identity of the God who is really God. It aims to answer the question: Which God? Gods are a dime a dozen in the history of religions. Which God are we talking about in Christian dogmatics? In light of the christocentric principle our answer is: This God is not the simple, solitary, and self-sufficient unit of radical monotheism. That would be the God of classical deism and unitarianism. The God of classical Christianity, in contrast, is the self-structuring reality of trinitarian faith, the One who antecedently differentiates the divine self as Father, Son, and Holy Spirit and is revealed as such in the economy of history and salvation.

Originally, the *doctrine* of the Trinity came about as a product of theological reflection on the revelation of God in the person of Jesus the Christ. At the heart of this development of the trinitarian dogma was the primitive Christian kerygma of God's identification with the death and resurrection of Jesus. Where faith in Jesus as the bringer of absolute salvation is set aside, there also trinitarian theology loses the fertile soil from which it has grown into its more fully developed dogmatic and liturgical forms. The doctrine of the

Trinity and the principle of christocentricity are mutually implicative. One reinforces the other. It is not by chance that the most christocentric of modern theologians, namely, Karl Barth, has also produced the most thoroughly trinitarian theology of them all.

Christianity is universally categorized as a monotheistic form of belief. This does not mean, however, that its doctrine of the Trinity and its confession of Christ arise subsequently at a lower level of symbolic meaning. There have been various forms of mystical, metaphysical, political, and moralistic monotheism which have relegated both the doctrine of the Trinity and belief in the uniqueness of Christ to secondary importance, making them appear dispensable.[7] In a dogmatic system of trinitarian monotheism the principle of christocentricity, far from being a function of subjective faith and traditional piety, operates as a criticism of every type of monotheism that would loosen the links between the identity of God and the person of Jesus the Christ.

NOTES

1. H. Richard Niebuhr discussed the idea of a unitarianism of the second person of the Trinity in "The Doctrine of the Trinity and the Unity of the Church," *Theology Today* 3 (1946): 371–84.

2. Cf. H. Urs von Balthasar, *Karl Barth: Darstellung und Deutung seiner Theologie*, 2d ed. (Cologne, 1962).

3. Eugene Te Selle, *Christ in Context* (Philadelphia: Fortress Press, 1975).

4. John Hick, *God and the Universe of Faiths* (New York: Macmillan Co., 1973).

5. Paul Knitter has provided an extensive critique of Protestant christocentricity in *Towards a Protestant Theology of Religions: A Case Study of Paul Althaus and Contemporary Attitudes* (Marburg: N. G. Elwert Verlag, 1974).

6. This form of pseudo-christocentricity was represented by William Hamilton, *The New Essence of Christianity* (New York: Association Press, 1961); Paul van Buren, *The Secular Meaning of the Gospel* (New York: Macmillan Co., 1963); Thomas J. J. Altizer, *The Gospel of Christian Atheism* (Philadelphia: Westminster Press, 1966).

7. Cf. Erik Peterson, "Der Monotheismus als politisches Problem," in *Theologische Traktate* (Munich, 1950), pp. 45–147; Eberhard Jüngel, *The Doctrine of the Trinity* (Grand Rapids: Wm. B. Eerdmans, 1976).

1

The Nature and
Method of Christology

Christology is the church's reflection on the basic assertion that Jesus is the Christ of God. Its aim is to construct a comprehensive interpretation of the identity and meaning of the person of Jesus as the Christ, under the condition of contemporary knowledge and experience.

WHAT IS CHRISTOLOGY?

Christology is the interpretation of Jesus of Nazareth as the Christ of God from the standpoint of the faith of the Christian church. The word "christology" means literally the *logos* about *Christos*, thought and speech about Christ. Christ is a title, and not the second name of Jesus. The title expresses the identity of Jesus of Nazareth, according to the apostolic witness and the catholic tradition. The question of Jesus' true identity was raised already in his own lifetime, as recorded in the Gospel of Mark (8:27–29). Jesus is reported to have asked his disciples on the way to Caesarea Philippi, "Who do men say that I am?" They replied, in effect, that people could not make up their minds about him. Some said he was John the Baptist, others Elijah, still others that he was one of the prophets. Then, turning to his disciples, Jesus asked, "But who do you say that I am?" Peter answered him, "You are the Christ." Peter's statement was a confession of his own personal faith. Other contemporaries of Jesus reached an opposite conclusion about who he really was. They said he was the Son of Satan!

Christology is not a scientific discipline which can be appropriately pursued apart from the discipleship of faith. Faith signifies an existential interest in the contemporary meaning of Jesus as the Christ of God. The experience of faith in Jesus as the living Christ means that christology is more than critical reflection on who Jesus was in his earthly existence. Jesus Christ can be the object of faith because he is not merely Jesus of Nazareth, an historical figure who lived and died once upon a time, but also the risen and living Christ who is presently embodied in the community of believers. Christology reflects on the meaning of Jesus the Christ now in the present encounters of Christian faith and action in the world.

Without the confession of faith in Jesus as the Christ, christology would be reducible to Jesuology. Faith is not a mere human performance, a work of the intellect, the will, or the emotions. No one can call Jesus the Christ purely as a result of historical scientific research. Traditional dogmatics has rightly stressed that faith is brought about through the inward witness of the Holy Spirit (*testimonium spiritus sancti internum*). This means that there is a dimension of mystery in the process of christological reflection. A fact-finding committee of scientifically trained historians could not prove that Jesus is the Christ. They could only show that this was the unanimous witness of believers in the early church, for which the New Testament stands as primary documentary evidence. The witness is clear. But was that witness true? The question of truth places every person before an either-or that cannot be decided without the power of faith and the witness of the Spirit.

The affirmation of the contemporaneity of Christ means that the Holy Spirit actualizes Christ's presence through faith, the receiving side of a real personal relationship. The Holy Spirit is the power to bring personal faith and Jesus who is the living Christ together now. This happens where and when it happens (*ubi et quando visum est deo*) by the power of the Holy Spirit, not when an investigating committee of historians issues the final report of their factual findings. It is the Spirit who raises the historical Jesus out of the remoteness of past history and situates him as the living Christ in the existential context of the present moment. The Holy Spirit does not, however, work in a direct, unmediated way. The Spirit is the inner power of the living voice of the gospel (the *viva vox evangelii*) which can be heard in, with, and under the preaching of the church. Christology would suffer from sterile historicism if its reflections were not nourished in a matrix of inquiry involving a complexity of vital factors including faith and the Spirit as well as preaching and the church.

The church as a community of believers is the appropriate context of responsible christological reflection. Faith in the living Christ is not a private mystical exercise between "Jesus and me." Apart from the gathered assembly (the *ecclesia*) of those who worship God in Jesus' name, there is no proclamation which has the power to awaken faith in Jesus as the living Christ of God. There are many forms of interest in Jesus of Nazareth which are powerless to mediate faith. Modern biographical and psychological speculations about the external and internal developments in the life of Jesus are the most notable examples of such faith-less interest.[1] The picture of Jesus the Christ which animates the preaching of the church is framed not by such arbitrary constructions of the imagination but by the christological creeds and confessions of the church. The purpose of the christological dogma of classical Christianity is to guide the church in faithfully representing the apostolic picture of Jesus as the Christ of God, so that its contemporary witness to the living Christ will not be a mirror in which the church idealizes itself or ideologizes its position in society. The christological dogma points beyond the church, ensuring that its Lord is the living Christ embodied in Jesus of Nazareth, and not an ahistorical myth, a metaphysical principle, a religious personality, or a moral virtuoso.

The authentic picture of the living Christ is given in the Bible; everything else is at best some kind of reproduction. Thus it will always be necessary for the church to test its christological interpretations by referring to the biblical picture of Jesus the Christ. The biblical picture of Christ, however, is not like a single snapshot. It is more like a montage of portraits sketched by several artists, from various angles and at different times and places. For this reason scholars now speak of a multiplicity of christologies in the New Testament. Nevertheless, all of them stem from the earliest witness of the apostles to Jesus of Nazareth, his life and teachings, and particularly his suffering, death, and resurrection.

We have shown that christology by its very nature moves between the poles of the contemporaneity of the Christ and the historicity of Jesus. If christology moves toward the pole of contemporaneity in a one-sided way, it veers off into subjectivism and modernism. We may speak of this in traditional terms as docetism: denial of the historicity of the Christ who is Jesus. If christology moves toward the pole of historicity in a one-sided way, it tends to fall back into either positivistic historicism or biblicistic fundamentalism. We may speak of these errors as ebionitism: denial of the presence of the living Jesus who is the Christ in the ongoing history of the church's proclamation of the word.

HISTORY, DOGMATICS, AND FAITH

The historian, the dogmatician, and the believer have their own ways of approaching the historical Jesus. Since the Enlightenment, Jesus of Nazareth has become the object of strictly historical scientific inquiry. Historical science first had to emancipate itself from dogmatic controls in order even to raise the question of the historical Jesus. Today scarcely anyone doubts the right of historians to inquire into the biblical sources for the most reliable information concerning the man Jesus as a figure of past history. But many scholars are skeptical of the possibility of uncovering the real Jesus of history behind the blanket of interpretations which the earliest believers laid on him. Theology has been posed a dilemma by the application of the historical-critical method to the Gospel sources. What is the dogmatic significance of the ongoing quest of the historical Jesus? By the "historical Jesus" we mean Jesus of Nazareth insofar as he can be made the object of historical-critical research. What is the relevance of the results of such research? Are they crucial for faith? Do they provide data for preaching? Or are they merely matters of endless debate among scholars, whose statements about history can never be advanced beyond a shadow of doubt? It is important to keep the boundary lines straight between historical science, dogmatics, and faith.

The critical historian can use the New Testament writings as source documents for the history of primitive Christianity. From these sources historians can reconstruct the beliefs and activities of the early church. Can they also penetrate these sources and reach back to the underlying facts concerning Jesus himself? The historian faces two kinds of difficulty. First, the Gospels present the history of Jesus as the Christ in forms of tradition that were written and transmitted under the impact of the resurrection faith. It has proved impossible to disengage naked facts of history from the interpretations in which they were embedded. Second, the modern historian can never approach the past without some kind of presuppositions. Some prior understanding about the nature of human existence and the meaning of religion will qualify all the statements a historian can make about the identity of Jesus of Nazareth. There is a philosophical or theological dimension of understanding implied in every use of the historical method to establish "what really happened." As historians proceed to a profound level of interpretation, it will become evident whether the results of their research are framed by the world view of a personalistic theist, a rationalistic deist, an immanentalist pantheist, a Marxist atheist, or whatever. There is no such thing as presuppositionless research.

In turning to the Gospel traditions concerning Jesus of Nazareth, the historical method of research can serve to raise the question of faith. All these traditions represent Jesus as the Christ of God. This is the irreducible minimum of the earliest apostolic witness. Either historians share the perspective of this witness to Jesus or they do not. There is no neutral ground. Historians who are believers, who confess Jesus as the Christ, the Savior of humankind, and the Lord of the world, are bound to read the Gospels differently from people who regard Jesus of Nazareth as an historical personality on the same level with all other human beings. The work of historical research can renew the age-old question: "Who do men say that I am?" The offense aroused by Jesus in his lifetime and the scandal of the apostles' preaching can be described by the historian in such a way as to renew the question of the true identity of Jesus. The answer to the question, however, is itself never purely a product of historical research. It involves a decision of faith.

Faith in Jesus as the Christ is not based on the results of historical-critical scholarship. Some dogmaticians have opposed the use of the historical method in biblical interpretation because they fear that faith will be made dependent on the shifting results of scientific research. This is the result of a misunderstanding. The results of historical inquiry do not form the basis and contents of Christian faith. It is the task of dogmatics to serve as the "defense attorney" for believers in face of the heteronomous claim of science to provide the contents or legitimate the basis of faith. The saving knowledge of Jesus as the Christ is passed on "from faith unto faith," not by publishing the latest results of historians or exegetes. An essential dependence of faith on the results of historical research would force believers to deliver their faith in trust to the authority of historical critics, as once it had to exist in bondage to an authoritarian church, a magisterial dogmatics, or an infallible Bible.

What then is the theological relevance of historical science, if faith is free of dependence on its most recently assured results? It is important to observe a distinction between dogmatics and faith. What is relevant for the constructive reflections of the theologian is not necessarily essential to the being or even the well-being of faith. Faith can exist very well without being caught up on the latest research, but dogmatics cannot ignore the ongoing process and results of historical-critical scholarship. Faith lives from the witness to Christ in the preaching of the church and the message of the Scriptures. Dogmatics is critical reflection that goes on in the church for the sake of a more mature understanding of faith, its foundations and contents. To this end dogmatics will help itself to every available means of acquiring knowledge about the historical events and interpretations which make up the living tradition that generates and sustains faith. The highly developed skills of historical research provide us with the best tools we have to ascertain what really happened in the past.

THE STARTING POINT
OF CHRISTOLOGY

One of the points at issue in contemporary theology concerns the right starting point of christology. Traditionally christology was done "from above," starting with the christological dogma of the ancient church. Both the medieval scholastic and the Protestant orthodox dogmaticians modeled their systems on Peter Lombard's *Four Books of Sentences*, beginning with the classical dogma of the two natures of Christ, divine and human. This christological dogma presupposed the dogma of the Trinity and the incarnation of the Son of God. Christology proceeded deductively from the eternal deity of Christ above to his human nature here below.

For a long time it seemed reasonable to begin christology with the dogma of the incarnation. It was the revealed doctrine of the church and the norm by which every heresy was to be anathematized. But once the dogma lost its status as the principle of authority in modern theology, it could no longer function as the starting point.[2] The christological dogma had to be justified as a legitimate interpretation of the New Testament picture of Jesus the Christ in the categories of the Hellenistic world of thought.

When the christological dogma was placed on the defensive by its modern critics, the attempt was made to salvage its meaning by concentrating on the kerygmatic Christ. This is a contemporary way of doing christology from above. It begins christology not with the traditional dogma of the two natures but with the kerygmatic picture of the Christ in apostolic Christianity. Christology then goes in search of the existential meaning of kerygmatic symbols, rather than the dogmatic truth of metaphysical concepts. We acknowledge a sympathy with this point of view, for two reasons. First, the actuality of faith in the living Christ is the condition of the possibility of doing christology today. Faith is the medium of christological reflection, even though history and not faith is the primal source of its data. Second, the New Testament is a collection of Easter stories that presuppose the faith of the apostolic community. Without that faith not a single story of Jesus would have been preserved for posterity. Yet we cannot be satisfied to assume the kerygmatic Christ as the starting point of dogmatic construction. The type of question put to the christological dogma can be transposed to the christological kerygma. What is its legitimating ground? What is the historical basis and content of the kerygma? The dogma does not rest on itself; neither does the kerygma.

There is now virtual consensus among theologians that christology must start from below. Here lies the deepest significance of the new quest of the historical Jesus. Scholars who participate in the new quest use various methods and reach different results, but most agree that it is historically possible and theologically necessary to penetrate behind the New Testament kerygma to traditions that convey some reliable knowledge about Jesus of Nazareth. Neither the dogma nor the kerygma is sufficient of itself to provide the basis and content of faith. Granted, there are no naked facts of history that can be shelled free of their husks of interpretation. That would be like looking for a nut inside an onion. Granted also that faith is not based on the results of any new quest of the historical Jesus. Faith is based rather on the preaching of the Easter kerygma, and certainly not on a modern scholarly reconstruction of the historical Jesus. Yet there is good reason to require that christology begin from below. This makes clear that both the christological dogma and the kerygmatic christology refer back to Jesus of Nazareth as the historical object of christology. Christology is based on the Christ to whom apostolic faith witnesses, and this Christ is none other than Jesus of Nazareth.

The dogma of the divine-human Christ and the kerygma of the risen Lord have to do with the history of Jesus. Christology seeks to understand the meaning and the connections between history, kerygma, and dogma. Kerygmatic and dogmatic interpretations are empty without grounding in the historical reality of Jesus. The other side of the dialectic is that historical facts are blind

THE NATURE AND METHOD OF CHRISTOLOGY

without the interpretative sequences in the kerygmatic and dogmatic formulations of the church.

The danger in starting christology from below is that it might end in a "low christology" of no use to the Christian faith. We define a "low christology" as an interpretation of Jesus which treats him as a mere man.[3] It converts the classical christological category of the "truly human" (*vere homo*) into the "merely human." This is a modernistic version of the ancient ebionitic heresy which taught that Jesus was only a man (*psilos anthropos*) and not the truly divine Son of God. On the other hand, starting christology from below with the historical Jesus need not preclude the development of a "high christology." A high christology treats the resurrection of Jesus and his unity with God as predicates belonging to the personal identity of Jesus the Christ, and not only as value judgments imposed on him from the arbitrary perspective of religious experience.[4]

Despite the current preference for doing christology from below, starting with what can be known about the historical Jesus, christological reflection is a hermeneutical process in which the movements "from above" and "from below" are not so much mutually exclusive as dialectically related in a comprehensive understanding of the identity and meaning of the person of Jesus the Christ. The process of interpretation extends from the contemporary act of faith in the believing community to the past-historical fact of Jesus interpreted by the apostolic kerygma as the Christ. This process of interpretation can be called a hermeneutical "circle" or "arc." The circular nature of this interpretation relativizes the distinction between starting "from above" or "from below." It is essential to acknowledge that the question of Jesus' identity cannot be separated from the engagement of faith and the Spirit. "No one can say 'Jesus is Lord' except by the Holy Spirit" (1 Cor. 12:3). The attempt to bracket out faith and proceed by reason alone is just as problematic as excluding reason and appealing to faith alone. The modern quest of the historical Jesus is eminently the work of historical reason. In abstraction from the total system of hermeneutical operations involved in christological thought, it cannot be regarded as the starting point. Within the horizon of an adequate hermeneutics, however, christology can begin with the question of how Jesus of Nazareth came to be called the Christ of God in the early church. Perspectives from the New Testament kerygma and the history of dogma may generate insight in the process of trying to understand how the historical Jesus can be the object of faith without violating the first commandment, "Thou shalt have no other gods before me."

For apologetic reasons christology today may choose to start with the appearance of the man Jesus and then lead up to the knowledge of his divinity through his death and resurrection. The divinity of Christ, it can be argued, no longer functions as a self-evident presupposition. Instead, modern historical consciousness looks on such a statement as a hypothesis that demands some sort of historical legitimation. But we should not allow our apologetic concerns to cross the boundaries of what can be seriously defended. The transition from the historical Jesus to the risen Christ of the apostolic kerygma or the divine Son of God of the ecclesiastical dogma cannot be explained and legitimated purely by historical argumentation. The effort to do so accounts for the trend in conservative New Testament scholarship to derive all the high christology of the later church from the lips of the historical Jesus. This means that the New Testament scholar must find all the seeds of later christological development in the teachings of Jesus. Failure to achieve this would mean that christology loses its origins in the real Jesus of history, shifting the basis and beginnings of christology to the creative developments in the early church.

If today dogmatics is to build on historical foundations, it will have to take the question of the origins of christology into consideration. Within the total hermeneutical framework, what do we understand to be the central datum of christology? Where is it to be found? How far back can we trace historically the rise of christology? How did it happen that the man Jesus who preached the coming of God's kingdom soon became the Lord of the kingdom in the kerygma of the church? Faith does not need an answer to these questions, but dogmatics will seek to understand the historical roots and ramifications of christology from its earliest origins to the present time.

First, some scholars locate the root of christology in the self-manifestation of Jesus himself. The christological predicates and titles in the apostolic kerygma are to be traced back to some aspect of the historical Jesus, whether his messianic self-consciousness, his claim to possess authority to forgive sins, his message of the coming kingdom, or his way with others. Scholars hold different opinions, but many agree that the roots of christology can be found in the historical person of Jesus.

Second, another group of scholars locate the central datum of christology in the historical event of Jesus' resurrection. The resurrection is something that really happened to the crucified Jesus. He was raised to a new mode of being beyond the fate of death. This Easter event is the presupposition for the primitive Christian proclamation of Jesus as the Christ of God. It is the key, finally, to the knowledge of Jesus' unity with God.

Third, there are those who ground christological faith neither in the earthly Jesus nor in his resurrection, but only in the kerygma of the early church. The resurrection is interpreted as the rise of faith in the disciples; the Easter kerygma is viewed as an interpretation of an otherwise unmessianic Jesus. The kerygma alone is the central datum of christology. Every attempt to inquire behind the kerygma to the underlying events of Jesus' life, death, and resurrection is ruled out as trying to establish proofs of faith.

There is no need for dogmatics to play off one of these lines of interpretation against the others. In our christological synthesis the person of Jesus Christ himself is not limited to the historical Jesus. The concept of the personal identity of Jesus Christ includes his earthly existence as well as his resurrected state of being. And the history of the interpretation of Jesus has a trajectory through the kerygmatic proclamations of the early church, the multiplicity of christologies assuming their embryonic form in the New Testament, and the creedal and dogmatic definitions of christology in church tradition. The historical Jesus, the kerygmatic Christ, and the christological dogma—these three are the stuff of which christology is made. The elimination of a single one of these factors deals a crippling blow to a christology that aims to serve the church in its preaching, life, and mission.

NOTES

1. This was the main point of Martin Kähler's attack on the "life of Jesus movement" of modern scholarship in *The So-Called Historical Jesus and the Historic Biblical Christ*, trans. Carl E. Braaten (Philadelphia: Fortress Press, 1964).

2. Cf. Wolfhart Pannenberg, *Jesus—God and Man*, trans. Lewis Wilkins and Duane Priebe (Philadelphia: Westminster Press, 1968), pp. 21ff.

3. As an example of this tendency, see *The Myth of God Incarnate*, ed. John Hick (Philadelphia: Westminster Press, 1977).

4. Pannenberg's *Jesus—God and Man* is an example of such a "high christology."

2

The Historical Jesus
and the Kingdom of God

The point of departure of the New Testament as a whole is the appearance of Jesus and his message of the kingdom of God. The explicit christology of the early church is founded on the historical and material transition from Jesus' preaching of the kingdom of God to the early church's Easter proclamation of Jesus as the Christ and the risen Lord.

JESUS' EXPECTATION
OF THE KINGDOM OF GOD

The "kingdom of God" was the central theme in the entire message of Jesus. All three synoptic Gospels picture Jesus as an itinerant preacher from Galilee announcing the good news of the kingdom of God (Mark 1:15; Matt. 4:23; Luke 4:43). Rudolf Bultmann states, "The dominant concept of Jesus' message is the Reign of God," [1] expressing a consensus among New Testament scholars. But the reign or kingdom of God was more than a concept in the mind of Jesus set forth in speech. It was the driving force of his whole career. It penetrated his sermons and sayings and motivated all his acts and miracles. Whatever Jesus performed in word and deed was depicted as a "sign" of the inbreaking rule of God. This is at once the most certain result of modern historical exegesis and the starting point for our constructive christological interpretation.

The consensus among scholars, however, breaks up the moment they begin to describe the meaning of the kingdom of God. In nineteenth-century Protestant theology, the kingdom of God was interpreted predominantly in moral terms, either personal or social. From Friedrich Schleiermacher to Albrecht Ritschl, the kingdom of God was conceived as an inner spiritual or an outward social moral force. The kingdom of God exists wherever people live according to the moral principles which Jesus taught, summarized especially in the Sermon on the Mount. This morality reached its zenith when Jesus exhibited the love of God by dying on the cross. Such a morality reveals the true essence of being human. Rightly understood, being a true Christian and an authentic person are one and the same thing.

This moral interpretation of the kingdom of God was shattered when in separate studies Johannes Weiss[2] and Albert Schweitzer[3] proved that the kingdom of God in Jesus' preaching was mainly an eschatological concept. The kingdom of God will not come as the cumulative result of human good works and historical progress. Rather, it is a miracle of God's power breaking in from beyond the realm of human potentiality. The research of Weiss and Schweitzer showed that the kingdom of God which Jesus expected in the near future was more like an apocalyptic end to the world than a paradise on earth gradually wrought by human means. Weiss dropped a bombshell in late-nineteenth-century Protestant theology, ruled at that time by the school of Albrecht Ritschl, when he wrote, "As Jesus conceived it, the Kingdom of God is a radically superworldly entity which stands in diametric opposition to this world. This is to say that there *can* be no talk of an *innerworldly* development of the kingdom of God in the mind of Jesus!"[4]

Neither Weiss nor Schweitzer did anything to make his own discoveries fruitful for Christian faith and theology. Neither could salvage Jesus from the wreckage of his apocalyptic-eschatological world view. What could such a view have to do with the evolutionary and progressive view of modern times? Better to cling to the modernized ethical construction of Jesus' message—although it rests on a misunderstanding—than try to retain his antiquated eschatological ideas. It is to the lasting credit of the dialectical theologians, Karl Barth, Rudolf Bultmann, Emil Brunner, Friedrich Gogarten, and others, that they sought to take seriously the eschatological hypothesis of Weiss and Schweitzer. In the name of eschatology they fought against the reduction of Christianity to a moralistic ideology.

In dialectical theology, however, eschatology took on a questionable meaning when it was transcendentally emptied of all concrete historical facts and temporal contacts, becoming instead a principle of radical otherness—the otherness of God standing against the world, of faith against reason, and of Christ against culture. The eschatological event comes like a sharp blade cutting into the present moment. Such an event can call one's life into question, cause a deep vibration in the soul, or generate a new self-understanding, but it tends to narrow the promises of the Bible that engender hope for changes in the real world of people and nations and the material conditions of their common life.

There is no way around the eschatological message of Jesus for any contemporary interpretation of his significance. The "new quest of the historical Jesus,"[5] pursued with such scholarly vigor in recent years, has slammed the door on any merely ethical appropriation of Jesus' relevance for modern times. But it was the "theology of hope"[6] that set in motion a new attempt to make good the aborted exegetical discoveries of Weiss and Schweitzer. At the same time, this movement has overcome the purely transcendental view of eschatology that dominated the dialectical and existentialist models of systematic theology. The result is that Jesus' proclamation of the kingdom of God is now placed at the very beginning of a historical reconstruction of the christology of primitive Christianity, and at the center of a systematic treatment of his significance in contemporary theology. Not so long ago it was thought that our chief problem in christology was that we know virtually nothing concerning the historical Jesus.[7] Now the problem is more that a massive amount of research has focused on Jesus' message of the coming kingdom, leaving us still unsure of how to interpret it. The problem has shifted from history to hermeneutics.

How can we follow Jesus in thinking of the *basileia* of God as an otherworldly reality of cosmic magnitude about to break in at any time? We moderns go on with our plans as though the world were to last forever, buying life insurance against that day when our own personal lives will come to an end. At best, people have an eschatological attitude as individuals, living as though each day were their last. Jesus related the coming of the kingdom to the world, as power to overthrow the dominion of Satan and to create a new world of lasting righteousness and happiness. He expected God to establish the power and glory of his rule in the *immediate* future. Instead the world has gone on without any real fulfillment for two thousand years. Was not Jesus' expectation of the coming kingdom proved wrong by the ongoing course of history? Is this not an error that touches the heart of his message, and not mere details of marginal significance? No wonder Adolf von Harnack gained a following when he separated an ethical kernel from the eschatological husk of Jesus' preaching.[8] According to Harnack the ethical teachings of Jesus are still valid, whereas his eschatological ideas are strange to modern time. If such a separation of Jesus' ethics from his eschatology is no longer tenable, how can we make the historical Jesus *cum* eschatology the point of departure for christological interpretation today?

The place to begin is with the question of what Jesus really meant by the kingdom of God. When Jesus spoke of the kingdom, he did not have in mind a realm in space and time. The word refers not to a spatial realm but to the dynamic rule of God. The kingdom is the kingly rule of God, God's unequaled power and sovereign authority. Perhaps we should say quite simply that the coming of the kingdom means the coming of God. The kingdom comes when God actually comes, when God seizes power and establishes dominion over all things. To expect the kingdom is to be open for *the coming of God*, nothing less.[9] But this has universal meaning, for when God comes in power, the world must change. Things cannot remain as they are. God's coming is the power to destroy all resistance to God's rule and freely to grant God's gracious kingdom to those in need of a new beginning—poor people, publicans, and prostitutes. God is not an idle sovereign sitting on a throne. God will act when he comes, both in works of judgment and in works of grace. The kingdom is not a condition of this world that can be brought about by human means. It is not a predicate of this world. As the rule of God it is inseparable from the actual being of God. The eschatological being and the historical acts of God are the inner and outer aspects of the same ultimate reality.

The kingdom of God becomes manifest in the ministry of Jesus through sign-events. A great reversal in the order of things is about to take place. According to Luke 6:20–21, the poor will become happy, the hungry will be satisfied, and those who weep will laugh. Only the coming of God's kingdom can generate the power to produce such a miraculous turnabout in the human world. But the purpose of such sign-events is to point to the coming of God and God's rule, not to focus on a new social order as an ultimate good in itself. The history of the kingdom of God in the West has made it practically synonymous with utopia. Utopias, however, are people-centered schemes, born of human imagination and run by human effort. Hence the Marxist humanist Ernst Bloch speaks paradoxically of a kingdom of God without God, for the true essence of the kingdom, he says, is nothing more than human fulfillment.[10]

This idea reduces the kingdom of God to anthropology. In Jesus' message *God* is the subject of ultimate concern when God comes with the kingdom. *God* is the essential condition of a radically new order. The kingdom of God is no longer the same thing when converted into a kingdom with humankind at the center. The cash value of the kingdom of God will be lost when exchanged for phrases like "realm of freedom" or "kingdom of peace." There is a surplus of meaning in the mystery of God that prevents God's kingdom from becoming a predicate of humankind or the world.

The kingdom of God never ceases to be mystery in Jesus' message. He never offered a definition or a straightforward description. He spoke in riddles and parables; he left hints and clues; his miracles and deeds could be taken several ways. The mystery lies hidden in the words he preached, the parables he told, and the miracles he did as signs of the rapidly approaching kingdom of God. Others—Pharisees and Zealots—were trying to bring in the kingdom of God, either through religious and moral good works or through revolutionary praxis. But Jesus, dismissing both techniques as human presumption, offered no direct formula for translating the kingdom into an earthly state of affairs. To be sure, Jesus did present ethical teachings—the ethics of the kingdom—but they could be comprehended only within the eschatological frame of his message as a whole. Nowhere did he teach common-sense moral principles that could be practiced by morally sensitive people in this kind of world. The ethics of Jesus are laden with eschatological presuppositions;[11] they make sense as a morality prefiguring the new reality of God's approaching kingdom. When Jesus' ethics are put to work in an earthly context, they are intended to function as signs of the coming kingdom. They were finally contradicted by the world in the violent language of the cross. The cross was the world's reply to the uncompromising love which Jesus poured into all his words and deeds. This means that the praxis of the kingdom invariably ends in the shape of a cross.

Jesus proclaimed the coming kingdom as an urgent appeal to his hearers. His point was not to pass on information about the kingdom, as other apocalyptic visionaries had done in colorful detail. It was rather to convince his audience that it was high time to get ready for the coming of God. His call to "repent and believe" was issued as if for the last time, as if soon it would be too late. He issued an invitation to be open to the mystery not of the being of God attained by mysticism and ecstaticism, as in Hellenistic religion, but of the coming of God which calls for repentance and faith in line with the Hebraic tradition.

One of the most heated debates in modern New Testament research has been whether Jesus expected the arrival of the kingdom in the very near future, or whether it was already being fulfilled in the present. There are passages that point in both directions.[12] Most scholars agree, however, that by far the majority of the passages which can be ascribed to the historical Jesus picture the kingdom of God as having drawn so near as to have a present impact. The kingdom is not yet fulfilled, but its coming is imminent and its initial impact is already being felt, at least so far as the present becomes a time to get ready and watch for signs of its actual arrival.

Why has it been so difficult for scholars to determine the exact nature of Jesus' expectation of the kingdom? The reason is that in producing the Gospels the early church mixed its own eschatological ideas into its picture of Jesus as the Christ. Shortly after Easter the church developed an eschatology balanced between two poles. The first pole was determined by the past appearance of Jesus as the Christ, the second by his future return on the day of judgment. Meanwhile the early church was enjoying life in the afterglow of Jesus' resurrection and filled by the outpouring of the Spirit. On this side of Easter and Pentecost the early church looked back to the time of Jesus as the source of the salvation it was experiencing in the present. Features of fulfillment due to Easter were written into the story of Jesus' own time. If Jesus looked ahead for salvation from the coming kingdom, the early church looked back to him as the Christ who had already made the kingdom present. Despite this orientation to the past, the early church also strained forward in expectation of a future fulfillment. Even some of these ideas of cosmic eschatology were read back into the message of Jesus (e.g. Mark 13). We are thus faced with at least three layers: first, Jesus' own expectation of the coming kingdom; second, the early church's conviction that the time of Jesus was pregnant with fulfill-ment; and third, its belief that Christ would return at the close of the age. New Testament scholarship has shown how these three layers of tradition were commingled after Easter and put back into the mouth of the historical Jesus. Apparently the early church sought historical legitimation for its dogmatic beliefs by grounding its own post-Easter eschatology in the earthly Jesus.

It now appears to be a firmly established result of critical Gospel research that Jesus of Nazareth did not think of the kingdom of God as already fulfilled in his ministry. Had he done so, that would have had the effect of drastically narrowing the meaning of the kingdom and rendering it impotent. Then its presence would have been so hidden in the world as to have had no power to change it. Then the meaning of fulfillment would have been so spiritual-ized as to be relegated to a supraworldly realm. But with Jesus it was different. His healing miracles and demon exorcisms were advance signs of the coming kingdom. His beatitudes and woes prove that he was fully aware that this world was still enthralled by evil powers. Obviously God's kingdom had not yet been established here and now. Now there are poor and hungry people. When the kingdom comes their misery will be lifted. Now they are suffering; soon they will rejoice. Jesus did not accept their fate as an everlasting condi-tion. He put all the weight of God's kingdom into his promise to change it.

Those who teach that the kingdom of God has already been realized in the time of Jesus make a farce of his love for the poor, the oppressed, the hungry, the bereaved, the sick, the overburdened, the alienated, the ostra-cized, the imprisoned, the accursed, and the sinful. To all these people, Jesus promised that the kingdom would soon come to change their lot. Moreover, there are no preconditions, qualifications, or moral requirements of any kind. It is enough that they are defenseless; they are prime candidates for the friend-ship of God. This message was good news to poor sinners, but a slap in the face of the righteous. It does not seem fair to people who have made a pro-fession of "full-time service for the Lord." But Jesus was operating with an eschatological transvaluation of moral values. Joachim Jeremias says that this was the unique thing in Jesus' message, the very thing that provoked the Pharisees to protest.[13]

But if Jesus promised the kingdom to the poor and the oppressed first, why did he do nothing to improve their condition? To be sure, he healed a few of them, but thousands became sick and died without his help. Most of the people in Palestine were left in their misery at the very time Jesus was preaching the kingdom, telling stories, and doing miracles. Some Christians, wanting to follow Jesus, have shared his vision but not his method. They have proposed the revolutionary method of putting the poor in office and the rich in jail. Even the sword and the guillotine have been consecrated for the serv-ice of the coming kingdom. Others of more liberal persuasion have created welfare programs and medical clinics to help the poor and the sick. But Jesus was neither a political revolutionary nor a social liberal.

Nor was Jesus a quietist, offering cheap consolation to those whose situation he deplored but did nothing about. There are Christians who want to take up the cross and follow Jesus, but have no hope to alter the conditions that create poverty and oppression. Enjoining patient suffering in this world, they promise a heavenly reward in the world to come. But Jesus was not a do-nothing quietist, directing all the traffic of the coming kingdom to a heavenly realm outside this world. Jesus used his leverage to bring the power of God's rule down to earth. His parables and miracles were concrete samples of the comprehensive salvation which the rule of God was about to establish for the world in general.

This brief sketch of Jesus' message of the kingdom of God does not enter into all its details. We are rather trying to catch that thread of his teaching about the kingdom that links up with the christology of the New Testament as a whole. The decisive question is not whether historians can reconstruct all aspects of Jesus' teaching, but what role he actually played in bringing about the kingdom he preached. The question is whether the beginning of christology as the New Testament sets it forth in a plurality of expressions reaches back to the central theme of Jesus' message—the kingdom of God. Or does christology spring *de novo* from the early church, with no material continuity with the historical Jesus?

THE GENESIS OF
CHRISTOLOGY IN THE NEW TESTAMENT

Christology cannot ignore the most heated debates going on in New Testament scholarship. Neither can it settle questions that still remain open in the field of critical historical research: Did Jesus understand himself as the Messiah? Did he identify himself with the coming Son of Man, taken in the eschatological sense? The wide-ranging difference between scholars on such questions can be easily detected by contrasting the methods and results of C. F. D. Moule's *The Origin of Christology*[14] with Willi Marxsen's *The Beginnings of Christology: A Study in Its Problems.*[15] They reach exactly opposite conclusions about whether Jesus believed he was the Messiah and the coming Son of Man, or whether these are titles which the early church transferred to him. The same contrast is visible with respect to other honorific titles applied to Jesus, such as Son of God and Lord. Dogmatics has no method of its own by which to resolve the strictly historical problems of New Testament research. But neither is it paralyzed by the failure of biblical scholars to reach a consensus on all the critical issues.

If Jesus did not explicitly refer to himself by any of the major christological

titles, how could the early church do so? How may we understand the genesis
and development of christology that makes a real difference to Christian faith,
so that what the early Christians said about Jesus does not flatly contradict
Jesus' own estimate of himself? If we take seriously Jesus' preaching of the
kingdom of God, then the question of how christology began is not first which
titles Jesus used about himself but whether he played a crucial role in bringing in the divine kingdom he proclaimed with such finality. The forerunner
of Jesus, John the Baptist, also preached the message of the coming kingdom,
announcing impending judgment and time for repentance. But Jesus was different. He was not the last prophet of the coming kingdom; he was the
medium of its arrival in beginning and in power. The realities of the kingdom
were already beginning to stir within history through the impact of Jesus'
ministry.

The root of christology in the ministry of Jesus is not located in a particular
title of honor he claimed for himself. What is important is that Jesus was
not only the proclaimer but also the bringer of the kingdom at the point
of its eruption. So Jesus could say, "But if it is by the finger of God that
I cast out demons, then the kingdom of God has come upon you" (Luke 11:20).
Even Rudolf Bultmann and members of his school who find no explicit
christology in Jesus' teaching strongly emphasize his authoritative claim as
the present mediator of the oncoming kingdom. In the words of Willi Marxsen, "the eschatological element is the primal datum of Christology." [16] Thus,
the genesis of christology lies in the fact that a person becomes related to
the coming kingdom by his or her decision for or against Jesus, as the occasion of its inbreaking in time. This eschatological role of Jesus is the basis
for speaking, with Bultmann and others, of an "implicit christology" in Jesus'
message.[17]

Whether Jesus was the Messiah, the Son of Man, the Son of God, or the
Lord depends not on finding these terms as self-designations on the lips of
Jesus but on whether the primitive community had good reason to apply these
titles to him as confessions of faith. What happened to bring the first believers
to such an awareness, if they did not simply read their christology from the
very words of Jesus?

Jesus was crucified and he was raised from the dead. His message had
aroused hope that God was coming soon in power and glory to put an end
to misery, poverty, and oppression, but instead Jesus got caught up in the
power struggles of passion week that led to the cross. So where was the fulfillment of Jesus' keen expectation of the coming kingdom? It was shattered on
the cross. The fulfillment did not come to pass as expected. Instead, the death
of Jesus by crucifixion took place, a gory substitute for the glory of the
kingdom. This means that either the kingdom of God emptied into the cross,
using it as a strange instrument of its way to fulfillment, or the kingdom finds

its fulfillment elsewhere, with no structural connection with the crucifixion of Jesus.

Many schools of theology do not look for the fulfillment of Jesus' expectation in the double ending of his life: cross and resurrection. Instead, quite different types of interpretation are offered, each in its own way avoiding the cross and its link to the coming kingdom. One type holds that the kingdom of God has not yet appeared; it is still future and otherworldly, not of this world. A second position views the kingdom as a call to decision here and now in the encounter with the message of Jesus; it is already present in every moment of existential decision. A third view sees the kingdom of God as something that lies in the historical future, coming by means of social and political transformations, either gradually and progressively or by means of revolutionary praxis. In none of these views is the crucifixion of Jesus integral to the arrival of the kingdom in history. Thus, they fail to connect Jesus' eschatological preaching of the kingdom to the early church's proclamation of Jesus as the crucified Christ in a fundamental way.

Jesus began his public ministry by announcing the coming kingdom with great expectation. He ended it by his death on the cross. The Gospel writers interpreted the death and resurrection of Jesus as the fulfillment of the kingdom whose coming he expected in the nearest possible future. But it was a fulfillment hidden under the sign of the cross, and therefore not manifest in all the power and glory that Jesus had expected. The one who had announced the coming of God with power to put an end to sin, death, and the power of the devil was condemned to die on the cross. This assassination could have been taken to mean that Jesus, self-deceived or betrayed by God, was simply proved wrong in his expectation of the kingdom. Instead, a great reversal of the disappointment on Good Friday took place. On the road to Emmaus the disciples had sighed, "But we had hoped that he was the one to redeem Israel" (Luke 24:21). But on the third day stories began to circulate that the crucified Jesus had appeared to some of his friends and disciples. These appearances of the living Jesus were interpreted by the first witnesses as evidence that God had raised Jesus from the dead and that this event was of an eschatological order, the beginning of the eschaton in the middle of history, a real fulfillment *in* Jesus of the expectation aroused *by* his message.

In the crucifixion and resurrection of Jesus the early church found the proof that Jesus was the expected Messiah, and further that he was the king of the kingdom he preached, crowned with a crown of thorns and enthroned on a cross, then granted a victory over the powers of evil in his resurrection from the dead. Here the Christ of faith and the Jesus of history prove to be one and the same Lord Jesus Christ. The primitive Christian community preached the kerygma of the crucified and risen Christ as the eschatological event that at least partially fulfilled the future eschatological kingdom which Jesus anticipated in all his preaching and activity. When the Catholic modernist Alfred Loisy said, "Jesus foretold the kingdom, and it was the church that came," [18] many Christians felt a crisis of contradiction between the preaching *of* Jesus and the early church's preaching *about* Jesus. Adolf von Harnack provided the classic statement of this supposed contradiction when he sharply contrasted the religion *of* Jesus with the religion *about* Jesus.[19] Ever since the time of the Enlightenment there has been the fear that a critical penetration of the sources will drive a wedge between Jesus and the church, separating the claims of apostolic faith in Christ from their roots in the Jesus of history. In fact, however, there is no such contradiction. The fear of sheer discontinuity between the historical Jesus and the kerygmatic Christ need not be nourished by a critical study of the Gospel sources. The basic claim of the gospel is that the identity of Jesus is revealed and the kingdom of God is fulfilled in the history of his death and resurrection. The validity of this claim explains how the early church could collect a plurality of christological titles from many quarters and transfer them to the historical Jesus in telling the whole story of his birth, life, death, and resurrection.

Faced with the events of Jesus' crucifixion and his Easter appearances, the early Christians began the history of christological interpretation that has now run for nearly two thousand years. But where has the church found its dominant symbols of interpretation? What has it used as a norm against an uncritical adoption of all novel interpretations? What has been the church's hermeneutical key to open the traditions of the past, to find new meanings in the present, and to gain new directions for the future? The earliest interpreters searched the Hebrew Scriptures, the Old Testament, and used its symbols and stories to point ahead to the events of "these last days" (Heb. 1:2) in which the promises of Yahweh were being fulfilled in the Son. The hermeneutics of promise and fulfillment can be traced in all the traditions of the New Testament, even in those most subject to Hellenistic influence. Thus, the cross of Jesus was interpreted as a sacrifice for sin in light of the Old Testament idea of atonement. The resurrection was interpreted as the dawning of a new era, the initial breakthrough of the new things prophesied in Isaiah 65—66. In reaching back to the Old Testament, however, the controlling norm was the apostles' belief that Jesus' message of the kingdom reached its apex in his death and resurrection, revealing that he was in person the Christ of God.

If the early church witnessed to the resurrection of Jesus as a fulfillment in line with Jesus' own kingdom expectation, this had a retroactive effect on its interpretation of the history of Jesus and the history of Israel as well. What the church came to believe about Jesus as the Christ was retrojected into the beginnings and then narrated as a story that unfolded according to a plot that was there all along. The story starts at the beginning and proceeds to the end. But in fact, hermeneutically speaking, the end of the story—the cross and resurrection of Jesus—was there from the beginning and guided the community in shaping the Gospel traditions. No wonder that the presence of the kingdom, experienced by the Christian community on account of the Easter fulfillment, could be traced back to the ministry of Jesus prior to Easter. Features from the Christ of Easter and the Jesus of history are interwoven in the Gospel narratives, since the church put them to use in its own kerygmatic and missionary career.

The church's interest was to concentrate on the person of Jesus as the Christ of God, for in him it had experienced eschatological salvation. Because this salvation was hidden in the crucified Christ and present through the Spirit in the risen Lord, faith was required from the beginning to acknowledge its reality. Faith is the only mode of access to the salvation which the coming of God with the kingdom works in the person of the crucified and risen Jesus. The coming of the kingdom in the cross keeps the kingdom hidden in history and can be seen only with the eyes of faith. If we leave faith aside and look to history with ordinary eyes, we find no convincing evidence that the kingdom of God has already come. The rabbis of Judaism taught that when the Messiah comes the world ought to look different.[20] And did not Jesus himself promise that when the kingdom comes there would be an end to suffering, oppression, poverty, hunger, and death? But history shows that these bitter realities continue; they have not diminished in even the slightest degree. Hence, if the early church's faith is true, its truth cannot be read off the open face of history, but lies hidden in the person of Jesus Christ and can be grasped through faith alone.

The primitive Christian faith kept two truths in tension. According to the truth of faith the kingdom of God has *already* arrived in Christ. This stands in tension with the truth about history that the kingdom has *not yet* come. Despite all the enthusiasm generated by Easter, the early Christians came to see that the kingdom of God was overlapping with the kingdom of this world, and that they had to live hopefully and realistically at the same time, citizens of two realms or ages still in conflict. The full reality of the kingdom of God was thus split into an *already* and a *not yet*. Easter is the sign of the already. But there is more to the story of the kingdom than Easter. Easter is only the first fruits. There is still the *parousia* to come, the final advent of Jesus to judge the living and the dead, the oncoming power of God's future in glory until God is all in all.

If the fulfillment of Easter were all there is to the coming of God's kingdom, there would not be much hope for the real world in which people live. The kingdom would be so spiritualized as to lose touch with the human struggles of life and death and of sin and suffering. There was perhaps from the beginning the temptation for Christians to allow their Easter faith to carry them into a gnostic type of spiritualized fulfillment, collapsing the two-dimensional kingdom of the *already* and the *not yet* into a one-dimensional present, beyond this world of nature and history. Some of the early Christians even tended to believe that their new life in Christ would place them beyond the pale of suffering and death. But soon they had to learn that the truth of the cross overlaps the fulfillment of the resurrection, as a sign that the struggles of history continue and hopes must be rekindled for a future fulfillment of the whole creation. When God comes with the kingdom, God comes to establish rule not only in the personal sphere of faith but also in the public realm in which the powers and principalities hold sway. Thus christology becomes related to eschatology as a down payment on a purchase to be paid in full only when the rule of God completely annihilates all the negativities of this life—the powers of sin, death, and the devil. Meanwhile, the lordship of Christ is hidden under the cross, guaranteed by the resurrection, alive in the Spirit, attested by faith, and at work through the church in contesting the powers that still rage against God in this world. But what is now hidden in history will be unveiled in glory when the world at last reaches its fulfillment in the final future of God's coming kingdom.

NOTES

1. Rudolf Bultmann, *Theology of the New Testament*, vol. 1, trans. Kendrick Grobel, (New York: Charles Scribner's Sons, 1954–55), p. 4.

2. Johannes Weiss, *Jesus' Proclamation of the Kingdom of God*, trans. R. H. Hiers and D. L. Holland (Philadelphia: Fortress Press, 1971).

3. Albert Schweitzer, *The Quest of the Historical Jesus*, trans. N. Montgomery (London: A. & C. Black, 1910).

4. Weiss, *Jesus' Proclamation*, p. 114.

5. Cf. James M. Robinson, *A New Quest of the Historical Jesus* (London: SCM Press, 1959).

6. Cf. Jürgen Moltmann, *Theology of Hope*, trans. James W. Leitch (New York: Harper & Row, 1967).

7. Rudolf Bultmann wrote in *Jesus and the Word*, trans. L. P. Smith and E. H. Lantero (New York: Charles Scribner's Sons, 1958): "I do indeed think that we can know almost nothing concerning the life and personality of Jesus, since the early Christian sources show no interest in either, are moreover fragmentary and often legendary; and other sources about Jesus do not exist" (p. 8).

8. Adolf von Harnack, *What Is Christianity?* trans. T. B. Saunders (New York: Harper & Brothers, 1957), pp. 55, 180.

9. Joachim Jeremias, *New Testament Theology*, trans. John Bowden (New York: Charles Scribner's Sons, 1971), 1:103.

10. Ernst Bloch, *Man on His Own*, trans. E. B. Ashton (New York: Herder & Herder, 1970). Building on Ludwig Feuerbach's idea that man is God to man (*homo hominis*

Deus), Bloch speaks of "God as the utopianly hypostasized and unknown human idea" (p. 208).

11. On the relation between eschatology and ethics in the teachings of Jesus, see Richard H. Hiers, *Jesus and Ethics* (Philadelphia: Westminster Press, 1968); Carl E. Braaten, *Eschatology and Ethics* (Minneapolis: Augsburg Publishing House, 1974); James M. Childs, *Christian Anthropology and Ethics* (Philadelphia: Fortress Press, 1978).

12. Werner G. Kümmel, *Promise and Fulfillment*, trans. Dorothea M. Barton (London: SCM Press, 1957).

13. Jeremias, *New Testament Theology*, 1:118–21.

14. C. F. D. Moule, *The Origin of Christology* (Cambridge: At the University Press, 1977).

15. Willi Marxsen, *The Beginnings of Christology: A Study in Its Problems*, trans. Paul Achtemeier (Philadelphia: Fortress Press, 1969).

16. Ibid., p. 33.

17. Cf. Rudolf Bultmann, "The Primitive Christian Kerygma and the Historical Jesus," in *The Historical Jesus and the Kerygmatic Christ*, ed. Carl E. Braaten and Roy A. Harrisville (Nashville: Abingdon Press, 1964), pp. 15–42.

18. Alfred Loisy, *The Gospel and the Church*, trans. Christopher Home (Philadelphia: Fortress Press, 1976), p. 166.

19. Adolf von Harnack's famous statement affirms: "The Gospel, as Jesus proclaimed it, has to do with the Father only and not with the Son." *What is Christianity?* p. 144.

20. Dorothee Soelle, *Christ the Representative*, trans. David Lewis (Philadelphia: Fortress Press, 1967), p. 108.

3

Classical Christology
and Its Subsequent Criticism

The christological dogma of the church succeeded in steering a middle course between heretical extremes to the right and the left, between the denial of the union of God and humanity in the person of Jesus and the denial of the duality of their respective natures. The formula "one person in two natures" preserved the central biblical message in the church that salvation comes from meeting the true God in the man Jesus Christ.

THE IDENTIFICATION
OF JESUS WITH GOD

There is a wide gulf between the messianic kerygma of the apostolic period and the trinitarian dogma of the ancient church. Most studies of New Testament theology do not even discuss the Trinity, the central doctrine of the patristic era. They proceed as if the New Testament were on the side of unitarianism. How is it possible, then, to move from the kingdom of God, the central datum of Jesus' message, to the dogma of the Trinity, which identifies the person of Jesus Christ with God? The motive for the transition is to be found in the Easter kerygma of the primitive Christian community.

The early church believed that the coming of God's kingdom took place in the crucifixion and resurrection of Jesus of Nazareth. For this reason Jesus was confessed as the King of the coming kingdom that he announced in the name of God. The early church faced a crucial theological problem. Was the death of Jesus a sign of failure or of fulfillment? The resurrection event made it possible to glimpse a hidden fulfillment of the kingdom in Jesus' own death on the cross. This belief in the hidden presence of eschatological fulfillment became the root cause of the early church's identification of Jesus with God. Without the resurrection there could have arisen no belief in the divinity of Jesus. But if God really came to establish the kingdom in Jesus' cross and resurrection, and if these events were actually a fulfillment of eschatological expectation, then God was truly identified with Jesus of Nazareth.

497

The coming of God and the coming of Jesus are thus unified in the experience of eschatological salvation. The logic of salvation demanded the identification of Jesus with God. The experience of Jesus' cross and resurrection as the definitive event of salvation generated a faith, centering on the person of Jesus Christ, that traditionally belonged only to God if idolatry were to be avoided. If salvation had really arrived through the person of Jesus, he must also have been God, because God and God alone is the power of salvation.

The transition from Jesus' message of the kingdom to the apostolic preaching of him as the Christ—from the proclaimer to the proclaimed (Bultmann)—is grounded in the faith-claim of the *ecclesia* that God has established the reality of the kingdom in the person of Jesus Christ through his death and resurrection. If for Jesus the kingdom was near, for the church it was already here—*in Christ.* The kingdom became history, bringing the power of God deep into the flesh and blood of Jesus the man. The preaching of Christ became the primary means of access to the mystery of the kingdom. The coming of the kingdom in Christ came to grips with the major powers that oppress humanity and the world in their depths.

In the cross of Christ, God was dealing victoriously with the *sin* of the world. In his resurrection, *death* was conquered and new life was made to last. In his ministry Jesus had challenged the rule of *Satan* by casting out demons. God had gained a victory in the encounter of Christ with sin, death, and the devil, precisely the kind of victory God was expected to win in the establishment of divine rule. These perspectives made clear why the early church could concentrate all its faith, hope, and love in the person of Jesus Christ and identify his coming with the advent of God's eschatological rule, in both judgment and grace.

The identification of Jesus with God was not at first the result of a dogmatic development. When Clement of Rome wrote early in the second century, "We must think of Jesus Christ as of God" (2 Clement 1:1), he was not passing on a dogmatic decree of a church council. He was, rather, summarizing in a few words what the primitive community had been expressing from the beginning in confessional, kerygmatic, and liturgical formulas.

The confession that "Jesus is Lord" (Rom. 10:9; 1 Cor. 12:3; Phil. 2:11) was not the product of a later hellenization of Christianity. This formula appeared already in the worship of the Palestinian community, placing Jesus on the line with God. Even though the title "Lord" was also frequently used at that time as a polite form of address, as in the expression "My Lord," its use in early Christian worship exalted the name of Jesus above every name (Phil. 2:9), because it was nothing less than the name of God. *Kyrios* was the Greek translation of the Hebrew *Adonai,* the favorite name for God among the Jews. Its application to Jesus in the context of worship could not be mistaken by people familiar with the rules of reverence due God's name in a Hebrew setting.

On the basis of faith in Jesus and the worship of him, the early church not only acknowledged Jesus as Lord but also transferred all the high divine titles and attributes to him. The exalted Lord Jesus Christ rules the world as only God can do. The Lordship of Jesus Christ is universal in scope, reaching beyond history and the church, encompassing nature and the creation, including all visible and invisible beings in heaven, on earth, and below the earth. The presupposition of the universal rule of Christ from his resurrection to the parousia is his identity with God in a preincarnate state and his role as the agent and medium of all creation (Col. 1:16ff.; Heb. 1:2). The dominion of Christ is not limited to the realm of redemption and the new creation. The New Testament concentrates the Lordship of Christ in soteriology, but actually the presupposition of his soteriological dignity is the role of Christ as mediator of all life in the original order of creation.

CHRISTOLOGICAL HERESIES[1]

The identification of Jesus with God did not take place without grave danger to the faith of the Christian church. The danger in stressing the divinity of Christ was that faith might lose sight of the real humanity of the man Jesus. Even in the New Testament period, and increasingly throughout the second century, there developed a tendency to see Jesus one-sidedly in terms of divinity. This one-sided view produced the heresy known as *docetism,* the perennial heresy of the "right wing" in christology. Docetism is the name of a christological teaching, circulating mostly in gnostic circles, that Jesus Christ only *appeared* to have a human body and only *appeared* to suffer and die. Docetism comes from the Greek word *dokein*, meaning "to seem." Marcion, the second-century heretic, was the most prominent theologian to popularize a docetic christology.[2] The gnostic influence, emanating in general from Oriental spirituality, regarded matter as evil and the flesh as unreal. Therefore, when God became man and the Word became flesh in the person of Jesus the Christ, this was only apparently so. For docetism the divinity of Christ posed no problem; it could hardly be emphasized enough. In its view, however, the Son of God could not really become human. The human life of Jesus evaporated into a cloud of divinity.

At the opposite pole there was *ebionitism,* the perennial heresy of the "left wing" in christology. "Ebionitism" is the name of a widespread christological teaching in the second century that presented Jesus as a mere man, denying his divinity altogether. We know of the Ebionites, as well as of the Docetists, not from their own writings but only through the polemics of their orthodox critics. Ebionitism was not named after a heretic called Ebion. The word comes from the Hebrew word *ebionim,* meaning "poor." The Ebionites stemmed mainly from Jewish circles, in contrast to the Hellenistic orientation of the Docetists. For the Ebionites, Jesus was certainly the Messiah, the Christ, but he was only a man. He could not be God. Impossible! They also denied the virgin birth. Jesus was born the natural son of an earthly father and mother, Joseph and Mary.

These christological heresies to the right and to the left seemed to be poles apart from each other. The one side enthusiastically affirmed the divinity of Christ, the other side denied it. The one side denied the real humanity of Jesus, the other side affirmed it. But these extremes were reverse sides of the same christological coin: a rejection of a real incarnation of God in the man Jesus.

The Docetists were bound to a Hellenistic concept of God as a timeless absolute who could not really change. Therefore, God's involvement in history, the realm of flux, could only be apparent. Because God is God, God is immutable. Thus there could be no real incarnation, no real change in an ontological sense, only an apparent one. The God of Greek metaphysics was completely in charge of the docetic christology.

The Ebionites were committed to a Jewish concept of God as totally other in transcendence and holiness. God is God and humanity is humanity; the infinite is not capable of entering the finite. The ontological separation makes a real incarnation of God unthinkable, even blasphemous. The God of Jewish monotheism was the controlling force behind the ebionitic christology.

These early docetic and ebionitic trends continued to develop in the ancient church and to generate more complex types of christological expression. The docetic line to the right can be seen in modalistic monarchianism, a third-century teaching advanced by Sabellius, bishop of Rome. The modalists were not docetists of the old style, for they acknowledged Jesus Christ to be a real man. However, the old spirit of docetism crept into the teaching of Sabellius. He taught that the One God (the divine monarchy) appeared as the Father in the Old Testament, as the Son in the life of Jesus, and finally as the Spirit in the church.[3] But these distinctions between Father, Son, and Spirit were more apparent than real. The human life of Jesus was a temporary mask of the One God in whom no differentiations could exist. The identity of Jesus as the Son of God was unmasked by Sabellius as the second mode of the divine self-manifestation, a temporary theophany, which in turn gave way to a third. This new type of docetism also made a real incarnation impossible, since that would violate the metaphysics of monotheism underlying the modalistic christology.

There was also in the third century a continuation of the ebionitic line to the left, in dynamistic monarchianism, represented by Paul of Samosata, bishop of Antioch. Adoptionism is the more common name for this type of christology.[4] It was not a repetition of the crass ebionitism which taught that Jesus was a mere man (*psilos anthropos*). In fact, the adoptionists could attack the ebionitic denial of the divinity of Christ. Christ was indeed divine; he was filled with the dynamism of the Spirit and uniquely was adopted by the Father as his only beloved Son. This was not an appearance of God from above as in modalistic monarchianism. On the contrary, in the adoptionist model Jesus Christ became divine from below by the indwelling of the Spirit and by his growth in godlike holiness. Adoptionist christology could not accept a real incarnation of God, a movement of the divine descending deep into the human. The movement went in the opposite direction, the human ascending by spiritual and moral development to the level of godlikeness.

The road to Chalcedon continued to bend now to the right and now to the left on the way to a definition of christology in which two truths could be affirmed at once: (1) the identification of Jesus as God in the interest of Christian worship and (2) the differentiation of the real humanity of Jesus from his divinity in fidelity to his Gospel picture. Christology to the right, with its stress on the divinity of Christ, was driven by the logic of the Christian liturgy in which Jesus Christ was exalted as God. Christology to the left, upholding the humanity of Jesus, was guided by the historical picture of Jesus in the synoptic Gospels. In general, theologians influenced by the great school of Antioch used a more historical-exegetical approach to the Bible and usually leaned to the left in christology. Theologians of the rival school of Alexandria applied a more speculative metaphysical method which postulated the divinity of Christ as the necessary condition of salvation, veering to the right in christology. These trends were typically illustrated in certain christological developments in the fourth and fifth centuries.[5]

At the time that Constantine became Pontifex Maximus (A.D. 321), Christianity was threatened by a serious attack from the left on the Christian confession of God's real presence in Jesus. The attack was led by Arius, who was influenced by the adoptionist theologians Lucian of Antioch and Paul of Samosata. Arianism, however, was a more complex denial of the divinity of Christ than we find in either ebionitism or adoptionism.[6] For Arius, Christ was more than a human being and more than the adopted Son of God. He was the Logos, the Son of God, who existed before God the Father created the world. But he was not God; he did not share the divine essence. The Logos was not eternal. The Arians chanted in a hymn, "There was when he was not." In the beginning there was God alone (the principle of monarchianism); then the Logos was created to assist God in the creation of the world. Because the Logos was a creature, he did not share God's metaphysical attributes of being immutable, impassible, and infinitely removed from time and history.

So the Logos could change, enter into history, unite himself with human flesh in the person of Jesus, even suffer and die. Thus the incarnation of the Logos was inferior to a real incarnation of the true essence of God.

Athanasius, the fierce opponent of Arius argued that Arianism was heresy because it called into question the whole reality of salvation.[7] If the Logos as the redeemer is ontologically inferior to God, as a creature is to the Creator, there can be no real salvation, for such a system places the burden of salvation on a creature. Athanasius asked how a being lower than God could raise human beings to the level of God. How could the mediator between God and humanity be less than fully divine and fully human? Is the gospel a story about a holy person ascending to God, or is it about a loving God condescending to humanity in a human way? Who mediates salvation? God, or some creature?

The fathers at the Council of Nicaea, A.D. 325, inserted an old word of gnostic origin, *homoousios,*[8] to expose the deficiency in the Arian christology. The *homoousios* affirmed the oneness of substance of the Son and the Father. This meant that the person of Jesus Christ would henceforth be confessed as "eternally begotten of the Father . . . true God from true God." Only on this basis could the worship of Christ make sense and the reality of the salvation of humanity and the world be secured.

The Nicene Creed became the fundamental statement of the church in the interpretation of the incarnation. It became the starting point for all who subsequently joined the christological debates on how the eternal Son of God, of the same substance as the Father, could become flesh in the person of Jesus Christ. The development of orthodox christology was accompanied by anathemas of precisely defined heresies. Our brief sketch of this development cannot enter into the labyrinth of historical questions that modern critical scholarship raises in connection with each of the ancient christological controversies. We cannot deal, for example, with the historical question whether the important leaders who lent their names to the classical heresies were in fact guilty as charged by their orthodox critics. When we speak of these heresies, we shall deal with them as "isms," following Friedrich Schleiermacher's suggestion that this is the appropriate way for dogmatics: "But these names are here intended only to denote universal forms which we are here going to unfold, and the definitions of which they are intended to remind us proceed from the general nature of the situation, even if, e.g., Pelagius himself should not be a Pelagian in our sense."[9]

Christology proceeded from its trinitarian connection to establish the relation between the divine Christ and the human Jesus. Apollinarianism, named after Apollinarius, bishop of Laodicea, began by affirming the high christology of the Nicene Creed.[10] As a friend of Athanasius, Apollinarius was thoroughly orthodox on the doctrine of the Trinity. He held that the Son is distinctly

other than the Father (against Sabellianism) but eternally shares the one
substance of the Father (against Arianism). But being right on the Trinity
by the standard of orthodoxy did not determine how a theologian might interpret the incarnation. Apollinarius moved in the direction of docetism when
he taught that the humanity of Christ assumed in the incarnation was
incomplete.[11] Surely the Logos in Christ was truly God; but in the incarnation he did not become wholly human. The Logos took upon himself the
body and soul of the man Jesus, but took the place of his human spirit.
Apollinarius' interest was to solve the problem of the unity of the person who
was both divine and human. How can two beings unite into one? Apollinarius
believed that a genuine union is possible only when the Logos, as the active
principle of self-consciousness and self-determination, substitutes himself for
the human spirit. The result is a truncated view of the human reality in Jesus
Christ. The union in Christ was a union of the perfect Logos with an incomplete
human nature. Apollinarius believed he had secured what was essential for
salvation, an integral divine-human person, a real God-Man, not just a godly
man.

Why was Apollinarianism condemned as heretical? The Council of Constantinople in A.D. 381 affirmed the completeness of Christ's human nature
and refused to accept any abbreviation of its faculties. The same logic which
called for the *homoousios* with the Father was at work to demand a comparable
homoousios with humanity. It was the logic of salvation. The operative principle was this: What was not assumed cannot be saved. If Christ was not fully
human, then the whole human person cannot be saved. The spirit in fact
constitutes the true essence of human being in the trichotomous scheme of
Platonism—body, soul, and spirit—within which Apollinarius worked. If the
human spirit is displaced by the divine Logos, the deepest spiritual dimension of human beings, enslaved by Satan, corrupted by sin, and condemned
to death, lies beyond the scope of salvation. The first church council to decide
against Apollinarianism declared, "If therefore the whole man was lost, it
was necessary that that which was lost should be saved" (Council of Rome,
A.D. 374–376). The church had struck one more blow against the heresy of
docetism.

The reaction to the docetic tendencies of Apollinarianism came swiftly from
the theologians of the Antiochian school, championed by Nestorius, patriarch
of Constantinople.[12] In earlier days the school of Antioch had been identified
with ebionitic or adoptionistic tendencies. The new school of Antioch accepted
the Nicene doctrine of the Trinity, namely, that Christ was fully God. But
the leaders of this school—Diodore of Tarsus, Theodore of Mopsuestia, and
Nestorius—retained the traditional Antiochian emphasis on the humanity
of Jesus. Jesus Christ was completely human, in body, soul, and spirit. One
of Nestorius' priests attacked the cultic term *theotokos* for Mary, meaning

that Mary was the "mother of God." The term seemed to detract from the human nature of Jesus, confusing it with the divine. For Nestorius, Jesus Christ was both fully God and fully man, but the divine and human natures must be kept distinct and unabbreviated in the incarnation. There must be two of everything—two natures, two substances, two wills, two sets of attributes—and therefore also two persons (*prosōpa*). If there were two natures in Christ, there had to be two persons. Nestorius could not imagine a nature without a person. Nature is what a thing essentially is and person (*prosopon*) is how it appears.

This doctrine of two persons joined in Christ became the defining mark of Nestorianism as a heresy. Here again we must remind the reader that we cannot deal with the modern historical question whether Nestorius was a Nestorian.[13] No matter what modern research may conclude about Nestorius' own teachings, Nestorianism denotes one of those "universal forms" to which Schleiermacher referred, which can contradict true Christian doctrine. The essential problem with Nestorianism is simple: It could not affirm a real incarnation. Its scheme was dualistic, stressing the divine and the human in their complete difference, thus failing to achieve a real incarnational union of God and humanity in the one person of Jesus Christ. The only type of unity which Nestorianism could allow was that of conjunction (*synapheia*), or a close communion of two persons enjoying a relation of mutual give and take.

The theologians of the school of Alexandria regarded Nestorianism as typical of the Antiochene tendency to teach that Jesus was a mere human being. The Nestorians offered a union of two persons living side by side in a fellowship of love and moral freedom. The Alexandrians insisted on a deeper ontological unity of God with the man Jesus. For Eutyches, patriarch of Constantinople, and Dioscuros, bishop of Alexandria, the most significant thing about Christ was his divine nature, not his humanity. The human nature was not denied so much as absorbed into the higher power of the divine nature, with the result that from the moment of the incarnation there remained only one nature. Hence this heresy is fittingly called *monophysitism,* meaning "one nature," and sometimes also Eutycheanism, after its one proponent.[14] The monophysites sacrificed the integrity of Jesus' humanity for the sake of his divinity. They missed the whole point of the incarnation: God's involvement deep in human history so that human beings might encounter God on a human plane and not have to search for salvation in the remoteness of God's heavenly being.

In the fifth century the church struggled between the Scylla of a divine Christ who was not really human (monophysitism) and the Charybdis of a human Jesus who was not really one with God (Nestorianism). At Nicaea (A.D. 325) the church condemned the Arian heresy for denying the full deity of Christ. At Constantinople (A.D. 381) the church rejected Apollinarianism for denying the complete humanity of Jesus. The emerging orthodox confession henceforth was to be that Jesus Christ was fully God and fully human. But how are the two related? This question preoccupied the church in the fifth century, as theologians struggled to integrate the diametrically opposed tendencies of Nestorius and Eutyches. Finally, at Chalcedon (A.D. 451) the council fathers formulated the christological dogma of two natures, divine and human, in the one person of Jesus Christ. Thus the church chose a middle course between the Nestorian and the Eutychean alternatives. Both extremes impaired the doctrine of the incarnation.

The final verdict pronounced by the Creed of Chalcedon reads:

> Following, then, the holy Fathers, we all with one voice teach that it should be confessed that our Lord Jesus Christ is one and the same Son, the Same perfect in Godhead, the Same perfect in manhood, truly God and truly man, the Same (consisting) of a rational soul and a body; *homoousios* with the Father as to his Godhead, and the Same *homoousios* with us as to his manhood; in all things like unto us, sin only excepted; begotten of the Father before ages as to his Godhead, and in the last days, the Same, for us and for our salvation, of Mary the Virgin *Theotokos* as to his manhood;
>
> One and the same Christ, Son, Lord, Only Begotten, made known in two natures (which exist) without confusion, without change, without division, without separation; the difference of the natures having been in no wise taken away by reason of the union, but rather the properties of each being preserved, and (both) concurring into one Person (*prosōpon*) and one *hypostasis*—not parted or divided into two persons (*prosōpa*), but one and the same Son and Only-begotten, the divine Logos, the Lord Jesus Christ; even as the prophets from of old (have spoken) concerning him, and as the Lord Jesus Christ himself has taught us, and as the Symbol of the Fathers has delivered to us.[15]

This is the famous Chalcedonian definition of the personal identity of Jesus Christ. We must first understand what the Chalcedonian Creed accomplished in its own time, before we examine it from the perspective of its modern critics. The main point of the creed was to affirm a true incarnation, not to explain its mystery. People who tried to explain the mystery, whether from the left (Nestorianism) or from the right (Eutycheanism), were anathematized. The Nestorian picture of a double personality and the monophysitic annulment of the human were both alike condemned. Against Nestorianism the creed asserted that between the two natures there was no division or separation, and against Eutycheanism that the two natures were not confused or changed one into the other. The two natures, though remaining distinct, were united in the one person of Christ. The creed did not, however, explain how two complete natures could be united in one person. It safeguarded the unity of the person as against Nestorianism and the completeness of the two natures as against Eutycheanism. It can be safely concluded that the council accomplished the negative purpose of condemning heresy, for a time building a protective fence around the mystery of the person of Jesus Christ. On the positive side it certainly left room for further development.

FROM THE CREED OF
CHALCEDON TO THE FORMULA OF CONCORD

Christological controversy did not end at Chalcedon. The pressures from the right and the left wings continued for more than a millennium, until in the sixteenth century the Lutheran and the Calvinist confessions placed their own characteristic and conflicting interpretations on the christological dogma. At the fifth ecumenical council in Constantinople (A.D. 553) an inference from Chalcedon was drawn, proposed by Leontius of Byzantium, affirming the "impersonal" humanity of Christ.[16] This is known as the doctrine of the *anhypostasia* and *enhypostasia*. Today it sounds strange to learn that orthodox christology entails the denial that Jesus was an individual human person. Docetism seems to have been thrown out by one council only to reappear in the next. The Council of Constantinople denied that Jesus had a human hypostasis, something that belongs to every other human being. Did this not conflict with the confession of Chalcedon that Jesus Christ was "*homoousios* with us as to his manhood; in all things like unto us"? Did not the doctrine of the anhypostatic nature of Christ rob him of something essential to every person: human personality and self-consciousness? This is the common view. Some critics have angrily dismissed this doctrine as the "beheading" of Christ; others have alleged that it represents the victory of monophysitism. Consider the sharp attack by Paul Althaus: "One cannot separate the nature from the person. Human personality is an essential constituent of human nature. Hence 'anhypostasia' abolishes the true humanity of Jesus, his believing and praying human ego, the truth of his being tempted."[17]

The decision for or against the doctrine of the *anhypostasia* depends on what it does to the truly human nature of Jesus Christ. Does this doctrine really violate the integrity of Jesus' complete humanity? Countering Althaus's criticism is Karl Barth's strong defense. Barth observes that *anhypostasia* as a negation must be linked with *enhypostasia* as an affirmation.[18] On the basis of the incarnation of the Word of God in the man Jesus Christ, what *anhypostasia* denies is that the human nature of Jesus existed or exists by itself outside the Word, and *enhypostasia* affirms that Jesus had personal existence but only in and through the Word. The humanity is not abolished or truncated but elevated and fulfilled in union with the person, the *hypostasis*, of the Word of God. Whether one sides with Althaus or Barth, it is clear that the council intended to draw a line once more against ebionitism, adoptionism, and Nestorianism, all of which viewed Jesus as an independent personality who lived a life of close spiritual fellowship with the Father.

In the seventh century, fear arose that christology had veered too far to the right in the direction of monophysitism. Insisting on *two* natures in line with Chalcedon, the dyophysites were confronted by a new edition of monophysitism in the teaching that only one "will" or one "energy" was operative in Christ. Hence this new style monophysitism was referred to as monenergism or monotheletism. At the sixth ecumenical council in Constantinople (A.D. 681) monothelitism was condemned, along with Pope Honorius I, who put down the whole controversy as a mere dispute about words.

The millennium between the six ecumenical councils of the ancient church and the christological controversies in the period of the Reformation was one of comparative barrenness. John of Damascus produced a scholastic synthesis in the tenth century that became normative for the future of Eastern Orthodoxy. It aimed to combine the various decisions of the ancient ecumenical councils. In the West there was scarcely any noteworthy development through the Middle Ages, except for a resurgence of adoptionism in eighth-century Spain. In this view Jesus, in his humanity, was the adopted Son by the grace of God (*adoptivus homo*). This teaching was condemned in various synods as a revival of the Nestorian impiety of dividing Christ into two sons, the eternal Son of God and the adopted Son of Man. In general, medieval scholasticism remained within the approved categories of Chalcedonian christology and turned its more creative energies from the doctrine of the person to the work of Christ.

The christological problem was raised again in the heated controversies between Lutherans and Calvinists on the doctrine of the communication of attributes (*communicatio idiomatum*).[19] Both sides claimed to stand on the basis of Chalcedon, which had taught that the attributes of the two natures were preserved in the personal union. Luther taught that at the Lord's Supper the whole Christ was really present, including his human nature, and therefore also his body and blood. Zwingli responded with his theory of *alloeosis*, which explains faith's language about the real presence as a figure of speech. Such verbal predications, Zwingli taught, strictly apply only to Christ's divine nature. The human Christ cannot be really present in the Lord's Supper, since he is finite and so can be present only one place at a time. Luther countered Zwingli's argument with his doctrine of ubiquity. Ubiquity or omnipresence is essentially an attribute of the divine nature, but is communicated to the human nature because of the incarnational union. Starting with the Lord's Supper, the controversy on the communication of attributes exploded into a full-scale war on christology between the Lutherans and the Reformed.

Lutherans and Calvinists both inherited standard Chalcedonianism from medieval scholasticism.[20] They agreed: (1) that in Christ there was one person in two natures, fully divine and fully human; (2) that there was a close inter-communion of the natures in a personal union; (3) that these natures kept their identities and were not commingled (against Eutycheanism) and yet did not exist separately in two different persons (against Nestorianism); (4) that the attributes of the natures were preserved, the divine being infinite and the human finite, the divine impassible and the human passible, etc.; (5) that nevertheless on account of the hypostatic union there was a communica-tion of attributes to the person of Christ, so that he possessed and used both divine and human powers. But just at this point there arose a difference. The Lutherans, taking a cue from Luther's doctrine of ubiquity in the Lord's Sup-per controversy, proposed a novel extension of the traditional understanding. Not only were the attributes of both natures communicated to the one per-son (acceptable to the Calvinists), but also the majestic powers of the divine nature were communicated to the human.

The Formula of Concord and later Lutheran dogmatics systematized the doctrine of the exchange of attributes in three genera, which the Lutheran fathers believed were supported by Scripture. First, there is the "idiomatic" genus: qualities of either nature may be ascribed to the entire person. Sec-ond, there is the "apotelesmatic" genus: actions of the one person may be ascribed to one or the other of the two natures. Third, there is the "majestatic" genus: divine qualities such as omnipotence and omnipresence are attributed to the human nature. This third type of communication of attributes, the *genus majestaticum,* [21] became the distinctive feature of Lutheran christology. The Calvinists remained loyal to the traditional limits of Chalcedon.

The ancient trends in christology were at work in the Reformed-Lutheran controversy.[22] The Reformed position was branded the child of Nestorianism, bearing a family resemblance to the ancient school of Antioch, and the Lutheran position the child of Eutycheanism, going back to the lineage of Alexandria. The Lutherans were eager to stress the *unity* of the divine-human person, running the monophysitic risk of mixing the natures. Their battle formula was *"finitum est capax infiniti,"* the finite is capable of the infinite. The human nature of Jesus Christ was capable of using the infinite powers of God, acting truly omnipresent, omnipotent, and omniscient at will. Did this picture of Christ remain within the classic limits of Chalcedon? The Reformed said "No!" They maintained a clear distinction between the two natures, so their counterslogan became *"finitum non capax infiniti,"* the finite is not capable of the infinite. Because the human nature of Christ was finite, it was not capable of being both at the right hand of the Father in heaven and present on earth in the bread and wine of holy communion.

The Calvinist zeal for the distinction of the natures was backed by the old-fashioned Nestorian logic. If the Logos is divine, then it could not limit itself to the flesh of Jesus. Accordingly, the Calvinists taught that the Logos, being infinite, must exist *extra carnem* (outside the flesh) and not be limited by its union with the flesh. The Heidelberg Catechism states: "Because the divinity is everywhere present, it must follow that it is indeed ouside its adopted humanity and yet none the less also in the same and remaineth in personal union with it." Among Lutherans this doctrine was dubbed the *extra-Calvinisticum*. It implied a very loose linkage between the Logos and the man Jesus of Nazareth and led to a theology of glory, opening the door to exalted language about the Logos apart from its enfleshment. The Lutherans countered with a theology of the cross, holding that the Logos can be known only in the flesh. So they coined the phrase *"totus intra carnem* and *numquam extra carnem"* (wholly in the flesh and never outside the flesh).

The christological issue that divided Lutherans and Calvinists, producing two confessional groups, erupted very early also within the Lutheran camp, creating two rival schools. Article VIII of the Formula of Concord (A.D. 1580) aimed at reconciling differences between the school of John Brenz (the Swabians) and the school of Martin Chemnitz (the Lower Saxons). Philip Melanchthon had written in his *Loci Communes* (1521) that "to know Christ is to know his benefits." He said that the mystery of divinity is more to be adored than investigated and complained of the *rabies theologorum* (the fury of theologians), which turned hairsplitting distinctions into polemical weapons. Melanchthon had little patience for analyzing the chemistry of the incarnation, determining how much divinity and how much humanity were operative in Christ and how their respective attributes were related to each other. But other Lutherans made these investigations their specialty.

The Formula of Concord tried to find balanced language to settle the disputes among Lutherans, but with little success. It looked for middle ground, but waffled on the issue of the divine attributes during the earthly life of Jesus. Did the Formula teach a doctrine of *"krypsis"* or *"kenosis"*? *Krypsis* means that the divine attributes were "hidden" in the incarnation, *kenosis* that they had been "laid aside." The combinations of these two alternatives were endless. Did the Formula teach that the person of Christ enjoyed full possession of the attributes but used them secretly? Or did it teach full possession and voluntary abstinence from use? Or did it teach full possession and partial arbitrary use? Or did it teach partial possession and partial use? Or partial possession and abstinence from use? And in the event of partial possession, with some degree of *kenosis*, which attributes were retained and which left behind in the incarnation?

The Formula of Concord did not achieve its aim of settling christological disputes. Instead the battle raged into the seventeenth century between the Lutheran dogmaticians of Giessen and of Tübingen. If the human nature of Jesus became ubiquitous, undergirding the real presence of the whole Christ in the Lord's Supper, was he also universal in an absolute sense in the whole world and in all creatures? Having started with a theology of the cross, stressing the grace of God in the concrete existence of the man Jesus, the Lutherans were drawn into a theology of glory by divinizing the flesh of Jesus, by glorifying the human with qualities of divinity. The Giessen theologians wanted to stress the state of humiliation (*status exinanitionis*), limiting the use of divine attributes in the earthly Jesus. The Tübingen theologians would tolerate no limitation of the divine in the human Jesus, but allowed that the powers were exercised in secret. They affirmed the doctrine of *krypsis* but no *kenosis*. Lutheran theology was threatened by an overdose of docetism. A settlement was reached, called the Saxon decision, which set limits to the Tübingen school and came out in favor of the partial kenotic theory of the Giessen theologians.

The christological problem lingered within confessional Lutheranism without finding a satisfactory solution. Only in the nineteenth century did some confessional Lutherans attempt a radically new point of departure, using the idea of *kenosis*, suggested by Phil. 2:6–7: "Who, though he was in the form of God, did not count equality with God a thing to be grasped, but emptied himself, taking the form of a servant, being born in the likeness of men." The kenotic christology of the nineteenth century was an attempt to remain faithful to the old Lutheran doctrine of the *communicatio idiomatum*. It occurred to Gottfried Thomasius that a fourth *genus* could be added to the *communicatio idiomatum*.[23] If the divine attributes were communicated to the human nature, why could not the reverse happen, with the human attributes being communicated to the divine nature? If the *finitum capax infiniti* is true, the reverse may also be true, the *infinitum capax finiti*. The infinite God may submit to the finite in the incarnation; the Logos may empty himself and take on a limited human form. To express this idea, Thomasius improvised the term *genus tapeinoticum*, from *tapeinos*, meaning "humble" and "lowly."

This kenotic christology affirmed that in becoming man the divine logos limited itself. According to Thomasius, the Son of God in becoming man abandoned those divine attributes which had to do with his cosmological or metaphysical role: omnipotence, omnipresence, and omniscience. He retained those personal moral attributes which identify him as God: truth, love, and holiness. His divine freedom and love made it possible to set aside his divine power and majesty during the days of his humiliation in the earthly Jesus.

Other kenotic theologians radicalized the notion of *kenosis*. H. R. von Frank spoke of a depotentiation of the consciousness of the Son in the person of Jesus. Gradually, he thought, the human consciousness of Jesus evolved into his self-consciousness as God. Wolfgang F. Gess went even further, completely abandoning the ancient idea of the immutability of God. Thus he paved the way for saying that the Son of God left behind all traces of his divinity in the incarnation. This raised the problem: If the Son of God became kenotically incarnate in Jesus in such a way that no traces of divinity were left, in what sense was Jesus really anything more than a mere man? How is a totally kenotic divinity different from no divinity at all? This could be tantamount to saying that in Jesus Christ, God had to become absent in order to be incarnate. In kenotic christology the content of the *vere deus* seemed to disappear to the vanishing point.

CRITICISM OF THE DOGMA

A widespread revolt against the classical dogma of the incarnation began in the period of the Enlightenment and continues virtually unabated in contemporary works on christology. Albert Schweitzer's indictment against the doctrine of the two natures was typical of many others: The life of Jesus was trapped in a dogma.

> When at Chalcedon the West overcame the East, its doctrine of the two natures dissolved the unity of the Person, and thereby cut off the last possibility of a return to the historical Jesus. . . . The formula kept the life prisoner and prevented the leading spirits of the Reformation from grasping the idea of a return to the historical Jesus. This dogma had first to be shattered before men could once more go out in quest of the historical Jesus, before they could even grasp the thought of His existence. That the historic Jesus is something different from the Jesus Christ of the doctrine of the Two Natures seems to us now self-evident.[24]

Oscar Cullmann, too, states that the Creed of Chalcedon shifted the categories of the New Testament from the function of Christ to a metaphysical problem about the two natures of his person.

> There is thus a difference between the way in which the first Christians and the later Church understood the Christological problem. . . . The Church fathers subordinated the interpretation of the person and work of Christ to the question of the "natures." . . . Their emphases were misplaced. . . . The discussion of "natures" is ultimately a Greek, not a Jewish or biblical problem.[25]

The attacks on the classical christology cover a wide range. To the extreme left there is the type of rationalistic criticism which wants to get rid of the Christ of the creeds in order to return to a historical Jesus whose moral principles, it is thought, would be directly relevant to modern times. The biography of Jesus is proposed as a fitting substitute for the christological dogma.[26] A more moderate approach argues that the philosophical language of the ancient christology is obsolete; whatever truth it contains must be translated into categories of modern thought. Schleiermacher shared this latter sentiment. He took the traditional formula that in Jesus Christ we have divine and human natures combined into one person to express the truth that Jesus was conscious of God in a perfectly complete way. He spoke of an "absolute potency of God-consciousness in Christ."[27] The term "divine nature," he argued, had been borrowed from pagan philosophy and was therefore ill-adapted to express the being of God in Christ. Further, the word "person" can only mean a life-unity, but this real unity is incompatible with the assertion of two natures, since every nature must have a will. There is another terminological difficulty in that the word "person" in the christological formulation does not harmonize with the way the same word had been used in the trinitarian language, where three persons were united in one essence or substance. If the individuality of Christ is one of the three persons in the Trinity, we are left with a tritheistic concept of God, or else the personality of Christ becomes unreal, yielding inevitably a docetic interpretation. Thus, for Schleiermacher the "two natures in one person" formula led to such contradictory statements in dogmatics that it finally proved to be of little service to the church.[28]

Adolf von Harnack expanded Schleiermacher's notion that the categories of classical christology stemmed from pagan philosophy. The dogmas were the product of the "hellenization" of Christianity.[29] They exhibit the acute intellectualization of faith in the New Testament sense. Harnack was aware that it could not have happened otherwise on Greek soil, especially if Christianity was to make good its claim to be a universal religion and to extend its mission into the world of Hellenistic culture. The corollary of this concession was, however, that modern dogmatics must undo the process of hellenization and recapture the essence of Jesus' message in terms relevant for today. The Trinity and the incarnation were the first dogmas to be sacrificed, being the most eminent examples of the transformation of Christianity into a system of intellectual doctrines.

In recent systematic theology, Paul Tillich developed a dialectical critique of the classical christological formulas.[30] He was able to say "yes" and "no" to them. This dialectical approach interpreted the creeds of classical Christianity in a more positive way. The church used the concepts of Greek philosophy and Hellenistic mysticism to interpret and defend the Christian message, not to substitute the concepts for the message itself. The message is Jesus Christ as the paradoxical appearance of essential God-manhood in existence. When this message was attacked by heresies, the church had to defend it, and in defending, had to define it in whatever language it found most adequate. It proved itself free to use nonbiblical philosophical terms to articulate a living message. The Council of Chalcedon was successful in defending the message, but it was bound to fail if forced to define the message for all generations to come. It could not have succeeded for all time, because the Greek concepts were culture-bound and not timelessly valid. Yet the church at Chalcedon was right in rejecting the heretical formulations of Eutycheanism and Nestorianism, as well as of Arianism and Apollinarianism. But its own "two natures—one person" formula is open to serious question as a positive statement. It gives rational form to an impossible myth which says that a divine person coming from heaven unites himself with an earthly person. For Tillich the essence of the incarnation is not this myth, but rather the paradox of the appearance of essential God-manhood. The potential eternal relationship of God and humanity appeared in Christ under the conditions of existence and history. Here Tillich is reaching back to Hegel's type of christology, which aimed to penetrate the external data of dogma, myth, and history to their inner meaning: the essential unity of God and humanity.

There is truth in each of the types of criticism we have summarized. Schweitzer was right; the dogma did tend to obstruct the view of the real historical life of Jesus. And every historian would agree with Cullmann's point about a shift of categories from the New Testament to the ecclesiastical creeds. Schleiermacher correctly pointed out terminological ambiguities in the trinitarian-incarnational complex of thought that have never been successfully cleared up. Harnack's slogan about the hellenization of Christianity may have been an exaggeration in its time, but it eloquently underscored how Christianity evolved into an intellectualized system of dogmas in the encounter with gnosticism. Finally, Tillich made several cogent points: first, the dogma is not the message, so to speak of faith in dogma would be a contradiction in terms, and second, the dogma combines elements of the myth of the incarnation in a seemingly rational way that is certainly open to question.

The criticism of the dogma of the incarnation is voluminous and unending. Yet when all the modern criticisms have been heard and measured, the church today still has good reason to retain continuity with the core of classical christology.[31] What is at stake is not the questionable philosophical terms and categories of Chalcedon, but quite simply the Christian confession that the person of Jesus Christ unites the reality of God with humanity in a way sufficient for salvation. The confession allows plenty of room for speculative analysis, but no room at all for finding in Jesus Christ something less than a real union of the true identity of God and the final definition of humanity. It is not necessary to know the precise philosophical meaning of such Greek terms as *homoousios, hypostasis, ousia, physis, prosōpon,* and *idiotes* to perceive even today in a totally different cultural setting that Chalcedon aimed to demarcate the boundaries beyond which the preaching of Christ cannot stray if it wishes to remain faithful to the apostolic kerygma of salvation. The issue today is not *whether* the classical christology is to be criticized, but *why?* Do the critics share the underlying faith that Chalcedon sought to defend, or do their quarrels with the ambiguous philosophical terms of the creed disguise their alienation from its fundamental content?

The dogma of the incarnation continues to warn the church against every solution of the christological paradox that stems from the ebionitic-adoptionistic left or from the docetic-monophysitic right. In predicating divine and human natures, as well as divine and human attributes, of the one Lord Jesus Christ, we are giving expression to the knowledge of faith that God has entered history as the power of final salvation of humanity and the cosmos. The dogma can help the church discern the difference between heresies to the right and to the left, past and present. It also positively aligns the church with the true preaching of Jesus Christ from the apostles to the present, making it possible to retrace the footsteps of orthodoxy. Hermeneutically, orthodoxy is always a sort of ex post facto construction. Only the future was able to tell whether the many christological proposals swimming in the sea of Nicaea or Chalcedon would be hooked on heresy or drawn into the nets of orthodox definition. Similarly, the multiplicity of modern christologies which have arisen in the nineteenth and twentieth centuries are being submitted to the test whether they "teach Christ aright" and prepare the way for the true preaching of the Word. The church will continue to use the Creed of Chalcedon in this process of testing, rejecting every view that tears God and human existence apart in the person of Jesus Christ and every view that separates the salvation of humankind from the person of Christ.

NOTES

1. For more extensive information about the christological developments treated in this section, consult the following works: Aloys Grillmeier, *Christ in Christian Tradition,* trans. J. S. Bowden (New York: Sheed & Ward, 1965), vol. 1; J. N. D. Kelly, *Early Christian Creeds* (1950; London: A. & C. Black, 1972); R. V. Sellers, *Two Ancient Christologies* (London: SPCK, 1940); H. A. Wolfson, *The Philosophy of the Church Fathers* (Cambridge, Mass.: Harvard University Press, 1956), vol. 1.

2. Adolph von Harnack, *History of Dogma,* 7 vols., trans. Neil Buchanan (New York: Dover Publications, 1961), 1:267–86.

3. It is customary to distinguish between the "economic Trinity" and the "immanent Trinity." Immanent Trinity means that the names of the Father, the Son, and the Spirit refer to real distinctions within God. Hence we also speak of the essential or ontological Trinity. Economic Trinity means that the distinctions arise from the three ways in which the one God has been manifested in the history of revelation (the divine economy). Ever since Friedrich Schleiermacher reopened the debate on Sabellius, scholars have questioned whether Sabellius actually taught that Father, Son, and Spirit refer merely to temporary and successive manifestations of God in relation to the world. (Friedrich Schleiermacher, "On the Discrepancy between the Sabellian and Athanasian Method of Representing the Doctrine of the Trinity," trans. with notes by Moses Stuart, *The Biblical Repository and Quarterly Observer* 6 [July 1835]: 1–116).

4. J. N. D. Kelly, *Early Christian Doctrines* (New York: Harper & Brothers, 1958), pp. 115–19.

5. See esp. Sellers, *Two Ancient Christologies.*

6. Kelly, *Early Christian Doctrines,* pp. 226–27.

7. Ibid., pp. 240ff.

8. Grillmeier, *Christ*, p. 269.

9. Friedrich Schleiermacher, *The Christian Faith*, ed. H.R. Mackintosh and J. S. Stewart (Edinburgh: T. & T. Clark, 1928), p. 97.

10. Charles E. Raven, *Apollinarianism* (Cambridge: At the University Press, 1923).

11. Wolfson, *Philosophy*, p. 599.

12. Friedrich Loofs, *Nestorius and His Place in the History of Christian Doctrine* (Cambridge: At the University Press, 1914).

13. On the modern debate whether Nestorius was a Nestorian, touched off by the discovery of a book Nestorius wrote in exile, *The Bazaar of Heracleides*, see Carl E. Braaten, "Modern Interpretations of Nestorius," *Church History* 32 (September 1963): 251–67.

14. Wolfson, *Philosophy*, p. 444.

15. This English version of the Creed of Chalcedon is quoted from R. V. Sellers, *The Council of Chalcedon* (London: SPCK, 1953), pp. 210–11.

16. Wolfson, *Philosophy*, pp. 409–15.

17. Paul Althaus, *Die Christliche Wahrheit* (Gütersloh: Bertelsmann, 1948), 2:225.

18. Karl Barth, *Church Dogmatics*, vol. 4/2, trans. J. W. Bromiley (Edinburgh: T. & T. Clark, 1958), pp. 49–50, 91–92.

19. Ian D. Kingston Siggins, *Martin Luther's Doctrine of Christ* (New Haven: Yale University Press, 1970).

20. Heinrich Schmid, *The Doctrinal Theology of the Evangelical Lutheran Church*, trans, Charles A. Hay and Henry E. Jacobs (Minneapolis: Augsburg Publishing House, 1875).

21. The *genus majestaticum*, the issue in the Lutheran-Reformed controversy, owes its name to the notion that the Son of God in the incarnation communicated his divine majesty to his assumed human nature.

22. Barth, *Church Dogmatics*, 4/2:73ff.

23. *God and Incarnation in Mid-Nineteenth-Century German Theology: Thomasius, Dorner, Biedermann*, ed. Claude Welch (New York: Oxford University Press, 1965).

24. Albert Schweitzer, *The Quest of the Historical Jesus,* trans. N. Montgomery (London: A. & C. Black, 1910), pp. 3–4.

25. Oscar Cullman, *The Christology of the New Testament*, trans. Shirley Guthrie and Charles Hall (Philadelphia: Westminster Press, 1959), p. 4.

26. Martin Kähler, *The So-Called Historical Jesus and the Historic Biblical Christ*, trans. Carl E. Braaten (Philadelphia: Fortress Press, 1964).

27. Friedrich Schleiermacher, *The Christian Faith*, ed. H. R. Mackintosh and J. S. Stewart (Edinburgh: T. & T. Clark, 1928), p. 385.

28. Ibid., pp. 391ff.

29. Harnack, *History of Dogma*, 4:219ff.

30. Paul Tillich, *Systematic Theology*, 3 vols. (Chicago: University of Chicago Press, 1951–63), 2:145ff.

31. See Karl Rahner's important essay "Chalcedon—Ende oder Anfang?" in *Das Konzil von Chalcedon*, ed. Aloys Grillmeier and H. Bacht, vol. 3 (Würzburg, 1954), pp. 3–49. In this essay Rahner argues that the Chalcedonian formula must be regarded more as a beginning than as an end.

4

The True Humanity
of Jesus Christ

Christian faith has an interest in the historicity of Jesus Christ that cannot be surrendered. The quest of the historical Jesus is a mark of taking seriously the full humanity of Jesus. The humanity of Jesus cannot be confined to his earthly state of existence, but is continuous with the postresurrection reality of Jesus Christ as the eschatological One.

THE HISTORICITY OF JESUS CHRIST

Two factors divide classical and contemporary christology: first, modern criticism of the metaphysics of the traditional trinitarian and incarnational dogmas, and second, the historical quest of the life of Jesus. In this chapter we will deal with the latter issue under the heading "The Historicity of Jesus Christ" and in the next chapter with the former as "The Historicity of God."

The critical study of the life of Jesus began in the Enlightenment with the application of the historical method of research as a tool of christological thinking. Hermann Samuel Reimarus was the first critical historian to attempt to portray the historical Jesus as he "really" was before the embellishments of faith and preaching exalted him to the level of divinity. For some of the more skeptical scholars, such as David Friedrich Strauss and Bruno Bauer, the historical Jesus exercised a negative function in theology. They probed the sources to discover a residual core of factual history, in order to prove their religious indifference to it. What mattered was the idea of the incarnation, the truth of the essential union of God and humanity, not its embodiment in the individual personality of Jesus. For more moderate scholars, such as Friedrich Schleiermacher and Alexander Schweizer, the historical Jesus had positive meaning, both as the source of faith and as the substance of christology. The historicity of Jesus Christ was basic to the Christian faith, not only as its starting point, but also as part of its essential content. The question of the *historicity* of Jesus Christ became the modern form of the debate over the classical assertion of his true humanity (the *vere homo*).

Just as classical christology had to steer its way between the Scylla of ebionitism and the Charybdis of docetism, so also in the nineteenth century these same two options reappeared as a challenge under the new conditions of the historical-critical approach to the Bible and Christian origins. The classical rivalry between the schools of Antioch and Alexandria was replayed on the ground of nineteenth-century theology. This rivalry is no less fierce in the twentieth century. The ebionitic left is exhibited in the modern attempt to replace the christological dogma with a biographical treatment of the life of Jesus. As the christological undercurrent of the main stream of the "Life of Jesus" movement, ebionitism was especially strong in eighteenth-century rationalism and in the later line of psychological analysis influenced by Schleiermacher. The aim of this approach was to describe the moral and religious consciousness of the man Jesus, and then to commend it as an exemplary model for human emulation. Scholars tried to discover timeless moral and spiritual values in Jesus, with great relevance for modern humanity. In fact, however, the substitution of the modern biography of Jesus for the classical dogma of the incarnation proved to be a deception. In pretending to be interested in history, rationalism reflected itself in the mirror of the past. It interpreted Jesus in the light of its own morality, not its morality in the light of Jesus. Albert Schweitzer was right in calling the bulk of these biographies totally unhistorical.

The docetic right flourished in the christologies influenced by the philosophical thought of the German idealists—Immanuel Kant, G. W. F. Hegel, Johann Gottlieb Fichte, and Friedrich Schelling. The christological dogma was not dissolved into a biography of the Jesus of history, but was translated into the Christ of faith as an abstract idea. Docetism became explicit in idealistic indifference to the historical Jesus as the basis and content of faith, substituting instead the idea of an essential unity of God and humanity related not to a specific individual but to generic humanity as a whole. This speculative metaphysical approach poured its own preferred ideas into the mold of christology and thus, like the rationalism before it, merited Schweitzer's verdict of a sovereign indifference to the real Jesus of history.

On the whole, however, the reinterpretation of christology in the nineteenth century was not dominated by the two extremes we have characterized as ebionitic (the more empirical psychological approach) and docetic (the more speculative metaphysical approach). Most biblical and systematic theologians took a mediating approach. Here the quest of the historical Jesus was assumed into the framework of a dogmatic christology. The conservative wing in Hegelian theology fought against its own school's docetic tendency to separate the universal idea of Christ from the historical facticity of Jesus. Similarly, many who wrote biographical and psychological treatments of the historical Jesus attempted to overcome the implicit ebionitism of the "Life of Jesus" movement, claiming that their project was the modern equivalent of taking the humanity of Jesus seriously. How could their scholarly interest in the Jesus of history be opposed to the intent of the christological dogma, since it too affirmed the true humanity (*vere homo*) of Jesus Christ? The quest of the historical Jesus was certainly legitimate as a venture of historical criticism; it was also theologically necessary as a motive of Christian faith. The mediating theologians were moderates. They worked both to establish points of contact between the quest of the historical Jesus and the classical dogma of the church and to minimize the areas of conflict that arose. Hence the historicity of Jesus Christ was an object of historical-critical research as well as a subject of faith and dogmatics.

It has become common to view the eighteenth- and nineteenth-century quest of the historical Jesus in a negative way. Albert Schweitzer's history of the movement testified to its failure, Martin Kähler's critique called it a dead end, and Karl Barth's renewal of classical dogmatics dubbed it a heresy of modern Protestantism. A more positive assessment is now possible. The quest for the historical Jesus was and continues to be christologically significant as an expression of faith's interest in the historicity of Jesus Christ.

THE HUMANITY OF JESUS CHRIST

The confession of the true humanity of Jesus was first elaborated in the writings of the antignostic fathers, Irenaeus, Hippolytus, and Tertullian, in the second century A.D. Their confession was not the result of the critical study of the life of Jesus, but rather the datum of a living faith handed down in the traditions of liturgy and preaching and firmly anchored in the Gospel narratives. In later orthodoxy, however, this confession became an ossified formula of ecclesiastical dogmatics. It is no wonder that many modern Christians were prepared to welcome the historical view of the life of Jesus as a liberation from christology's conceptual bondage to an abstract dogmatism. Hoskyns and Davey exclaimed in their *Riddle of the New Testament*, "Whatever else Jesus may be, He is a man."[1] The full humanity of Jesus has become as important to modern believers as it was to earlier Christians who struggled against gnosticism and its variant docetic derivations.

The contemporary emphasis on the historicity of Jesus Christ has renewed the meaning of the ancient phrases of Chalcedon, "perfect in manhood . . . truly man . . . of a rational soul and a body . . . *homoousios* with us as to his manhood . . . in all things like unto us." It has reinforced Luther's statement that Jesus came as "one of the hoi polloi"[2] or that he was "bone of our bone, flesh of our flesh." The soteriological thrust of these assertions is unmistakable.

But what about the "sinlessness" of Jesus? The ancient creeds, echoing the

New Testament witness, claimed Jesus to be in all respects as we are, "except without sin." He "committed no sin" (1 Pet. 2:22), and he was tempted, "yet without sin" (Heb. 4:15).

The sinlessness of Jesus has been called into question by theologians who believe that sinning is implied in the full humanity of Jesus.[3] They regard the idea of sinlessness as a docetic cancer spreading into the earliest attempts to picture the life of Jesus. The "Life of Jesus" movement as a whole found the idea bothersome, because it calls into question the principle of analogy underlying every attempt to write a biography or to psychoanalyze Jesus. Here the principle of analogy allows our modern knowledge of the stages of human development and forms of human behavior to be applied in reconstructing the life of Jesus from the Gospel sources. But if Jesus was sinless, he was unique. How could we hope to explain the unique development of this man in terms of principles that apply to common human experience? In writing against the biographical and psychoanalytic "Lives of Jesus," Martin Kähler stated the problem clearly:

> Is this method justified in writing about Jesus? Will anyone who has had the impression of being encountered by that unique sinless person, that unique Son of Adam endowed with a vigorous consciousness of God, still venture to use the principle of analogy here once he has thoroughly assessed the situation? We must not think that we can solve the problem with a pantograph, reproducing the general outlines of our own nature but with larger dimensions. The distinction between Jesus Christ and ourselves is not one of degree but of kind. . . . Sinlessness is not merely a negative concept. The inner development of a sinless person is as inconceivable to us as life on the Sandwich Islands is to a Laplander.[4]

The ambiguity is clear. If Jesus was like us in all respects, the principle of analogy would seem to apply in his case as much as in the study of other great personalities of the past. But if he was sinless, the method of analogy is seriously limited, if not altogether invalid.

What, then, is the logic of asserting the sinless humanity of Jesus? Is it a result of research or a presupposition of faith? How do we know that Jesus was sinless? Does Jesus' sinlessness really contradict the assumption that he was entirely human? Some scholars have recently exploited every imaginable hypothesis in taking seriously the humanity of Jesus. They have speculated about his sexuality, his marital status, and his psychological hang-ups.[5] Since the Gospel sources contain no such data, the imagination must run riot and generate its phantasies *ex nihilo*. But to what end? Some defend these speculations as taking the humanity of Jesus seriously and getting rid of the last vestiges of docetism. A less than fully human Jesus would be of no value to us. The ring of the ancient logic of salvation can be heard. Jesus must have been wholly what we are.[6] But here the logic turns against itself. If he was entirely like us, *with no difference*, he would have been in the same predicament as everyone else, with no power to save. How could a common sinner be the savior of humankind? The ancient logic of salvation was two-dimensional. Jesus Christ must be wholly what we are, so that we may become wholly what he is. In sharing our human lot, he is not reduced to its sinful condition. This statement is not the result of historical research, but the vivid impression of the total impact of Jesus' person on his followers' memory injected in the stream of apostolic interpretation. Every layer of tradition in the New Testament witnesses to the confession of Jesus' sinless humanity. This is an historical judgment, but whether or not a person or the church today assents to its truth is a matter of faith and dogmatic interpretation.

The sinlessness of Christ does not diminish his solidarity with the fallen condition of human existence. Classical dogmatics became the victim of a deductive type of logic, concluding to the sinlessness of Christ from the hypostatic union. With seemingly flawless logic it was reasoned that if Christ was the Logos, the divine Son of God, he must have been sinless. Even the possibility of sin (*posse peccare*) must be excluded, because God is opposed to the nature of sin, and God cannot be self-contradictory. The modern impact of the historical picture of Jesus has done much to blunt the force of such logic from above. Starting with the story of Christ's temptation, it has been inferred that Christ must have been able to sin. To be human is to be tempted, and real temptation presupposes the possibility of sin. Here the logic of inferential reasoning proceeds from below, arguing from the humanity of Christ to the reality of temptation and the ability to sin. Whether coming from above or from below, however, this type of logical reasoning contributes little to christological insight.

It is better not to indulge in a logical overkill. The biblical story of Christ's temptation is presented in terms of a real struggle. According to the principle of analogy, which we, along with Kähler, have already called into question, our common human experience of real conflict in temptation is invariably associated with a sense of standing at the crossroads and the possibility of taking the wrong turn, of sinning. If these connections hold for us, they must logically hold for Christ. But by what kind of logic? It is the psycho-logical law of experience under the conditions of our fallen human nature. Does it apply to Christ in the same way? Schleiermacher pronounced an emphatic "no," but paid the price of eliminating the element of conflict from Christ's perfectly God-conscious and sinless life.

Docetism hangs like a dark cloud over such a reading of the temptation stories. The temptations involved real conflict. They were profoundly experienced by Jesus as a pull away from the Father's will. We are not dealt a psychological card with which to trump the story and take away its existential seriousness. We are given no theory about whether he could have sinned or could not have sinned. He was tempted and he did not sin. He prayed in the crisis of temptation. He fled for strength to his Father and put Satan behind him. His sinlessness lay in doing the Father's will, in taking up the cross of the kingdom.

We can say this much: Jesus could not have sinned and really been the One he was revealed to be in his cross and resurrection. This is not a logical inference from the hypostatic union or the preexistent Logos. It is a retroactive type of judgment based on the role of Christ in the mission of God's approaching kingdom. There is a dimension of mystery in the life of Christ, seen on this side of Easter. The proposition of the great tradition that he could not have sinned (*non posse peccare*) was an unfortunate explanation of this mystery. It converted the mystery of Christ's person into a metaphysics of his nature. The New Testament points to this dimension of mystery in the wilderness temptations, speaking symbolically of Christ being filled with the Holy Spirit and of his self-consciousness as the Son of God. Could he have sinned? The question cannot be answered from above by a metaphysics of the incarnation or from below from the psychology of common human experience. The story is written to point to the mystery of Christ in the special context of his messianic identity and mission.

A related question has occupied the minds of theologians: Did Jesus' consanguinity with the human race mean that he shared the nature of humanity before the fall or that he inherited the fallen nature along with all others? In late medieval theology, Jesus' birth of the Virgin Mary settled the issue. Sin was transmitted by the male sperm in the sexual act; therefore, Jesus was exempt, having been born of a virgin and conceived by the Holy Ghost. This explanation is another pseudotheological example of deductive reasoning, not to mention outdated biology. The confession that Jesus was not a sinful man does not place him in a kind of existential demilitarized zone beyond the limits of our fallen human existence.

Jesus shared the existential condition of our fallen human nature. Perhaps few have stressed the human experience of Jesus more dramatically than Luther. Luther said, "He ate, drank, slept, worked, suffered, and died like any other human being." He added, "He had eyes, ears, mouth, nose, chest, stomach, hands, and feet, just like you and I have. He took the breast; his mother nursed him as any child is nursed."[7] It is impossible to exaggerate Jesus' solidarity with our common human experience—with this single exception, that he did not fall into sin. He knew the feelings of hunger, fatigue, fear, anger, grief, and sadness. Luther stressed the agony of the suffering and dying man forsaken by God and all his friends. Of course, this emphasis on the humanity of Christ was pointless to Luther, unless the Christ who was so utterly human was at the same time qualitatively different from all others. The humanity by itself was not able to accomplish anything, apart from the power of divinity that came through it. Jesus became our brother that God might become our Father; he condescended to assume our flesh and bone, our body and soul, this "poor bag of worms," in order that God might have mercy on all the wretched people of this world. The homiletical force of this vision of Christ makes sense only on the christological premise that Jesus is at once "very God and very man."

THE IDENTITY OF THE
EARTHLY JESUS AND THE RISEN CHRIST

There is a type of interest in the historical Jesus that possesses no fundamental meaning for Christian faith. The apostle Paul referred to it as a knowledge of Christ "from a human point of view" (*kata sarka*) (2 Cor. 5:16). We adopt such a point of view whenever we seek to learn about Jesus as merely Jesus, abstracting him from the total evangelical picture as the risen Christ. The naked facts about Jesus do not speak for themselves. They require a framework of meaning to be grasped. The preaching of Jesus as the risen Christ influenced the shape of the history that was narrated in the Gospels. The Gospels give us a character sketch of Jesus, depicting him as a real historical person and as human in the fullest sense.

If we take the New Testament message as our criterion, we cannot reduce the historicity of Jesus to the narrow limits of positivistic historicism, nor his humanity to the limits of naturalistic humanism. The history of Jesus and his humanity cannot be interpreted within the limits of an historical empiricism. The historiographical goal of discovering the empirical truth about the Jesus of history by means of a presuppositionless research has been doomed in modern hermeneutics but still hangs on in some historical circles. The empirical truth does not exhaust what we mean by the historical truth.

The historical truth about the reality of Jesus cannot be separated from the living impression he made on those who gave us the only sketch we possess of his being and meaning. To look for his historicity apart from his meaning is like trying to locate the Kantian *Ding an sich*. The meaning of a person is the key to understanding whatever is true and real about him or her. So it is with Jesus of Nazareth. Jesus means Christ; Jesus means Savior; Jesus means Lord; Jesus means Son of God; and so forth. The point is that apostolic interpretation of the meaning of Christ is the transparent medium of the historical truth and reality of Jesus—if we are no longer to regard him *kata sarka*.

The resurrection of Jesus is an essential element of his total picture. It belongs to his history; it has a factual side. Otherwise, it disappears into the quicksand of arbitrary interpretation. After his death by crucifixion Jesus appeared to some of his friends, and they spread the news about what they had witnessed in two words: Jesus lives! They did not say merely that his cause lives on. Theirs was not a mere belief in the immortality of Jesus' influence. The resurrection of Jesus was not a postulate of faith, nor an expression of the hidden meaning of his life, nor an existential interpretation of his death on the cross. Faith was not the basis of the resurrection; the resurrection was the basis of faith. The event of Jesus' resurrection, then, explains the transition from Jesus as the announcer of the kingdom to Jesus as the announcement itself.

The earthly Jesus and the risen Christ are one and the same person. The personal identity of Jesus Christ includes both his earthly existence and the exalted mode of his being and acting. It is not the case that Jesus is fact and all the rest myth, legend, or fiction. That would spell the end of Christian faith. Yet the personal equation of the earthly Jesus and the risen Lord is not open to a process of verification which suspends the factors of faith, worship, prayer, and preaching. There are no proofs of the Easter event. We have only the testimonies of witnesses, all of whom were believers. They are no longer available for cross-examination. The experience of being grasped by faith and the power of the Spirit, however, can liberate the mind to be receptive to the evidences of the resurrection—eyewitness accounts of the appearance of the risen Christ and the empty tomb—and to make a judgment in their favor. Faith and reason work together in the act of confessing that the risen Lord encountered in faith is identical with the earthly Jesus nailed to the cross.

JESUS CHRIST AS
THE ESCHATOLOGICAL ONE

The event of the resurrection made Jesus God's eschatological representative for the whole of humankind. The resurrection of Jesus belongs to his humanity. It cannot be subtracted from his history without cutting him off from the future which God granted him on "the third day." In raising Jesus from the dead, God incorporated the dimension of eschatological fulfillment into the definition of human being. The resurrection is a symbol of hope for a fulfilling future of life beyond the annihilating power of death. The message of the resurrection makes sense only within the horizon of our own most certain existential destiny, of having to die. Other religions offer different solutions to the problem of death. Christianity proclaims the resurrection of Jesus as God's answer to the human question whether death is the eschaton of life.

The resurrection is a unique event; it is the only event in human history in which the power of death has been challenged and its claim to finality discredited. The resurrection of Jesus was the "first fruits," to be followed in the end by a universal resurrection. The destiny of Jesus in the resurrection reveals a future for humanity that carries the promise of fulfillment beyond death.

We have underscored the historicity of the true humanity of Jesus Christ. We now stress that the resurrection expands the definition of his humanity to include an eschatological destiny beyond death. The new life of Christ beyond death is an element of the image of God (*imago dei*) which he represented perfectly—without sin.

Much of the Christian tradition has taught that Jesus Christ restored the image of God in humanity to its state of integrity before the fall. The damage caused by the fall of the first Adam has been undone by Jesus as the second Adam, by his obedience, by his sinlessness, and by his victory over death. Irenaeus used the idea of *recapitulation* to speak of Jesus going over the ground covered by Adam, "so that what we had lost in Adam—namely, to be according to the image and likeness of God—that we might recover in Christ Jesus."[8] But Irenaeus' idea of recapitulation did not entail a mere restoration of the broken image to its state before the fall. Something *new* happened in Jesus.[9] He did, of course, bring about a renewal of the image, but at the same time actualized a fulfillment to the highest possible state of perfection. Irenaeus taught that Adam's innocence before the fall was enjoyed in a state of immaturity. He was "unfinished man."[10] He was like a child who had yet to become a mature person. Christ was the new Adam. He was all that Adam failed to become, on account of the fall. Adam was not created perfect all at once. His completion was something to be realized in the future of humanity. Jesus Christ has been revealed as that new human being of the future, as the final measure of the nature and destiny of humankind.

Irenaeus located the event of the recovery of the image of God in the incarnation rather than in the resurrection. He said,

> Man is created for the Son, and he attains his perfection in the Son. His destiny was realized only when the image of God took human life in the Incarnation and took up into himself the man who had been created in the image of God. The Incarnation and its benefits had no reality when man was first created; man, therefore, is a child, son, whose goal and objective is full growth.[11]

It is doubtful, however, that Irenaeus recaptured Paul's way of picturing Jesus Christ as the image of God. For Paul, the newness in Christ was an eschatological reality that occurred in the resurrection and became representatively valid on that basis for the whole of humanity.

The risen Christ is the future destiny of all humankind. The goal of human development is to become mature in the perfect image of God as it became realized in the exalted and resurrected humanity of Jesus Christ. We can point to its incarnational presence in the life of Jesus only because of prior knowledge of eschatological fulfillment in the resurrection victory of Christ over death. If death had been the end of Christ, if the resurrection had not put an end to death, the New Testament could not have begun to speak of the incarnation of the image of God in the man Jesus. Death would have swallowed up the life of Jesus forever. Instead, he became the person embodying the good news of a fulfilling future beyond the fate of personal and cosmic death.

NOTES

1. Edwyn Hoskyns and Noel Davey, *The Riddle of the New Testament* (London: Faber & Faber, 1936), p. 209.

2. Quoted in Ian D. Kingston Siggins, *Martin Luther's Doctrine of Christ* (New Haven: Yale University Press, 1970), p. 36.

3. See G. C. Berkouwer, "The Sinlessness of Christ," in his *The Person of Christ* (Grand Rapids: Wm. B. Eerdmans, 1954), pp. 239-304.

4. Martin Kähler, *The So-Called Historical Jesus and the Historic Biblical Christ*, trans. Carl E. Braaten (Philadelphia: Fortress Press, 1964), p. 53.

5. E.g., William A. Phipps, *Was Jesus Married?* (New York: Harper & Row, 1970); Tom Driver, "Sexuality and Jesus," *USQR* 20 (March 1965): 235–46.

6. The classic axiom in traditional christology affirms: *Quod non est assumptum non est sanatum*. This means: "What has not been assumed [in the incarnation] is not saved."

7. Siggins, *Martin Luther's Doctrine of Christ*, p. 199.

8. Quoted in James M. Childs, *Christian Anthropology and Ethics* (Philadelphia: Fortress Press, 1978), p. 20, n. 9.

9. See Gustav Wingren's definitive study on Irenaeus, *Man and the Incarnation*, trans. Ross Mackenzie (Philadelphia: Fortress [Muhlenberg] Press, 1959).

10. Ray Hart, *Unfinished Man and the Imagination* (New York: Herder & Herder, 1968).

11. Quoted in Childs, *Christian Anthropology and Ethics*, p. 95.

5

The True Divinity
of Jesus Christ

The truth of the incarnation is that God took on a truly human
reality, so that in Jesus Christ he stands on both sides of the boundary separating the Creator from the creation. The confession that
Jesus in his person is truly God means that God's decisive and final
word for the world has been communicated once for all in his Word
made flesh.

THE STORY OF GOD INCARNATE

The doctrine of the incarnation was the pillar of orthodox christology from
the Council of Chalcedon to the age of the Enlightenment. This pillar has
been shattered by the blows of modern criticism. Nineteenth-century studies
in the history of dogma (Adolf von Harnack) linked the christology of the
ancient church to the process of hellenization. In the twentieth century, form-
critical analysis of the Gospel traditions has shown that the incarnation was
not part of the earliest preaching of the apostles. In the beginning was the
Easter kerygma; the motif of the incarnation entered at a subsequent stage
of development. Finally, the history and phenomenology of religions have
called our attention to the mythic character of the incarnation. The notion
of the preexistent Son of God becoming a human being in the womb of a
virgin and then returning to his heavenly home is bound up with a mythological picture of the world that clashes with our modern scientific world view.
    There are two opposite reactions to the discovery of the mythic character
of the incarnation. The conservative reaction is to reject the discovery in defense
of traditional faith. In its simplest form, this view argues that the Bible contains truth, not myth.[1] The incarnation was a real event of history. The Son
of God really became human in the person of Jesus. Calling the incarnation
a myth detracts from its truly historical character. Would that not turn the
incarnation into a universal truth equally applicable to all human experience
and likely to be enshrined in all the great religions? Myth abhors being tied
to a concrete historical event or to a unique historical person. Myth deals with

527

recurrent patterns and archetypal notions valid wherever they may be found. But the incarnation is bound to what happened at one point in space and time—the concrete life of the historical Jesus. Therefore myth is an inappropriate category to apply to the incarnation of the Son of God.

The liberal reaction is to acknowledge the discovery of the mythic character of the incarnation, and then to demythologize the Christian faith to make it relevant to the contemporary world. In this view the story of the incarnation is not essential to the Christian faith. The myth can be eliminated and other concepts more compatible with the modern mind can be found to express the significance of Jesus Christ for us.

Arguments in favor of demythologizing the story of Christ are numerous. Let us summarize some of the most common. (1) The very concept of an incarnate person being both divine and human is not really intelligible. (2) It is intellectually impossible to accept the incarnation as literally true and to equate Jesus ontologically with God. (3) The incarnation was a bad myth to begin with. Such mythical speculations draw attention away from the real Jesus of history, his role and agency in representing God for us. (4) The essence of the myth can be stated in nonincarnational terms; for example, in Jesus we encounter God's claim on us, or in Jesus the meaning of God for our lives has been disclosed in an existentially significant way. We moderns can more easily use existential and ethical categories in formulating the meaning of Christ for life in our time.

Neither the conservative denial of myth in the New Testament nor the liberal approach of demythologizing has proven adequate for constructive Christian theology. A third approach is possible:[2] an interpretation of the myth as story, without taking its symbolic elements literally but also without eliminating its historical aspects. Rudolf Bultmann was right in his observation that the New Testament kerygma was proclaimed within the framework of mythology. There were three levels in the mythical picture of the world: heaven above, hell below, and earth between. There were beings—angelic beings, demonic beings, and human beings—passing from one level to the other. God was in heaven, humankind on earth, and the demons in the underworld. Divine and demonic forces were engaged in a cosmic struggle, producing effects in the inner life of human beings and the outer world of nature.

The story of the incarnation took place within the structure of such a mythological universe. The preexistent Son of God came down from heaven, entered earthly existence by means of virgin birth, worked miracles on nature, sacrificed himself for the sins of the world, overcame the power of demons by his resurrection, descended into hell to preach his victory, ascended to heaven to sit at the right hand of God the Father, and finally promised to come again in a blaze of glory to judge the world. The main statements of the Apostles' Creed are so bound up with its mythological form that to get rid of the myth would destroy the creed *in toto*. Can modern people still be expected to accept the creed, with its mythological elements? We know that in the scientific picture of the world, the categories "above" and "below" do not make sense. Therefore the story of the descent of the Son of God to earth and his ascent into heaven cannot be taken literally. The question is whether the meaning of the myth of the incarnation can be saved without taking it literally, yet without getting rid of its mythic structure. Can it be interpreted in a way that both grasps the essence of the Christian message and does not misplace the scandal of the gospel?

Bultmann proposed the method of existentialist interpretation to salvage the kerygma in the myth, so that modern men and women will not take offense at outdated myth and miss the saving message. The truth of the myth, he said, lies in its existential meaning for each individual.[3] The New Testament message of Christ is overlaid by mythical elements from Jewish apocalyptic eschatology and gnostic dualistic cosmology. Bultmann challenged theology to demythologize the New Testament, in order to lay bare the existential meaning of the kerygma enshrined in the myth. The story of Christ in the Gospels is a mixture of historical events and mythological symbols. The purpose of the myth is to interpret the significance of the events. Today we must search the myth for the existential meaning of the events, and not take the myth at face value. We must ask about the existential significance of the myth of the preexistent Christ and of his cross and resurrection. To accept these as objective descriptions of a supernatural realm of happenings is to miss the point of the myth: to relate the apostolic kerygma to human existence.

Bultmann's project of existentialist interpretation was too narrowly conceived to sustain itself in the field of biblical hermeneutics. The sole purpose of the myth cannot be to interpret the *existential* significance of the events on which the kerygma is based. The kerygma speaks of the *act of God* in Christ. God cannot be reduced to a term of human existence. Theology cannot be translated into anthropology without remainder. To speak of God acting in history is at the barest minimum a piece of symbolic mythology. There is no way to demythologize the New Testament kerygma by means of existentialist interpretation without losing its transcendent reference to God. The kerygma does not only speak of the possibilities of human existence; it speaks first and foremost of the history of the acts of God, not literally but in symbolic terms.

Myth and its symbols are indispensable to express the reality of God in the person of Jesus. Myth is an appropriate form of language for expressing the events and meanings of God's revelation in history. Even Bultmann's definition of myth makes this clear. He defines myth as "the use of imagery to express the otherworldy in terms of this world and the divine in terms of human life, the other side in terms of this side."[4] The story of the incarnation offers a perfect illustration; it speaks of God entering time and space in the person of Jesus. God was in Christ. This points to a real event that affected the inner life of the divine Trinity. Although this is a symbolic way of speaking, it counters a subjectivist interpretation of the myth which sees the incarnation either as the revelation of a hidden potential of common human experience or as the objectification of humanity's longing to be reconciled with God. The very truth and word of God, God's own grace and love, entered the history of humankind and the world with the appearance of Jesus Christ. The myth of the incarnation is, therefore, not reducible to its existential core of meaning. When an existential criterion of meaning is strictly applied, elements of the myth which are not considered to be existentially relevant are eliminated, such as the preexistence of Christ or the story of the virgin birth. We would be well advised not to allow the existentialist—or any reductionist—mode of interpretation to acquire a monopoly on the categories used in christology.

THE HISTORICITY OF GOD

The story of the incarnation is a mixture of mythical and historical categories. Because the incarnation affirms that the *Son of God* is Jesus, mythical language is essential; because it claims that *Jesus* is the Son of God, historical categories must be used. The early church did not simply repeat the story of Christ in the two languages of myth and history. Already in the second century the church borrowed ontological categories from Greek philosophy to interpret the myth of God becoming human, of the Logos becoming flesh. Terms like *ousia, hypostasis, physis, prosōpon,* and *idioma* are nonbiblical categories coming from the Greek philosophers. The bridge from the mythological language of the Gospels to the ontological statements of the creeds could be found, the church fathers believed, in the New Testament itself. When John's Gospel says that "the Logos became flesh," the church fathers exegeted this statement in ontological terms. In ontologizing the incarnation, they may have had the purest intention of remaining biblical, but they introduced an ontology into their christology that was alien to its fundamental meaning. If the myth of the incarnation must be set forth in ontological speech, the question becomes: What kind of ontology? What ontological assumptions about the nature of God, humanity, and the world should be applied in the interpretation of the reality and truth of the incarnation of Jesus Christ?

There is a sharp contrast between the idea of God in Greek ontology and the picture of God reflected in the biblical story of the incarnation. The God of the Greek philosophers was not a dynamic, living, acting, self-communicating subject who became freely involved in the world of space and time, of physical matter and human flesh. There could be no coming or becoming, no motion or emotion, no pain or plurality in the God of Greek metaphysics. How could the static transcendence of an immutable and impassible deity be correlated with christology without contradicting the gospel of God's *coming* and of the Logos *becoming* flesh in the person of Jesus? The church fathers worked with the only ontology they had at their disposal, transforming it to fit their biblical faith. They were by no means uncritical in assimilating ideas from Greek metaphysics.[5] They stressed the biblical motifs of the living power and gracious freedom of God in their doctrines of creation and providence, involving God deeply in the world of matter and the flux of history. They stressed these in sharp contrast to the Greek concept of an absolutely unaffected and eternally remote God. It would therefore be erroneous to charge the church fathers with having made the Christian faith captive to the principles of Greek philosophy. The use of Greek ontology was the *aggiornamento* of the church's theology in that time.

In retrospect, however, it is possible to see that the theological transformation of Greek ontology was not carried through radically enough. The problem of using the Greek philosophical concept of God came to a head in the formation of christological doctrine. The absolute God of Greek metaphysics was heartless, graceless, and faceless. That God could not suffer, because suffering meant lack, and God does not lack anything. God must be beyond the pale of human suffering. God must be impassible, apathetic, and without compassion. The picture of Christ in the New Testament, by contrast, is full of suffering. Jesus Christ suffered what every human being suffers: hunger and thirst, fatigue and loneliness, disappointment and betrayal, and finally death. There was suffering in body, soul, and spirit. This was not, however, merely the suffering of the man Jesus or of the human nature of Christ, far removed from the being and life of God. In the New Testament, passages abound which involve the Son of God, and indirectly therefore also the Father, in the destiny of Christ's suffering. "God sent forth his Son, born of woman, born under the law" (Gal. 4:4). First Corinthians 2:8 claims that the rulers of this age "crucified the Lord of glory," and Acts 3:15 that they killed "the Author of life." The classical passage is Phil. 2:6–8: "Who, though he was in the form of God, did not count equality with God a thing to be grasped, but emptied himself, taking the form of a servant, being born in the likeness of men. And being found in human form he humbled himself and became obedient unto death, even death on a cross."

Against the background of Greek metaphysics the idea of God would have to be kept far removed from involvement in the suffering of Christ. A God who suffers cannot really be God. There were two heretical ways of relating God to the problem of the suffering of Christ. The one way was that of the ebionites and the adoptionists: affirm the suffering of Christ but then make sure he was only a human. The sufferings could be accepted as real because Christ was merely human. The reality of his sufferings proves that he was not truly God, because God cannot suffer. The underlying axiom came not from the Bible but from the Greek ontological concept of God. The other way was that of the docetists and the monophysites: affirm the divinity of Christ but then make sure the sufferings were not real. Christ was God beyond doubt. This proves that the sufferings referred to in the Gospels were only apparent. Christ did not really suffer, because he was truly God, and God cannot suffer. Again, the underlying axiom was the impassible God of Greek metaphysics, not the living God of the Bible.

The God of Israel, the Father of Jesus Christ, was no apathetic being, an anonymous essence infinitely removed from the pain and suffering of creation. The Father suffered along with the Son. God was not bound to suffer as an essential predicate of his being. Rather, God was free to suffer as a function of divine love. Suffering cannot be predicated of God as a metaphysical attribute implied by God's immanence in the world process, nor as an ontological limitation of God's own being and nature, out of the need to be fulfilled. The Greeks were right; there is no deficit in God. But they wrongly concluded that for this reason there can be no pain in God.[6] The Father of Jesus Christ suffered, not from any lack in being but from the abundance of love. "For God so loved the world that he gave his only Son" (John 3:16).

Orthodox christology denied that the Father suffered when it rejected patri-passianism as a heresy in the Sabellian controversy. Sabellianism claimed that the Father suffered because it collapsed any real personal distinction between the Father and the Son. Orthodoxy reacted to this modalistic view by attributing suffering only to the Son. Only one of the Trinity suffered. We today are not threatened by the Sabellian problem; we are thus able to reach a different conclusion about the suffering of God. The Father did not personally suffer through some ontological lack, but rather through the compassion that the Father had for a Son who took the destiny of humankind into his own life. Even on orthodox grounds it does not make sense to divorce the suffering of Christ from the Father. Christ suffered in his person, and this person (*hypostasis*) is God the Son, of one being (*homoousios*) with the Father. If God was in Christ, then suffering became a part of the experience of God. "For in him the whole fulness of deity dwells bodily" (Col. 2:9). The incarnation would not be real if the Father's heart were not open to the suffering of his beloved Son. The distinction between the Father and the Son can be maintained without denying the Father a share in the incarnate fate of his Son Jesus Christ. If the dispassionate God of Greek metaphysics is supplanted by the compassionate God of Israel, the Father of Jesus Christ, a major barrier has been removed to a constructive interpretation of the myth of the incarnate Son of God. The myth does not need to be denied. It calls for interpretation with the help of an ontology different from that of Greek metaphysics. Only a suffering God can be harmonized with the picture of Christ in the Gospels. The suffering of Christ was a shaft deeply driven into the heart of God. The revelation of God, therefore, includes the negativities of Christ's human experience in this world from birth unto death.

The Greek idea of the impassibility of God made a real incarnation of the Son of God intellectually offensive; the immutability of God made it impossible. The Creed of Chalcedon called Mary the Mother of God, "*theotokos*." The term provoked heated opposition from the side of the Nestorians, who argued that Mary was only the Mother of Christ, "*Christotokos*." The advantage of the *theotokos* formula is that it underscored that the subject of the incarnation was actually God—God the Son. If the Son of God was not born of Mary, he could not truly be the One who lived, suffered, and died. Then only Jesus, a mere human, carried the full burden of salvation, contradicting our two initial christological statements: *God* was in Christ and the *Logos* became flesh.

The gospel narrative of God becoming one with humanity in Jesus the Christ conflicts sharply with an ontology of divine immutability in which God simply is what he is in static identity. An absolutely immutable God is not able to become the subject of incarnational predicates, making the history of human existence his own history and assuming the reality of the world's becoming into his own reality as the Logos of God. An ontology constructed in the light of faith in the gospel will speak not of the utter impassibility and immutability of God but rather of the historicity of God and God's coming-to-be in the humanity of Jesus the Christ.

The classical doctrine of the exchange of divine and human attributes (*communicatio idiomatum*) in the one person of Jesus Christ represented in principle a break with the Greek metaphysical doctrine of God. The absolute of Greek metaphysics was ontologically incapable of acting in a state of humiliation, in the flux of history, and under the conditions of finitude. The christology of the ancient church, however, did not succeed in drawing out all the consequences of its own conciliar decisions at Nicaea, Constantinople, and Chalcedon for its concept of God and the incarnation.[7] The categories of ancient metaphysics found their way into the theology of the church fathers and to a large extent replaced the biblical categories of historical and eschatological thinking.

It was Martin Luther who made the most complete break with the hybrid system which the Christian tradition had developed out of Greek metaphysics and biblical faith. His theology of the cross (*theologia crucis*) meant that the philosophical idea of God would have to be radically transformed in light of the cross. He said that a theologian worthy of the name is one who perceives the mystery of God through the suffering and cross of Christ, and not by speculating on the essence of God from the way things are. Luther struck the first blow against the medieval doctrine of the analogy of being (*analogia entis*),

533

which lay at the heart of medieval natural theology. For Luther, the hidden God is revealed in the cross. In the light of the crucified Christ we understand the true being of God and of humankind. God's self-revelation was *sub contrario*, in terms that seem contrary to God's nature as such. In drawing out the implications of the exchange of attributes between the two natures in Christ, Luther began the construction of a new christology, which is still in the process of being developed. The living God did not exclude but embraced the opposite in a process of exchanging qualities of nature and destiny. In exchange for death God gave life, in exchange for foolishness God gave wisdom, in exchange for bondage God gave freedom, in exchange for sin God gave righteousness, in exchange for weakness God gave power, and so on. Consequently, in exchange for God's own glory, God assumed humility; in exchange for eternity, God entered time; in exchange for God's love, God absorbed hatred.

In an eloquent passage Luther said:

> What does it mean that the Son of God should be my servant, and so utterly debase Himself that He should take the burden of my misery and sin—Yes, the whole world's sin and death? He says to me, "You are no longer a sinner, but I am. I step into your place—you have not sinned, but I have. The whole world is in sin, but you are not in sin—I am. All your sins are to lie on Me and not on you."[8]

Luther's interest in what he called the "happy exchange" (*fröhliche Wechsel*) between God and God's people in Christ was not primarily speculative but soteriological. His emphasis on the humanity of God in Jesus was for the sake of humanity. This accounts for such realistic language as "Mary makes broth for God." "Mary suckles God with her breasts, bathes God, rocks and carries Him; moreover, Pilate and Herod crucified and killed God." His concern was for the integrity of the worship of Christ as God in the flesh and for the presence of God in Christ "for us men and for our salvation."[9]

THE DIVINITY OF CHRIST

The starting point for a new ontological interpretation of the identity of Jesus Christ lies in the worship of the Christian church from earliest times until now. The early church responded to the apostolic proclamation of God's redemptive act in Christ in the language of prayer, praise, and thanksgiving. This language customarily refers not only to the *acts* of God in history but also to the *being* of God who is eternally free in power and love. The original language of faith points to the eternal glory, holiness, wisdom, love, and power of God. This is the primary language of faith and confession. Its supreme form is doxology, the sheer praise of God for being God. As a second step the church appropriated ontological concepts to help explicate the doxological utterances about the being, nature, and attributes of God. The dogmatic statements of the ancient church, its trinitarian and christological definitions, represent a grand interweaving of doxological and ontological terms.[10]

Although these doxological-ontological statements refer ultimately to the being of God, they are rooted in the soil of redemptive historical events. They cannot be uprooted and taken as abstract speculative theses about the essence of God. Doxology has its basis in the message of God's activity and presence in the history of Jesus. The ontological interpretations similarly intend to serve the church's worship of the mystery of God.

The tendency in modern christology, from Ritschl and Harnack to Cullman and Bultmann, to eliminate the ontological in favor of functional statements in christology failed to observe the doxological source of ontological thinking. Not even in the New Testament can we reduce christology to purely functional historical categories. There is no full-blown ontology, to be sure, but there are statements that clearly imply an ontological understanding of the status of Jesus as the Son of God, even as actually *God*. Ernst Käsemann, master exegete of the New Testament, wrote in his commentary on Romans, "A metaphysical sense of the divine Sonship of Jesus is clearly presupposed by the whole of the New Testament."[11]

Ontological christology is most evident in the Fourth Gospel. The mission of Jesus is obediently to carry out his ontological divine Sonship, to reveal the being of God in him and with him. There is no divorce here between his being and his mission; ontological and functional statements are united in the mission of Jesus to set forth the Father's love in history.

The total impact of the New Testament leads to the conclusion that Jesus Christ is not only the Son of God in some subordinate sense, but is actually God. At the center is the Easter confession that Jesus is *kyrios*, the Greek translation of the Old Testament name of God, *Adonai*. The confession of Jesus as God is rooted in the liturgy of the early church. Jesus as the Christ "reflects the glory of God and bears the very stamp of his nature" (Heb. 1:3). Nothing less than an ontological equation of Jesus with God is implied in all these New Testament descriptions of Jesus' relation to the Father and of his saving function. His being and his mission are mutually implicative. His function as Savior without his being as God would be powerless and baseless; his being as God without his saving mission would be abstract and empty. Ontological-doxological statements belong together with functional-historical statements in a comprehensive christology.

It has been recently suggested that the classical christology of the two natures of Christ in the Creed of Chalcedon was not about two natures at all. Rather, says R. A. Norris, the creed is about two languages. "The *Definition* is not talking about Jesus; it is talking about Christian language about Jesus."[12] In line with this statement is an earlier one by P. T. Forsyth, "The mighty thing in Christ is His grace and not His constitution,"[13] here echoing unmistakably Philipp Melanchthon's famous saying that to know Christ is simply to know his benefits.[14] These are examples of the modern inclination to play off the functional significance of Christ against his ontological status. We believe this is an understandable but mistaken tendency.

The best way to overcome the bad effects of Greek metaphysics on classical christology is to find a better one, not to opt for none at all. When existentialist christology speaks of Christ as a possibility of existence or when the approach of linguistic analysis explains christology as a descriptive grammar of the language of faith, both fail to formulate the ontological relation of Jesus to God, of the Son to the Father. The language of Chalcedon about two natures and two sets of attributes in Christ is not merely offering rules for the language of faith and preaching. That would beg the question of why such rules should be binding for the church in all ages. The creeds of Nicaea and Chalcedon make definite assertions concerning two dimensions of reality in Christ because there *are* two dimensions. It is not enough for the language of faith to be logically correct. There is an ontological dimension which is the condition of the truth and meaning of the language of faith.

Christology is free to use modern categories from existentialism, language-analysis philosophy and the philosophy of history to explain the duality implied in the two-natures doctrine of the Chalcedonian definition. Nothing is to be gained by forever binding the church's christology to the ontological concepts of Platonic and Aristotelian philosophy. We wish to say the same thing in reworking christology into a new system of concepts. We certainly do not want to say anything less. If we say there are two natures in Christ, a divine *physis* and a human *physis*, this is language that has to be explained. What is meant is not nature as natural physical substance, but nature as the essence of what something is. The expression "the divine nature" of Christ means that whatever it is that makes God God and not something else is really present in the person of Jesus Christ. "Human nature" means that whatever it is that makes humans essentially human is fully actual in them. The quest for an adequate definition of what it is that makes God and humans what they are will continue in the history of philosophy. These definitions will, in turn, continue to be tested and transformed in light of Jesus Christ who represents God to humanity and humanity to God in his own person.

In the nineteenth century, Protestant theologians tried every new metaphysical and epistemological approach to explain the Christian confession that Jesus Christ is "very God and very man." Schleiermacher certainly intended to affirm the uniqueness of the Redeemer and to assert that in some sense we can speak of a "real existence of God" in Christ. The philosophies of Immanuel Kant, Friedrich Schelling, and G. W. F. Hegel[15] triggered numerous attempts to rethink the old christological formula on the new ground of modern critical thought. In the twentieth century, too, the thought of every major philosopher has been exploited for the sake of new christological construction. Martin Heidegger in Germany, Ludwig Wittgenstein in England, and Alfred North Whitehead in the United States are three of the most noteworthy philosophers whose methods and concepts have been used in the revision of christology. Currently attempts are being made to go back to some earlier philosophers to rediscover old ideas with new significance, such as Thomas Aquinas in Roman Catholic theology, Karl Marx in Latin American liberation theology, and G. W. F. Hegel in Protestant eschatological theology.

Not all philosophies are equally successful in expressing what the church meant to confess in its formula "very God and very man." In principle they have not had so much difficulty providing categories to explicate the true humanity of Jesus, although even here they have tended to idealize, moralize, or romanticize the picture of the man. Trouble surfaces when they turn to the confession of the true divinity of Christ. Karl Barth once contrasted Wilhelm Herrmann's christology with orthodox christology in this fashion: "Orthodox christology is a glacial torrent rushing straight down from a height of three thousand meters; it makes accomplishment possible. Herrmann's christology, as it stands, is the hopeless attempt to raise a stagnant pool to that same height by means of a hand pump; nothing can be accomplished with it."[16]

Thomas's confession of Jesus Christ, "My Lord and my God!" is an immediate analytic judgment of faith that one either makes or does not make. If one prefers to call it a judgment of reason, it is in any case a reason emancipated by the power of the Spirit and faith. This is not a retreat to subjectivism. In confessing the divinity of Jesus Christ, we do not attribute to him a notion of deity which we have derived beforehand from our own philosophical speculations. We do not look at Jesus and call him God because he conforms so remarkably to our preconceived idea of what a God must be. Jesus is not the fulfillment of our prior notion of God. He *is* God for us. We apprehend the final meaning of God in Jesus, and nowhere else. The whole spectrum of reality in Jesus Christ, his life, death, and resurrection, is the locus of God's self-definition. Christian faith looks to Jesus Christ and confesses, "There is no other God."

We do not approach the biblical picture of Christ armed with a sufficient idea of God derived from an autonomous metaphysics, laying our own mantle of divinity on him, as it were; but neither do we call Jesus God as an inference derived from our own religious experiences. To borrow Barth's metaphor, that would be like trying to raise the level of Lake Michigan with a hand pump. This approach has led to the idealizing and deifying of Jesus as a great man.

But God is not humanity raised to the *n*th degree. Making Jesus into the hero of a Christian cult does not warrant calling him God. Neither the metaphysical approach from above nor the experiential approach from below escapes the charge of arbitrary subjectivism. If our confession of the divinity of Jesus is based on a prior conception we hold of God or on the fact of our religious experience, we are confronted with a Jesuology thinly disguised by superlatives of our own making. The alternative is to discover the divine and human dimensions of reality in the one person of Jesus Christ in the act of his self-manifestation.

Faith is brought to the confession of God in Christ, not on the strength of reason (philosophy) or religion (experience), but solely by the power of the Holy Spirit. "No one can say 'Jesus is Lord' except by the Holy Spirit" (1 Cor. 12:3). The Holy Spirit mediates the relation of faith to the person of Christ and generates the understanding that Jesus is not merely Jesus; he is the Christ in whom *God* is present and active. The divine-human reality of Jesus Christ becomes a living presence to faith through the preaching of the Word. This Word is a representation of the Christ who reveals himself through the Scriptures. When preaching is faithful to the Scriptures, Jesus is proclaimed as the Christ, the Savior, the Lord, the Logos who was with God, who was God, and who became flesh (John 1:1, 14).

It is well and good that the confession of the true humanity of Jesus has come into its own in contemporary christology, perhaps more persistently than at any time in the history of theology. But all this would amount to nothing in the cause of the world's salvation if the divine Sonship of Jesus were not the power to back it up. In confessing the true divinity of Jesus Christ, we are saying that in Jesus God is revealed as the finally valid answer to all our ultimate questions about the meaning of existence and the future of life. As the exclusive medium of God's final word of judgment and hope, Jesus is the one through whom the knowledge of ultimate salvation enters history. He represents the final hope of each individual and the future of the cosmos. There is simply no need for another revelation of God, because Jesus is God's unsurpassable self-revelation. The world still awaits, however, the realization of what has been revealed—fulfillment of life's potential in the eschatological kingdom of God.

Jesus can be our God because the power of God's absolute future— *basileia*—was shown to be effectually present in his person and ministry. Whoever is united with Jesus in faith is assured, therefore, of an everlasting future with God. This presence of the power of God's future eschatological kingdom in the person, miracles, parables, sayings, and above all in the death and resurrection of Jesus constitutes the meaning of the confession that God is one with Jesus and that Jesus is very God for us. The essential unity of God with Jesus of Nazareth is manifest in Jesus' unlimited love for God and his absolute devotion in representing God's unconditional love for the world. The heart of the final and future kingdom of God is the unrestricted freedom to have life in the plenitude of love. The classical confession of the *homoousios* of Jesus as God's Son with the Almighty Father is rooted in this agapeic union of God and Jesus.

AN ONTOLOGICAL
INTERPRETATION OF THE INCARNATION

The special task of an ontological interpretation of the incarnation is to explicate the relationship between God and Jesus, between divinity and humanity in the one person of Jesus. Its task is to characterize the kind of unity effected in the life of Jesus between divinity and humanity, to analyze the *locus divinitatis* in him. How does this unity between Jesus and his Father differ in principle from the unity between God and humanity in general, expressed in the notion that God created humankind in the divine likeness and image (*similitudo et imago dei*)? Is the incarnation here the actualization of a potential human union with God, or is it a miraculous transcendent act from beyond the immanent potentialities of nature and history? All these considerations aim to illuminate the confessional answer to the question: Who is Jesus Christ?

In trying to understand the unity of the divine and the human in the one person of Jesus, we can approach the matter from two sides, from above or from below. From below means from the human side, and from above means from the divine side. Both sides are manifest in the personal history of Jesus of Nazareth. From below, from the human side, we can say that Jesus' unity with the Father represents a perfect realization of the humanity of humankind. The original unity between God and humanity lost in the fall is restored in the perfect actualization of Jesus' humanity in union with the Father. The incarnation seen from below reveals the truth that humanity realizes the true essence of human being only by becoming one with the Father. Seen from below, that is, from the perspective of the Gospel story, "Jesus increased in wisdom and in stature, and in favor with God and man" (Luke 2:52). Throughout life he maintained a perfect union with the Father, showing no trace of sin and unbelief, but only perfect love to God and obedience to God's will. The more human he showed himself to be, the more radically did his unity with the Father become manifest.

From the divine side we can do no better than say that the eternal love which flows freely between Father, Son, and Spirit overflows the circle of divine being, positing a world in which God can communicate divine love in a human way. The classical doctrine of the hypostatic union means that Jesus is the unique event of God's loving self-communication.

539

In this section we shall propose a historical revision of ontology in light of the biblical understanding of the eschatological future kingdom of God appearing in the history of the person of Jesus the Christ. The metaphysical ontology of the Greek philosophers not only hindered the understanding of the incarnation but also blocked an eschatological interpretation of historical events. In an eschatological interpretation of historical reality the truth belongs to the whole. Only from the end does it appear what the whole truth of reality is. The final meaning of history can be disclosed only from its future end. Jesus the Christ as a figure of history is presented in the New Testament as the true revelation of the future end of all reality. The total biblical picture of Jesus as the Christ is a fusion of two sets of symbols. Both incarnational and eschatological symbols are interwoven in the ealiest traditions which tell of the identity and meaning of Jesus the Christ. Eschatology and incarnation join in the interpretation of the history of Jesus as the locus of divine presence and activity.

Paul Tillich once suggested that the ancient discussions of the unity of two natures and two wills in Christ must be transformed in our present situation into the problem of the interpretation of history and its relation to the kingdom of God. The ontological dimension in christology retains its validity, but it must be an ontology broken open by eschatology and history, and no longer determined by the Greek spatial myth of origin and its metaphysics of substance. It must become an ontology revised in light of the historical-eschatological framework of the Bible.[17]

The union of two histories, the history of *God's* coming within the personal history of *Jesus* of Nazareth, is an event which calls for an ontological interpretation. Paul Tillich reached back to the categories of German idealism, particularly to Schelling and Hegel, to discover conceptual tools that might facilitate an ontological interpretation of the incarnation. The modern opposition to Hegel—partly because of his own later development, partly because of his left-wing disciples, Strauss, Feuerbach, and Marx—has been so vehement that his potential contribution to a new historically determined ontology has been overlooked until very recently. Karl Barth, in his history of theology in the nineteenth century, closed his chapter on Hegel with this enigmatic valediction: "We must therefore be content to understand him as the man he was: as a great problem and a great disappointment, but perhaps also a great promise."[18] It is the promise of Hegel that interests theology today.[19] The promise lies in a new interpretation of the Trinity and of the incarnation in light of an historical revision of ontological thought, thus overcoming the ahistorical metaphysics of Greek philosophy. For Hegel the absolute was not unmoved substance but acting subject, which expresses itself in a dynamic way through what is other than itself. For him it was not metaphysical nonsense but dialectical truth that Being Itself would mediate itself through its opposite: life through death, love through wrath, fulfillment through negativity, and the divine through the human. The Infinite is capable of embracing itself and the finite in a dialectical unity of opposites. How do we know? Because it has happened. This is not a matter of *a priori* speculative knowledge which the philosopher can derive from the logic of reality in general. Rather, it is *a posteriori* theological reflection based on the event of the incarnation and its transparent structure in the biblical picture of Jesus the Christ.

Our knowledge of God has been mediated through the Christ-event. How can we express the self-revelation and self-manifestation of God in the person of Jesus? How can we best understand the identity of Jesus Christ in ontological terms? Taking a clue from Hegel, we have said that it belongs to the nature of ultimate reality to express itself dialectically through what is other than itself, expressing identity in difference. This is an abstract interpretation of the Johannine statement: God is love. If there is only one, in static identity, the occurrence of love cannot take place. It is the nature of love to unite two who can be differentiated, to overcome the difference, to reconcile through self-emptying. This vision of God as love is projected from the concrete history of Jesus Christ, his relation to his Father, and his death on the cross.

What happened in Jesus Christ, through his human experience of suffering love and sacrificial death, was nothing less than the coming and history of God. The truth of the incarnation is that God is identified with this one man, communicating the divine Word through this man's particularity and the deepest love in the event of the cross. God who does not need to change to be fully divine has become someone utterly human out of the fullness of love and freedom, not out of any lack in God's being or fatal necessity. Birth, death, change, history, and negation no longer happen only on the human side of the ontological abyss between God and the world.

The incarnation of love in the history of Jesus Christ is thus an ontological event. For the love God has communicated in the history of Jesus Christ is the love which is the very nature of God's own being. God *is* love. The ontological meaning of this statement has been explained in the doctrine of the Trinity. The inner relations between the members of the triune God are characterized by the eternal dynamics of love. The good news of the incarnation is that this love has come to be in the person of Jesus, reconciling the world and humanity to their eternal source in God. God's coming in Christ has taken human history and the world's becoming into the divine life. God entered the world of time and space, reestablishing the whole creation as the realm of God's rule. The incarnation is God's self-emptying of everything that separated the Creator from the creation, to embrace the entire cosmos as an acceptable part of the kingdom of God. In the act of *kenosis*, self-emptying, we see the self-surrender of God to others in order to win them back. God was able to do this because of the freedom of divine love. The power of love by which God created the world in the first place is the same power by which God showed freedom for self-emptying and self-humiliation in Jesus Christ, entering the conditions of human existence, and thus claiming the history of humanity and of the world as the means of divine self-communication.

NOTES

1. See *The Truth of God Incarnate*, ed. Michael Green (Grand Rapids: Wm. B. Eerdmans, 1977), which was an instant response to *The Myth of God Incarnate*, ed. John Hick (Philadelphia: Westminster Press, 1977).

2. See Paul Tillich, "The Meaning and Justification of Religious Symbols," in *Religious Experience and Truth*, ed. Sidney Hook (New York: New York University Press, 1961), pp. 3–11.

3. Rudolf Bultmann, *Jesus Christ and Mythology* (New York: Charles Scribner's Sons, 1958).

4. Rudolf Bultmann, "New Testament and Mythology," in his *Kerygma and Myth*, ed. Hans W. Bartsch, trans. R. H. Fuller (London: SPCK, 1954), p. 10.

5. Wolfhart Pannenberg, "The Appropriation of the Philosophical Concept of God as a Dogmatic Problem of Early Christian Theology," in his *Basic Questions in Theology*, vol. 2, trans. George H. Kehm (Philadelphia: Fortress Press, 1971), pp. 119–83.

6. See Kazoh Kitamori, *Theology of the Pain of God* (Richmond: John Knox Press, 1965).

7. See Werner Elert, *Der Ausgang der altkirchlichen Christologie* (Berlin: Lutherisches Verlagshaus, 1957).

8. Ian D. Kingston Siggins, *Martin Luther's Doctrine of Christ* (New Haven: Yale University Press, 1970), p. 241.

9. Ibid., p. 232.

10. See Edmund Schlink, "The Christology of Chalcedon in Ecumenical Discussion," in *The Coming Christ and the Coming Church* (Edinburgh: Oliver & Boyd, 1967), pp. 87–95.

11. Ernst Käsemann, *An die Römer* (Tübingen: J. C. B. Mohr [Paul Siebeck], 1973), p. 3.

12. R. A. Norris, "Toward a Contemporary Interpretation of the Chalcedonian Definition," in *Lux in Lumine: Essays to Honor W. Norman Pittenger*, ed. R. A. Norris (New York: Seabury Press, 1966), p. 78.

13. P. T. Forsyth, *The Person and Place of Jesus Christ* (London: Independent Press, 1909), p. 10.

14. "Hoc est Christum cognoscere, beneficia eius cognoscere." Philipp Melanchthon, *Loci Communes, CR* 21:85.

15. See James Yerkes, *The Christology of Hegel* (Missoula, Mont.: Scholars Press, 1978).

16. Karl Barth, *Theology and Church*, trans. Louise Pettibone Smith (New York: Harper & Row, 1962), p. 265.

17. See Paul Tillich, "A Reinterpretation of the Doctrine of the Incarnation," *CQR*

147 (January 1949): 113–148; also, *The Interpretation of History* (New York: Charles Scribner's Sons, 1936).

18. Karl Barth, *Protestant Thought: From Rousseau to Ritschl*, trans. Brian Cozens (New York: Harper & Row, 1959), p. 305.

19. See Hans Küng, *Menschwerdung Gottes, Eine Einführung in Hegels Theologisches Denken als Prolegomena zu einer Künftigen Christologie* (Freiburg: Herder Verlag, 1970).

6

The Humiliation and
Exaltation of Jesus Christ

The story of the incarnation of Christ is told in images and symbols
as a passage back and forth between two states of being, the state
of exaltation and the state of humiliation. The essence of the story
is the participation of God in the human condition for the salvation of humanity and the fulfillment of the world.

THE PREEXISTENCE OF CHRIST

The preexistence of Christ is an integral part of the myth of the incarnation.
References to the preexistence of Christ (or the Logos or the Son of God) can
be found in the epistles of Paul and the Gospel of John.[1] Their intention is
to be understood soteriologically. They say that Jesus is the eternal Son of
God because the salvation he delivered to humankind has its origin in God.
If the One who lived, suffered, and died for our salvation is not eternally
from God, there is no real and certain salvation. Jesus and Yahweh must share
the same eternal ground if the salvation Jesus has wrought for us is to count
as equally valid for God. God sent the Son into the world in human form.
The mythological structure may be transparent on its surface, but its essential meaning is basic to the gospel. The implicit argument is soteriological.
Jesus is the acknowledged Savior of humankind. But only the eternal God
can grant salvation. Therefore the ultimate identity of Jesus must derive from
the eternal life of God.

Arianism was rejected as heresy because it left a gap between Jesus and
Yahweh of an ontological order, thereby undermining the basis of salvation.
For this reason Luther referred to Arius as Narrius,[2] "Narr" being the German for "fool." It would be foolish for Christians to reopen a gap between
Jesus and Yahweh if they are in earnest about the salvation they claim to have
received through Jesus himself. Jesus must have always been one with God
if the salvation he brought is divinely authorized. The idea of preexistence
means that Jesus never was an individual person apart from the event of the
incarnation of the Son of God. If Jesus truly represented God for us, there

never was when he was not divine. He was not an afterthought in the divine plan for the world. He was the eternally begotten Son of God, not only the historically born son of Mary.

THE VIRGIN BIRTH

In the Apostles' Creed we confess that Jesus was conceived by the Holy Spirit and born of the Virgin Mary. Since the Enlightenment, this has become one of the most disputed doctrines. In contemporary theology Emil Brunner denied the virgin birth of Christ in his book *The Mediator*. He called it a "biological curiosity"[3] and saw a possible connection with docetism because it made the Holy Spirit usurp the function of the human father. How could Jesus be like us *in all respects* if he did not actually have a human father? Karl Barth dismissed Brunner's arguments as "a bad business."[4] Wolfhart Pannenberg sides with Brunner and asks whether Barth's arguments for the virgin birth do not put him "on the path of Roman Mariolatry?"[5] For Pannenberg, "the story of the virgin birth bears all the marks of a legend."[6] He concludes: "Theology cannot maintain the idea of Jesus' virgin birth as a miraculous fact to be postulated at the origin of his earthly life. To that extent it is problematic that the virgin birth found entry into the Apostles' Creed."[7]

The primary interest of dogmatics is to interpret the virgin birth as a symbol and not as a freakish intervention in the course of nature. Scientific inquiries into the frequency of parthenogenesis in the world of nature are beside the point. They contribute nothing to deeper insight into the revelatory reality to which the story of Jesus' birth points. It is possible to hold to the virgin birth as a biological fact and miss its point. It is also possible to make the same point without reference to the virgin birth, as the writings of Paul and John prove by not mentioning it. It is important, then, not to let the story get bogged down in biology, but to read it as a symbol witnessing to the truth of the kerygma. The truth of the conception by the Holy Spirit is that God was the author of salvation through Christ from the beginning, not first in his resurrection, nor on the cross, nor at the baptism, but from the moment of his conception by Mary. The story reinforces the idea of the preexistence of Christ and serves the same purpose of grounding the history of salvation in the eschatological reality that is prior to the world itself. The story works against an adoptionistic christology by engaging the power of the Spirit in the birth of Jesus prior to anything he might have done to merit adoption. The story vindicates a theology of grace alone by attacking the root of works-righteousness at the base of christology itself.

The exclusion of a human father in the birth of Jesus has become more problematic to modern Christians than it was in ancient times. Originally the confession of Jesus' birth from the Virgin Mary was a sign of his real humanity, pointing away from the docetic denial of his solidarity with the human race.[8] The fact that Jesus was born of a woman like every other child was proof that he was a real human being. The point of the story was to work against docetism. Unfortunately, the symbol of the virgin birth no longer has a clear antidocetic ring for modern ears. We cannot imagine how the story could concretize the interest of faith in the real humanity of the Savior. Why should the absence of human paternity make the truth of God's presence in the incarnation more apparent? Is God the Father in competition with the role of our human father? Did not God create fatherhood and look upon it as "very good"? Why then should human fatherhood be eliminated in the work of salvation? If we grasp the original intention of the story to witness to the real humanity of Jesus, we must not allow a shift in the situation from ancient times to the present to play a trick on us, which it would do if we were to use the story apologetically to prove the divinity of Christ or to explain the sinlessness of Jesus. The story has become increasingly ambiguous because our natural tendency is to take it to mean the opposite of what it originally intended.

THE CRUCIFIXION OF JESUS

The descent of the Son of God into the womb of Mary and his birth in history as a Hebrew baby have been theologically discussed as the transition from glory to a state of humiliation. It forms the heart of the notion of *kenosis*—self-emptying. The descent into the human depths of humiliation continued in the ministry of Jesus and came to a climax in his suffering and death. The crucifixion of Jesus was an historical event, the outcome of a political trial in which all the powers of the establishment conspired to put an innocent man to death. The crucifixion, however, was more than an event of past history with ripple effects on the subsequent course of world history. The historicity of the cross of Jesus must be maintained against every possible tendency to dissolve its once-for-allness in an existentialist interpretation that stresses its timeless quality as an ever-present possibility of self-understanding. Such an interpretation would stand closer to gnosticism than to the gospel.

Before the cross can be seen in its relation to existential experience, it must be grasped as an event of past history. Otherwise it has nothing to do with the cross of Jesus Christ. The crucifixion of Jesus happened only once and will never happen again. Nevertheless, the meaning of the historical cross was transmitted in the suprahistorical language of mythological symbolism. The cross is not a fact of history that interprets itself. The New Testament writers used a rich variety of symbols taken from the world of ancient Jewish and gnostic mythology to interpret the meaning of the cross. When the cross is viewed mythologically, and not simply as one historical event alongside others, it receives redemptive significance of cosmic proportions. It is the task of the doctrine of the atonement to explicate the dogmatic meaning of the cross. Here we need only include it as one further stage in the kenotic self-abasing movement of the Son of God from the heights of glory to the depths of humiliation in a death by crucifixion under Pontius Pilate, a death whose universal redemptive significance has been interpreted according to Jewish ideas of atonement (sacrifice and satisfaction) and the gnostic myth of redemption (death and resurrection).

JESUS' DESCENT INTO HELL

The downward curve of the incarnational line reached its lowest point in Jesus' descent into hell. In the seventeenth century, Lutheran and Reformed dogmaticians debated whether Jesus' descent into hell was the extreme limit of his humiliation or the initial step toward triumph and exaltation. We are including it under the state of humiliation, because the descent into hell is a symbol which conveys the truth that Jesus' victory over the enemies of man (sin, death, and the devil) was attained by first suffering the negation they introduced into the world.

The phrase in the Apostles' Creed "He descended into hell" unites two different ideas. Hell is a translation of the Greek word "hades," designating the abode of the dead. Later in church usage, hell was equated with the place of the damned. The verse in 1 Pet. 3:19 states that after his death Jesus "went and preached to the spirits in prison," and verse 4:6 makes clear that on this trip "the gospel was preached even to the dead." Originally it was thought that when people died they want to hades, a waiting room for the dead until the last judgment. A shift in meaning occurred in later theology, so that when people died they went directly to heaven or hell, except for those who went to purgatory to be cleansed of their impurities. The transition from a descent to hades to a descent into hell is easy to explain. Hell is the sphere of Satan's dominion. If Christ is to free also those who have died, he must declare his victory in the stronghold of Satan himself.

The theological significance of Christ's descent into hell/hades is twofold. First, insofar as we emphasize that Christ descended into hell—the place of the damned—we are stressing the depth-dimension of his suffering and humiliation for our sakes. At one and the same time he suffered and overcame through his suffering the torment of hell as separation from God. Jesus did not only suffer the wrath of God in his conscience, not only anxiety about his calling, not only temptation to compromise his loyalty to the kingdom; he also suffered the deepest distress of humanity all the way to the cross, subjecting himself to the alienating powers of death, Satan, and hell. The meaning of this symbol is that the deepest humiliation of Christ happened so that as the Lord of hell he might vanquish once for all the existential power that hell holds over our future. Second, insofar as we confess Christ's descent to hades as the realm of the dead, we are claiming that his work of salvation is universal and reaches beyond the limits of those who preach and hear the gospel in this life. Nations and generations of people who lived before the coming of Christ and who have never been confronted with the preaching of salvation in his name are not eternally lost. Christ goes even to the dead, so that he might be acclaimed the Lord of the living and the dead.

THE RESURRECTION

Three days after his death Jesus appeared again to a small circle of friends. The crucified Jesus revealed himself as the living, risen, exalted Lord who had triumphed over death and the devil. The raising of Jesus was an act by which God put an end to his humiliation and exalted him above all the enemies of humankind, and without it our faith is in vain (1 Cor. 15:14). Mythological symbolism contributed to the interpretation of the event of the resurrection. The question has become acute in modern theology whether in the resurrection we are dealing only with a myth or with a truly historical event.

Some theologians dismiss the resurrection as of little importance. Consider this statement by a "process" theologian: "Christian faith (as I understand it) is possible apart from belief in Jesus' resurrection in particular and life beyond bodily death in general, and because of the widespread skepticism regarding these traditional beliefs, they should be presented as optional."[9] Other theologians are doubtful about the possibility of verifying the resurrection as a specific, historically definable event, but would still wish to speak about it as a way of interpreting the real significance of the cross. So Bultmann writes: "Belief in the resurrection is simply and exactly the same as belief in the cross as 'salvation event!' "[10] The cross is the historical fact, the resurrection its symbolic meaning. On the other side, there are theologians who share Wolfhart Pannenberg's view that the resurrection of Jesus was an historical event and that it must so be proved by historical reason. He writes:

> There is no justification for affirming Jesus' resurrection as an event that really happened, if it is not to be affirmed as a historical event as such. Whether or not a particular event happened two thousand years ago is not made certain by faith but only by historical research, to the extent that certainty can be attained at all about questions of this kind.[11]

Paul Althaus split the difference between Bultmann and Pannenberg, arguing with Pannenberg that the resurrection was truly an event of history, empty tomb and all, but agreeing with Bultmann that it cannot be verified by the critical methods of the historian. Althaus wrote in his dogmatics *Die*

Christliche Wahrheit: "That Jesus was raised from the dead and appeared to his disciples as the Risen One is something we can only know for sure by faith under the impact of all the witnesses to Jesus, his life and message and death, as well as his resurrection."[12]

All the modern scholarly differences on the historical problem of the resurrection should not overshadow the prevailing exegetical consensus that from the point of view of the whole New Testament the resurrection of Jesus was an event that really happened in time and space, that eyewitnesses were prepared to vouch for it, and that the earliest Christians believed it to be a firmly established truth. Unfortunately scholars are in much greater agreement on what the resurrection *meant* in the New Testament than on what it *means* to Christian faith today. The degree of consensus that exists at the historical level does not prevail in systematic theology. Other factors intervene, such as the nature of an historical event, the meaning of history, the relation of faith to facts, and the relevance of believing in life beyond death.

An historian's presuppositions may determine for him or her that the resurrection did not really happen because such a thing could not happen. But who knows beforehand the limits of what is historically possible? If what is "humanly possible" is the measure of what is historically possible, the resurrection of Jesus must be regarded as impossible. In the biblical view, what is historically possible is always weighed within the horizon of a world that is ever open to the activity of the living God. Nature and history are not closed in on their own inherent possibilities. In face of *a priori* denials of the resurrection of Jesus, it is necessary for theology to become critical of criticism, to free the mind and prepare the way for an unprejudiced hearing of the witnesses.

However, no matter how positive the results of historical research may ever be in verifying the earliest testimonies to the resurrection of Jesus, we can never dispense with the role of faith in responding to the message of Easter. The preaching of the risen Christ goes on in the context of the church's celebration of his real presence. This preaching and the faith it generates cannot take the place of historical-critical examination of the texts. On the other hand, no historian can convert historical statements with their higher or lower degrees of probability into a personal decision of faith in Jesus as the living Lord. The judgment of historians is likely to lean in favor of the historical reliability of the resurrection reports only if they already approach the reports with the bias of belief that Christ is risen indeed. They need not be apologetic about their faith. Would it not be absurd to argue that lack of faith enhances the skills of an historian in cross-examining the witnesses with a critical eye?

Faith does not close the eyes of reason; it may open them to see things that seem to contradict all analogies from ordinary human experience. The report that a dead man has been raised from his grave and lives a new life beyond the reach of death is without analogy in history. It is *sui generis*—so far the only event of its kind. There is therefore no conflict here with natural science, as often presumed. Conflict with natural science arises only if the resurrection entails suspension of the so-called laws of nature. But this is not the case, since such laws function in the natural world all the way to death. Jesus' death was no exception. Whether beyond death there is another kind of story to tell in the language of myth and symbol or legend and metaphor does not lie within the purview of the natural sciences to prove or disprove.

We cannot summarize here the exegetical results of modern scholarship regarding the Easter traditions. Suffice it to recall that the gospel of Easter was conveyed through two strands of early tradition, the older one dealing with the appearances of the risen Lord, the other with the discovery of the empty tomb. In both traditions the irreducible minimum was the conviction that Jesus is no longer dead but alive. We can call the resurrection an historical event because it happened in a particular place, in Palestine, and at a definite time, a few days after his death and prior to Pentecost. The knowledge of this event depends on witnesses who passed on the reports of what they heard and saw. On the other hand, the nature of the reality that appeared to the witnesses was more than historical. It was an eschatological event. The witnesses reported that they had seen Jesus alive and the tomb empty. Immediately they interpreted this event as the first instance of the widely anticipated eschatological event of resurrection from the dead. The New Testament refers to the resurrection of Jesus as the "first fruits" of the new world that dawns with the coming of God's kingdom. This dual character of the resurrection— that it is at once an event within the horizon of history and an eschatological event—accounts for the fact that some theologians are willing, others unwilling, to call the resurrection an historical event. The event and the reports which transmit the knowledge of the event occurred within the framework of history, but when we turn to the meaning of this event, we see clearly what it means to speak of the resurrection as an eschatological event.

Christianity is based on the gospel of the resurrection of Jesus of Nazareth, because in this event God vindicated the claim of Jesus to be the prime representative of his coming kingdom. Christianity could not have had a beginning if the crucifixion had been the absolute end of Jesus. The cause of Jesus would have perished with him.

In raising Jesus from the dead, God raised the cause for which he lived and died to the highest power in the history of salvation. By ratifying Jesus' claim to be the authoritative mediator of God's kingdom, the cause of the kingdom itself gained a promising future in world history. The church of Jesus Christ entered at this point as a creation of the Spirit to announce the eschatological breakthrough in the new and deathless form of life which Jesus' inherited through the resurrection.

THE ASCENSION

The exaltation of Jesus Christ moves from his resurrection on the third day through the forty days of his self-manifestation to the day of his "ascension." The mythical features of this trajectory of exaltation are obvious the moment we ask where Jesus went when he ascended to heaven. Christian art has depicted the ascension as a visible movement of Jesus' body through the clouds, with the disciples standing by, looking up and watching him disappear. In some realistic paintings all one can see is the feet, the rest of the body having been enveloped by clouds. The need to demythologize the story should not, however, weaken our sense for the message it contains.

The story of the ascension is preceded by a period of forty days after the resurrection. The symbolic significance of the number forty was already firmly established in the biblical history of salvation. We can recall Moses' forty days and forty nights on top of the mountain (Exod. 24:18), or Elijah's sojourn on Mount Horeb forty days and forty nights (1 Kings 19:8), or Israel's wandering in the wilderness forty years, or Jesus' fasting and temptations in the wilderness forty days. The forty days between the resurrection and the ascension was a time in which the risen, exalted Christ revealed himself to those who still had to live and preach the message under the old conditions of this world of transiency and death. It was eminently a time qualified by the self-revealing presence of Jesus on his way from humiliation to exaltation.

The ascension of Jesus came at the end of the forty days. It signified the end of the time in which Jesus himself was the revealing subject of revelation and the beginning of the time in which the Spirit through the Word and the sacraments conveys him as the revealed subject matter of revelation. The ascension prepared the way for the time of the church which takes place between the ascension of Christ and his return at the end of time. Not only Rudolf Bultmann but before him Martin Luther ridiculed the literalistic images of the ascension common in popular piety as childish ideas. If we ask, "Where did Jesus go?" we can only answer, "He went to the Father." Even the scholastic theologians did not interpret the ascension in a purely spatial way. To be sure, they took the myth literally, visualizing Jesus going up into the clouds of heaven. But this was only an outer sign of an invisible ascension to the throne of God which is not located in a particular place but represents the omnipresent rule of God. Karl Barth similarly referred to the ascension of Jesus as the homecoming of the Son who had wandered into a far country, a homecoming to the Father's house.

In one respect the content of Easter and the ascension are one and the same. They both mean that God exalted Jesus. In the earliest Christian preaching the resurrection of Jesus from the dead was itself interpreted as an act of exaltation (Acts 2:33; 5:30–31; Phil. 2:9). Yet there are good reasons for distinguishing the two events in the church year, separated by forty days, even though dogmatics would be hard pressed to justify these distinctions with sound historical arguments. The end of Jesus' time on earth is like the beginning. It is a mystery clothed in the language of myth and symbol. History does not give us a key to unlock it.

The ascension marked the beginning of something new in history. John quotes Jesus as saying, "It is to your advantage that I go away" (John 16:7). The absence of Christ according to the flesh (*kata sarka*) opened the possibility of a new form of presence according to the Spirit (*kata pneuma*).

At first it seems that the ascension draws the Christian faith into the vortex of the myth of eternal recurrence, in denial of the historical structure of the gospel as a message of events that never repeat themselves. It seems that the Son ascends to exactly the same place from which he descended. Origen enunciated the formula "The end is always like the beginning." This was an axiom taken from Neo-Platonic philosophy and applied as an hermeneutical key to open the mysteries of biblical revelation. But actually the ascension was an advance, not a return to the *status quo ante*, to the previous place of the Son with the Father. It was an advance to a new epoch of history, to the sending of the Spirit and the mission of the church in world history.

THE SESSION AT
THE RIGHT HAND OF GOD

Jesus was exalted to the right hand of the Father. The "right hand" was a symbol in the ancient East for a position of power exercised in the name of the ruler. The Christian confession that Jesus was exalted to the place of power at the right hand of God was an adaptation of a statement in Ps. 110:1: "The Lord says to my lord: 'Sit at my right hand, till I make your enemies your footstool.'" Originally this saying was God speaking to the king of Jerusalem. When, in the early church, Jesus was called "Lord," the saying was interpreted as God speaking to Jesus. Between the time of Jesus' earthly ministry and his return at the end of time to judge the world, Jesus rules now as the Lord of history and the church.

The confession that Jesus is sitting at God's right hand is not to be taken in a literal sense as referring to a definite place. This became a topic of major dispute in Luther's controversy with Zwingli on the Lord's Supper. Zwingli argued that since Christ ascended and sits at the right hand of God in heaven, he cannot at the same time be really present at every altar on earth. Luther argued that this is precisely the point of the phrase "at the right hand of God." The right hand of God refers to God's power to fill heaven and earth; it refers to royal omnipotence and majesty; it is the efficacious dominion by which God is everywhere governing, controlling, and administering all things.

Therefore, when Christ sits at God's right hand, it means that he participates in the divine power, glory, and dominion over all things in heaven and on earth. It is a statement acknowledging the present Lordship of Jesus Christ.

The older dogmaticians (Martin Chemnitz, John Andrew Quenstedt, John Gerhard, David Hollaz) interpreted the "right hand of God" in a broad sense to refer to the Lordship of Christ in terms of three ways in which he rules in the world. First there is the "rule of grace" (*regnum gratiae*). Jesus participates now in the power of God's Spirit to rule in the hearts of humankind. Because Jesus sits now at the right hand of God, he is no longer bound to the limits of his earthly ministry. He shares in a suprahistorical freedom to be universally present to all generations everywhere and at all times. For this reason he can be the Lord of the one ecumenical church dispersed among the nations. Because he sits at the right hand of God, he can keep his final promise: "Lo, I am with you always, to the close of the age" (Matt. 28:20).

Jesus exercises his rule of grace by means of the church's ongoing witness to his earthly life and ministry according to the Gospels. The living Christ who sits at the right hand of God does not create faith by a direct "I-Thou" kind of mystical relationship apart from the mediation of the Word and the sacraments. Individuals who claim to have mystical visions of the living Christ do not thereby acquire new knowledge of revelation on which the church as a whole can act.

The Lordship of Christ in the New Testament is not limited in scope to his rule of grace in and through the church. The center of gravity, to be sure, is Christ's Lordship of the church. This is clear from the idea that the church is the body of Christ and that Christ is the head of the church. As the body of Christ, the church plays a special role in the rule of Christ. The church is where the Lordship of Jesus Christ is acknowledged. But the Lordship of Christ is not restricted to the church. It is universal in scope, extending beyond his spiritual rule in the hearts of believers, beyond his rule in the church through Word and sacraments, and reaching the outer circumference of creation, including everything that lives and moves in nature and history. All powers—political, economic, social, national, and international—have been in principle submitted to the Lordship of Christ, who exercises his dominion at the right hand of God. The older dogmaticians referred to this as the "rule of power" (*regnum potentiae*). Nineteenth-century German theology, with some twentieth-century Lutheran theologians, have said that this aspect of the Lordship of Christ is exercised from the "left hand of God." They defend it on the basis of Luther's doctrine of the two kingdoms. But this notion of the "left hand of God" is not a concept that can be found in the New Testament. The "left hand" is not a biblical symbol for the way that God relates to the world of history and nature. Instead, God's political rule of power as well as God's reconciling rule of grace are functions of the dominion of Christ who sits at the "right hand" of God. The theology of "the left hand of God" produced a dichotomous nonchristological approach to contemporary social and political ethics and should be replaced, on the basis of the New Testament, by a christocentric theology of the session of Jesus Christ at God's right hand.

The church fathers—Ignatius, Justin, Irenaeus, and Origen—carried forward the New Testament witness to the cosmic Lordship of Christ. All things were created through Christ, and for him and in him all things cohere and have their meaning (Col. 1:16–17). The church fathers taught that invisible powers are working behind the back of all the visible powers on earth. There are powers, principalities, angels, thrones, dominions, authorities, and eons that are the real rulers of history. The church fathers declared, on the basis of the cosmic christology of the New Testament, that all these hierarchies in heaven and on earth have had to succumb to the superior dominion of Christ. The victory of Christ counts against all the invisible superpowers which are the directing forces behind the earthly powers: the nations, the world rulers, the empire, and so on. The *regnum potentiae* of Christ at the right hand of God is one of the foundation stones of a Christian political ethic.

The third aspect of the Lordship of Christ at God's right hand was referred to by the old dogmaticians as the "rule of glory" (*regnum gloriae*). It is the eschatological dimension which can be more clearly dealt with in connection with the expectation of the return of Christ as the future judge of the world.

THE COMING IN GLORY

The Lordship of Christ has an eschatological dimension which makes clear that the world is still struggling in a state of separation from its promised future fulfillment. The glory of Christ and the misery of the world stand in sharpest contrast to each other. The hope that was born at Easter for the world has not yet been realized in history. The hope for the new humanity and the new world still awaits a future in which the victory of Christ over his enemies—sin, death, and the devil—will be established beyond doubt. Primitive Christianity expressed this hope for final victory in the symbol of the coming again of the risen Lord to fulfill the rule of God which Jesus had proclaimed in his earthly ministry. The picture of Jesus returning in the clouds of heaven through which he left the earth in his ascension cannot be taken literally. What it points to, however, is that the world faces an ultimate judgment and that the earthly Jesus is the revelation of the ultimate standard by which the world will be judged. Nobody will escape being judged by the standard of life which Jesus inaugurated in his own ministry. The expectation of the return of Christ in glory is a sober reminder that this life is moving toward ultimate accountability. Jesus is the Lord who will exercise judgment by the authority of God. Yet Christians face this judgment with hope for themselves and the world, for the eschatological judge is none other than Jesus, who revealed the absolute love and mercy of God. If we ask why Jesus should be the judge in the end, the answer is that Jesus is the essence of what it means to be fully human. Humans will not be judged by a heteronomous law alien to their very being. Jesus is the final revelation of the essence and future of humanity. The return of Christ in glory is awaited as the future realization of the humanity of humankind and the fulfillment of the world, passing through judgment to an eternity in which God will be all in all.

NOTES

1. See the study of the idea of preexistence in the New Testament by R. G. Hamerton-Kelly, *Pre-Existence, Wisdom, and the Son of Man* (Cambridge: At the University Press, 1973).

2. Ian D. Kingston Siggins, *Martin Luther's Doctrine of Christ* (New Haven: Yale University Press, 1970), pp. 194–95.

3. Emil Brunner, *The Mediator*, trans. Olive Wyon (Philadelphia: Westminster Press, 1947), p. 326.

4. Karl Barth, *Church Dogmatics*, vol. 1/2 (Edinburgh: T. & T. Clark, 1936–77), p. 184.

5. Wolfhart Pannenberg, *Jesus—God and Man*, trans. Lewis Wilkins and Duane Priebe (Philadelphia: Westminster Press, 1968), p. 149.

6. Ibid.

7. Ibid.

8. See the most comprehensive study on the virginal birth of Jesus in the primitive Christian traditions by Raymond E. Brown, *The Birth of the Messiah* (New York: Doubleday & Co., 1977).

9. David Griffin, *Process Christology* (Philadelphia: Westminster Press, 1973), p. 12.

10. Rudolf Bultmann, "New Testament and Mythology," in his *Kerygma and Myth*, ed. Hans W. Bartsch (London: SPCK, 1954), p. 41.

11. Pannenberg, *Jesus—God and Man*, p. 99.

12. Paul Althaus, *Die Christliche Wahrheit* (Gütersloh: Bertelsmann, 1948), p. 269. (Translation mine.)

7

The Uniqueness and Universality of Jesus Christ

God has been revealed in the particular history of Jesus Christ, to embrace the universal future of the church and the world. The claim of the gospel is that the uniqueness of Jesus lies in his universal meaning, that this concrete person in history holds in himself the key to the universal fulfillment which God intends for all.

THE HERITAGE OF EXCLUSIVENESS

The true identity of Jesus Christ has been mediated to us in texts and traditions which unanimously confess that he is the exclusive medium of eschatological salvation. Acts 4:12 is the classical locus of this christological exclusiveness: "And there is salvation in no one else, for there is no other name under heaven given among men by which we must be saved." Christian exclusiveness has found several ways of manifesting itself. Traditionally, the Catholic type of exclusivism has focused on the church. "Outside the church there is no salvation." The statement first appeared in one of Cyprian's letters in the third century. It was reiterated in the papal bull *Unam Sanctam* of Boniface VIII in 1302: "We believe that there is one holy catholic and apostolic church . . . outside of which there is no salvation. . . . We declare that it is necessary for salvation for every human creature to be subject to the Roman Pontiff."[1] Traditionally, the Protestant type has felt uncomfortable with the ecclesiocentric form of exclusivism. It has focused instead on faith, quoting passages like John 3:18: "He who believes in him is not condemned; he who does not believe is condemned already, because he has not believed in the name of the only Son of God." Also Rom. 10:17: "So faith comes from what is heard, and what is heard comes by the preaching of Christ."

The heritage of Christian exclusiveness runs deep into the New Testament and dominates the tradition from earliest times to the present. But from the beginning the same tradition has created loopholes to provide people outside the Christian circle with the chance of salvation. Catholics of the most exclusive type conceded that people outside the church can be saved through the loopholes of "invincible ignorance" or "baptism by desire." Protestants in the older line of dogmatics appealed to 1 Pet. 3:19, which states that Christ preached to the spirits in prison, as proof that people who did not encounter Christ and believe in this life would be given a "second chance" on the threshold of the future life. Sometimes they also talked about the invisible church whose limits are unknown, and thus presumably might also include some "noble pagans." The judgment that reservations will be taken in heaven only for Christians, only for those who accept Christ by faith in this life or belong to his church, has seemed too harsh to be taken in a strictly literal sense.

Currently there are voices raised against every sort of Christian exclusivism, including all the loopholes which continue to reinforce the underlying premise. The question is now whether there is full and equal salvation through the non-Christian religions. The loopholes only provided an exceptional way of salvation. What is said to be needed now is a full acknowledgment of the other major religions as valid ways of salvation. We are living in one world with a plurality of cultures, religions, and ideologies. Either we acknowledge the legitimacy of this pluralism, or we threaten the possibility of living together in a peaceful world. We expect governments, corporations, and other agencies to do their part to cooperate in establishing conditions that drive toward the unity of the human world without diminishing the plurality of its forms. Why should not the religions of the world do their part? Christianity has begun to open up channels of dialogue with people of other religions. But many feel that the exclusivistic premise which it brings to the dialogue clogs the channels and makes a real exchange impossible.

Professor John Hick of Birmingham, England, has taken the lead among Protestants in calling for a "Copernican revolution"[2] which aims to overturn the christological dogma at the bottom of all Christian exclusivism. It is not enough to broaden the way of Christian salvation by speaking with Tillich of a "latent church" or with Rahner of "anonymous Christianity." Those are the convenient modern loopholes. He calls them "epicycles." So Hick goes deeper and lays the axe at the christological roots of exclusivism. He says, "For understood literally the Son of God, God the Son, God-incarnate language implies that God can be adequately known and responded to *only* through Jesus; and the whole religious life of mankind, beyond the stream of Judaic-Christian faith is thus by implication excluded as lying outside the sphere of salvation."[3] Pluralism is compatible with the unity of all humankind if we acknowledge that the various streams of religion in the world carry the same waters of salvation leading to eternal life with God. God is at the center of the universe of faiths; Jesus is only one of the many ways—the Christian way—that leads to God. He is not the one and only Son of God, Lord of the world, and Savior of humankind. Each religion has its own and does the job in its own way. In this way John Hick has rooted out the last vestige of exclusivism.

On the Catholic side the leftwing of Rahner's school has also abandoned the Christian claim that Jesus Christ is "different," "decisive," "unique," "normative," or "final," toppling the pillar on which the traditional claims to exclusiveness lean. For surely it makes no sense to argue that believing in Jesus Christ or belonging to his church are essential for salvation, if he is ultimately only one among many founders pointing the way to God. Paul Knitter has made the clearest case among Catholics for a revision of the traditional claim that Jesus Christ is the one and only Savior of humankind, that he is the once-for-all revelation of God's eschatological salvation in store for the whole world. In "A Critique of Hans Küng's *On Being a Christian*,"[4] Knitter like Hick lays his axe at the roots not only of the christological dogma but also of the apostolic kerygma. His motive is the same: to pave the way for dialogue with other religions that won't be "hamstrung"[5] by the exclusivist mindset. He writes, "Intellectually and psychologically is it not possible to give oneself over wholly to the meaning and message of Jesus and at the same time recognize the possibility that other 'saviors' have carried out the same function for other people?"[6] He answers "yes" and argues "that the claim for Jesus' exclusive uniqueness does not form part of the central assertions of Christian texts."[7] The claim that salvation takes place only in Jesus can be chalked up to "the historically conditioned world view and thought-patterns of the time."[8] Knitter concludes that there is no exclusive claim that belongs to the core of the Christian message. He would agree with Harnack that the exclusive element is not part of the kernel, but only the husk of the gospel.

Far to the right of this antiexclusivist position, we find a new affirmation of the heritage of exclusiveness among the neoevangelicals, who are conducting a vigorous campaign against every form of universalism. The idea that there is salvation in the non-Christian religions is denied point-blank. At Lausanne the evangelicals declared dogmatically that "it is impossible to be a biblical Christian and a universalist simultaneously."[9] They now teach as dogmatic truth and as a criterion of faithfulness to the gospel of Jesus Christ that all those who die or who have died without conscious faith in Jesus Christ are damned to eternal hell. If people have never heard the gospel and have never had a chance to believe, they are lost anyway. The logic of this position is that children who die in infancy are lost, the mentally retarded are lost, all those who have never heard of Christ are lost. Nevertheless, evangelicals cling to this view as the heart of the gospel and the incentive to mission.

THE UNIQUENESS
OF JESUS CHRIST

The texts and traditions that tell us about Jesus of Nazareth represent him as the expected Messiah of Israel, God's only Son, the Lord of creation, and the Savior of all humanity. We have no nonchristological picture of the historical Jesus. Every recollection of his identity is penetrated by an identification that raises his significance to the highest possible power. If one should subtract all the special titles of identification, one would not be left with the identity of Jesus who is really Jesus. One is rather left with the question whether Jesus of Nazareth ever existed or with an empty assertion of his naked historicity. But what of his meaning? What about his true identity?

When John the Baptist wondered about the true identity of Jesus, he asked, "Are you he who is to come, or shall we look for another?" (Matt. 11:3; Luke 7:19). The answer of the early church was clear: Jesus is the One who was to come. He is the Messiah. Similarly, when Jesus asked his disciples on the way to Caesarea Philippi, "Who do men say that I am?", Peter answered, "You are the Christ, the Son of the living God" (Mark 8:27; Matt. 16:16). The New Testament abounds with titles that serve to identify the uniqueness of Jesus. The historical Jesus probably did not designate his true identity by such titles of honor as Christ, Son of God, Lord, Savior, Logos, and so on, but the early church did without any shadow of doubt. These titles were conferred on Jesus in the light of faith in the risen presence of Jesus. They are titles which in the same writings are bestowed on God. Both God and Jesus are spoken of as Savior. Both God and Jesus are spoken of as Lord. Jesus is the Savior because he will save his people from their sins. Jesus is the Lord because God has raised and exalted him above all others. Jesus is the subject of names that are above all other names, because they are the names of God. They speak eloquently of the uniqueness of Jesus.

New Testament theologians argue whether these titles of honor go back to the historical Jesus himself, or whether they have been written back into the Gospel texts from the post-Easter situation of faith. In one sense it does not matter, for both sides must agree that the Jesus of history is represented to us in texts and traditions which describe his uniqueness. He is depicted not as a son of God but as *the* only begotten Son of God, not as *a* savior but as *the* Savior, not as *a* lord but as *the* Lord, and so on. These designations of Jesus as Lord and Savior identify him as the foundation of divine salvation. They are not name tags loosely attached to the personal reality to which they refer. There is no nominalism intended in the transference of high titles of honor to Jesus of Nazareth.

If we strip away the names that are above all the names which generally apply to other human beings, we have no way to speak of the meaning of Jesus. We can speak of him in the symbols of the texts and traditions, or we cannot speak of him at all, unless we fabricate our own image of Jesus and arbitrarily call him what we will. Nothing is clearer in the New Testament and the Christian tradition than the uniqueness of Jesus in whose name alone there is salvation, before whom every knee should bow and every tongue confess that he is Lord to the glory of God the Father (Phil. 2:10–11).

One of the earliest symbols of Christianity was the fish. In Greek the letters that spelled fish—IXTHUS—represented an ancient christological confession: Jesus Christ Son of God Savior. By what other names can Jesus be known? These are symbols that participate in the reality to which they refer, to use Tillich's definition of a symbol. Christian faith has no knowledge or interest in Jesus as Jesus, minus the names which symbolize his unique meaning. These symbols have a prehistory in the religions of that time, but when transferred to Jesus they crown him with a significance that underscores his uniqueness. They do not mean that Jesus is unique as every individual is unique. Although he is truly human, these titles place him in a class by himself. He is the one and only Christ, or he is not the Christ at all. He is the one and only Son of God, or he is not God's Son at all. He is the one and only Savior, or he is no Savior at all. The exclusive claim is not a footnote to the gospel; it is the gospel itself. Not part of the husk, it is the kernel itself. The answer of the gospel to John the Baptist's question "Are you he who is to come?" is "Yes, and we shall not look for another" (Matt. 11:3).

All the christological titles of the texts and traditions of historic biblical and catholic Christianity intend to lift up the uniqueness of Jesus as the living Christ, the risen Lord, and the eschatological Savior of the world. They alone can legitimate the role that Jesus came to assume as the cultic center in primitive Christian worship. Without these titles that acclaim the exclusive uniqueness of Jesus, he loses the vehicles of interpretation by which he is no mere dead hero of the past, buried in the ruins of his own time and place, but the living presence of God in the flesh. These titles—and they alone— tell us what the earliest believers in Jesus thought he was all about. They reveal the true identity of Jesus; at the core of this revelation is the exclusive uniqueness of Jesus in relation to God and his coming kingdom, in relation to the church, and in relation to the entire world of history and nature. If we do not use these christological titles as our linguistic access to the knowledge of Jesus' identity and meaning, then we shall have to find some other way of speaking about him, unless we are to remain silent. Who would we then say that he is, if he is not the one whom the earliest texts and traditions identify as the only true embodiment of God's Word in history?

What is the essence of the uniqueness of Jesus? It does not lie in the fact that he was an historical individual who lived once upon a time in Palestine. Every one of us is a unique individual in the sense that none of us has a duplicate. But the uniqueness of Jesus is *sui generis*. He died as a unique historical individual at one time and place, under Pontius Pilate just outside the gate, but he was raised to be the living presence of God in every new age and every strange place. The issue of Jesus' uniqueness finally has to do with the resurrection. "God raised him up, having loosed the pangs of death" (Acts 2:24).

When we confess the uniqueness of Jesus, we do not mean merely that he was a concrete individual human being, which he was. We mean that he is the concrete embodiment of universal meaning. The true identity of Jesus was revealed to his disciples only after the resurrection, or at least only then could they begin to understand what he had been disclosing step by step along the way. If we could turn back the reel of history to the days before Easter, if we could find some tapes or pictures of the man Jesus, if we could read the obituaries that appeared in the *Galilean Gazette*, we would hardly gain a deeper insight into the true identity of Jesus. The true identity of Jesus is something which in the last analysis "flesh and blood" cannot reveal to us. More historical information will not solve the riddle of Jesus' personal identity. If people look into the abundant texts and traditions of the Christian past and conclude that Jesus is not the one he is said to be, they may invent other names and labels to transfer to Jesus, but in doing so they are not adding to the fund of our knowledge about the historical Jesus, but only telling the world where they personally stand in relation to him. For the christological titles which the apostles applied to Jesus were not projected on an objective screen of history. They were born in the struggles of following Jesus, of preaching the kerygma of his cross and resurrection and taking the gospel to the gentiles. A christological title is a dialectical statement that lives in the polar tension between subject and object. It says something about Jesus, but also about the person making the confession. No one can call Jesus Lord unless he or she has been grasped by the Holy Spirit (1 Cor. 12:3). The statement is not a product of objectifying analysis. Peter's confession "You are the Christ, the Son of the living God" was an ecstatic statement, a miracle of the mind (Tillich).

The true identity of Jesus can be acknowledged only by faith in him as the risen Lord and the living Christ. We do not expect that anyone will confess the uniqueness of Jesus, in the special sense implied by the sum of the christological titles, by means of a reconstruction of the historical Jesus. That Jesus is dead and buried and will always remain sealed in the tomb to people who do not believe that he now lives freely beyond the limits of his own earthly fate.

THE UNIVERSALITY
OF JESUS CHRIST

The uniqueness of Jesus belongs to the core of the Christian gospel. What is unique about Jesus, however, is precisely his universal meaning. This particular and concrete man, Jesus of Nazareth, is unique because of his universal significance. His uniqueness lies in his universality. If Jesus is the Savior, he is the universal Savior. I cannot confine him to being my personal Savior, merely the focus of my own experience of God.

We are back to the beginning. If Jesus is the unique and universal Savior, how can there be a dialogue with other religions? Are not Christians bound to say that theirs is the only way of salvation, that non-Christians will be saved either by being evangelized here and now or by some loophole or other? We seem to be confronted with a dilemma. If Jesus is the unique and universal Savior, there is no salvation in the non-Christian religions. If there is salvation in the non-Christian religions, then Jesus is not the unique and universal Savior. Theology is facing this dilemma.

Christians should not be afraid of dialogue with other religions. The religions are part of the universal context in which the true identity of Jesus must find new expression. The christological titles did not descend on Jesus all at once and ready-made. There was a development in which new titles were discovered for Jesus in the hermeneutical process of transmitting the traditional texts within the horizon of new contexts. Every christological title had to be born again in history, in the process of encountering the story of Jesus in a new religious context. We do not yet fully know how we shall confess Jesus in the future of dialogue with other religions. We shall continue to confess him in the language of our familiar texts and traditions. But the universality of Jesus means that he will live in the medium of symbols which may still seem strange to us. Churches and theologians are calling us to a new dialogue with the world religions. It is therefore urgent that we know what we mean by the uniqueness and universality of Jesus Christ.

We have spoken about the uniqueness of Jesus, guided by the import of the major christological titles applied to him after Easter. But how shall we understand the universality of Jesus?

Christians believe in the universality of salvation in Jesus' name. It is God's will that all people shall be saved and come to the knowledge of the truth (2 Tim. 2:4). Evangelicals generally accept universal salvation in this sense, as valid in principle for all people. But they restrict salvation in the end to those who actually hear the gospel and put their faith in Christ.[10] Under this restriction the rift that has been opened up in the world through sin will widen to an eternal chasm, splitting the one world of God's creation into two unreconcilable halves, only God's half will be much smaller than the devil's, in fact, only a remnant of the whole. There is not much for the angels to sing about, if the evangelicals get what they expect—a heaven sparsely filled with only card-carrying Christians.

Biblical universalism transcends the particularist eschatology of the evangelicals. There are stern warnings in the New Testament threatening eternal

563

perdition. There are reservations; there are qualifications of the universal hope. But these are addressed more to those inside with apparently the right credentials than to those outside. "This people honors me with their lips, but their heart is far from me" (Matt. 15.8; Mark 7:6). "Not every one who says to me, 'Lord, Lord,' shall enter the kingdom of heaven" (Matt. 7:21). The New Testament warns of the spiritual danger of using the right evangelical words and ecclesiastical doctrines as the basis of trust and hope. There is spiritual danger in reducing the power and future of the universal Christ to the pinhole size of the believer's faith or the church's confession here and now.

New Testament universalism, however, is always a predicate of the uniqueness of Jesus Christ, not a metaphysical attribute of the world in process (as in the Origenistic doctrine of *apokatastasis ton panton*), nor of a saving potential inherent in the world religions, nor of an existential possibility universally available to every person in a moment of decision. The uniqueness Christians claim for Jesus as World-Savior lies in the revelation of his eschatological identity, constituted by his resurrection victory over death as the "last enemy" of humankind. The uniqueness of Jesus is not a function of our Christian *blik*. It belongs to him by virtue of his enthronement as the Lord of the coming kingdom. A particularist eschatology can be constructed only by picking particular passages and choosing to ignore others.

What about the universalist thrust in the Pauline theology? As in Adam all men die, so also in Christ shall all be made alive" (1 Cor. 15:22). "For in him [Christ] all the fulness of God was pleased to dwell, and through him to reconcile to himself all things, whether on earth or in heaven, making peace by the blood of his cross" (Col. 1:19–20). "For he has made known to us in all wisdom and insight the mystery of his will, according to his purpose which he set forth in Christ as a plan for the fulness of time, to unite all things in him, things in heaven and things in earth" (Eph. 1:9–10). "That at the name of Jesus every knee should bow, in heaven and on earth and under the earth, and every tongue confess that Jesus Christ is Lord, to the glory of God the Father" (Phil. 2:10–11). "When all things are subjected to him, then the Son himself will also be subjected to him who put all things under him, that God may be everything to every one" (1 Cor. 15:28). "And he is the expiation for our sins, and not for ours only but also for the sins of the whole world" (1 John 2:2). These verses create a total impression of the universalizing tendencies in the New Testament.

Christian theologians are debating the question whether there is salvation in other religions and taking sides on the issue, without first making clear the model of salvation they have in mind. What is the salvation theologians expect to find or not to find in other religions? Vastly different things are meant by salvation. If salvation is whatever you call it, there is no reason for a Christian to deny that there is salvation in other religions. We may speak of salvation on two levels, phenomenologically and theologically. On a purely phenomenological level, there are numerous models of salvation and there are ways of delivering each of the models and making them work. When the nomads needed a land for their salvation, they were promised a land by their God, and they got it, and have suffered ever since. When the slaves in Egypt needed deliverance from oppression for their salvation, God called Moses to lead the exodus out of Egypt. When the wandering people of God needed food for their salvation from hunger, God supplied them with daily manna from above. And the history of salvation went on, creating different models for its expression, but always pointing forward to new dimensions generated by the experience of fundamental lack. Land is needed, but it is not enough. Freedom is needed, but it is not enough. Food is needed, but it is not enough.

If we are told there is salvation in the other religions, there is no *a priori* reason to deny the claim. It depends on what is meant by salvation. If salvation is the experience of illumination, then the Buddha can save. If salvation is the experience of union with God, then Hinduism can save. If salvation is being true to the ancestors, then Shintoism can save. If salvation is revolution against the overlords and equality for the people, then Maoism can save. If salvation is liberation from poverty and oppression, then Marxism can save. If salvation is psychological health, there is salvation not only outside the church but outside the religions as well. If salvation is striving for humanization, for development, for wholeness, for justice, for peace, for freedom, for the whole earth, for whatnot, there is salvation in the other religions, in the quasi-religions and in the secular ideologies. The reason Christians are confused and have appeared so smug about salvation is that they imagined they held a monopoly on salvation. Then when they have discovered virtues and values that match or excel what they find among Christians, they are prepared to accept the doctrine of salvation in non-Christian religions, perhaps even to the point of surrendering every version of the *solus Christus*.

On a theological level, salvation is not whatever you want to call it, the fulfillment of every need or the compensation for every lack. We do not deny that we may also speak of salvation in this extended phenomenological sense, with the warning that it has generated much of the confusion in which our topic languishes. Salvation in the Bible is a promise that God offers the world on the horizon of our expectation of personal and universal death. The gospel is the power of God unto salvation because it promises to break open the vicious cycle of death. Death is the power that draws every living thing into its circle. Here we cannot enter into the mystery of death. But if anyone denies the reality of death and its power to insinuate itself as the eschaton of all life, which threatens the very conditions of the possibility of meaningful existence, we should take a patient "wait and see" attitude. It is just a question of time before death will punctuate everybody's personal story with its own annihilating force. We cannot derive a final meaning for life on this side of death. We can gain the partial salvations we are willing to pay for, but no techniques of salvation can succeed in buying off death.

Salvation in the New Testament is what God has done to death in the resurrection of Jesus. Salvation is what happens to you and me and the whole world in spite of death, if only the resurrection of Jesus means what the apostolic kerygma and the catholic dogma have interpreted it to mean. The story of salvation is a drama of death and resurrection, whatever other human personal and social problems the word might trade on. The gospel is the announcement that in one man's history death is no longer the eschaton, but was only the second-to-last thing. It has now become past history. Death lies behind Jesus, qualifying him to lead the procession from death to new life. Since death is what separates humankind from God in the end, only that power which transcends death can liberate humanity for eternal life with God. This is the meaning of salvation in the biblical Christian sense. It is eschatological salvation, because the God who raised Jesus from the dead has overcome death as the final eschaton of life. Our final salvation lies in the eschatological future when our own death will be put behind us. This does not mean that there is no salvation in the present, no realized aspect of salvation. It means that the salvation we enjoy now is like borrowing from the future, living now as though our future could already be practiced in the present, because of our union with the risen Christ through faith and hope.

Theologians who speak of salvation in the non-Christian religions should tell us if this is the same salvation which God has promised the world by raising Jesus from the dead. The resurrection gospel is the criterion of the meaning of salvation in the New Testament sense. When Chistians enter into dialogue with people of other religions, they must do their utmost to communicate what they mean by the assertion that Jesus lives, and explain how this gospel intersects the hopes and fears of every person whose fate is to anticipate death as the final eschaton. If the dialogue should show that other religions are not much moved by the problem of death, that the problem of death is limited to a particular way of viewing the human predicament, we would have to say that the encounter with Christianity itself becomes the occasion for everyone to see that the problem of death arises out of the structure of existence itself. The gospel falls on the human situation and illuminates the universal existential problem. This is the hypothesis that Christians bring into interreligious dialogue.

The new challenge to christology is to speak of the identity of Jesus Christ in the context of the world religions and secular culture. In the past, theology has dealt with the religions from afar, giving us a Christian interpretation of the non-Christian religions from a ready-made theological point of view.

In a sense this is all we can do prior to the event of dialogue. But if we really believe that the uniqueness of Jesus lies in his universality, that his identity is always being mediated through the concrete events of history, then we should be open to exploring what the non-Christian religions can contribute to our understanding of the universal identity of Jesus Christ. The history of the religions once contributed all the christological titles to the interpretation of the Jesus-event. Some of them were rooted in the ancient Hebrew traditions, others not, but all of them were transformed in the process of being assimilated to the traditions about Jesus. That process is still going on in the openness of world history, engendered by the universal missionary witness to Jesus as the Christ, the Lord and Savior of the world.

The identity of Jesus cannot be limited to the particular contexts of our past. Christology is not static. New contexts have made it possible for new meanings to blossom on old texts. They relate to the concrete struggles of people for life, health, wholeness, fulfillment, salvation. In India, Jesus is pictured by some as the Avatar. To us this means practically nothing, but in India it may mean a great deal. In many parts of the Third World, Jesus is the liberator. Liberation has become the focal image of a whole new christology. To us it may also mean something, but not exactly the same as to people suffering the conditions of poverty, exploitation, and oppression. In the patristic era Jesus was called the Logos, and that carried a metaphysical meaning quite different from the same word in the Gospel of John. In Nazi Germany, Martin Niemöller preached about Jesus as the true *Führer*. In the context of Western atheism and the trend to depersonalization in technological society, Dorothy Soelle has animated the theme of Jesus as the "representative." Similar titles such as "advocate," "delegate," and "deputy" have been used to speak of the meaning of Jesus for modern people, and perhaps soon, if not already, someone in the Far East will suggest "chairman." Every culture has to ask of Jesus in its own way, "Are you the One who is to come, or do we look for another?" Every people will have to answer, "Who do you say that I am?" in a language they can understand. The crucifix of Jesus as a tortured Peruvian Indian on the cover of Gustavo Gutierrez's *Theology of Liberation* could not have been sculpted in our part of the world.

The point we have been making is that the exclusive uniqueness of Jesus, mediated by the texts and traditions that announce his resurrection as the living Lord, drives us to discover his universal significance, not in another world after this one but in the real contexts of ongoing history. His true identity is still being disclosed in the encounter of the gospel with the world religions. The gospel does not meet the world religions on a one-way street, giving them the traditional symbols of christology and receiving nothing back. The dialogue will be a two-way street, in which the condition of openness to the other religions will be motivated by knowledge that they also somehow speak of Jesus Christ. The Old Testament is the paradigm case of how one religion of another time and place can speak of Jesus Christ in a proleptic way. If the apostles and the church fathers could find anticipations of Christ in the Old Testament, we have a right to expect a similar thing in the texts and traditions of other religions. For God is not without witnesses in these religions.

We have steered a course between the Scylla of an evangelicalism without the universality of Jesus Christ and the Charybdis of a universalism without the uniqueness of Jesus Christ. But ours is not essentially a middle position that combines elements at random from the right and the left. Rather, the right and the left are splinters of a holistic vision of the eschatological Christ whose uniqueness lies in his concrete universality. This universality is being worked out in the world mission of the church. The ultimate horizon of this historically mediated universality is hope for an eternal restitution of all things in God. We have a universal *hope* in Christ, not a universal gnosis. It is a hope that engenders the actions of witness and mission in history, not a knowledge that pretends to know the final outcome of things in advance. It is a hope that the Lord of the church will finally rule as the Lord of the world, inclusive of its religions. Meanwhile, we can witness and work as though God is at work behind the backs of the plurality of world religions, pushing them forward into a final unity that has become proleptically incarnate for all in Jesus Christ. There are not two ways of salvation.[11] There is one salvation and one way of salvation. That is the eschatological salvation valid for all through the One who came that all might find life, who died that the world might be reconciled, who was raised that hope might live for the victory of God and the restitution of all things in God.

NOTES

1. Quoted in Robert L. Wilken, "The Making of a Phrase," *Dialog* 12 (Summer 1973): 174.

2. John Hick, *God and the Universe of Faiths* (New York: Macmillan Co., 1973), pp. 121ff.

3. John Hick, "Jesus and the World Religions," in *The Myth of God Incarnate,* ed. John Hick (Philadelphia: Westminster Press, 1977), p. 179.

4. Paul F. Knitter, "A Critique of Hans Küng's *On Being a Christian,*" *Horizons* 5/2 (1978): 151–64.

5. Ibid., p. 156.

6. Ibid., p. 153.

7. Ibid.

8. Ibid., p. 154.

9. *Let the Earth Hear His Voice*, ed. J. D. Douglas (Minneapolis: World Wide Publications, 1975), p. 76.

10. See Harold Lindsell, "Universalism," in *Let the Earth Hear His Voice*, pp. 1206–13.

11. The notion of two ways of salvation has been clearly proposed by H. R. Schlette, *Colloquium salutis—Christen und Nichtchristen heute* (Cologne, 1965); also "Einige Thesen zum Selbstverständnis der Theologie angesichts der Religionen," *Gott in Welt II*, ed. J. B. Metz (Frieburg: Herder Verlag, 1964), pp. 306–16.